Oman

WORLD BIBLIOGRAPHICAL SERIES

General Editors:
Robert G. Neville (Executive Editor)
John J. Horton

Robert A. Myers   Ian Wallace
Hans H. Wellisch   Ralph Lee Woodward, Jr.

John J. Horton is Deputy Librarian of the University of Bradford and currently Chairman of its Academic Board of Studies in Social Sciences. He has maintained a longstanding interest in the discipline of area studies and its associated bibliographical problems, with special reference to European Studies. In particular he has published in the field of Icelandic and of Yugoslav studies, including the two relevant volumes in the World Bibliographical Series.

Robert A. Myers is Associate Professor of Anthropology in the Division of Social Sciences and Director of Study Abroad Programs at Alfred University, Alfred, New York. He has studied post-colonial island nations of the Caribbean and has spent two years in Nigeria on a Fulbright Lectureship. His interests include international public health, historical anthropology and developing societies. In addition to *Amerindians of the Lesser Antilles: a bibliography* (1981), *A Resource Guide to Dominica, 1493-1986* (1987) and numerous articles, he has compiled the World Bibliographical Series volumes on *Dominica* (1987), *Nigeria* (1989) and *Ghana* (1991).

Ian Wallace is Professor of German at the University of Bath. A graduate of Oxford in French and German, he also studied in Tübingen, Heidelberg and Lausanne before taking teaching posts at universities in the USA, Scotland and England. He specializes in contemporary German affairs, especially literature and culture, on which he has published numerous articles and books. In 1979 he founded the journal *GDR Monitor*, which he continues to edit under its new title *German Monitor*.

Hans H. Wellisch is Professor emeritus at the College of Library and Information Services, University of Maryland. He was President of the American Society of Indexers and was a member of the International Federation for Documentation. He is the author of numerous articles and several books on indexing and abstracting, and has published *The Conversion of Scripts, Indexing and Abstracting: an International Bibliography* and *Indexing from A to Z*. He also contributes frequently to *Journal of the American Society for Information Science, The Indexer* and other professional journals.

Ralph Lee Woodward, Jr. is Professor of History at Tulane University, New Orleans. He is the author of *Central America, a Nation Divided*, 2nd ed. (1985), as well as several monographs and more than seventy scholarly articles on modern Latin America. He has also compiled volumes in the World Bibliographical Series on *Belize* (1980), *El Salvador* (1988), *Guatemala (Rev. Ed.)* (1992) and *Nicaragua (Rev. Ed.)* (1994). Dr. Woodward edited the Central American section of the *Research Guide to Central America and the Caribbean* (1985) and is currently associate editor of Scribner's *Encyclopedia of Latin American History*.

VOLUME 29

Oman
Revised and Expanded Edition

Frank A. Clements

Compiler
Head of Learning Resources,
College of St. Mark and St. John, Plymouth

CLIO PRESS

OXFORD, ENGLAND · SANTA BARBARA, CALIFORNIA
DENVER, COLORADO

British Library Cataloguing in Publication Data

Oman – 2 Rev. ed. – (World bibliographical
series; vol. 29)
I. Clements, Frank A.   II. Series
016.95353

ISBN 1–85109–197–1

Clio Press Ltd.,
Old Clarendon Ironworks,
35A Great Clarendon Street,
Oxford OX2 6AT, England.

ABC-CLIO,
130 Cremona Drive,
Santa Barbara,
CA 93116, USA.

Designed by Bernard Crossland.
Typeset by Columns Design and Production Services Ltd, Reading, England.
Printed and bound in Great Britain by
Bookcraft (Bath) Ltd., Midsomer Norton

THE WORLD BIBLIOGRAPHICAL SERIES

This series, which is principally designed for the English speaker, will eventually cover every country (and many of the world's principal regions), each in a separate volume comprising annotated entries on works dealing with its history, geography, economy and politics; and with its people, their culture, customs, religion and social organization. Attention will also be paid to current living conditions – housing, education, newspapers, clothing, etc.– that are all too often ignored in standard bibliographies; and to those particular aspects relevant to individual countries. Each volume seeks to achieve, by use of careful selectivity and critical assessment of the literature, an expression of the country and an appreciation of its nature and national aspirations, to guide the reader towards an understanding of its importance. The keynote of the series is to provide, in a uniform format, an interpretation of each country that will express its culture, its place in the world, and the qualities and background that make it unique. The views expressed in individual volumes, however, are not necessarily those of the publisher.

VOLUMES IN THE SERIES

Contents

Contents

Contents

Introduction

The Sultanate of Oman had, for the Western world, remained relatively unknown until the bloodless coup of 1970 that saw the assumption of power by Sultan Qaboos bin Said bin Taimur. Until this event the country had remained in self-imposed isolation, a backwater in what had become a region flowing with the wealth from oil. If it had not been for the communist-backed insurrection in Dhofar province and the outside assistance received by the Sultan, it is doubtful whether the name of Oman would have appeared in the international press.

Prior to the coup the Sultanate had been firmly rooted in the past, remaining cut off from the rest of the world in self-imposed exile. The society, to Western eyes, was akin to that of the European Middle Ages: the country had no system of general education, an almost total absence of health services, poor internal communications and a pattern of petty restrictions imposed on personal freedom, though some cautious steps towards modernization were taking place.

However, it would be wrong to assume, as some writers have, that Oman was of no significance before the discovery of oil and the coup which placed the country firmly on the road to development and modernization. Indeed the Sultanate has an important history in relation to the Arabian Peninsula, East Africa, the development of maritime techniques and world trade, and, in particular, the historical development of the Ibadhi sect of Islam.

The Sultanate lies at the extreme south-west of the Arabian Peninsula, occupying a land area of some 120,000 square miles. It is bordered on the north by the United Arab Emirates, by the Rub' al-Khali of Saudi Arabia in the north and west and by the newly united Yemen in the extreme west. However, this new found unity is in danger with civil war breaking out between the North and South, indicating that the basic differences between the two ideologies have not been resolved. It has a coastline of some 1,000 miles from the Strait of Hormuz in the north to the Yemen border, although the Musandam Peninsula in the north is separated from the main part of Oman by a strip of land belonging to the United Arab Emirates.

It is the geography of Oman that has affected its history and its people, both of which have developed separately from the rest of the Peninsula. The differences in development from her other Arab neighbours having been accentuated in Oman by the influx of Africans, which resulted from Omani involvement in East Africa and the slave trade, and a strong Indian merchant community in Muscat.

The history of the Sultanate has still to be studied in detail, especially the prehistoric period, although in the past two decades some work has been undertaken by teams of Danish, British and American archaeologists. There is evidence of settlement in the third millennium BC, and links are known to have existed with Sumeria through the export of copper to the cities of Ur and Chaldes, at the time when Oman was known as Makkan. This connection was first explored by Bibby in *Looking for Dilmun* which largely substantiated the claims, but in recent years further scientific study has confirmed the connection. The period before the arrival of the Arabs is largely undocumented and the only available sources are unreliable.

During the first centuries AD the coastal districts fell under Persian rule, and this foreign dominance was to become a feature of Omani history though at no time did a foreign presence ever totally control the Sultanate. The Persian presence left two main legacies to the Sultanate, the first being the introduction of the *qanat* and *aflaj* systems of irrigation and the second the development of trading links to Africa, India and China. Indeed it has been recorded that 'The propinquity of Oman to India, its incomparable position and its convenient ports and creeks combined to make it a cradle of navigation, and the Omanis became the pioneers and chief carriers of commerce by sea in the oriental world' (S. B. Miles, *The countries and tribes of the Persian Gulf*. London: Cass, 1966, p. 355-56).

The arrival of the Arabs into Oman is also badly documented and partially lost in legend. It has been ascribed dates varying from the 2nd to the 6th century AD, and it is likely that there were several different migrations during this period. The migrations came from the Yemen, attributed to the breaching of the Marib dam and the diverting of the spice routes from overland to the sea, and from the north through Buraimi. At first the Arab presence was outside the areas under Persian control and some form of accommodation was reached between the two peoples.

Oman had the distinction of being one of the first countries to be converted to Islam during the life of the Prophet Muhammed in about AD 630. The immediate outcome was the expulsion of the Persian ruling class and the assumption of power by the Arabs. From this point the history of Oman becomes confused and obscure, as the centre of activity was elsewhere in the Arab world. However, this period saw the establishment of the Ibadhi sect of Islam resulting from a rift in the Caliphate and the arrival of the Kharajji refugees in the northern part of the Sultanate. This was to lead to the creation of the Imamate in interior Oman, an event that was to have such an important impact on the internal politics of Oman and was to cause a rift between the interior and the coastal regions. The development of the Imamate is well covered by J. C. Wilkinson's *The Imamate tradition of Oman* and other articles by the same author.

The next significant development was the onset of European influence with the arrival of the Portuguese at the beginning of the 16th century. Although their influence never really extended into the interior, the Portuguese presence lasted until 1649, and was characterized by continual conflict between the Arabs and their rulers until at last the Portuguese were forced out of Oman, though their legacy of military fortifications at Muscat and Sohar still remain.

The war against the Portuguese was also waged at sea following success in Oman, and from this time the Omanis became a maritime power of some significance, obtaining a foothold in Zanzibar and the East African mainland. There was a parallel development in trade, with the Omanis becoming involved in carrying slaves, gold, and ivory from East Africa to Mocha and the Persian Gulf, spices and rice from the Malabar coast, and cloth from Surat. In return, dates and coconuts from Dhofar were shipped for sale in the towns of the Persian Gulf, and dates, pearls, fish and horses were taken to Surat and other Indian ports. Trade links were also established with the Malay Peninsula and, through Chinese merchants, to China itself. At the same time raids were carried out against Portuguese ships and settlements in East Africa and India.

After an era of power and prosperity the Sultanate went into a period of economic decline, largely as a result of British suppression of the slave trade. The suppression was the subject of treaty agreements and enforcement was gradually increased by the presence of British naval ships. Additionally, the East India Company impinged on the Arabian Gulf trade with India and on the commercial activities of the Omani merchants in East Africa. The position within the Sultanate was further complicated by periods of internal dispute with conflicts over the Imamate question and the form of succession. These resulted in armed conflict between the major tribal groups of the Hinawi and Ghafiri. The decline was not arrested and eventually led to a rift between the Sultanate and Zanzibar, with the latter breaking away from the rule of Oman and further weakening Oman's economic base.

Introduction

At the beginning of the 19th century Britain began to become heavily involved in the affairs of the Sultanate, mainly through the Indian Government. This accounts for the large numbers of descriptions of exploration and travel undertaken during the period by British officials and military personnel. The involvement became economic as well as political and military when Britain, through the Indian Government, became responsible for the payment of the annual Canning Award which was supposed to be paid by Zanzibar as compensation to the Sultan for loss of revenues. The payment of the award was used as a threat on more than one occasion to ensure that the Sultan followed policies approved by Britain.

During the 19th century Oman became agitated and introspective, being completely immersed in internal power struggles between the Sultan and the Imam. The situation became such that the writ of the Sultan did not extend beyond the coastal regions; the interior, or Oman proper, was the province of the elected Imam and subject to its own internal power struggle. At the same time the Sultanate was subject to external pressures, particularly from Britain concerning the suppression of the slave trade and from the Wahhabis with designs on the Buraimi Oasis area.

The Canning Award, paid by Britain from 1871, amounted to 40,000 Maria Theresa dollars and formed a significant proportion of the Sultanate's budget. It did not, however, arrest the decline and in addition it made the ruler dependent on Britain and increased the tension between the coastal area and the interior. By the last quarter of the 19th century Oman had sunk into a subsistence economy, and the signing of the anti-slavery treaty by Sayyid Turki increased the economic problems and resulted in further significant migration to Zanzibar.

Internal unrest was the by-product of this general debility and armed attacks from the interior became a regular event. The Sultan retained his power only by 'buying off' the attackers, thus increasing his dependence on Britain and on the merchant community from whom the money had to be borrowed. In 1883 Sayyid Turki was succeeded by his son Sayyid Faisal whose government was so weak that only internal disputes in the interior prevented him from being overthrown.

Finally, in 1913, the tribes revived the office of Imam and a joint tribal revolt took place in May of that year. Faisal died in the month of October, to be succeeded by Taimur who had been cultivated by British officials and who was considered a suitable ruler. Despite the change of ruler it was only British forces in the form of Baluchi troops that prevented the Imamate forces taking Muscat. However, no follow-up action was allowed by British officials and the effort merely restored the status quo.

The situation lasted for five years until, at the instigation of the British Political Agent in Muscat, the Treaty of Sib was concluded in 1920. The treaty was an exchange of letters which had four articles relating to the people of Oman: that they would be at peace with the Sultan; they would have full right of movement and security in the coastal towns; and claims against them by the merchant community would be settled by Islamic law. In return the Sultan agreed not to interfere in tribal matters and the coastal population were to be permitted to enter Oman on lawful business or for commercial purposes. The treaty brought some measure of stability to the area, but it was an uneasy truce and the basic problems still remained unresolved.

The British government attempted to assist the Sultan in swallowing the blow to his pride that the treaty had caused, by means of a loan from the Indian Government to be repaid over ten years, and this was sufficiently large to pay off all of his debts. Despite the short-term services of a British financial adviser the Sultan was heavily in debt again by 1924. The following year saw the appointment of Bertram Thomas. He was allotted for five years to try to reorganize the financial structure and the administration, but he was no more successful than his predecessor, and Thomas spent much of his time travelling the country and writing for the Royal Geographical Society.

In 1932 Sultan Taimur abdicated. He was succeeded by Said bin Taimur who inherited a divided and heavily indebted country. A great deal has been written of his rule, which was characterized by a lack of development and by financial constraint, which did, however, clear the administration of all its debts. However, this financial constraint and an unwillingness to delegate power led to serious economic and social hardships and political unrest.

It had been a considerable achievement for Sultan Taimur to restore the country's finances – the result of prudent financial management and a determination to contain government expenditure. As a result, there was little development within the Sultanate despite the beginning of revenues from the export of oil. Early studies of Oman following the 1970 *coup d'état* had focused on the radical changes that had taken place but later research has questioned whether the pre-1970 regime had been as bad as conventional wisdom had deemed. Some studies are now arguing that the period since 1970 has been one of continuity in government matters rather than radical change.

The period of Sultan Taimur's rule was still beset by problems and worsening relations with the interior. The situation worsened following the Second World War when oil exploration began again in earnest and when Saudi Arabia revived her claim to the area around Buraimi Oasis. Thus began a period of real crisis, with the Imam flirting with Saudi

Arabia and trying to secure recognition for the independence of the Imamate through the Arab League and the United Nations. Although the Sultan succeeded in establishing a presence in the interior, armed revolt broke out in 1957 and was quelled only by the use of Trucial Oman Scouts led by British officers. The remnants of the dissidents were not defeated until 1959.

At last the Sultan ruled over a unified territory, the power of the Imamate had been broken, the Treaty of Sib was a casualty of war, and administrative control over the country was increased. However, the Sultan lost his opportunity to unite the country by returning to his palace at Salalah, continuing his policy of financial restraint and autocratic rule, maintaining a system of petty restrictions, and blocking all but the most modest attempts at progress. This was despite the production of oil which had come on stream in 1967, radically improving the financial position of the administration.

Once again unrest was the by-product, only this time it arose in the southern province of Dhofar in 1963. It began as a manifestation of political and social unrest among Dhofaris returning from employment in Oman's richer neighbours, Saudi Arabia and the United Arab Emirates. By 1967 the revolt had taken on a Marxist bias, and had become a revolutionary movement aimed at overthrowing the established order throughout the Gulf States and, over the years, the movement changed its name to reflect its changing objectives.

It soon became clear that the revolt could not be contained by the Sultan's forces, especially when it received backing from the newly independent People's Democratic Republic of Yemen along with Russian and Chinese involvement in terms of training facilities, equipment and logistics. As a result, the Sultanate was again dependent upon outside assistance for survival, with Britain providing training, equipment and seconding or contracting personnel to the Sultan's armed forces, and Iran and Jordan providing armed forces. In the case of Iran this was quite significant, being used by the Shah as a means of giving his forces battle experience and fulfilling his perceived role as policeman of the Gulf. This outside intervention succeeded in containing the revolution but the root causes were still present, and it was evident that the Sultan was not adaptable to the new situation and that the revolt would continue.

This resulted in the *coup d'état* of 1970, led by Said bin Taimur's son Qaboos who had been under virtual house arrest in Salalah since his return from British military training at Sandhurst. The timing was such that many of the Sultan's advisers were out of the country on summer leave and the coup was the work of a small number of carefully picked men. The strategic position of Oman, the perceived threat to the other

Gulf States, and the safety of Western oil supplies led Britain to indicate that it would not stand in the way of a change of ruler.

Despite recent research showing that the rule of Said bin Taimur was not as bad as first indicated in works written immediately after the coup, there was no doubt that the change of leadership brought about a new lease of life for Oman. The new ruler revoked the petty restrictions imposed by his father, and embarked upon a programme of social and economic modernization and development and government reform. One significant development was the Civil Aid Programme targeted at Dhofar province and this strategy had an immediate effect: the original grievances of the rebels were removed, leaving only the hard-core Marxist element with a real will to fight. The struggle was to last a further six years, relying on outside assistance, but the vital battle for the hearts and minds of the Dhofari people had been won, assisted by the fact that Sultan Qaboos has a Dhofari mother.

At the same time the Sultan was pursuing a policy of bringing Oman within reach of the modern world, by the introduction of education, health and welfare services, and a programme of economic expansion and social justice. In addition, Oman began to establish relations with her Arab neighbours and took steps to become a member of the international community. All of this was achieved by the use of oil revenues and deficit budgeting for a number of years. However, Oman has limited reserves and the revenue must be used effectively in order to achieve an economic and social stability which will last when the oil era has ended.

A great deal has been achieved since 1970, but Oman is not without problems, particularly in relation to the succession, future economic prospects and the stability of society. However, the Sultan has been successful to date in maintaining economic and social progress whilst pursuing a largely independent foreign policy as evidenced by the granting of access to military facilities to the United States. A major problem for the economy is the expenditure on defence which, although reduced of late, still accounts for about one-third of government expenditure and has had a detrimental effect on development policies at times of economic turndown.

Oman is a member of the Gulf Cooperation Council and it is here that the future should lie in regional terms. The GCC is still in the early stages of development and many of the initial goals have still to be achieved. However, in an extremely volatile region, and with Iran and Iraq as neighbours – both have had territorial designs on various islands in the Arabian Gulf and, in the case of Iraq also on the state of Kuwait – some form of regional collective security is essential. It is evident that collective security without outside assistance is beyond the scope of the member states, because of both the size of the populations and an apparent inability to agree on a common foreign and defence policy. Under these circumstances the Sultanate's defence expenditure and largely independent approach is understandable.

The economy has been assisted by the increase in gas reserves which have risen from 9.8 trillion cubic feet at the beginning of 1990 to 17 trillion cubic feet by the end of 1992 and, it is expected that the figure will increase substantially by the year 2000, with gas production becoming equal to that of oil. The policy of restricting gas consumption to internal use is being reversed with the introduction of a liquefied natural gas plant and the Far East as a potential export market. The company will be state owned but with minority private enterprise shareholding. Coal has also been found in southeastern Oman and an estimated 36 million tonnes will be sufficient to fuel a generating plant to supply the total electricity requirements of the region.

Present government policy is the creation of a national economy based on private enterprise with suitable incentives and tax advantages. The private sector has been encouraged by interest-free loans from the Oman Development Bank, exemption from import duties on equipment and raw materials required for production purposes, tariff protection and exemption from income tax for five years, renewable for a further five years. In addition, industrial estates have been developed for the establishment of factories and Oman now manufactures textiles, furniture, electrical goods, food and paper products and fabricated metal goods.

Prospects for the immediate future are good, with reserves of oil and gas providing a revenue well into the next century. Oman also has the advantage of an agricultural and fishing base with development potential, and mineral resources not found elsewhere in the Gulf. The future of the economy is not wholly dependent upon oil but development can be sustained only if economic diversification is maintained, thus enabling the economic and social aspirations of the population to be met.

The long and involved history of Oman gives rise to a large amount of literature covering its early history and its early exploration by Europeans. Much material has also appeared on the Dhofar War, and the present programmes of development and of investment in agriculture, copper mining and industrial diversification have resulted in a new wave of articles and books about the Sultanate. Recent events in the Horn of Africa, Iran, Afghanistan, Iraq and Kuwait, have highlighted the strategic significance of the country and ensured that it will remain in the forefront of regional politics and the international stage.

The bibliography

This bibliography makes no claim to completeness, but the material listed should provide a comprehensive picture of Oman for the general reader, the librarian or the researcher. It needs to be used in conjunction with the first edition as most of the material has not been transferred into this edition. Arrangement is by broad subject heading, and within that breakdown is alphabetical by author or title. Cross-references have been used where necessary to refer the user back to the main annotated entry. As is the case with all bibliographies, my aim has been objectivity, but inevitably a subjective element is present.

The compilation of a bibliography on Oman has presented certain problems in trying to present a comprehensive picture of the country. Some of the sections are rather brief, and a lack of material on subjects such as art galleries and museums or political parties has meant that no sections exist for them – the odd item available has been located in the most appropriate section. This apparent imbalance is easily understood by a reading of the introduction, which provides an essential background to the bibliography, where the historical outline of the Sultanate will serve to provide evidence for Oman's special characteristics.

As a deliberate policy all the general trade and national bibliographies have been excluded, and, in the main, only English-language, translated items, or items with an English summary have been listed. The treatment of the Omani presence in Zanzibar and East Africa has also been selective because it is not a feature of contemporary Oman: only major works have been listed or references made from items listed for other reasons. Similarly, the treatment of the Dhofar War has been kept within reasonable limits by the exclusion of the majority of newspaper reports, inclusion of which would have made the bibliography unwieldy and distorted its balance.

Only a selected number of treaties have been included, and these are normally to be found in their appropriate subject sections. However, a special section on treaties has been included for items showing the links between Great Britain and Oman and the problems of the suppression of the slave trade, and for internal treaties illustrating the delicate power structure of 19th- and early 20th-century Oman.

In the introduction I have alluded to the significance of the Gulf Cooperation Council both to Oman and the region. A certain number of items relating to Oman and its membership of the GCC have been included, particularly in the sections on economy and regional security. However, the section is extremely selective and the reader is directed to *Arab Regional Organizations*, Clio Press 1992, which has significant coverage of the GCC.

I cannot recommend too highly the use of other bibliographies listed

Introduction

in this volume, particularly the works by Shannon and Duster, and the general reference books, in particular the various Middle East yearbooks and the *Index Islamicus.*

Frank A. Clements
Plymouth, England
June 1994

The Country and its People

1 **Oman: the modernization of the Sultanate.**
Calvin H. Allen.   Boulder, Colorado: Westview Press, 1987. 142p.
bibliog.
An overview and analysis of Oman's political history which presents a good
introduction to the Sultanate following the 1970 *coup d'état*. Despite its title the
author does not present the present regime as modernist but seeks to demonstrate the
historical continuity of the regime and similarities in style between Sultan Qaboos
and his father in terms of reliance on expatriate advisers and personal isolation.
Although he gives a sympathetic description of Oman, the author is critical of the
problems of corruption and cult of personality and considers the specific problems of
the succession and regional alignments.

2 **A separate place.**
Calvin H. Allen.   *Wilson Quarterly*, vol. 11, no. 1 (1987), p. 48-63.
A review of the history of Oman from 750 to 1987, focusing on the influences and
impacts of various European nations on the politics, culture and society of Oman.
The economic importance of the oil industry from the 1950s to the 1980s is also dealt
with.

3 **Historical and cultural dictionary of the Sultanate of Oman and the
emirates of Eastern Arabia.**
John Duke Anthony.   Metuchen, New Jersey: Scarecrow Press, 1976.
135p. bibliog. (Historical and Cultural Dictionaries of Asia, no. 9).
A useful publication which provides, in dictionary form, a brief account of the
various issues, personalities and events of significance to the area. A handy
publication for the beginner because a great many of the available publications
assume prior knowledge and this dictionary helps provide a background.

4   **The Aramco reports on Al-Hasa and Oman, 1950-1955.**
London: Archive Editions, 1990. 120p. maps.

A collection of the various reports produced by the Arabian American Oil Company
which in the case of Oman centred on Saudi Arabian support for the Imamate and its
right to independence, and the Saudi Arabian claim to the Buraimi Oasis. Aramco
obviously had a vested interest in presenting the Saudi case as all the disputes had the
possible presence of oil at their centre.

5   **Oman: the reborn land.**
Frank. A. Clements.   London: Longman, 1980. 182p. maps.

Examines the Sultanate since 1970. However, a significant proportion of the book
deals with the historical and geographical background, which is more than just a
backcloth to present-day Oman. The major part of the book deals with post-1970
developments: the growth of an infrastructure, the legal system, social changes, health
services and communications. The Dhofar War is considered, although the emphasis
is on post-war reconstruction which will determine the future of the province.
Education and youth are seen as the future of Oman, and agriculture and fishing are
discussed at length because of their significance to the economy when oil revenues
run out. The future potential for oil, natural gas, and mineral resources is also
examined. The final chapter deals with the strategic position of Oman, its relations
with the People's Democratic Yemen Republic, Soviet influences and the question of
the Strait of Hormuz.

6   **Muscat: capital city of Oman.**
Ray L. Cleveland.   *Middle East Forum*, vol. 35, no. 9 (1959), p. 27-29.

A description of the city and everyday life prior to the urban development brought
about by the oil revenues and the subsequent development programmes.

7   **Concept Omanica: a comprehensive guide to Oman.**
Ruwi, Oman: International Printing Press, 1984. 162p. maps.

A general review of Oman covering all aspects of the country and its people. It also
includes an alphabetical and classified listing of companies with addresses, telephone
and telex numbers, key personnel and activities.

8   **Musandam.**
Paola M. Costa.   London: Immel, 1991. 252p.

A review of the scenery, unique culture, settlement patterns and traditional building
techniques of the Musandam Peninsula. The area is one of the least accessible parts of
the Sultanate and the area has developed separately from the rest of the Sultanate. This
is very informative, well illustrated and readable but not an in-depth academic study.

9   **The last corner of Arabia.**
Michael Darlow, Richard Fawkes.   London: Namara Publications,
1976. 128p. maps.

A book which emerged as a by-product of a documentary film, and as such is mainly
concerned with the author's experiences in Oman while filming. The book lacks any real
depth but it gives an introduction to the Sultanate and is supported by excellent
photographs.

10 **Forts of Oman.**
Walter Dinteman. London: Motivate Publishing, 1993. 128p.

A highly illustrated account of the role of the fort in Oman's history since the 16th century which covers Portuguese and Omani fortifications. The remains of these structures represent an important part of Oman's cultural heritage and the coloured photographs are an excellent pictorial record.

11 **Oman: a new dawn.**
T. Eigeland. *Aramco World Magazine* (May-June 1983). 40p.

This booklet, by a variety of authors, was produced to coincide with the visit of Sultan Qaboos to the United States. A series of articles cover all geographical aspects of the country. Topics include history of Oman, the terrain, development, the people, ports, frankincense, the *falaj* system [irrigation channels; plural, *aflaj*], craftsmen, seashells, and the mountains of Musandam.

12 **The Omanis: sentinels of the Gulf.**
Liesl Graz. London: Longman, 1982. 202p.

An examination of the strategic position of Oman and the possibility that Oman might be used as a land from which United States forces could operate in time of war. The work also has a section on pre-1970 Oman and the economic consequences of the ban on the slave trade and Western incursions into the trade normally carried out by Arab dhows. An extremely valuable section is that dealing with the daily life of women, with information on divorce, education and employment.

13 **Doctor in Arabia.**
Paul W. Harrison. London: Hale, 1943; New York: John Day, 1940. 303p.

The author was a missionary and the book reflects his calling. It is a valuable source of information on the interior and has descriptions of health conditions, social conditions and economics.

14 **Oman and its renaissance.**
Donald Hawley. London: Stacey International, 1977. Reprinted 1980.

This well-produced and lavishly illustrated book is informative and to be recommended as an introductory work. The author has successfully placed the renaissance of Oman in the context of the country's long history and sophisticated culture.

15 **This strange eventful history: memoirs of earlier days in the UAE and Oman.**
Edward Henderson. London; New York: Quartet Books, 1988. 184p. maps.

The author was one of the pioneers of southeastern Arabia in the pre-oil days, firstly as an employee of the Iraq Petroleum Company in 1948, and subsequently as a member of the British Foreign Office, becoming Britain's first ambassador to Qatar. The book focuses on two events in which the author played a crucial role. The first was the military action in 1984 to secure the Sultan's authority in interior Oman, primarily so that the oil company could explore the geologically promising Jabal Fahud area. Henderson was accompanied by a small force of Omani levies under a British officer together with a collection of shaikhs who had been deposed by the Imam and the expedition moved from village to village evicting the Imam's garrisons and extracting expressions of loyalty to the Sultan from the local authorities. The second incident was the expulsion of the Saudis from Buraimi Oasis. Having been seconded to the British Government as a political officer, Henderson negotiated a cease-fire and was responsible for overseeing the expulsion of the Saudi forces and their local supporters. The book is also valuable for an observation of life in the pre-oil era, the local personalities and events such as the return of the last pearling fleet to Dubai.

16 The Sultanate of Oman: a heritage.
Ann Hill, Darryle Hill. London: Longman, 1977. 168p. maps.

This book draws on a considerable period of time spent by the authors making documentary films in the Sultanate. It is excellently produced and beautifully illustrated, but the text is slight by comparison.

17 Muscat precis, 1892-1905.
India Foreign and Political Department. Simla, India: Government Printing Office, 1906. [n.p.].

A digest of official material relating to British interests in the Sultanate which, at that time, were administered through the Indian Government.

18 Minister in Oman: a personal narrative.
Neil McLeod Innes. Cambridge, England; New York: Oleander Press, 1987. 292p. maps. bibliog.

The author had been hired by Sultan Said bin Taimur to be his foreign minister from 1953 to 1958 and this book provides detailed accounts of the administration, the unification of Oman, and a survey of Omani society and politics. Innes was in charge of the Muscat Infantry but also had responsibility for the one school, the basic medical system and a variety of other duties not connected with foreign affairs. The bulk of the work deals with political and military aspects of the unification process, the revolt in the interior between 1957 and 1959, and the Buraimi Oasis dispute.

19 A new dawn?
Mark N. Katz. *Wilson Quarterly*, vol. 11, no. 1 (1987), p. 64-77.

An examination of the political leadership of Sultan Qaboos in the first seventeen years of his rule and the successful transformation of the country. Also considered is the strategic geographical position of Oman and the political implications of the control of the Strait of Hormuz.

20 Enchanting Oman.
Shirley Kay. London; Abu Dhabi: Motivate Publishing, 1992. 112p. map.

This well-illustrated introduction to Oman, covering all aspects of the country, is really designed for the general reader with an interest in the Sultanate. The strength of the book is in its 160 coloured photographs. The same author has also contributed the section on Oman (p. 60-85) in *The Arab Gulf Cooperation Council* (London; Abu Dhabi: Motivate Publishing, 1991. 166p.).

21 Oman: a new dawn.
J. Lawton, P. Lunde, B. Wace. *Aramco World Magazine*, vol. 34, no. 3 (1983), p. 1-41. map.

A review of the reawakening in Oman, this article covers history, geography, economic development, fortifications, the *falaj* system, naval protection of the Strait of Hormuz, traditional crafts and culture.

22 The Sultanate of Oman: a forgotten Empire.
John M. Mackenzie. *History Today*, vol. 34 (Sept. 1984), p. 34-39.

A survey of the history of Oman from the early seventeenth century: the ending of Portuguese rule, the Imamate and its power struggle with the Sultan's rule on the coast, the East African Empire, British suppression of the slave trade and subsequent political involvement in the Sultanate. The security of Oman's borders were determined by British power and British aid had assisted the modernization policies of the present regime.

23 Sultan in Oman: venture into the Middle East.
James Morris. London: Faber & Faber, 1957. 146p.

A readable history of Oman with geographical descriptions by province, together with a consideration of Omani society. Morris also deals with the question of oil exploration, the Buraimi Oasis dispute and the sovereignty of the Sultanate.

24 Dhofar – What made it different?
Miranda Morris. In: *Oman: economic, social and strategic developments*, edited by B. R. Pridham. London: Croom Helm, 1987, p. 51-38.

A study of the Dhofar province of Oman. It is different from the rest of Oman, with its early history bound up with that of Arabia on account of the trade in frankincense, myrrh and other gums and aromatics. This has led to the area and its inhabitants being clouded with myth and legend. This study deals with the very early history, frankincense and the early twentieth-century travellers, as well as the later twentieth-century travellers to the region. The article then focuses on present-day Dhofar and deals with the people, the geographical differences from the rest of Oman and the distinctive Dhofari languages. The point is made that many puzzles still remain to be dealt with in Dhofar, particularly with regard to the early history of the province and the origin of its inhabitants; these need to be resolved before the development process blurs the differences which still exist.

25 Oman.
Mark Nicholson, Khazam Merchant. *Financial Times* (London) (30 Nov. 1991), p. i-iv. map.

A special supplement containing a survey of Oman which covers the following topics: the need to diversify from oil; problems of excess banking capacity; defence and security policies and expenditure; foreign policy; and key facts on the oil and agriculture industries.

26 A day above Oman.

John Nowell. London: Motivate Publishing, 1992. 128p.

A pictorial representation of daily life in Oman, with landscapes, people, and photographs of everyday activities. The book has 179 coloured photographs with some striking aerial photographs.

27 Oman 1986.

Sultanate of Oman: Ministry of Information, 1986. 127p.

An introduction to the country and people of Oman, covering all aspects of Oman's history, geography and social conditions.

28 The Gulf States and Oman.

Christine Osborne. London: Croom Helm, 1977. 208p. maps.

The section on Oman, p. 130-55, begins with a brief historical introduction leading to the assumption of power by Sultan Qaboos. It goes on to deal with the importance of oil and minerals to the economy of the Sultanate and the moves towards industrial diversification and economic development. Osborne also briefly surveys improvements in education, health facilities, agriculture and communications, the war in Dhofar and the development in the provinces resulting from the Civil Aid Programme. Although not specifically related to Oman, the sections on social change among the Bedouin and on costume and jewellery are of interest.

29 Unknown Oman.

Wendell Phillips. London: Longman; New York: McKay, 1966. 319p. maps. bibliog.

The results of a large-scale expedition mounted by the author, which produced data on the social structure of Oman, the culture and customs, Ibadhism, health and archaeology.

30 Oman: change or continuity?

B. R. Pridham. In: *Arabia and the Gulf: From traditional societies to modern states*, edited by Ian Richard Netton. London: Croom Helm, 1986, p. 132-55.

This contribution challenges the hitherto accepted view that 1970 was a watershed in Omani history and that no development had been in place prior to the coup by Sultan Qaboos. The various claims and counter-claims are examined and the case is argued for the post-1970 era to be regarded as one of continuity rather than change. The general conclusion of the study is that conditions prior to 1970 were not as bad as conventional wisdom has deemed and that post-1970 has not been as good as has been made out 'and that there is a strong theme of continuity in governmental matters which reflects the new Oman image'.

31 Oman: economic, social and strategic developments.
Edited by B. R. Pridham.   London: Croom Helm, 1986. xx+234p.

Oman in an important country as far as the West is concerned both as an oil exporter and as a key ally because of its strategic position at the entrance to the Arabian Gulf and its control of the Strait of Hormuz. This work aims to provide an overview of recent economic, social, and political developments in Oman covering the historical and geographical background, the Dhofar War and the problems of the interior. Economic developments in the oil and non-oil sectors are considered as is Oman's contribution to the economic integration of the region through the Gulf Cooperation Council. The question of regional security is dealt with, particularly with regard to the close relationship with the United States. Education and cultural issues are also covered. References and annotations to specific contributions are to be found in the relevant sections of this bibliography.

32 Where time stood still: a portrait of Oman.
Duchess of St. Albans.   London: Quartet, 1980. 242p. maps.

This account of Oman is based on the author's journeys in the late 1970s, and is largely a personal impression of Oman and the changes that had taken place since the coup of 1970. It traces the history of the Sultanate from 3500 BC, and covers the internal tribal conflicts, the slave trade, foreign invasions and the Dhofar War. Consideration is also given to the socio-economic development programmes of the government, the agricultural sector, and the petroleum-based economy. The work is also interesting because of the accounts of social life based largely on the author's conversations with the Omani people throughout the Sultanate.

33 Dawn over Oman.
Pauline Searle.   Beirut: Khayat, 1975; London: Allen & Unwin, 1979. 146p. map.

An extremely readable book on Oman by an author who lived in the Sultanate for nine years and who obviously has a great affection for the country. The book covers Oman's early history, geography, natural history, society, culture and current developments. It succeeds in conveying a wealth of information in an entertaining manner. This is an extremely useful book which provides a good starting point, especially for anyone who knows little or nothing about the Sultanate.

34 Oman: politics and development.
Ian Skeet.   London: Macmillan, 1992. 195p. maps. bibliog.

A study of the transformation of Oman since 1970 into a modern oil-producing nation building on a base of rudimentary social and economic infrastructure. Following an introductory section, the first part of the book gives an impression of modern-day Oman, the winning of the Dhofar War and the early period of development which was undisciplined and, at times, chaotic. Section two deals with the economic development between 1976 and 1990, a period of controlled development in contrast with the earlier years. The second section also deals with Oman's position within the region and the growing relationship with the United States. Amongst other topics considered are the changes in Omani society, the role of women, conservation of the historical heritage and the environment. The final section deals with the decade to 2000, and considers the problems likely to be faced by the Sultanate, dealing particularly with water resources, economic diversification, employment, government, foreign affairs, and internal relations and the unity of the state. This is an extremely well-researched study of Oman over a period of two decades and follows on from the author's earlier work *Muscat and Oman: the end of an era.*

35   A speech by Sultan Qaboos bin Sai'd on the occasion of Oman's national anniversary.
Journal of the Gulf and Arabian Peninsula Studies, vol. 7, no. 26 (April 1981), p. 173-79.

The full Arabic text of a speech delivered by the Sultan of Oman in December 1980, in which he reviewed Oman's achievements in the 1970s. Areas covered include education, social services and administration. Development projects to diversify the economy are outlined and the speech also stresses the need to preserve Oman's culture and traditions.

36   The Arabs of Oman.
W. H. Storm, Paul W. Harrison.   *Moslem World*, vol. 24, no. 3 (1934), p. 262-70.

An account by two missionaries who were also responsible for medical provisions administered from a hospital in the Capital Area. It deals with the social aspects of Oman, the lack of basic public services and utilities, and the evils of slavery.

37   This is Oman.
London: Stacey International in co-operation with Dowa, Rogerson Ltd and Wadlaw Grosvenor Ltd, 1985. maps.

A volume of 235 photographs issued by the government of the Sultanate of Oman as part of the fifteenth National Day celebrations in November 1985. The photographs illustrate Omani topography, national culture and modern development, and are well produced.

38   Oman: the making of the modern state.
John Townsend.   London: Croom Helm, 1977. 212p. maps.

This was one of the first books to appear on the Sultanate following the 1970 coup, other than government publications and coffee-table books. The author was economic adviser to the Omani government in 1972-75, an important period of social and economic development. Because of its timing and the background of the author, this work is important for an understanding of the first five years of the reign of Sultan Qaboos. However, the author is highly critical of the mistakes that were made and of the early development of the new infrastructure, without giving a great deal of credit for social and economic improvements.

39   Oman.
Esther Webman.   In: *Middle East Contemporary Survey, 1981-82,* edited by Colin Legum, Haim Shaked, Daniel Dishan.   New York: Holmes and Meir, 1984, p. 510-18.

A review of the domestic and foreign affairs of Oman in 1981-83 with special coverage of economic affairs, security and the armed forces. Consideration is also given to the establishment of a 45-man Advisory Council to counter criticism of the Sultan's autocratic rule.

40 **Behind the veil in Arabia: Women in Oman.**
Unni Wikan. Baltimore, Maryland: Johns Hopkins University Press, 1982. 314p. bibliog.

The women used as a case-study for this work are those of Sohar. The author makes use of comparative evaluations with a theoretical underpinning, but reflecting her personal preferences and prejudices. The research has produced a significant amount of data about an area of society in which little accurate information is available. One interesting area of study is the analysis of the *burqa*, the distinctive facial mask worn by women, which is seen as enhancing women's beauty and erotic appeal, signalling adherence to the code of sexual modesty. However, further study needs to be made regarding its status in society, particularly in terms of the nature of authority and power in Arab society, and as an indicator of the autonomy of women in Omani society.

41 **The Imamate tradition of Oman.**
John C. Wilkinson. Cambridge, England: Cambridge University Press, 1987. 415p. maps.

This work focuses on interior Oman which was a tribal society governed by an elected Imam according to the rules of Ibadi Islam. The author examines the Ibadi tradition, the development of the Imam as a law enforcer and one feature of the Imamate, that of exclusive ownership of agricultural land with property documents attesting to such ownership. Also considered in detail is the establishment of Al Bu Sa'id rule and the struggles between the area controlled by the Sultan and the interior which aspired towards independence and courted links with Saudi Arabia and the Arab League. The book is extremely detailed and well researched, using classical Omani texts, official records and Western works on the area, and also reflects the author's involvement in the Sultanate over a period of time. The work is essential to any study of the Imamate and will be regarded as the definitive work on the history of the Imamate.

Oman and East Africa.
See entry no. 463.

Oman in General Works on the Middle East

42 **The United Arab Emirates: a modern history.**
Muhammad Morsy Abdullah.   London: Croom Helm; New York: Harper & Row, 1978. 365p. maps.

This authoritative work on the United Arab Emirates has various references to Oman, with whom the UAE shares a common frontier. The author considers the question of the Imamate and internal dissent in Oman, the problem of Saudi Arabian involvement and the Buraimi Oasis, and relations with Great Britain.

43 **Annual Register of World Events. Section V: the Middle East and North Africa.**
London: Longman; New York: St. Martin's Press. 1758- . annual.

This is an account of significant events in Oman and other countries of the Arab world; and is produced annually.

44 **The pirate coast.**
Charles Dalrymple Belgrave.   London: Bell, 1966; Beirut: Librairie du Liban, 1972. 200p. maps. bibliog.

A useful introduction to the history of the lower Gulf States, including Oman, dealing with the arrival of the Portuguese, increasing European influence and internal disturbances in Oman. The work is based on the diary of Francis Lock, Commander of HMS *Eden*, and discusses naval operations in the area during th period 1818-21.

45 **The past and present connection of England with the Persian Gulf.**
Thomas Jewel Bennett.   *Journal of the Royal Society of Arts*, vol. 50 (13 June 1902), p. 634-52.

A detailed survey of British involvement in the Gulf, dealing with the role of the Indian government as the authority for British policy in the area. Also considered are the presence of the Portuguese, Anglo-French rivalry and the naval actions against 'pirates' operating from the Trucial States.

46 The Middle East in global strategy.
Edited by Aurel Brown.   London: Mansell; Boulder, Colorado: Westview Press, 1987. 274p.

A study of the strategic interests of the superpowers in the Middle East as part of the link between international politics and strategy. Oman is largely dealt with in the fourth part of the book *The Gulf: the other Middle East* which covers the geopolitical impact of the Iranian revolution on the Gulf, the Soviet Union and the Gulf, and United States strategic concerns in the Gulf region.

47 Britain in the Indian Ocean.
Alistair Buchan.   *International Affairs* (London), vol. 42, pt. 2 (1966), p. 184-93.

The author examines British interests in the area – including the Persian Gulf, Oman and the Yemen – in relation to Britain's role as a former world power. He concludes that the Gulf States should be encouraged to become less dependent on Britain or else Arab nationalism of the Egyptian brand could spread there. Buchan also stresses the necessity for the various states to settle their border disputes.

48 The Gulf: A portrait of Kuwait, Qatar, Bahrain and the UAE.
John Bulloch.   London: Century Books, 1984. 224p. bibliog.

This is a wide-ranging analysis of the region, by the Middle East correspondent of the *Daily Telegraph*, which covers the history of the region, the effects of oil revenues on the economic and social structure, and the problems associated with migrant labour. Despite its title, there are numerous references to Oman, particularly with regard to early European interests through the arrival of the Portuguese, British interests in the area and the historical importance of Oman as a mercantile nation. Also considered are the Dhofar War and relations with Saudi Arabia especially in connection with boundary disputes and the Buraimi Oasis.

49 Britain, India and the Arabs.
Briton Cooper Busch.   Berkeley, California; London: University of California Press, 1971. 522p. maps. bibliog.

Primarily concerned with the Arab revolt, the peace settlement and the conflicting interests of the British Foreign Office and the Indian government. Relations with the other Gulf States and Oman are also considered. The work is useful for an understanding of the level of British involvement.

50 Military forces in the Persian Gulf.
Alvin J. Cottrell, Frank Bray.   Washington, DC: Georgetown University, Center for Strategic and International Studies with Sage Publications, 1978. 71p. map. (Washington Papers, vol. vi, no. 60).

Pages 47-50 outline the strength of Oman's armed forces and of foreign military personnel in the Sultanate.

51 **The Middle East reader.**
Edited by Michael Curtis. New Brunswick, New Jersey; Oxford, England: Transaction Books, 1986. 485p.
This is a selection of articles drawn from the *Middle East Review*. Amongst other topics, they cover: the Middle East political environment, economic factors, the role of the superpowers, and relations with the external world. The articles are mainly general in nature and relevance to Oman is as part of the regional context.

52 **Southern Arabia.**
Brian Doe. London: Thames & Hudson, 1971. 267p. maps. bibliog.
A well-illustrated account of the archaeology and early history of the area, with references to present-day Oman.

53 **Money rush**
Andrew Duncan. London: Hutchinson, 1979. 384p. map.
This work has a large number of references to Oman, dealing in particular with the Dhofari rebellion, relations with Saudi Arabia, the Buraimi Oasis dispute and Iranian military assistance. Also considered are the history of the Sultanate, the reign of Sultan Said bin Taimur, and the *coup d'état* of 1970 with the subsequent upsurge of economic and social development. A chapter entitled 'Sweets for the children' includes an interview with Sultan Qaboos and some of the ministers concerned with development and social progress.

54 **The United Arab Emirates: an economic and social survey.**
K. G. Fenelon. London: Longman, 1976. 2nd ed. 164p. map. bibliog.
Although primarily about the United Arab Emirates the work includes a consideration of Oman as part of Trucial Oman and also deals with the question of the Buraimi Oasis dispute.

55 **The Middle East: a history.**
Sydney Nettleton Fisher. Westminster, Maryland: Knopf, 1978; London: Routledge & Kegan Paul, 1971. 2nd ed. 749p. maps. bibliog.
Oman is considered in relation to the development of Islam and its split into two main branches. Greater coverage is given in the section entitled 'Oil and Arabia' and in passages on inter-Arab relations, such as the development of the Arab League.

56 **The turbulent Gulf.**
Liesl Graz. London; New York: I. B. Tauris, 1990. 312p. bibliog.
This work examines the Arabian Gulf during the period 1982-90 but was finished prior to the Iraqi invasion of Kuwait. The author presents the case for considering the Gulf States as being diverse in nature, with Oman regarded as a special case because of its cultural, religious and political traditions. In considering the Iraq–Iran war the Shi'i population of Oman did support the Khomeini regime but there were no open demonstrations of support. The work concludes with a consideration of the role of the Gulf Cooperation Council and the future of the region. Appendices provide vital statistics and the text of the UN resolution 598 calling for a ceasefire between Iran and Iraq.

57 A handbook of Arabia.

Great Britain. Admiralty, Naval Intelligence Division. London: HM
Stationery Office, 1917. 709p. maps. (Geographical Handbook Series).

Chapter IX (p. 237-84) treats Muscat and Oman. Information is given on products,
population and social structure, currency and geography.

58 The affairs of Arabia.

Great Britain. Foreign and Commonwealth Office. Edited by Robin L.
Bidwell. London: Cass, 1971. reprint. 2 vols.

An indispensable reference source and a basic tool for any consideration of British
involvement in the affairs of the Sultanate. The reprint has a valuable introductory
section by Robin Bidwell which discusses the text, gives biographical outlines of
people mentioned and provides an overview of events and items covered in the book.
However, specific documents can be located easily only if their full details are
known, otherwise a detailed examination of the contents list is necessary.

59 The Trucial States.

Donald Hawley. London: Allen & Unwin, 1970. 379p.

An excellent work which deals with Oman as part of the Trucial States, though it
pre-dates many of the significant political events that have taken place in the region.
Oman is given the least amount of coverage as the work is mainly concerned with the
countries now known as the United Arab Emirates.

60 The Persian Gulf States.

Rupert Hay. Washington, DC: Middle East Institute, 1959. 160p.

A consideration of the whole Gulf region, with sections on geography, history and the
economy. The author was British Resident in Muscat, 1941-49.

61 Farewell to Arabia.

David Holden. London: Faber & Faber, 1967; New York: Walker,
1966. 268p. maps.

Although mainly concerned with events in the present-day Yemen, the book gives a
detailed account of relations between Oman and Great Britain and of the internal
situation in the Sultanate. The author was chief foreign correspondent of the *Sunday
Times* and an outstanding journalist and writer on the Arab World.

62 The Gulf: Arabia's western approaches.

Molly Izzard. London: Murray, 1979. 327p. map.

An excellent introduction to the Gulf area, with numerous references to the Sultanate
of Oman which are both informative and readable. The work considers the following
aspects of Oman: general history, including Zanzibar; Omani–Wahabi rivalry; the
slave and arms trades; oil production; early health services; and social change.

13

63 **Arabia, the Gulf and the West.**
John Barrett Kelly.   London: Weidenfeld & Nicolson, 1980. 530p.
maps. bibliog.

A critical examination of the governments and peoples of the Arabian Gulf, the uses
to which oil wealth is being put and attitudes towards the West. Argues that Britain
had committed an act of folly in abandoning the Gulf in 1971, the inadequacy of
United States policy in attempting to fill the vacuum and the corrupting effects of oil
wealth on the societies of the Middle East. Oman is dealt with throughout the book,
but Chapter Three deals specifically with Oman and covers the problems of the
Imamate, internal unrest and the Dhofar War, and relations with Saudi Arabia and the
People's Democratic Republic of Yemen (PDRY). Oman's relations with Great
Britain, Iran, Iraq, Saudi Arabia and the United Arab Emirates are examined, as are
prospects for the future of the Sultanate which are coloured by the Marxist presence
in the PDRY and possible future internal disturbances.

64 **Britain and the Persian Gulf, 1795-1880.**
John Barrett Kelly.   London: Oxford University Press, 1968. 911p.
maps. bibliog.

An indispensable work for any consideration of Britain's role in the Gulf during the
period in question. Although wider in coverage than the present-day Sultanate, past
events in the area were very interrelated and British policy was a crucial element in
the politics and history of the region.

65 **The United Arab Emirates: unity in fragmentation.**
Ali Mohammed Khalifa.   London: Croom Helm; Boulder, Colorado:
Westview Press, 1979. 246p.

Although primarily concerned with the United Arab Emirates, this book has sections
of relevance to Oman, particularly in its discussions of the Dhofari rebellion, the
question of the Imamate, territorial disputes over the Buraimi Oasis, and regional
relationships in general.

66 **A short history of the Middle East, from the rise of Islam to
modern times.**
George E. Kirk.   London: Methuen, 1948. 301p. maps. bibliog.

Covers the early history of the area and, in particular, the rise of British power in the
Gulf States, Oman and Aden.

67 **The Middle East in world affairs.**
George Lenczowski.   London; Ithaca, New York: Cornell University
Press, 1980. 4th ed. 863p. maps. bibliog.

Useful for a study of Oman in relation to the strategic importance of the area and
relations with Yemen.

68 **Encyclopaedia of Islam.**
Edited by B. Lewis, J. Schacht.   Leiden, The Netherlands: Brill;
Atlantic Highlands, New Jersey: Humanities Press, 1953- . in progress.

Indispensable for any study of the Middle East, with many relevant articles, each contributed by an expert. Particularly relevant for a study and understanding of the various Islamic sects, including Ibadhism.

69 **The Persian Gulf: an introduction to its peoples, politics and economics.**
David E. Long.   Boulder, Colorado: Westview Press, 1967. 172p. maps.

Examines US policies towards the Gulf States, particularly in relation to the politics and social structure of the area. These policies had undergone a radical change following the 1973 oil crisis which brought recognition of the strategic significance of the area.

70 **The Middle East: a social geography.**
Stephen Hemsley Longrigg, J. Jankowski.   London: Duckworth, 1970. 2nd ed. 291p. maps. bibliog.

Considers the early history of South Arabia and the Persian Gulf States, including Oman.

71 **Gazetteer of the Persian Gulf, Oman and central Arabia.**
J. G. Lorimer.   Farnborough, England: Gregg International, 1970. 4693p. maps. bibliog. (6 vol. reprint of original published in 2 vols, Calcutta, 1915).

A significant study of the area, although Oman forms only a section of the work. It was originally designed as a working tool for British officials in the Gulf and as such is easy to use because of the excellent indexing. The historical section covers three volumes in the reprint, dealing first with the area as an entity, the individual states and a series of appendixes on slave trading, gun running, etc. However, it should be borne in mind that this was an official work for use by officials and the viewpoints expressed are as seen through British eyes with the object being the furtherance of British policy interests in the region. The work was commissioned by Lord Curzon, Viceroy of India, and the compilation was highly selective and misrepresented the history of the Arabian Peninsula and the Gulf. Nevertheless, as this work was based on the relevant source documents the view purveyed has prevailed.

72 **The Arab state.**
Edited by Giacomo Luciani.   London: Routledge, 1990. 484p.

This study attempts to provide a balanced and convincing view of the complex reality of contemporary Arab politics, arguing against the widely held view that Arab states are arbitrary creations lacking historical or present legitimacy. Oman is dealt with throughout the text particularly in relation to Ibadhism and the Imamate, the use of migrant labour and development policies.

73 **The Middle East: a political and economic survey.**
Edited by Peter Mansfield. Oxford, England: Oxford University Press, 1980. 5th ed. 448p. maps.

A significant work divided into three main sections, the first introductory, the second consisting of thematic studies, and the third a country-by-country survey. The first section provides a very useful introduction to the region as a whole, giving a brief historical and political outline, treating religious questions and the various Islamic sects, and offering a brief economic and social survey, and offering a brief economic and social survey. The country-by-country survey covers all aspects of Oman, its history, geography, society, agriculture and oil industry.

74 **The Middle East and North Africa.**
London: Europa Publications. 1948- . annual.

One of the standard reference tools, and for many years the only one available. It is divided into four parts, the first being a general survey containing articles on various aspects of the Middle East. The second section deals with the work of organizations in the area, including the various operations of the United Nations and other bodies. The third section deals exclusively with the various countries, covering their physical and social geography, history, economic affairs and statistics, and providing a directory and a short bibliography. The last section covers other reference material, and includes a brief biographical section, details concerning calendars and weights and measures, research bodies, and a listing of general bibliographies.

75 **Middle East Yearbook.**
London: Middle East Magazine, 1977- . annual.

The four sections of this reference book cover various background features, the Middle East in relation to the rest of the world, the economy of the area and give a country-by-country survey. The country survey comprises the bulk of the volume and is prefaced by an introductory article giving an outline of the history, economy, etc. Brief facts are then given on geography, climate, population, education, public services, etc., while statistics are provided on production, oil, and budgets. The work is enhanced by numerous maps, showing oil production and refining, agriculture, population and so on. The specialist articles are also of value.

76 **The countries and tribes of the Persian Gulf.**
Samuel Barrett Miles. London: Harrison & Sons, 1919. Reprinted Frank Cass, 1966. 644p.

One of the earliest standard works on the area, particularly for the early history of Oman when the Sultanate had a great deal of influence in the area, though even then it was on the wane. The author was British Consul at Muscat during the period 1872-87, and would have had an important role in the country, because his post was influential and powerful and reinforced by British subsidies to the regime.

77 **The Cambridge Encyclopaedia of the Middle East and North Africa.**
Edited by Trevor Mostyn. Cambridge, England: Cambridge University Press, 1988. 504p. maps. bibliog.

A major reference work on the countries of the Middle East and North Africa, organized in six parts and covering: Lands and people; History; Societies and economies; Culture; Countries; and Inter-state relations. The country survey of Oman is on pages 395-99 but there are references also elsewhere in the text.

78 **Remarks on the tribes, trade and resources around the shore line of the Persian Gulf.**
Lewis Pelly. *Transactions of the Bombay Geographical Society*, vol. 17 (1863), p. 32-112.

Deals mainly with the conduct of trade and the development of markets run by Indian traders in Persia and the Arabian Gulf States. The Indian community was the main merchant sector in Oman and this is still the case in contemporary Oman.

79 **The Arabian Peninsula in modern times: a historiographical survey.**
John Everett Peterson. *American Historical Review*, vol. 96 (Dec. 1991), p. 1435-49.

A survey of the historical development of the Arabian Peninsula states and the literature which has appeared on the region. Until recent times this consisted largely of the accounts of explorers or government officials, principally British, stationed in the area. Oman is dealt with in the context of the split between the Imamate and the coastal region, the weakening of the country through the loss of the East African Empire and the significance of oil. Brief assessments of the material available on each of these subjects are included. The author concludes that the foundation of the region's modern history is still *terra incognita* and that exploration is needed to 'sort out the correct balance between change and continuity and to reach reliable conclusions about the nature of state formation in the Arabian Peninsula'.

80 **Neglected Arabia 1892-1962.**
Reformed Church of America. Farnham Common, England: Archive Research, 1988. 4600p. 8 vols.

This is a reprint of the complete run of the journal of the Arabian Mission of the Reformed Church of America, and provides valuable insight into the history of the Gulf region. The journal reveals something of the social, medical and educational development of the area. The activities of the Mission are particularly relevant to Oman prior to 1970, especially in terms of medical facilities.

81 **Britain and the Arab States: a survey of Anglo-Arab relations.**
M. V. Seton-Williams. London: Luzac, 1948. 330p. maps. bibliog.

This useful handbook for a consideration of British interests in the area, including Oman, is supplemented by documents and maps.

82 The Middle East: Oil, conflict and hope.
Edited by A. L. Udovitch. Lexington, Massachusetts: Lexington Books, 1976. 557p.

This work is volume 10 in a series entitled 'Critical choices for Americans' aimed at understanding and projecting present trends to assist in the formation of United States policies. Oman is considered at relevant points throughout the text covering economic growth, population, its role in inter-Arab relations and relations with Iran and Saudi Arabia. Political developments are covered in the contribution entitled 'Saudi Arabia and the Gulf States' by J. B. Kelly which is annotated elsewhere in this bibliography (see item no. 741).

83 Area handbook for the peripheral states of the Arabian Peninsula.
United States, Department of the Army. Washington, DC: Government Printing Office, 1971. maps.

Part of a series produced by Stanford Research Institute for the American army. Although dated 1971, the compilation was made prior to the coup of 1970. A separate chapter devoted to Oman deals with the political geography, population, social structure and the economy.

84 Area handbook for the Persian Gulf States.
United States, Department of the Army. Washington, DC: Government Printing Office, 1977. 448p. maps. bibliog.

A comprehensive coverage of the Gulf States, surveying all aspects of life in the area. The treatment is by area and topic, then country by country. The section on Oman is on pages 341-409.

85 The kingdom of oil: the Middle East, its people and its power.
Ray Vicker. New York: Scribner, 1974; London: Hale, 1975. 264p.

Brief consideration is given to the development of oil concessions in Oman and the government's growing control of Petroleum Development (Oman) Ltd. Reference is also made to the Dhofari rebellion and the problem that this type of insurrection poses for the future of the oil industry.

86 The Near East since the First World War.
M. E. Yapp. London: Longman, 1990. 528p. bibliog.

Yapp covers the modern history of the area, with treatments of Egypt, Iraq, Iran, Israel, Turkey and all of the states of the Arabian Peninsula, including Oman. This is a useful introductory survey of each of the countries covered.

87 The making of the modern Gulf States: Kuwait, Bahrain, Qatar, the United Arab Emirates and Oman.
Rosemarie Said Zahlan. London; Boston, Massachusetts: Unwin Hyman, 1989. 180p.

An extremely readable account of the contemporary socio-economic and political developments in the Gulf States, including Oman. This is a useful digest of the secondary studies available on the area and attempts to provide a coherent summing of the contemporary scene in Arabia. Oman is specifically dealt with between pages 106 and 115.

88   **The golden milestone: reminiscences of pioneer days fifty years ago in Arabia.**
       Samuel Marinus Zwemer, J. Continue.   New York: Fleming H. Ravell, 1938. 157p.

An account of the missionary activities of the Dutch Reformed Church of America which provided the only medical treatment in pre-war Oman. The general perception of Arabia is somewhat limited.

Exploration and Travel

General

89 Travellers in Arabia.
Robin L. Bidwell.   London: Hamlyn, 1976. 224p. maps.

A work which brings together the major explorations of Arabia, covering Oman on pages 192-220. A valuable introduction for the general reader and a useful refresher for the specialist.

90 Far Arabia: explorers of the myth.
Peter Brent.   London: Weidenfeld & Nicolson, 1977. 239p. maps. bibliog.

An extremely readable study of exploration in Arabia, including Oman. It discusses the effects of explorer's accounts on the Western image of Arabia, an image which was often far removed from reality.

91 Explorers of Arabia: from the renaissance to the end of the Victorian era.
Zahra Freeth, H. V. F. Winstone, H. Victor.   London: Allen & Unwin, 1978. 308p. maps.

A collection of extracts illustrating the travels of nine explorers of Arabia. Two are of relevance to Oman: Carsten Niebuhr (p. 61-90), and William Gifford Palgrave (p. 153-92).

92 Travels in Oman: On the track of the early explorers.
Philip Ward.   Cambridge, England: Oleander Press, 1987. 571p. maps.

A compendium of travel accounts on Oman, this volume covers the works of the significant travellers, explorers, adventurers and wanderers. The opening chapter reviews contributions from travellers who visited Muscat and the immediate environs but not the interior. The explorers and travellers covered are Bent, Cole, Cox, Eccles, Geary, Haines, Hamdani, Hamerton, Ibn Battuta, Kaempfer, Loyd, Miles, Pengelly, Stiffe, Bertram Thomas, Ward, Wellsted and Whitelock. The book is organized by region covering the Capital Area, east from Muscat, Sharqiyah, Jabal Al Akhdar and Dhahirah, Batinah coast, Musandam Peninsula and the Dhofar province.

Before 1900

93 **Explorations of the frankincense country, southern Arabia.**
J. Theodore Bent. *Geographical Journal*, vol. 6, no. 2 (1895), p. 109-34.
This account of exploration in Dhofar covers all aspects of the province, including geography, social structure, crafts, flora and fauna, and history. The article also gives a useful background sketch of the history of the Sultanate of Oman in general.

94 **Bibliographical notes on European accounts of Muscat 1500-1900.**
Robin L. Bidwell. *Arabian Studies*, vol. 4 (1978), p. 123-59.
A very valuable guide to the various accounts of explorations, travel and observations on Muscat during the period in question.

95 **Account of an overland journey to Meskat and the 'free mountains' of Oman.**
C. S. D. Cole. *Transactions of the Bombay Geographical Society*, vol. 8 (Jan. 1847-April 1848), p. 106-19.
Cole's account of travel in the area is particularly interesting because of the visit to the Jabal Al Akhdar (Green Mountains) which were largely independent from the coastal area and have a history of separate development.

96 **The Kooria Mooria Islands.**
Stafford B. Haines. *Nautical Magazine*, vol. 26 (1857), p. 385-89.
One of the earliest descriptions of these islands off the southern Oman coast, which were then of economic importance as a source of guano fertilizer.

97 **Memoir of the south-east coasts of Arabia.**
Stafford B. Haines. *Journal of the Royal Geographical Society*, vol. 15 (1845), p. 104-60.
The author was an officer in the Indian Navy, in charge of surveying the Oman and South Arabian coasts during the 1829-35 period These detailed accounts of the surveys represent early European viewpoints on the Sultanate of Oman at that time. Much of the account is concerned with the recording of details of relevant to naval and general shipping requirements.

98   **Second part of Captain S. B. Haines' memoir of the south and east coasts of Arabia with his remarks on winds, currents etc.**
Stafford B. Haines.   *Transactions of the Bombay Geographical Society*, vol. 11 (July 1852-Dec. 1853), p. 60-211.
A continuation of the previously cited work (q.v.).

99   **A new account of the East Indies, being the observations and remarks of Captain Alexander Hamilton, who spent his time there from the year 1688 to 1723, trading and travelling, by sea and land, to most of the countries and islands of commerce and navigation between the Cape of Good Hope, and the island of Japan.**
Alexander Hamilton.   Edinburgh: J. Masmon, 1727. 2 vols. maps.
The first volume contains an interesting account of early 18th-century Muscat and the position of the Imams of interior Oman and was used extensively by Lorimer (q.v.). Various reprints have appeared over the years.

100   **Oman through English eyes.**
Ruth Mallas.   *Middle East*, no. 130 (Aug. 1985), p. 52-53.
A description of British travellers to Oman in the 19th and early 20th centuries, covering the travels of James Wellsted, Major Percy Cox and Bertram Thomas.

101   **Across the Green Mountains of Oman.**
Samuel Barrett Miles.   *Geographical Journal*, vol. 18, no. 5 (1901), p. 465-98. map.
An extremely detailed and informative account of a journey made by the author in 1876 across the Jabal Al Akhdar, or Green Mountains, which lie sixty miles southwest of Muscat at the centre of the mountain chain which begins in the Musandam Peninsula. The article gives a very good description of the area in terms of physical geography, and also covers the local wildlife, water resources and economy. The author also considers the history of the tribes of the Jabal Al Akhdar and deals with the architectural features of their houses and fortifications. Although over a hundred years old, this detailed article is still of great value as an early record of exploration.

102   **Journal of an excursion in Oman.**
Samuel Barrett Miles.   *Geographical Journal*, vol. 7, no. 5 (1896), p. 522-37.
Another useful account of exploration in the interior, full of information and constituting a good background for an understanding of contemporary Oman.

103   **On the border of the great desert: a journey in Oman.**
Samuel Barrett Miles.   *Geographical Journal*, vol. 36, no. 2 (1910),
p. 159-78; vol. 36, no. 4 (1910) p. 405-25. map.
This account is of a journey made twenty-five years before publication. The two
papers contain a wealth of detail on the populations, social structure, flora and fauna,
culture and topography and represent one of the first real accounts of Oman's interior.

104   **The coast of Arabia felix from the journal of H.M.S. *Levan.***
W. F. W. Owen.   *Nautical Magazine*, vol. 26 (1857), p. 180-91.
A topographical account of the coastline as observed from a British Royal Navy ship
cruising off Aden and the Dhofar province. Provides a variety of information as
recorded in the ship's log, with precise locations for each observation.

105   **Narrative of voyages to explore the shores of Africa, Arabia,**
Madagascar.
W. F. W. Owen.   London: Bentley, 1833. 2 vols. maps.
The voyages were largely concerned with mapping the coastlines and hydrographic
work. This account includes material on the coast of Oman.

106   **Personal narrative of a year's journey through central and eastern**
Arabia, 1862-63.
William Gifford Palgrave.   London: Macmillan, 1868. Reprinted,
Farnborough, England: Gregg International, 1969. 421p. maps.
This account of a journey financed partly by Napoleon III was well received on
publication. Doubt has since been cast on the veracity of the account and on its
descriptions of interior Oman. Wendell Phillips remarked that 'all places where he
stayed have apparently disappeared from the maps'.

107   **Embassy to the eastern courts of Cochin China, Siam and Muscat;**
in the U.S. sloop-of-war *Peacock* . . . during the years 1832-3-4.
Edmund Roberts.   New York: Harper, 1837. 432p.
An account of his travels written by the first US representative to Oman. One result
was the first American treaty with Muscat in 1833. See also *Treaties and*
international acts of the United States of America, item no. 441.

108   **Narrative of a journey into the interior of Oman.**
James Raymond Wellsted.   *Journal of the Royal Geographical*
Society, vol. 7 (1837), p. 102-13.
One of the earliest accounts of European exploration in the interior of Oman
presenting an interesting series of observations on the topography and peoples of the
Imamate.

109 **Travels in Arabia.**
James Raymond Wellsted. London: John Murray, 1938. 2 vols. maps.

The author was the first European to visit the Green Mountains and the interior of Oman – in the early 1830s – and this is an account of his travels. The book deals with the geography of the area and discusses life in Oman, the dhow trade, Oman's involvement in the slave trade and Oman's relations with the outside world.

110 **Arabia: the cradle of Islam; studies in the geography, people and politics of the peninsula, with an account of Islam and mission work.**
Samuel Marinus Zwemer. New York: Fleming H. Ravell, 1900; London: Oliphant, 1912. 634p. maps. bibliog.

The author was a missionary of the Dutch Reformed Church of America, which was instrumental in providing much-needed medical assistance to Oman. The book covers life in Arabia as seen through the eyes of a missionary.

20th century

111 **Oman: land of frankincense and oil.**
Robert Azzi. *National Geographic*, vol. 143, no. 2 (1973), p. 204-29. map.

A well-illustrated introduction to the process of modernization in the Sultanate of Oman, this article is designed for the general reader.

112 **Some excursions in Oman.**
Percy Z. Cox. *Geographical Journal*, vol. 66, no. 3 (1925), p. 193-227.

An excellent account of travels undertaken by the author at the turn of the century whilst serving in Muscat as Political Agent of the government of India. His first journey was from Abu Dhabi to Buraimi, then across the desert side of the Jabal Al Akhdar, and finally to Muscat through the Wadi Samail. The second journey was from Ras al-Khaimah to Buraimi, from where he travelled directly to the coast at Shinas and then along the coastline of Sohar. The article also deals briefly with the natural history of the Sultanate.

113 **The Sultanate of Muscat and Oman, with a description of a journey into the interior undertaken in 1925.**
G. J. Eccles. *Journal of the Royal Central Asian Society*, vol. 14, pt. 1 (1927), p. 19-42. map.

An interesting account of the western Hajar mountain range by an Indian army officer in command of the Muscat levies, acting as escort to the D'Arcy Exploration Company on survey.

114 A visit to Trucial Oman.
Harry Luke. *Geographical Magazine* (Sept. 1954), p. 243-47.

A readable, but not detailed, account of travels in the United Arab Emirates and the Buraimi Oasis of Oman.

115 The sand kings of Oman.
Raymond O'Shea. London: Methuen, 1947. 209p. maps.

An interesting account of the Sultanate written by a Royal Air Force Officer during a period of duty in Oman. It is useful because it gives an account of the last vestiges of the slave trade, observations on the fishing industry and the fishing communities, and a description of the flora and fauna. The book covers the period between 1944 and 1945 and is a day-to-day account of O'Shea's life in the Sultanate. He makes many interesting observations on the social life, customs, inter-tribal rivalry and border disputes.

116 The Empty Quarter, being a description of the great south desert of Arabia known as Rub' al-Khali.
H. St. John Philby. London: Constable; Norwood, Pennsylvania: Norwood Editions, 1933. 433p. maps.

Philby's account of his explorations from east to west across the Empty Quarter is one of the classic descriptions of this ill-defined border between Oman and Saudi Arabia.

117 Rub' al Khali.
H. St. John B. Philby. *Geographical Journal*, vol. 81, pt. 1 (1933), p. 1-26.

This further account of Philby's travels in the Empty Quarter is of topographical and anthropological interest.

118 The Southern gates of Arabia: a journey into the Hadramaut.
Freya Stark. London: John Murray, 1936. 328p.

An illustrated account of general history and travel mainly in the Hadramaut, but with numerous references to Oman, especially the province of Dhofar.

119 Across the Empty Quarter.
Wilfred P. Thesiger. *Geographical Journal*, vol. 111, pt. 1 (1948), p. 1-21.

An account of the explorer's journey from Salalah in Dhofar province across the Rub' al-Khali to Liwa and back, a distance of some 2,000 miles. The journey was undertaken between October 1946 and May 1947 on behalf of the Middle East Anti-Locust Unit. The account is interesting because the travel was by camel and represents an early authoritative narrative of exploration in an area previously closed to Europeans.

120 **Arabian sands.**
Wilfred P. Thesiger. London: Allen Lane, 1977. 347p. maps.

This must rank as one of the finest travel books about Arabia. While being extremely readable, it is full of detailed information about the topography, flora and fauna and society of the area. Thesiger's journeys were made by camel among Bedouin who had not been exposed to the effects of an oil-based economy or urbanization, and who maintained a society based on personal freedom and self-discipline. The journeys were made when Oman was a closed society, especially as far as the Western world was concerned, and so Thesiger's work has additional significance on that account.

121 **Desert borderlands of Oman.**
Wilfred P. Thesiger. *Geographical Journal*, vol. 116, nos. 4-6 (1980), p. 137-71. map.

One of the classic travel accounts of Oman, based on a journey undertaken during the years 1948-49. The journey began at Abu Dhabi and continued westwards to the Liwa Oasis and then southwards to the quicksand area of Umm al-Samim. From there the author travelled through the Gharbaniat sands and across the Hugaf depression to Masirah Island. The second part of the journey was along the eastern Hajar and then to Muwaigh by way of the edges of the Oman mountains. The main objective was to collect data for a more accurate mapping of the area by Royal Geographical Society cartographers. As one would expect, the article is full of detailed information and observations, presented in an extremely readable and entertaining manner.

122 **A further journey across the Empty Quarter.**
Wilfred P. Thesiger. *Geographical Journal*, vol. 113, no. 1 (1949), p. 21-46. map.

In 1947 the explorer travelled through the western part of the Rub' al-Khali to Liwa and the Buraimi Oasis. As with his other accounts, this article contains a wealth of information conveyed in an engaging style.

123 **A new journey in southern Arabia.**
Wilfred P. Thesiger. *Geographical Journal*, vol. 108, nos. 4-6 (1946), p. 129-45. map.

An account of a three-month journey from Salalah to the southern edges of the Rub' al-Khali. As with all of Thesiger's work this contains a wealth of detail on the topography, flora and fauna, society and customs. Enjoyable as much for its literary style as for its wealth of detail.

124 **Alarms and excursions in Arabia.**
Bertram Thomas. London: Allen & Unwin; Indianapolis, Indiana: Bobbs-Merrill, 1931. 296p. maps.

The author travelled extensively in Oman and this is an interesting and readable account of his experiences. In addition to being an explorer, the author served as financial adviser to the Sultan following the First World War. This must be ranked with Thesiger's works as one of the classic accounts of Oman in the early twentieth century.

125 **Arabia Felix: across the Empty Quarter of Arabia.**
Bertram Thomas. London: Cape, 1932. 304p.
Comparable to the work of Thesiger as a major description of the exploration of
Arabia. The detailed description of Thomas's journey, his companions and the
various tribesmen encountered, presents a valuable portrait, both sympathetic and
objective, of the area.

126 **A camel journey across the Rub' al-Khali.**
Bertram Thomas. *Geographical Journal*, vol. 77, no. 3 (1931),
p. 209-42.
An account of a camel journey from Dhofar province across the Empty Quarter to
Qatar in 1930, made without official approval and relying on friendships made on
previous journeys. As one has come to expect from Thomas, the article contains a
wealth of information presented in a readable and entertaining manner. The
appendices are particularly useful, dealing with: regional sands and water holes of the
Rub' al-Khali (their locations, depth, nature of water and distances, in terms of days
between waterholes); and natural history collections, presenting brief notes made by
the staff of the British Museum on the specimens collected by Thomas.

127 **A journey into Rub'al-Khali the southern Arabian desert.**
Bertram Thomas. *Geographical Journal*, vol. 77, no. 1 (1931),
p. 1-31.
An extremely valuable contribution to early knowledge of the parts of the Sultanate in
the Rub' al-Khali, containing a considerable amount of detailed observation.

128 **The south-eastern borderlands of Rub' al-Khali.**
Bertram Thomas. *Geographical Journal*, vol. 73, pt. 3 (1929),
p. 193-215.
Although primarily concerned with the area now within the boundaries of Saudi
Arabia, the account also considers parts of the Sultanate of Oman which were then the
ill-defined boundaries between the two states.

129 **Ubar – the Atlantis of the sands of Rub' al-Khali.**
Bertram Thomas. *Journal of the Royal Central Asian Society*,
vol. 20, pt. 2 (1933), p. 259-65.
An account of a journey to find the city of Ubar which was supposed to exist in the
southern part of the Empty Quarter somewhere in the region of the Yemen. Thomas
provides an interesting general description of the area, including the northern borders
between Dhofar province, the Yemen and Saudi Arabia.

130 **Mountain of the sun.**
Stephen Thomas. *Aramco World Magazine*, vol. 28, no. 2
(March-April 1977), p. 12-15.
An account of a journey made through the interior of Oman from Muscat to Misfoa,
with commentaries on social customs and various settlements. The author also

describes the *falaj* system. The article is well illustrated by the author, who is also a professional photographer.

131 **From Hasa to Oman by car.**
Desmond Vesey-Fitzgerald. *Geographical Review*, vol. 41 (1951), p. 544-60.

An interesting account of a journey made by the author in 1948 during his period of service as a field officer for the Anti-Locust Research Unit. The author gives a detailed account of the route in terms of distances, travelling conditions, surfaces and natural discomforts. Incidental to this account is a brief description of the various places visited in Oman in the section from Sharjah and thence along the Batinah coast to Muscat.

132 **Three journeys in northern Oman.**
Samuel Marinus Zwemer. *Geographical Journal*, vol. 19, pt. 1 (1902), p. 54-64. map.

An interesting historical account of travels in northern Oman, including the present-day United Arab Emirates. Written by a missionary of the Dutch Reformed Church of America, it also includes an account of the Batinah coast.

Geography

Regional and physical

133 **Sand dune dynamics and sand sea evolution.**
R. J. Alison. *Landscape Research*, vol. 13, no. 2 (1988), p. 7-11.
Discusses the suitability of the Wahiba Sands in Oman for the investigation of the spatial and temporal evolution of sand dunes. The Wahiba Sands are regarded as a perfect example of a sand sea.

134 **The ophiolite–radiolarite belt of the north Oman mountains.**
Franz Allemann, Tjork Peters. *Eclogae Geologicae Helvetiae*, vol. 65, pt. 3 (1972), p. 657-971. map.
An extremely detailed discussion of the organic history of the north Oman mountains, based on investigations in the Emirate of Al-Fujairah and the Jabal Al Akhdar in the Sultanate of Oman. The article deals with the geological composition of the mountains, and reconstructs the physical history of the mountain range on the basis of known stratigraphical and petrographical data. A valuable contribution, but aimed very much at the specialist.

135 **The study of and a contribution to the geomorphology of the Arabian Gulf.**
Taiba A. Al-Asfour. In: *Change and development in the Middle East*, edited by John I. Clarke, Howard Bowen-Jones. London: Methuen, 1981, p. 174-88. maps.
A study of the more recent geomorphological history of the Gulf, including Oman, considering the creation of island sabkhas, alluvial erosion and other physical characteristics of the region.

136 **Sand formations in southern Arabia.**
R. A. Bagnold. *Geographical Journal*, vol. 117, pt. 1 (1951),
p. 78-86. map.
Discusses the formation, growth and movement of dunes in the light of the need for
roads, airports, oil installations and pipelines.

137 **The deep structure of the east Oman continental margin:
preliminary results and interpretation.**
P. J. Barton (et al.). *Tectonophysics*, vol. 173, nos. 1-4 (1990),
p. 319-31.
Describes the preliminary results of a coincident normal incidence and wide-angle
seismic experiment across the east Oman continental margin north of the Masirah
Island ophiolite. The survey revealed a deep offshore basin dammed oceanwards by a
ridge which the authors interpret as a related fault block. Rapid changes in crustal
thickness across the margin were also revealed by the survey.

138 **Geology of the Arabian Peninsula.**
Z. R. Beydoun, United States Geological Survey. Washington DC:
Government Printing Office, 1966. 49p. (Professional Paper 560).
Section D of the paper deals with Dhofar and has a geological bibliography.

139 **Mantle flow patterns at an oceanic spreading centre: the Oman
periodotites record.**
G. Ceuleneer (et al.). *Tectonophysics*, vol. 151, nos. 1-4 (1988),
p. 1-26.
The mantle section of the Oman ophiolite is the longest piece of the uppermost
oceanic mantle exposed at the earth's surface. As a result, extensive mapping of the
region has been conducted in order to unravel mantle processes which are associated
with the oceanic lithosphere.

140 **The use of digitally-processed spot data in the geological mapping
of the ophiolite of northern Oman.**
S. Chevral (et al.). In: *Ophiolite genesis and evolution of the oceanic
lithosphere*, edited by T. J. Peters. London: Kluwer, 1991, p. 853-73.
A discussion of the geological mapping of the Shinas area in the north Oman
mountains on the border with the United Arab Emirates, covering the Semail
ophiolite which is fully exposed in an area which is not easily accessible.

141 **Oman, including the Trucial Coast.**
Ronald A. Codrai. *Canadian Geographical Journal*, vol. 40, pt. 4
(1950), p. 185-92. map.
A well-illustrated brief sketch of the Sultanate, mainly for the general reader.

142   **Southern Arabia: a problem for the future.**
Carleton S. Coon.   *Papers of the Peabody Museum of American
Archaeology and Ethnology* (Harvard University), no. 20 (1943),
p. 187-220.
A review of the geography and culture of southern Arabia, which deals largely with
the Yemen but also includes the southern province of Dhofar.

143   **Circulation and upwelling off the coast of south-east Arabia.**
R. I. Currie.   *Oceanologica Acta*, vol. 15, no. 1 (1992), p. 43-60.
Currie presents the results of a series of observations made during the International
Indian Ocean Expedition. The expedition provides observational data on summer
circulation on the upper 500 metres of the Western Arabian Sea.

144   **The Oman Wahiba Sands project.**
R. W. Dutton, Nigel Winser.   *Geographical Journal*, vol. 153, no. 1
(1987), p. 48-58.
The Wahiba Sands Sea study by the Royal Geographical Society is significant
because as an isolated unit it is a living laboratory of old and new sands, together with
a rich diversity of flora and fauna. The article briefly considers the structure of the
area, the Bedu way of life and the environment.

145   **The effect of weathering minerals on the spectral response of rocks
in Landsat Thematic Mapper imagery (Oman).**   In: *Advances in
digital image processing. Proceedings Remote Sensing Society's 13th
annual conference held at the University of Nottingham, 1987.*
Nottingham, England: Remote Sensing Society, 1987, p. 849-58.
Digitally enhanced Landsat Thematic Mapper images of the Oman mountains were
used as an asset to fieldwork in chosen areas. The spectra of samples collected during
the fieldwork are compared to those of similar types in the available literature in order
to delineate the absorption features present and to relate these to surface mineralogy.

146   **National report about the geologic and mineral activities in the
Sultanate of Oman.**
Ismail Mudathir Elboushi.   Muscat: Ministry of Development,
Directorate General of Petroleum & Minerals, 1974. [n.p.]. maps.
A résumé of past activities and an assessment for the future, especially the prospects
for the development of the copper-mining industry, together with an account of the
geology of the Sultanate.

147   **Some features of the upwelling off Oman.**
A. J. Elliott, G. Savidge.   *Journal of Marine Research*, vol. 48, no. 2
(1990), p. 319-33.
Hydrographic data were collected in the coastal waters of Oman during the monsoon
season in summer 1987. The minimum surface temperatures were found close to the

coast and in the region of the Kuria Muria Islands, while strong surface gradients
were found near Ras al Hadd at the entrance to the Gulf of Oman.

148   **The Musandam Expedition 1971-72. Scientific results: part 1, II.**
       Vertical and horizontal earth movements.
       N. L. Falcon. *Geographical Journal*, vol. 139, pt. 3 (1973),
       p. 404-49.

A study of the vertical and horizontal crust movements of the region around the
Musandam Peninsula, which are relevant to the scientific details concerning crustal
tectonic processes and continental drift. The significance of the area for this study is
that the limestone promontory of Musandam is part of a geological feature known as
the Oman Line, and it is thought that the influence of this feature may extend as far
north as the Rural Mountains.

149   **The Musandam, Northern Oman, Expedition, 1971-72.**
       N. L. Falcon. *Geographical Journal*, vol. 139, pt. 1 (1973), p. 1-19.
       maps.

The condensed account of the Royal Geographical Society expedition, whose main
objective was to obtain data on the Quaternary history of the area. Additional
objectives were to study the geology of the area and conduct hydrographical surveys,
as well as topographical and biological studies. Contains a wealth of information
distilled from the main report deposited with the library of the Royal Geographical
Society.

150   **Derivation and orthography of Rub' al Khali.**
       Nabih Amin Faris. *Journal of the Royal Central Asian Society*,
       vol. 44, pt. 1 (1957), p. 28-30.

A discussion of the term Rub' al-Khali, used to describe the Empty Quarter. The
author concludes it is of modern derivation and not used by the Bedouin in the area,
and suggests that it may be derived from *al-rub'al-Kharab*, or ruined quarter, or
al-rub'al-muhtariq, or scorched quarter, as used by early Arab geographers to
describe the unknown and unexplored desolation of the area.

151   **The geology and mineral resources of Dhofar province, Muscat**
       and Oman.
       Cyril S. Fox. Calcutta India: Baptist Mission Press, 1947. 78p.

In this brief geological account of the Sultanate, Fox also deals with the agriculture of
Oman and its industrial potential.

152   **Ophiolite in the Oman: the Open University Project.**
       I. G. Gass (et al.). *Episodes*, vol. 8, no. 1 (1985), p. 13-20.

A review summary of the development and scientific results obtained by an Open
University Research team working on the ophiolites of Oman. The Oman mountains
are dominated by the Semail ophiolite nappe which represents a section of 'normal'
oceanic lithosphere formed at a spreading axis in a major ocean basin.

153 **Geology of the Oman mountains.**

K. W. Glennie, M. G. Boeuf, M. C. A. Clarke. *Geologisch Mijnbouwkundig Genootschop*, vol. 31 (1974), 432p.

An extremely detailed study of the geology of the mountain structure in Oman augmented by tables, charts and maps.

154 **Late Precambrian–Cambrian sediments of Huqf Group, Sultanate of Oman.**

G. E. Gorin (et al.). *American Association of Petroleum Geologists Bulletin*, vol. 66, no. 12 (1982), p. 2609-27.

A study of the five formations of the Huqf group and the Huqf basin which is traditionally considered part of a belt of evaporitic basins and intervening carbonate platforms which stretched across the Pongea landmass.

155 **Geology and mineral resources of the Trucial Oman range.**

J. E. G. W. Greenwood, P. E. Loney. London: Institute of Geological Sciences, 1968. 108p.

A study of the geological structure of the Jabal Al Akhdar and the potential mineral resources of the area and their commercial prospects.

156 **Outlines of the stratigraphy and structural framework of southern Dhofar (Sultanate of Oman).**

T. R. Hawkins (et al.). *Geologie en Mijnbouw*, vol. 60, no. 2 (1980), p. 247-56.

At the time of writing, deep water wells drilled in Southern Dhofar produced new evidence for the geological structure of the area. The article discusses the geological characteristics of the area based on the new information.

157 **The Kuria Muria Islands.**

Rupert Hay. *Geographical Journal*, vol. 109 (1947), p. 279-81. map.

Although brief, this article is useful because very little is written about these islands. They ceased to be of importance once the guano deposits had been exhausted, that is, by about 1860.

158 **The Musandam limestone (Jurassic to Lower Cretaceous) of Oman, Arabia.**

R. G. S. Hudson, M. Chatton. *Notes et Mémoires sur le Moyen-Orient*, vol. 7 (1959), p. 69-93.

A geological study of the Musandam Peninsula, one of the least accessible parts of the Sultanate because of its mountainous interior.

159 **The structure of the Jabal Haqab area, Trucial Oman, Arabia.**
R. G. S. Hudson (et al.). *Quarterly Journal of the Geological Society* (London), vol. 110, no. 1 (1954), p. 121-52.
A geological outline of the mountain area of Haqab, including a structure map of the area on a scale of 1:60,000.

160 **The geology and tectonics of Oman and of parts of S. E. Arabia.**
G. M. Lees. *Quarterly Journal of the Geological Society* (London), vol. 84, no. 4 (1928), p. 585-670. maps. bibliog.
A detailed study of the structural geology of the interior of the Sultanate and its geological links with other parts of the peninsula.

161 **The physical geography of south-eastern Arabia.**
G. M. Lees. *Geographical Journal*, vol. 71, no. 5 (1928), p. 441-70. maps.
An account of an expedition to Oman in 1925-26, organized to explore the coastal area as far as Dhofar, the area to the north of the Jabal Al Akhdar, but not the range itself. The main body of the article is restricted to the physical geography of the area, but three appendices deal with specimens brought back by the expedition, including flints, birds and insects. These are considered in the relevant sections under the name of the author of each specialist report.

162 **The Musandam Expedition 1971-72. Scientific results: part 2, VI. Al Mahsar tidal appreciation.**
H. P. May. *Geographical Journal*, vol. 140, pt. 1 (1974), p. 102-3.
As part of the Royal Geographical Society expedition in 1971-72, a hydrographic survey was undertaken to establish the feasibility of a canal through the al-Mahsar isthmus. This article reports on the survey, which involved comprehensive tidal observations on both sides of the isthmus to determine mean sea level and tidal characteristics. One conclusion drawn from the survey is that any canal would need a lock due to the difference in water levels, and that long-term observation on an annual basis, together with the recording of meteorological data, would be necessary for detailed planning.

163 **Ophiolite genesis and evolution of the oceanic lithosphere.**
Edited by T. J. Peters, A. Nicholas, R.G. Coleman. London; Boston, Massachusetts: Kluwer Academic, 1991. 903p. maps.
This volume presents the proceedings of the Ophiolite Conference, held in Muscat, Oman, 7-18 January 1990. The proceedings are divided into sections: processes at spreading centres; magmatic ores; hydrothermalism; tectonics of emplacement and metamorphism and palaeographic setting of the Oman ophiolite; palaeoenvironment of other ophiolites; and mapping ophiolites. The study of the Oman ophiolite has been a major geological activity but the majority of the 42 papers are too specialized to annotate separately within this bibliography.

164   **Proceedings, scientific results, Ocean Drilling Program, leg 117, Oman margin/Neogene package.**
W. L. Prell.   Texas: A&M University, College Station, 1991. 638p.

A collection of papers resulting from the Ocean Drilling Programme at 12 locations on the Oman continental margin. The work is divided into the following sections: bio-, litho- and magnetostratigraphy; sedimentology; palaeoceanography; inorganic chemistry; and organic geochemistry. Subject and palaeontological indexes are provided. The work consists of 32 papers which are too specialized to be annotated separately in this bibliography.

165   **Geology of the Musandam Peninsula (Sultanate of Oman) and its surroundings.**
R. Ricateau, P. H. Riche.   *Journal of Petroleum Geology*, vol. 3, no. 2 (1980), p. 139-52.

A detailed geological examination of the Musandam Peninsula which is a vast outcrop of platform carbonate rocks of Permian to Middle Cretaceous age.

166   **The geology of the Persian Gulf–Gulf of Oman region: A synthesis.**
D. A. Ross, E. Uchupi, R. S. White.   *Review of Geophysics*, vol. 24, no. 3 (1986), p. 537-56.

In the Mesozoic most of the Arabian Peninsula, Persian Gulf, south-western Iran, and eastern Iraq constituted the Arabian platform. The article discusses how geological changes over the years have shaped the contemporary physical structure of the region.

167   **Royal Geographical Society Musandam Expedition: report on a marine geophysical survey on the Musandam Peninsula, northern Oman.**
Boreham Wood, England: Hunting Geology & Geophysics, 1972. [4]+21p. maps.

A geophysical examination of one of the least accessible parts of Oman which had significance because of the potential for offshore oil development.

168   **The monsoon-induced upwelling system of the southern coast of Oman.**
G. Savidge (et al.).   *Marine Biology*, vol. 104, nos. 1-4 (1992), p. 390-91.

Few detailed observations are available of the upwelling region off the southern coast of Oman in contrast to the other major coastal upwelling areas of the world. This account is based on an oceanographic survey by the RSS *Charles Darwin* made in August 1987 during the monsoon season when wind conditions favour upwelling.

169 **A shore-based survey of upwelling along the coast of Dhofar region, southern Oman.**
G. Savidge, G. Lennon, A. J. Mathews. *Continental Shelf Research*, vol. 10, no. 3 (1990), p. 259-75.

A shore-based survey of hydrographic variables along the southern Oman coast was carried out during the monsoon season between August and November 1985. Strong evidence of upwelling was found, based on temperature and nutrient data for the eastern half of the survey area which had a severe coastal relief and a steeply shelving bathymetry. Distinct increases in chlorophyll were also apparent within the Salalah Bay at the boundary between stratified and upwelling water.

170 **The scientific results of the Royal Geographical Society's Oman Wahiba Sands Projects, 1985-1987.**
Muscat, Oman: Office of the Adviser for Conservation of the Environment, Diwan of Royal Court, 1988. x+576p. (*Journal of Oman Studies* Special Report, no. 3).

This volume contains fifty-one reports covering the scientific aspects of the Royal Geographical Society's expedition to the Wahiba Sands, a unique desert area with abundant flora and fauna. The reports are grouped under the headings; Earth sciences; Biological resources; and Economy and society. The coverage is extremely detailed and reports include: Agriculture and human resources; Traditional crafts: Products and techniques; and Markets and marketing: Interdependence and change in the local economy. For an account of the expedition, see *The sea of sands and mists: Desertification-seeking solutions in the Wahiba Sands* by Nigel Winser (item no. 185).

171 **Structure of the Musandam culmination (Sultanate of Oman and United Arab Emirates) and the Straits of Hormuz syntaxis.**
M. P. Searle. *Journal of the Geological Society* (London), vol. 145, no. 5 (1988), p. 831-45.

A geological survey of the Musandam Peninsula which falls within the Sultanate of Oman and the United Arab Emirates, detailing the various geological structures found through the length of the Peninsula.

172 **Structure of the Hawasina window culmination, central Oman mountains.**
M. P. Searle, D. J. W. Cooper. *Transactions of the Royal Society of Edinburgh: Earth Sciences*, vol. 77, no. 2 (1986), p. 148-56.

The results of detailed mapping, stratigraphical logging and structural analysis of the Hawasina window in the central Oman mountains reveals an extremely complex thrust geometry and structural history. A model is proposed for the structural evolution of the window supported by four cross-sections of the window and a map.

173   **The John Murray Expedition to the Arabian Sea: Part I,**
      Physical-chemical examination of areas, including Gulf of Oman.
      R. B. Seymour-Sewell.   *Nature*, vol. 133, no. 3351 (1934), p. 86-89.
A report on the hydrological survey of the Gulf of Oman which found an absence of
bottom life over large areas due to the presence of sulphuretted hydrogen.

174   **The John Murray Expedition to the Arabian Sea: Part II.**
      Hydrographic results of areas including Gulf of Oman.
      R. B. Seymour-Sewell.   *Nature*, vol. 133, no. 3366 (1934), p. 669-72.
The major purpose of the expedition was to map the sea bed off Oman and to measure
the circulation of currents.

175   **The John Murray Expedition to the Arabian Sea: Part III. Final**
      traverse.
      R. B. Seymour-Sewell.   *Nature*, vol. 134, no. 3392 (1934), p. 685-88.
A further report of the hydrological survey of Oman, which aimed to map the sea
floor, survey the geological structure of the sea bed and measure the circulation of
currents.

176   **Regional setting and petrological characteristics of the Oman**
      ophiolite in north Oman.
      J. D. Smewing.   *Ophiolite, Special Issue*, no. 2 (1980), p. 335-78.
The Omani ophiolite forms the major part of a 700 km arcuate mountain chain
flanking the south coast of the Gulf of Oman. This account describes the field
relationships and petrology of the ophiolite units in north Oman in order to determine
the petrogenesis of the region.

177   **The Musandam Expedition 1971-72. Scientific results: Part 1, III.**
      Pre-Quaternary geology.
      D. South.   *Geographical Journal*, vol. 135, pt. 3 (1973), p. 410-14.
A consideration of the stratigraphy and structure of the Musandam Peninsula
following the reconnaissance mapping of the area by the expedition. The article
relates findings to earlier survey work undertaken by oil company exploration teams.

178   **Post-pluvial changes in the soils of the Arabian Peninsula.**
      J. H. Stevens.   In: *The environmental history of the Near and Middle*
      East since the last Ice Age, edited by William C. Brice.   London:
      Academic Press, 1978, p. 263-73.
Deals with the environmental factors influencing soil formation in the Arabian
Peninsula, including Oman, at the time when climatic conditions were more moist and
before present conditions restricted development.

179 **The general geology of Oman.**
R. H. Tschopp. In: *Proceedings of the Seventh World Petroleum Congress*, Mexico, 1967. Barking, England: Elsevier, 1967, vol. 2, p. 231-42.

A survey of the geology of Oman, particularly in relation to prospects for future petroleum exploration and discovery.

180 **Burial and thermal history of Proterozoic source rocks in Oman.**
W. Visser. *Precambrian Research*, vol. 54, no. 1 (1991), p. 13-36. map.

A geological and thermal history of the Proterozoic sedimentary basin of Oman using present-day data to reconstruct the history, with the objective of determining the time of hydrocarbon generation in the area. Visser concludes that in north-west Oman generation occurred in the Mesozoic, whilst generation in the centre and south-east ceased some 400 million years ago.

181 **The Musandam Expedition 1971-72, Scientific results: Part 1, IV. Late Quaternary subsidence.**
Claudio Vita-Finzi. *Geographical Journal*, vol. 139, pt. 3 (1973), p. 414-21. maps.

The hydrographic and geophysical work of the expedition indicated a tilting of the peninsula towards the north-east during the Late Quaternary, and the evidence indicates that 'the vertical displacement of the north and east coasts appear to have exceeded 60m during the last 10,000 years'. The article develops the theme of the relative importance of subsidence and eustatic submergence in producing the present coastline of Oman.

182 **The Wahiba Sands – a museum of aeolian paleogeomorphology.**
A Warren, R. Cooke. *Geography Review*, vol. 4, no. 1 (1990), p. 35-38.

A description of a geomorphological study in the Wahiba Sand Sea as part of the Royal Geographical Society expedition. Considers the origin of the desert sand, formation of aeolonite ancient dunes, the formation of linear dunes and the evidence for climatic change. The authors conclude that climatic change and strengthening monsoons will accelerate dune formation in the area.

183 **The Oman ophiolite, some critical stratigraphic and structural relationships and a possible method of emplacement.**
M. J. Welland. *Mineralogical Association of Canada. Annual Meeting Programme Abstracts* (1974), p. 97.

A geological study of the serpentine rock in Oman with accounts of its existence, particularly in the Jabal Al Akhdar range. As the ophiolite is exposed to a great extent it has been the object of extensive research.

184   **The occurrence of geodes in Dhofar, Oman.**
       J. M. Wills. *Journal of Oman Studies*, vol. 8, pt. 1 (1985), p. 75-80.
       maps.

The geodes in Oman are of sedimentary origin. Scattered through several wadis of western central Dhofar, they vary from walnut size to approximately football size. The geodes have a knotty opaque outer skin of chalcedony, and within, a drusy lining of crystal quartz often with secondary crystal growth of calcite or gypsum. The article provides a physical description of the geodes, their mineral composition, and their mode of formation. The geodes' locations are detailed on a map of Dhofar and illustrations are provided of the various types.

185   **The sea of sands and mists: Desertification-seeking solutions in the Wahiba Sands.**
       Nigel Winser.   London: Century, 1989. xxii+199p. maps. bibliog.

An account by the project organizer of the scientific expedition of the Royal Geographical Society in 1986 in the Wahiba Sands. The aim of the project was to explore and report on the Wahiba Sands, a unique desert area of sand dunes, forests, night mists and an abundance of wildlife and plants. The book describes the preparations for the project, the uses of computer technology for mapping purposes and the close relationship forged with the Bedu of the area whose skills and knowledge were of paramount importance to the project. The team made some new scientific finds and the flora and fauna of the area was recorded in detail. In essence, the study was also about understanding the region with a view to its preservation, and the project team was conscious of the fact that any plans for the area would have to include the Bedu as partners if they were to be successful. This is an extremely well-written and entertaining account of an expedition which is also covered by specific articles throughout this work.

186   **The floor of the Arabian Sea.**
       John D. H. Wiseman, R. B. Seymour-Sewell.   *Geological Magazine*,
       vol. 74 (1937), p. 219-30.

A geological survey which is much wider in coverage than the Sultanate, although the latter is geologically connected to the Indian Ocean. The mapping was carried out in four sections, the relevant one being that from Aden to Karachi and including an interesting account of the Kuria Muria Islands.

Origin of crude oils in Oman.
See item no. 949.

Chromite-rich and chromite-poor ophiolites: the Oman case.
See item no. 966.

Climatology

187 **Currents in the Persian Gulf, northern portions of Arabian Sea, Bay of Bengal.**
E. W. Barlow.   Part 1: Summary of previous knowledge, *Marine Observer*, vol. 9, no. 99 (1932), p. 58-60; Part II: The south-west monsoon period, *Marine Observer*, vol. 9, no. 105 (1932), p. 169-71; Part III: The north-east monsoon period and general summary, *Marine Observer*, vol. 9, no. 108 (1932), p. 223-27.

This article is relevant because of the effect that the monsoons have on the climate of Dhofar province, the Jabal Al Akhdar, and the importance of information on currents for shipping and fishing.

188 **The assessment of rainfall in north-eastern Oman through the integration of observations from conventional and satellite resources.**
E. C. Barrett.   Rome: Food and Agriculture Organization, 1977. 55p. maps. (FAO Access no. 37482).

One of a series of reports on rainfall in Oman designed to provide essential data for agricultural planning and development prospects for the sector.

189 **Paleoclimate reconstruction in northern Oman based on carbonates from hyperalkine groundwaters.**
I. D. Clark, J. C. Fontes.   *Quaternary Research* (Canada), vol. 33, no. 3 (1990), p. 320-36.

This palaeoclimate reconstruction for the past 35,000 years in northern Oman uses an unusual approach involving travertines and fracture calcites associated with hyperalkine springs. The technical results of the reconstruction are compared against those for the Rub' al-Khali of Saudi Arabia, the monsoon record of East Africa, and the Arabian Sea with remarkably good results.

190 **Climate of the Batinah.**
P. M. Horn, J. B. Nielson.   Rome: Food and Agriculture Organization, 1977. 27p. (FAO Access no. 39621).

Covers the period 1973-77 and is extremely relevant to the prospects for agriculture in the area and the problem of water resources on the Batinah coast caused by the declining water table and dangers of desalination.

191 **Climate of Jebel Akhdar.**
P. M. Horn, J. B. Nielsen, I. A. Manthri, S. Salaam.   Rome: Food and Agriculture Organization, 1977. 19p. (FAO Access no. 40095)

Particularly concerned with the area around Saiq where the terraced agriculture benefits from the moisture of the edges of the monsoons.

192 **Rainfall in Dhofar to 1977 inclusive.**
P. M. Horn.   Rome: Food and Agriculture Organization, 1978. 23p.
(FAO Access no. 39622).
A study of the plain of which Salalah is part and which benefits from being on the edge of the monsoons.

193 **Rainfall in the Muscat area.**
P. M. Horn.   Rome: Food and Agriculture Organization, 1976. 34p.
(FAO Access no. 39620).
One of the series of surveys undertaken for the Sultanate by the Food and Agriculture Organization designed to assist with agricultural planning and development. All of the surveys contain tabular data.

194 **A study of weather over the Arabian Peninsula.**
W. S. Kuo.   *Meteorological Magazine*, vol. 11, no. 2 (1965),
p. 25-35.
A useful introductory article which treats Oman as part of the regional survey.

195 **Some features of the synoptic meteorology of south-west Asia.**
S. Mazumdar.   *World Meteorological Organization Technical Notes*,
no. 69 (1965), p. 117-40.
A general account of weather in the area, including the Sultanate of Oman.

196 **The climate of interior Oman.**
D. E. Pedgley.   *Meteorological Magazine*, vol. 99 (1970), p. 26-37.
The analysis of the weather patterns of the Oman interior and the Hajar range covers wind, monsoons and rainfall.

197 **Cyclones along the Arabian coast.**
D. E. Pedgley..   *Weather*, vol. 24, no. 1 (1969), p. 456-68.
Considers the incidence, pattern and effect of cyclone conditions along the coast of the Yemen and Oman. At various times, cyclones have led to considerable damage, particularly in the Salalah area and on Masirah Island.

198 **Fog moisture and its ecological effects in Oman.**
M. R. S. Price (et al.).   In: *Arid lands*, edited by E. E. Whitehead
(et al.).   London: Belhaven Press, 1988, p. 69-88.
Fog moisture is experienced in the Dhofar mountains and the Jiddat al Harasis plateau and these are used as case-studies to demonstrate the benefit of such precipitation to the ecosystems. The measurement techniques are described, as are the climatic conditions causing the precipitation and calculations as to the amount of water that can be extracted. The effects on the human ecology and vegetation are described to show how the plant communities have evolved in response to the climate creating ecosystems not found elsewhere in Arabia.

199 **Summary of synoptic meteorological observations, southwest Asian coastal marine areas.**
Washington, DC: United States Department of Defense, 1971.
The meteorological data on the Sultanate of Oman appears in volume 5 of this set.

200 **Los neblinas costeras de Chile y Oman. Similitudes y diferencias.**
(The coastal fogs of Chile and Oman: Similarities and differences.)
P. Cereceda Transcesco (et al.). *Revista Geográfica de Chile Terra Australis*, vol. 33 (1990), p. 49-60.
This Spanish-language article, with an English summary, focuses on the similarities and differences in atmospheric conditions in Oman and Chile which lead to the formation of high-level fogs. The results of the conditions are that Oman has a high fog water collection rate, but for only two or three months of the year, whereas in Chile the duration is throughout the year but with a low collection rate. The uses to which both countries can put the water are also similar.

201 **Persian Gulf region: a climatological study.**
K. R. Walters, W. F. Sjoberg. Scott Air Force Base, Illinois: Air Force Environmental Technical Applications Center, 1990. 73p.
A study describing the climatology of the Persian Gulf, the Strait of Hormuz, the Gulf of Oman and the adjacent land areas for a radius of 150 nautical miles. Chapters are also devoted to the geography of the areas studied, the phenomena of the monsoon climate, particularly relevant for Oman, and the four major geographical subdivisions: the Persian Gulf proper, the Strait of Hormuz, the Gulf of Oman and the Omani Arabian Sea coast.

202 **Northern Oman flood study.**
H. S. Wheater, N. C. Bell. *Proceedings of the Institution of Civil Engineers*, vol. 75, pt. 2 (1983), p. 453-73.
A study in Northern Oman of a depth–duration–frequency relationship for short-duration rainfall based on the station-year method. The relationship is proved to be consistent with the frequency distribution from records at Muscat and with similar records in Saudi Arabia.

The monsoon-induced upwelling system of the southern coast of Oman.
See item no. 168

Water resources

203 Renewable natural resources in the Middle East.
J. A. Allan. In: *Change and development in the Middle East*, edited by John I. Clarke, Howard Bowen-Jones. London: Methuen, 1981, p. 24-39.

This contribution considers the renewable natural resources of the region, particularly water, and the need for surveys and the development of proper management techniques. The treatment is regional in nature and Oman features throughout the statistical tables which show levels of rain in relation to rainfall and percentages of agricultural land.

204 Water resources and boundaries in the Middle East.
Ewan W. Anderson. In: *Boundaries and state territory in the Middle East and North Africa*, edited by G. H. Blake, N. Schofield. Wisbech, England: Menas Press, 1987, p. 85-98.

Although oil has dominated the geopolitics of the Middle East it has been prophesied that towards the end of the century the politics of the region will be shaped more by water than oil. In dealing with Oman, this contribution deals with the significance of the *falaj* system of irrigation, the construction of dams on the Batinah coast to protect losses and improve recharge, and the significance of sub-surface water in north-western Oman and the Buraimi Oasis.

205 Traditional method of groundwater utilization in the Middle East.
Peter Beaumont. *Groundwater*, vol. 11, pt. 5 (1973), p. 23-30.

Although confined to Iran, this article is relevant for its detailed technical treatment of the *qanat* system of irrigation. The discussion of the system and the diagrammatic explanations are equally relevant to Oman and to the associated *falaj* system.

206 Water resources and their management in the Middle East.
Peter Beaumont. In: *Change and development in the Middle East*, edited by John I. Clarke, Howard Bowen-Jones. London: Methuen, 1981, p. 40-72. maps.

A survey of water resources in the Middle East and problems of management covering rainfall, groundwater and irrigation. The article also includes a cross-section and plan of a *falaj* in Oman.

207 The Awamir: specialist well and *falaj* diggers in northern interior Oman.
John Stace Birks, Sally E. Letts. *Journal of Oman Studies*, vol. 2 (1976), p. 93-100.

A consideration of the Awamir tribe, whose tribal area lies within the Sharqiya, with their capital Qala'at Al-Awamir near Izki. The tribe has become the specialist well and *falaj* diggers, employed by landowners wealthy enough not to need to maintain their own irrigation systems. Due to the nature of their work, nearly 250 men of the tribe are semi-permanently away working on water supplies throughout Oman, returning home during Ramadam or possibly on one other occasion during the year. The group of men tend to work together and often in the same area, sometimes becoming share-croppers at the end of their well-digging.

208 Sib water supply, actual production and expectation.
W. Bolliger.   Muscat: Petroleum Development (Oman) Ltd, 1991. [n.p.].

A survey of the water supply available in the Seeb area, current production and usage and the possible output necessary to cope with urban development.

209 Water: satellite images show up potential resources.
Alison Brown.   *Middle East Economic Digest, Special Report* (Nov. 1980), p. 16-17.

Satellite scanning is being used to locate potential sources of additional water for development in agriculture and growing urban demands. Attempts are also being made to coordinate exploration and to control water use and the drilling of wells.

210 Modern and fossil groundwater in an arid environment: A look at the hydrogeology of Southern Oman.
I. D. Clark (et al.).   In: *Isotope techniques in water resources development. Proceedings of an International Symposium held March-April 1987.*   Vienna: International Atomic Energy Agency, 1987, p. 167-87.

Agriculture in Oman had been undergoing a period of sustained expansion but with a heavy reliance on groundwater sources for irrigation. The Public Authority for Water Resources has developed a considerable knowledge of groundwater availability and quality through a comprehensive programme of exploration. The programme included a national survey of environmental isotopes in groundwater, surface waters and precipitation, with the objective of determining the mean residence times of groundwater and defining their recharge sources.

211 Origins and age of coastal groundwaters in northern Oman.
I. D. Clark, P. Ravenscroft, P. Fritz.   In: *Proceedings of 10th Salt-water Intrusion Meeting.*   Ghent, Belgium: Geologisch Institut R.V.G., 1989, p. 75-84.

The area of northern Oman is the most heavily cultivated part of the Sultanate but heavy extraction from the alluvial aquifers has led to increased salination and a deterioration in the groundwater. Saline intrusion is now occurring in both the shallow and deep coastal groundwaters and the study is an attempt to understand the mechanisms and frequency of the aquifers recharge.

212 Qanats, karaz and foggaras.
George B. Cressey.   *Geographical Review*, vol. 48, no. 1 (1958), p. 21-44. map.

A general consideration of this form of irrigation, known in Oman as the *falaj* system, of relevance because the applications are basically the same wherever the system is used. An extremely useful explanation of their construction, operation and economic importance.

213   **Desalination: The solution to Oman's thirst.**
A. A. Dawood, R. W. Leidholdt. *Journal of the American Water Works Association*, vol. 78, no. 7 (1986), p. 80-85.

Oman has limited water resources and rapid development has increased the demand for fresh water, resulting in the introduction of desalination facilities which are also linked into electric power generation. The authors discuss the history of Oman's water supply, water resources, transmission facilities, the distribution system and future plans for the sector. The particular problems of the capital area and Muscat are also evaluated.

214   **The origins and spread of *qanats* in the old world.**
P. W. English. *Proceedings of the American Philosophical Society*, vol. 112 (1968), p. 170-81.

Wider in coverage than the Sultanate and dealing with the *qanat* system of irrigation first designed in Persia. The same system in Oman is known as the *falaj* system.

215   **Sweetwater for the hottest land.**
Ranulph Fiennes. *Geographical Magazine* (Sept. 1976), p. 889-93. map.

A consideration of the *falaj* system of Oman, dealing briefly with the history of its development and the communal maintenance it requires.

216   **Groundwater supply and advanced water treatment in Oman.**
D. H. F. Gamble, C. M. Biggin. *Journal of the Institution of Water Engineers and Scientists*, vol. 41, no. 1 (1987), p. 55-74.

Examines the water resources assessment and development in Oman which was carried out in four phases over a two-year period; initial investigations; further investigations; groundwater exploration; and groundwater development. The second part of the paper deals with water treatment and supply and discusses existing plant and proposed extensions: design criteria, proposed plant, fluoride removal, and economy and operation.

217   **Water research needs in the Arabian Gulf area.**
A. Al-Hamoud (et al.). *Desalination*, vol. 72, nos. 1-2, p. 3-7.

A study of the priority goals for water resources research in the Gulf Cooperation Council states, followed by suggestions of ways to attain these goals. The goals for the member states, including Oman, cover the preservation and protection of aquifers, improved distribution and efficiency of use, reducing production costs, securing supply sources to meet future demands, centralized data collection, and national training programmes.

218 **Water resources of Salalah Plain. An interim appraisal.**
P. M. Horn. Rome: Food and Agriculture Organization, 1978. 32p.
(Field Document, no. 8. FAO Accession no. 39624).

A survey to measure the surface water balance and the effect on the balance of
agricultural expansion and urbanization.

219 **Development and management of fossil groundwater resources for
purposes of drought mitigation.**
K. W. F. Howard. In: *Greenhouse effect, sea level and drought.
Proceedings of a workshop held at Fuerteventura in 1989*, edited by
R. Paepe (et al.). London: Kluwer for NATO AS1 Series, 1990,
p. 495-512. (Series C, 325).

Wider in coverage than Oman – it covers North Africa and the whole of the Arabian
Peninsula – this work is included because of the significance of groundwater in
Oman, particularly on the Batinah coast, and problems of salination. The contributors
argue that as these are finite resources an appropriate management strategy must be
developed which rejects the traditional safe-yield theories and recognizes
groundwater mining as an acceptable alternative. They conclude that groundwater
mining is acceptable provided: it is positively planned and realistically evaluated in
advance; close control over production is exercised; and there is a clear and feasible
plan for alternative supplies once the groundwater is exhausted. Any development
programme will need to be flexible to respond to data and the effects of groundwater
pumping and must include intense monitoring and a constant upgrading of resources
and economic assessments.

220 **Results of test drilling for water in northwestern Sharqiya area,
Sultanate of Oman 1983-1984.**
J. R. Jones. Muscat: Public Authority for Water Resources, 1986.
(Report no. 85-21).

A report of water resource surveys undertaken in the Sharqiya area of northwest
Oman designed to assist with development planning in the areas of agriculture and
social facilities. The availability of water in this area is seen as critical to the
maintenance of this oasis-based society.

221 **Friday's water: Water rights and social hierarchy in Sharqiya,
Sultanate of Oman.**
G. C. Le Cour. *Etudes Rurales*, nos. 93-94 (Jan.-June 1984), p. 7-42.

A French-language study of the hierarchical organization surrounding the ownership
of, and access to, water in the Sharqiya oasis. Ownership is a matter of private
property with access being derived from the purchase of weekly rights to irrigation
water purchased at auction on Fridays. The author considers the *falaj* system of Oman
which is crucial to that country and which ensures all members of the community can
have access to water, thus perpetuating the cohesion of the village community.

222   **Attitudes to *falaj* water and their importance.**
      S. E. Letts, John Stace Birks.   Durham, England: Durham University,
      1973. (Field Statement no. 2).

Part of the Durham Oman Project which looks at the importance of the *falaj* system to agriculture but which also deals with the social structure that has evolved to manage the system.

223   **Raised channel systems as indicators of paleohydrologic change; a
      case study from Oman.**
      J. Maizels.   *Paleography, Paleoclimatology, Paleoecology*, vol. 76,
      nos. 3-4 (1990), p. 241-77.

Aims to determine the extent to which 'raised' channel systems may be used as indicators of long-term palaeohydrological change and thus of broader palaeoenvironmental changes. The paper reviews the palaeohydrological significance of former drainage systems in interior Oman and demonstrates the application of palaeohydrological methods to the analyses of the long-term evaluation of 'raised' channel systems.

224   **Factors affecting the flow of *aflaj* in Oman: a modelling study.**
      Y. P. Parks, P. J. Smith.   *Journal of Hydrology*, vol. 65, no. 4 (1983),
      p. 293-312.

A study of the *aflaj* of Oman examining factors affecting their flow, their response to recharge and their impact on the surrounding aquifers. Considers the significance of the *aflaj* as important sources of water supply.

225   **Oman's unfailing springs.**
      L. T. Simarski.   *Aramco World*, vol. 43, no. 6 (1992), p. 26-31.

An account of the *aflaj* system of irrigation and the well and canal engineering works which deliver 70 per cent of Oman's water supply.

226   **Coastal salination: a case history from Oman.**
      G. Stanger.   *Agricultural Water Management*, vol. 9, no. 4 (1986),
      p. 269-86.

A report on the problems of salination in the coastal area of Oman particularly in the Batinah area. Problems have arisen because of the increased usage of water to develop agriculture in the area, resulting in a decrease in the water table and increasing the dangers of salination.

227   **Changing drainage patterns in a semi-arid area and their effects
      on groundwater resources.**
      S. E. Sutton.   *Earth Surface Processes and Landforms*, vol. 12, no. 5
      (1987), p. 567-70.

A study of a group of wadi bottom alluvial aquifers in northern Oman which shows that the magnitude of groundwaters is poorly correlated, possibly due to progressive water-gap captures across a limestone ridge.

228 **On Omani *aflaj* and the Madrid water supply system.**
Francisco Utrey.   *Journal of Oman Studies*, vol. 6, pt. 1 (1982),
p. 173-76.

A study of the origins of the Omani system of *aflaj* and the Madrid water system
which shows distinct similarities and a possible link with Moorish settlement in
Spain. The study also looks at the phonological evidence of similar systems in the
Middle East and the Mediterranean and uses this to demonstrate the technological
intercommunication which must have taken place. It is stressed that further research
is needed in the area, particularly the legal provisions regulating water distribution,
through a study of unpublished Omani and Spanish manuscripts.

229 **Temperature, salinity and density of the world's seas – Arabian
Sea, Persian Gulf and Red Seas.**
P. E. La Violete, T. R. Fronterec.   Washington, DC: United States
Oceanographic Office, 1967. 105p.

Useful for a consideration of the problems of salinity in places like the Batinah coast,
where the water table is falling due to the development and mechanization of the
agricultural sector, together with improved methods of water extraction.

230 **Water resources survey of northern Oman.**
Muscat: Sir Alexander Gibb and Partners, with International Land
Development Consultants, 1975. [n.p.]. maps.

A survey of water resources in northern Oman, with a view to assessing supplies for
future agricultural and urban development.

231 **The organization of the *falaj* irrigation system in Oman.**
J. C. Wilkinson.   Oxford, England: University of Oxford, School of
Geography, 1974. 24p. (Research Paper no. 10).

A paper which deals with the *falaj* system of irrigation, but also considers the social
organization associated with its use and maintenance.

232 **The origins of the *aflaj* of Oman.**
John C. Wilkinson.   *Journal of Oman Studies*, vol. 6, pt. 1 (1983),
p. 177-94. bibliog.

Water supply in all of the main settlements of Oman has been based on groundwater,
and the country can be divided into two hydrological areas: the coastal area relying on
wells; and the interior on the system of *aflaj*, supplemented by the use of wells. The
article is an attempt to reconstruct the history of *aflaj* or *qanat* building in Oman. The
introduction deals with the arguments for assuming an early Iranian origin for the
Omani system. This argument for a pre-Islamic origin of the system is further
substantiated by a study of Omani society in central Oman, for that society does not
fit the centralized administration needed to construct, maintain and develop such a
system of irrigation. Nor does the present population of Oman have any real technical
knowledge of *qanat* building or any knowledge of the history of the *qanat*. Next, the
author discusses the history of *qanat* construction and the development of the *aflaj* in
the Islamic period, before going on to a consideration of the archaeological evidence
for prehistoric settlement in Oman and the communities' role in the construction of

*qanat*s in the seventh or eighth centuries BC. These conjectures are based on field studies in the Julfar region. The author stresses that further research is still needed, and that his conclusions may need to be revised as further archaeological evidence becomes available, since conditions may have varied at different periods in the past.

233 **Water and tribal settlement in south-east Arabia: a study of the**
aflaj **of Oman.**
J. C. Wilkinson.   London: Oxford University Press, 1977. 276p.
maps. bibliog.

An indispensable work for the study of Oman, particularly important for its coverage of water supply to tribal settlements. Wilkinson handles a complex subject in an authoritative manner, with a clear understanding of his subject and of the Sultanate, and the study is valuable both for its historical treatment and its relevance to present conditions. The main areas covered are: the geographical and regional background; water resources and climate; the impact of the Imamate government; population and social structure; agriculture; and social change. The extensive bibliography covers both European and Arabic sources, and the work is well indexed.

234 **Water mills of the Batinah coast of Oman.**
T. J. Wilkinson.   *Proceedings of the Seminar for Arabian Studies*,
vol. X (1980), p. 127-32. map.

The water supply system and distribution through the *aflaj* has been the subject of a lot of research but little has been written on their use on the Batinah coast to operate water mills. This article describes the construction of these water mills and the skills used by the engineers to accommodate variations in terrain. The known locations of water mills in the Gulf and the Arabian Peninsula are summarized in order to place the Omani mills into context in terms of chronology within the region. Evidence shows that the Omani water mills were from the 8th to the 10th century AD and were in use during the Abbasid period, but that they have been disused for centuries.

The reaction of rural populations to drought: a case study from South-East Arabia.
See item no. 989.

Maps, atlases and gazetteers

235 **Mapping in the Oman ophiolite using enhanced Landsat Thematic Mapper images.**
M. J. Abrams, D. A. Rothery, A. Pontine.   *Tectonophysics*, vol. 151,
nos. 1-4 (1988), p. 387-401.

Prior to the Landsat facility, mapping of the Oman ophiolite had produced maps of internally inconsistent quality. The use of the short-wavelength infrared spectrum by Landsat enabled consistent mapping of the ophiolite by using the distinctions in the spectral reflectances of different rock types and their weathering products. The data produced were valuable for the mapping of similarly exposed terrains in arid and semi-arid regions.

236 Thematic mapping for developing countries using metric camera imagery (Oman).

H. Asche. In: *Mapping from modern imagery. Proceedings of a Symposium of ISPRS Commission IV and RSS, Edinburgh. International Archives of Photogrammetry and Remote Sensing*, vol. 26, pt. 4 (1986), p. 278-82.

Metric camera mapping photography is regarded as a major breakthrough for precision topographical and thematic mapping. Asche discusses results of medium-scale pilot maps from the Sultanate of Oman using the systems which were designed for use in connection with regional planning applications.

237 Trigonometric survey of the harbours of Muttra and Muscat on the coast of Arabia.

G. B. Brucks, S. B. Haines. London: James Horsburgh, 1831.

This map was based on surveys carried out by these two officers in 1828, on a scale of 7.7 inches to a mile. It is a detailed plan of the shoreline, with schematic views of the two cities.

238 Survey of the shores and islands of the Persian Gulf 1820-1829.

Edited by A. S. Cook. London: Oleander Press, 1989. 1 vol. text, 378p. 4 boxes of charts in volume format.

A collection of the first complete survey of the Gulf coast and islands by the Bombay Marine representing the first British portrayal of coastal settlements, with harbour plans, water-colour paintings and supporting text. Muscat harbour was one of those surveyed.

239 Charting the Wahiba Sand Sea.

R. Cooke. *Geographical Magazine* (May 1985), p. 268-73.

Outlines the logistics of the Royal Geographical Society's research project to study the Wahiba Sand Sea of south-east Oman as a complete environment, together with the lifestyle of the inhabitants. Some preliminary findings are also outlined.

240 Memoir of a chart of the east coast of Arabia from Dofar to the island of Maziera. From an eye-draught taken by Captain John S. Smith in December 1781.

Edited by Alexander Dalrymple. London: Bigg, 1787. 2nd ed. vi+11p.

A description of one of the earliest Western-produced charts of the coast of the Sultanate from Dhofar province to Masirah Island.

241 **Evaluation of Spacelab photography for small scale mapping.**
M. Davison. *Photogrammetric Record*, vol. 11, no. 66 (1985),
p. 695-97.
Hunting Surveys Ltd had carried out mapping on a scale of 1:100,000 of part of
Oman, based on photography done in 1981. Stereoscopic cover of the area was
available from Spacelab, enabling comparisons to be made with the existing mapping.

242 **Landsat surveys of southeastern Arabia.**
J. R. Everett, D. R. Russell, D. A. Nichols. In: *Desert and arid
lands*, edited by F. El-Baz. Dordrecht, The Netherlands:
Kluwer-Nijhoff, 1984, p. 171-94.
Deals with land use and terrain analysis in north Oman, using satellite imagery
covering groundwater studies, and petroleum exploration through an analysis of the
regional geological structure.

243 **The Persian Gulf Pilot, including the Gulf of Oman.**
Great Britain. Admiralty. London: Hydrographic Department,
1864- .
An indispensable tool for all mariners, it has continued to appear in different editions
since 1864. At times the title has varied slightly.

244 **Gulf of Aden Pilot.**
Great Britain. Admiralty Hydrographic Office. London: HM
Stationery Office, 1932. 540p. maps.
An invaluable source of data for mariners: complements the *Persian Gulf Pilot* (see
item no. 243).

245 **Vegetation evaluation in the arid zone: case studies from Landsat
in the Middle East.**
R. Harris. In: *Remote sensing for rangeland monitoring and
management. Proceedings of a Conference held at Silsoe, 1983.*
Reading, England: Remote Sensing Society, 1983, p. 134-37.
Uses case-studies from Iran, Kuwait and Oman to illustrate the value of Landsat
imagery to evaluate vegetation patterns in the Middle East.

246 **Space photography and nautical charting.**
A. R. Kilbride. In: *Mapping from modern imagery. Proceedings of a
symposium of Remote Sensing Society held in Edinburgh in 1986.*
Nottingham, England: Remote Sensing Society, 1986. *International
Archives of Photogrammetry and Remote Sensing*, vol. 26, part 4,
p. 183-91.
Discusses the use by the British Hydrographic Department of space photography to
resolve longstanding positional discrepancies on Admiralty charts. The use of
Spacelab photography represents an important new source for small-scale chart
revision and compilations with the areas covered by a single frame and the clarity of

coastal zones enabling reefs and islands to be accurately positioned. Results of large-format camera photography of southern Oman are discussed.

247 **Mapping Arabia.**
John Leatherdale, Roy Kennedy. *Geographical Journal*, vol. 141, no. 2 (1975), p. 240-51.

Describes the work of Hunting Surveys Ltd in the mapping of Arabia, including Oman. The article considers the surveying techniques and methods of operation, particularly in the desert areas. Prime motivation for all these activities was the need for accurate surveys for oil exploration, but the programme has now moved into the area of topographical mapping. The role of aerial and satellite photography in this area is also discussed.

248 **Maps of south-western Asia.**
Washington, DC: United States Army Map Service, Corps of Engineers. irregular.

The maps, on a scale of 1:250,000, are part of the K502 series and show political and man-made features as well as physical features. The maps are revised from aerial photography. Oman is covered by the NF-40 sub-series from Khabura to the south, and NG-40 for northern Oman.

249 **Musandam Peninsula.**
London: Royal Geographical Society, 1973.

A map on a scale of 1:100,00 issued after the Royal Geographical Society's Musandam Expedition of 1971-72.

250 **A comparison of Landsat images and Nimbus thermal-inertia mapping of Oman.**
Howard A. Pohn. *Journal of the United States Geological Survey*, vol. 4, no. 6 (1977), p. 661-66.

A mapping technique especially useful in remote inaccessible areas to resolve ambiguous identification of rock formations by a combination of thermal-inertia maps and satellite photographs.

251 **The Robertson Group plc: GIS within a worldwide natural resource and environmental consultancy.**
Mapping Awareness and GIS Europe, vol. 5, no. 5 (1991), p. 34-37.

Describes the operation of the Geographical Information System (GIS) and remote sensing unit in the Robertson Group which is a large natural and environmental consultancy. Also describes the activities of the unit in the areas of geoscientific mapping, database design, consultancy and training, and image processing. Amongst the sample projects outlined are some in Oman and the Yemen.

252 **The Musandam Expedition 1971-72. Scientific results: part 2, V.**
Land survey.
G. P. Robinson. *Geographical Journal*, vol. 140, pt. 1 (1974),
p. 94-102. maps.

A condensed version of a report on the Royal Geographical Society's expedition to
the Musandam Peninsula in 1971-72 which deals with the survey work undertaken
primarily for geodetic and topographical mapping purposes. This is very important
research, but the content is specialized.

253 **A new map of southern Arabia.**
C. B. Serjeant, H. von Wissman. *Geographical Journal*, vol. 124,
pt. 2 (1958), p. 163-71.

Discusses the compilation of the Royal Geographical Society's new map of Aden,
Oman and the southern edge of the Rub' al-Khali. The first part of the article by Von
Wissman deals with cartographic aspects, whilst the contribution by Serjeant is
concerned with problems of transliteration and standardization of place-names.

254 **Mission to earth: Landsat views the world.**
Nicholas M. Short (et al.). Washington, DC: Government Printing
Office, 1976. 459p. (National Aeronautics and Space Administration,
SP-360).

A collection of Landsat photographs, including some of the Arabian Peninsula, with
accompanying notes on land forms, ophiolites and geological features.

255 **Arabia in the fifteenth-century navigational texts.**
G. R. Tibbetts. *Arabian Studies*, vol. 1 (1974), p. 86-101. maps.

An interesting article which examines the various references to the Omani coastline in
navigational texts, and the significance of the coastal features in the area's trade.

256 **Oman, official standard names approved by the United States**
Board of Geographic Names.
United States Defense Mapping Agency Topographic Center.
Washington, DC: Government Printing Office, 1976.

The gazetteer lists some 5,600 entries for Oman, with the names of most settlements,
physical features and cultural entities. Also listed are the various maps on which the
gazetteer is based.

257 **Persian Gulf Pilot: Comprising the Persian Gulf, Gulf of Oman**
and the Makran Coast.
United States Navy Hydrographic Office. Washington, DC:
Government Printing Office. irregular.

Descriptive data supplementing the various nautical charts; frequently revised and
updated.

258 **Sailing directions for the Persian Gulf: includes Gulf of Oman and northern shore of Arabian Sea eastward to Ras Muria.**
United States Oceanographic Office.   Washington, DC: Government Printing Office, 1960. 351p. maps.

Designed to serve the mariner, this publication reviews the coastal areas, offshore areas, port facilities and the settlements that can be seen from ship. As this is a working tool for mariners, the detail is continually being revised, hence the loose-leaf format.

259 **Series map production by 42 Survey Engineer Group.**
A. J. M. Vickers.   *Photogrammatic Record*, vol. 12, no. 70 (1987), p. 429-41.

Describes the production of part of a new series of maps of Oman on a scale of 1:100,000 by soldiers of 42 Survey Engineering Group. The detail of the mapping operation is described as are the problems caused by the barren nature of the terrain and the use of advanced technology.

Narrative of voyages to explore the shores of Africa, Arabia, Madagascar.
See item no. 105.

Dissertations

260 **Foraminifer evidence of monsoon upwelling off Oman during the Late Quaternary.**
David Morrill Anderson.   PhD thesis, Brown University, 1991. 306p. (Available from University Microfilms, Ann Arbor, Michigan, order no. AAD92-04824).

A study of the variations in upwelling through the use of plankton fossils and other sediments to reconstruct the history of coastal upwelling off the coast of Oman.

261 **Groundwater recharge studies (Cyprus, Oman).**
C. A. C. Konteatis.   PhD thesis, University of Nottingham, England, 1987. 780p.

This is a study of artificial groundwater recharge which can be applied only where the hydrogeological conditions permit. The author has had extensive experience in the design and execution of such schemes in Cyprus and Oman from 1981. The sections of relevance to Oman are: Chapter 3 which deals with background on water resources, geology and hydrogeology as related to groundwater recharge and its advantages; Chapter 4 which deals with the Wadi Quryat Experimental Groundwater recharge scheme in the interior; and Chapter 5 which deals with the Wadi Samail Groundwater recharge scheme on the Batinah coast.

262 **Use of satellite remote sensing of cloud and rainfall for selected operational applications in the fields of applied hydrology and food production.**
Clare Power. PhD thesis, University of Bristol, England, 1989. 588p.
(Available from University Microfilms International, Ann Arbor, Michigan, order no. AADDX-89379).

The first part of the dissertation deals with the literature on the use of remote sensing in the fields of cloud, rainfall, vegetation and food production monitoring and assessment. Part two includes specific projects and case-studies, including three in the Sultanate of Oman.

263 **The hydrogeology of the Oman mountains.**
Gordon Stanger. PhD thesis, Open University, Milton Keynes, England, 1986. 418p. (Not available from University Microfilms).

A study of the groundwater resources of northern Oman, an arid area almost entirely dependent upon groundwater recharged by a highly sporadic rainfall. The nature of the geology and pattern of groundwater is studied and Stanger points out that the buried alluvial channels facilitate efficient interception and recovery by the *falaj* system of irrigation. The point is made that on the Batinah coast increased usage of water for agriculture has led to moderate-to-severe salination.

Environment

264 Omanian land-based oil inputs to the Gulf of Oman.
H. Awad, M. A. Al Moharamy, S. A. Al Eissa. *Oil and Chemical Pollution*, vol. 6, no. 2 (1990), p. 91-99.

Part of a world-wide project to estimate oil inputs from coastal refineries to the marine environment. This account is concerned with the Omani refinery and the adjacent waters in the Gulf of Oman. It is estimated that 160.4 tons of crude oil wastes and refined products are added annually to the waters, to which must be added 140 tons from a neighbouring tank farm. An examination of the petroleum residues in the water indicate a high rate of dispersal and dilution, more than 200 times less than the concentration of oil in the discharge itself.

265 Hydrocarbons in seawater, sediment, and oyster from the Omani coastal waters.
M. I. Badawy, F. Al-Harthy. *Bulletin of Environmental Contamination and Toxicology*, vol. 47, no. 3 (1991), p. 386-91.

Hydrocarbons in seawater, sediment and oysters were determined as part of the Omani marine monitoring programme with samples being obtained at Musandam, Muttrah, Masirah and Raysut. Analysis were conducted using ultraviolet (UV) fluorescence analysis, with samples from Masirah and Raysut being relatively contaminated whilst that from Muttrah, near an oil terminal, was relatively clean. However, samples from all sites showed evidence of oil pollution in sediments and system samples showed the presence of petroleum hydrocarbon pollution at all stations.

266 Sources of pollution of Mina al Fahal coastal area.
M. I. Badawy (et al.). *Bulletin of Environmental Contamination and Toxicology*, vol. 49, no. 6 (1992), p. 813-20.

A study of the pollution in the sea area off the Mina al Fahal oil refinery to determine the sources of hydrocarbons and wastewater emissions in the Gulf of Oman.

267 **Tar loads on Omani beaches.**

M. I. Badawy, F. T. Al-Harthy. *Bulletin of Environmental Contamination and Toxicology*, vol. 47, no. 5 (1991), p. 732-77.

The results of a study of the incidence of tar balls on Omani beaches and the source of the oil pollution to which Oman is vulnerable due to its geographical position and length of coastline along the Arabian Sea. The study took place between 1985 and 1988, using methods specified by UNESCO, and the results showed that most tars were pitch black, accumulated in bands, but with less being found in the Salalah region. The differences in oil compositions indicated that they were from different origins, and samples from northern Oman were completely derived from foreign sources.

268 **Geo-constants in Oman.**

Howard Bowen-Jones. In: *Oman: economic, social and strategic developments*, edited by B. R. Pridham. London: Croom Helm, 1987, p. 118-33.

This contribution argues that certain geographical constants have not only affected the historical past but continue now (and will do in the future) to affect the course of development in Oman. The first of the constants considered is water, particularly groundwater. This is followed by regional habitats which are considered so influential as to have determined the structure of Omani regional life and activity between regions. The final constant considered is that of the location of Oman, because the external relationships – economic, cultural and political – have been of great importance, and are likely to remain so in the future.

269 **Survey of tar, hydrocarbon and metal pollution in the coastal waters of Oman.**

K. A. Burns (et al.). *Marine Pollution Bulletin*, vol. 13, no. 7 (1982), p. 240-47.

Beach sampling after the monsoon season in 1982 showed standing stocks of tar, with amongst the highest values reported for anywhere in the world, and a trend of increasing levels of oil pollution in the Strait of Hormuz area. Data collected would seem to support the theory that tanker deballasting is the major source of oil pollution on Omani coasts. However, heavy metal and chlorinated hydrocarbon concentrates were low compared to those in more industrialized areas.

270 **Oil pollution in the southern Arabian Gulf and Gulf of Oman.**

H. S. Emara. *Marine Pollution Bulletin*, vol. 21, no. 8 (1990), p. 399-401.

This paper produces the results of surveys to measure oil pollution in the southern Arabian Gulf and Gulf of Oman based on cruises in the region between 16 February and 3 March 1987, and on other research by the same author in 1984, 1985 and 1986.

271 **Coastal zone management planning and marine protected areas.**

R. V. Salm. *Parks*, vol. 12, no. 1 (1987), p. 18-19.

A coastal zone management plan has been completed in Oman to ensure that areas of sensitive or valuable coastal environment are not neglected and that coastal areas are properly managed.

272 **Horizontal and vertical distribution of oil pollution in the Arabian Gulf and Gulf of Oman.**
M. I. El Samra, K. Z. El Deeb. *Marine Pollution Bulletin*, vol. 19, no. 1 (1986), p. 14-18.

An examination of the sea area of the Arabian Gulf and the Gulf of Oman divided into three zones according to the sources of oil pollution and the method of its transport. The effects of offshore oil fields as sources of pollution are discussed in horizontal and vertical scales. The survey showed lower values of oil concentrations in the coastal waters zone.

273 **Monsoon cloudwater chemistry on the Arabian Peninsula.**
R. S. Schemenauer, P. Cereeda. *Atmospheric Environment*, Part A, 26A(9), 1992, p. 1583-87.

Samples of cloudwater were collected near the Dhofar coast between 2 and 30 July 1990. Chemical analysis demonstrated that the cloudwater was very clean.

Dissertation

274 **A contribution towards the conservation of Dhofar, Southern Oman, using remote sensing techniques for determining ecological zones.**
F. M. S. Al-Lamki. MPhil thesis, University of Edinburgh, Scotland, 1988. (Available from British Library, Document Supply Centre, Boston Spa, Wetherby, West Yorkshire, United Kingdom).

Development in Dhofar since 1975 has led to exploitation of its natural resources, thus revealing a fragile and sensitive ecosystem. Ecological zones within Dhofar province have been determined by interpretation of remote sensing imagery in terms of aerial photographs, space photographs and digital space imagery, augmented by fieldwork. The province is considered of environmental significance: it is unique in the more arid Arabian Peninsula in having an annual three months of light rain produced by the monsoons.

Flora and Fauna

275 Lizards with northern affinities from the mountains of Oman.
E. N. Arnold. *Zoologische Mededelingen*, vol. 47, (1972), p. 111-28.
Traces the origins of lizards in Oman which are not unlike a species found in the extreme north of the Arabian Peninsula.

276 The sea birds of the southwest coast of Arabia.
Roger Bailey. *Ibis*, vol. 108, no. 2 (1986), p. 224-64. maps.
The result of a study carried out by the author in 1963-64 as part of the International Indian Ocean Expedition. Following an outline of the geography and marine life of the area, it presents studies and documentation of sea-birds, covering the coast from Ras Fortak to Ras al-Hadd in Oman, and a 200-square mile area of sea from that coast. The survey is supported by location maps, and tables list the birds recorded and the physical characteristics of those which were collected and ringed.

277 Flora Arabica.
E. Blatter. *Records of the Botanical Survey of India*, vol. 8, nos. 1-6 (1919-36). 519p.
An official publication of the Government Printing Office of Calcutta, which includes records of the flora of Oman as part of its survey.

278 An account of the fishes obtained by Surgeon Major A.S.G. Jayakar at Muscat, east coast of Arabia (Parts 1, 2 and 3).
G. A. Boulanger. *Proceedings of the Zoological Society of London* (1887), p. 653-67; (1889), p. 236-44; (1892), p. 134-36.
The author (who also studied Omani dialects) was based at Muscat where he collected these specimens. The articles are illustrated and very informative, but specialist in nature.

279 **Arabian seabirds.**

W. A. Bourne. *Ibis*, vol. 133, no. 1 (1991), p. 136-37.

A report on sea-birds off the southern coast of Oman based on the author's observations during the period November 1987 to February 1988 and in August 1988 whilst on the RFA *Tidespring*. An abundance of northern sea-birds were observed in the inshore coastal waters of Oman outside of the monsoon periods and a list of the birds and locations are provided.

280 **Notes on birds observed in South Arabia.**

P. W. P. Browne. *Ibis*, vol. 92 (1950), p. 52-65.

A listing, with brief data, of both native and migratory birds observed in the area.

281 **The distribution of the damage potential of the desert locusts.**

F. T. Bullen. London: Anti-Locust Research Centre, 1969. 44p.

(Anti-Locust Memoir no. 10).

One of a series of reports produced by the Anti-Locust Research Centre, which also covers Arabia.

282 **The Musandam Expedition 1971-72. Scientific results: part 1, I. Biological aspects.**

P. F. S. Cornelius. *Geographical Journal*, vol. 139, pt. 3 (1973), p. 400-3. map.

Virtually the first account of the flora and fauna of northern Oman, with the emphasis on marine life. The article also briefly considers the type and volume of inshore fishing along the peninsula. This is an abbreviated account of the much fuller report housed in the Royal Geographical Society library, which lists fully the specimens collected on the expedition, now deposited with the British Museum.

283 **Seasonal breedings and migrations of the desert locust in north eastern Africa and the Middle East.**

D. E. Davies. London: Anti-Locust Research Centre, 1952. 57p.

(Anti-Locust Memoir no. 4).

One of a series of publications issued by the Anti-Locust Research Centre, dealing with breeding seasons and migration patterns.

284 **The zoogeography of the mammal fauna of southern Arabia.**

M. J. Delahy. *Mammal Review*, vol. 19, no. 4 (1989), p. 133-52.

A review of the mammal fauna of the coastal areas of Saudi Arabia, in the Red Sea southwards from Taif, the Yemens and Oman. The classifications of the various species are listed and brief physical, climatic and vegetational descriptions of the regions are provided.

285 **Breeding of the desert locust over southern Arabia following a tropical cyclone in May 1959.**
J. M. Denton. London: Anti-Locust Research Centre, 1969. 4p. (Occasional paper no. 15).
An examination of breeding results following cyclone conditions in the Oman area.

286 **Environmental conditions and phytoplankton distribution in the Arabian Gulf and Gulf of Oman, September 1986.**
M. M. Dorgham, A. Moftah. *Journal of the Marine Biological Association of India*, vol. 31, nos. 1-2 (1989), p. 36-53.
A study of the environmental conditions and the characteristics of the phytoplankton population during September 1986 in the Arabian Gulf and the Gulf of Oman. Marked regional variations were observed in the nutritional conditions of the surface water, and in the levels of salinity which decreased from the Gulf of Oman to the Arabian Sea.

287 **An ecological study of the rocky shores of the southern coast of Oman.**
Geneva: United Nations Environmental Programme, 1985. 18p. (UNEP Seas Report Study, no. 71).
This report is an account of a study of the littoral and immediate sublittoral ecology of Oman with special attention given to rocky shore communities occurring in the Salalah region of Dhofar. A brief outline of physical and environmental factors isincluded to explain some of the factors which may influence the seasonal distribution of plants and animals.

288 **Long day's vigil in Oman.**
Deborah Forester, Timothy Tear. *International Wildlife*, vol. 20, no. 2 (1990), p. 18-24.
The Arabian oryx, a rare wild antelope, has been protected since 1972 when it neared extinction due to hunting and poaching. In 1990 more than 100 animals roam within an area of 7,000 square miles in the Jabal Al Akhdar and it is hope that the herd will rise to 300 by the end of the decade.

289 **Foraging behaviour and identification of Upcher's warbler.**
C. H. Fry. *British Birds*, vol. 83, no. 6 (1990), p. 217-21.
An account of the habitat and ground foraging of Upcher's warbler which is a regular spring passage migrant in Oman between late April and mid-May. Its habitat is a one-kilometre patch of *Acacia* woodland on the coast 40 kilometres west of Muscat.

290 **The birds of Oman.**
Michael D. Gallagher, Martin W. Woodcock. London: Quartet, 1980. 310p. maps. bibliog.
An essential work for a study of the birds of Oman. The work begins with a background survey of the geography, climate and water resources of the Sultanate. The authors then look at the bird life in detail, and there is a large section of coloured

plates with descriptive text. They also provide a section on observations of the birds and conclude with lists of new species, ringed birds recovered in Oman, species still requiring confirmation, and a checklist. Gallagher was assistant to the adviser for the conservation of the environment and Woodcock is a specialist in Asian ornithology.

291 **Notes on birds collected and observed in Oman and Hadhraumat.**
    K. M. Guichard, D. Godwin. *Ibis*, vol. 94, no. 2 (1952), p. 294-305.
A series of brief notes on birds sighted and collected in Oman and present-day Yemen.

292 **The south Arabian unicorn.**
    R. A. B. Hamilton. *Folk Lore*, vol. 54 (1943), p. 261-62.
The unicorn of folklore is in fact the Arabian oryx which was once abundant in Oman and which from a distance often appeared to have only one horn. After being hunted into extinction, the oryx has been successfully been reintroduced from captive breeding stock.

293 **Remote sensing support for the Omani White Oryx Project.**
    R. Harris. In: *Remote sensing for rangeland monitoring and management held at Silsoe, 1983*. Reading, England: Remote Sensing Society, 1983, p. 17-24.
Landsat images were used to produce terrain cover and geomorphology maps of the Jiddat al Harasis region to support the reintroduction of the white oryx into the central desert of Oman.

294 **Satellite remote sensing for resource management in the central Oman desert: a case study of the White Oryx Project.**
    R. Harris. In: *Proceedings of a National Conference on Resource Management, San Francisco, 1983*, edited by Y. M. Schiffman (et al.). Springfield, Virginia: CERMA, 1984, p. 43-52.
Landsat imagery of the central desert of Oman was used to provide environmental information to assist the resource management of the reintroduced Arabian oryx in the Jiddat al Harasis region.

295 **The mammal fauna of Oman with special reference to conservation and the Oman Flora and Fauna Survey.**
    David Lakin Harrison. *Journal of Oman Studies*, vol. 6, no. 2 (1983), p. 327-39.
Argues the case for conservation of Oman's flora and fauna as an important part of the Sultanate's national heritage. The article discusses the nature of conservation, why it is necessary, how it should be undertaken and the special areas of concern in Oman. The mammal fauna of the Sultanate comprises some 56 known species of which 34 are of conservation interest, 8 are considered to be threatened with local extinction and one species is extinct locally but has been saved in captivity and could be restored to its wild state. This is the Arabian oryx (see other articles on its reintroduction into Oman, for example, items 288, 292-294, 308-309, 325). Preservation of the habitat is seen as important as a protection from hunting, and it is

considered that the ultimate success of any conservation policy must depend on education. A number of publications in both English and Arabic, and sponsored by the government, are furthering this cause.

296   The mammals of Arabia.
David Lakin Harrison.   London: Benn, 1964-72. 3 vols.

Volume 1. is entitled Insectivora, chiroptera, primates; volume 2. Carnivora, ortiodactyla, hydrochoeridae; and volume 3. Lagomorpha, Rodentia. This is a comprehensive study of mammal animal life in Arabia, with detailed descriptions, illustrations and considerations of habitat and breeding. It includes Oman.

297   Mammals obtained by the expedition with a checklist of the mammals of the Sultanate of Oman.
David Lakin Harrison.   In: *Scientific results of the Oman Flora and Fauna Survey, 1975.   Journal of Oman Studies Special Report*, no. 1 (1977), p. 13-26.

A description of the mammals found during the flora and fauna survey of 1975 together with a checklist of the known species of mammals present in the Sultanate. The survey was sponsored by the government in order to obtain evidence to enable conservation planning to take place.

298   The mammals obtained in Dhofar by the 1977 Oman Flora and Fauna Survey.
David Lakin Harrison.   *Journal of Oman Studies Special Report*, no. 3 (1980), p. 387-97.

A description and listing of the mammals observed and recorded in Dhofar province during the flora and fauna survey which was sponsored by the government. The objective was to document the mammal population of the region to assist with future conservation policy.

299   Observations on a wild goat from Oman, eastern Arabia.
David Lakin Harrison.   *Journal of Zoology*, vol. 151, no. 1 (1967), p. 27-30.

An article about the tahr goat of the Jabal Al Akhdar, which at that time was in danger of extinction.

300   The Oman Flora and Fauna Survey, 1975.
David Lakin Harrison.   *Journal of Oman Studies*, vol. 1 (1978), p. 181-86. map.

A report of a survey of the flora and fauna of the Jabal Al Akhdar range, within the boundaries of a proposed national park. The scientific reports based on the survey cover a large body of botanical and zoological specimens and are intended for specialist use.

301 **On a collection of birds made in Oman.**
David Lakin Harrison. *Bulletin of the British Ornithologists' Club*,
vol. 76 (1956), p. 34-36, 46-51.
A listing and description of birds collected by the author, who has written a great deal
on the flora and fauna of the Sultanate.

302 **On a collection of mammals from Oman, with the description of
two new bats.**
David Lakin Harrison. *Annals and Magazine of Natural History*, vol.
12, no. 8 (1955), p. 897-910. bibliog.
A useful introduction to the mammal life of Oman, much of which had not been
systematically recorded. This is evidenced by the identification of two new bats.

303 **A park to save the Arabian tahr.**
David Lakin Harrison, Michael D. Gallagher. *Oryx*, vol. 12, no. 5
(1974), p. 547-49.
Discusses the plans of the Sultan to create a national park in the Jabal al Akhdar as a
reserve for the Arabian tahr, a mountain goat which was in danger of extinction.

304 **Plans for reserves in Oman.**
David Lakin Harrison, Michael D. Gallagher. *Oryx*, vol. 13, no. 3
(1976), p. 287-88.
Outlines the government's plan for the creation of national reserves in Oman, one of
which was to be sited in the Jabal Al Akhdar to cater for the reintroduction of the
Arabian oryx and to provide protection for the tahr wild goat.

305 **Plans to save the Arabian tahr.**
David Lakin Harrison. *Asian Affairs*, vol. 63 (Feb. 1976), p. 33-34.
An account of the plans to protect the tahr goat in a wildlife reserve in the Jabal Al
Akhdar using local tribesmen as game wardens.

306 **Protecting Oman's wildlife.**
David Lakin Harrison. *Middle East International*, no. 70 (April
1977), p. 25-27.
A brief article on the need for conservation in Oman, where various animals,
especially the tahr mountain goat, are unique to the area. In the light of this problem,
an expedition was mounted, with the support of the Sultan, to survey the Jabal Al
Akhdar with a view to creating a national park. The author believes the prospects
encouraging, as in Oman 'there is a clear realisation that the essential ingredient for
ultimate success lies in the education of the youth of the country in their own national
heritage of flora and fauna'.

307 **Arabian oryx: a desert tragedy.**
D. S. Henderson. *National Park and Conservation Magazine*, vol.
48, no. 5 (1974), p. 18-21.
Describes the hunting and poaching which led to the oryx being extinct in Oman,
together with a description of its biology and habitat.

308 **The Arabian oryx: Its distribution and former habitat in Oman and its reintroduction.**
Hartmut Jungius. *Journal of Oman Studies*, vol. 8, pt. 1 (1985),
p. 49-64. map.
This paper deals with the feasibility study on the project to reintroduce the Arabian
oryx into Oman using part of the breeding herd established in American and Europe
in 1962/63 for this purpose. The feasibility study examined the natural history, status
and human use of the former habitat of the oryx and compiled data on the basic
ecological requirements of the oryx. In addition, the study aimed to identify the most
suitable area for reintroducing the oryx and to prepare a reintroduction strategy and
technique. The study concluded that the Jiddat al Harasis was the ideal area for the
reintroduction of the oryx but it needed to be designated as a wildlife sanctuary and
an administration and guard force established to ensure law enforcement. Also an
education/information programme needed to be mounted to inform people inside and
outside of the area about the reasons for the project. Finally, an infrastructure needed
to be established to administer the project and to assess the adaptation of the released
animals in the wild, to identify problems and to advise on solutions.

309 **Plans to restore Arabian oryx in Oman.**
Hartmut Jungius. *Oryx*, vol. 14, no. 4 (1978), p. 328-36.
The Arabian oryx had been exterminated in the Arabian Peninsula as a result of
indiscriminate hunting and their habitat and biology are described. However, the oryx
had been bred in captivity and was to be reintroduced into its natural habitat in Oman,
The tribesmen of the Jiddat al Harasis, where the last known oryx had been killed,
had agreed to act as game wardens to the reintroduced species.

310 **On some birds from the Oman peninsula.**
N. B. Kinnear. *Bulletin of the British Ornithologists' Club*, vol. 48,
no. 1 (1927), p. 11-12.
Observations on the collection of birds made by the geologist G. M. Lees, including a
description of a hitherto unknown sandgrouse.

311 **Report on collection of birds, appendix IV of *The physical geography of south-eastern Arabia.***
N. B. Kinnear. *Geographical Journal*, vol. 71, no. 5 (1928),
p. 465-66.
A report from the Natural History section of the British Museum on the collection of
twenty-three specimens brought back by an expedition. The report lists the species of
birds and adds expert comment where necessary.

312 **Fishes of Saudi Arabia: freshwater fishes of Saudi Arabia and adjacent regions of the Arabian Peninsula.**
F. Krupp. *Fauna of Saudi Arabia*, vol. 5 (1983), p. 568-636.
Divides the Arabian Peninsula into three sub-provinces based on the distribution and affinities of primary freshwater fishes. One sub-province is the Oman mountains, with three species closely related to or co-specific with Iranian Cyprinides.

313 **Butterflies of Oman.**
Torben Larsen, Kiki Larsen. Edinburgh; Muscat: Government of Oman and Bartholomew, 1980. 80p.
A comprehensive catalogue of the butterflies of Oman including their descriptions, food and habitat.

314 **The zoogeographical composition and distribution of the Arabian butterflies (Lepidoptera Rhopalocera).**
T. B. Larsen. *Journal of Biogeography*, vol. 1, no. 2 (1984), p. 119-58.
There are 148 species of Rhopalocera and two-thirds of these are of Afrotropical origin. Dhofar province and northern Oman are classified as belonging to that region for the incidence of butterflies.

315 **In search of Arabian oryx.**
Michael Lloyd. *Geographical Magazine*, vol. 37 (April 1964), p. 898-906.
An expedition to Oman to locate and photograph the Arabian oryx, which was in danger of becoming extinct due to the activities of hunters over a number of generations.

316 **Oman adventure.**
Kenneth Mackinnon. *Blackwood's Magazine*, vol. 269, no. 1628 (1981), p. 481-94.
The author was a locust officer in the Arabian Peninsula. During the winter of 1949-50 he made a visit to Oman as a naturalist and in this article he details the various flowers and birds to be found in the Sultanate. This was a period when European influence in Oman was discouraged, especially in the interior; the author's account of his exploration is therefore especially interesting.

317 **Arabia: Sand, sea, sky.**
Michael McKinnon. London: BBC Books, 1990. 224p. bibliog.
A study of the complete flora and fauna of the Arabian Peninsula and the present ecological transformation and its effects on the future of the inhabitants and the wildlife. References to flora and fauna in Oman are scattered throughout the text, including a consideration of the Arabian oryx as part of a conservation project.

318 **Wild flowers of Northern Oman.**
James Mandeville.   London: Bartholomew, 1978. 64p.

A publication arising out of the Oman Flora and Fauna Survey begun in 1975, which concentrates on the Jabal Al Akhdar, and gives a selection of flowers which are of significance or of beauty in the area. Each plant's habitat is given along with the Arabic name and any interesting facts. The pictures, made on location by Dorothy Boway, are an accurate botanical record.

319 **Descriptions of 68 new Gastropoda from the Persian Gulf, Gulf of Oman and North Arabian Sea dredged by F. W. Townsend, 1901-3.**
J. C. Melville.   *Annals and Magazine of Natural History*, vol. 7, no. 12 (1903), p. 289-324.

The samples were dredged by Townsend during operations for the Indo-European Telegraph.

320 **The Mollusca of the Persian Gulf, Gulf of Oman and Arabian Sea.**
J. C. Melville, R. Staden.   Part I: 'Cephalopoda, Gastropoda, Scophopoda', *Proceedings of the Zoological Society*, vol. 2, no. 2 (1941), p. 327-460. bibliog.; Part II: 'Pelecypoda', *Proceedings of the Zoological Society*, vol. 7, no. 2 (1906), p. 783-848. bibliog.

An examination of the distribution of molluscs and the species to be found in these areas, based on the collections made by F. W. Townsend from 1893 to 1906 during operations for the Indo-European Telegraph. The collections contained specimens of hitherto unknown species.

321 **Plants of Dhofar.**
Anthony G. Miller, Miranda Morris, illustrated by Susanna Stuart-Smith.   Muscat: Office of the Advisor for Conservation, 1988. xxvii+361p. maps. bibliog.

This volume deals comprehensively with the plants of Dhofar and their environment. The first section, by Miller, deals with the topography and climate of Dhofar province together with a brief description of its flora and fauna, and the geological character of the area. The second section, by Morris, describes the plants in some detail and their uses in food, the tanning industry and in pharmacology as medicinal herbs, both in terms of formal Arabic medicine and folk medicine, the latter knowledge being the purview of Omani women. The rest of the book deals with the plants; these are listed alphabetically by their Latin botanical names and their local Arabic equivalent both in Dhofar and Jibbali.

322 **The ecology of the Arabian tahr (*Henitrogus* Jayakari Thomas 1894) and a strategy for the conservation of the species.**
Paul N. Munton.   *Journal of Oman Studies*, vol. 8, pt. 1 (1985), p. 11-48. maps.

This work is based upon the results of two years' fieldwork in the Wadi Surin reserve in the mountains of Oman. It deals in detail with a number of topics, including: the climate of the study area; the flora of the habitat in Wadi Surin; the diet of the Arabian tahr; the use of the Oman mountains by the tahr; a survey of the mountains of northern Oman and the varieties of flora in the area; and the populations of the Arabian tahr. The final part of the article outlines a conservation strategy for the Arabian tahr which includes the necessity for the tahr to have access to the optimum habitat, ungrazed by domestic stock and where hunting and poaching can be controlled. Also the laws governing protected areas need to be examined to ensure continuity with traditional practices and of particular need is the re-enforcement of ancient laws on tree cutting to protect the high cover of small trees in the country.

323 Locust survey in Oman, 11 January to 3 March 1968.

G. B. Popov.   London: Anti-Locust Research Centre, 1968. 7p.
(Occasional report no. 13).

One of a series of specialist reports forming part of the centre's research programme into the control and eradication of the locust.

324 New grasshoppers from Oman and its neighbours.

George B. Popov.   *Journal of Oman Studies*, vol. 8, pt. 1 (1985), p. 65-74.

The Flora and Fauna Surveys of 1975 and 1977 have generated interest in Oman from collectors and naturalists, and the article describes a new species and two subspecies of grasshopper in Oman, together with a new long-horn grasshopper discovered by the author in the People's Democratic Republic of Yemen. The article provides a detailed description of the caterpillars, with diagrams and illustrations, together with references to collections made by other naturalists since the flora and fauna surveys were undertaken.

325 Animal re-introductions: the Arabian oryx in Oman.

M. R. S. Price.   Cambridge: Cambridge University Press, 1989. 291p.

The Arabian oryx became extinct in its native area in 1972 as a result of over-exploitation by tribesmen and game hunters. This work describes the reintroduction of the Arabian oryx into central Oman, using zoo-bred animals with great success. The genus Oryx is described in detail, paying attention to its biology, history and the background to its extermination in the wild. An account then follows of the breeding process in captivity, the planning for reintroduction, the chosen area, the management of the herd and the role of the Harasis tribe in its conservation.

326 The Bedu minds the oryx.

M. R. S. Price.   *Geographical Magazine*, vol. 57, no. 12 (1985), p. 644-45.

The oryx has been reintroduced into the Jiddat al Harasis in Oman, largely as a result of the involvement of the local Harasis tribe as protectors of the oryx, and through the offering of social and economic benefits.

327 **Desert locust migrations and synoptic meteorology in the Gulf of Aden area.**
R. C. Rainey, Z. Waloff. *Journal of Animal Ecology*, vol. 17, no. 2 (1948), p. 101-12.
Discusses the influence of the weather on the migratory habits of the locust.

328 **Seasonal and longer-period changes in the desert locust situation with a note on a tropical cyclone affecting southern Arabia in 1948.**
R. C. Rainey. *World Meteorological Organization Technical Notes*, no. 69 (1968), p. 255-64.
A further consideration of the link between weather conditions and the breeding and migration of locusts.

329 **Cretaceous and Paleogene echinoids from Dhofar (Sultanate of Oman) and connections between the Indian Ocean and Mediterranean basins.**
J. Roman (et al.). *Bulletin of the Geological Society of France*, vol. 5, no. 2 (1989), p. 279-86.
A rich fauna has been collected in Dhofar, suggesting connections with three of the western Mediterranean echinoids and with fauna of the Indian Ocean. The relationships show that formal migrations between the two areas had become difficult well before interruption in the Lower Miocene.

330 **Adult sex ratios in the green sea turtle.**
J. P. Ross. *Copeia*, no. 3 (1984), p. 174-76.
This study of sea turtles, *Chelonia mydas*, in the waters of the Sultanate of Oman consistently suggested greater proportions of females amongst the population.

331 **Birds of Oman and Muscat.**
Rodolphe Meyer de Schauensee, S. Dillon Ripley. *Proceedings of the Academy of National Science*, vol. 105 (1953), p. 71-90. map.
An account of a collecting and observing visit to the Sultanate in 1951. The article lists and locates 144 species of birds, and also records three new types of babbler, lark and warbler. The field notes record sightings by date and place.

332 **The scientific results of the Oman Flora and Fauna Survey 1975: a *Journal of Oman Studies* special report.**
Muscat: Ministry of Information and Culture, 1977. 267p. maps. bibliog.
A very important report on the flora and fauna of Oman, surveyed on behalf of the Sultanate by a number of specialists including David Lakin Harrison and J. P. Mandaville. This work is essential for any specialist study of the flora and fauna of Oman.

333 **Reef and coral communities of Oman, with a description of a new coral species** (Order Schoractina, genus Acarthastrea).
C. R. C. Sheppard, R. V. Salm. *Journal of Natural History*, vol. 22, no. 1 (1988), p. 263-79.

Three areas off the mainland of Oman support corals, separated by stretches of shallow sandy or muddy sublittoral. Three categories of coral reef are recognized and described. Some 91 coral species are identified, and comparisons show the Oman fauna to be similar to that of the Arabian Gulf with a 63 per cent match, but relatively dissimilar to that in other areas of significant coral in the Arabian Sea.

334 **The Arabian Oryx Oryx-Leucoryx re-introduction project in Oman 10 years on.**
J. A. Spalton. Toulouse, France: Institut de Recherche sur les Grands Mammifères, 1992, p. 343-47.

This paper was presented at an international symposium on ungulates held at Toulouse in September 1991. The author is an adviser on the Arabian Oryx Project in the conservation office of the Diwan Royal Court. The article reviews the Arabian Oryx Project in the Jiddat al Harasis National Park, and covers the problems faced in the ten years the programme had been running, the growth of the herd, management techniques and the specific problem of inbreeding.

335 **The Arabian oryx.**
D. R. M. Stewart. *East African Wildlife Journal*, vol. 1 (1963), p. 103-17.

A study of the Arabian oryx, which was in danger of becoming extinct, and its relationship with the African branch of the species.

336 **Role of social theory in reintroduction planning: a case study of the Arabian oryx in Oman.**
Timothy H. Tear, Deborah Forester. *Society and Natural Sources*, vol. 5, no. 4 (1992), p. 359-75.

This article examines the reintroduction of the Arabian oryx into Oman, using a social theory to assess the programme in the context of a conceptual model. The system used proposes that the reintroduction programme is a resource system composed of events which can be analysed from ecological, ethnological and economic perspectives.

337 **The Sultan and the oryx.**
Ray Vicker. *International Wildlife*, vol. 10, no. 3 (1980), p. 4-11.

The ruler of Oman, Sultan Qaboos, has been very supportive of wildlife conservation and measures were taken to protect the oryx and the goat-like tahr. Local tribesmen had agreed to leave the animals undisturbed in the wild but oryx had also been sent abroad to zoos in an attempt to foster a breeding programme to enable reintroduction of the animals at a future date.

338 Note on the occurrence of *Dolium variegatum* Lamarck, at Muscat
with consideration on its geographical distribution at the present
day and in former geological times.
E. W. Vredenberg. *Journal of the Royal Asiatic Society of Bengal*,
vol. 14 (1918), p. 449-59.
A specialist article on fauna which, according to the Lamarck theory, shows evidence
of genetic inheritance and its incidence in the Muscat area, both past and present.

339 **Arabian locust hunter.**
G. F. Walford. London: Hale, 1963. 176p. maps.
An account of the extremely important work of the anti-locust unit operating in the
Arabian Peninsula, including Oman, in an attempt to eradicate the locust and prevent
its periodic destruction of crops.

340 **The Omani camels.**
M. F. Warden. *International Symposium on Agricultural
Development, Muscat, Oman 14-19 October 1989.* Damascus, Syria:
Arab Centre for the Study of Arid Zones and Dry Lands, 1990. 19p.
An Arabic-language paper, with English summary, on the status, usage and value of
the camel in Omani husbandry and in the overall life of the nomadic population.

341 **Humpback whale songs from the North Indian Ocean.**
H. Whitehead. *Investigatio. Cetacea*, vol. 17 (1985), p. 157-62.
Humpback whale songs were recorded off Oman in January 1983 and in the Gulf of
Manner, Sri Lanka, in February and March 1983 and these songs were similar to one
another, but very different from songs recorded in the North Atlantic or North Pacific.
These recordings and other evidence suggest that a small number of humpbacks spend
the year within the North Indian Ocean.

342 **The distribution of organic carbon and nitrogen in sediments from
the Arabian Sea.**
J. D. H. Wiseman, H. Bennett. *Scientific Reports from the John
Murray Expedition*, vol. 3, no. 4 (1940), p. 193-320.
This is an important contribution to the study of Arabian Sea flora and to the
palaeontology of the area but it is intended for the specialist reader.

Prehistory and Archaeology

343 **Explorations in Dhofar, Oman.**

Frank P. Albright. *Antiquity*, vol. 29, no. 113 (1955), p. 37-39.

A brief note to record the four archaeological digs undertaken in Dhofar province in 1952 and organized by Wendell Phillips. Preliminary excavations of earlier settlements indicated that a great deal more investigation and recording needed to be undertaken.

344 **Qurum: a case study of coastal archaeology in northern Oman.**

P. Biagi (et al.). *World Archaeology*, vol. 16, no. 1 (1984), p. 43-61.

Qurum is providing evidence of prehistoric coastal settlement through an archaeological investigation of a cluster of shell-middens. These relate to a small population of fishermen of the 5th and 4th millennium BC with a marine-based culture. Stock breeding of goats and cattle was also practised, however, showing early contact with farming groups.

345 **Looking for Dilmun.**

George Bibby. New York: Knopf, 1969; London: Collins, 1970. 383p.

Although mainly concerned with Bahrain and the Al-Ain oasis in Abu Dhabi and the archaeological work there over a period of fifteen years, this work is relevant because of Bibby's theory about the origins of the lost civilization of Dilmun which he concluded was sited in present-day Bahrain. The link with Oman is through the copper trade based in Makan, which Bibby concludes would be found in the area of Buraimi Oasis and the Oman mountains.

346 **Excavations and survey in Oman, 1974-1975.**
Beatrice De Cardi, Stephen Collier, D. S. Doe. *Journal of Oman Studies*, vol. 2 (1976), p. 101-87. maps.

The report is in three parts: the first discusses the excavations and the surveys; the second part is a gazetteer; and the third consists of a series of plates. The report discusses the excavations and surveys of sixty-two sites near 'Amiah in the Wadi al-'Ayn, which showed great similarity to sites at Umm an-Nar off Abu Dhabi and at Hili in the Al-Ain oasis.

347 **The rock art of Oman 1975.**
Christopher Clarke. *Journal of Oman Studies*, vol. 1 (1975), p. 113-22. maps.

A study of the rock art of Oman undertaken during 1973-74. It is a preliminary work because the collected evidence has still to be documented and assessed, though the author stresses that the art (both human and animal representations) is difficult to date and to place into historical perspective.

348 **Preliminary report on archaeological soundings at Sohar.**
Ray L. Cleveland. *Bulletin of the American School of Oriental Research*, vol. 153, pt. 1 (1959), p. 11-19. map.

A report on initial excavations carried out at Sohar in January 1958, when three sites produced a range of pottery dating back to the 6th or 7th century. Initial soundings confirmed extensive occupation during Abbasid times – a possibility also indicated by geographical accounts – as well as trading links between Oman and the rest of the Islamic world and the Far East.

349 **The copper mining settlement of Arja: A preliminary survey.**
P. M. Costa. *Journal of Oman Studies*, vol. 4, pt.1 (1978), p. 9-14.

A preliminary survey of the copper-mining settlement at Arja in the northern Oman mountains, with a view to assessing its historical and economic significance. This was part of a series of archaeological studies being undertaken on behalf of the Omani government, and it includes a study of the economic pattern of settlement activity designed to support mining activity.

350 **Notes on traditional hydraulics and agriculture in Oman (archaeological data).**
P. M. Costa. *World Archaeology*, vol. 14, no. 3 (1983), p. 273-95.

Archaeological work in Oman has led to a growing collection of data on water exploitation and agriculture which has provided a wider knowledge of ancient Near Eastern hydrology and land utilization. The investigations have also shed light on art and architecture and sites in Oman are discussed in relation to their architectural value and their implications for settlement patterns. The architecture of an Omani garden is also presented using Masjid al-Luqta, near Muscat, as a case-study.

351 **Treasure of Ophir.**
Charles Edward Vercher Crauford. London: Sheffington, 1929.
287p. maps.

An attempt to place the biblical site of Ophir in present-day Dhofar. Speculation about its location still continues and some geological surveys in Saudi Arabia seem to have produced evidence for its siting. However, the general information in this book is still of interest.

352 **Ancient and modern man in south western Arabia.**
Henry Field. Coral Gables, Florida: University of Miami Press, 1956. 342p.

A detailed review of recorded archaeological sites, with a few introductory notes to each area. Oman is considered on pages 110-15; the detail is largely based on the work of Wilfred Thesiger and Bertram Thomas.

353 **A study of ancient slags from Oman.**
U. M. Franklin, J. C. Grasjean, M. J. Tinkler. *Canadian Metallurgical Quarterly*, vol. 15, no. 1 (1976), p. 1-7.

Although primarily an archaeological study of mining in ancient Oman, this study also has relevance to current mining prospects and proposals.

354 **Archaeological investigations in the Oman peninsula: a preliminary report.**
Karen Frifelt. *Kuml: Arbog for Jysk Arkaeologisk Selskab* (1968), p. 170-75.

An initial report on the work of the Danish archaeological expedition, which was largely centred in the area of the Buraimi Oasis.

355 **Evidence of a third millennium BC town in Oman.**
Karen Frifelt. *Journal of Oman Studies*, vol. 2 (1976), p. 52-73.

A further report of the work of the Danish archaeological expeditions of 1975-76, in the Bat area of Ibri. The report outlines the evidence for the theory that a large settlement existed in the area. It is backed by plans and photographs of the site and drawings of the various artefacts.

356 **A possible link between Jamdat Nasr and the Umm an-Nar graves of Oman.**
Karen Frifelt. *Journal of Oman Studies*, vol. 1 (1975), p. 58-80. map.

This report of a Danish archaeological survey of 1972-73 considers the possible relationship between Bronze Age settlements found on the island of Umm an-Nar off the Abu Dhabi coastline and mainland settlements in the Sultanate of Oman, particularly around Buraimi and the western Hajar. One conclusion to be drawn from the archaeological evidence is that the excavated communities at Umm an-Nar were wealthy and organized to an extent which would exceed that brought about by fishing or date growing at Buraimi. Possible this prosperity was based on metals and minerals found in the mountains and valleys of Oman; this possibility is further substantiated by the discovery of Umm an-Nar graves along the Wadi Jizzi, and especially in the Ibri area.

357 A preliminary discussion of ancient mining in the Sultanate of Oman.

G. W. Goettler, N. Firth, C. C. Houston. *Journal of Oman Studies*, vol. 2 (1976), p. 43-55.

The basis for this article was a survey of mineral exploration undertaken in 1973 by Prospection (Oman) Ltd, which discovered vestiges of at least forty-four ancient mining sites. The discoveries to date seemed to confirm the hypothesis put forward by Geoffrey Bibby, that the location of ancient Makan was in northern Oman. Being the by-product of a modern mining survey, this is not primarily an archaeological account, but it is useful for its description of the sites and the mining methods apparently used there, and includes illustrations of the locations.

358 Oman in the third millennium BC.

A. Hastings, J. M. Humphries, R. H. Meadow. *Journal of Oman Studies*, vol. 1 (1975), p. 9-56. maps.

An extremely valuable article giving an initial picture of conditions in Bronze Age Oman. The article is a report of the work of the Harvard Archeological Group during 1973 and 1974, when it located and documented seventeen settlements. The article is extremely detailed in coverage, giving location maps, illustrations and records of the items uncovered at each site, together with plans of the sites and archaeological deductions associated with the discoveries.

359 Third millennium BC copper production in Oman.

A. Hauptmann, Gerd Weisgerber. *Proceedings of the 20ième Symposium d'Archométrie*, Paris (26-29 March 1980).

Examines the significance of copper production to Oman's economy and influence.

360 Harvard Archeological Survey of Oman 1973: II – some later prehistoric sites in the Sultanate of Oman.

J. H. Humphries. *Proceedings of the Seminar for Arabian Studies*, vol. 4 (1974), p. 49-77.

An extremely important study of the early history of the Sultanate which had hitherto not been systematically investigated and documented.

361 The copper mountain of Magan.

Harold Peake. *Antiquity*, vol. 2, no. 8 (1928), p. 452-57.

The question of Makan and the supply of copper to the Sumerians puzzled archaeologists for some time, but following the work of George Bibby *Looking for Dilmun* (see item no. 345) it is generally accepted that Makan was located in Oman.

362 **Quest for Sheba.**
N. S. Pearn, V. Barlow. London: Nicholson and Watson, 1937. 258p. map.

Investigates the various possible locations of the country ruled by the Queen of Sheba, of which Oman, particularly Dhofar province, is one possibility.

363 **Qataban and Sheba: exploring the ancient kingdoms on the biblical spice routes of Arabia.**
Wendell Phillips. New York: Harcourt Brace, 1955. 362p.

Extremely valuable for a description of archaeological sites, excavations and ruins in the Dhofar province. As a explorer for oil and a representative of the Sultan, the author had free access to the area.

364 **An introduction to the anthropomorphic content of the rock art of Jabal Akhdar.**
Keith Preston. *Journal of Oman Studies*, vol. 2 (1976), p. 17-38. map.

An article based on a survey of sites in the northern mountains of Oman undertaken in 1975, to illustrate the stylistic and iconographic variations found with the anthropomorphic representations. It was discovered that the art appears mainly in concentrated sites on the limestone walls of the narrow wadis of the Jabal Al Akhdar. The art is of an uncertain age, though some is certainly 1,500 years old. It has a high anthropomorphic content, featuring mounted and unmounted figures, but also includes representations of animals, weapons, vehicles and signs. The article goes on to discuss the content, style, techniques, size and iconography of the art, with diagrams and photographs to illustrate the points raised.

365 **Harvard Archeological Survey of Oman 1973: I – flint sites in Oman.**
J. Pullar. *Proceedings of the Seminar for Arabian Studies*, vol. 4 (1974), p. 33-48.

A presentation of evidence of settlement discovered during the survey.

366 **New Neolithic sites in Oman.**
George H. Smith. *Journal of Oman Studies*, vol. 2 (1976), p. 189-98.

A description of stone implements collected at various sites in central Oman. The article lists the various tools collected at each site and includes life-size diagrams.

367 **Report on the collection of flint implements: appendix III of *The physical geography of south-eastern Arabia.***
Reginald A. Smith. *Geographical Journal*, vol. 71, no. 5 (1928), p. 464-65.

A brief report which identifies the flint specimens as artefacts, but with no real indication of what purposes they might have served. Smith concludes that they can be regarded only as a subject for further research.

368 **The dating of the Umm an-Nar culture and a proposed sequence for Oman in the third millennium BC.**
Maurizio Tosi. *Journal of Oman Studies*, vol. 2 (1976), p. 81-92. maps.

The author considers the Umm an-Nar culture of Abu Dhabi and attempts to date archaeological discoveries in Oman by providing an absolute chronology of the Umm an-Nar settlements.

369 **The emerging picture of prehistoric Arabia.**
Maurizio Tosi, edited by B. J. Siegel (et al.). *Annual Review of Anthropology*, vol. 15 (1986), p. 461-90.

A consideration of the growth of civilization in Arabia in three stages: a formative stage; an initial stage of food production; and a developed farming economy. Eastern Arabia and Oman are considered to have reached higher levels of social aggregation by the second half of the third millennium BC.

370 **Notes on the distribution and exploitation of natural resources in ancient Oman.**
Maurizio Tosi. *Journal of Oman Studies*, vol. 1 (1975), p. 187-206. maps.

A report on a preliminary survey of northern Oman to produce evidence of the early economic determinants, with a view to assisting other archaeological and historical investigations and enabling the Department of Antiquities to have a useful instrument for planning future activities. Each section provides a general survey of the settlements and activities in the early history of Oman and contains recommendations for future research activity.

371 **Evidence of ancient mining sites in Oman: a preliminary report.**
Gerd Weisgerber. *Journal of Oman Studies*, vol. 4, pt. 1 (1978), p. 15-28. map.

This is a preliminary survey of ancient copper-mining sites in Oman which provides details as to locations and evidence pointing to such activity. This article is very much a preliminary to further work undertaken by the author and other archaeologists in particular defined sites.

372 **A new kind of copper slag from Tawi 'Arja, Oman.**
Gerd Weisgerber. *Journal of the Historical Metallurgy Society*, vol. 12, no. 1 (1978), p. 40-43.

A study of the mining spoils from an ancient mining site in Oman, aimed at providing evidence for a study of the settlements associated with mining activity.

373 **The archaeology of Oman: a preliminary discussion of the Islamic periods.**
Donald S. Whitcomb. *Journal of Oman Studies*, vol. 1 (1975), p. 122-57. maps.

A consideration of the archaeological materials for the entire Islamic era, resulting from a reconnaissance of archaeological sites on the Batinah coast and in the southeast as far as Ras al Hadd. The survey was carried out in 1975 by a team from Harvard. The article uses a few representative sites to illustrate historical periods and geographical situations in northern Oman. The presentation is in three sections: the early Islamic (630-1055 AD); the middle Islamic (1055-1500 AD); and the late Islamic (1500-1750 AD). Each period is illustrated by a description of selected sites, together with photographs, plans and details of artefacts.

Farming communities of the Oman Peninsula and the copper of Makkan.
See item no. 959.

History

General

374 Records of Oman 1867-1960.
Edited by Ronald W. Bailey. Farnham Common, England: Archive
Research, 1992. 8000p. 12 vols.

This collection of facsimiles from original political archives traces the history of the
Al Bu Said dynasty, considers the tribal affairs of Oman including the question of the
Imamate, territorial questions including the Buraimi Oasis dispute, and political
developments within the Sultanate. This is an extremely important documentary
source for the history of the Sultanate of Oman.

**375 A collection of texts dealing with the Sultanate of Muscat and
Oman and its international relations 1790-1970.**
Robin Bidwell. *Journal of Oman Studies*, vol. 6, no. 1 (1983),
p. 21-33.

This paper presents references to international agreements concerning Oman from the
period covered by Aitchinson's *A collection of treaties, engagements and sanads
relating to India and neighbouring countries* (item no. 421), to the accession of
Sultan Qaboos. The dates of the texts are given – together with details of the
signatories, where appropriate – a summary of the contents, and references as to
where the texts can be found. The objective has been to provide references useful to
researchers, and as a result Bidwell has also included concessions, proclamations,
Orders in Council and the Treaty of Sib.

376 **European powers and south-east Africa: a study of international relations on the south-east coast of Africa, 1796-1856.**
Mabel V. Jackson Haight. London: Longmans Green, 1942. Rev. ed., Routledge & Kegan Paul, 1967. 368p. maps. bibliog.

The early contact with East Africa, the slave trade and relations between Zanzibar and Muscat are covered, together with the wider international significance. Of relevance also are the consideration of British and Portuguese interests and rivalry in the area.

377 **Arabian Gulf intelligence: Selections from the records of the Bombay Government. New Series No. XXIV, 1856.**
Edited by Thomas R. Hughes. London: Oleander Press, 1985. xxvii+687p. maps.

This volume reproduces the various intelligence reports produced by British representatives and political residents in the area. Areas covered are Arabia in general, the Gulf States and Oman.

378 **The legal and historical basis of the British position in the Persian Gulf.**
John Barrett Kelly. In: *St Antony Papers No. 4*. London: Chatto & Windus, 1958, p. 118-40.

An extremely useful survey by an authority on the subject. It provides essential background to British influence in the area by presenting a succession of treaties and understandings with Oman and the Gulf Sheikhdoms.

379 **Oman and the Trucial Coast.**
E. C. B. Mackinnon. *Australian Quarterly*, vol. 30, pt. 1 (1958), p. 65-76.

Considers the geography of the Sultanate and the early history and politics, particularly the founding of the Ibadhi sect of Islam in the 9th century. Also considers the period of Portuguese rule, the Omani struggle for independence, and the increasing British influence. The question of the Imamate, the various armed insurrections and Britain's role as a supporter of the Sultan are also examined.

380 **References to Oman in the literature on Arabian geography.**
Manuela Marin. *Journal of Oman Studies*, vol. 6, no. 1 (1983), p. 59-64.

A survey of the available literature on Arabian geography, with references to Oman covering the period up to the fifteenth century. The study is concerned with material relating to Oman's commercial activity which is due to its significance in trading between the Arab countries and the Far East, Africa and other regions. It is pointed out by Marin that the information is fragmentary, imperfect, and rarely based on first-hand experience, but it is important to present the view that the Arab world had of Oman's commercial activities. The activities are discussed, as are the various sources which clearly demonstrate the importance of Oman in the international trade of the Arab world and the significance of the port of Sohar. The article also discusses the qualities of Omani seamanship and problems of navigation in the areas around Oman.

381 **The Persian Gulf administration reports 1873-1957.**
Farnham Common, England: Archive Research, 1986. 7700p. 11 vols.

A collection of the annual reports from the British political officers in the Gulf Residency and Agencies in Bushire, Bahrain, Muscat and Kuwait. This is a primary source of information for Gulf history covering political, social and economic development in the region. The reports are often supplemented by memoranda on specific local matters. Important for an understanding of Britain's role in Oman during a crucial period of its history.

382 **Persian Gulf naval reports, 1829-1955.**
Great Britain, Admiralty. Farnham Common, England: Archive Research, 1992. 10,000p. 16 vols.

A collection of naval reports from the Gulf which includes details of early surveying voyages, naval actions, observations on tribes and settlements of the area and encounters with Arab traders. Also provides information on encounters with Arab 'pirates' and reports on the Gulf arms traffic and blockade between 1909 and 1914.

383 **Oman: a history.**
Wendell Phillips. London: Longman; New York: Reynal, 1967. 246p. maps.

An extremely readable general history of the Sultanate by one of the world's biggest individual oil concessionaires. The author also served as economic adviser and director of general antiquities to Sultan Said bin Taimur, but his influence declined after the *coup d'état.*

384 **The traditional state of 'Uman: a sketch.**
Richard Preece. *School of Advanced International Studies Review,* vol. 10, no. 1 (1965), p. 26-32.

Traces the history of the Sultanate to date and considers the Wahhabi (later Saudi Arabia) involvement in the politics of the interior with particular reference to support for the Imamate in its quest for independence.

385 **History of the Imams and Sayyids of Oman from AD 661-1856, translated from the original Arabic, and edited, with notes, appendices, an introduction, continuing the history down to 1870, by George Percy Badger.**
Salil Ibn Razik. New York: Burt Franklin, 1963. 435p. map. bibliog. (Originally published by Hakluyt Society, 1871. First Series, no. 44).

A valuable source of detail about the early history of Oman, especially the period after 1741. There are some reservations concerning Badger's datings, the translation of certain portions, and the question of original authorship. The introduction by Badger cites a number of sources of the period, and this is bibliographically valuable. Badger was a member of the commission set up to arbitrate between Oman and Zanzibar which resulted in the Canning Award providing a subsidy to Oman for the loss of its East African Empire and the lucrative slave trade.

386 Muscat and Oman: the end of an era.
Ian Skeet. London: Faber & Faber, 1974. 224p. map.

Although published four years after the 1970 coup which brought about great change in Oman, this book deals only with the period which ended with the rule of Sultan Said bin Taimur. The author provides an historical appreciation of the Sultanate beginning with the influence of the Portuguese and continuing through the various internal dissensions and the Zanzibar Empire to the 20th century and the reign of Said bin Taimur. The latter part of the book deals with the archaic form of administration and the petty restrictions imposed by the Sultan, but the author also emphasizes the positive side, mainly the rescuing of the Sultanate from debt.

387 Arabian assignment.
David Smiley. London: Cooper, 1975. 248p. maps.

The author was commander of the Sultan's forces at Muscat, on secondment, and the first part of the book presents a general history of Oman, including British relations with the Sultanate and the war in Dhofar. The second part deals with the situation in the Yemen.

388 The Omani manuscript collection at Muscat. Part 1: a general description of the MSS.
G. R. Smith. *Arabian Studies*, vol. 4 (1978), p. 161-90.

Based on research carried out in Oman in 1976 on the invitation of the Minister of National Heritage to examine some recently collected Arabic manuscripts which were to form the basis of a National Museum and Library collection. The article lists the manuscripts by categories and, wherever possible, provides author, title, date of copying, and the Ministry accession number. In some cases only the number of manuscripts within a category is listed because of lack of time to investigate further. The object of the article is primarily to advise scholars as to the existence of the material.

389 Arabian treaties 1600-1960.
Edited by Penelope Tuson, Emma Quick. Farnham Common, England: Archive Research, 1992. 2200p. 4 vols.

A comprehensive handbook of international treaties, agreements and undertakings relating to the Arabian Gulf and Peninsula. Coverage is of Oman, Bahrain, Kuwait and Iraq. This volume is designed to update the work of Aitchison (see item no. 421)

390 The records of the British Residency and agencies in the Persian Gulf.
Penelope Tuson, Joan C. Lancaster. London: India Office Library and Records, 1979. xx+188p. map. bibliog. (India Office Records. Guide to Archive Groups IOR r/15).

A valuable guide to the official British documentation on the affairs of the Gulf States, including Oman. These records are vital to any historical study of the region and this guide is a useful key to the material available in the India Office Library collection.

Early history and Portuguese rule

Early history

391 The formation of the Omani trading empire under the Ya'aribah dynasty (1624-1719).
Abdul Aziz El-Ashban. *Arab Studies Quarterly*, vol. 1, no. 4 (1979), p. 354-71.

An examination of the action taken between 1624 and 1719 by the Ya'aribah Imamate to restore Oman's economic prominence through the development of both maritime and caravan trade, and backed by strong central leadership. This period was ended by the decline of the Ya'aribah Imamate; internal dissension led to its being overthrown by the Portuguese.

392 The coinage of Oman under Abu Kalyer the Buwayid.
A. D. H. Bivar, S. M. Stern. *Numismatic Chronicle* (1958), p. 147-56.

A consideration of the small number of coins from this period of Oman's history, when the country came under the rule of the Buwayids during the 10th century. The evidence of the coins is used to supplement other contemporary historical evidence.

393 The prehistoric graveyard of Ra's al-Hamra (RH5): (A short preliminary report on the 1981-83 excavations).
A. Coppa (et al.). *Journal of Oman Studies*, vol. 8, pt. 1 (1985), p. 97-102.

The archaeological excavation of the settlement and graveyard at Ra's al-Hamra began in January 1981 and, at the time of this article, the fourth and final excavation was about to take place. Up to 1984 57 burials involving 80 individuals had been brought to light from an area of some 140 square metres. The article describes the types of graves discovered and their contents, including a study of the remains to determine the health conditions of the prehistoric population – the dental remains proved valuable in this analysis. A histogram is produced to show the distribution by age at death and the 21-25 age group is by far the largest, about 21 per cent of the total.

394 A third millennium kiln from the Oman Peninsula.
K. Frifelt. *Arabian Archaeology and Epigraphy*, vol. 1, no. 1 (1990), p. 4-15.

Reports on the excavation of a pottery kiln dating from the third millennium BC at Hili, which is part of Al-Ain in the United Arab Emirates and close to the border with Oman. The kiln and its contents have provided valuable information on prehistoric economic production in the Oman Peninsula.

395   Zufar in the Middle Ages.

R. Guest. *Islamic Culture*, vol. 9, pt. 4 (1935), p. 402-10.

A consideration of the early history of Dhofar province, dealing with relations between the area and Hadhramaut, the specific language of the people, and the agricultural basis of the economy.

396   Some surprising aspects of Omani history.

Donald Hawley. *Asian Affairs*, vol. 12, no. 1 (1982), p. 28-39.

A survey of the early history of Oman from the trade links with Sumeria in 2500 BC through to the domination of commerce in East Africa and trade with China. The Al bu Said dynasty came to power in 1744 and is the oldest ruling tradition in the Middle East, though the history of Oman from 794 BC has been dominated by dynastic families. Oman, due to its geographical situation, now guards the Strait of Hormuz through which the bulk of the Western world's petroleum is shipped.

397   Relations between China and the Arabs in early times.

Zhang Jun-Yan. *Journal of Oman Studies*, vol. 6, no. 1 (1983), p. 91-109.

A discussion of historical events related to links between the Chinese and the Arabs from the 2nd century BC to the 17th century AD, based largely on Chinese sources. The article is divided into five periods, as follows: relations before the 7th century AD; contacts between the 7th and 9th centuries AD; relations from the 10th to the 13th century AD; relations from the end of the 13th and 14th century; relations from 15th to 17th century. The relations were largely based on trade, and this is dealt with in each section, as is the transfer of technology such as paper making.

398   The Sinaw hoard of early Islamic coins.

N. Lowick. *Journal of Oman Studies*, vol. 6, no. 2 (1983), p. 199-230. maps.

Reports on the discovery, in September 1979, of an earthenware pot containing some 948 coins from the Sassanian and early Islamic periods. The coins were sent to the British Museum for cleaning, conservation and identification, and the article is based on these findings. The hoard was by a water course at Sayh al-Tashkit, one kilometre west of the village of Sinaw in the interior; the earliest coin was struck in 590 AD and the latest coin is dated 840 AD. It is possible that the hoard was buried because of a tribal disturbance or the fear of revolution. This is the first of its period reported in Oman, and only the second such discovery in the Arabian Peninsula. The article gives details as to the dynastic composition of the collection, the regional distribution of the minting, details of fragmentary coins and pierced coins. Pages 211-30 are a catalogue of the coins.

399   The early relationship between Arabia and India.

S. S. Nadvi. *Islamic Culture, the Hyderabad Quarterly Review*, vol. 11, no. 2 (1973), p. 172-79.

Deals largely with the important early trading links which eventually resulted in military operations against the Portuguese presence in India, both at sea and with raids on coastal settlements.

400 **Arms manufacture and the arms trade in south-eastern Arabia in the early Muslim period.**
David Nicolle. *Journal of Oman Studies*, vol. 6, no. 2 (1983), p. 231-38.

A study of arms and armour manufacture and trade in Oman, Bahrain and the Yemen largely during the 10th century AD. It is considered that the leather of Yemen and the copper of Oman could have been significant, particularly in the Bronze Age manufacture of arms. However, there is a lack of archaeological data to confirm or deny its usage and the available evidence is largely circumstantial. The article goes on to describe: various items of arms and armour in the region during the period; and relics discovered, including finds in Iran, Iraq and Syria. Consideration is also given to the international trade that passed through Oman which, at that time, was the major entrepôt centre of the Arab world; raw materials were imported and finished products exported, together with arms produced in Mosul, mainly to Ceylon and India, though perhaps also to the Malay Peninsula. In all of this the significance of Omani copper production was probably greater than hitherto realized.

401 **Preliminary epigraphic survey of Islamic material in Dhofar.**
Giovanni Oman. *Journal of Oman Studies*, vol. 6, no. 2 (1983), p. 277-90.

The Ministry of National Heritage and Culture has sponsored research into the ancient city of Zafar, nowadays called al-Balid, and the epigraphic survey of the Salalah area is part of this research. A complete survey had already been undertaken of the visible burial grounds of al-Balid and the epigraphic material found has been numbered and photographed. The survey also intends to locate other burial grounds and other sites of ancient mosques and monuments where Arabic inscriptions could possibly be found. The article includes sketches of the various burial grounds where the inscriptions have been noted, and examples of the types of inscription.

402 **From Qade to Mazun: four notes on Oman, c 700BC to 700AD.**
D. T. Potts. *Journal of Oman Studies*, vol. pt. 1 (1985), p. 81-96.

The history of Oman from the middle of the first millennium to the Islamic conquest is not well known and this article provides an insight into this period. It is stressed that events in Oman cannot be appreciated in isolation from their broader historical context. The article traces the changes in name by which present-day Oman was known ranging from Qeda in Mesopotamian times to Mazun in 700 AD, the latter being a toponym and probably Persian in origin.

403 **Persian Gulf seafaring and East Africa: ninth–twelfth centuries.**
Thomas M. Ricks. *International Journal of African Historical Studies*, vol. III, no. 2 (1970), p. 339-57. maps.

At the time of writing, little was known of medieval commercial relations between the Persian Gulf States and East Africa, apart from occasional references by Arab and Iranian geographers. However, archaeological research in East Africa and research by Iranian historians has thrown new light on the trade links between the Persian Gulf and East Africa. The bulk of the article is concerned with Iranian seafaring links and trade with East Africa but the rise of Muscat and Aden led to an increasing role for Oman and the Yemen in this trade.

404 Political theory and institutions of the Khawarij.

Elie Adib Salem. Baltimore, Maryland: Johns Hopkins University Press, 1956. 117p. (University Studies in Historical and Political Science, vol. 74, no. 2).

Deals with the foundations of the Ibadhi movement in interior Oman through a study of its political structure.

405 Masqat in the Arab lexicographers and geographers.

G. Rex Smith. *Journal of Oman Studies*, vol. 6, no. 1 (1983), p. 145-48.

The author examines the possible origins of Masqat (Muscat), now the present-day capital of Oman, in terms of the meaning of the name and the various accepted possibilities including an abbreviation for *masqat al-ra's* which means place of birth, or as a geographical description of the area being a place where sand falls and comes to an end, or possibly an origin is to be found in Persian connections. In examining references to Muscat in accounts of medieval Arab geographers the writer found a paucity of material indicating that, at that time, the town was not as important as Sohar, Dhofar and Aden, and that its rise to prominence began with the arrival of the Europeans in the 16th century.

406 Arab–Persian land relationships in late Sassanid Oman.

J. C. Wilkinson. In: *Proceedings of the Sixth Seminar for Arabian Studies*. London: Seminar for Arabian Studies, 1972, p. 40-51.

This paper concentrates on late Sassanid rule in Oman during the 6th century AD, when the Arabs evicted the Sassanid ruling classes following the arrival of Islam and thus gained real control over the land. The writer examines the social structure during the period of Sassanid rule, and considers the hypothesis that the system of land utilization and irrigation was well established before the Arabs took over: 'maintaining their tribal organizations and bedu attitudes, there is no reason to suppose that the Arabs did anything to expand the prosperity of the land or create new settlements in pre-Islamic times any more than they did when they became masters of the land'.

407 Bio-bibliographical background to the crisis period in the Ibadi Imamate of Oman (end of 9th to end of 14th century).

J. C. Wilkinson. *Arabian Studies*, vol. 3 (1976), p. 137-64.

An examination of the Imamate crisis caused by the deposing of Imam al-Salt bin Malil al-Kharusi at the end of the 9th century, through a study of primary Omani sources from the *ulama* [teachers] of the Rastaq and Nizwa schools. The crisis had political repercussions which lasted until the end of the 14th century and nearly caused the decline of Ibadhism. The author notes that this is 'a highly confused and deliberately distorted period of Omani history' and that these primary sources provide a starting point for further research.

408 **The Julanda of Oman.**
J. C. Wilkinson. *Journal of Oman Studies*, vol. 1 (1975), p. 97-108.
A consideration of the Julanda who were the prominent tribe in Oman from the time of the second wave of Arab immigration into Oman to the establishment of the Ibadhi Imamate at the end of the 8th century. The history of the tribe is traced from the migration and its relationship with the Persians to its dominant role in the eventual Arab state. Their period of dominance ended in 822 AD after an unsuccessful attempt to topple the Imam, and the tribe now consists of herdsmen mainly in the Sharqiya.

409 **The origins of the Omani state.**
J. C. Wilkinson. In: *The Arabian Peninsula: society and politics*, edited by Derek Hopwood. London: Allen and Unwin, 1972. p. 67-88.
This contribution deals with the early history of the Omani state from the first Arab migrations. The author also deals with the Ibadhi form of Islam and the growth of alienation between Muscat and Oman.

410 **A sketch of the historical geography of the Trucial Oman down to the beginning of the sixteenth century.**
J. C. Wilkinson. *Geographical Journal*, vol. 130, no. 3 (1964), p. 337-49. map.
This article has a wider coverage than the area of the Sultanate of Oman, dealing also with the remainder of the Gulf States which formed the Trucial Oman area.

Portuguese rule

411 **Commentary of Roy Freyre De Andrada in which are related his exploits from the year 1619, in which he left the kingdom of Portugal: as General of the Sea of Oman, and coast of Persia, and Arabia, until his death.**
Roy Freyre De Andrada. London: Routledge, 1992. 326p. maps.
Despite the leadership of Andrada who succeeded in turning defeat into victory, Portuguese fortunes were too low to save and they were expelled from Oman and from their East African possessions by the Omanis. Additionally their presence in India was under attack by the Omanis as was their shipping in the Indian Ocean and the Arabian Sea.

412 **The book of Duerta Barbosa, an account of the countries bordering on the Indian Ocean and their inhabitants.**
Duarte Barbosa. Lisbon: [n.p.], 1554. Reprinted 1812; London: Hakluyt Society, 1918. 2 vols. map.
This work is thought to have been completed in 1518 and is of interest for the accounts of the Portuguese travellers in the area and their dominant position in Oman. The work also provides descriptions of the Portuguese settlements, fortifications and defences.

413 **Some notes on the Portuguese in Oman.**
C. F. Beckingham. *Journal of Oman Studies*, vol. 6, pt. 1 (1983),
p. 13-20.

A brief consideration of Portuguese sources relevant to Omani history. These sources
are considered to be of great importance to a study of Oman due to the paucity of
Arabic materials relating to the period when the country was under Portuguese
control during the sixteenth and seventeenth centuries. Various sources are examined
to illustrate their significance to researchers, but it is also pointed out that they are of
little use for a study of interior Oman – largely because Portuguese influence was
restricted to the coastal area.

414 **New light on the relations between the Portuguese and the
Omanis, 1613-1633.**
C. R. Boxer. *Journal of Oman Studies*, vol. 6, no. 1 (1983), p. 35-40.

The first part of the paper deals with the capture of Sohar by the Portuguese in 1616.
Sohar had been under the control of Mohammad bin Muhenna and operating as a very
successful entrepôt and cutting into the trade of Hormuz and Muscat. The second part
deals with the attitude of Roy Freyre De Andrada's attitudes to the Arabs and
Iranians, as seen through the autobiography of Toral y Valdes in 1635, and by the
chronicles of Antonio Bocarro entitled *Decada XIII da Historia de India* published in
Lisbon in 1876. The latter account also considers the rule of Nasir ibn Murshid who
had successfully expelled the Portuguese from the mountains of Oman and had
captured Julfar in 1633.

415 **Anglo-Portuguese rivalry in the Persian Gulf, 1615-1635.**
Charles Ralph Boxer, E. Prestage. In: *Chapters in Anglo-Portuguese
relations*. Watford, England: Voss and Michael,1935, p. 46-129.

A survey of the power struggle for influence in the area, including Muscat and Oman.

416 **The commentaries of the great Afonso Dalboquerque, second
Viceroy of India.**
Translated and edited by Walter de Gray Birch. London: Hakluyt
Society. First series, nos. 53, 55, 62, 69 (1875-84). Reprinted, New
York: B. Franklin, 1970. 4 vols.

The early part of the work is concerned with the Spanish attack on Hormuz in 1508
and the subsequent assaults on Muscat. The first volume also deals with the
fortifications and defences of the area and includes a plan of Hormuz.

417 **Struggle between the Portuguese and the Arabs of Oman for
supremacy in the Persian Gulf and the Indian Ocean.**
Jamal Zakariya Qasim, Abdul Ali. *Hamdard Islamicus* (Pakistan),
vol. 9, no. 4 (1986), p. 75-80.

Assesses the role of Oman in the unseating of Portuguese economic domination of the
Persian Gulf and the Indian Ocean and the expulsion of the Portuguese from the
Sultanate. This role is seen as crucial to the process which also involved other Arab
and European powers. The work originally appeared in 1973 in Arabic.

418   **Omani naval activities off the Southern Arabian coast in the late
       11th/17th century, from Yemeni chronicles.**
       R. B. Serjeant.   *Journal of Oman Studies*, vol. 6, no. 1 (1983),
       p. 77-89.
This account of Omani naval activities off the southern Arabian coast is based on
Yemeni sources. The activities of the Omanis were largely directed against coastal
areas from the Red Sea to Mocha and, although motivated by a desire for revenge
against the Portuguese, the acquisition of plunder was also a major factor. The
appendices deal with the issues of security for Indian shipping using Yemeni ports,
and with the situation in Dhofar province at that time.

419   **The Portuguese off the south Arabian coast: Hadrami chronicles
       with Yemeni and European accounts of Dutch pirates off Mocha in
       the seventeenth century.**
       R. B. Serjeant.   London: Oxford University Press, 1963. 233p. maps.
Included because of the significance of the Portuguese presence for the Sultanate, and
the subsequent war waged against them by the Omanis on land and sea in the
Sultanate, East Africa and on the trade routes. The appendices include a section on
Arabic shipping terms and details of the inscriptions at the Merani fort in Muscat.

16th-19th centuries

Muscat and Oman

420   **The first Sa'udi dynasty and Oman, 1795-1818.**
       Muhammad Morsy Abdullah.   In: *Proceedings of the Fourth Seminar
       for Arabian Studies*.   London: Seminar for Arabian Studies, 1970,
       p. 34-41.
Deals with the rise of the Saudi dynasty at the end of the 18th century, which resulted
in the conquest of the Najd and thus paved the way for confrontation between the new
rulers and Oman. The author examines early Saudi expeditions into Oman; the
political and religious state of Oman at the end of the 19th century; Saudi–Omani
relations during the 1800-18 period; British and Saudi relations in Oman; and Omani
attitudes towards the Saudis.

421   **A collection of treaties, engagements, and sanads relating to India
       and neighbouring countries: revised and continued up to the
       1st June 1906.**
       Compiled by Charles Umpherston Aitchinson.   Calcutta, India:
       Government Printing Office, 1909. 13 vols. maps.
The volume of main relevance is volume 12. It is divided into three sections. The first
part contains agreements with Oman, beginning with that of 12 October 1798, which
was the earliest British agreement with Oman. Part 2 is broader in context as it cites

material concerning the Persian Gulf, Bahrain, the Wahhabis and Trucial Oman. Part 3 covers the Sultanate and Sohar.

422   **The State of Masqat in the Gulf and East Africa, 1785-1829.**
Calvin H. Allen, Jr.   *International Journal of Middle East Studies*, vol. 14, no. 2 (1982), p. 117-27.

An examination of the history of Muscat both in the Arabian Gulf and East Africa between 1785 and 1829. The article takes issue with the view of Omani history which maintains that the establishment of the capital at Muscat was an expression of a unified state and a change in the basis of ruling power from the land to the sea. The author argues that Hamad bin Said Al Bu-Said had in effect established an independent state in Muscat which enabled him to profit from trade with the interior whilst, at the same time, being free from the tribal opposition which met any attempts to unite the coast and the interior. Freed from this, Hamad and his successors were able to pursue an aggressive military and political policy in the Arabian Gulf between 1785 and 1820 and in East Africa from 1820 and 1829, the latter being designed to create a commercial empire centred on Muscat. The success of the policy was based on no interference in the affairs of Oman. The article discusses these two periods of history in some detail, and indicates that in 1829 the concept of the commercial empire was abandoned by Sayyid Said who left Muscat for Zanzibar, leaving the rulers of Muscat to become involved in Omani politics rather than commercial affairs.

423   **Maritime trade and Imamate government: two principal themes in the history of Oman to 1728.**
R. D. Bathurst.   In: *The Arabian Peninsula: society and politics*, edited by Derek Hopwood.   London: Allen and Unwin, 1972, p. 89-106.

This is an important and useful assessment of the early period of Oman's history from the arrival of Islam to the early 18th century. The article deals with the complex period in a succinct but informative manner and is subdivided as follows: From Islam to the arrival of the Portuguese; The Portuguese period, 1507-1650; Maritime power and Imamate government, 1650-1719; Civil war, 1719-28.

424   **Muscat.**
J. Theodore Bent.   *Contemporary Review*, vol. 68, no. 360 (1895), p. 871-82.

A survey article on the history of Oman and eventual British interest in the area. The article was motivated by the Muscat insurrection of tribesmen against the Sultan's rule, and the increasing significance of the area for the Persian Gulf and sea routes to Egypt, India and the Far East.

425   **Southern Arabia.**
J. Theodore Bent, V. A. Mabel.   London: Smith Elder, 1900. 455p. map.

Bent visited southern Arabia in 1889 and 1890, interviewing Sultan Faisal, and returning in 1895. He was the first European to explore the mountains in Dhofar behind the Salalah plain. The Muscat area and the history of the Sultanate are likewise considered.

426 **Oil interests and the formation of centralized government in Oman, 1920-1970.**
Thomas Bierschenk. *Orient* (Berlin), vol. 30, no. 2 (1989), p. 205-19.

This article argues the case that the transformation of Oman from theocracy to monarchy can be understood only in the context of changes in world market forces. It is argued that the Omani–Saudi border disputes and the dispute between the Sultan and the Imam in the 1950s can be interpreted accurately only if two external factors are taken into account. The first of these was the shift in British interest away from protecting sea routes to India to the safeguarding of oil production and exploration in the Gulf; the second was the dissolution of British hegemony as a result of rivalry with the United States. The article examines the situation prior to 1920, when no unified state existed; the 1920 Treaty of Sib; British and American oil interests after the First World War; oil and Sultan Said's attempts to reunify the state between 1930 and 1945; post-Second World War history; the Buraimi Oasis dispute and the Imamate revolt; and concludes with the emergence of the Oman *rentier* state between 1958 and 1970.

427 **The diary of a Mocha coffee agent.**
Peter Boxall. *Arabian Studies*, vol. 1 (1974), p. 102-18.

This article discusses the trade in coffee with the East India Company. It is based on the diary of Francis Dickinson who represented the company in Mocha covering the year 1793. Although dealing with present-day Yemen, the article is of interest for its consideration of: the significance of Indian trade with Arabia; the difficulties encountered; the relations between the company and the region in relation to the terms under which the trade was undertaken; and the difficulties faced by Europeans operating in the area.

428 **Britain and the Persian Gulf, 1894-1914.**
Briton Cooper Busch.   Berkeley, California: University of California Press, 1967. 432p. maps. bibliog.

Valuable for a consideration of British and French influence in the area, and in particular French attempts to obtain a foothold in the Sultanate. Busch also produces trade statistics for Muscat for this period.

429 **Convention of commerce and navigation between Great Britain and Muscat, signed at Zanzibar, 31 May 1839.**
British and Foreign State Papers, vol. 28 (1839). 1080p.

It is interesting to note that this agreement was concluded in Zanzibar, where the Sultan spent the greater part of his time.

430 **Great Britain in the Indian Ocean: a study of maritime enterprise, 1810-1850.**
Gerald S. Graham.   London: Oxford University Press, 1967. 479p.

A discussion by a naval historian of the slave trade, the activity of 'pirates' and the Royal Navy's role in trying to suppress both activities. The suppression of the slave trade was to have a devastating effect on the economy of both Oman and Zanzibar.

431 **The life of Sir Percy Cox.**
Philip Percival Graves. London: Hutchinson, 1941. 350p.
This biography has a great deal of material on the Gulf area and Oman, where Cox
was Consul and Agent during the period 1899-1904. He also held the important post
of Political Resident for the Persian Gulf in 1909.

432 **Historical and other information, connected with the province of
Oman, Muscat, Bahrain and other places in the Persian Gulf.**
Selections from the Records of the Bombay Government, no. 24
(1856), p. 1-40.
One of a series of research papers based on Indian government records. They contain
information relevant to studies of historical, economic and sociological aspects of
Oman.

433 **Precis on the slave trade in the Gulf of Oman and the Persian
Gulf, 1873-1908, with a retrospect into previous history from 1852.**
Indian Government. Foreign and Political Department. Calcutta:
Government of India, 1906.
An important source of information on Oman's involvement in the slave trade, which
resulted from her interests in Africa. The involvement of the British Government in
attempts to suppress the trade in the region are also considered.

434 **Report on the administration of the Persian Gulf Political
Residency and Muscat Political Agency for the year 1873-4 to
1903-4.**
India Government. Foreign and Political Department. Calcutta:
Superintendent of Government Printing. annual.
Accounts of relations between the Sultanate and Great Britain during the years in
question, when British affairs in the area were handled from India. The Political
Agent played a significant role in the Gulf, influencing events and directing policies.

435 **Paper relative to the measures adopted by the British government,
1820-1844, for affecting the suppression of the slave trade in the
Persian Gulf. To which are appended copies of the engagements
entered into with the British government, 1822-51; by His
Highness the Imaum of Maskat, the Arab chiefs of the Persian
Gulf, and the government of Persia, for the attainment of the
above object.**
Arnold Burrowes Kemball. *Selections from the Records of the
Bombay Government*, no. 24 (1856), p. 635-87.
A valuable source of basic data on the question of the suppression of the slave trade
and British pressure in the Sultanate to cease activity in the trade which was the main
factor in the economic success of the country.

436   **The dismemberment of Oman and British policy towards the Persian Gulf.**
Ravinder Kumar. *Islamic Culture*, vol. 36 (1962), p. 8-19.
The author deals in depth with British influence in the Sultanate (which began in 1798) up to the period of the Canning Award and the dismemberment of Oman and Zanzibar which marked the end of the maritime empire. He also examines internal problems in the Sultanate linked with the question of the Imamate and the Wahhabi invasions of the country. The question of the dismemberment and the compensation paid by the Canning Award are considered of prime importance as 'thereafter Oman ceased to be a maritime power and its destiny revolved more and more around the insular politics of mainland Arabia and the Persian Gulf'.

437   **India and the Persian Gulf region, 1858-1907: a study in British imperial policy.**
Ravinder Kumar.   Bombay, India: Asia Publishing House, 1965.
259p.
Wider in coverage than Oman, but useful for an understanding of British interests in the region which were mainly looked after by the India Office.

438   **The menace of Muscat and its consequences in the late 17th and early 18th centuries.**
Laurence Lockhart. *Asiatic Review*, n.s., vol. 42, no. 112 (1946),
p. 363-69.
An examination of the growth of Omani power, particularly in relation to the military threats to Portuguese holdings in East Africa and India. The author also deals with the rivalries between the European powers over spheres of influence in the area, and notes how internal troubles reduced Oman's power, especially in the early 18th century.

439   **Nadir Shah's campaigns in Oman and Central Arabia, 1737-1744.**
Laurence Lockhart. *Bulletin of the School of Oriental and African Studies*, vol. 8, no. 1 (1935-37), p. 157-71.
A study of the Iranian campaigns in Oman. These were unsuccessful mainly because the supreme command went to Taqi Khan, who was corrupt as an administrator and inefficient as a military leader. From the Omani viewpoint the campaign was expensive in terms of hardships and casualties, 'but they led in the end to the suppression of the decadent Yariba dynasty by that of the Al Bu Saids, which rules Muscat to the present day'.

440   **History of Seyd Said, Sultan of Muscat . . . by Shaikh Mansur . . .who became commander of the forces of the Sultan of Muscat against the Geovasseam and Whabees pirates.**
Vincento Mauryi.   London: J. Booth, 1819. 174p. map.
A consideration of the rule of Said bin Sultan, 1791-1856, with first-hand observations of some sea battles, but dealing largely with the question of 'piracy' from 1805 and the threat from the Wahhabis. The work also has a map of Muscat showing the fortifications of the city and the surrounding area.

441 **Treaties and international acts of the United States of America, vol. 3.**
Edited by Hunter Miller. Washington, DC: Department of State, Government Printing Office, 1933.
The treaty of 1835 appears on pages 789-810; it was actually concluded in 1833.

442 **The pirates of Trucial Oman.**
Herbert Moyse-Bartlett. London: MacDonald, 1966. 256p. maps. bibliog.
Deals mainly with 'pirate' activity along the coasts of Trucial Oman though the definition of such activity was a British one and has been challenged by Arab sources (see Al-Qasin *The myth of Arab piracy in the Gulf*, item no. 443). Moyse-Bartlett also deals with Omani and British efforts to suppress the slave trade at the beginning of the 19th century and with the trial of Captain T. Thompson for his disastrous military expedition against the Bani Bu Ali tribe in the district of Ja'lan, south of Muscat, in 1820. He lists various relevant treaties between Britain and the Imam of Muscat and the Arab tribes of the Persian Gulf.

443 **The myth of Arab piracy in the Gulf.**
Sultan Muhammad Al-Qasini. London: Croom Helm, 1986. 344p. bibliog.
The British were the dominant power in the Arab Gulf in the late eighteenth and early nineteenth century and the conventional view was that British imperialist expansion was justified because of the need to suppress Arab piracy. This book is significant in that it challenges the myth of Arab piracy and argues that the threat was created by the East India Company in order to take over the trade with India at the expense of the Arab traders. As the East India Company did not have the warships to defeat the Qawasin traders it was necessary to create a threat in order to persuade the British government to send warships to the area. The defeat of the Qawasin and the storming of Ras al-Khaimah opened the door to British expansion in the remainder of the Trucial States and Oman. Based on extensive use of the Bombay Archives (which had not been used before) this book provides a reinterpretation of a crucial period in Gulf history.

444 **Oman and Muscat: An early modern history.**
Patricia Risso. New York: St. Martin's Press, 1986. 258p. bibliog.
This work provides a brief geographical and historical background to Oman before dealing with the subject of Ibadhism and the ideological basis for the Imamate form of government during the period 1749-1840. A further area of study which is of interest in the shift from the Imamate to a secular Al Bu Said regime. The work is based on India Office records, travel accounts and Arabic primary sources providing a useful, detailed account of Oman's early history.

445   **Dates and references of the history of the Al Bin Said dynasty**
      1741-1856.
      Rudolph Said-Ruete.   *Journal of the Royal Central Asian Society*,
      vol. 18, pt. 3 (1931), p. 233-85.

A very useful article outlining the main events of the period both in the Sultanate and
in the Zanzibar settlements. This was a crucial period in the history of the dynasty as
it saw the dismemberment of the Omani Empire in 1856 with the independence of
Zanzibar and a subsequent decline in maritime power.

446   **Said bin Sultan, 1791-1856, ruler of Oman and Zanzibar: his place**
      in the history of Arabia and East Africa.
      Rudolf Said-Ruete.   London: Alexander Ouseley, 1929. 200p. maps.
      bibliog.

In addition to the biographical coverage of his grandfather's rule, the author covers
the early history of Oman and Zanzibar, the question of the Imamate, and relations
with Britain and France.

447   **Ancient trading centres of the Persian Gulf: Maskat.**
      Arthur W. Stiffe.   *Geographical Journal*, vol. 10, no. 6 (1897),
      p. 608-18.

Mainly an account of the port of Muscat and its trading influences as a centre for
shipping to India and Zanzibar. The history of Oman is covered without too much
detail, as is the Portuguese occupation and expulsion.

448   **Arab rule under Al bu Sa'id dynasty of Oman 1741-1937.**
      Bertram Thomas.   *Proceedings of the British Academy*, vol. 24, no. 1
      (1938), p. 27-53.

A general review of Omani history and particularly the rise of the interior and the
growth of Muscat as the capital of the Sultanate. Also discussed is the growth of
Omani power at sea and the rise of the maritime empire. That period was followed by
one of decline brought about by the end of the slave trade and the subsequent general
decline of the Sultanate, all of which led, at that time, to economic ruin.

449   **The birth of Saudi Arabia: Britain and the rise of the House of**
      Sa'ud.
      Gary G. Troeller.   London: Cass, 1976. 287p. map. bibliog.

This work is relevant to a consideration of Wahhabi designs on Oman during the mid-
19th century and at intervals during the early development of Saudi Arabia. The
situation was complicated by intrigue prior to the First World War and the conflicting
interests of the British Foreign Office and the Indian Government.

450 **Historical sketch of the rise and progress of the government of Muskat; commencing with the year 1694-1695, and continued to the year 1819.**
Francis Warden (et al.). *Selections from the Records of the Bombay Government*, no. 24 (1856), p. 167-234.
A useful background to the history of the Sultanate during the period in question. At that time it had several links with India in terms of trade, maritime rivalry with the Portuguese and raids on their coastal settlements in Goa.

451 **The Omani manuscript collection at Muscat. Part 2: the early Ibadi fiqh works.**
J. C. Wilkinson. *Arabian Studies*, vol. 4 (1978), p. 191-208.
A useful introduction to essential primary source material for a study of the early history of Oman and the Ibadhi movement, particularly in the Imamate.

East African empire

452 **Muqdisha in the nineteenth century: a regional perspective.**
Edward A. Alpers. *Journal of African History*, vol. 24, no. 4 (1983), p. 441-59. map.
Mogadishu had been a thriving and wealthy community but by 1970 this had changed due to the ascendancy of the Omani empire over the Banaadir coast and rivalry between Mogadishu's two townships Shingaani and Xamarweyn. The rivalry allowed Omani Zanzibar an influence as a mediator which in turn secured Omani dominance over the economy of the region.

453 **A history of the Arab state of Zanzibar.**
Norman Robert Bennett. London: Methuen, 1978. viii+804p.bibliog.
A history of Zanzibar which was for several centuries part of the Omani empire and of central importance to East Africa's growing contact with the international economy. The important trade sectors were slaves, ivory and cloves and the economic success of Zanzibar was a major factor in the economy of Oman. British interests in the western Indian Ocean also brought about a close relationship with the Al Bu Said rulers particularly during the period from 1820 to 1880.

454 **Trade and empire in Muscat and Zanzibar: the roots of British imperialism.**
M. Roda Bhacker. London: Routledge, 1992. 224p.
An examination of the role of Oman in the Indian Ocean, the maritime empire, trade, and the slave trade prior to British domination in the region. British interest in Africa led to the demise of Omani power in 1856 with the Canning Award compensating the Sultan for the loss of Zanzibar.

455 **Zanzibar: city, island, coast.**
Richard Francis Burton. London: Tinesley, 1872. 2 vols. map.
Written following an 1857 expedition led by Burton to Zanzibar, when Omani authority there was in decline.

456 **East Africa and its invaders, from the earliest times to the death of Seyyid Said in 1856.**
Sir Reginald Coupland. Oxford, England: Oxford University Press, 1938; New York: Russell, 1965. 583p. maps.
A useful consideration of the Omani economic penetration of East Africa from Zanzibar, rivalry with the Portuguese, and the development of the slave trade with the ancillary trade in ivory and cloves.

457 **The exploitation of East Africa, 1856-1890: the slave trade and the scramble.**
Sir Reginald Coupand. London: Faber and Faber, 1968. 507p.
Useful for a consideration of the Omani economic penetration in East Africa to 1871 and the development of the slave trade. Also deals with the rivalry between the Zanzibari Arab rulers and the Portuguese for control over the area's economy and the scramble of the European powers for a stake in East Africa.

458 **A history of East and Central Africa to the late nineteenth century.**
Basil Davidson. New York: Anchor Books, Doubleday, 1969. 358p. bibliog.
A useful study of the Omani presence in East Africa, dealing with the arrival of the Arabs in Zanzibar, the expulsion of the Portuguese, and the growth of the slave trade. Also considers Arab influence in the development of the history of East Africa through the period in question and the significance of the spread of Islam in the region.

459 **Ahmad bin Na'aman's mission to the United States in 1840, the voyage of Al-Sultanah to New York City.**
Hermann Frederick Eilts. *Essex Institute Historical Collections*, vol. 98, no. 4 (1962), p. 219-77.
An interesting account of trade developments between Oman and the United States, formalized by an 1835 treaty which was actually concluded in 1833. This article is connected with the voyage of an Omani ship from Zanzibar to America and the West Indies.

460 **History of Zanzibar, from the Middle Ages to 1856.**
Sir John Milner Gray. London: Oxford University Press, 1967. 314p.
A good history of Zanzibar for the period ending with the death of Seyyid Said. It has a useful bibliography, and is relevant to a study of Omani influence in East Africa through the growth of empire in Zanzibar, the slave trade and the spread of Islam.

461 **Aspects of Indian culture in nineteenth century Zanzibar.**
Jagdish S. Gundara. *South Asia* (Australia), vol. 3, no. 1 (1980),
p. 14-27.

A study of the social position and economic activities of the Indian merchants who migrated to Zanzibar in the 19th century. The community were in a non-Hindu culture but were protected by the liberal regime of Sultan Said (1791-1856) and flourished due to favourable economic conditions. The economic interests of the Indian community broadened beyond cross-Indian Ocean trade and this dilution of interests led to the weakening of the Omani empire and increased the vulnerability of the community. Gundara also examines some of the leading Indian families and the gradual decline of their businesses by the end of the 19th century.

462 **Princes of Zinji: the rulers of Zanzibar.**
Genesta Hamilton. London: Hutchinson, 1957. 272p.

An account of the reign of Seyyid bin Sultan, with background information on the social life and customs of the island under Omani influence.

463 **Zanzibar: its history and its people.**
W. H. Ingrams. London: Cass, 1967. 527p.

Chapters 7 (p. 73-85) and 9 (p. 96-121) deal with Omani emigration to the island and eventual settlement on the mainland. Also of relevance is *Oman and East Africa* by Ahmed Hamoud Al-Maamiry (New Dehli, India: Lancers Publishers, 1980. 2nd ed. 151p. bibliog.) which discusses the relations that existed between East Africa and Oman from an Omani viewpoint. The work concludes with a consideration of the rule of Said Bin Taimur, the Dhofar War and the early period of the reign of Sultan Qaboos.

464 **The early history of Oman in East Africa.**
James Kirkman. *Journal of Oman Studies*, vol. 6, no. 1 (1983),
p. 41-58. maps.

Connections between Oman and East Africa go back to the time of the Julanda in the first century of Islam and fall into three distinct periods. The first period covers the early presence to the expulsion of the Portuguese from Mombasa, the second the period of remote sovereignty from the end of the seventeenth century to 1837, and the third the direct rule of Seyyid Said. This article covers the first two periods but the point is made that the history is poorly documented in Omani and East African sources and that even Portuguese sources are limited in quantity and scope. The history of the Omanis in East Africa is interwoven with the history of Omani trade and both are largely unrecorded. The available sources are discussed, as are the principal trading commodities and the contacts with the various tribes in East Africa and their relations with the Arab merchants. The appendices reproduce details of the Sultans in East Africa and genealogical tables.

465 **Zanzibar: background to revolution.**
Michael Lofchie. Princeton, New Jersey: Princeton University Press, 1965. 316p.

The opening chapters deal with the historical background to the Omani presence in Zanzibar and its effects on the social structure.

466 **The Swahili coast: politics, diplomacy and trade in the East African littoral, 1798-1856.**
Christine Stephanie Nicholls. London: Allen & Unwin, 1971. 419p.
(St. Antony's College Oxford, Publication no. 2).
This book describes the Omani presence in East Africa from the viewpoint of the African inhabitants and is stated by the author to be a study of 'the aggressive maritime group, the Omani Arabs, on the peoples of the Swahili coast' at the beginning of the 19th century. It focuses on Omani imperialism in Zanzibar and East Africa and, in particular, Said bin Sultan's involvement in trade and the development of Zanzibar's mercantile community.

467 **Zamani: a survey of East African history.**
B. A. Ogst, J. A. Kieran. London: Longman, 1968. 407p. maps.
bibliog.
Contains a section entitled 'Omani Arab period, 1700-1950', on pages 131-38.

468 **History of East Africa.**
Roland Oliver, Gervase Mathew. London: Oxford University Press, 1963. 3 vols.
The first volume of this three-volume set begins with the Stone Age and covers the period to the end of the 19th century. It contains numerous references to Omani rule in Zanzibar.

469 **Memoirs of an Arabian princess from Zanzibar.**
Emily Ruete. New York: Markus Wiener Publishing, 1989.
xxii+298p.
The author was the daughter of the Sultan of Zanzibar. Having married a German national, she became involved in the competition between Germany and Britain for control over Zanzibar. The work is also useful for a female perspective of palace life and details of schooling, foods, religious festivals, medicine and slavery. The book was originally published in 1888 in German and translated into English in the same year.

470 **Slaves, spices and ivory in Zanzibar: Integration of an East African commercial empire into the world economy 1770-1873.**
Abdel Sheriff. Athens, Ohio: Ohio University Press, 1987. 297p.
During the period of the study Zanzibar was part of the Omani empire and the role of Said bin Sultan's rule (1806-56) is examined in terms of the economic development of the island. The work studies economic dynamism within East Africa, in a global context but with a particular interest in the slave trade. The focus of the work is on the evolution of commercial communities in East Africa which were entirely dependent upon foreign interests and the exploitation of imperialism, including that of Oman.

471 **East Africa through a thousand years: a history of the years
A.D. 1000 to the present day.**
Gideon S. Ware, Derek A. Wilson.   New York: Africana Publishing,
1970. 344p.

This work has many references relevant to Oman, including information on the dhow
trade, Omani rule in Zanzibar, the growth of the slave trade, and economic and
religious penetration of Africa.

472 **British imperialism and the East African slave trade.**
Richard D. Wolff.   *Science and Society*, vol. 36, no. 4 (1972),
p. 443-62.

A review of the slave trade and British involvement, which also includes a section on
Omani rule in Zanzibar.

20th century

General

473 **The Indian merchant community of Masqat.**
Calvin H. Allen.   *Bulletin of the School of Oriental and African
Studies*, vol. 4, no. 1 (1981), p. 39-53.

A survey of the social and economic history of the two principal Indian merchant
communities in Oman which date from the fifteenth century. The Hindu Bhattias of
Muscat migrated to Muscat in the 15th century from the Sind and played a major role
in the Indian Ocean trade under Arab, Portuguese and British domination. The
original migration was reinforced by a second wave from Kutch during the 19th
century. The other principal community is the Shiite Moslem Luti, which settled in
Matrah in the late 18th and early 19th centuries. Both communities have experienced
some political and religious harassment over the years but they have survived to
become a major commercial and financial élite within Oman, with extensive property,
banking and trading interests throughout the Arabian Gulf and the Indian Ocean.

474 **Warlords of Oman.**
P. S. Allfree.   London: Hale, 1967; New York: Barnes, 1968. 191p.
map.

The author served in the Trucial Oman Scouts and also on the Intelligence staff of the
Sultanate. The work is a readable account of events and personalities and covers the
problems of the Imamate, internal insurrections and the Buraimi Oasis dispute.

475 **Records of Oman 1867-1947: Why, how and wherefore?**
Ronald Bailey.   *Asian Affairs*, vol. 21, no. 2 (1990), p. 131-43.

The Records of Oman from 1867 to 1947 are based on British Consular and Political
Office records deposited in the India Office Library and provide an important

commentary on economic and foreign relations during the period in question. This article is based on a lecture given at the Royal Society for Asian Affairs in London in November 1989 and deals largely with the editorial work related to the completion and publication of the eight volumes in the series.

476 The winds of morning.
Hugh Boustead.   London: Chatto and Windus, 1971. 240p. maps.

An interesting British assessment of the early moves towards development in Oman under Sultan Said bin Taimur. The author was Director of Development from 1958 to 1961, prior to becoming Political Agent in Abu Dhabi.

477 Footsteps in the sand: The Gulf in transition, 1953-1958.
Bernard Burrows.   Salisbury, England: Michael Russell Publishing, 1990. 175p. maps.

The author was British Political Resident in the Gulf during the period in question and this account is based on personal recollections and access to official records in the Public Records Office. The Buraimi Oasis dispute is considered at some length, though Burrows' involvement began only when the arbitration process was about to begin. Oman is specifically dealt with between pages 112 and 121, concentrating largely on the problems associated with the re-occupation of the interior by the Sultan, the actions of the Oman Liberation Army with support from Saudi Arabia, and British involvement in the campaign. The views of the Political Resident at the time are also expressed in a memorandum in Annexe 1, dated 1949 and reviewing 'the Arab Sheikhdoms of the Persian Gulf'.

478 British defence policy east of Suez, 1947-1968.
Philip Darby.   London: Oxford University Press, for the Royal Institute of International Affairs, 1973. 366p. maps.

A useful consideration of British involvement in Oman during the period in question. Britain acted as a supporter of the Sultan's authority and had responsibility for representing Oman in external matters.

479 Britain's feudal friends in Oman.
Faris Glubb.   *Venture*, vol. 18, pt. 9 (1966), p. 14-16.

The author, secretary of the Committee for Rights of Oman, argues for the independence of Oman, true democracy for the Sultanate and the replacement of the Sultan. The policy of Britain in supporting the Sultan against the aspirations of the people, especially in the interior, is seen as encouraging a resistance movement linked with the South Yemen movement.

480 Foreign Office annual reports from Arabia 1930-1960.
Great Britain, Foreign Office.   Farnham Common, England: Archive Research, 1993. 2100p. 4 vols.

Reproduces the annual reports from British diplomatic representatives in the Arabian Peninsula, including Oman, with material from Ambassadors, Ministers and the Political Resident in the Gulf. All available reports and surveys are included.

481 **Political diaries of the Persian Gulf 1904-1958.**
Great Britain, Foreign Office. Farnham Common, England: Archive
Research, 1991. 1300p. 20 vols.
This collection comprises all surviving diaries and intelligence reports that could be
located which had been submitted by British political officers in the Gulf region
covering Bushire, Kuwait, Bahrain, Qatar, Muscat and the Trucial States. It is a
valuable source of information on British activity in the area, being particularly
relevant to Oman and especially questions of the Imamate, the Buraimi Oasis and
border disputes with Abu Dhabi and Saudi Arabia. It is also of relevance to British
relations with the Sultans of Oman and the Sheiks of the Trucial States, and a prime
source of information on British policy in the various states and in the region.

482 **The Gulf States and Oman in transition.**
Frauke Heard-Bey. *Asian Affairs*, n.s., vol. 59, no. 3 (1972),
p. 14-22.
A consideration of the political prospects for the Gulf and Oman following British
withdrawal from the area, and the need for the Gulf States to secure their own
independence. Much of the article is not specifically related to Oman, but the author
does examine the administrative machinery of the Sultanate, which is by decree of the
Sultan, and the regional network of *walis* [regional governors]. Mention is also made
of the insurrection in Dhofar, which the author sees as arising from the weakness of
the Gulf area following British withdrawal. Although military solutions may be
necessary, the main problems are social, and must be tackled at that level.

483 **Muscat: the way ahead.**
Richard Johns. *Middle East International*, no. 6 (Sept. 1971),
p. 7-12.
A consideration of the prospects for the Sultanate following the coup, and of the plans
for economic and social development.

484 **Politics and religion in 'Uman: A historical review.**
Nabil M. Kaylani. *International Journal of Middle East Studies*,
vol. 10, no. 4 (1979), p. 567-79.
A review of the development of religion and politics in Oman from the 8th century AD
to 1979. Ibadhism was adopted as the religion of Oman in the 8th century, an event
which resulted in detachment from the Caliphate and separate development within the
country. Kaylani examines the internal struggle between the interior and the Sultans
of Muscat, vulnerability to foreign influences – particularly British – the uniting of
the country, and the end of the Imamate. He concludes that in the 1970s social
progress had been made and the country was enjoying a period of political stability.

485 **The Arab states and the Arab League: a documentary record.**
Muhammad Khalil. Beirut: Khayat, 1962. 2 vols.
A collection of the major policy statements, international agreements and debates,
which are of great relevance. Coverage of Oman is in volume 2, dealing with the
question of the Imamate, the slave trade and its cessation and various international
agreements over Zanzibar, Kuria Muria and the Treaty of Sib.

486 **New direction in Oman.**
Michael Lake. *Venture*, vol. 22, no. 9 (1970), p. 20-24.
An appraisal of the possible implications of the accession of Sultan Qaboos, particularly with regard to development policy and an end to Oman's self-imposed introspection.

487 **International relations of Arabia: the dependent areas.**
Herbert J. Liebesny. *Middle East Journal*, vol. 3, no. 3 (1947), p. 148-68.
Discusses the internal structure of Oman and the international question of the status and independence of the Sultanate.

488 **The Persian Gulf in the twentieth century.**
John Marlowe. London: Cresset Press, 1962. 278p. maps. bibliog.
An extremely valuable work on developments in the area during the 20th century, a crucial period in terms of both oil and political development. Oman is mentioned at intervals throughout the text, dealing briefly with the early history and Portuguese influences, the growth of British influence, and the question of oil. Although Oman does not figure prominently in this work, the fortunes of the Sultanate were very much interwoven with the affairs of the Gulf, and for this reason the book is extremely relevant.

489 **Political geography of Trucial Oman and Qatar.**
Alexander Melamid. *Geographical Review*, vol. 43 (1953), p. 194-206.
This article deals with a wider geographical area than Oman, as it includes the United Arab Emirates and Qatar. The changes brought about by the oil industry are thought by the author to offer 'an unusual insight into the evolution of states and their territorial and maritime sovereignty'. Consideration is given to the boundary problems between the various states which, as oil exploration is intensified, will need to be solved.

490 **Recent developments in the Sultanate of Oman.**
R. P. Owen. *The World Today*, vol. 26, pt. 9 (1970), p. 379-83.
An account of the coup of 1970 which brought Sultan Qaboos to power. As background, the author deals with the reign of Said bin Taimur, both its credits and debits, and the war in Dhofar.

491 **The Persian Gulf Gazette.**
London: HM Stationery Office, vol. 1, no. 1 (Oct. 1953); vol. 20, no. 1 (May 1972); supplements no. 1-58 (Oct. 1953-Aug. 1968).
Issued by the British Political Residency in the Persian Gulf, these issues contain various references to Britain's relations with Oman since the early 1950s and cover topics such as the Buraimi Oasis dispute.

492 **Oman and the Persian Gulf, 1858-1949.**
Edited by J. D. Porter. Chapel Hill, North Carolina: Documentary Press, 1982. 90p.

A collection of letters, reports, interviews and documents written between 1835 and 1949, and taken from previously unpublished United States diplomatic archives. The documents have been selected to throw light on United States interests and activities in the area.

493 **Recueil des actes et protocoles concernant le différent entre la France et la Grande Bretagne à propos des beutres de Mascate, soumis au Tribunal d'Arbitrage constitué en vertu du compromis arbitral conclu à Londres le 13 octobre 1904 entre les puissances susmentionnées.** (Collection of papers and documents relating to the differences between France and Great Britain concerning the Muscat dhows, concluded by virtue of arbitration at London on 13 October 1904 between the aforementioned persons.)
The Hague: Permanent Court of Arbitration, 1906. 81p.

The official record of the *Muscat Doro* case over the use of the French flag on local vessels. It was in part an attempt by the Sultan to reduce his dependence upon Britain and the judgment affirmed the independence of the Sultanate. The documents are in English and French, and a full list of those used in the litigation is also produced. An important case which strengthened British influence in the area.

494 **Arabian adventure.**
Anthony Shepherd. London: Collins, 1961. 256p. maps.

This personal account of service with the Trucial Oman Scouts is relevant to a study of Omani history during the difficulties with the Imamate and the Buraimi Oasis dispute.

495 **The word of Sultan Said bin Taimur, Sultan of Muscat and Oman, about the history of the financial position of the Sultanate in the past and what it is hoped it will be in the future, after the export of oil.**
Sultan Said bin Taimur. Muscat, 1968. [n.p.].

A review by the Sultan of the measures taken to rectify economic problems prior to the discovery of oil, and the measures envisaged by the ruler for developing his country when the oil revenues began. An important paper for an understanding of the contemporary history of the Sultanate, especially the background to the situation leading to the coup in 1970. This statement is reproduced as appendix 1 of *Oman: the making of the modern state* (q.v), p. 192-98.

Imamate question

496 **The Arab war: confidential information for general headquarters from Gertrude Bell; being despatches reprinted from the secret** *Arab Bulletin.*
Gertrude Bell.   London: Golden Cockerell Press, 1940. 50p. (Limited Edition).
Includes a paper entitled 'The rebellion against the Sultan of Muscat. May 1913 to July 1916' (p. 28-30). In it, Gertrude Bell outlines the establishment of the 20th-century Imamate and the trouble between the Sultan and Imam at that time.

497 **The Arabian Peninsula: the protectorates and Sheikhdoms.**
Jasper Y. Brinton.   *Revue Egyptienne de Droit International*, vol. 3 (1967), p. 25-38.
A review, by a judge, of the legal aspect of the conflict between the Imamate and the Sultan. He concludes that the latter has not compromised either the internal or external sovereignty of the Sultanate.

498 **Report of the Special Committee on the situation with regard to the implementation of the declaration of the granting of independence to colonial countries and peoples. Chapter XIII: Oman.**
S. M. Chada.   New York: United Nations General Assembly (25 Nov. 1970). 13p. (A/8023 Part II).
Part of the continuing consideration of the problem of Oman's recognition by the United Nations, either as the Sultanate of Muscat and Oman or with the Imamate as a separate entity.

499 **From theocracy to monarchy: authority and legitimacy in inner Oman, 1935-1957.**
Dale F. Eickelman.   *International Journal of Middle East Studies*, vol. 17, no. 1 (1985), p. 3-24.
An examination of the origins and workings of the Ibadhi Imamate from 1935 to1955. The shift from theocratic rule to rule by the Sultan between 1955 and1957 was largely on the assumption that Sultan Said would preserve much of what was Islamic in the political life of the interior.

500 **Report on the Special Committee with regard to the implementation of the declaration on the granting of independence to colonial countries and peoples. Chapter XIII: Oman.**
Mohsen S. Esfendiary.   New York: United Nations General Assembly (15 Nov. 1967). 16p. (A/6700/Add.12).
Deals with the question of the request by the Imamate to be treated as an independent state.

501 **Controversy over Oman.**
Ezeldin Foda. *Egyptian Economic and Political Review*, vol. 4, no. 4
(1958), p. 12-14.
An attack on British support for the Sultan in 1957 military actions against the
Imamate. The writer argues that the revolt in Oman could not be classed as an internal
struggle because the Imamate of Oman was a sovereign state with a greater claim to
legitimacy than the Sultanate of Muscat. The terms of the Treaty of Sib of 1920 are
used to support this premise.

502 **Report of the Special Committee on the situation with regard to
the implementation of the declaration on the granting of
independence to colonial countries and peoples. Chapter XIV:
Oman.**
Abdul Samed Ghaus. New York: United Nations General Assembly
(11 Nov. 1969). 12p. (A/7623/Add.5)
A consideration of the question of the Imamate's request to be treated as a separate
independent state.

503 **Report of the Special Committee on the situation with regard to
the implementation of the declaration on the granting of
independence to colonial countries and peoples. Chapter XVII:
Oman.**
Abdul Samad Ghaus. New York: United Nations General Assembly
(8 Nov. 1968). 18p. (A/7200/Add.8)
Deals with the question of the request by the Imamate to be treated as an independent
state.

504 **Great Britain's relations with Yemen and Oman.**
Rupert Hay. *Middle Eastern Affairs*, vol. 11, no. 5 (1960), p. 142-49.
Primarily an assessment of the rift between the Sultan and the Imam, and Britain's
role in supporting the Sultan, but Hay also considers the strategic significance of
Oman in relations to the Gulf. Much of the article deals with the Yemen and border
disputes and insurrections.

505 **Arabian extremities.**
M. L. Heath. *Journal of the Royal Central Asian Society*, vol. 47,
no. 3-4 (1960), p. 260-69.
The author was commander of the British forces in the Arabian Peninsula, and this is
a survey of the various countries for which Britain had defence responsibility. Heath
looks briefly at the internal history of Oman, the Treaty of Sib and the Imamate, and
the significance of the Sultanate in terms of its strategic position.

506 **Sultanate and Imamate in Oman.**
John Barrett Kelly. London: Oxford University Press, for the Royal
Institute of International Affairs, 1959. 20p.
A brief survey concentrating on the events in the 1950s and presenting the official
pro-Sultan view of actions against the Imamate.

507 **British aggression against the Imamate of Oman.**
M. Tathalla El Khatib. New York: Arab Information Centre,
Research Section, 1958. 13p. (Information Paper 6b).
A paper supporting the Imamate against the Sultan, and by implication censuring
Britain for military support given to the Sultan in quelling the revolt in the interior.

508 **Disturbances in Oman.**
Hans Kruse. *International Studies Quarterly*, vol. 7, no. 4 (1966),
p. 589-94.
A consideration of the conflict between the Sultan and the Imamate in 1957 over the
attempt by the Imamate to secure independence for interior Oman, with Saudi
Arabian backing, whilst Sultan Said bin Taimur was attempting to secure his control
throughout Muscat and Oman. The article also considers Britain's involvement in the
struggle, the political effect of the conflict in the rest of the Arabian Peninsula, and
the significance of the Ibadhi religious adherence in the situation.

509 **British attitudes toward the Ibadiyya revivalist movement in east
Arabia.**
Ravinder Kumar. *International Studies*, vol. 3, no. 4 (1962),
p. 43-50.
A consideration of the support given to the Sultan in the face of the revived Imamate,
which was seeking independence for the interior through armed revolt. The Sultan
was supported by British forces from the Trucial States.

510 **The United Nations and the politics of the Arabian Peninsula.**
Marc Lee, Geoffrey Matthews. *Contemporary Review*, vol. 211,
no. 1222 (Nov. 1987), p. 230-34.
Includes references to United Nations deliberations on the claim of the Imamate to be
considered as a separate state.

511 **Riding the storm 1956-1959.**
Harold Macmillan. London: Macmillan, 1971. 786p.
Presents the official British view regarding military presence in Oman to support the
Sultan against the Imamate (p. 270-71) and the Buraimi Oasis dispute (Chapter 8).

512 **The question of Oman.**
Abid A. al-Marayati. *Foreign Affairs Reports* (India), vol. 15, no. 8
(1966), p. 99-109.
An examination of the conflict between Said bin Taimur, Sultan of Muscat and Oman,
and Ghalib ibn Ali, Imam of Oman who sought to acquire jurisdiction over Oman.
This claim was resisted by the Sultan and the United Kingdom, but supported by the
Arab states, in particular the United Arab Republic (UAR), Saudi Arabia and Iraq.
This assessment stresses that the United Kingdom support for the Sultan was
motivated by oil and political interests. The latter part of the article traces the
progress of the conflict through the United Nations, where the Arab states sought to
obtain a ruling against the United Kingdom and a decision in favour of the Imam.

513 **The situation in Oman: a geopolitical analysis.**
Ram Nordan. *Patna University Journal*, vol. 18, pt. 3 (1963),
p. 1-17.
Examines British interventions in Oman on behalf of the Sultan against the
insurrection of the Imamate, which the author considers to be unwarranted
interference. The article deals with the historical background to the Imamate,
particularly with regard to the situation in the 1950s. Also considered are the politics
of oil and the operation of the concessions system, and American influence in this
system in the Arabian Peninsula, particularly Saudi Arabia.

514 **Oman: report of ad hoc committee.**
United Nations Monthly Chronicle, no. 2 (March 1965), p. 28-31.
A review of the United Nations actions regarding the question of the Imamate and the
sovereignty of Oman. It includes the views of the opposing factions.

515 **The Oman war, 1957-1959: a critical history.**
Popular Front for the Liberation of Oman and the Arabian Gulf
Committee, 1974. 24p. map. (9th June Studies).
A publication issued by the political office of the Dhofari guerrillas, examining the
internal struggle between the Sultan and the Imam, with British political and military
support going to the Sultan.

516 **Britain and 'The Oman War': An Arabian entanglement.**
John Everett Peterson. *Asian Affairs*, vol. 63, no. 3 (1976), p. 285-98.
A study of British involvement in the struggle for interior Oman which followed the
death of the Imam in May 1954 and resulted in rebellion against the Sultan and aided
by tribesmen from Saudi Arabia. The situation was further complicated by unrest at
Buraimi Oasis which was claimed by Saudi Arabia, Abu Dhabi and Oman. The author
considers the involvement and tactics of British air and land forces in the Jabal al-
Akhdar and the role of the United Nations in resolving these conflicts. Oman was
admitted to the United Nations in October 1971.

517 **The revival of the Ibadi Imamate in Oman and the threat to
Muscat, 1913-1920.**
John Everett Peterson. *Arabian Studies*, vol. 3 (1976), p. 165-88.
A study of the unrest in the interior of Oman, which resulted in the revival of the
Imamate and its threat to the Sultan. The threat to the Sultanate was only partially
solved by the Treaty of Sib in 1920.

518 **Petition from the Imam of Oman concerning Oman.**
New York: United Nations General Assembly (2 June 1969), 1p.
(A/AC. 109/PET 1059).
The final attempt by the Imamate to gain recognition as an independent state.

519   **Report of the proceedings of the 17th session of the General**
      Assembly of the United Nations on Oman.
      London: HM Stationery Office, 1962. (Command no. 2087).
The British account of the Oman deliberations at the United Nations.

520   **The question of Oman, an analysis of the British Omani dispute.**
      New York: Arab Information Centre, 1960. 24p. (Information Paper,
      no. 13).
A view of the Imamáte question which supports the independence of Oman from
Muscat, with the dependence of the latter on Britain. Also reproduces the text of the
Treaty of Sib.

521   **Oman and the southern shore of the Persian Gulf.**
      Edited by George Rentz.   Cairo: Arabian-American Oil (ARAMCO),
      1952. 326p. maps.
The text is in both English and Arabic and was prepared by the Research Division of
the oil company's Relations Department. The work covers historical and geographical
topics, the tribal structure, politics and economics, and the Ibadhi sect. As one might
expect of its Saudi Arabian-based sponsor company, the volume deals with the
interior of Oman and sees the Imamate as a separate entity from the Sultanate of
Muscat.

522   **The cause of Oman: historical background and statehood as**
      outlined in the statement before the fifteenth General Assembly of
      the United Nations.
      Ahmed al-Shuqayrai.   Cairo: Bureau of Oman, Imamate, 1961.
A restatement of the case presented to the United Nations for recognition of the
Imamate as an independent state.

523   **Muscat and Oman.**
      David Smiley.   *Journal of the Royal United Services Institution*,
      vol. 108, no. 617 (1960), p. 29-47. maps.
An account of military activity in Oman over the question of the Buraimi Oasis and
the revolt in the interior by the Imamate against the Sultan. The author was appointed
Chief of Staff of the Sultan's armed forces in 1958 and the article describes the
military campaign against the Imam with the objective of securing control over the
whole of the territory of Muscat and Oman for the Sultan. The key role of the Special
Air Service (SAS) in the campaign is also discussed, as is the future role of the
Sultan's armed forces following the withdrawal of the British units from the
Sultanate.

524   **The status of Oman and the British Omanite dispute: an analysis based on official documents.**
New York: Arab Information Centre, 1957.
Argues the case for the Imamate and the independence of the interior. Discusses the background to British involvement in the Sultanate and reproduces various papers, such as the Treaty of Sib.

525   **Question of Oman: report of the special representative of the Secretary-General on his visit to Oman.**
United Nations General Assembly.   New York: United Nations, 1963. 49p. maps. (A/5562).
This is also known as the de Ribbing Report, after the UN special representative who was sent on a fact-finding mission concerning the question of the Imamate. His visit was made in 1963 and the resulting report found that the Imamate was no longer a viable entity and should not be brought before the United Nations. This conclusion was not, however, accepted by a number of Arab states who had supported the cause of the Imamate.

526   **Question of Oman: report.**
United Nations. General Assembly. Ad Hoc Committee on Oman.
New York: United Nations, 1965. 222p. maps. (A/8846).
A major international report on the question of Omani representation in the United Nations and the vexed question of the Imamate. The report details the work of the Committee, reproduces the reports of the various inspection trips, and covers the history of the area and representatives from the Sultan and the Imam. The report also reproduces the Treaty of Sib and lists the major international treaties and agreements relating to the Sultanate.

527   **Not in the limelight.**
Ronald Evelyn Leslie Wingate.   London: Hutchinson, 1959. 232p.
The memoirs of a diplomat from the Indian Political Service who was instrumental in ending the seven-year Imamate revolt in 1920 and was involved in the negotiations leading to the Treaty of Sib.

528   **The United Kingdom–Muscat treaty of 1951.**
Richard Young.   *American Journal of International Law*, vol. 46, no. 4 (1952), p. 704-8.
An account of the above treaty in relation to the affairs of the area and the question of the Imamate.

Buraimi Oasis dispute

529 **Arbitration agreement regarding the Buraimi Oasis with an exchange of notes, Jeddah: 30 July 1954.**
In: *Saudi Memorial*. Cairo, 1955, vol. 2, p. 1-14. (English edition).
The English text of the agreement between Britain and Saudi Arabia over the Buraimi Oasis dispute.

530 **Arbitration for the settlement of the territorial dispute between Muscat and Abu Dhabi on one side and Saudi Arabia on the other: memorial of the government of Saudi Arabia.**
Cairo: al-Maaref, 1955. 3 vols. maps.
The official Saudi case for the territory of Buraimi Oasis presented at the arbitration hearing which ended in failure. This item should be read in conjunction with United Kingdom memorial: *Arbitration concerning Buraimi and the common frontier between Abu Dhabi and Saudi Arabia* (q.v.), issued by the British Foreign Office.

531 **Buraimi, a study in diplomacy by default.**
Howard Bushrod, Jr. *Reporter* (23 Jan. 1958), p. 13-16.
A consideration of the support given by Saudi Arabia to the Imam and Saudi claims to the Buraimi Oasis, ostensibly the result of long-standing border disputes, but more importantly . . . 'a struggle between American and British oil interests'. Britain felt at the time that the dispute was fostered by the ARAMCO oil corporation to increase its concession area, and Bushrod produces evidence to substantiate this view.

532 **Conflict and tension among the states of the Persian Gulf, Oman and Saudi Arabia.**
Joseph Churba. Montgomery, Alabama: Maxwell Air Force Base, 1971. 74p. (Documentary Research Division, Aerospace Studies Institute, AV-204-71-1PD).
A military viewpoint of Gulf politics, dealing with Oman, the Buraimi Oasis dispute, the war in Dhofar and the Imamate question.

533 **Arbitration agreement between the government of the United Kingdom acting on behalf of the ruler of Abu Dhabi and His Highness the Sultan Said bin Taimur, and the government of Saudi Arabia. Jeddah: 30 July 1954.**
Great Britain, Foreign and Commonwealth Office. London: HM Stationery Office, 1954.
The official agreement to arbitration with Saudi Arabia over the Buraimi Oasis dispute.

534   The Buraimi dispute: contemporary documents 1950-1961.
Great Britain, Foreign and Commonwealth Office.   Farnham
Common, England: Archive Research, 1992. 6000p. 10 vols.

A companion to the Buraimi memorials providing detailed evidence based on the original political files of the 1950s. Extremely valuable for a study of the Buraimi Oasis dispute and relationships between Oman, Saudi Arabia and the United States.

535   United Kingdom memorial: arbitration concerning Buraimi and the common frontier between Abu Dhabi and Saudi Arabia.
Great Britain, Foreign and Commonwealth Office.   London: HM
Stationery Office, 1955.

The arbitration proceedings of 1955 were abortive and this account assesses the difficulties that prevented settlement of the territorial dispute between Abu Dhabi, Saudi Arabia and the Sultanate of Oman. The dispute became very heated at one stage, and almost led to war between the Sultanate and Saudi Arabia as relations were already strained due to Saudi support for the Imamate in its struggle against the Sultan. This item should be read in conjunction with the Saudi Arabian government's memorial on the subject, *Arbitration for the settlement of the territorial dispute between Muscat and Abu Dhabi on one side and Saudi Arabia on the other* (item no. 530).

536   The Persian Gulf States and their boundary problems.
Rupert Hay.   *Geographical Journal*, vol. 120, pt. 4 (1954), p. 433-45. map.

In dealing with Oman, the author briefly considers the boundary problems in the Musandam Peninsula and between Oman and the present United Arab Emirates. He also examines in slightly more detail the tripartite dispute between Saudi Arabia, Abu Dhabi and Oman over the Buraimi Oasis.

537   The Buraimi Oasis dispute.
John Barrett Kelly.   *International Affairs*, vol. 32, pt. 3 (1956),
p. 318-26.

An excellent account of the Buraimi Oasis dispute between Saudi Arabia on the one hand, and the Sultan of Oman and the Sheikh of Abu Dhabi on the other, with Britain acting on behalf of the latter parties. The author, an expert on politics in the Gulf, deals with the historical background to the dispute, the significance of the oasis, and contemporary events leading to the reawakening of the dispute.

538   Eastern Arabian frontiers.
John Barrett Kelly.   London: Faber and Faber; New York: Fernhill
House, 1964. 319p. maps.

The second part of this book, concerned with events following the Second World War, deals extensively with the Buraimi Oasis dispute during 1952-55, and the various claims and counter-claims. This is an extremely valuable work and essential reading for understanding the border disputes in the Arabian Peninsula at that time and their historical background.

539 **Sovereignty and jurisdiction in eastern Arabia.**
John Barrett Kelly. *International Affairs*, vol. 34, pt. 1 (1958),
p. 16-24.

A further consideration, by an expert in the field, of the various problems of spheres of influence and frontiers in eastern Arabia. In essence, claims to disputed territories are based upon one or both of two grounds: past or present occupation, or current exercise of jurisdiction. The Buraimi Oasis dispute is examined from these standpoints and the author concludes that until the various disputes, including Buraimi, are solved, 'King Saud will continue to feel free to challenge the authority of the Sultan of Muscat and Oman and that of the rulers of the Trucial Sheikhdoms in the western marches of their dominions'.

540 **Boundaries and petroleum in southern Arabia.**
Alexander Melamid. *Geographical Review*, vol. 47, pt. 4 (1957),
p. 589-91.

A consideration of the various border disputes including the Buraimi Oasis and the ill-defined Rub' al-Khali frontier between Saudi Arabia and the Sultanate of Oman. The boundary problems are discussed in relation to the complexities of exploration and oil concessions in a volatile area.

541 **The Buraimi Oasis dispute.**
Alexander Melamid. *Middle East Affairs*, vol. 7, no. 2 (1956),
p. 56-63.

This article seeks to explain the involved background to the dispute, which eventually went to unsuccessful arbitration in 1955. The dispute was long-standing, originally because of the presence of water, without which the tribes on either side could not survive, and then because of the possible presence of oil in the area. An additional factor in the conflict was the internal Oman dispute between the Sultan and the Imam, with the latter receiving support from Saudi Arabia.

542 **The economic geography of neutral territories.**
Alexander Melamid. *Geographical Review*, vol. 45, pt. 3 (1955),
p. 359-74.

Discusses whether economic growth effects the status of neutral territories or vice versa. Problems related to the Middle East and the unresolved Buraimi Oasis dispute are examined on pages 363-69.

543 **Geographical boundaries and nomadic grazing.**
Alexander Melamid. *Geographical Review*, vol. 55, pt. 2 (1965),
p. 287-90.

An interesting article on the problems of geographical boundaries, which have become important in Arabia because of oil, in relation to traditional areas of tribal influence as defined by grazing rights. This has been an important consideration in the Buraimi Oasis dispute.

544 **Oil and the evolution of boundaries in eastern Arabia.**
Alexander Melamid. *Geographical Review*, vol. 44, pt. 2 (1954),
p. 295-96.
A consideration of the Buraimi Oasis dispute in relation to the possible presence of
oil in the area.

545 **Anglo-American rivalry in the Middle East: The struggle for the
Buraimi Oasis 1952-1957.**
Tore Tingvold Petersen. *International History Review* (Canada),
vol. 14, no. 1 (1992), p. 71-91.
An examination of the diplomatic and economic consequences for Great Britain and
the United States – because of the significance of the oil deposits – when Saudi
Arabia occupied the Buraimi Oasis. Although Buraimi was governed by Oman her
foreign affairs were represented by Great Britain and, as a result, Great Britain was
involved in the crisis. The events caused a deterioration in Anglo-American relations
with British accusations of US neo-imperialism and United States criticisms of
British security policy in the Middle East.

546 **The Buraimi dispute, the British armed aggression.**
A. S. Sahwell. *Islamic Review*, vol. 44 (April 1956), p. 13-17.
Presents the Saudi case for claiming the Buraimi Oasis in the dispute with Abu Dhabi
and Oman. Because Britain still held responsibility for the foreign affairs of the
Trucial States and Oman, it handled negotiations with Saudi Arabia on their behalf. In
addition, the British-officered Trucial Oman Scouts provided the military presence in
the area.

547 **Buraimi Oasis.**
Wilfred P. Thesiger. *Illustrated London News*, no. 225 (3 July 1954),
p. 19-20.
Deals with the Buraimi Oasis dispute between Saudi Arabia and Oman, and the
involvement of Great Britain, presented here in the role of protector of the Sultanate.

Dhofar War and reconstruction

548 **The secret war.**
David C. Arkless. London: Kimber, 1988. 244p.
The personal memoir of Arkless describing his service as an air-drop crew member in
counter-guerrilla operations in Dhofar between 1971 and 72. A very detailed account
of experiences of air sorties and ground operations against dissident communist
forces in Dhofar.

549 **Armed struggle in Arabia.**
London: Gulf Committee, 1976. 35p. map. bibliog. (Gulf Studies, no. 1).
A statement on the continuance of the Dhofar insurrection despite its military defeat and the official declaration of victory by the Sultanate.

550 **South Arabia: violence and revolt.**
J. Bowyer Bell. London: Institute for the Study of Conflict, 1973. 14p. maps. (Conflict Series, no. 40).
Deals largely with the internal situation, but also discusses the Dhofar War – which is seen as a means of exporting revolution throughout the region – and the question of Soviet and Cuban involvement.

551 **Cuban intervention in Africa and Arabia.**
Wolfgang Berner. *Aussenpolitik* (English Edition), vol. 27, no. 3 (1976), p. 328-35.
Deals with the role of Cuban mercenaries in the Yemen and in the Dhofar rebellion.

552 **British intelligence and covert action.**
Jonathon Bloch, Patrick Fitzgerald. London: Junction Books, 1983. 284p. bibliog.
A detailed, hostile review of British special operations around the world since the Second World War. There are numerous references to Oman, covering operations against the Imamate and in the Dhofar War.

553 **British troops in Oman.**
New Left Review, no. 92 (July-Aug. 1975), p. 105-12.
A critical examination of the role of the British military advisers and contracted personnel in the Sultan's armed forces with regard to the Dhofar War.

554 **Rebellion in Dhofar: the spectre of Vietnam.**
R. M. Burrell. *New Middle East* (March-April 1972), p. 53-58.
An examination of the origins of the Dhofar rebellion. Burrell looks at the political development of the guerrilla movement and British involvement in the war to protect Western interests in the area, and states that 'the priority of this struggle to the politically unstable but economically vital Persian Gulf may, in the long run, render this remote Arabian war more decisive for, and detrimental to, Western interests than the better known struggle in South-East Asia'.

555 **Revolution in Dhofar: Sultanate of Oman.**
Ray L. Cleveland. *Middle East Forum*, vol. 47, no. 3-4 (1971), p. 93-102.
Discusses the war in Dhofar, mainly from the strategic and political aspects, and examines the involvement of China and Russia in the struggle. The author considers that 'Dhofar has become a major battlefield in the struggle to control Arabian oil, and

the outcome of the conflict has great political significance for the future history of the Arabian Peninsula'.

556 **Oman and the Dhofar rebellion.**
Victor J. Croizat. *Marine Corps Gazette*, vol. 59, no. 2 (1975), p. 18-22.

An account of the strategies adopted by the Sultanate against the rebels which were gradually beginning to become effective towards the mid-1970s.

557 **Annual of Power and Conflict: a Survey of Political Violence and International influence.**
Brian Crozier. London: Institute for the Study of Conflict, 1973- . annual.

Each volume until 1976 contained a section on Oman relating to the war in Dhofar and its military implications.

558 **Secret war number eleven, slavery and oil are the stakes on the Arabian Peninsula.**
Claude Deffarge, Gordon Troeller. *Atlas*, vol. 18, no. 3 (1969), p. 32-37.

An analysis of the Dhofar War, seen as a war against slavery in the Sultanate and involving the economic potential of oil.

559 **Dhofar: Britain's colonial war in the Gulf.**
Gulf Committee. London: Crest Press, 1972. 72p. maps.

A critical and biased assessment of Britain's role in the Dhofar War with the Sultanate being regarded as a colony of Britain and being used as an instrument to preserve and further British interests in the region.

560 **Evidence of PDYR aggression against the Sultanate of Oman.**
Muscat: Government Printing Press, [n.d.]. 8p.

The Sultanate's case to prove Yemeni involvement in the Dhofar War. It covers the supply of arms, the provision of training facilities and bases, and involvement in cross-border incursions.

561 **Where soldiers fear to tread.**
Ranulph Fiennes. London: Hodder and Stoughton, 1975. 256p. map.

Covers two aspects of the war in Dhofar, dealing from first-hand experience with the fighting, and also with the changes that had taken place in the three years following the accession of Sultan Qaboos. Consideration is given to the use of oil wealth to pursue objectives in Dhofar, and the oil price rises which enabled programmes of economic and social development to take place through the Civil Aid Programme.

562 **Who dares wins.**
Tony Geraghty.   London: Arms and Armour Press, 1980; Nashville,
Tennessee: The Baltey Press, 1980. [Published as *Inside the SAS*],
249p. maps. bibliog.
A review of operations of the Special Air Services in the period following the Second
World War. There are numerous references to the Dhofar War and campaigns in
Oman, with the main section being on pages 117-37.

563 **Class struggle in the Arab Gulf.**
Fred Halliday.   *New Left Review*, no. 58 (Nov.-Dec. 1969), p. 31-37.
An analysis of the politics and objectives of the Dhofari rebels. Their cause is seen as
a class struggle against the Sultan and the established order, with the latter being
supported by British imperialism.

564 **Counter insurgency old and new: the case of Oman.**
Fred Halliday.   *Gulf Studies*, vol. 1, no. 1 (1976), p. 13-35.
A view of the war in Dhofar and its outcome, mainly from the viewpoint of the
Dhofari rebels. Halliday views the war as a popular class struggle against the
autocratic established order which was no longer relevant to the modern Arab world
but which was receiving Western support, especially from Britain, to protect Western
imperialistic interests in the area and to safeguard Arab oil supplies.

565 **Interview with Tala Saad and Said Seif on the political situation in
Oman and Dhofar.**
Fred Halliday.   *New Left Review*, no. 6 (March-April 1971), p. 53-58.
The two persons named in the article were, respectively, members of the General
Council of the Popular Front for the Liberation of the Occupied Arabian Gulf
(PFLOAG) and the Popular Revolutionary Movement. The article represents a pro-
revolutionary view of the conflict in Dhofar.

566 **Oil and revolution in the Persian Gulf.**
Fred Halliday.   *Ramparts*, vol. 9, pt. 9 (1971), p. 52-54.
An analysis of the Dhofar revolt which had evolved a Marxist–Leninist ideology. The
author examines the maturation of the revolt and the necessity for it to spread to other
Gulf States in order to be successful.

567 **Soviet policy towards the rebellion in Dhofar.**
Howard M. Hensel.   *Asian Affairs*, vol. 13, no. 2 (1982), p. 183-207.
Hensel surveys the changes in the policy of the Soviet Union towards the rebellion in
Dhofar from 1962 to 1977. Initially, support was given to the rebellion channelled
through the People's Democratic Republic of Yemen, but the coup of 1970 and
resultant reforms and development policies reduced the motivation of the tribal rebels
and dissidents. Soviet interest in the Dhofar War began to decline and was overtaken
by an interest in the Iranian situation and other strategic concerns in the region. The
petering out of the rebellion in the latter part of the 1970s was welcomed by the
Soviet Union.

568 **A contract officer in Oman.**
Alan Hoskins. London: Costello, 1988. 192p. bibliog.
A highly personal account of life in Oman for an officer on contract to the Sultan of
Oman's armed forces who spent four years as a staff officer at the Omani Ministry of
Defence. The account largely centres on the day-to-day problems associated with the
running of affairs in a country so alien to British contracted staff.

569 **Interview with Abdul Aziz al-Qadi, Chairman of the PFLO
Central Executive Committee.**
News from Oman and South Arabia, no. 38 (May 1981), p. 1-6.
This interview with the Chairman of the Popular Front for the Liberation of Oman
was held in February 1981, and covers the PFLO's revolutionary programme set out
in 1976 and achievement by the time of the interview. Al-Qadi voices optimism about
the success of the armed struggle against the regime of Sultan Qaboos. He condemns
the United States ties with Oman and the Camp David Accords, whilst the Soviet
Union is regarded as an ally.

570 **SAS Operation Oman.**
Tony Jeapers. London: Kimber, 1980. 247p.
An account of Special Air Services special operations, intelligence gathering,
propaganda and counter-insurgency activities in Oman between 1971 and 1976.

571 **Red guerrillas of the Arabian Gulf.**
B. Karabuda. *Eastern Horizons*, vol. 9, no. 5 (1970), p. 48-54.
Deals with the communist backing for the Dhofari rebels from both China and the
USSR, and the change of control in the rebel movement.

572 **Revolutionary transformation in the Arab world: Habash and his
comrades from nationalism to Marxism.**
Walid W. Kazziha. London: Knight, 1975. ix+118p.
Kazziha is concerned with the move to the left in the revolutionary politics of the
Arabian Peninsula. The question of Dhofar and Oman is considered in the context of
the wider political organization outside the Sultanate.

573 **Hadramaut, Oman, Dhofar: The experience of revolution.**
John Barrett Kelly. *Middle Eastern Studies*, vol. 12, no. 2 (1976),
p. 213-20.
The Federation of South Arabia was established in 1963 by Great Britain but
excluded Hadhramaut, Oman and Dhofar. The article analyses the reasons for their
exclusion and the impact of the federation on both members and non-member states
and on the surrounding region. Kelly also examines economic conditions in the area,
the complexities of the tribal structures, Marxist influence in Southern Yemen, the
influence of Islam, and the role of Great Britain in the area.

574   **The Dhofar insurgency: an overview.**
       M. A. Saleem Khan.   *Journal of the United Service Institute of India*,
       vol. 105, no. 438 (1975), p. 28-34.

The rebellion in Dhofar began in 1965 against the rule of Sultan Said bin Taimur and continued for over a decade but the coup of 1970 placated a number of the rebels. However, a hard core had come under the influence of the Marxist regime of the People's Democratic Republic of Yemen (PDRY) and continued the war with backing from the PDRY, Iraq and China. Aid to Oman came from Great Britain and Iran; it succeeded in containing the rebels, and by 1975 China had withdrawn support from the insurgents.

575   **The lion and the mistletoe.**
       H. J. Lockhart.   *Blackwood's Magazine*, vol. 313, no. 1896 (1973),
       p. 361-69.

The war in Dhofar was begun by a section of the population who had formed the Dhofar Liberation Front but by 1968 the movement was being supported by Chinese communists through the provision of arms and equipment shipped through Aden. Training was also provided for the leaders of the movement in Aden, Peking and Dhofar. Operation Lion was an operation mounted in 1972 to blockade supply routes from the People's Democratic Republic of Yemen and starve the newly formed Popular Front for the Liberation of the Occupied Arabian Gulf. The author was personally involved in this operation.

576   **Regional military involvement: a case study of Iran under the Shah.**
       Maqsud Ul Hasan Nuri.   *Pakistan Horizon*, vol. 37, no. 4 (1984),
       p. 32-45.

Examines Iran's adoption of the role of protector of the Persian Gulf following Britain's withdrawal from the region. One manifestation of this role was the involvement of Iranian troops in the Dhofar War from 1972 to 1977 at the request of the Omani governments. This served Iran's military strategy and provided a good training ground for Iranian troops in battle conditions.

577   **Air power in low-intensity conflict in the Middle East.**
       William J. Olson.   *Air University Review*, vol. 37, no. 3 (1986),
       p. 2-21.

An examination of the effective use of air power in low-intensity warfare, using the Dhofar War, Afghanistan and the 1982 Israeli invasion of Lebanon as case-studies.

578   **Revolutionary warfare in Oman: a strategic appraisal.**
       Bard E. O'Neill, William Bundage.   *Middle East Review*, vol. 10
       (Summer 1978), p. 48-56.

An analysis of the Dhofar uprising and the likely outcome in view of the government's reforms and counter-insurgency policy. Ultimate success for the PFLO is seen as dependent on precarious outside support which seems unable to respond to disunity within the ranks caused by government reforms.

579   **The rebellion in Dhofar: a threat to Western interests in the Gulf.**
      R. P. Owen.   *The World Today*, vol. 29, no. 6 (June 1973), p. 266-72.
Deals with the significance of the Dhofar War, particularly in relation to the danger to
the West of the possibility of a communist presence in the area, and the threat to
future oil supplies.

580   **Moscow and the Persian Gulf countries 1967-1970.**
      Stephen Page.   *Mizon*, vol. 13, no. 2 (1971), p. 72-88.
Deals with the growth of Soviet interest and influence in the Gulf and the use of the
People's Democratic Republic of Yemen as a base for revolutionary activities,
particularly in Oman.

581   **The USSR and Arabia: the development of Soviet policies and
      attitudes towards the countries of the Arabian Peninsula, 1955-
      1970.**
      Stephen Page.   London: Central Asian Research Centre, 1971. 152p.
Wider in context than the Sultanate of Oman, but valuable for a consideration of
Soviet and Chinese involvement in Oman through the provision of support for the
Dhofar insurgents by supplying arms and training facilities.

582   **Oman 1975: The year of decision.**
      K. Perkins.   *Journal of the Royal United Services Institute for
      Defence Studies*, vol. 124, no. 1 (1979), p. 38-45.
The rebellion in Dhofar in 1975 developed into a war against the new Sultan,
threatened the stability of the regime and was backed by the Soviet Union and China.
Using British personnel and equipment, a conventional war and counter-insurgency
was waged in Dhofar by the Sultan of Oman's armed forces. The success of the
campaign demonstrated that civilian as well as military control was needed, in tandem
with development policies and a restoration of political rule. The author was
commander of the Sultan's armed forces.

583   **Guerrilla warfare and ideological confrontation in the Arabian
      Peninsula: The rebellion in Dhofar.**
      John Everett Peterson.   *World Affairs*, vol. 139, no. 4 (1977),
      p. 278-95.
This examination of how the insurrection in Dhofar became an ideological and
military struggle is used as an example of an ideological confrontation between
traditional and progressive regimes, something which has become a factor in Arab
politics since the Second World War. The military aspects of the war are examined,
as is the battle that was taking place for the hearts and minds of the people and the
restoration of the Sultan's remit throughout the country.

584 **The British army: the Dhofar campaign, 1970-1975.**
J. Pimlott. In: *Armed forces and modern counter-insurgency*, edited
by I. F. W. Beckett, J. Pimlott. London; New York: St. Martin's
Press, 1985, p. 16-45.

An examination of the role of the British army in the Dhofar rebellion. It was
concerned both with training Omani personnel and with providing specialist forces
under contract to the Sultanate of Oman or on secondment. This avoided direct
British government involvement in the conflict, but the provision of highly trained
anti-terrorist personnel was not impaired by these constraints.

585 **Documents on the national struggle in Oman and the Arabian
Gulf.**
Popular Front for the Liberation of Oman. London: Gulf Committee,
1974. 107p. map. (9th June Studies).

A presentation of the Popular Front's cause through accounts of their various
congresses and the resolutions that were passed. Expressions of support from outside
Oman are also included.

586 **Gulf liberation manifesto.**
Popular Front for the Liberation of the Occupied Arabian Gulf. In:
National liberation fronts, 1960-70, edited by D. C. Hoges, R. E. Abu
Shanab. New York: Morrow, 1972. p. 143-45.

A reproduction of the PFLOAG's manifesto, aimed at political and social change
throughout the Gulf and based on Marxist principles.

587 **Oman: insurgency and development.**
D. L. Price. London: Institute for the Study of Conflict, 1975. 19p.
map. (Conflict Studies, no. 53).

An account of the war in Dhofar both from the military viewpoint and from that of
the Civil Aid Programme. The geopolitical situation of the Sultanate within the larger
region is also considered.

588 **Military press brief: Dhofar.**
Sultanate of Oman. Muscat: Ministry of Information, 1976. 12p.
map.

A brief yet succinct account of the causes, progress and conclusion of the war in
Dhofar, issued by the Ministry after the main military struggle was considered ended.
The work of the Civil Aid Department and its role as an instrument of change are also
dealt with.

589 **The rescuers: The world's top anti-terrorist units.**
Leroy Thompson. Boulder, Colorado; London: Paladin Press, 1986.
241p.

This survey of the major counter-terrorism forces of the non-Soviet bloc covers
weapons, equipment, organization, training and a summary of their major activity.

The author describes the Sultanate of Oman's Special Forces, their activities against the Dhofari rebels and the war in the province.

590   **The liberation of Dhofar.**
Fawwaz Trabilsi.   *Middle East Research and Information Project Reports*, vol. 1, no. 6 (1972), p. 3-11.
A view of the conflict in Oman from the viewpoint of the Popular Front for the Liberation of Oman.

591   **End of a ten year's war.**
Penelope Tremayne.   *Journal of the Royal United Services Institute for Defence Studies*, vol. 122, no. 1 (1977), p. 44-48.
An assessment of the significance of the defeat of the rebels in Dhofar which prevented Soviet control, by proxy, of the Gulf States and their oil production. Discusses Soviet support for the dissidents, the training facilities provided by the People's Democratic Republic of Yemen, and British and Iranian support for the Sultan of Oman's armed forces.

592   **From resistance to revolution.**
Penelope Tremayne.   *Army Quarterly and Defence Journal*, vol. 103, no. 1 (1975), p. 46-50.
Discusses the guerrilla warfare in the Dhofar province of the Sultanate of Oman from 1964 to 1975 with its development from a limited internal protest to a movement aimed at revolution throughout the region.

593   **Guevera through the looking-glass: A view of the Dhofar war.**
Penelope Tremayne.   *Journal of the Royal United Services Institute for Defence Studies*, vol. 119, no. 3 (1974), p. 39-43.
The Dhofar rebellion began in 1964 as a localized insurrection against the Sultan but was later penetrated by the Marxist leadership of the People's Front for the Liberation of the Occupied Arabian Gulf. By 1970 the initiative had passed to the rebels, but by 1974 the initiative had been lost, thanks to the reforms initiated by Sultan Qaboos and more effective counter-insurgency tactics adopted by the Sultan's armed forces.

594   **Turmoil in Southern Arabia.**
Lewis B. Ware.   *Military Review*, vol. 59, no. 11 (1979), p. 51-54.
A brief survey of political instability in Oman and the Yemen Arab Republic during the 1960s and 1970s. Ware focuses on the role of the People's Democratic Republic of Yemen in initiating and fostering instability.

Oman and East Africa.
see item no. 463.

Conflict and tension among the states of the Persian Gulf, Oman and Saudi Arabia.
See item no. 532.

Treaties

With Great Britain

595 **Cowinamah, or written engagement from the Imam of Muscat for the exclusion of the French from his territories.**
In: *A collection of treaties, engagements and sanads relating to India and neighbouring countries,* edited by Charles Umpherston Aitchinson. Calcutta, India: Superintendent of Government Printing, 1933, vol. 7, p. 110.
This agreement, signed in Muscat on 12 October 1798, was instrumental in securing British influence in the Sultanate to the exclusion of other European powers.

596 **Agreement entered into by the Imam of the state of Oman for the residence of a British Agent at Muscat.**
In: Aitchinson (q.v.), vol. 7, p. 88.
This agreement, signed in Muscat on 18 January 1800, enabled Britain, through its Political Agent to exercise considerable influence over the affairs of the Sultanate.

597 **Treaty with the Imam of Muscat for the suppression of the slave trade in his dominions.**
In: Aitchinson (q.v.), vol. 7, p. 89-91.
Signed in Muscat on 4 September 1822, with an additional article agreed on 9 September 1822. This was one of a series of treaties designed to halt the slave trade which had resulted from the Arab presence in East Africa.

598 **Additional articles regarding the suppression of the foreign slave trade entered into by His Highness Saeed Syud bin Sultan, the Imam of Muscat.**
In: Aitchinson (q.v.), vol. 7, p. 99.
Signed in Muscat on 17 December 1839, this agreement was a further attempt to halt the slave trade from East Africa and to provide for enforcement by the British Royal Navy.

599 **Agreement between Her Majesty the Queen of the United Kingdom of Great Britain and Ireland and His Highness Syud Saeed bin Sultan, the Sultan of Muscat, for the termination of the export of slaves from the African dominions of His Highness the Sultan of Muscat.**
In: Aitchinson (q.v.), vol. 7, p. 101.
This agreement, signed at Zanzibar on 2 October 1845, gives an indication of the ineffectiveness of previously concluded treaties and agreements which were causing the Sultan grave economic problems.

600 **Deed of cession of the Koria Moria Islands executed by His Highness the Imam of Muscat in the presence of Captain Freemantle, commanding Her Majesty's Ship *Juno*.**
In: Aitchinson (q.v.), vol. 7, p. 102.

Signed in Muscat on 14 July 1854. At the time the islands were economically important because of their natural fertilizer resources. The cession of the islands allowed Britain to exploit these resources.

601 **Exchange of notes between Lord Canning, Governor-General of India, and His Highness Syud Thowaynee bin Saeed bin Sultan, Sultan of Muscat, regarding the arbitration between Muscat and Zanzibar: 1. Letter to His Highness Syud Thowaynee bin Saeed bin Sultan, dated Fort William, 2 April 1861; 2. Letter from Syud Thowaynee bin Saeed bin Sultan to Lord Canning, dated 15 May 1861.**

These letters set out the terms of the Canning Award and the Sultan's acceptance. Following arbitration by Lord Canning, this important agreement compensated the Sultan for the loss of Zanzibar. The agreement assumed even greater importance when Zanzibar defaulted and Britain assumed responsibility for the payment. This strengthened British control in Oman, since the award was a major part of the Sultan's income.

602 **Agreement concluded with the Sultan of Muscat for the construction of telegraph lines within His Highness' territory. Signed at Birka on 17 November 1864, and sealed at Muscat on 18 November 1864.**
In: Aitchinson (q.v.), vol. 7, p. 107.

An indication of the British presence, in political terms, in the affairs of the Sultanate and the increasing reliance of the Sultan on British advice and expertise.

603 **Convention concluded between the British government and the Sultan of Muscat for the extension of the electric telegraph through the dominions subject to the sovereignty of the Sultan of Muscat in Arabia and Mekran.**
In: Aitchinson (q.v.), p. 107.

Signed in Muscat on 19 January 1865, this convention provided for a further extension of the network (both by cable and wireless) for internal and external communications.

604 **Treaty between Her Majesty the Queen of the United Kingdom of Great Britain and Ireland and His Highness the Sultan of Muscat for the abolition of the slave trade.**
In: Aitchinson (q.v.), p. 108.

Signed in Muscat on 14 April 1873, this was a further attempt to suppress the slave trade which, although drastically reduced, had not been completely eradicated.

605 **Agreement entered into by the Sultan of Muscat relative to the jurisdiction of the British Political Agent and Consul over subject of native states in India residing in the Muscat dominions.**
In: Aitchinson (q.v.), vol. 7, p. 109.

This agreement, signed in Muscat in 1873, placed responsibility for the large Indian community with the British Agent and outside the jurisdiction of the Sultan's government.

606 **Exchange of letters between Her Britannic Majesty's Political Agent and Consul at Muscat regarding the levy of duty from distressed vessels putting into the ports of Muscat: 1. Letter from the Political Agent and Consul to the Sultan, 2 February 1875; 2. Letter from the Sultan of Muscat to the Political Agent and Consul, 10 February 1875.**
In: Aitchinson (q.v.), vol. 7, p. 110.

The regulations established by the Sultan regarding duties to be charged on the cargoes of ships putting into Omani ports.

607 **Treaty of friendship, commerce and navigation between Great Britain and Muscat.**
In: *Great Britain: British and Foreign State Papers*. London: HM Stationery Office, 1891, vol. 83.

Signed in Muscat on 19 March 1891, this was the forerunner of a series of treaties between the two countries which have renewed this original treaty for varying periods of time. The terms of this treaty and the subsequent renewals have set the pattern of relationships between the two states.

608 **Agreement regarding the cession of territory by the Sultan of Muscat and Oman.**
In: Aitchinson (q.v.), vol. 12, p. 24-41.

This agreement, signed in Muscat on 20 March 1891, prevented the Sultan for ceding territory without the approval of the British government.

609 **Proclamation issued by the Sultan of Oman regarding the suppression of the illegal importation of arms into Persia and British India.**
In: Aitchinson (q.v.), vol. 12, p. 240-41.

This tripartite agreement, dated 13 January 1898, shows Oman's position at the centre of an arms trade. The agreement was designed to stem the supply of arms to dissidents in the two countries.

610   **Notification issued by the Sultan of Muscat respecting the transportation of arms . . . to those portions of the African coast which are under the British Protectorate, and also to those parts which are under the Italian Protectorate.**
In: *Great Britain: British Foreign and State Papers.*   London: HM Stationery Office, 1905, vol. 96, p. 665-66.
Aimed at preventing the supply of arms through Oman to dissidents operating in the areas. It was issued in Muscat on 17 October 1903.

611   **Treaties and undertakings in force between the British government and the Sultan of Maskat and Oman, 1845-1914.**
Indian Government. Foreign and Political Department.   Calcutta: Government Printing Office, 1914. 2 vols.
A useful collection, in English and Arabic, of the various treaties and agreements from the period in question.

612   **Civil air agreement between the United Kingdom and the Sultanate of Oman. Bahrein: 5 April 1947.**
In: *Great Britain: British and Foreign Office State Papers.*   London: HM Stationery Office, 1947, vol. 147, p. 928-31.
The text of the agreement allowing Great Britain sole right to establish an airport and air services in Oman.

613   **Agreement concluded between Her Majesty's government in the United Kingdom and the Sultan of Muscat and Oman modifying the exchange of letters between the United Kingdom and Muscat regarding extra territorial jurisdiction, Muscat, 20 December 1951, and thereby transferring to the Sultan of Muscat and Oman jurisdiction over Indian nationals.**
In: *Great Britain: British and Foreign Office State Papers.*   London: HM Stationery Office, 1958, vol. 163, p. 490.
Signed in Muscat on 25 April 1957 and 10 March 1958, this nullified the agreement of 1873 (q.v.) whereby responsibility for the Indian nationals in Oman had been vested in the British Political Agent.

614   **Exchange of letters between the United Kingdom and the Sultanate of Oman concerning the Sultan's armed forces, civil aviation, Royal Air Force facilities and economic development in Muscat and Oman.**
London: HM Stationery Office, 1958. (Treaty Series, no. 28).
The formal exchange of letters allowing for the use of Masirah Island by the Royal Air Force, and detailing plans for further development of civil aviation and economic assistance and development.

615 **Treaty of cession between Her Majesty in respect of the United Kingdom of Great Britain and Northern Ireland and the Sultan of Muscat and Oman relating to the Kuria Muria Islands, Salalah, 15 November 1967.**
London: HM Stationery Office, 1968. (Treaty Series, no. 8).
The treaty by which Great Britain returned the Kuria Muria Islands to the Sultanate of Oman.

The legal and historical basis of the British position in the Persian Gulf.
See item no. 378.

Internal

616 **Treaty of peace between His Highness Syud Saeed bin Sultan, The Imam of Muscat, and Syud Humood, the Chief of Sohar.**
In: Aitchinson (q.v.), vol. 7, p. 110.
Signed in Muscat on 23 December 1839, this treaty is an illustration of the internal situation in the Sultanate which was fraught with dissent.

617 **Engagement entered into by Syud Syf bin Humood, Chief of Sohar for the abolition of the African slave trade in his ports, 22 May 1849.**
In: Aitchinson (q.v.), vol. 11, p. 89.
A further attempt by the British government to abolish the slave trade; it illustrates the fragmentary nature of control within the Sultanate.

618 **Treaty of alliance, offensive and defensive, between His Highness Syed Soweynee, Governor of Muscat, and Abdullah ben Fysul, son of the Wahhabi Chief and Commander of the Wahabee expedition into Oman, 9 May 1853.**
In: *India Office: Enclosures to Bombay Secret Letters*, vol. 117, no. 258.
Enclosure to secret letter 69 of 28 November 1853, Kemball to Malet, 13 September 1853. An attempt to reach an agreement with the Wahhabis who claimed sovereignty over areas of northern Oman, particularly in the Buraimi Oasis area.

619 **Declaration of the Wahabee Ameer regarding the territorial integrity of the British protected sheikhdoms and of the Kingdom of Maskat, given to the British Political Resident in the Persian Gulf.**
In: Aitchinson (q.v.), vol. 10, p. 116.
An agreement concluded by the Wahhabis in Bushire, Iran, on 21 April 1866, after a series of incursions into Oman. By signing this treaty they effectively recognized British influence in the area.

620 **Agreement of Sib, 1920.**
In: *Oman and the twentieth century*, edited by J. E. Peterson.
London: Croom Helm, 1978, p. 174-75.

This agreement was an attempt to end the hostilities between the Imamate and the
Sultan and was the result of delicate negotiations conducted by and through the
Political Agent at Muscat. It takes the form of two letters sent to the Political Agent
by the Sultan's government and by the Omani tribes, both agreeing to the terms
arranged through the mediator. The negotiations were all conducted and letters all
written in Arabic, and only translated versions appeared in English as part of the India
Office records and correspondence, from which this version was taken.

Dissertations

621 **Roots of domination and dependency: British reaction towards the
development of Omani commerce at Muscat and Zanzibar in the
nineteenth century.**
M. Reda Bhacker. DPhil thesis, University of Oxford, 1988. 401p.
(Available from University Microfilms, Ann Arbor, Michigan, order
no. AADD-97224).

The rise of Zanzibar in the nineteenth century was largely attributed to the activity of
Muscati mercantile communities as a result of challenges to their traditional Indian
markets from the British. The suppression of the slave trade led to expansion into
traditional commercial activities such as ivory and textiles and into plantation
economies, notably cloves and dates. However, Britain intensified its anti-slavery
campaign and succeeded in challenging Omani domination of the market largely
because of the weakness of the regime in Oman which relied on British aid against
outside aggression.

622 **British maritime contacts with the Persian Gulf and Gulf of
Oman, 1850-1900.**
Nigel Robert Dalziel. PhD thesis, University of Lancaster, England,
1989. 442p. (Available from University Microfilms, Ann Arbor,
Michigan, order no. AADDX-91578).

A study of British informal imperialism in the Gulfs of Persia and Oman dealing
specifically with Oman, the Trucial States, Qatar, Bahrain and Kuwait, as these states
were particularly susceptible to British maritime power because of their dependence
upon the sea. The eventual dominance of Britain due to its maritime power is
examined, as are the economic links and cooperative developments which began to
emerge during the period in question.

623 **The influence of the environment on pre-Islamic socio-economic organization in southwestern Arabia.**
Abdul Kareem Abdulla S. Al-Ghamedi. PhD thesis, Arizona State University, 1983. 310p. (Available from University Microfilms, Ann Arbor, Michigan, order no. AAD83-15793).

South-western Arabia is considered to be important archaeologically for a study of the pre-Islamic period. Any find is of significance because little is known about the area during this period. Also, the rainfall and climate rendered the area suitable for agriculture, and this was particularly the case with Oman. However, other factors were disruptive forces: flash floods; cyclical droughts; limited arable land; and socio-economic conflicts.

624 **A history of Omani–British relations, with special reference to the period 1888-1920.**
H. B. A. S. Y. H. Al-Mousawi. PhD thesis, University of Glasgow, Scotland, 1990. (Available from the British Library, Document Supply Centre, Boston Spa, Wetherby, West Yorkshire, United Kingdom).

The study begins by surveying the development of Omani relations with Great Britain from the 1620s. However, the main concentration of the study is on the reign of Sultan Faisal, 1888-1913 but technically extended to 1920, when British policy in the area was determined by the need to defend the North-West Frontier of India. Muscat was of crucial importance because it was the nearest port to India, and for the sea route between England and India. Also Muscat had become a centre for the arms trade in the region and was supplying arms to the rebel tribes in India, thus causing Britain to desire more control over the Sultanate. A further excuse was the offering of protection to Indian citizens in Muscat but the arms trade was in reality the crucial issue. The whole relationship with Britain at that time led the Sultan to open relations with France for protection; these are studied, particularly with regard to the flying of the French flag by Omani ships, a dispute settled by arbitration in 1905. The arms trade continued to flourish and became big business, such that by 1908 most European powers wished for the trade to be suppressed. Continued British pressure on the Sultan over the suppression and control of the arms trade led to a revolt against the Sultan in 1913 in order to elect a ruler sympathetic to Omani needs. The revolt lasted until 1920 and Oman was effectively partitioned, with the Sultan ruling the coastal area, and the elected Iman ruling the interior with a capital at Nizwa.

625 **Eastern Arabia in the sixth and seventh centuries A.D.**
Hassan Muhammad Al-Naboodah. PhD thesis, University of Exeter, England, 1988. 298p. (Available from University Microfilms, Ann Arbor, Michigan, order no. AADDX-86825).

This study presents a geographical, political and economic survey of Bahrain and Oman during the pre-Islamic and early Islamic years, focusing primarily on the principal tribes of the region.

626 **The Resident in the Gulf: British power in transition 1858-1872 (Persian Gulf).**
Omer Saleh Al-Omery. PhD thesis, University of Essex, England, 1989, 319p. (Available from University Microfilms, Ann Arbor, Michigan, order no. AADD-88503).

This study examines the development of British control in the area, growing out of the presence of the East India Company and a greater involvement of the Crown in Indian affairs. Chapters four and five are specifically related to the often turbulent relations between the Residency and Oman.

627 **The Qawasim and British control of the Arabian Gulf.**
Mubarak Al-Otabi. PhD thesis, University of Salford, England, 1989. 200p. (Available from University Microfilms, Ann Arbor, Michigan, order no. AADD-91406).

A study of the growth in British control in the Persian Gulf, beginning in 1820 with a series of agreements with local leaders in the area which led to the various sheikhdoms becoming known as the Trucial States. The actions taking against the Qawasim of Ras al Khaimah was justified as the putting down of 'piracy' but this version of events is now being challenged by scholars. The author argues also that not enough attention has been paid to the role of Wahhabism and Anglo-French rivalry in the determining of British policy in the Trucial States, including Oman.

628 **Legacy of Dilmun: The roots of ancient maritime trade in Eastern coastal Arabia in the 4th/3rd millennium B.C.**
Constance Maria Piesinger. PhD thesis, University of Wisconsin, Madison, 1983. 1224p. (Available from University Microfilms, Ann Arbor, Michigan, order no. AAD84-00508).

Although a study of the Eastern Province of Saudi Arabia during the late 4th-3rd millennium BC, this dissertation does consider the nature and mechanisms of interregional networks in the region. This includes links with Oman and Southern Mesopotamia through Bahrain which was deemed to be the site of Dilmun; Oman was the site of the copper mountains of Makan.

629 **American foreign policy toward the Sultanate of Oman, 1977-1987.**
Wallace Lynn Rigsbee. PhD thesis, University of Cincinnati, 1990. 184p. (Available from University Microfilms, Ann Arbor, Michigan, order no. AAD91-08671).

An examination of United States foreign policy towards Oman between 1977 and 1987, with Oman becoming a crucial player in US central strategic planning for the Middle East. In addition to trade, which was the traditional cornerstone of the relationship, military cooperation has also grown both in terms of military sales and the use of facilities.

630 **The evolution of national boundaries in the southeastern Arabian Peninsula: 1934-1955 (Volumes I and II) (Buraimi, Gulf States, Saudi Arabia, Qatar, United Arab Emirates, Oman).**
Abdulrahman Rashid Al-Shamlan. PhD thesis, University of Michigan, 1987. 484p. (Available from University Microfilms, Ann Arbor, Michigan, order no. AAD87-12065).

A study of the formation of the Arabian Peninsula in the twentieth century, and in particular the definition of Saudi Arabia's south-eastern boundaries. This has been largely reflected in the dispute over the Buraimi Oasis which involved Saudi Arabia, Oman and the United Arab Emirates, and Great Britain acting on behalf of the latter states. The situation was complicated by British colonial policy in the area and by the presence of oil in the region.

631 **British foreign policy toward the Sultanate of Muscat and Oman, 1954-1959 (Muscat).**
G. Lawrence Timpe. PhD thesis, University of Exeter, England, 1991. 453p. (Available from University Microfilms, Ann Arbor, Michigan, order no. AADDX-95849).

British efforts to secure interests in India and Kuwait included, as part of the strategy, the establishment and maintenance of the Al Bu Said dynasty in Oman. The signing of the anti-slavery treaties were seen as designed to destroy Oman as a regional economic threat and the separation of Zanzibar from Oman was also a 'divide and rule' device. In addition, the study examines the growing dependence on military aid from Britain to secure Oman against foreign incursions from Saudi Arabia.

Population and Social Structure

632 Sohar: Culture and society in an Omani town.

Frederik Barth. Baltimore, Maryland; London: Johns Hopkins Press, 1983. 264p. maps. bibliog.

A portrait of life and society in Sohar and an analysis of cultural pluralism and its maintenance. The first part deals with Sohar's geography, its position in the tradition of Arab culture, links with the outside world and its administrative structure. The second part considers the cultural diversity of the city, dealing with the various ethnic mixes within the community and religious, occupational and social patterns. Part three examines daily life in Sohar, discussing behaviour, family life, social interaction and economics, and concluding with profiles of twelve Sohari residents. The final part is the author's theoretical explanation of the process of continuity and change within the cultural diversity of Sohar. The book is almost totally based on interviews and observations in Sohar between March-August 1974 and December-January 1975-76.

633 The geographical mobility of a rural Arab population: some implications of changing patterns.

John Stace Birks. *Journal of Tropical Geography*, vol. 48 (1979), p. 9-18.

A study of patterns of mobility in the rapidly evolving community of Khadi on the slopes of the Hajar mountains. The village had a population of 244, with agriculture being the main activity. However, 25 per cent of the population were absent from the village, with 82 per cent of the absentees being male; these figures reflect the movement of labour to the more economically developed areas of the Arabian Peninsula. In contrast almost 32 per cent of the women had never left their village and most of their travel was restricted either to the harvesting of dates in larger settlements or to attendance at hospital.

634 **Some aspects of demography related to development in the Middle East, with special reference to the Sultanate of Oman.**

John Stace Birks. *Bulletin of the British Society for Middle Eastern Studies*, vol. 3, no. 2 (1976), p. 79-88.

The results of a sample demographic and housing survey, designed as a basis for planning, and forming part of a research project at Durham University. It was demonstrated that a high rate of migrant absenteeism is affecting the birth rate and also causing a decline in the agricultural section of the economy. The author concludes that the social development and the people's rising expectations are both a contributory factor to the migration and a result of it.

635 **Trucial Oman in the 16th and 17th centuries.**

Beatrice De Cardi. *Antiquity*, vol. 44, no. 176 (1970), p. 188-95.

Examines the social structure and settlement pattern in north-western Oman during the time of the Portuguese occupation.

636 **Notes on the Janabat of Oman.**

John Carter. *Addorah*, vol. 4, no. 2 (1978), p. 19-43.

The Janabat tribe of Oman live in the interior of Oman, in the desert area on the border of the Rub' al-Khali, a region which is now part of the operating area of Petroleum Development (Oman) Ltd.

637 **Tribal structures in Oman.**

John Carter. In: *Proceedings of the Tenth Seminar for Arabian Studies*. London: Seminar for Arabian Studies, 1977, p. 11-68. bibliog.

A sound introduction to the social structure and tribal divisions within the Sultanate. These are a very complex pattern of interwoven and interdependent relationships, but they nevertheless retain distinctiveness.

638 **Tribes in Oman.**

J. R. L. Carter. London: Scorpion Communications and Publications, 1982. 176p. maps. bibliog.

A study of the Bedouin and settled tribes in Oman and Dhofar province through the utilization of detailed genealogies of tribes, sub-tribes and families, together with lists of sub-sections, war cries, camel brands and other facts to explain tribal society. The mass of detail is often difficult to handle, particularly as the genealogies often lack dates or reference points, and the relationship of family details to those of the sub-tribes and sub-tribes to tribes is fraught with difficulty. The author remains aware of the transitional nature of the facts presented within the genealogies, their function within tribal society and the attempts of informants to supply facts even when none were available. This is an attempt to record the oral traditions within tribal society as they relate to family and tribal structures. It is accompanied by 32 pages of coloured plates.

639 **Notes on settlement plans in traditional Oman.**
P. M. Costa. *Journal of Oman Studies*, vol. 6, pt. 2 (1983),
p. 247-68.

A study of the origins and development of traditional settlement in Oman. To produce
it, Costa will work in collaboration with the Department of Antiquities and the
Ministry of National Heritage and Culture. For each settlement, the research will
include an analysis of its plan prior to recent expansion, a study of its quarters, their
origins and socio-economic organization. The research will be based on classical
Arabic sources, Omani historical material and local written and oral material as well
as foreign written material. Wherever possible, parallel field research will be
undertaken with a study of water supply and land use, archaeological surveys and
excavations. This article deals only with the first stage of the research, that of the
physical layout of the settlements which has relied heavily on the work of Lorimer in
1915, Miles in 1919 and Wilkinson in 1977 and has included use of aerial
photographs, ground reconnaissance, and surveys and excavations. Here, Costa
covers the general characteristics of the settlements, describes the architecture and
economic activity, and plans are produced of oasis, coastal and mining settlements.

640 **The Shihuh of northern Oman: a contribution to cultural ecology.**
Walter Dostal. *Geographical Journal*, vol. 138, pt. 1 (1972), p. 1-7.
map.

The Shihuh are to be found largely in the Musandam Peninsula, but also in Ras
al-Khaimah. They are thought to be of Baluchi origin, with an Arab component and
possibly another from the 'Ard of Oman. This paper, based on fieldwork carried out
in the area during 1970-71, discusses the relationships between environment and
culture, using the Shihuh as a case-study. The article also deals briefly with the
physical geography of the area, climate, agriculture, religion, and the customs of the
tribe.

641 **Two south Arabian tribes; al-Qara and al-Harasis.**
Walter Dostal. *Arabian Studies*, vol. 2 (1975), p. 33-41.

A consideration of two tribes, one of whom, the al-Qara, reside in the interior and are
at variance with the rule of the Sultan, whilst the al-Harasis tribe are nomadic and
found mainly on the coast of Batinah. The article discusses the social structure of
each tribe, their customs, dress, and economic life.

642 **The merchants: the big business families of Saudi Arabia and the
Gulf States.**
Michael Field. Woodstock, New York: The Overlook Press, 1985.
371p.

A collection of family stories designed to give an insight into the workings of Arab
society, and using nine of the great merchant families as case-studies. The family
histories are used within more general descriptions of society, the inter-relationship
between the merchant families and the rulers, the consumer society, the history of
pearling and the rise of modern Arabia. In the case of Oman, the Sultans are the
selected merchant family and the complex relationship between the merchant families
and the rulers is a valuable section of this work.

643 **Nomads in the Sultanate of Oman: Tradition and development in Dhofar.**
Jorg Janzen. Boulder, Colorado; London: Westview Press, 1986. 315p. bibliog.

A study of nomadic society in Dhofar province based on field research carried out between January and August 1977, and January to May 1978. Although the Dhofar War was officially over in 1975, Janzen found that the tribal feuds remained endemic in remote areas and that foreigners were mistrusted. This study represents a valuable collection of material on the social and economic activities of the province, assessing the impact of the post-1970 government development programmes. A further objective was to provide as much ethnographic and geographical information on the province as possible. The work was originally published in 1980 in German.

644 **The racial characteristics of the southern Arabs.**
Arthur Keith, W. M. Krogman. In: *Arabia Felix*, by Bertram Thomas. London: Cape, 1932, p. 31-33.

An anthropological study of the head and stature measurements made by Thomas. Comparisons are drawn between these characteristics and those of African and Indian peoples.

645 **Rich countries, poor countries: hidden stratification among the Omani Arabs in Eastern Africa.**
Grandmaison C. Le Cour. *Africa*, vol. 59, no. 2 (1989), p. 176-84.

The Arab tribes of Oman, and the Omani tribes who have settled in East Africa, are egalitarian within the tribes by law and reality, though there are social divisions within the tribal organization. However, there is a hidden internal hierarchy between sections which has been caused by economic, political and historical factors. The following topics are discussed in this context: the conditions of 19th-century East Africa, and their impact on the Omani tribes; the evolving divisions between coastal planters and caravan traders; the factors and social strategies which have maintained the divisions and strengthened the internal hierarchies.

646 **Demographic change in the Arab Gulf States: recent trends and implications for the future.**
Robert E. Looney. *Scandinavian Journal of Development Alternatives*, vol. 9, nos. 2-3 (1990), p. 103-15.

The significance of demographic change in the region, in terms of its economic and political implications, is discussed. Census data from the various states, including Oman, are used. The Gulf States are characterized by low participation by nationals in the labour force, because of the ill-defined localization policies, reduced costs from use of non-nationals, decreased income in the private sector, and a civil service system that hinders competition. Future trends indicate a reduction in unskilled expatriate labour but an increased demand for, and retention of, professional and higher-skilled workers, particularly in the service and maintenance sectors.

647 **Notes on the tribes of Oman.**
Samuel Barrett Miles. Calcutta, India: Administrative Report of the
Persian Gulf, 1880-81, p. 19-44 (Selections from the Records,
no. 181).
The article lists 135 tribes, together with information about settlements, population
and tribal afflictions.

648 **Society and state in the Gulf and Arab Peninsula.**
Khaldoun Hasan, Ali Naqeeb. London: Routledge, 1990. 206p.
This work has been translated from the Arabic and presents valuable material for a
study of the Arabian Peninsula. It deals with nomadic society, traditional trade and
trade routes, and the effects of Western imperialism on the national economy. In this
context the role of the East India Company is discussed, as is the suppression of the
slave trade and the effects on the economy of the region – they were particularly
severe in Oman. The Ibadhi expansion towards Muscat and the Wahhabi movement
towards Buraimi and Oman are seen as internal resistance against Western
encroachment. During the 17th and 18th centuries Muscat emerged as a regional
commercial power, and its decline is seen as a result of outside interference, with the
role of Britain being regarded as a 'grand imperial design'. The work concludes with
a study of authoritarian rule in the region and argues for the development of
democratic institutions, but holds out little hope for such development.

649 **Nomadism on the Arabian Peninsula: a general appraisal.**
P. G. N. Peppelenbosch. *Tijdschrift voor Economische en Sociale
Geografie*, vol. 49, pt. 6 (1968), p. 333-46. maps.
Although the bulk of the article deals with the nomads of Saudi Arabia, the country
which has the largest percentage in its population, the work in fact covers the whole
peninsula, and a great deal of what is written about the Bedouin of Saudi Arabia is
relevant to the Bedouin as a whole. The author begins by discussing the accepted
image of the nomad, which is based mainly on the accounts of early explorers, and
follows this by a consideration of nomadism as a phenomenon, defining five main
requirements necessary for true nomadism. Nomadic life is at a crisis stage because
traditional life is changing; this is due to the decreasing demand for camels, the end
of raiding or protection as a source of revenue, the attractions of cash employment,
and the process of sedentarization.

650 **Oman: a class analysis.**
Popular Front for the Liberation of Oman and the Arabian Gulf.
London: Gulf Committee, 1974. 20p. map. (9th June Studies).
An appraisal of the social structure of the Sultanate, designed to reveal the
inequalities and oppression which have given rise to the rebel movement against the
government.

651 **Memorandum on the tribal divisions in the principality of Oman with a map showing the general distribution of the tribes, and a table showing the genealogy of the ruling dynasty of Muscat.**
Edward Charles Ross. *Transactions of the Bombay Geographical Society*, vol. 19 (Jan. 1868-Dec. 1873), p. 188-98 (published 1874).
Valuable for an understanding of the social and tribal structure of Oman, the areas of dispute and the spheres of influence of the various tribes. A more detailed, complex description can be found in Carter's *Tribes in Oman* (see item no. 638).

652 **A taste of paradise.**
Hussein Shehadeh. *Middle East*, no. 121 (Nov. 1984), p. 37-38.
A description of the village of Misfah in Oman, located about 75 miles from Muscat in the mountains. The population of 300-400 grow dates, bananas and limes for market and the community is largely self-sufficient. Development had reached the village in the form of television, but village life was largely unchanged.

653 **Some social aspects of the Trucial States.**
In: *The Arabian Peninsula: society and politics*, edited by Derek Hopwood. London: Allen and Unwin, 1973, p. 219-30.
This contribution deals with the social position of women in the Trucial States, which for this purpose include Oman. Hopwood examines the situation in general and attempts to assess the impact of oil wealth on a social structure which has existed for centuries.

654 **The central Middle East: a handbook of anthropology and published research on the Nile Valley, the Arab Levant, southern Mesopotamia, the Arabian Peninsula and Israel.**
Edited by Louise Sweet. New Haven, Connecticut: Human Relations Area Files Press, 1971. 323p.
The chapter on the Arabian Peninsula has a section on Oman covering ethnology and geography. There is an annotated bibliography of significant research.

655 **The Bedu of southwest Arabia.**
Wilfred P. Thesiger. *Journal of the Royal Central Asian Society*, vol. 37, no. 1 (1950), p. 53-61.
The text of a lecture given to the Society in 1949, dealing with the Bedouin of the Empty Quarter. Thesiger describes their social life, tribal laws, and struggle for survival against the environment. The tribes of that area respect no political barriers and move between Saudi Arabia and Oman.

656 **Among some unknown tribes of south Arabia.**
Bertram Thomas. *Journal of the Royal Anthropological Institute*, vol. 62 (1932), p. 83-103.
Observations on the Hadara tribes of Dhofar, based on notes made by Thomas during the year 1928.

657 Anthropological observations in south Arabia.

Bertram Thomas. *Journal of the Royal Anthropological Institute*, vol. 62 (1932), p. 83-103.

Based on research undertaken by Thomas during his explorations. He used skull measurements, etc., to illustrate differences between the various native races.

658 Musandam Peninsula and its people the Shihuh.

Bertram Thomas. *Journal of the Royal Central Asian Society*, vol. 16, no. 1 (1929), p. 71-86.

The Shihuh are critically different from the remainder of the Sultanate, and they are thought to be the last of the original inhabitants of south-east Oman who fled to the Musandam Peninsula in the wake of the Arab migrations.

659 Bayasirah and Bayadir.

J. C. Wilkinson. *Arabian Studies*, vol. 1 (1974), p. 75-85.

This article considers two distinct social classes in Oman; the Bayasirah have been excluded from Arab tribal groups, while the Bayadir have been completely assimilated. The Bayasirah were not assimilated mainly because they had no known racial origins and were regarded as inferior, therefore having client status in relation to the dominant Arab tribes. As a group, however, they form a numerically important part of the population, retaining their own clan structure, but have been more or less rejected by later settlers. In contrast, the Bayadir were assimilated into the Arab population, becoming agricultural workers with clearly defined duties. The duties varied according to the locality where they worked, and are a survival of pre-Islamic times and village organization. They have remained unchanged since Sassanid times.

The Bedouin of Central Oman.

See item no. 667.

The Harasis: Pastoralists in a petroleum exploited environment.

See item no. 669.

Studies on the built environment of the Batinah.

See item no. 1131.

Social Change

660 Arab women meeting the challenge.
Middle East (Aug. 1990), p. 3-10.

Discusses the role of women in regional development and includes interviews with members of the Women's Society of Oman.

661 Complications of geography, ethnology and tribalism.
Fredrik Barth. In: *Oman: economic, social and strategic developments*, edited by B. R. Pridham. London: Croom Helm, 1987. p. 17-30.

This study of the geography, ethnology and tribalism in Oman's past examines these aspects which are still relevant to contemporary Oman. With regard to geography, it is concluded that physical aspects of the environment still endure, but that many aspects are changing rapidly, such as distances in terms of travelling time, communications, and the domestic environment. The cultural aspects of ethnology and tribalism are far more volatile. No longer can tribalism be seen as a major force but cultural pluralism is very marked and represents a major aspect of contemporary Oman. The author concludes that 'the task of nurturing and transferring cultural traditions that are still vital should not be insuperable'. If successful, such a policy would ensure the continued, beneficial effects of those aspects of the past far into the future of Oman.

662 Development of decline of pastoralists: the Bani Quitab of the Sultanate of Oman.
John Stace Birks. *Arabian Studies*, vol. 4 (1978), p. 7-19. map.

A study of the problems facing Oman with regard to the possible decline of agriculture, the changes in social structure through employment in the oil industry, and the attractions of urbanization. The author uses the Bani Quitab as a case-study.

663 **Diqal and Muqaida. Dying oases in Arabia.**
John Stace Birks, Sally E. Letts. *Tijdschrift voor Economische en Sociale Geografie*, vol. 68, no. 3 (1973), p. 141-51. maps. bibliog.
A study of the changes brought about in traditional oasis-based societies by a multiplicity of external forces.

664 **The impact of economic development on pastoral nomadism in the Middle East: an inevitable eclipse?**
John Stace Birks. In: *Change and development in the Middle East*, edited by John I. Clarke, Howard Bowen-Jones. London: Methuen, 1981, p. 82-94.
A general consideration of the decline of pastoral nomadism in the Middle East, dealing with the effects of development policies, sedentarization programmes, and the significance of water resources. However, all the arguments are equally relevant to the position in Oman, where men from northern Oman still travel to other Gulf States and Saudi Arabia as migrant labourers or to enlist in the armies of the capital-rich states. The major problem to be faced in the future is that there will be no recourse to a local economy in the traditional nomadic areas should the demand for migrant labour fall.

665 **The Shawawi population of northern Oman: a pastoral society in transition.**
John Stace Birks. *Journal of Oman Studies*, vol. 2 (1976), p. 9-16.
This paper examines the Shawawi peoples, the pastoralist section of Omani society living in dispersed households outside villages in order that their sheep and goats do not damage crops. The families live in temporary camps known as *firqan* (sing. *fariq*) between which they move on a semi-regular basis. Although they may also own palm-trees and gardens, the Shawawi do not consider themselves to be farmers, and arable plots are never the main part of their occupation. The article is divided into three sections, the first dealing with the mountain Shawawi, who form about fifty-five per cent of the population and because of their remoteness retain a scarcely changed society. The second section covers the Shawawi of the Dhahira lowlands, who constitute only about five per cent of the population and must be more mobile than their mountain counterparts because of the scarcity and nature of watering places. The last section deals with the impact of migrant labour movement upon the Shawawi, this being considered in some detail because of the importance of pastoral farming in Oman.

666 **Women: work prospects broaden horizon.**
Alison Brown. *Middle East Economic Digest Special Report* (Nov. 1980), p. 34-35.
Analyses the impact on women of the encouragement to actively participate in employment, education and specialist training. It is recognized that it will be some time before women contribute equally to the country's development.

667   **The Bedouin of central Oman.**
Dawn Chatty.   *Journal of Oman Studies*, vol. 6, no. 1 (1983),
p. 149-62.

The Bedouin of central Oman can be characterized as mobile kin units sharing a harsh
and difficult terrain, with their society being based on animal husbandry of camels
and goats. The links between the units are loose but the practice of pastoral nomadism
has evolved over the years into a dynamic part of the general culture of the Middle
East. Pastoral nomadism had become an integral part of a society described as an
'ecological trilogy' of three mutually dependent communities – urban, rural and
pastoral – which, although separate, each contribute to the support of the others, and
thereby contribute to the maintenance of the total society. The objective of this paper
is to examine the changes that have taken place in Oman as a result of the economic
and social developments resulting from the exploitation of oil. In particular, the
analysis concentrates on the impact on pastoral nomadism of contact with the legal,
economic and bureaucratic forces of the oil companies, and whether change was a
process of adaptation to the changed environment or if the tribes allowed themselves
to be moulded into categories which suited the modern apparatus. The author also
considers the settlement pattern of central Oman, with migrations from the southern
coast of Arabia and the northern gateway of the Buraimi Oasis, as a background to
the contemporary situation, together with an examination of the various tribes, the
role of the paramount sheikh in regulating nomadic life, and developments prior to
the arrival of the oil companies. The main part of the article concentrates on relations
with Petroleum Development (Oman) Ltd, the impact that the oil companies had on
the tribes with which it made contact, and the effects on the traditional tribal
organization, tribal society and economic life. Despite changes in the economy and
society, the author hopes that the inevitable drift to the town can be reversed with
enlightened planning and the provision of services responsive to their traditional
needs: mobile health services, education facilities and welfare services. Failure to do
so could result in the pastoral nomads swelling the ranks of the displaced landless
poor in the urban areas of Oman.

668   **The Bedouin of central Oman: adaptation or fossilization.**
D. Chatty.   *Studies in Third World Societies*, vol. 18 (1982), p. 13-32.

An historical analysis of the complex impact of Petroleum Development (Oman) Ltd
(PDO) and Western bureaucracy, legal and economic forces on the Bedouin of central
Oman. Economically, the Bedouin showed great adaptability but the once-fluid
lifestyle was altered by PDO's actions in establishing administrative boundaries,
territorial rights, and the selection of tribal elders.

669   **The Harasis: Pastoralists in a petroleum exploited environment.**
Dawn Chatty.   Paper presented at the 1987 Annual Conference of the
British Society for Middle Eastern Studies, 12-15 July 1987, at the
University of Exeter. 11p. maps.

A study based on 24 months of fieldwork carried out amongst the Harasis tribe in
Central Oman. The twin aims were to assess the needs and aspirations of the tribe and
to devise a programme to meet those needs. The government's objective was to raise
the standard of living of the population 'without undermining the traditional way of
life'. A major investment was made in primary healthcare, educational facilities,
veterinary services and welfare services, and a tribal centre was established at Haima
to develop an administrative focus for the area. The result was the rapid decline of a

strong tribal society and the beginnings of a national identity amongst the tribe. The paper covers, amongst other topics, the traditional tribal economy, domestic life, petroleum exploration and development, the pastoral economy, and water resources.

670 **Women's component in pastoral community assistance and development: a study of the needs and problems of the Harasis population, Oman: Project findings and recommendations.**
D. Chatty, E. Mitchell. New York: United Nations, 1984. 106p. (Restricted document TCD/OMA-80-WO1/1).

The report of a project designed to extend Oman's programmes in health, education, agriculture and social services to the pastoral nomads, the Harasis of the Jiddat al-Harasis. The target population is briefly reviewed and the needs of the population in health, education, welfare and water are considered in detail. The report describes the implementation of an immunization scheme for women and children set out by the World Health Organization, and identifies allied problems in the area of social welfare. Recommendations are made in each area, with the objective of inducing the tribe to seek assistance from the Tribal Administration Centre without adversely affecting their traditional way of life.

671 **The islands of Kuria Muria: a civil aid project in the Sultanate of Oman administered from Salalah, regional capital of Dhofar.**
Frank A. Clements. *Bulletin of the British Society for Middle Eastern Studies*, vol. 4, no. 1 (1977), p. 37-39.

A brief look at the social changes being implemented on these islands as part of the Civil Aid Programme instituted in the Dhofar province. The programme was also an attempt to ensure that the islands remained populated despite the attractions of the mainland.

672 **Bedouins, wealth and change: a study of rural development in the United Arab Emirates and the Sultanate of Oman.**
Rainer Cordes, Fred Scholz. Tokyo: United Nations University, 1980. 65p. (NRTS-7-UNUP-143).

A consideration of the changes in traditional bedouin society brought about by the influence of the oil economy. These include the attraction of the oil industry as an employer, and the rural development made possible by oil revenues.

673 **A rural community development project in Oman.**
Roderic W. Dutton. In: *Change and development in the Middle East*, edited by John I. Clarke, Howard Bowen-Jones. London: Methuen, 1981, p. 199-212.

This contribution discusses the surveys undertaken by the University of Durham in the rural areas of Oman which revealed that rural communities were in disarray as a result of having lost the feeling of mutual dependence, the skilled use of local resources, and the interdependence of the communities. This is considered important because of the post-oil future and the need to fall back on agriculture and fishing. The chapter then continues by discussing the Khabura Development Project which was established at the instigation of Petroleum Development (Oman) Ltd. Dutton considers that 'This is not the only path of rural progress but much of the Khabura experience is fundamentally relevant to rural community development elsewhere in the Middle East and the world'.

674 **Women and community in Oman.**
Christine Eickelman. New York: New York University Press, 1984. 251p.

This book is based on research conducted in Hamra, an oasis in the interior of Oman, in 1979 and 1988. In it, Eickelman examines women's everyday roles from the perspective of the women themselves. Hamra has been undergoing major changes, with the men leaving the oasis for work and returning once a week or month, and with local trade and agriculture in decline. At the same time new educational and health facilities have been introduced by the government. The activities and social relations of women are discussed within the context of the household, extended family, neighbourhood and the community, together with the variations between women of different status. The research also found that economic improvements resulted in changes in social practice but that the basic values remain. Also of relevance is an article by the same author 'Fertility and social change in Oman: Women's perspectives' (*Middle East Journal*, vol. 74, no. 4 (1993), p. 652-66) which examines the highly active role played by women in sustaining the social position of their household. Status and prestige are closely linked to their reproductive roles, with high birth rates and postpartum visiting being deliberate personal strategies for maintaining family and household status, and for the enhancement of status in other areas.

675 **Development surveys in the Middle East.**
W. B. Fisher, H. Bowen-Jones. *Geographical Journal*, vol. 140, pt. 3 (1974), p. 454-66. maps.

A preliminary report on a four-year study undertaken by Durham University on progress in northern Oman, though the article also considers similar work in the Mediterranean and other areas of the Middle East. The objectives for the programme were to record the different regions, to collect observational data, and to assist Oman's Ministry of Agriculture and Ministry of Development Organization in the interpretation and utilization of the results.

676 **Rural change in the Sultanate of Oman.**
Tom Gabriel. *Asian Affairs*, vol. 19, no. 2 (1988), p. 154-63.

Gabriel examines the pattern of social change in the rural areas of Oman brought about by increased oil revenues and growing urbanization. As a result of development, changes have occurred in the usage of resources, the agricultural sector and the use of water. In the desert areas of northern Oman the social structure is complex as the villagers and farmers co-exist with the nomads.

677 **Social change in the Gulf States and Oman.**
Frauke Heard-Bey. *Asian Affairs*, vol. 59, no. 3 (1972), p. 309-16.

An analysis of the political, economic and social changes in the Gulf States and Oman achieved through the development of oil resources. One development which has impacted on all areas has been the use of migrant labour to service the manpower demands of the oil industry and infrastructural development. Inequalities had emerged within, and between states, and, at the time of writing, governments seemed incapable of efficiently and equitably distributing the new wealth.

678 **Oman: a difficult break with the past.**
V. Isaev. *Aziaa i Afrika Segodnia* (USSR), vol. 4 (1989), p. 30-32.
Describes Oman's development from 1964 to 1988, with concentration on the post-1974 era and the benefits from oil wealth. Isaev discusses the problems faced in adapting ancient traditions to the new economic and social realities.

679 **Oman since 1845: disruptive modernization in a traditional Arab society.**
Robert Geran Landen. London; Princeton, New Jersey: Princeton University Press, 1967. 463p. maps. bibliog.
This work makes extensive use of Omani chronicles and archival material, and deals with modernizing influences which affected the Sultanate from 1845 to the discovery of oil in 1963. Deals first with the position in Oman in relation to the Gulf States prior to changes caused by European influences and predating early modernizing influences. A large section of the study deals with the growth of European and British economic interests in Oman and the Gulf States, together with the Sultanate's attempts to come to terms with the 20th century.

680 **Women and revolution in Oman.**
Oman Solidarity Campaign/Gulf Committee. London: Gulf Committee, 1975. 43p. map.
Discusses the role of women on the side of the anti-government forces in Dhofar.

681 **An urban profile of the Middle East.**
Hugh Roberts. London: Croom Helm, 1979. 239p. maps.
Studies the transitional nature of the area given the development of new urban communities and the changing of traditional ones. In this study, the population and social structure are examined, and projections are made concerning population growth and its impact on urban development. Roberts also considered the patterns of communication within the Sultanate and their possible effect on future population distribution and social development, with much stress being placed on the relatively sophisticated (by Middle East standards) public transport network.

682 **Oman leaps into the 20th century.**
Barbara Wace. *Geographical Magazine*, vol. 44, no. 10 (July 1972), p. 681-86. maps.
Examines the problems faced by the Sultanate following the coup of 1970 in the move towards modernization.

683 **Traditional Arab communities in the modern world.**
W. Montgomery Watt. *International Affairs* (London), vol. 44, pt. 3 (1968), p. 494-500.
The author examines the phenomenon of Arabism and its interaction with the modern world, through a study of Oman and Yemen and using standard works on the area to explore the societies of the countries.

684 **The Al Wahiba: Bedouin values in an oil economy.**
R. Webster. *Nomadic Peoples*, vol. 28 (1991), p. 3-17.
Bedouin life in Oman is illustrated by using the Al-Wahiba as a case-study because they still follow a semi-nomadic herding life in north-eastern Oman. The form of agriculture is still traditional, small-scale and with extremely low productivity, but it possesses cultural goals and values which are in danger of being undermined by oil prosperity. About half of the Omani population are engaged in agriculture, fishing and pastoralism, often on a part-time basis, but 50 per cent of the country's gross domestic product (GDP) is from oil which provides 80 per cent of government revenue. The danger is that prosperity from oil will critically undermine pastoral activity and destroy the cultural goals and values associated with it unless conservation measures are taken.

685 **Tyrant or pet canary – The role of women in two Arab societies.**
Unni Wikan. *Tidsskrift for Samfunnsforskning* (Norway), vol. 16, no. 4 (1975), p. 29-32.
A Norwegian-language study of the role of women in Arab/Muslim culture, using data from field studies conducted in Cairo and Sohar in Oman. Cairo women were found to be independent, assertive and dominant, whereas Omani women were more submissive and respectful and seen as a reflection of the husband's ability to provide for her. The study also showed that the ambitions of the Omani husband made him vulnerable to sanctions from his wife and, in some cases, this stress has led to Oman men resorting to transvestism.

686 **Problems of oasis development.**
John C. Wilkinson. Oxford, England: University of Oxford School of Geography, 1978. 40p. bibliog. (Research Paper, no. 20).
The thesis of this paper is that there has been a general decline in oasis life, with a breakdown of old ways and the rural economy due to sedentarization. The author advances suggestions for reversing this trend by a process of dynamic planning, with a view to reintegrating pastoral and cultivator societies. The paper examines the traditional pattern of nomadic bases, agriculture, crafts, the problems of social change and modernization.

687 **Rural pattern of living destroyed by change.**
John C. Wilkinson. *Financial Times* (London) (28 Jan. 1980), p. 7.
An examination of the degree to which traditional Omani life in the interior is being changed by the oil-based economy. Wilkinson discusses the resultant change in infrastructure and the loss of traditional village and tribal democracy. Many of the changes are inevitable, but, in a country of perhaps three-quarters of a million people, 'there is no room for complacency in this decline of the agricultural economy'.

The reaction of rural populations to drought: a case study from South-East Arabia.
See item no. 989.

Language

688 **Notes on the Mahrah tribe of southern Arabia, with a vocabulary of their language, to which are appended additional observations on the Gara tribe.**
H. J. Carter. *Journal of the Bombay Branch of the Royal Asiatic Society*, vol. 3, no. 11 (1847), p. 339-70.
The language of the Mahra tribe is different from most Omani dialects and is now in danger of becoming a lost language.

689 **The sociocultural dimension of TEFL education: the Omani file.**
Jane Jackson Fahmy, Linda Bilton. *Journal of Multilingual and Multicultural Development*, vol. 13, no. 3 (1992), p. 269-89.
A study of the motivations and attitudes of TEFL (teaching English as a foreign language) students enrolled at the Sultan Qaboos University. Sociocultural, linguistic and educational background data were obtained through a questionnaire, and proficiency in English was assessed through the Comprehensive English Language Test. It was found that most of the students had a positive view on the use of English and did not fear Westernization as an outcome of their studies.

690 **Courtesies in the Gulf area: a dictionary of colloquial phrase and usage.**
Donald Hawley. London: Stacey International, 1978. 96p. maps.
A useful guide for the businessman and traveller, but it does assume some knowledge of Arabic. It also illustrates how different the Sultanate is from the rest of the Gulf.

691 **Towards a dialect geography of Oman.**

Clare Holes. *Bulletin of the School of Oriental and African Studies*, vol. 52, no. 3 (1981), p. 446-62. maps.

A study of the phonology and morphology of the Omani Arabic dialects and an attempt to place them within the geography of Oman. The work was based on an analysis of conversational data, tape-recorded between 1985 and 1987 in rural locations in northern Oman. The speakers were largely men and women aged over 35 with little or no formal education who were, or had been, engaged in traditional occupations. The research was a by-product of research being undertaken on behalf of the Omani Ministry of Health into rheumatic disease amongst a sample of 2000 adults. Examples of the various dialects are reproduced.

692 **The code languages of Oman.**

D. H. Insall. *Journal of Oman Studies*, vol. 6, no. 1 (1983), p. 111-21.

A discussion on coded versions of languages used in Oman. These were based on the colloquial dialect of areas, thus rendering them unintelligible to the outsider and unrecognizable as a form of Arabic. The research into this area of linguistics was prompted by an interview and tape-recording made in 1977 of an elderly Shaikh of Siya in the eastern Hajar region of northern Oman who was using a coded language. The article seeks to set out the framework, and discover the extent to which codes were used, as a basis for future research, because the accumulation of information on codes has indicated that they are more widespread and actively used than was ever envisaged when the first recording was made in 1977.

693 **The O'manee dialect of Arabia.**

A. S. G. Jayakar. *Journal of the Royal Asiatic Society*, n.s., no. 2 (1889), p. 811-89.

An extremely detailed study of the dialect used in Oman, which contains traces of Persian and Indian (the latter when trade is involved) and Arabic words significantly changed in meaning from their use elsewhere in the Arabic-speaking world. The vast differences in the Oman dialect are attributed largely to a lack of education, a total lack of local literature and a departure from the standard rules of grammar.

694 **Diminutive patterns in modern south Arabian languages.**

Thomas Muir Johnstone. *Journal of Semitic Studies*, vol. 10, no. 1 (1973), p. 98-107.

This article is for the linguistic specialist and considers the structure of the various languages still used in southern Arabia, including Oman.

695 **Folk-tales and folk-lore of Dhofar.**

Thomas Muir Johnstone. *Journal of Oman Studies*, vol. 6, no. 1 (1983), p. 123-26.

Describes the content of a corpus of stories collected by the author over a period of ten years in Dhofar. They give little sociological information about Dhofar, but a further collection of true stories and oral historical narratives do provide background social information on the inhabitants of the mountains and their values. The stories are all in the Mahri and Jibbali languages, and the author's motives for collection were as examples of linguistic texts.

696   **The language of poetry in Dhofar.**
Thomas Muir Johnstone. *Bulletin of the School of Oriental and African Studies*, vol. 38, pt. 1 (1972), p. 1-17.
A specialized examination of poetry written in Dhofar by speakers of Sheri, a mixture of the ancient Sheri and Mehri languages no longer in common use. The article examines a series of poems to illustrate this poetic language.

697   **The modern south Arabian languages.**
Thomas Muir Johnstone. *Afroasiatic Linguistics*, vol. 1, no. 5 (1975), p. 1-29. bibliog.
A very specialized examination of the modern south Arabian languages which are now confined to Dhofar and Socatra: Mehri, Sheri and Socatri. This work begins with a survey of the speakers, followed by an examination of the phonological system, morphology and notes on syntax.

698   **Bibliography of the modern south Arabic languages.**
Wolf Leslau. *Bulletin of the New York Public Library*, vol. 50, no. 8 (1946), p. 607-33.
One of the few specialist bibliographies in this field. It is valuable for a study of the linguistics in the area which includes Oman.

699   **The position of the dialect of Curia Muria in modern south Arabia.**
Wolf Leslau. *Bulletin of the School of Oriental and African Studies*, vol. 12, no. 1 (1947-48), p. 5-19.
The dialect has almost been lost because all but one of the islands has been abandoned.

700   **Some preliminary remarks on a collection of poems and songs of the Batahirah.**
M. J. Morris. *Journal of Oman Studies*, vol. 6, no. 1 (1983), p. 129-44.
This article presents the results of a preliminary examination of a collection of poems and songs of the Batahirah tribe recorded by the author in Dhofar between 1976 and 1980. The language used by the Batahirah is not written, and the poems and songs have all been committed to memory, with texts changing over the years. Also, younger members of the tribe are vague about the exact meaning of words or of the events that the song or poems portray. The Batahirah live along the littoral of the Kuria Muria bay and number about 300. They rely on fishing for their livelihood and have benefited materially and socially from the government's investment in the fishing industry. Such development and easier communications may result in the loss of the Batahirah language though the female conservative influence maintains its importance with the young children. The author reproduces extracts from various songs and poems, together with a brief explanation as to their meaning and their

intentions. The author also stresses the need for continued collection of such material before the traditional way of life and language of the Batahirah and other similar groups disappears with further economic and social development.

701 **Four strange tongues from central south Arabia – the Hadra group.**
Bertram Thomas. *Proceedings of the British Academy*, vol. 23 (1937), p. 231-31. maps.
Includes a consideration of the Jebali language of Dhofar province.

702 **The Kumzari dialect of the Shihuh tribe, Arabia, and a vocabulary.**
Bertram Thomas. London: Royal Asiatic Society, 1930. (Asiatic Society Monographs, no. 21).
The dialect of the Shihuh is thought to pre-date the Arab migrations into Oman, and the tribe, which inhabits the Musandam Peninsula, is thought to be the last survivor of the original inhabitants of the area.

Dissertation

703 **The morphonology of Muscat Arabic.**
Bonnie Carol Glover. PhD thesis, University of California, Los Angeles, 1988. 300p. (Available from University Microfilms, Ann Arbor, Michigan, order no. AAD88-22312).
Describes the morphology and phonology of Muscat Arabic, based on data collected from men and women in the old city and focusing on certain phonological characteristics of the dialect.

Religion

704 **The origins of the Islamic state, being a translation from the Arabic, accompanied with annotations. Geographic and historic note of the *Kitb futuh al-buldan*.**
Ahmed ibn Yahya al-Baladhumi. New York: Columbia University Press, 1916; Beirut: Khayat, 1968. 2 vols. (vol. 1 translated by Philip Khuri Hitti; vol. 2 by Francis Clark Murgotten).
An important work for understanding the spread of Islam and the beginnings of Arab statehood. It includes a section on Oman and the introduction of Islam to the country.

705 **Ibadism and the sectarian perspective.**
Dale F. Eickelman. In: *Oman: economic, social and strategic development*, edited by B. R. Pridham. London: Croom Helm, 1987, p. 31-50.
This study – based on extensive fieldwork in Oman begun in 1978 – looks at the transformation of Ibadhism in Oman since the 1950s and attempts to portray the main trends of contemporary religious discourse and identity. Because of the significance of the Imamate to the interior of Oman and the country's isolation up to the year 1970, the process of modernization gives the country's encounter with Islamic thought and politics a distinct Omani flavour. This account concentrates principally on sectarian identity which has manifested itself through a scale of perceived social action, a wider sense of Islamic community and the implementation of a modern educational system, all of which have led to a profound change in religious sensibilities. However, the interior Ibadhi community is likely to continue to play a vital, if reinterpreted, role in the future of Oman.

706 **Religious knowledge in Inner Oman.**
Dale F. Eickelman. *Journal of Oman Studies*, vol. 6, pt. 1 (1983),
p. 163-72.
The twentieth-century Imamate in Oman was one of the world's last theocracies and,
in principle, was the ideal Muslim state as the governors of the Imam were ordered to
'command that which is legal and forbid that which is not, to rule with justice, to take
that which is due from oppressors and to give to the oppressed, to protect the weak
from violent and negligent uses of power and to give counsel . . . just as the Prophet
Muhammad gave counsel to his community' (from a manuscript by Abri Shaykh
Ibrahim Said al- entitled 'Kitab tabsirat al-ma'tabirin fita 'rikh al-abriyn, written in
1958). The implication of this view of society was that the nominated Imams had to
have an extensive knowledge of the Koran and of Islamic traditions and only a few
could understand the intricacies of Islamic law and tradition, thus men of learning in a
largely illiterate population were in a position of power. This article discusses the
relationship between the men of learning and the wider population as a basis for
understanding the realization of the just society of the Imamate and the gaining of
popular legitimacy. Due to the paucity of written material on the twentieth-century
Imamate this study is based on extensive field research, including interviews with
individuals who lived in the Imamate, participated in its administration or who dealt
with it from the coastal areas, letters, accounts of the Imamate's public treasury, and
documents in private libraries.

707 **Religious tradition, economic domination and political legitimacy:
Morocco and Oman.**
Dale F. Eickelman. *Revue de l'Occident Musulman et de la
Mediterranée* (France), no. 29 (1980), p. 17-30.
The study of traditional Islam in Oman is influenced by the fact that attitudes to
religion are strongly influenced by traditions and the complex tribal structures of the
interior with its Imamate tradition. The article is based on a survey of the available
literature and field studies, with the situation in Morocco being used as a comparative
study to reinforce the complexities of the Omani situation.

708 **A description of new Ibadi manuscripts from North Africa.**
A. K. Ennami. *Journal of Semitic Studies*, vol. 15, no. 1 (1970),
p. 63-87.
Valuable for a study and understanding of Ibadhism which is found only in Oman and
parts of North Africa.

709 **The Ibadites in Arabia and Africa.**
Tedeuoz Lewicki. *Journal of World History*, vol. 13, no. 1 (1971),
p. 51-130. map.
A valuable article on the tenets, significance and development of Ibadhism, of which
Oman is now the main centre.

710 **A Sultanate asunder.**
George Rentz. *Natural History*, vol. 83, no. 3 (1974), p. 57-68.

At first Rentz is concerned with the possible effects of the oil economy on the Ibadhi sect of Islam, but his article develops into a consideration of the relationship between the other Islamic sects in Oman.

711 **The Ibadis.**
R. Rubinacci. In: *Religion in the Middle East. Three religions in concord and conflict*, edited by A. J. Arberry. Cambridge, England: Cambridge University Press, 1969. vol. 2: Islam, p. 302-17.

A compact, informative study of the Ibadhi Islamic sect.

712 **Oman: An Ibadhi–tribal monarchic syndrome.**
M. A. Saleen-Kahn. *Islam in the Modern World*, vol. 5, pt. 1 (1974), p. 71-90; vol. 5, pt. 2 (1974), p. 52-70.

A detailed study of Ibadhism during its medieval and modern history in Oman. Discusses the religious and political codes of Ibadhism and the history of its development in Oman and, in particular, the relationship between the elective Imamate and the interests of the Sultanate as a monarchic institution. Oman is particularly relevant to a study of Ibadhism as it is the only country with an Ibadhi majority which represents a much mellowed and moderate branch of the Kharijis of the first Muslim century. The Kharijis are examined to determine the development of contemporary Ibadhism, and this is followed by an account of its spread into Oman, the development of the Imamate and the struggle for political power between the Imamate and the Al Bu Said dynasty.

713 **The majesty that was Islam: the Islamic world 661-1100.**
W. Montgomery Watt. London: Sidgwick & Jackson, 1974. 276p. bibliog.

References to Oman are limited but this work is relevant to a study of the establishment of Ibadhism and the early conflict between the Caliphs and the Omanis.

714 **The Ibadi Imamate.**
John C. Wilkinson. *Bulletin of the School of Oriental and African Studies*, vol. 39, pt. 3 (1976), p. 535-51.

A consideration of Ibadhism and the Imamate. The article aims to cover the 'basic principles about the nature of the contract which the Ibadhi community enters into when it elects an Imam, and to study it specifically from the Omani point of view'. The second part considers how the Imam was elected from the 8th to the 20th century, using contemporary historical sources.

Politics and religion in 'Uman: A historical review.
See item no. 484.

Dissertation

715 **Early Islamic Oman and early Ibadism in the Arabic sources.**
A. Ubaydii.   PhD thesis, Cambridge University, England, 1990.
(Available from British Library, Document Supply Centre, Boston
Spa, Wetherby, West Yorkshire, United Kingdom).

The object of this study is to describe the accounts of early Islamic Oman and the
early Ibadism in the Arabic sources. The study makes use of newly discovered Ibadhi
manuscripts in Oman and tries to avoid the parochialism and dogmatism of these
sources and the one-sided representation by Muslim historians. The author has
attempted to provide a critical evaluation of these sources and to provide background
information on Omani society and tribal structure.

Health

716 **Diabetes mellitus in the Sultanate of Oman.**
M. G. Asfour (et al.). *Diabetic Medicine*, vol. 8, no 1 (1991),
p. 76-80.

In February 1990 a World Health Organization consultancy was undertaken to assess the incidence of diabetes mellitus in Oman. Investigations during the consultancy suggested that 9 per cent of all adult hospital admissions and 12 per cent of adult hospital bed occupancy were associated with diabetes. As a result it is considered that diabetes must become a priority area in Oman's health strategy and that there must be an emphasis on epidemiological research, education and the acquisition of appropriate technology.

717 **Report on the food and nutrition situation (with particular reference to children) in the Sultanate of Oman.**
M. Autret, S. Miladi. Cairo: Food and Agriculture Organization,
1979. 31p. (FAO Access no. 42618).

A report by the Food and Agriculture Organization for the United Nations Children's Fund on the health services and nutrition programmes needed in the Sultanate. The authors consider vitamin deficiency needs, vaccination programmes and other preventive medicine.

718 **Acute purulent pericarditis in Oman children.**
N. Ballal (et al.). *Journal of Tropical Pediatrics*, vol. 37, no. 5
(1991), p. 232-34.

A study of eight children admitted to the Royal Hospital in Muscat with purulent pericardial effusions, six of the patients being under two years of age. The study showed that early diagnosis, surgery and antibiotics helped to prevent the high morbidity and morality usually associated with this condition in developing countries.

719 **Malaria in Muscat.**
C. A. Gill. *Indian Journal of Medical Research*, vol. 4, no. 2 (1916), p. 190-235.
A detailed survey of the incidence of malaria in the Sultanate. At the time of writing, the disease was endemic.

720 **Rural health time.**
Liesl Graz. *World Health* (Feb.-March 1981), p. 22-27.
A discussion of the activities of rural health teams in Dhofar. These visited desert communities to try to reduce the incidence of bronchitis and tuberculosis which were prevalent in the region at that time. In the course of such visits, the rudiments of healthcare are taught to the villagers so that they are able to treat their own patients.

721 **Teaching clinical skills to new medical students: the Oman experience.**
B. M. Linder, A. Saha, G. F. Heseltine. *Medical Education*, vol. 26, no. 4 (1992), p. 282-84.
An account of an initiative by the College of Medicine at Sultan Qaboos University to move away from a didactic emphasis in the teaching of family and community healthcare by involving students actively, as early as possible, through the acquisition of relevant clinical skills. The success of the initiative has led to family- and community-based clinical exposure for all classes.

722 **Family and community health in a new medical school.**
J. P. Musgrove. *Medical Education*, vol. 24, no. 2 (March 1990), p. 124-28.
Discusses the evolution of the curriculum on family and community health programmes for the medical school of the Sultan Qaboos University.

723 **Nutrition country profile: Oman.**
Rome: Food and Agriculture Organization, Food Policy and Nutrition Division, 1990. 14p. (FAO Accession no. XF 90-295703).
A study of food consumption and the nutritional value of the diet of Omanis, including nutrient deficiencies and the incidence of disease.

724 **Musculoskeletal pain in Omanis, and the relationship to joint mobility and body mass index.**
G. Pountain. *British Journal of Rheumatology*, vol. 31, no. 2 (Feb. 1992), p. 81-85.
The results of a house-to-house survey of representative areas of Oman, with 920 adults responding to a questionnaire about musculoskeletal pain. Back pain was reported in 42 per cent of the females and 25 per cent of males, knee pain in 15 per cent of females and 18 per cent of males, and hip pain in only three females and one male. In rural communities musculoskeletal pain was more common and less anatomically localized. The results of the survey were similar to those in Africans and Indians, but higher than those reported for Europeans.

725 **The prevalence of rheumatoid arthritis in the Sultanate of Oman.**
G. Pountain. *British Journal of Rheumatology*, vol. 30, no. 1 (Feb. 1991), p. 24-28.

The results of a house-to-house survey in representative areas of Oman. It involved 1925 Omani adults aged 16 and over, and aimed at assessing the incidence of rheumatoid arthritis. Seven cases are studied and these indicated a statistical prevalence of 3.6 per thousand adults. Adjusted for the population structure of the whole country, the prevalence was 8.4 per thousand adults. Complementary data were also obtained from rural health centres.

726 **A controlled trial of surgery for trachomatous trichiasis of the upper lid.**
M. H. Reacher (et al.). *Archives of Ophthalmology*, vol. 110, no. 5 (1992), p. 667-74.

This study of surgery trials on trachomatous trichiasis of the upper eyelid in Oman provides success rate statistics for various techniques and varying degrees of severity. The research is extremely relevant because of the incidence of such eye diseases in Oman, particularly in the interior.

727 **Survey of infection in babies at the Khoula Hospital, Oman.**
A. Rejab, J. De Lowois. *Annals of Tropical Paediatrics*, vol. 10, no. 1 (1990), p. 39-43.

A survey carried out in the special care baby unit at Khoula Hospital in Muscat, covering 1265 babies admitted to the unit from the 8720 born in the hospital. In 190 cases the babies satisfied the criteria for infection, with the most common clinical presentation being pneumonia. A variety of other infections were also identified and are discussed in the article. The results of the survey show that in developing countries unsophisticated research can be of value both in identifying infection and in recognizing possible solutions.

728 **Oman: leaping across the centuries.**
R. Smith. *British Medical Journal*, vol. 297 (20 Aug. 1988), p. 540-44.

A review of development in the health services of Oman since 1970, including: factors affecting healthcare provision; primary care; hospital care; the introduction and use of high technology; and medical education based on the Sultan Qaboos University.

729 **Sultanate of Oman: health project.**
Washington, DC: World Bank, Health and Nutrition Department, Division 3, 1987. 74p.

A review of the health project in Oman which has various policy objectives: the reduction of mortality and morbidity particularly in the rural al-Batinah region; the strengthening of the infrastructure to manage the health sector; and to prepare the way for a more efficient implementation of the health service. The background to the current health service provision is also provided.

730 **Target 'health 2000'.**
World Health Forum, vol. 2, no. 2 (1981), p. 174-76.
Examines the actions of two member states of the World Health Organization, Norway and Oman, to achieve the official target of health for all by the year 2000. The Omani programme was designed to achieve simple preventive medicine for all, such as a mass vaccination programme.

731 **Striking success in control of disease.**
Penelope Turing. *The Times* (London) (9 May 1980), p. 5.
A report on the remarkable improvement in the standard of health provision in the Sultanate, a provision which was almost non-existent prior to 1970. In particular, the article looks at the campaign against malaria and trachoma, which has been very successful.

732 **Beliefs and practices related to health, nutrition and child rearing in two communities in Oman.**
UNICEF. Abu Dhabi: UNICEF Gulf Area Office, 1973. [n.p.].
Deals with traditional diets, nutrition, health and healthcare in Nizwa, the old interior capital, and Sohar, a major fishing community. Also considers the traditional beliefs relating to child rearing and the use of folk medicine.

733 **Man becomes woman – transvestism in Oman.**
Unai Wikan. *Tidsskrift for Samfunnsforskning* (Norway), vol. 17, no. 4 (1976), p. 318-34.
A Norwegian-language study of the incidence of institutionalized transvestism; the implications of this for society are explored. The transvestites retain male names and gender but are socially classified as females in terms of relationships between the sexes. At the time of the fieldwork (1975) about 1 in 50 males were identified as transvestites and homosexual prostitutes but Omani society regarded such behaviour with tolerance and would view interference in the relations and activities of others as illegitimate.

734 **Wildlife rabies in Oman and the United Arab Emirates.**
World Health Organization. *Weekly Epidemiological Record*, vol. 67, no. 10 (1992), p. 65-68.
Rabies was confirmed in Oman in 1990 when a child died following a fox bite and 200 further cases were reported in the first nine months of 1991. The article details the laboratory analysis of infected foxes and other animals and discusses control methods.

Politics

735 **Offshore politics and resources in the Middle East.**
Gerald H. Blake. In: *Change and development in the Middle East*,
edited by John I. Clarke, Howard Bowen-Jones. London: Methuen,
1981, p. 113-29. maps.
This contribution studies the political problems associated with offshore boundary
delimitation and considers that the numerous offshore disputes could well add a new
dimension to an extremely volatile region. Oman has a coastline of 1861 kilometres, a
territorial limit of 12 nautical miles and an exclusive fishing zone of 200 nautical
miles. The situation is considered in relation to the potential for offshore oil and gas,
fishing potential, and the strategic and military significance which, in the case of
Oman, relates to the Strait of Hormuz.

736 **The Gulf War and the new world order.**
Edited by Haim Bresheeth, Nira Yuval-Davis. London; Atlantic
Highlands, New Jersey: Zed Books, 1991. 293p.
This book represents a series of contributions aimed at describing and analysing the
underlying causes, reasons and likely effects of the Gulf War. Oman is only briefly
dealt with in this text, being on the periphery of the conflict, but consideration is
given to political vulnerability caused by the use of migrant labour and the lack of
developing democratic institutions. In the contribution on the environmental impact
of the Gulf War Oman is considered to have suffered environmental degradation due
to the presence of the military in the area.

737 **Politics and participation where Britannia once ruled.**
R. M. Burrell. *New Middle East* (Dec. 1972), p. 32-36.
A general overview of the situation in the Gulf twelve months after British
withdrawal and the then political prospects for the area. The article ranges wider than
the Sultanate, but all of this is relevant to the geopolitical situation in the Sultanate at

the time. The article also reviews the Dhofar War and the progress being made by the Oman government against the rebels.

738 The emergence of nation-states in the Arabian Peninsula.
John Everitt. *Geojournal*, vol. 13, no. 3 (1986), p. 197-200.

Until the development of oil resources political authority in the region rested with the decentralized tribes, except for the Yemen and Oman. British presence in the area encouraged the creation of national identities and subsequent external political events have encouraged moves towards co-ordination, leading, eventually, to the creation of the Gulf Cooperation Council.

739 Arabia without Sultans.
Fred Halliday. London: Penguin Books, 1974; New York: Random House, 1975. 527p. map.

This work deals with political unrest in Arabia and offers a left-wing viewpoint of the situation. Much of the book is devoted to the civil war in the Yemen and the insurrection in Dhofar province. Halliday aims at showing the state of the working class in the authoritarian regimes of Arabia, the divisions in Arabian society, and the capitalist influence in the economies and politics of the Arabian Peninsula.

740 A prevalence of furies: tribes, politics and religion in Oman and Trucial Oman.
John Barrett Kelly. In: *The Arabian Peninsula: society and politics*, edited by Derek Hopwood. London: Allen and Unwin, 1972, p. 107-41.

An important contribution to understanding the two forces that have been instrumental in shaping and directing the political life of Oman. The first is the division between the Ibadhi and Sunni inhabitants and the second the Hinawi–Ghafiri factionalism question. The author dates this from the early wars fought in the 18th century over the succession to the Ibadhi Imamate, when the two main tribes were on opposing sides and tended to draw other tribes into the conflict.

741 Saudi Arabia and the Gulf States.
John Barrett Kelly. In: *The Middle East: Oil, conflict and hope*, edited by A. L. Udovitch. Lexington, Massachusetts: Lexington Books, 1976, p. 427-62.

This contribution traces the political developments within Saudi Arabia and the Gulf States and relations between the Gulf States. In the case of Oman, an historical outline is provided. It covers particularly the question of the Imamate, the rise of the Al Bu Said dynasty, and internal politics associated with the tribal nature of Oman and the various political factions. Also considered are relations with Saudi Arabia, which were considered delicate, and those with the People's Democratic Republic of Yemen in relation to the Dhofar War.

742 **Political stability in the Gulf Cooperation Council states: challenges and prospects.**
Emile A. Nakhleh. *Middle East Insight*, vol. 6 (Winter 1989), p. 40-46.
Examines the sources of legitimacy of the ruling families of the member states of the Gulf Cooperation Council (GCC), the concept of regional cooperation as represented by the GCC and the challenges faced by the organization. The article includes a list of the ruling families in each of the GCC states, including Oman.

743 **Legitimacy and political change in Yemen and Oman.**
John Everett Peterson. *Orbis*, vol. 27, no. 4 (1984), p. 971-98.
A comparative analysis of legitimacy and political change in Oman and the Yemen Arab Republic from the nineteenth century to the 1980s. Traditionally their political systems were based on the Zaydi and Ibadhi sects who maintained the loose cohesion of the various tribes. However, pressure for modernization created new traditional rulers who increased centralization but could not survive the test of legitimacy and were overthrown. In contemporary Oman the Sultan is deemed to have, at best, personal legitimacy whilst the rulers of the Yemen Arab Republic lack legitimacy.

744 **Oman in the twentieth century: political foundations of an emerging state.**
John Everett Peterson. London: Croom Helm, 1978. 286p. maps. bibliog.
One of the few major academic works to have appeared on the Sultanate, concentrating on events since 1970 and the accession of Sultan Qaboos. An examination of the perennial themes of Omani politics and external influences, and how these have changed during the 20th century. The author also deals with the problems of the Imamate, especially during the rebellion in the mountains during 1913-20, and the Dhofar War, and with the reactions of the Sultanate to their impact. This is an extremely valuable work, providing an understanding of a complex period in the Sultanate's history and development.

745 **Oman's odyssey: from Imamate to Sultanate.**
John Everett Peterson. In: *Oman, economic, social and strategic development*, edited by B. R. Pridham. London: Croom Helm, 1987, p. 1-16.
An examination of the transformation that has taken place in Oman's politics from the nineteenth century onwards. The traditional form of Oman's politics had three principal themes: tribalism; the Ibadhi Imamate; and maritime trade. Tribalism and the Imamate were inextricably intertwined, whilst maritime trade flourished when the other two were in decline or in disarray. The tribally based Imamate was always in tension with the maritime trade which was centred on the coast. The Imamate began to disintegrate at the end of the Yarubi era in 1744 and was replace by the Sultanate but only as a result of other forces: British interference in the traditional political pattern; the process of modernization; and the discovery of oil.

746 **The political status of women in the Arab Gulf States.**
John Everett Peterson. *Middle East Journal*, vol. 43, no. 1 (1989),
p. 34-50.
The status of women in the member states of the Gulf Cooperation Council, including Oman, is discussed in order to assess women's potential for political participation through an examination of the changing economic and social climates. Progress in women's status has occurred in three places: increased government employment; growth in the number of women in senior positions; and socio-political change. However, these prospects are balanced by an examination of the trend towards neo-conservatism among Gulf women which is also a threat to overall development.

747 **Tribes and politics in Eastern Arabia.**
John Everett Peterson. *Middle East Journal*, vol. 31, no. 3 (1977),
p. 297-312.
A consideration of the political change which has taken place in Eastern Arabia with the evolution of political authority from the decentralized tribal basis to a number of independent states. The author traces the political development of the various Gulf States, including Oman, and Britain's role in fostering such development. He also examines the use by the rulers of oil revenues both to consolidate and delegate political powers, a device which has meant tribal leaders having to develop interests in trade and property in order to retain influence.

748 **Political prisoners in the oil states: Oman, Bahrain, Saudi Arabia, Iran.**
London: Gulf Committee, 1974. 32p. map.
A treatise arguing against political oppression of left-wing opposition in the named states.

749 **The Sultanate was real and not a legal fiction.**
R. Rizvi. *Journal of the Pakistan Historical Society*, vol. 28, no. 1
(1980), p. 33-41.
An examination of the position of the Sultanate as a concept within Islam and in relation to *sharia* law. The Muslim state from 700 to 1200 AD led the world in power, order, standard and extent of government, literature, science, philosophy and religious tolerance. The Sultan had responsibilities towards the people, with a duty to pursue Islamic tenets and to protect the weaker members of the community. Although not strictly about Oman, this exposition of the legal status of a Sultanate is extremely relevant for an understanding of the legitimacy of the state.

750 **Monarchic institutions in the face of modernization.**
Ghassane Salama. *Politica Internazionale*, vol. 2, no. 1782 (1981),
p. 8-18.
An analysis of the monarchies of the Gulf States, including Oman, in the light of the
overthrow of the Shah and the attack on Mecca in 1979. Salama considers that the
most forceful opposition is likely to come from the emerging middle class who will
not be able to tolerate exclusion from power. Historically, the ruling class had
concentrated power through modernization of the economy and society and by
ignoring the aspirations of traditional religious groups.

Politics and religion in 'Uman: A historical view.
See item no. 484.

Women in politics: A global view.
See item no. 1124.

Law and Constitution

751 **Oman.**
Abdel Moncim Attia. Dobbs Ferry, New York: Oceana Publications, 1974. 450p. (Constitutions of the World Series).
A descriptive account of the constitution of Oman.

752 **Oman.**
Husain Muhammed al Baharna. In: *International encyclopaedia of comparative law.* Dobbs Ferry, New York: Oceana Publications, 1972. Vol. 1: National Reports, p. 1-2.
A commentary on the constitutional framework of Oman.

753 **Register of the laws of the Arabian Gulf.**
William M. Ballantyne. London: Graham &Trotman, 1991. 780p.
This register of the laws of the Arabian Gulf is a compilation of the written laws and regulations of the Arabian Gulf States from promulgation to the present day. Also included are laws passed during the British presence in the Gulf which have survived to this day and also ancient laws which predate the codification process but remain in force. Oman is covered in section D of the work, with the contents organized by 19 subject categories and indexed chronologically. The format is loose-leaf and there is a quarterly updating service.

754 **Business laws of Oman.**
London: Graham & Trotman, 1987. 700p. 2 vols.
A compilation of the business laws of Oman covering all aspects of economy and trade within the Sultanate. The publication is issued in loose-leaf form and is updated quarterly.

755 **Decree concerning the territorial sea, continental shelf and exclusive fishing zones of the Sultanate of Oman, 17 July 1972.**
In: *National legislation and treaties relating to the Law of the Sea.*
New York: United Nations Legislative Series, 1974. 23p.
(ST/LEG/Ser. B/16).

A reproduction of the Sultan's decree concerning territorial waters and fishing rights.

756 **Economic development law/1975.**
Sultanate of Oman. *Official Gazette*, no. 75 (15 March 1975).

This law specifies the terms of reference for the Development Council and the rules for the annual development planning budget. It also details the exceptions to the regulations which can be granted only by decree of the Sultan.

757 **Insurance companies law of Oman (A translation from Arabic into English of the Insurance Companies Law of Oman, Sultan Decree 12/79).**
Edited by M. H. Hall. London: Graham & Trotman, 1986. 56p.

An English translation aimed at businesses wishing to operate in Oman or to trade with the Sultanate.

758 **Commercial laws of the Middle East, 1983.**
Edited by Allen P. K. Keessee. Dobbs Ferry, New York: Oceana Publications, 1982.

An English translation of various Omani commercial, business and trade laws including the Conflict of Interest Ordinance of 1974, the Banking Ordinance of 1974, and the Banking Secrecy Ordinance of 1977. Produced in loose-leaf format (in a binder) for an updating service.

759 **The laws of the Sultanate of Oman. The Maritime Law of 1974 as amended through May 31, 1975.**
Dobbs Ferry, New York: Oceana Publications, 1975.

A reproduction of the maritime law on territorial waters.

760 **Muscat dhows arbitration in the Permanent Court of Arbitration at the Hague: grant of French flag to Muscat dhows.**
London: Harrison, 1905. 3 vols.

1. The case on behalf of His Britannic Majesty and of His Highness the Sultan of Muscat. 2. The counter-case on behalf of His Britannic Majesty. 3. Argument on behalf of His Britannic Majesty. The documentary evidence to prevent the French from being ceded rights by the Sultan.

761 **Oman: marine pollution control law.**
In: *National legislation and treaties relating to the Law of the Sea.*
New York: United Nations Legislative Series, 1976, p. 76-85.
(ST/LEG/Ser. B/18).
This law was mainly necessitated by the increase in oil activity at Port Qaboos.

762 **The general principles of Saudi Arabian and Omani company laws.**
Nabil Salah.   Plymouth, England: Macdonald & Evans, 1981. 338p.
bibliog.
A guide to the general principles of Oman's company law designed for use by the businessman aiming to do business in the Sultanate or proposing to set up joint ventures with Omani partners.

763 **Traditional concepts of territory in South East Arabia.**
John. C. Wilkinson.   *Geographical Journal*, Vol. 149, no. 3 (1983),
p. 301-15.
A detailed study of the concept of territory in Oman and the United Arab Emirates from pre-Islamic times to the 20th century. Islamic law which declares water, vegetation and fire to be common property is basic to nomadic law. Points of dispute between nomads and villagers are discussed, as are legal sources, marine law and tribal differences. In the twentieth century the question of territoriality has come to the fore again, this time based on the presence and importance of oil.

Marine delimitation in the Persian Gulf and the right of passage in the Strait of Hormuz.
See item no. 817.

Passage of warships through the Strait of Hormuz.
See item no. 819.

Oman's new bankruptcy code – Part I: Application, supervision, commercial firms.
See item no. 902.

Administration and Local Government

764 **Kings and people: Oman's State Consultative Council.**
Dale F. Eickelman. *Middle East Journal*, vol. 38, no. 1 (1984),
p. 51-71.

The article begins by considering the question of the status of absolute monarchies
and the concept of Consultative Councils, before considering the situation in Oman.
The State Consultative Council (SCC) began as a concept in November 1980 and
came into being in October 1981 as a result of a Royal Decree establishing the SCC
and appointing its first members. The SCC is very much a consultative body and can
make recommendations only to the Sultan for approval or rejection, a measure which
avoids conveying any diminution in royal authority. The article discusses the
composition of the SCC and analyses the location of the delegates, age range and
educational level, together with its development of a role as an effective advisory
body. Public reaction to the SCC is also discussed, but it is emphasized that reliable
means of assessing public reaction are non-existent and that only informal evidence
can be gathered. The article concludes with an assessment of the future of the SCC
which could be developed to allow for more effective domestic consultation and
possibly even wider participation in decision-making. In October 1983 the Sultan
announced that the SCC would be charged with discussing and revising laws, and
introducing amendments before they were endorsed by Royal Decree.

765 **The establishment and composition of the Development Council.**
Sultanate of Oman. *Official Gazette* (1 Dec. 1974). (Royal Decree
41/74).

The decree establishing the Development Council, which comprised the main finance
ministries and the Directorate-General of Finance.

766   **The establishment of the Water Resources Council.**
Sultanate of Oman.   *Official Gazette* (1 Oct. 1975). (Royal Decree 45/75).
The decree established a Water Resources Council charged with maintaining and improving water resources for development purposes.

767   **The government of the Sultanate of Oman.**
Muscat: Petroleum Development (Oman) Ltd, 1972. 6p.
A brief account of the infrastructure created after the 1970 coup. The infrastructure was still in an embryonic state when this work was published.

768   **Gulf States.**
Robert Geran Landen.   In: *The Middle East: its government and politics*, edited by Abid A. al-Marayati (et al).   Belmont, Massachusetts: Duxbury Press, 1972, p. 295-316.
The government and infrastructure of the Sultanate is dealt with generally, as one of the Gulf States.

769   **The Arab Gulf States: steps towards political participation.**
John Everett Peterson.   London: Praeger, 1989. 155p.
An analysis of the role of national councils in Oman, Bahrain, Qatar, the United Arab Emirates and Saudi Arabia. The author considers the structure of government, participation, and political parties and allegiances.

770   **Text of the law concerning organisation of government administration.**
Sultanate of Oman.   *Official Gazette* (28 June 1975). (Royal Decree 26/75).
This decree established the pattern of administration, with a Council of Ministers, ministries and specialist councils. The terms of references are given for each, along with the legal and administrative limits of their power.

Foreign Relations

771 **Oil power and politics: conflict in Arabia, the Red Sea and the Gulf.**
Mordechai Abir. London: Cass, 1974. 221p. maps.
Deals with relations between the Arab states and the degree of intervention from outside powers resulting from the presence of oil. The sections of relevance to Oman are largely those concerned with the war in Dhofar, and relations with Saudi Arabia, particularly over the Imamate and the Buraimi Oasis.

772 **The Arabian Gulf States: Their legal and political status and their international problems.**
Husain Muhammad al Baharna. Beirut: Librairie du Liban, 1975. 2nd rev. ed. lxii+428p.
Deals with the emergence of the Gulf States, including Oman, as independent states, and considers the various boundary disputes and outside influences.

773 **The legal status of the Arabian Gulf States: a study of their treaty relations and their international problems.**
Husain Muhammad al Baharna. Manchester, England: University of Manchester Press, 1968. 351p. maps. bibliog.
An important work for understanding the role of Britain in the Arabian Gulf, the boundary disputes between the states and the international implications of the situation. The scope of the work is much wider than Oman itself, but it is valuable because of the interconnected problems of the area. Of particular relevance to Oman are the analyses of British treaty relations with Muscat, the British–Saudi controversy over Buraimi Oasis, Oman's internal disputes, and the Treaty of Sib.

774 **Security in the Persian Gulf.**
Edited by Shahram Chubin. London: International Institute for
Strategic Studies; Totowa, New Jersey: Allenheld Osmun, 1981-82.
4 vols.

Volume 1 covers the domestic political factors contributing to Gulf security and the economies of the various states, including Oman. The remaining volumes examine the relations between the various states, development programmes, political developments and the role of outside powers, mainly dealing with the post-1973 period. Discussion also centres on superpower interaction in terms of competition and the management of regional conflicts.

775 **Continental-shelf boundary: Iran–Oman.**
In: *United States: Department of State International Boundary Study
Series A: Limits of the Seas*, no. 67 (1967), 7p. map.

One of a series of publications designed to detail agreements for measurement of the continental shelf and territorial water. The boundary here is the Strait of Hormuz.

776 **Muscat and Aden peace bid falters.**
John Dimsdale. *Eight Days*, vol. 3, no. 26 (1981), p. 16-17.

A survey article covering the continuing problems between Oman and the People's Democratic Republic of Yemen, both of which filed complaints in 1981 with the Arab League, each accusing the other of border incursions and armed aggression. The United Arab Emirates and Kuwait were involved in mediation and indirect tripartite talks had been established but peace talks were halted because of the border skirmishes.

777 **The protectors.**
Paul Eedle. *Monday Morning*, vol. 10, no. 465 (18 May 1981),
p. 56-57.

An appraisal of the debate on America's rapid deployment force in the Gulf with some states opposed to its presence, whilst Oman had already provided military facilities to the United States.

778 **Guardians of the Gulf.**
Economist, vol. 279, no. 7188 (6 June 1981), p. 24-25.

An appraisal of the political and strategic role of the Sultanate of Oman which in 1981 was firmly allied to the West and had provided military facilities to the United States. Due to the threat posed by the People's Democratic Republic of Yemen, about half of the Sultanate's budget was spent of defence. The economic significance of oil and gas is briefly reviewed.

779 **Iran–Oman agreement on the continental shelf.**
International Legal Materials, vol. 14, no. 6 (1975), p. 1478-79.

This agreement defines the sea boundaries between the two countries in the Strait of Hormuz.

780 **Oman, a rock in the sands.**
L. Johnson. *Defense Foreign Affairs*, vol. 7, no. 6 (1979), p. 6-11.
A consideration of the military capabilities of the Sultanate, its strategic position and its role as an ally of the West.

781 **Oman: critical to the Western world's oil supply.**
Thomas M. Johnson. *Armor* (Jan. 1981), p. 42-45.
An analysis of Oman's strategic importance to the Western world because of the Strait of Hormuz through which one half of the oil used by the Western world is shipped. The significance of Oman became internationally apparent as a result of the outbreak of the Iraq–Iran war. The geography of Oman is briefly described.

782 **Soviet policy in the Gulf Sates.**
Mark N. Katz. *Current History*, vol. 84, no. 498 (Jan. 1985),
p. 25-28, 41.
An assessment of Soviet policy in the mid-1980s with regard to the pro-Western economies of the Gulf Cooperation Council states which have been seen as possible targets for Soviet aggressive policy. However, the article argues that the inter-state settlement of local disputes and the oil price rises in 1973 diminished Soviet influence, because living conditions within the GCC rose and so reduced the impetus to revolution. The Soviet Union changed its policy towards the cultivation of friendly relations but, apart from Kuwait, the policy was largely successful.

783 **Oman and the world.**
Joseph A. Kechichian. *American Arab Affairs*, no. 35 (1990-91),
p. 135-50.
This article deals with the emergence of Oman from over one hundred years of political isolation. Sultan Qaboos, on his accession in 1970, undertook to pursue a multi-pronged foreign policy aimed at: regaining control over the Dhofar province; introducing development projects; and improving Oman's strategic position in the region and taking her place as part of the world community. The article briefly considers the following topics: settlement of border disputes; the Dhofar rebellion; Oman's view of Gulf security and the Gulf Cooperation Council; relations with Iran, France, Great Britain, the United States and the Soviet Union. Kechichian concludes that long-term prosperity is dependent upon regional security and that Oman must be able to cope with the political situation in the region following the liberation of Kuwait and the rising military power of Iran.

784 **Embargo busting: Arab oil deliveries to South Africa.**
Arthur Jay Klinghoffer. *Middle East Review*, vol. 22, no. 2 (Winter
1989/90), p. 25-29.
A study of the oil embargo of South Africa which, the author argues, is being breached by a number of Arab states, including Oman, despite public advocacy for the sanctions. The violations were covered by South Africa's non-publication of oil import statistics. The author contends that Israel should disclose figures for this trade and improve the quality of its statistical data.

785 **Arms and allies on the Arabian Peninsula.**
Thomas L. McNaugher. *Orbis*, vol. 28, no. 9 (1984), p. 489-524.
This analysis of the security situation in the Arabian Peninsula in 1984 examines the role of outside nations in the region and the prospects for cooperation amongst members of the Gulf Cooperation Council. Data are provided on the military strengths of Oman, Saudi Arabia and the two Yemens, the populations and military strengths of the Middle East states and the coastal, land and air defence forces of the Gulf Cooperation Council.

786 **Importance of the Strait of Hormuz discussed.**
Abd-al-Ghani Muruwwak. *Al-Mustaqbal* (3 May 1980), p. 85-89.
An Arabic-language report on the strategic significance of the Strait of Hormuz due to the flow of oil exports to the Western world and Japan. With 1,700 kilometres of shoreline to be protected, the burden for Oman is significant in defence expenditure.

787 **Oman and Gulf security.**
B. K. Narayan. New Delhi: Lancer Publishers, 1979. 192p. bibliog.
An assessment of Oman's strategic importance to Gulf security, particularly because of the Strait of Hormuz, her pro-Western stance within the region, and the importance of continued political stability within the Sultanate.

788 **Oman: a wary north eye.**
Economist, vol. 293, no. 7372 (15 Dec. 1984), p. 50-52.
A review of Oman's security problems. These are accorded a high priority by the government, being allocated 40 per cent of the budget. Additional funds were provided by the Gulf Cooperation Council in recognition of Oman's strategic importance. Relations with Iran had improved, but Oman was still guarded in relations with the Iranian government and there was internal concern about the Palestinians who were regarded as dangerous radicals.

789 **An appraisal of US strategy in the Indian Ocean.**
Rasul B. Rais. *Asian Survey*, vol. 23, no. 9 (1983), p. 1043- 51.
The United States had neglected the Persian Gulf and the Indian Ocean until the oil crisis of 1973 forced the government to recognize the area's geopolitical significance. The article discusses the changes in the strategic planning and defence policies relating to the region and possible links with NATO and Japan regarding the region. The base facilities in Oman are discussed in this context.

790 **Iran's foreign policy, 1941-1973, a study of foreign policy in modernising nations.**
Rouhollah K. Ramazani. Charlottesville, Virginia: University Press of Virginia, 1975. 507p. maps. bibliog.
Deals with Iranian policy toward the Gulf in general, Oman, and the Dhofar War. In the latter case, Iranian military support was supplied at the request of the Sultan and was used by Iran as a means of training its troops in war and counter-insurgency conditions.

791 **The Persian Gulf and the Strait of Hormuz.**
Rouhollah K. Ramazani. Alphen aan den Rijn, The Netherlands:
Sijthoff & Nordoff, 1979. 141p. (*International Straits of the World*,
vol. 3).
A survey of the rivalry in the area between various powers and superpowers,
concluding that the key to real security rests with the local states themselves.
However, the book was written prior to the Islamic revolution in Iran and must be
viewed in this context. Ramazani also deals with the question of the Dhofar rebellion,
Soviet influence in the People's Democratic Republic of Yemen, and the strategic and
economic significance of the Strait of Hormuz in relation to the passage of oil.

792 **The Persian Gulf: Iran's role.**
Rouhollah K. Ramazani. Charlottesville, Virginia: University Press
of Virginia, 1972. 157p.
An important study of the position of Iran in the Persian Gulf at the time of the Shah
– he saw Iran's role as the policeman of the Gulf. The work includes a consideration
of the economic and strategic importance of the Strait of Hormuz which is shared by
Oman and Iran and critical to the passage of oil.

793 **US military interests in area explained.**
Najib Riyadh. *Al-Mustaqbal* (3 May 1980), p. 80-84.
An Arabic-language appraisal of United States military and economic assistance to
Oman in return for the granting of land, sea and air facilities. In terms of economic
aid, Oman was to be granted 45 million dollars in 1981/82 and 95 million dollars in
1982/83.

794 **Saudi Arabia: the ceaseless quest for security.**
Nadav Safran. Cambridge, Massachusetts, Harvard University Press,
1985. 892p. bibliog.
An extremely comprehensive examination of the Saudi Arabian policy towards
internal security and regional defence. This is evidenced by the major financial
investment made in terms of military build-up and the facilities provided for members
of the armed forces and security forces. References to Oman are scattered throughout
the text but particular emphasis is placed on relations with Iran, problems of Dhofar
and the People's Democratic Republic of Yemen, and the dispute over the Buraimi
Oasis.

795 **Arabian boundaries: primary documents 1853-1960.**
Edited by Richard Schofield, Gerald Blake. Farnham Common,
England: Archive Research, 1992. 16,000p. 30 vols.
The definitive collection of documents and maps determining the history of national
boundaries in the Arabian Peninsula, including Oman, Saudi Arabia and Abu Dhabi,
and the political relations between the states. Amongst the documents are
correspondence, treaties, telegrams, memoranda and notes, including diplomatic
assessments. The introduction by the editors is especially helpful and the
comprehensive notes are essential to an understanding of boundaries and their
definition.

796　**Arabian boundary disputes.**
Edited by Richard Schofield.　Farnham Common, England: Archive
Research, 1992. 13,000p. 20 vols.

A further collection of primary source material which is broader than the foundation
work *Arabian boundaries: primary documents 1853-1960* (q.v.) in terms of
geographical area and time-scale. Aims at presenting the historical background to
border disputes and the current position regarding them, with each being examined in
turn.

797　**Special press release by Abdul Aziz al-Rowas.**
Journal of the Gulf and Arabian Peninsula Studies, vol. 6, no. 24
(1980), p. 184-88.

An interview with Abdul Aziz al-Rowas, Minister of Information and Youth Affairs,
which outlines Oman's foreign policy – particularly its support of the
Egyptian–Israeli peace treaty – and Oman's position in relation to the Palestinian
cause. Also discussed was Oman's view on Gulf security and the need for the Gulf
states to be responsible for their own collective security.

798　**A special press release by Ali Naser Mohamed, President of the
People's Democratic Republic of Yemen.**
Journal of the Gulf and Arabian Peninsula Studies, vol. 6, no. 24 (Oct.
1980), p. 182-84.

An interview with the President of the People's Democratic Republic of Yemen
which focuses on the PDRY's relations with Oman, Iraq and North Yemen. In respect
of Oman, the interview concentrates on Kuwaiti mediation between the two countries
in 1980 which was aimed at changing Oman's stand on the Camp David Accords.

799　**Admission of new members to the United Nations: application of
the Sultanate of Oman for admission to membership in the United
Nations. Note by the Secretary-General.**
United Nations.　New York: United Nations General Assembly,
2 June 1971. 2p. (Document A/8320).

A background note by the Secretary-General on the Sultanate's application for
membership of the United Nations.

Dissertations

800 **International politics of the Persian Gulf States from a subsystemic core perspective.**
William Leroy Dowdy. PhD thesis, Tulane University, New Orleans, 1982. 571p. (Available from University Microfilms, Ann Arbor, Michigan, order no. AAD82-26691).

An in-depth study of the underlying characteristics of the states bordering the Persian Gulf, including Oman, which examines the relations between them over the period from 1970. The study tests the hypothesis that the area constitutes an emerging core of the long-conceived Middle East subsystem of global politics, and seeks to evaluate this approach to the study of regional political relationships.

801 **The Gulf Cooperation Council: Arabia's model of integration.**
Ghalib Tulhab Etaibi. PhD thesis, Boston College, Massachusetts, 1984. 269p. (Available from University Microfilms, Ann Arbor, Michigan, order no. AAD85-10684).

An analysis of the foundations and emergence in 1981 of the Gulf Cooperation Council (GCC) which is regarded as a unique case amongst contemporary integrative schemes. The thesis identifies the relevant local, regional, and international factors which helped to shape the GCC.

802 **Relations between Oman and the states of Eastern Arabia 1804-1856: as shown in the *Kitab Badr al-Tamam fi Sirat Sa'id bin Sultan* of Ibn Ruzayq.**
S. M. al-Hashimy. MPhil thesis, University of Leeds, England, 1990. (Available from British Library, Document Supply Centre, Boston Spa, Wetherby, West Yorkshire).

A study of the relationships between Oman and the states of Eastern Arabia as shown in *Kitab Badr al-Tamam* by Ibn Ruzayq in the reign of Sultan Said bin Sultan (1804-56). The work discusses Oman's relationships with the Al-Qawasim of Ras al-Khaima, the Utub of Kuwait and Bahrain, and the Wahhabis of present-day Saudi Arabia. The relationships have been affected by a variety of factors, including: Omani tribes' cooperation with outside powers; the strengths and weaknesses of these external forces; internal problems faced by Sultan Said; and the attempts of foreign powers to obtain influence in Omani ports.

803 **USSR–Gulf States relations since the British withdrawal from East of Suez in 1971 (Saudi Arabia, Kuwait, Qatar, Oman, Bahrain).**
Mishel Abdullah Al-Mosaed. PhD thesis, University of Denver, 1990. 299p. (Available from University Microfilms, Ann Arbor, Michigan, order no. AAD90-30082).

A study of the changing relations between the Gulf States, including Oman, following British withdrawal from the Gulf in 1971. Although relations had significantly improved over the years it was concluded that the Soviet Union had not seriously challenged United States in a region of vital importance to the West because of oil. In the case of Oman, relations in the 1970s had been coloured by Soviet support for the Dhofar rebellion and the People's Democratic Republic of Yemen. The study also shows that the West's dependence upon oil has led to a degree of interdependence between the Gulf States and the West, whilst at the same time allowing the Gulf States a degree of independence in foreign relations.

Regional Security

804 **Gulf States efforts to ensure collective security.**
A. Acharya. *Pacific Defence Report*, vol. 12, no. 10 (1986), p. 11-13.
Examines the role of the Gulf Cooperation Council in trying to establish a defence policy and an integrated military command structure in order to provide for their collective security. A measure of disagreement was the question of the use of outside forces such as the United States.

805 **The Sultanate of Oman and American security interests in the Arabian Gulf.**
Calvin H. Allen Jr. In: *The Arabian Peninsula: Zone of ferment*, edited by Robert W. Stookey. Stanford, California: Hoover Institution Press, 1984, p. 1-16.
A study of Oman as the United States' oldest friend in the Arabian Peninsula and a valuable ally following the June 1980 agreement allowing the United States access to military installations in Oman. The article also examines perceived liabilities in the relationship, with doubts about the legitimacy of the ruling dynasty, the problem of an unclear succession, and Oman's ethnic diversity.

806 **Oman, the Gulf and the United States.**
John Duke Anthony. In: *Oman, economic, social and strategic developments*, edited by B. R. Pridham. London: Croom Helm, 1986, p. 177-94.
This contribution deals with the strategic significance of Oman and its membership of, and enthusiasm for, the Gulf Cooperation Council as a factor in ensuring regional security. The essay also deals with Oman's close relations with the United States and cooperation over military matters, including the provision of facilities.

807 **Leave it to us.**
Sue Bolton. *Middle East International*, no. 151 (5 June 1981), p. 4-5.
A report on the summer meeting of the Gulf Cooperation Council (GCC) held on 25 May 1981. At this summit the leaders of the GCC states claimed sole responsibility for Gulf security and rejected defensive alliances with the West. Despite Oman's arguments for military coordination between member states no decision was reached because of Oman's decision to grant the United States both air and naval facilities.

808 **Oman: an energetic approach to regional security.**
Alison Brown. *Middle East Economic Digest Special Report* (Nov. 1983), p. 2-5.
A report submitted in November 1983 on Oman's military and economic situation. The strategic position of the Sultanate was recognized by the Gulf Cooperation Council by a grant of 1,800 million dollars in July 1983 to help meet Oman's military expenses. Some of the military facilities are described, as are those granted to the United States.

809 **Moderation and stability in the Gulf.**
John Christie, Joseph Wright Twinan. *American Arab Affairs*, no. 18 (Autumn 1986), p. 1-32.
This article is divided into two parts: the first part provides a brief overview of the history and development of the Gulf Cooperation Council; the second focuses on the achievements of the Gulf Cooperation Council, with particular reference to Bahrain, Qatar and Oman.

810 **Military strategy and regional security in the Gulf: The options for the West and the moderate Gulf States.**
Anthony H. Cordesman. In: *Oman: economic, social and strategic developments*, edited by B. R. Pridham. London: Croom Helm, 1987, p. 209-48.
Cordesman argues that the West and the moderate Gulf States must develop some form of common strategy as neither can create a structure of regional deterrence or defence on their own. The West cannot maintain its own security without a sure supply of oil and must secure local cooperation in order to maintain stability within the region. Tables provide data on the size of Gulf forces, battle-tank strength, aircraft strength, military expenditure, relative size of defence efforts, and arms sales to the Gulf.

811 **Defence projects bear brunt of spending cuts.**
Middle East Economic Digest Business Feature, vol. 30, no. 51 (20 Dec. 1986), p. 56-58.
An overview of political and economic events in Oman in 1988. In order to offset reduced oil revenues, defence spending was significantly reduced and the riyal devalued by 10 per cent against the US dollar. Oman shares the concern of the other Gulf States about the effects of the Iraq–Iran war but had ensured that links with Iran were maintained.

812 **Nuclearisation of the Middle East.**
Anoushiravan Ehteshami. London: Gulf Centre for Strategic Studies
for Brassey's, 1989. 199p.

A study of the possible dangers of nuclear war in the Middle East through the
proliferation of nuclear weapons and technology seen against the wider issues of the
region. Oman features at various points throughout the text, but particularly in
relations with the United States and access to military facilities.

813 **Gulf Cooperation Council: the security policies.**
Laura Guazzone. *Survival*, vol. 30, no. 2 (March 1988), p. 134-47.
map.

The Gulf Cooperation Council (GCC) had established a joint military committee to
coordinate defence and to develop a joint arms purchasing policy and military
manoeuvres. Guazzone indicates that the GCC saw the perceived threats at that time
(1988) as flowing from the outcome of the Iraq–Iran war but with other possible
security threats being perceived as coming from Israel, Ethiopia, the People's
Democratic Republic of Yemen and the Yemen Arab Republic.

814 **Arabia imperilled: the security imperatives of the Arab Gulf
States.**
Mazher A. Hameed. Washington, DC: Middle East Assessments
Group, 1986. 188p. bibliog. (Published by Croom Helm as *Saudi
Arabia, the West and the security of the Gulf*).

A very detailed examination of the security implications of the area, with references
to Oman throughout the text. It covers, amongst other topics: the geopolitics of Gulf
security; the security environment; the threat profile; the security resources of the
Gulf states; problems of security and gaps in provision; and United States interests in
the Gulf. An important contribution to the literature, with the Gulf seen as one of the
critical areas affecting Western strategic interests because it is threatened by radical
pressures, internal tensions and Soviet interests, and since it also possesses fifty per
cent of proven oil reserves.

815 **Omani navy: operating in troubled waters.**
T. Johnson, R. Barrett. *Naval Institute Proceedings*, vol. 108 (March
1982), p. 99-103.

A survey of the Omani navy and its operations particularly in relation to the patrols in
the Strait of Hormuz protecting the shipping routes for the oil tankers from the
Arabian Gulf. The fleet consists largely of small coastal patrol vessels operating
mainly from bases in the Capital Area.

816 **The elusive quest for Gulf security.**
Abd al-Hadi Khalaf. *Middle East Report* (Sept. 1987), p. 19-22, 32.

An assessment in 1987 of the progress made by the Gulf Cooperation Council with
regard to the question of Gulf security. Attempts to coordinate security and military
cooperation had, in the opinion of the author, failed due to mutual distrust and
unresolved border disputes. The attitudes towards the Iraq–Iran war has also been
fragmented, ranging from official neutrality to open support for Iraq.

817 **Marine delimitation in the Persian Gulf and the right of passage in the Strait of Hormuz.**
U. Leanza. *Marine Policy Report*, vol. 1, no. 3 (1989), p. 217-35.
A survey of the complicated geopolitical situation in the region, including the right of passage through the Strait of Hormuz. The article focuses on the legal problems arising from the inconsistency between the applicability of customary law in relation to the continental shelf and Article 16, paragraph 4 of the 1958 Geneva Convention and the applicability of articles 34, 37 and related articles of the 1982 Law of the Sea Convention.

818 **Security in the Persian Gulf: 2. Sources of inter-state conflict.**
Robert Litwak. London: Gower, for the International Institute for Strategic Studies; Totowa, New Jersey: Allanheld Osmun, 1981. 103p. maps.
This work deals with the complex problem of the interrelationship between the various states in the area. Chapter 3, 'The lower Gulf states' examines the questions of boundaries in the region and in relation to Oman the section of interest is that dealing with the Buraimi Oasis dispute. Chapter 4, 'Southern Arabia' deals with relations between Oman and the People's Democratic Republic of Yemen.

819 **Passage of warships through the Strait of Hormuz.**
S. Mahmoudi. *Maritime Policy*, vol. 15, no. 5 (1991), p. 338-48.
Oman's policy of rejecting transit passage as a right for flag states in the Strait of Hormuz is seen as contradictory to the Law of the Sea Convention of 1982, as article 310 prohibits ratifying states from making such conclusions.

820 **Policy implications of boundary disputes in the Persian Gulf.**
Lenore G. Martin. *Middle East Review*, vol. 15, nos. 1-2 (Fall/Winter 1982), p. 28-32.
Argues that United Sates policy in the Gulf has tended towards military preparedness rather than political, and has appeared to focus on external effects when the main threat was likely to come from internal border disputes. Amongst the disputes examined is that between the People's Democratic Republic of Yemen and Oman which had the increased sensitivity of control over the Strait of Hormuz. The various options open to US policy-makers are examined and it is considered that a Gulf States Defence Organization on the lines of the North Atlantic Treaty Organization (NATO) would be the most viable option for protecting oil supplies.

821 **The Gulf Cooperation Council: policies, problems and prospects.**
Emile A. Nakhleh. New York: Praeger, 1986. 128p.
An introductory survey of the GCC which attempts to assess its impact on the security and stability of the Gulf region. The work begins with a background description of the six member states, including Oman, and a consideration of the regional role of the organization through the perceptions of the six leaders. The volume also contains a summary of development issues in the member states covering publicly owned projects, bureaucracy, industry, education, and demographic questions.

822 **Omani ships reflect Gulf War lessons.**
International Defence Review, vol. 25, no. 6 (1992), p. 617.
A discussion of the design, construction and armaments systems of two corvettes ordered by the Royal Omani Navy from the British shipyard Vosper Thorneycroft. The final equipment fit reflected the tactical lessons of the Gulf War. This type of article is common in connection with defence procurement, and can be found in this journal and other titles such as *Jane's Defense Weekly* and *Jane's Intelligence Review*.

823 **Defending Arabia.**
John Everett Peterson. New York: St. Martin's Press; London: Croom Helm, 1986. 275p. bibliog.
A study of the policies of the Gulf Cooperation Council (GCC) states, Britain and the United States with regard to Gulf security in the light of the historical background. The main conclusion is that the GCC will always be dependent on external assistance for defence and that advances in non-military areas will become increasingly important to the continued security of the Gulf States. Also considered, in some detail, are the origins of, and the impetus for, the establishment of the GCC and the common interests of the member states. Britain's involvement in the Dhofar War is also examined, as are the defence capabilities of Oman, and US access to military facilities.

824 **The GCC and regional security.**
John Everett Peterson. *American Arab Affairs*, no. 20 (Spring 1987), p. 62-90.
An assessment of the military capabilities of the Gulf Cooperation Council in the late 1980s and of the individual member states. Saudi Arabia and Oman are the strongest of the GCC states in military terms but their forces are constrained by small populations. The GCC states are still reliant on foreign assistance and are really dependent on the United States to deter any major attack.

825 **The Gulf Cooperation Council: search for unity in a dynamic region.**
Erik R. Peterson. Boulder, Colorado; London: Westview Press, 1988. 346p. bibliog.
A comprehensive and systematic account of the Gulf Cooperation Council's development and its progress towards political and economic integration. The first part of the work considers the historical links and rivalries between the member states, common links in terms of political structures and common institutions, as well as the role of regional instability in the formation of the GCC. Part two examines the ideological reasons for cooperation amongst the member states, including the role of Arabism and the tendency of the Gulf States to support pan-Arab interests. The final section catalogues and analyses the activities and achievements of the GCC, covering political, economic and military aspects of cooperation and integration. Also considered are the effects of both the Iranian revolution and the Iraq–Iran war on the region. Oman features throughout the text, but with particular coverage on economic development, governmental infrastructure, oil development, military development, physical infrastructure, relations with the superpowers and Great Britain and Saudi Arabia, and the GCC's role in rapprochement in ties with the People's Democratic Republic of Yemen.

826 **The Gulf Cooperation Council: record and analysis.**
R. K. Ramazani. Charlottesville, Virginia: University Press of
Virginia, 1988. 240p. bibliog.
A balanced and comprehensive account of the establishment of the Gulf Cooperation
Council and an assessment of its record to date. The book records the reasons for the
establishment of the GCC in 1981 – the need to strengthen the security of member
states and improve their ability to cope with terrorism, and the desire to make
progress towards the development of economic ties and the coordination of
diplomatic policies. Ramazani also considers the effect of the Iraq–Iran war on the
solidarity and effectiveness of the GCC and the fact that the end of the war and the
return of Iraqi attention towards the Gulf could cause problems for the GCC, a
prediction that was to come true with the invasion of Kuwait in 1991. References to
Oman appear throughout the text.

827 **Oman's role in the Gulf Cooperation Council and the region.**
Riad N. El-Rayyes. In: *Oman, economic, social and strategic
developments*, edited by B. R. Pridham. London: Croom Helm, 1987,
p. 195-208.
Begins with a consideration of Oman's strategic position both in relation to the
Arabian Gulf and the Gulf of Aden/Red Sea route, before considering the
establishment of the Gulf Cooperation Council. The article then deals with the
concept of a Gulf Deterrent Force, the economic agreement within the GCC, and
attitudes towards foreign policy. Oman has its own priorities in foreign policy but has
continued to persevere with the GCC in the belief that Gulf security would become
stronger through the combined development of the organization.

828 **The Gulf Cooperation Council: moderation and stability in an
interdependent world.**
Edited by John A. Sandwick. Boulder, Colorado: Westview Press;
Washington, DC: American-Arab Affairs Council, 1987. 289p.
bibliog.
A collection of nine essays (which first appeared as a series of articles in
American-Arab Affairs) all of which stress the significance of the Gulf Cooperation
Council and the strengths it possesses as a result of the common background of its
member states, as well as religion, language and traditions. The subjects dealt with
include: finance; economic integration; oil policies; regional security; superpower
interests in the Gulf; the historical background; the position of smaller states within
the GCC; and changes in the legal systems of the member states. The conclusion
assesses the progress of the GCC towards integration and considers that progress in
the context of the construction of a global Islamic political society. It is asserted,
however, that the conservative Arab Gulf monarchies cannot really be deemed to
have the capacity to create a building block in any global sense. As a key member of
the GCC there are numerous references to Oman throughout the text.

829 **Strategic significance focuses attention on stability – Oman.**
Arab Economics, vol. 14, no. 151 (1982), p. 37-40.
Examines the question of the stability of the Omani regime in the light of its strategic
significance in relation to the Strait of Hormuz.

830　**The Sultan and the Strait.**
Monday Morning, vol. 12, no. 12 (1985), p. 94-103.
An interview with Sultan Qaboos covering a variety of topics of regional concern.
Amongst the topics covered are: the independence of Oman despite its pro-Western
stance; the maintenance of free passage through the Strait of Hormuz; the importance
of the Gulf Cooperation Council; attempts at mediation in the Iraq–Iran war; and the
need to find a peace formula acceptable to the Arabs and Israel.

Dissertations

831　**The Gulf Cooperation Council (GCC) and regional integration:
An analysis of cultural origins, political evolution and collective
security.**
Abdul-Jaleel Kassim Ali.　PhD thesis, Catholic University of
America, 1988. 268p. (Available from University Microfilms, Ann
Arbor, Michigan, order no. AAD88-14933).
An examination of the establishment of the Gulf Cooperation Council which, the
author suggests, was partially motivated by the Iraq–Iran war, and the Soviet invasion
of Afghanistan. He concludes that the GCC was created in response to external
changes in the Gulf and could not have been formed had it not been for regional
pressures. The author also asserts that local efforts towards integration had been
encouraged by the strategic vulnerability felt by the member states and by
revolutionary turmoil in Iran, as well as by political terrorism.

832　**The Gulf Cooperation Council: reasons and challenges, critical
and analytical study.**
Abdulla Meshail A. Al-Anzi.　PhD thesis, Claremont Graduate
School, Claremont, California, 1986. 296p. (Available from University
Microfilms, Ann Arbor, Michigan, order no. AAD86-19072).
The Gulf Cooperation Council was established to cope with regional tensions because
the individual states were unable to deal effectively with these local problems
themselves. Stability and regional security were threatened by the Iranian revolution,
the Iraq–Iran war and unrest within the member states caused by radical Islamic
movements. The author asserts that the difficulties facing the GCC at this time (ca.
1986) stemmed from: the lack of political development within the member states; the
existence of conflict in and between ruling families; the economic problems faced by
the member states because of their overdependence on oil; population problems; and
border disputes.

833   **The Gulf Cooperation Council: search for security in the Persian Gulf.**
Joseph Albert Kechichian.   PhD thesis, University of Virginia, Charlottesville, Virginia. 1985. 596p. (Available from University Microfilms, Ann Arbor, Michigan, order no. AAD86-15597).

The conservative governments of the Arabian Gulf States were encouraged to form the Gulf Cooperation Council by outside factors, such as the Iraq–Iran war and the Soviet invasion of Afghanistan. This study analyses the search for regional security in the Gulf and the future prospects for the GCC as a vehicle for regional security. Also considered are the reactions of the GCC to perceived threats such as the Iraq–Iran war, the Arab–Israeli conflict, the threat from the Soviet Union, and potential sources of dissidence within member states.

834   **The Gulf Cooperation Council: a study in integration.**
Rashid A. Al-Makhawi.   PhD thesis, University of Salford, England, 1990. 230p. (Available from University Microfilms, Ann Arbor, Michigan, order no. AAD90-91355).

The Gulf Cooperation Council was established in 1981 and at the time Western observers determined that regional security was the prime consideration though it is not mentioned in the charter. Indeed the initial moves were towards economic integration and other forms of cooperation between the member states. This study examines the development of the GCC largely as an instrument of Arab unity, but at the same time reflects on Western theories of integration based on the concept of a security community.

Economy

835 The Arab Gulf economy.

Harby Mohammed Mousa Arikat. Durham, England: University of Durham, Centre for Middle Eastern and Islamic Studies, 1987. 66p.

An economic and demographic profile of the Gulf States, including Oman, in 1987. It stresses the necessity for regional cooperation and integration to develop industrially. Statistical tables are included.

836 Economic developments and migrant labour movement.

John Stace Birks, G. Mackay. *Orient*, vol. 20, no. 2 (1979), p. 101-5.

Deals with the problem of labour migration from Oman to more lucrative employment in the United Arab Emirates and Saudi Arabia, and the resulting effects on development in Oman.

837 The Gulf Cooperation Council: Achievements and challenge.

Abdulla Yacoub Bishara. *American Arab Affairs*, no. 7 (Winter 1983), p. 40-44.

An adaptation of a speech delivered by the Secretary-General of the Gulf Cooperation Council in September 1983 at a conference on United States diplomacy in the Gulf. Amongst the topics discussed were regional security, economic integration, the Iraq–Iran war, and tensions between Oman and the People's Democratic Republic of Yemen.

838 Oman: the party's over.

J. Bodgener. *Middle East Economic Digest* (8 March 1986), p. 6-8.

Oman had increased oil production in the face of falling prices to maintain the development momentum. However, the oil price slide in 1988 led to a devaluation of the Omani riyal, resulting in the deferment of large projects and the scaling down or cancellation of others. Other austerity measures were likely to be introduced in order to balance the budget.

839 **Oman.**
J. Bodgener, R. Allen. *Middle East Economic Digest* (Dec. 1984), p. 1-24.

A survey of the Omani economy which discloses that it had not been subject to the recession facing other producers as a result of prudent planning and careful expenditure. This result has also been achieved by rising oil production which was essential if the development momentum was to be maintained.

840 **Oman.**
J. Bodgener, R. Allen. *Middle East Economic Digest Special Report* (1986). 23p.

A reappraisal of the third Five-Year Development Plan, 1986-90, forced by a sudden economic downturn. All the aspects of the plan are discussed and statistics are provided for 1969-86.

841 **Oman 1970-1985.**
J. Bodgener, R. Allen. *Middle East Economic Digest* (Nov. 1983), p. 1-25.

A review of Oman's economy and development between 1970 and 1985 as the country moved into its third five-year development plan. The authors consider that the economy is in a healthy state and that the second plan which ended in 1985 had met the majority of its targets despite falling oil prices. The latter had been countered by increasing output and sales.

842 **Major companies of the Arab World 1992/93.**
Edited by G. Bricault. London: Graham & Trotman, 1992. 16th ed. 1120p.

The leading annual directory of over 6500 of the most important companies in the Arab world, including Oman, with full contact data on each company, financial data and areas of commercial activity.

843 **Expand and diversify.**
Gulf States Newsletter, no. 213 (1 June 1987), p. 9-12.

Oman's economy in 1987 had performed rather better than her neighbours in terms of riding out the economic recession caused by low oil prices. A contributory factor had been the government's reluctance to invest in large-scale public industry, preferring instead to concentrate on the encouragement of small-scale private enterprise. Tables are included, showing the structure of trade in 1985, the balance of payments from 1982 to 1985, government revenues from 1982 to 1984, and major trading partners in 1985.

844 **Oman emerges from the shadows.**
Roger Hardy. *Middle East*, no. 133 (Nov. 1985), p. 7-10. map.

A survey of Oman's economic development between 1970 and 1985, illustrated by statistical comparisons: a rise in teachers from 30 in 1970 to 9,236 in 1985; a rise in the number of telephones from 557 to 23,000 over the same period; and an increase in gross national product (GNP) by 25 per cent per year from 1976 to 1980. The Five-Year Development Plan for 1981-85 has emphasized diversification from oil and several small and medium-sized industries were established. The plan for 1986-90 placed an emphasis on agriculture in order to counter the migration from the rural areas to the capital.

845 **The Gulf economic crisis and its social and political consequences.**
Shireen T. Hunter. *Middle East Journal*, vol. 40, no. 4 (Autumn 1986), p. 593-613.

Discusses the economic crisis in the oil-producing Gulf states, including Oman, following four years of oil surplus and falling revenues. The author considers the effects of the recession on social and religious tensions and the economic effects in the overall business sector. Economic adaptability is considered to be limited because of weaknesses in the infrastructure and the tendency of the oil states to deny the full extent of the problems. The effects on the demands for expatriate labour are also considered.

846 **A jump of centuries: a survey of the Arabian Peninsula.**
Economist, vol. 235, no. 6615 (1970), p. 1-28.

A general survey of modernization and development in the area, including Oman, concentrating on the quantum leap taken by the Arab states and made possible by oil wealth.

847 **More than 12,000 Omani companies and institutions.**
Al-Tijari (Oman), (July 1981), p. 4-7.

A report on Oman's growth from 1970 to 1981 which showed that 12,000 companies and institutions had been established by 1981. The first five-year development plan had achieved a number of its goals and a Development Council was established in 1975 to administer central economic planning. Foreign investment had played a significant part in this period of development.

848 **Economic liberalization in the Middle East.**
Edited by Tim Niblock, Emma Murphy. London: I. B. Tauris, 1992. 288p.

A discussion of the crucial questions of social, political and economic liberalization in the Middle East as advocated by the Western powers and the International Monetary Fund (IMF). It is considered that many of the conditions imposed by organizations such as the IMF are inappropriate to the socio-economic structure of the Arab countries and succeed only in worsening the situations that they seek to resolve. Case-studies are presented of Egypt, Tunisia, Israel, Oman and Yemen.

849 Oman.
Pakistan and Gulf Economist, vol. 2, no. 30 (July 1983), p. 10-43.
map.

An economic survey of Oman covering oil, agriculture, water, industry, banking, healthcare and education in relation to the objectives of the second five-year development plan. Also discussed are Pakistan–Oman relations. Statistical data is provided covering 1967-85.

850 Oman.
Al Markazi (Central Bank of Oman), vol. 8, no. 7 (1983), p. 5-32.

This survey of economic development in Oman from 1976 concentrates on the oil and gas resources, rates of extraction, and the significance of the sector to the government's budget. The implementation of development projects continued despite the drop in oil prices and the banking sector had performed better than the same sector in other countries. The Oman Development Bank had also become well established and the Sultan Qaboos University project was on target. Statistical data from 1976-82 are provided.

851 Oman diversifies.
Gulf States Newsletter, no. 291 (14 July 1986), p. 6-8.

A consideration of Oman's attempts in 1986 to cope with declining oil revenues. The 1986-90 Five-Year Development Plan had a growth target of only 4 per cent, state spending was cut by 10 per cent, the riyal devalued, and the emphasis placed on diversification from oil. However, new oil pipelines were also planned, as was an expansion of refining capacity. Plans were also announced to increase agricultural output and copper mining. An import table for 1984 is included.

852 Oman: dramatic improvement in economy provides opportunity to invest oil wealth in long-delayed major projects.
Business America, vol. 3, no. 14 (1980), p. 28-29.

An increase in oil production in 1980 was designed to earn at least $2.7 million in that year and to enable a number of new projects to be started to stimulate the economy. Government policy was to diversify away from oil by developing human and natural resources in the country and encouraging the private sector to invest in joint ventures. Mention is made of the copper-mining development, highways construction and fisheries.

853 Oman – How to diversify?
An-Nahar Arab Report and Memo, vol. 9, no. 23 (2 Aug. 1985), p. 4-7.

An examination of Oman's attempts to diversify its economy in 1985 in order to create a productive economy for the post-oil era. The economic climate at the time had been affected by the decline in oil prices which had resulted in the reduction of development projects and the raising of a 300m Eurodollar loan.

854 **Oman: planned growth pays off.**
Eight Days, vol. 3, no. 2 (17 Jan. 1981), p. 6-11.
A review of Oman's second Five-Year Development Plan, 1981-85, which forecast double the expenditure of the 1975-80 plan. Defence and security were scheduled to receive the bulk of the expenditure, with communications, electricity and water the priorities for the civil ministries.

855 **Oman: recent economic developments and prospects.**
Washington, DC: World Bank, Europe, Middle East and North Africa region, Country programme department 2, 1986. 65p. maps.
A report on recent economic development projects with the emphasis on production structure and government measures, and with special emphasis on the oil and gas sectors, mining, agriculture and non-petroleum manufacturing.

856 **Oman starts second decade of progress under Qaboos.**
Arab Economist, vol. 13, no. 136 (Jan. 1981), p. 22-24.
A report on the economic development of Oman as foreseen under the second Five-Year Development Plan, 1981-85. The plan provided for defence and security as priority areas.

857 **Oman: steady growth of economy.**
Petroleum Economist, vol. 49, no. 11 (1982), p. 451-52.
Interest in Oman seems to be more than is justified by its oil reserves, largely due to its strategic position on the southern side of the Strait of Hormuz. Oman has been profiting from the interest shown by the oil-importing countries by to using their aid and investment to develop the economy and safeguard its territory.

858 **Oman – Sultanate cuts wide strides towards development.**
Middle East News Economic Weekly, vol. 25, no. 52 (25 Dec. 1985).
The overview of Oman's development from 1969 onwards shows significant investment in agriculture, a major expansion in education, and greatly enhanced industrial development, with a rise in units from 10 to 2,300 and copper exports of 8,385 tons.

859 **Oman's five-year plan.**
Middle East Newsletter, no. 152 (15 Dec. 1980), p. 14-16.
A discussion of the 1981-85 Five-Year Development Plan, the prime objective of which was to secure economic diversification. Priority was to be given to infrastructure projects such as electricity and water services, roads, public utilities, housing and social welfare. In addition, education was to be expanded and the total budget was put at 20 million dollars over five years.

860   **Oman's second Five-Year Development Plan (1981-85).**
Middle East Economic Survey (Nicosia), vol. 25, no. 6 (23 Nov. 1981),
p. 1-11.
An overview of the second Five-Year Development Plan, considering the targets and
objectives, sources of funding, investment by sectors, and expenditure by ministries.
There are seven pages of statistics covering the period 1981-85.

861   **Oman's second five-year plan.**
Al-Tijari (Oman), (July 1981), p. 16-18.
A description of Oman's second Five-Year Development Plan, 1981-85, including a
statistical summary of the development budget of the civilian ministries. The
conservation of oil resources and the expansion of the fishing industry are accorded
priority status. Plans are laid out for the construction of a copper smelter by 1982,
with processing of 100 million tons by 1983.

862   **Oman today.**
Middle East News Economic Weekly, vol. 24, no. 47 (22 Nov. 1985),
p. 16-19.
A survey of Oman's economy in 1985 on the fifteenth anniversary of Sultan Qaboos'
reign. Oil production had been increased to 416,00 barrels per day, diversified
industries had been introduced and imports reduced by an increase in refining
capacity and the manufacture of cement. As a result of the Iraq–Iran war traffic in
Oman's ports rose, with a 900 per cent increase in the transhipment of goods between
1984 and 1985.

863   **Oman today.**
Middle East News Economic Weekly, vol. 24, no. 50 (13 Dec. 1985),
p. 18-21.
A review of developments in telecommunications, education, health and housing. A
new telecommunications centre had been opened at Muscat and a satellite link was
planned for the end of 1985. A state university, with medical faculty, was scheduled
for opening in 1986, and fifteen hospitals and nineteen health centres had been
established, with 35 mobile health teams to serve the rural areas. Housing provision
was to be increased by the building of six new satellite towns in the Muscat area.

864   **Privatise, diversify and 'Omanise'.**
The Middle East, no. 157 (Nov. 1987), p. 29-30.
An interview, held in November 1987, with the President of the Oman Chamber of
Commerce and Industry, Maqbul ibn ali Sultan. Government measures to encourage
private industry and diversification of the industrial base away from oil are discussed,
as is the need for the private sector within the Gulf Cooperation Council to cooperate.
Expatriate labour in Oman amounts to some 33 per cent of the workforce but
advances in education, particularly in technical areas, will benefit Omani
employment.

865 **Quarterly Economic Review of Bahrain, Qatar, Oman, the Yemens.**
London: Economist Intelligence Unit. (Quarterly with annual supplements).

A valuable guide to economic developments in Oman, beginning with general overviews of the region and followed by the country surveys. Information is brief but current, and the reviews are a useful source of statistical data.

866 **Problems and prospects of development in the Arabian Peninsula.**
Yusif A. Sayigh. *International Journal of Middle East Studies*, vol. 2, pt. 1 (1971), p. 40-58.

An important paper on development in the Arabian Peninsula. Although discussion of Oman forms only part of the paper, it is useful for comparative purposes. After a brief introduction, the article is divided into two main sections which consider problems (p. 41-52) and prospects (p. 53-58). The text is supported by excellent statistical tables.

867 **The second Five-Year Development Plan, 1981-1985.**
Muttrah, Oman: Sultanate of Oman Development Council, 1981. 286p.

Reviews the economic development of Oman under the first development plan and details the aims and objectives of the second plan. Details are provided of the source and usage of government revenues and the plans of all the ministries are described. Statistical data are provided for the period 1970-85.

868 **Aspects of economic dualism in Oman, 1830-1930.**
M. Speece. *International Journal of Middle East Studies*, vol. 21, no. 4 (1989), p. 495-515.

Describes the two different types of economic organization which had developed in Oman between 1830 and 1930. The coastal region had evolved a system of rent capitalism, with many of the absentee landlords being foreign merchants who controlled most of the coastal trade. In the interior, trade links with the coast were weak and the markets were not part of a wider market but functioned largely as centres for the local exchange of goods across ecological and political boundaries.

869 **Sultan Qaboos outlines Oman's development strategy.**
Middle East Economic Digest, vol. 29, no. 50 (14 Dec. 1985), p. 8-11.

An interview with Sultan Qaboos in December 1985 about the 1986-90 Five-Year Development Plan. Priority is to be given to education, health, road construction, electrification and water. Oil production was scheduled to be maintained at 500,000 barrels per day. Other topics discussed were: the abolition of the rural councils due to their ineffectiveness; the establishment of diplomatic relations with the USSR; and the Soviet presence in the People's Democratic Republic of Yemen.

870 **Sultanate of Oman business directory 1989/90.**
Ruwi, Oman: Apex Publishing, 1989. 9th ed. 336p.

A directory of companies in Oman, providing full identification details and data about key personnel and activities. The listing is both alphabetical and classified, and there is an index of products and services.

871 **The first Five-Year Development Plan, 1976-1980.**
Sultanate of Oman. Muscat Development Council. 1976. ix+130p.

The plan reviews the period from 1970 and details the aims and objectives for development for the period 1976-80. It also discusses resources, projects, policies and procedures, and investment by ministry and region. An essential document for a study of projected development in all sectors of the Oman economy.

872 **Country programme of Oman: UNDP assistance requested by the government of Oman for the period 1977-1981.**
United Nations. New York: United Nations Development Programme (UNDP) Governing Council, 1979. (Governing Council Jan. 1979 meetings DP/GC/OMA/R.2).

The case for funding development projects needed by Oman which cannot be wholly financed from oil revenues. The report was based on research work undertaken in various sectors of the economy and the infrastructure.

873 **The Middle East in the coming decade: from wellhead to well-being.**
John Waterbury, Ragaei El Mallakh. New York: McGraw Hill, 1978. 219p. bibliog.

This book was produced for the 1980s Project of the Council of Foreign Relations and aims at charting the course of economic and political development in the Middle East. References to Oman are largely contained in the first half of the book which considers 'The Middle East and the New World Economic Order', dealing largely with the effects on the economy of oil revenues, and the labour market with its reliance on expatriate labour. Coverage is also given to the Dhofar War, relations with Iran and Saudi Arabia, and Oman as part of a sub-region of the Gulf consisting of the oil-producing nations.

874 **Oman.**
J. Whelan, A. Brown, J. Wallace. *Middle East Economic Digest Special Report* (18 Nov. 1980), 37p.

An interview with Sultan Qaboos on the economic development of Oman in relation to the second Five-Year Development Plan. In addition to the objectives of the plan the interview covers the priority areas of Dhofar and the Musandam Peninsula, the culture of Oman, contract law, female employment, and relations with the United States.

875 **Oman: a MEED practical guide.**
Edited by J. Whelan. London: Croom Helm for *Middle East Economic Digest*, 1984. 2nd ed. 248p. maps.

This guide to the legal and practical aspects of doing business in Oman provides information on all of the various sectors of the economy. Information is also given on the financial and taxation regulations, customs and duties, visas, hotels, etc. Designed for the business person with little knowledge of Oman.

876   **Oman: self help is the order of the day.**
John Whelan.   *Middle East Economic Digest*, vol. 25, no. 25 (19 June 1981), p. 26-27.

A review of Oman's second Five-Year Development Plan (1981-85). The main feature of the plan is a self-help policy designed to improve industry and the expansion of the private sector. Total expenditure under the plan is forecast as 21,319 million dollars, depending upon oil revenues.

Development

877 **The impact of oil revenues on Arab Gulf Development.**
M.S. El Azhary. London: Croom Helm; Boulder, Colorado:
Westview Press, 1984. 203p.

The proceedings of a symposium held at the University of Exeter in October 1982
that examines the oil economies of the Arabian Gulf states that are heavily dependent
upon large oil reserves and virtually no other natural resources. Areas covered include
agriculture, industry, banking, population and manpower. Oman is considered as part
of this general study.

878 **Ancient Oman is transformed.**
Howard Bowen-Jones. *Geographical Magazine*, vol. 102, no. 4
(1980), p. 286-93. map.

The article begins with a brief historical and geographical introduction to factors
which have affected the social, economic and political development of the Sultanate.
The bulk of the article deals with developments since 1970 in the fields of agriculture,
education, oil, minerals, and transport and communications. It is stressed that the
creation of a modern state is not being pursued at the expense of the ancient cultural
identity of the Sultanate.

879 **Development planning in Oman.**
Howard Bowen-Jones. *Arab Gulf Journal*, vol. 2, no. 1 (1982),
p. 73-79.

This article considers the first two Five-Year Development Plans which cover the
periods 1976-80 and 1981-86. The author concludes that Oman had been fortunate in
that revenues had increased more rapidly than expected, thus sustaining development.
However, dependence on hydrocarbon resources remained and a broad-based,
self-sustaining economy was essential for the future.

880   **Oman: doors open to foreign tourists.**
Alison Brown.   *Middle East Economic Digest Special Report* (Nov. 1983), p. 8-10.

An examination of tourism in November 1983 which had not been possible before the February of that year as the country was closed to foreign tourists. However, tourism in unlikely to be a major revenue earner for two reasons: the inhospitable climate, and the dislike of foreign tourists by the religious community. Although money has been spent on developing hotels and other amenities for tourists not enough has been spent on restoring antiquities.

881   **Oman: traditional and modern adaptations to the environment.**
Christine Drake.   *Focus* (New York), vol. 38 (Summer 1988),
p. 15-20. map.

A consideration of the development policies of the Omani government. These had transformed the country since 1970, but in a sensitive manner with due regard to its history and cultural heritage. Oman was selective about the outside influences that were accepted and tourism was strictly controlled and not actively promoted.

882   **Interdependence, independence and rural development in Oman: the experience of the Khabura Development Project.**
R. Dutton.   *Journal of Oman Studies*, vol. 6, no. 2 (1983), p. 317-27.

This article provides the background to the rural communities in Oman before the discovery of oil, and reviews the interdependence necessary in such communities for them to survive. The effects of oil wealth have had a profound effect on rural Oman, primarily because it was a source of cheap and plentiful labour. The dangers were recognized by the government and, with the aid of Petroleum Development (Oman) Ltd, a research project was set up by Durham University to investigate a typical area of northern Oman. The team was asked to recommend ways in which rural resources could be developed to promote greater self-reliance and economic independence through improved productivity. The study examined a cross-section of northern Oman from al-Khabura on the Batinah coast over the mountains to Ibri and the al-Zahira. The survey revealed that the indigenous rural communities were in disarray and that there was a need for rural community development in Oman. The government asked Durham University to undertake a pilot project in the village of al-Khabura, dealing with the small-farm livestock system, water resources, honey production, and extension work based on the development of independent skills to further the community.

883   **Gulf region.**
K. Emonts.   *Geschaftsreise*, vol. 22, nos. 13-14 (1984), p. 7-11.

A series of articles on tourism in the Middle East covering transportation, communications, hotels, and general conditions for foreigners. Oman is considered to have declined as an important business tourism destination at the time of the oil boom to a situation where the supply of tourist infrastructure far exceeds demand.

884   **A crack in the wall.**
Don Graff.   *Travel Holiday*, vol. 171 (March 1989), p. 77-81.
In 1989 Oman had begun to take the first steps towards tourism after years of isolation – it was only following the coup in 1970 that modern facilities were built which would support a tourist industry. Oman is conscious of its historical heritage and is pursuing a policy of development, but tailored to a programme of conservation. The embryonic tourist industry aimed at attracting people with an interest in culture and history, and was to be carefully controlled to avoid overdevelopment.

885   **Development potential and policies in the South Arabian ountries: Yemen Arab Republic, People's Democratic Republic of Yemen, Sultanate of Oman.**
Michael Hoffman.   Berlin: German Development Institute, 1982.
152p. maps.
Oman is dealt with between pages 69 and 86, and after a survey and consideration of the government the work deals with: the macroeconomic trends; the infrastructure; and sectoral developments in agriculture and fisheries, oil and mining. The study concludes with a consideration of the question of foreign aid.

886   **Oman: the past, the present and the potential of the development of the country.**
S. A. Ibragim.   *Geografiya*, vol. 2, no. 1 (1988), p. 72-77.
Considers the potential for development in Oman and diversification from oil in the areas of agriculture and copper mining. However, major problems are identified in the training of nationals for the Omani labour market and the need to introduce democracy into Omani society.

887   **Arab resources: The transformation of a society.**
Edited by Ibrahim Ibrahim.   Washington, DC: Georgetown University Center for Contemporary Arab Studies; London: Croom Helm, 1983.
304p. maps.
This work considers development in the Arab world in relation to the imbalance between human and natural resources. A range of factors affecting development are considered, as are the sectoral resources, the development infrastructure, and the range of problems faced by the Arab countries with their development programmes and the transformation of Arab society. Contributions of direct relevance to Oman are separately listed and annotated in the relevant sections.

888   **Reducing dependence through investment in human capital: an assessment of Oman's development strategy.**
R. E. Looney.   *Socio-economic Planning Sciences*, vol. 24, no. 1 (1990), p. 65-75.
An assessment of post-1970 efforts at developing human capital in Oman, together with a consideration of the factors likely to impede such progress. The main finding of the study is that impressive gains have been made in education but that these may be threatened by the continuing priority given to defence expenditure, and the

military's competition for non-financial resources might slow down job creation in other sectors, to the extent that the demand for education is reduced.

889 Economic requirements for development, Oman.
Ragaei El Mallakh. *Middle East Journal*, vol. 26, no. 4 (1972), p. 415-27.

Examines the factors necessary for economic development, both qualitative and quantitative. The oil-based economy receives much attention, as do the early stages of progress in education and social welfare. The position of agriculture and the need to increase production are also considered, as is the need for a phased programme of industrial diversification and a skilled indigenous labour force to carry it out.

890 Interior Oman.
Alexander Melamid. *Geographical Review*, vol. 76, no. 3 (1986), p. 317-21.

The interior of Oman had been independent but was incorporated into the rest of the Sultanate by 1956. Melamid describes the distribution of oil revenues in the area which raised the standard of living of the estimated population of 200,000. The changing lifestyles of the interior are examined, including the nomadic population, as are specific government projects, including the copper mine and smelter which has had only a minimal impact.

891 Oman: overcoming the obstacles to development.
Jennifer Robb. *Middle East Economic Digest Special Report* (Nov. 1983), p. 18-21.

An examination – carried out in 1983 – of Oman's regional development policy in the Musandam Peninsula where the majority of the population are involved in fishing. The various development projects include electrification, water desalination, construction of a fishing harbour and improved road communications.

892 Aviation in the Arabian Gulf.
P. Sheppard. *Travel and Tourist Analyst*, no. 4 (1991), p. 5-19.

The Gulf States have been a traditional refuelling stop for airliners flying to the Far East but new long-range aircraft could endanger this business. The article discusses the strategies being pursued to promote the region, the airport facilities, and the hospitality infrastructure. The business prospects for the region and tourism development strategies are also examined. Oman and the Yemen are considered as long-term tourism prospects, but stability needs to be restored to the region before such development can become effective.

893 The need for rural development in the southern sub-region of the Arabian Peninsula.
Abdel Aziz El Sherbini. *Dirasast Natural Sciences*, vol. 7, no. 1 (1980), p. 65-74.

Examines the options for development amongst the rural areas in Oman and the two Yemens. The author considers what needs to be achieved in the areas of health, education and the rural infrastructure. Oman is considered to be advantaged because of its oil-based economy. Characteristics of the rural poor are detailed though it is pointed out that data were difficult to gather.

894 Oman.

Ian Skeet. *Geopolitics of Energy*, vol. 13, no. 7 (1991), p. 1-4.

An examination of the problems and prospects for development measured against the 1991-95 Five-Year Plan and Oman's dependence upon oil revenues and therefore the international price of oil. Oman is also dependent upon expatriate labour for the provision of services at all levels but, at the same time, faces problems of providing employment for an increasingly educated population. The financial problems faced are the high costs of maintaining the infrastructure and social services provision – while still devoting 36 per cent of total expenditure to defence – and the instability of oil prices and production levels. Skeet also considers the strategic position of Oman and the after-effects of the Gulf War, relations with Saudi Arabia, and problems of democracy.

895 Development in Oman 1970-1974.

Sultanate of Oman. Muscat: Ministry of Development, National Statistical Department, 1975. [n.p.].

A survey of development in the first few years of the reign of Sultan Qaboos in all areas of government activity,. A large amount of statistical data is included.

896 Oman's development strategy.

John Whelan. In: *Oman: economic, social and strategic development*, edited by B. R. Pridham. London: Croom Helm, 1987, p. 134-44.

This contribution examines Oman's development strategy. It had begun slowly prior to the 1970 coup, but had accelerated afterwards, such that by 1975 a budgetary crisis arose which was solved only by the creation of a Supreme Development Council chaired by the Sultan. The country's oil revenues are the mainstay of the development strategy and proven reserves will guarantee production well into the next century. Neverthless, exploration still continues, especially in Dhofar. Measures to diversify the economy are also considered since oil revenues accounted for 86 per cent of the budget, but some success had been achieved in exports of food and livestock, copper and fish. Traditional exports of dates, fruit and vegetables were also on the increase. Development is constrained by the lack of skilled Omani manpower and, at the time of writing, Omanis accounted for only 35 per cent of the workforce. Finally, consideration is given to the role of the private sector; it is favoured by the government as a vehicle for economic development and the government has therefore been active in its support for private ventures. Increased liberalism has also come to the market through entrance on to the international scene and membership of the Gulf Cooperation Council.

897 Oman stands up to be counted.

Jeannie Yamine. *An-Nahar Arab Report and Memo*, vol. 10, no. 29 (1985), p. 4-5.

A review of Oman's development which has led it to become a viable force in the Arab world. The government has successfully developed oil production and copper mining and evolved an infrastructure for economic development projects and essential services.

Finance and Banking

898 Annual Report of the Central Bank of Oman.
Muscat: Central Bank of Oman, 1978- . annual.
The report of the bank's activities, a survey of the economy and statistical data, in
Arabic and English.

899 Another lean year forecast for Oman.
Gulf States Newsletter, no. 329 (25 Jan. 1988), p. 11-13.
A report on the 1988 budget and economic policies designed to reduce the budget
deficit. Austerity measures were designed to achieve a balanced budget for 1988.
However, one-third of the budget was still earmarked for defence.

**900 Arabian currency arrangements seen evolving in the context of
rapid change.**
Michael E. Edo. *International Monetary Fund Survey*, vol. 3, no. 23
(9 Dec. 1974), p. 374-77.
Edo considers the development of currency and financial arrangements in the Arabian
Peninsula, including Oman, and discusses the establishment of the currency boards
and central monetary institutions, which did not happen in Oman until 1970. The
Muscat Currency Authority was established in 1970, and replaced in 1972 by the
Currency Board. Unlike some of the other currency boards in the area, Oman's was
given a limited role in the licensing of commercial banks.

**901 An analytical study of payments of the G.C.C. countries,
1970-1983.**
F. I. Al-Habib, M. M. Metwally. *Asian Profile* (Hong Kong), vol. 14,
no. 1 (1986), p. 61-72.
An analysis of the balance of payments and other economic factors in the Gulf
Cooperation Council, including Oman, during the years 1970-83 in which oil prices

increased and declined, and discussing the effects of these fluctuations. The article also suggests that further cooperation is needed between the member states and that controls may have to be introduced.

902   **Oman's new bankruptcy code – Part 1: Application, supervision, commercial firms.**
J. Alasdair Jeffrey. *Middle East Executive Reports*, vol. 13, no. 12 (Dec. 1990), p. 14-16.

A description of the bankruptcy code included as part of the country's new law of commerce and the procedures to be followed. In essence, any commercial company can be declared bankrupt if its financial affairs are in disorder and it ceases to pay its debts. This does not apply to joint venture firms.

903   **Lending – World Bank to Arab countries.**
Syrie et Monde Arabe, vol. 34, no. 408 (Feb. 1988), p. 21-25.

A report on World Bank lending to Arab countries in the 1987 financial year, which, with the International Development Agency, amounted to 10 per cent of the world commitments. Oman received 18 World Bank loans, totalling 1,511 million dollars.

904   **Income tax in Oman.**
David Mosey. *Financial Law Review*, vol. 9, no. 2 (1990), p. 35-36.

Income tax was introduced in September 1980 for wholly Omani-owned local companies and other business establishments. The new law has eliminated the double taxation of profits experienced by contractual joint ventures.

905   **Muscat stock market coming soon.**
Middle East Executive Reports, vol. 11, no. 9 (1988), p. 20-21.

A report on progress towards establishing the Muscat Stock Exchange following the Royal Decree no. 53 of 1988. Initially stocks traded will be Omani, but Gulf Cooperation Council and foreign stocks may be introduced at a later stage.

906   **Oman: State master budget for 1985.**
Middle East Newsletter, vol. 10, no. 261 (6 May 1985), p. 12-14.

A report on Oman's budget for 1985/86. It totalled 1,919 million Omani riyals, of which 717 million was allocated to defence and security. Increased allocations were also given to education, communications, electricity and water.

907   **Oman: the budget is cut. Now what?**
Middle East Executive Reporter, vol. 11, no. 2 (1988), p. 11-13.

A review of Oman's budget for 1988 with a projected expenditure of 4.2 billion dollars and revenue of 3.5 billion dollars. Defence and security were scheduled to receive the bulk of the expenditure, having been allocated 1.4 billion dollars. Major development projects were in the areas of power generation and water supplies.

908 **Omani banks find favour.**
John Wilson. *Banker*, vol. 135, no. 718 (1988), p. 111-12.
A review of the Omani banking system which was mainly concerned with domestic finance and rarely participated in international loan syndications. The article reviews the banks' various assets and loans, the latter pegged to 85 per cent of a bank's assets.

Prospects for the world oil industry.
See item no. 938.

Dissertations

909 **Monetary and financial integration of the Gulf Cooperation Council (GCC) for the Arab States of the Gulf.**
Abdulrahman Abdulmohesen Al Kalaf. PhD thesis, University of Kentucky, 1991. 231p. (Available from University Microfilms, Ann Arbor, Michigan, order no. AAD91-22833)
This study evaluates the feasibility of establishing a currency area amongst the GCC states; four theories are discussed. The author argues that some form of monetary arrangement should be supported but that it must be preceded and supported by fiscal, monetary and regulatory co-ordination.

910 **Financial policy in a small open oil-exporting developing country: The case of Oman.**
Mohamed Abdulaziz Kalmoor. PhD thesis, University of Colorado at Boulder, 1988. 231p. (Available from University Microfilms, Ann Arbor, Michigan, order no. AAD89-12198).
A study of the role of financial policy in small open oil-exporting countries, using Oman as a case-study. The study focuses on interests rates, inflationary financing and the question of the optimal exchange rate peg.

Trade

911 **An assessment of the trade and restructuring effects of the Gulf Cooperation Council.**
Michael Cain, Kais Al-Badri. *International Journal of Middle East Studies*, vol. 21, no. 1 (1989), p. 57-69.
Examines the finance, economy and trade amongst the countries of the Gulf Cooperation Council, including Oman. Amongst topics covered are: income structures and gains in gross domestic product; output; structure of trade within the GCC; imports; and exports. There are supporting tables and projections to the year 2000.

912 **Marketing in Oman.**
Claude Clement. Washington, DC: United States Department of Commerce, International Trade Administration, 1988. 48p.
This survey of marketing prospects in Oman covers transportation, trade regulations, employment, taxation, investment regulations, and guidance for the business traveller.

913 **Arab trade with Indonesia and the Malay Peninsula from the 8th to the 16th century.**
R. R. Di Meglio. In: *Islam and the trade of Asia*, edited by D. S. Richards. Oxford: Bruno Cassirer, 1970, p. 105-36.
This examination of early Arab contacts with the Far East during the period in question. These were based largely on the Persian Gulf ports and Oman. Sohar was a significant contributor to this trade which also led to links with China.

914 **The China trade.**
Nancy Jenkins. *Aramco World Magazine*, vol. 26, no. 4 (July-Aug. 1975), p. 24-31.
Includes a consideration of the dhow trade of Oman and Basra with China at least 500 years before the voyage of Marco Polo.

915 **The ocean-going dhow trade to East Africa.**
D. N. McMaster. *East African Geographical Review*, vol. 4, no. 1 (1966), p. 13-26.
A study of the historical dhow trade to East Africa from Oman which was of great economic significance until the middle of the nineteenth century. The trade with East Africa mainly consisted of dried fish, salt, foodstuffs, carpets, henna and earthenware pots, until the growth of the slave trade assumed dominance in the economy of Zanzibar and the coastal regions of East Africa.

916 **Cargoes of the East: the ports, trade and culture of the Arabian Seas and western Indian Ocean.**
Esmond Bradley Martin, Chryssee Perry Martin.　London: Elm Tree Books, 1978. 24p.
An essential work on the dhow trade of the Middle East and, in particular, Oman. It is beautifully illustrated, extremely readable and highly informative. It is of great value for the study of early trade patterns with East Africa and India, the slave and spice trades, the Omani presence in East Africa and wars with the Portuguese. The book also contains a great deal on the traditions and cultures of the sailors and merchants, and on the construction of their ships.

917 **Muscat Trade Report.**
Simla, India: Government of India Press. annual.
The official trade report with statistics of activity. It was issued by the Indian Political Agent in Muscat until 1947 when India ceased to be responsible for the affairs of the area.

918 **Commercial relations of India with Arabia.**
S. S. Nadvi. *Islamic Culture*, vol. 7 (1933), p. 281-308.
Wider in coverage than Oman, but that country receives considerable attention because of its long-standing trade with the Indian sub-continent.

919 **The Persian Gulf trade reports 1905-1940.**
Farnham Common, England: Archive Research, 1987. 4000p. 8 vols.
This collection covers the whole of the Persian Gulf, including Oman, providing narrative reviews of each year's events covering banking, customs, pearl fishing, fishing and general trade. It includes tabular shipping returns and export and import tables listing commodities, quantities, values, and countries of origin and destination.

920 **Oman: new bilateral agreements to aid business prospects.**
Karl S. Reiner. Washington, DC: United States Department of
Commerce, Overseas Business Reports, 1980. 9p.

A report issued in September 1980 on the prospects for American exporters in Oman.
Opportunities are identified in the areas of foodstuffs, air conditioners,
telecommunication equipment, cars and computing equipment. In 1979 United States
exports to Oman totalled 88 million dollars.

921 **Marketing in Oman.**
Mark Roth. Washington, DC: US Department of Commerce,
International Trade Administration, 1981. 35p.

A report covering economic trends in Oman in the 1980s and providing information
on commerce, banking, transportation, trade regulations, foreign investment and
customs regulations. Roth points out that specialization in trade is not common in the
private sector as most firms combine the functions of importer, wholesaler and
distributor. Information is also provided on Oman's legal system.

922 **The role of Eastern Arabia in the third and second millennium
Arabian Gulf trade.**
M. Speece. *Paper presented at the Second International Symposium
on Studies in the History of Arabia–pre-Islamic Arabia*, University of
Riyadh, Saudi Arabia, 1979. 15p.

An examination of the role of eastern Arabia in the international trade network since
prehistoric times. Oman was able to develop subsistence agriculture but could supply
only raw materials to the network.

923 **Steady demand for agricultural inputs in the Gulf States.**
Middle East News Economic Weekly, vol. 26, no. 3 (16 Jan. 1987),
p. 16-22.

An examination of agricultural inputs in the Gulf States, including Oman, which
showed that agrochemical imports to the Gulf States had increased steadily to 40
million dollars in 1985, with agricultural chemical imports reaching 10 million
dollars. This clearly demonstrated that there was an emphasis on agricultural
expansion.

924 **Gulf trade and finance: Trade and market prospects.**
Rodney Wilson. London: Graham & Trotman, 1987. 125p. maps.

A general survey of Gulf trade at that time which includes a country-by-country
survey of economic performance from 1970. The work has extensive computer-
generated charts of statistical data and economic forecasts.

**The formation of the Omani trading empire under the Ya'aribah
dynasty (1624-1719).**
See item no. 391.

Oil

General

925 **Annual report to His Majesty, the Sultan of Oman.**
Minas al-Fahal: Petroleum Development (Oman) Ltd, 1968- .

The report of the operating company in Oman, covering all aspects of its activities, with a large statistical and financial section. In each report over the years, the company has also recorded various changes in control, which now rests with the government, with PD(O) as an operator.

926 **The petroleum geology and resources of the Middle East.**
Z. R. Beydoun, H. V. Dunnington. Beaconsfield, England: Scientific Press, 1975. 99p. maps. bibliog.

Deals with geology in general terms, before considering the conditions specifically related to oil-bearing strata. The second part of the study discusses petroleum reserves in a global context and then goes on to examine the region specifically. The areas of Oman considered are Dhofar, Gulf of Oman, Strait of Hormuz to the southern Gulf, interior Oman and the eastern Rub' al-Khali.

927 **Oman: prospects good for export refinery.**
Alison Brown. *Middle East Economic Digest Special Report* (Nov. 1983), p. 27-31.

A report on Oman's oil and gas resources in 1983 which indicated that Oman could produce 400,000 barrels per day into the 21st century. Increases in production, however, would be dependent on upgrading the pipelines to the refinery. Details are given of the production of oil and gas by Petroleum Development (Oman) and Elf Aquitaine.

928 Oman: moving towards the major league.
J. Cranfield. *Petroleum Economist*, vol. 54, no. 3 (1987), p. 961-63.
Oman's oil production had risen from 284,000 barrels per day (b/d) in 1980 to 550,000 b/d in 1986. Petroleum Development (Oman) announced that eight new oilfields were due to come on stream in 1987. Associated natural gas had been rapidly developed to meet the needs of local industry, with planned production due to rise to 600 million cubic feet per day by 1990.

929 Proterozoic salt basins of the Persian Gulf area and their role in hydrocarbon generation.
H. S. Edgell. *Precambrian Research*, vol. 54, no. 1 (1981), p. 1-14.
The role of Proterozoic sediments as source rocks for oil in the Arabian Peninsula has assumed an importance not previously realized. This paper demonstrates their importance to the origins of oil in Eastern Arabia and, in particular, Oman.

930 The decline of Arab oil revenues.
Edited by Abdel Majid Farid, Hussein Sirriyeh. London: Croom Helm, 1986. 200p.
A survey of the effects on the Arab economies of the decline in oil revenue following the decline in oil prices since 1981. The contributors also review how lower oil revenues have affected Arab countries and the oil industry in general. Oman is dealt with at various points throughout the text, and in the context of the Gulf Cooperation Council and its significance to the region.

931 Oman oil finds bring winds of change.
Ann Fyfe. *The Middle East*, no. 52 (Feb. 1979), p. 78-80.
A consideration of the oil finds in Dhofar, originally thought to have been a compensation for the decline in northern output. Subsequent investigation shows that the output will mean a real increase in oil production and revenues will be maintained.

932 Higher Omani oil output is hedge against Gulf closure.
An-Nahar Arab Report and Memo, vol. 8, no. 4 (23 Jan. 1984), p. 16-17.
A report on Oman's crude oil production which had increased to 400,000 barrels per day during 1983. Oman sells 60 per cent of its crude oil to Japan and its export terminals are south of the critical area of the Strait of Hormuz. The possibility of a second oil refinery and a Gulf Cooperation Council pipeline terminating in Oman are also discussed.

933 Oil in Oman – A short historical note.
Francis Hughes. In: *Oman: economic, social and strategic developments*, edited by B. R. Pridham. London: Croom Helm, 1987, p. 168-76. map.
A brief survey of the development of Oman's oil industry which was first discovered at Fahud in north Oman in the 1950s but exports did not begin until 1967. The survey considers exploration and production, the pipeline system, refining and the associated

natural gas pipeline. Hughes also provides a survey of historical events in the oil industry and tables of production. He concludes that the key to the future is continuing exploration and investment in techniques of enhanced oil recovery.

934 **Oman's crude oil production capacity to be stepped up to over 700,000 B/D in 1987.**
Elizabeth Legros. *Arab Oil and Gas*, vol. 16, no. 374 (16 April 1987), p. 31-36.

A review of Oman's oil production which was expected to rise from 489,000 barrels per day in 1985 to 710,000 b/d by mid-1987. Exploration was still continuing, and ten new small fields had been brought on stream at the end of 1985. About 90 per cent of production is exported from the terminal at Mina al-Fahal.

935 **The oil industry in the Middle East.**
Keith McLachlan. In: *Change and development in the Middle East*, edited by John I. Clarke, Howard Bowen-Jones. London: Methuen, 1981, p. 95-112. map.

This contribution examines the oil industry in the Middle East, in particular Iran, Iraq, Saudi Arabia and the Gulf States, including Oman. The author considers the evolution of the industry, the location of resources in terms of geology and the effects and impact of the oil industry. Amongst other topics are: the industry's effects on development; reserves and production levels; exports; and new developments and ownership of the industry. Despite national control of oil operations there is still reliance on the international oil industry for oilfield expertise, transfer of crude and refined oil, and export operations.

936 **Energy watchers: – Shadow OPEC: New element for stability and a 'reintegrated' oil industry: implications for supply, marketing, pricing and investment.**
Edited by Dorothea El Mallakh. Boulder, Colorado: International Research Center for Energy and Economic Development, 1990. 122p.

A consideration of the non-OPEC (Organization of Petroleum Exporting Countries) oil producers and their role in the international oil industry which is seen as a possible stabilizing influence. Their role in guaranteeing continuity of supply, marketing, pricing policies and the effects on the OPEC cartel are discussed. Oman's role is considered in the OPEC/non-OPEC cooperation.

937 **Power play, oil in the Middle East.**
Leonard Mosley. New York: Random House, 1973. 457p.

The work deals generally with oil in the Middle East, its political implications, and the role of the oil companies as multinational influences. Mosley also considers the Buraimi Oasis dispute, the Oman coup of 1970, and the work of early oil developers in Oman.

938 **Prospects for the world oil industry.**
Edited by Tim Niblock, Richard Lawless.   London; Dover, New
Hampshire: Croom Helm, 1985. 160p.

The proceedings of a *Symposium on the Energy Economy* held at the University of
Durham on 9-10 May 1984. Topics of interest are 'Industrialization in the Arab States
of the Gulf' and 'Income Illusion of Petroleum Exports: The case of the Arab Gulf
Cooperation Council Members'.

939 **Oman trying to become OPEC's 14th member.**
Mideast Markets, vol. 14, no. 6 (1987), p. 9-11.

Oman is not a member of the Organization of Petroleum Exporting Countries (OPEC)
and has always followed an independent pricing policy which has sometimes brought
it into conflict with OPEC. Production had risen to 620,000 barrels per day by August
1986 and reserves at that time were estimated at 4.032 billion barrels whilst gas
reserves were estimated at 7.5 billion cubic feet. Development was being
concentrated on finding more fields and in proving reserves. A table shows production
levels from 1980 to 1986.

940 **Oman's crude oil production capacity to be stepped up to over
700,000 B/D in 1987.**
Middle East News Economic Weekly, vol. 16, no. 374 (1987), p. 31-36.

An assessment of Oman's oil production capacity, with ten new small fields raising
capacity to 489,000 B/D in 1985. It was anticipated that this would increase to
710,000 by mid-1987. Over 80 per cent of the output would be exported through the
terminal at Mina al-Fahal. Further exploration was still under way and several
discoveries had been made between 1985 and 1986.

941 **Oman: the emergence of a new oil era.**
Jan Seymour.   *Middle East Economic Review*, vol. 11, no. 43
(23 Aug. 1968), p. 1-32.

Discusses the impact of the oil finds on the economy of Oman and the prospects for
development, although this development was not to materialize in real terms until
1970.

942 **Oil production outside the Gulf 1981-1986.**
A. E. Sieminski.   *Geopolitics of Energy*, vol. 13, no. 7 (1991),
p. 4-10.

The article provides data on the oil production levels of the non-OPEC countries,
non-Gulf OPEC production, and Gulf OPEC production. Information is provided on
the oil-related developments of the non-OPEC producers, including Oman, with
figures for levels from 1988 to an estimated figure for 1996 on a tabular basis.

943 **Development of the Fahud field.**
R. H. Tschopp. In: *Proceedings of the Seventh World Petroleum Congress*, Mexico, 1967. Barking, England: Elsevier, 1967, vol. 2, p. 243-50.
An account of the discovery and development of the Fahud field, the first to be brought on stream by Petroleum Development (Oman) Ltd.

944 **European interests and Gulf oil.**
Valerie Yorke, Louis Turner. London: Gower for Royal Institute of International Affairs, 1986. 125p. bibliog.
A study of European interest in Gulf oil as a crucial element in international relations despite the relative reduction in dependence on oil imports following 1980 and the decline in oil prices. Oman is dealt with in the sections covering 'The Economic Environment of the Gulf' and 'The Political Environment of the Gulf' within the auspices of the Gulf Cooperation Council.

Exploration, developments and concessions

945 **Arabian Gulf oil concessions 1911-1953.**
Farnham Common, England: Archive Research, 1989. 7000p. 12 vols.
Provides a documentary record of negotiations between Gulf rulers, the oil companies and the British government over oil concessions in the region. It includes the texts of the first land-based oil concession agreements for Oman, the United Arab Emirates, Kuwait and Bahrain.

946 **The evolution of oil concessions in the Middle East and North Africa.**
Henry Cattan. London; Dobbs Ferry, New York: Oceana Publications, 1967. 173p. maps.
The standard work on this very complex area, and invaluable for an understanding of the subject, both generally and in relation to Oman.

947 **Stratigraphy and rock unit nomenclature in the oil-producing area of interior Oman.**
M. W. Hughes Clarke. *Journal of Petroleum Geology*, vol. 11, no. 1 (1988), p. 5-60.
A description of the various sedimentary rock sequences in the oilfield areas of interior Oman, together with major gaps which punctuate a subdivision into 11 major rock units with 7 impermeable sealing units. Commercial hydrocarbon accumulations

are retained by these seals, but in southern Oman reservoirs are commonly in units that are much older than the seals which overlie them.

948 **Middle East oil money and its future expenditure.**
Nicholas Fallon. London: Graham & Trotman, 1975; New York: International Publications Service, 1976. 240p. maps. bibliog.

Begins by discussing the oil crisis of 1973-74 and its effects on oil prices and politics, projecting these developments into the 1980s. The author examines the major development and expenditure sectors, and highlights prospects and problems such as the lack of a middle-management resource. A country survey of development plans is also given, and Oman is covered on pages 172-74.

949 **Origin of crude oils in Oman.**
P. Grantham (et al.). *Journal of Petroleum Geology*, vol. 11, no. 1 (1988), p. 61-80.

A review of the geological history of Oman and a placing of petroleum geochemistry within the geological context. The oils found in Oman are classified into five groups and related to the geology of the area. A petrochemical description of each of the oils is provided.

950 **The history of Oman's Fahud Geodetic Datum.**
M. H. B. Jenson. *Land and Minerals Surveying*, vol. 3, no. 10 (1985), p. 520-22, 524-33.

Examines the background of the Fahud Geodetic Datum in Oman, ranging from its origins with the operations of Petroleum Development (Oman) between 1950 and 1960 and by Shell from 1960. The basis of most survey work in Oman is based on the Fahud Datum.

951 **Oil bearing sediments of Gondwana glaciation in Oman.**
B. K. Levell (et al.). *American Association of Petroleum Geologists Bulletin*, vol. 72, no. 7 (1988), p. 775-96.

Significant deposits of oil have been found in the Al Khlata formation of the Permian–Carboniferous lower Haushi Group in south Oman. At least three glacial phases can be recognized from examination of the log data from some 500 wells with shales; variable laminations and dropstones and tillites are all diagnostic of glacial deposits.

952 **The oil companies and the Arab World.**
Giacoma Luciani. London: Croom Helm, 1984. 197p.

An examination of the relationship between the various oil companies and the Arab world. Amongst topics dealt with are: the disintegration of the international oil industry; the policy of producing countries with regard to relations with the oil industry; and the global strategies of the international oil companies and their attitude towards the Arab countries. Oman is dealt with at relevant points throughout the text and in the numerous statistical tables.

953 **New oil from Arabia.**
Alexander Melamid. *Geographical Review*, vol. 78, no. 1 (1988),
p. 76-79.

Provides details of new discoveries and production plans on the Arabian Peninsula,
particularly in North Yemen and Oman. Neither country is a member of OPEC but as
a result of close relations with Saudi Arabia they may conform to OPEC policies.
Future problems could arise if attempts are made by OPEC to curtail new sources of
production.

954 **Oil activities are still expanding in Oman but revenues are down
to 2.9 billion dollars.**
Arab Oil and Gas, vol. 13, no. 304 (16 May 1984), p. 27-31.

Oil revenues accounted for 90 per cent of Oman's revenues which in 1983 totalled 2.9
billion dollars. Oil reserves had an anticipated life of twenty years at 1983 production
levels. Gas reserves are also significant and development was under way in 1984 to
exploit the resources more fully. A brief outline is given of the 1981-85 development
plan and a table of oil production statistics, exports and revenues from 1968 to 1983
is provided.

955 **Oman today: oil and gas.**
Middle East News Economic Weekly, vol. 24, no. 48 (29 Nov. 1985),
p. 13-17.

Omani production at the end of 1984 had risen to 416,000 barrels per day, increased
from 1983 to counter falling oil prices. The production policy was to pump only
enough oil to finance development and oil reserves had been raised to 4 billion barrels
by the discovery of new fields. An exploration programme had been launched to find
new sources of natural gas to meet the needs of the domestic, industrial and public
utilities sectors.

956 **The preliminary oil concessions in Trucial Oman 1922-1939.**
Rosemarie J. Said. *International Interactions*, vol. 3, no. 2 (1977),
p. 113-34.

A reconstruction of the history of oil concessions in Trucial Oman from 1922 to 1939
and the policies pursued by the British government to ensure that the concessions
were given to companies selected by the British government, all achieved without the
use of force or at any cost to the Treasury. The author discusses the negotiation
towards concessions and the subtle pressures used by Britain to enhance British
interests and to exclude American oil companies from the region.

957 **Three firms acquire Omani concession in Persian Gulf.**
Oil Gas Journal, vol. 83, no. 11 (1985), p. 59.

An announcement relating to concessions granted by Oman in the Persian Gulf in an
area of 159,000 acres off the Musandam Peninsula. The three companies are North
South Resources Ltd, International Petroleum Ltd, and Peninsula Petroleum
Corporation.

Burial and thermal history of Proterozoic source rocks in Oman.
See item no. 180.

Dissertation

958 **Viability of industrial integration within the Gulf Cooperation
Council: The case of petrochemical industries (Middle East).**
Mohammed Salem Al-Sabban.   PhD thesis, University of Colorado at
Boulder, 1983. 288p. (Available from University Microfilms, Ann
Arbor, Michigan, order no. AAD83-17636).

The formation of the Gulf Cooperation Council in 1981 was a major step towards the
comprehensive economic development of the region but diversification from oil is
seen as difficult due to a lack of natural resources. The situation with regard to
petrochemical industries is seen as different because of the availability of cheap
energy supplies, and plans were in hand for joint petrochemical production and
marketing.

Minerals and Mining

959   **Farming communities of the Oman Peninsula and the copper of Makkan.**
Thiery Berthoud, Serge Clenzion.   *Journal of Oman Studies*, vol. 6, no. 2 (1983), p. 239-46. map.

This article attempts to continue the studies of Oman's mining activities in order to try to substantiate the works of Peake and Bibby and determine whether Oman was the Makkan quoted in the cuneiform texts of Mesopotamia. Two sets of data are considered necessary to confirm the hypothesis. The first consists of devising an archaeological programme to confirm the chemical correspondence between copper objects found in Mesopotamia and the ore of the Omani mountains, the correlation of such data with other possible Middle East sites, and the chronology of imports from Oman into Mesopotamia. The second set of data was the archaeological investigation of settled communities in Oman without which mining activity could not have existed and local subsistence was essential for the survival of such communities. Twenty years of archaeological study in Oman has produced evidence of settled farming communities in areas of mining activity, evidence of copper mining and smelting, and possibly the manufacture of objects for export. Additionally, the chemical evidence also links the copper of Oman with objects found in Mesopotamia but shows it was involved in a much more complex trading pattern than had been previously thought. Questions still remain, particularly with regard to control of the trade, the associated social structure and the spread of the networks.

960   **Oman: Sohar stages a copper revival.**
Alison Brown.   *Middle East Economic Digest Special Report* (Nov. 1983), p. 32-34.

A report on the activities of Oman's copper mines which produced 6,700 tonnes in 1983, a figure which was anticipated to rise to 20,000 tonnes in 1984. The mine at Sohar contains enough copper to sustain 11-12 years of full production but deposits at Dams and Rakah could not be exploited because the infrastructure was not in place.

961 **Petrography, geochemistry and structural development of a large number of chromite occurrences in the Oman ophiolite.**
K. P. Burgrath (et al.). In: *Metallurgy of basic and ultrabasic rocks*, edited by M. J. Gallag. Hanover, Germany: Institute of Mining and Metallurgy, 1986, p. 199-216. maps.

A mineral survey in the Oman ophiolite, southwest of Muscat, revealed a large number of chromite occurrences which were subsequently studied. About 32.7 per cent of the chromite ores fell within the industrial limits for refractory ore without upgrading.

962 **Geology and mineral resources of the Oman mountains: A reconnaissance survey of parts of the Sultanate of Oman.**
J. N. Carney, M. J. Welland. London: Institute of Geological Sciences (Overseas Division), 1974. (Report no. 27).

Extremely relevant in view of the plans to resume copper mining activity after a series of proving surveys.

963 **Copper: A catalyst for northern Oman.**
Charles Gudron. *Middle East*, no. 191 (Sept. 1985), p. 24-25.

The mining operation in Sohar have been the catalyst for the urban and industrial development of northern Oman. The mines at Lasayl and Sayda produce 3,000 tonnes of ore per day which are processed to produce 99.98 per cent pure copper cathodes.

964 **Beyond the oil era? Arab mineral resources and future development.**
M. S. Khawlie. London: Mansell, 1990. 132p.

An investigation of the economic potential of the Arab world's natural mineral resources when oil resources are no longer viable. Khawlie surveys the mineral resources present in the region, including Oman, the efforts being put into developing the sector and the position of mineral resources in the social structure, together with policies and financial factors affecting mineral resource development. The appendix is a geological synopsis of the Arab world.

965 **The mineral industry of Qatar, Trucial States, Muscat and Oman, Federation of South Arabia and Yemen.**
United States. Department of the Interior. In: *Mineral Yearbook*. Washington, DC: Government Printing Office, 1964- . annual.

One section of this annual provides world-wide reports, including Oman, on the mineral industry and its prospects.

966 **Chromite-rich and chromite-poor ophiolites: the Oman case.**
A. Nicolas, H. Al Azri. In: *Ophiolite genesis and evolution of the oceanic lithosphere*, edited T. J. Peters (et al.). London: Kluwer, 1991, p. 261-74. map.

A survey of chromite deposits in Oman. These belong predominantly to the concordant structural types; that is, those which have been deformed by plastic flow and tectonical rotation. Chromite deposits have been found in restricted areas and some parts of Oman are totally devoid of deposits. The Oman ophiolite is the largest and best exposed in the world, hence the geological interest in the area, but it is comparatively poor in chromite deposits.

967 **On the genesis and composition of natural pyroaurite.**
R. M. Taylor (et al.). *Clay Minerals*, vol. 26, no. 3 (1991),
p. 297-309.
The samples of the mineral pyroaurite which were found in the desert regions of Oman varied in colour according to location, primarily due to the differing conditions in the hydrological environment.

968 **Copper production during the third millennium BC in Oman and the question of Makan.**
Gerd Weisgerber. *Journal of Oman Studies*, vol. 6, pt. 2 (1983),
p. 269-76. map.
Examines the question of Makan and its location in relation to Mesopotamia which had an impressive metal industry but no raw materials, except for clay. It is concluded that no definite conclusions can yet be drawn but some archaeological evidence and deductions do point to Oman being the source of the Sumerian copper. The author lists the requirements for the geographical location of Makan and studies the known evidence in Oman to substantiate the link between the two countries, concluding that, for a variety of reasons, the mountains of Oman are most probably to be recognized as the mountains of Makan.

National report about the geologic and mineral activities in the Sultanate of Oman.
See item no. 146.

Geology and mineral resources of the Trucial Oman range.
See item no. 155.

The copper mining settlement of Arja: A preliminary survey.
see item no. 349.

A study of ancient slags from Oman.
See item no. 353.

A preliminary discussion of ancient mining in the Sultanate of Oman.
See item no. 357.

Evidence of ancient mining sites in Oman: a preliminary report.
See item no. 371.

Arms manufacture and the arms trade in south-eastern Arabia in the early Muslim period.
See item no. 400.

Industrial Diversification

969 Industry: encouraging the private sector.
Alison Brown. *Middle East Economic Digest Special Report* (Nov. 1983), p. 31-33.

A report on the Omani government's policy of encouraging the private sector as a means of ensuring industrial diversification. As part of the Ministry of Commerce and Industry's budget some 60.2 million dollars were allocated for the development of the Rusayl Industrial Estate, with 11 of the 77 units opened in 1984. Small businesses were being encouraged to occupy the units through land offers, soft loans, import duty exemptions and feasibility studies.

970 Oman: recovery keeps contractors busy.
Alison Brown. *Middle East Economic Digest Special Report* (Nov. 1983), p. 24-26.

A report on the recovery in the construction industry and in the development of industrial projects following a slowdown in 1982. Various projects are described and the work of Omani and foreign contractors is detailed.

971 Oil, industrialization and development in the Arab Gulf States.
Atif A. Kubursi. London: Croom Helm, 1984. 144p.

A study of the interrelationship between oil production, industrialization and development in the Arab Gulf States, including Oman. Of particular interest is that of the potential for growth in agriculture and the non-oil industries, and the role of the Gulf Cooperation Council in the future of the member states.

972 An economic assessment of Oman's industrial diversification efforts.
R. E. Looney. *Orient*, vol. 32, no. 2 (1991), p. 217-35.

An assessment of Oman's experience of industrial diversification; in particular: factors responsible for Oman's progress, problems encountered with the process and the strategies available to the government to overcome impediments to industrial growth. Looney concludes that a large potential still exists for import substitution in some manufacturing areas and service sectors, with the main threat to development being the expenditure on military development plans. A further possible threat is that competition for resources could create an inflationary environment which will not be conducive to domestic production.

973 **Structural and economic change in the Arab Gulf after 1973.**
Robert E. Looney. *Middle Eastern Studies*, vol. 26, no. 4 (1990),
p. 514-35.

A study of the push for industrialization in the Gulf States, including Oman,
following the oil price rises of 1973/74. Four motives are discerned as being
responsible for these structural changes: diversification from oil; use of new-found
wealth for economic development; increased profit from downstream activities; and
control over the international oil industry through creation of their own structures.
The work is supported by twelve detailed statistical tables, providing evidence of
structural changes in the economy.

974 **Oman Manufacturers' Directory 1989/90.**
Ruwi, Oman: Oman Chamber of Commerce and Industry, 1989.
2nd ed. 171p.

Directory of manufacturing companies, listing full identification details together with
products manufactured and production capacity. The lists are alphabetical, by name
and activity. Information is also provided on the investment climate in Oman and the
developments in the manufacturing sector.

975 **The Gulf.**
F. Jamal Shahida, Mohammed Ali. *Pakistan and Gulf Economist*,
vol. 4, no. 38 (1985), p. 42-46.

An overview of the industrial sector in Oman and Bahrain. The industrial sector in
Oman is small in relation to the GDP but after a 5 per cent growth in 1983 it grew by
11 per cent in 1984. The government has encouraged the private sector through tax,
land and infrastructure incentives, and the opportunity to buy shares in previously
wholly government-owned businesses.

Prospects for the world oil industry.
See item no. 938.

Agriculture and Fishing

976 **Agricultural policy of Oman.**
Khartoum: Arab Organization for Agricultural Development, 1983.
133p.
A review of agricultural policy in Oman, covering all sectors and providing statistical data for the range of economic activity in the sector and in the rural economy.

977 **Agriculture and industry record rapid progress.**
Al-Tijari (Oman), (July 1981), p. 10-11.
A report on agriculture within the framework of the first Five-Year Development Plan covering 1976-80. Under the plan, experimental farms have been established, research stations and extension services founded, and farmers encouraged to adopt new farming methods. Also twenty-one schemes for the development of fish production have been instituted. The sector contributed 5.4 million Omani riyals to the GNP in 1976-77.

978 **Agriculture development in the Sultanate of Oman.**
Rural Reconstruction, vol. 21 (July 1988), p. 25-32.
Examines the various intensive studies being carried out in the Sultanate on land use and water resources. Among the topics considered are land distribution, water management, soil management and government loans to farmers.

979 **Agriculture – still important (Oman).**
Arab Economist, vol. 7, no. 74 (1975), p. 30-36.
Discusses the state of agriculture in Oman in terms of the need to increase the cultivated area, to improve productivity and to diversify. A national Farm Economic Survey was being carried out and a Water Resources Centre established, using funds provided in 1974 by the United Nations Development Programme (UNDP) and the Food and Agriculture Organization (FAO).

980 **Oman. Techno/economic feasibility study of utilizing mesopelagic fish for the production of fish meal and fish oil in the Sultanate of Oman.**

E. Arnesen, J. Shaerfe. Rome: Food and Agriculture Organization, 1986. 55p.

Provides an account of the mesopelagic fish resources of Oman and their fisheries together with an economic analysis of fish meal and fish oil manufacture from these resources. In order to ensure technical and economic feasibility of the industry, procedures essential for its success are detailed.

981 **Rabies in the Sultanate of Oman.**

F. A. Ata (et al.). *Veterinary Record*, vol. 132, no. 3 (1993), p. 68-69.

Describes the spread of rabies in Oman from the first cases reported in August 1990 in the north to all regions by October 1991. It was determined that foxes were largely responsible for the transmission of the disease and a control programme had been activated, including vaccination of registered domestic animals and destruction of stray animals.

982 **Ancient beekeeping in the Sultanate of Oman.**

S. J. Bailey. *Bee Craft*, vol. 74, no. 5 (1992), p. 145-49.

A study of the tradition of beekeeping in the Sultanate of Oman and its significance in rural society.

983 **Review of national fisheries for the Sultanate of Oman.**

R. B. A. Al Barwani. In: *Collective volume of working documents presented at the expert consultation on stock assessment of tunas in the Indian Ocean*, Mauritius, 23-27 June 1986, p. 262-64. (FAO Report No. FAO-FI-INT/86/016).

A review of the fishing industry in Oman which considers tuna resources, collection of data on fish stocks and catches, diseases of fish stocks and the fishing industry infrastructure.

984 **Review of national fisheries for the Sultanate of Oman. IPTP expert consultation on stock assessment of tunas in the Indian Ocean.**

R. B. Al Barwani. *Collective volume of working documents, Vol. 3, presented at the expert consultation on stock assessment of tunas in the Indian Ocean.* Moka, Mauritius, 1989, p. 262-64.

A discussion of tuna stocks in Oman's coastal waters considering yellow fin, longtail and kawakawa. The development programmes of the government are also discussed, particularly in the area of the collection of statistical data.

985 **Status report of Oman. IPTP Workshop on small Tuna, Seerfish and Billfish in the Indian Ocean.**
R. Al Barwani. Report of a workshop on small Tuna, Seerfish and Billfish in the Indian Ocean, Colombo, Sri Lanka, 1988. (FAO/UNDP IPTP/87/GEN/13).

Provides landing statistics for the artisanal fisheries of Oman, covering the period 1985-86 and including kingfish and tuna. Methods of fishing included drift gillnets, trawl lines and handlines.

986 **Agricultural development in the Middle East.**
Edited by Peter Beaumont, Keith McLachlan. Chichester, England: Wiley, 1985. xii+349p.

Examines the recent history of land and water use in agriculture in the Middle East to provide a background to contemporary developments. The second part of the book covers systematic topics of agricultural development from livestock to planning, covering the region as a whole. The third section considers individual countries, including Oman, discussing the question of agricultural change. A concluding chapter surveys trends in Middle East agriculture.

987 **Prospects of agriculture and fisheries' development in GCC member states.**
F. H. Bescisu. *Journal of the Gulf and Arabian Peninsula Studies*, vol. 10, no. 38 (1984), p. 125-68.

An Armenian-language article exploring the features and prospects in agriculture and fishing in the member states of the Gulf Cooperation Council. Oman is considered, along with Saudi Arabia, to be one of the most favoured in terms of agriculture and fishing, but it is considered that there is a need for cooperation in the areas of research, conservation and pollution controls.

988 **The mountain pastoralists of the Sultanate of Oman: reactions to drought.**
John Stace Birks. *Development and Change*, vol. 9, pt. 1 (1978), p. 71-86. map.

By the winter of 1974-75 the Wadi al-Kabir area had experienced four years without rain, and the conditions of pasture were the worst for twenty years. As a result of livestock foraging, naturally occurring fodder was extremely scarce and had reached a critical stage. This paper deals with the ways in which the pastoralists coped with the drought conditions, and the implications of the drought conditions in a wider context. The article also deals briefly with the social structure of the pastoralists, their patterns of mobility and the daily life pattern in the mountains.

989 **The reaction of rural populations to drought: a case study from South-East Arabia.**
John Stace Birks. *Erdkunde*, vol. 31, no. 4 (1977), p. 229-305.

An account of a particularly severe drought experienced in the Western Hajar mountains between 1973 and 1975. A case-study is made of the village of Ghayzayn where water flow was reduced to 2.5 per cent of the 1973 volume, crops were abandoned, the date harvest was very poor and the economic wealth of the village suffered. The water flow was not increased as there was dispute as to whether the drought would be short-lived and, if not, no action could ameliorate its effects. The outcome of the drought was a growth in temporary and permanent migration from the village, a breaking of the community spirit and an aggravation of the dissatisfaction with agriculture and a desire to seek cash employment outside the village.

990 **Some problems of agricultural development in the Sultanate of Oman.**
John Stace Birks, Sally E. Letts. *Journal of the Gulf and Arabian Peninsula Studies*, vol. 5, no. 18 (1979), p. 157-69.

Oman's income from oil is modest and because of her large rural population agriculture must feature heavily in future development. However, there had been a decline in the cultivated area, with the population favouring employment in the non-agricultural sector, a change which resulted in Oman having to import substantial quantities of food. The main effort needs to be concentrated on the improvement of existing land holdings into commercially viable units. Agricultural extension services have been introduced to provide effective aid to farmers and to try to reawaken an interest in the land. The authors conclude that to be successful agriculture must be accorded priority within the scheme of national planning.

991 **Agricultural production and/or rural development?**
Howard Bowen-Jones, Roderic Dutton. *Arab Gulf Journal*, vol. 4, no. 1 (April 1984), p. 51-64.

An examination of the conflict in the Arab Gulf States between increasing agricultural production and the need for rural development. The pressure was increasing because of reduced oil revenues and a desire to ensure rural stability. In Oman's case, rural development projects had been given priority because of the large rural population.

992 **Agriculture in the Arabian Peninsula.**
Howard Bowen-Jones, Roderic Dutton. London: Economist Intelligence Unit, 1983. (Special Report, no. 145).

A survey of agriculture in the area, including Oman, covering land and water resources, changes in usage, production in the 1970s, the structure of food production, import dependence and future trends. The main trends in the agricultural sector are discussed and recommendations made for improvement.

993 **The effect of water stress on growth and dry matter distribution in juvenile *Sesbania sesban* and *Acacia nilotica*.**
M. Bradbury. *Journal of Arid Environments*, vol. 18, no. 3 (1990), p. 325-33.

An experiment in the growing of *Sesbania sesban* and *Acacia* from seeds in northern Oman to determine the effect of water stress on the plants. Those not subject to such stress achieved a greater area of leaf growth and a greater overall growth rate. The conclusion was that leguminous species from arid areas may be more suitable alone or used as a multipurpose tree and shrub within tropical agriculture.

994 **Isolation and identification of arboviruses from the Sultanate of Oman.**
S. M. Al-Busaidy, P. S. Mellor. *Epidemiology and Infection*, vol. 106, no. 2 (1991), p. 403-14.
An account of the use of sentinel herds and vector surveillance systems to identify the presence of the arboviruses in Oman. At least three strains of virus were identified in goat herds, whilst one came from *Culicoides imicola*, the first such case in Arabia.

995 **Report on a mission to the Dhofar (Sultanate of Oman). Project identification. Animal husbandry; sheep; goat; dromedary; pastures technical aid.**
N. Chabeuf. Maisons-Alfort, France: Centre de Coopération Internationale en Recherche Agronomique pour le Développement, 1984. 31p.
A report on a mission to Dhofar, conducted on behalf of the Omani Ministry of Agriculture and Fisheries to advise on a development programme for animal husbandry including foodstuff improvement, and also a veterinary programme to improve the quality of the livestock.

996 **Report on a mission to the Dhofar (Sultanate of Oman). Project identification. Animal husbandry; sheep; goat; dromedary; pastures technical aid.**
N. Chabeuf. Maisons-Alfort, France: Centre de Coopération Internationale en Recherche Agronomique pour le Développement, 1984. 11p.
See item no. 995 for annotation.

997 **Commercial fisheries in Oman.**
Final report. Washington, DC: NTIS, 1988. 43p. (Report No. AID-PN-ABC-046).
A report commissioned by the Omani–American Joint Commission for Economic and Technical Co-operation in Muscat and the Agency for International Development in Washington on the activities and potential of the Oman fishing industry. The report concludes that the potential exists for a major expansion of the fishing industry, but that the main constraint is the lack of appropriate government action. Up to 1988 development had concentrated on coastal fisheries and an investment of $10.5 million had been made in small vessels. accounting for 70 per cent of the fishing fleet. The report also notes that the private sector had responded by investing in a fish processing plant and export facility, utilizing a government programme that had installed refrigeration facilities in the fishing villages.

998 **Developing Oman's interior desert.**
Middle East News Economic Weekly, vol. 26, no. 12 (18 March 1988), p. 21-24.
A pilot farm was established by Petroleum Development Oman and Booker Agriculture International in 1986 in the interior desert at a site at the south-western

end of the Marmul oilfield. The aim was to test a wide variety of crops, and research was conducted into soil conditions, irrigation requirements and climate.

999 **Developing Oman's interior desert.**
Middle East News Economic Weekly, vol. 26, no. 14 (1 April 1988), p. 21-24.
A description of part of an agricultural research programme on land reclamation in the interior desert. This aspect was concerned with seeding techniques and problems of high soil density and rapid surface desiccation. Rhodes grass proved the best for reclamation and a variety of vegetables and fruit proved successful in terms of volume of production and quality. Crops planted on the sites of old ant colonies proved the most successful because of the soil enrichment.

1000 **Developing Oman's interior desert.**
Middle East News Economic Weekly, vol. 26, no. 16 (15 April 1988), p. 12-16.
An account of part of Oman's development project for the interior desert area dealing with the testing of the marketability of quality crops. Rhodes grass was used for land reclamation and the best crops were found to be Rhodes grass, Italian rye grass and alfalfa. The next stage of the project was the refining of Rhodes grass production and the study of soil–crop–water interactions.

1001 **Development of small-scale fisheries (Arabian Sea).**
Rome: Food and Agriculture Organization, Fisheries Dept, 1984. 7p. (Report no. FAO-FI-IOFC/DMG/84/3).
A brief summary of the development of artisanal fishing in the area of the Persian Gulf, Gulf of Oman and the Arabian Sea. This sector of the industry is significant in the economy and the social structure of Oman. The report is in Arabic and English.

1002 **Enterprise and innovation in an indigenous fishery: The case of the Sultanate of Oman.**
William Donaldson. *Development and Change*, vol. 11, no. 3 (1980), p. 479-95.
A review of the process of modernization of the Omani fishing industry from the 1960s which demonstrated that fishermen have adopted innovations in craft, equipment and marketing best suited to the needs of the industry. This pragmatic development is in contrast to the somewhat grander schemes proposed by the Ministry's foreign consultants.

1003 **Fisheries of the Arabian Peninsula.**
William J. Donaldson. In: *Change and development in the Middle East*, edited by John C. Clarke, Howard Bowen- Jones. London: Methuen, 1981, p. 189-98.
A survey of the importance of fishing in the Arabian Peninsula which had not really changed in terms of the methods used for centuries, until the middle of the twentieth century. The introduction of commercial fishing has had mixed results, but Oman's participation agreement with Japan and subsequently Korea has not been successful

as the companies have not met their targets. The comparison is made with the artisanal fisheries which have been regarded as unproductive and inefficient, but in fact have proved to be reproductive in terms of the use of capital and labour, with their flexibility proving to be a distinct advantage. The author also stresses the important social significance of these close-knit traditional communities. This contribution is based on data collected since 1974 as part of the University of Durham Oman Research Project.

1004 **Management of the Indo-Pacific Spanish mackerel,**
Scomberomorus commersoni, in Oman.
R. G. Dudley (et al.). _Fish Research_ (Amsterdam), vol. 15, nos. 1-2 (1992), p. 17-43.
A study of the mackerel fish in Oman, aimed at enabling preliminary management recommendations to be made. Data were collected on the growth rate of the fish and it was determined that protection of the young growing fish could have significant benefits for the fishery. Such protection could be achieved by instituting moderate mesh regulations.

1005 **Agricultural policy and development: Oman, Bahrain, Qatar and**
the United Arab Emirates.
R. Dutton. In: _Agricultural development in the Middle East_, edited by P. Beaumont, K. McLachlan. Chichester, England: Wiley, 1985, p. 227-40.
Oman is the best placed of the countries surveyed with regard to the presence of renewable and fossil water and the best endowed land. It has a distinct rural population and agricultural tradition but the farming practices in 1985 were not relevant to the changing circumstances. Attention has been focused on plans to bring more land into production but the author's view is that the concentration should be on increasing productivity on those units already in existence.

1006 **Durham University Khabura Development Project. Findings and**
recommendations. No. 1. Cultivation using a 2 wheel tractor on
the Batina.
R. W. Dutton. Durham, England: Durham University, Department of Geography, 1979. 10p.
The project found that problems of soil cultivation on small farms in Oman was the greatest single restriction on development and that the use of a two-wheel tractor could make an important impact on these problems. The recommendation was that ten two-wheel Howard Gem tractors should be introduced at Khabura to test the theory and a report should be made to the Ministry of Agriculture so that further action could be considered.

1007 **Honeybees in Oman.**
Edited by R. W. Dutton (et al.). Muscat, Oman: Office of the Adviser for Conservation of the Environment, 1982. 38p.
A largely pictorial account of beekeeping and wild honeybees in Oman, based on research carried out by the Ministry of Agriculture and the University of Durham.

1008   **Updating agriculture and associated rural enterprises.**
R. W. Dutton.   In: *Oman, economic, social and strategic developments*, edited by B. R. Pridham.   London: Croom Helm, 1987, p. 94-117.

The agricultural and rural craft base in Oman is seen as under threat from the economic and social change brought about by oil wealth. The author argues that it is essential for rural resources to be conserved to ensure their long-term usefulness, and water resources are deemed to be a critical concern. The infrastructure is in place to ensure that effective development can take place, but there is a need to ensure that it runs smoothly and efficiently to ensure a balance between conservation and development.

1009   **Soils of the Arabian Peninsula.**
S. M. Elgawhary.   Riyadh, Saudi Arabia: Ministry of Agriculture and Water, 1987. 69p.

A bibliographical listing of 155 references to the soils and land resources of Saudi Arabia, the Gulf States, Oman and the two Yemens published between 1944 and 1983.

1010   **Effect of planting density on growth and yield of irrigated maize *Zea mays* in the Batinah coast region of Oman.**
H. A. Esechie.   *Journal of Agricultural Science*, vol. 119, no. 2 (1992), p. 165-69.

The results of a field study in 1989 and 1990 to investigate the effect of planting density on the growth and yield of maize under irrigation in the Batinah coast region. Two maize cultivars were grown in varying densities, and leaf area and grain yield were measured.

1011   **Evaluation of present status and potential development of animal feed resources in the Arab countries, pt. 20. The Sultanate of Oman.**
Khartoum, Sudan: Arab Organization for Agricultural Development, 1982. 102p. (Report no. AOAD-MF-82-CO-OM-003).

A report on the foodstuff provision for livestock in the Sultanate of Oman, with recommendations for the development of foodstuffs and the enhancement of natural grazing facilities.

1012   **Livestock development.**
D. E. Faulkner.   In: *Current problems and prospects for agricultural development in the Sultanate of Oman*.   Rome: Food and Agriculture Organization, 1973. 24p.

A report prepared for the United Nations Development Programme Preparatory Assistance Mission to provide data on possible developments to be financed by the programme.

1013 **Fisheries policies and cooperation among Gulf countries.**
Rome: Food and Agriculture Organization, Fisheries Dept, 1984.
12p. (Report no. FAO-FI-IOFC/DMG/84/10).
A review of the fisheries policies of the various Gulf States and the moves towards
cooperation and coordination amongst the member states of the Gulf Cooperation
Council. The article is in Arabic and English.

1014 *Acacia tortilis* and *Prosopis cineraria* **leguminous trees for arid
areas.**
P. J. Gates, K. Brown. *Outlook on Agriculture*, vol. 17, no. 2
(1988), p. 61-64.
Presents the results of a study of physiological and genetic characteristics of *Acacia
tortilis* and *Prosopis cineraria* in the woodlands of the Wahiba Sands in Oman. The
study was particularly concerned with foliar water uptake and salt tolerance. The
results are used to determine the effectiveness of these plants for reafforestation
programmes in arid regions in relation to root growth, drought tolerance and the
ability to take in water through leaf surfaces from nocturnal dew.

1015 **Alfalfa collecting in southern Arabia.**
L. Guarino. *Plant Genetic Resources Newsletter*, no. 80 (Dec.
1989), p. 33-39.
A consideration of the role of alfalfa in the rural economy of southern Arabia,
including Oman. The article covers the genetic problems of the plant, production,
breeding and the place of alfalfa as a renewable resource. The project was also
concerned with the collection of plant genetic resources between April and July 1987.

1016 **Crop collecting in the Sultanate of Oman in the context of the
Arabian Peninsula.**
L. Guarino. *Plant Genetic Resources Newsletter*, no. 77 (March
1989), p. 27-33.
Deals with the place of crop cultivation in the agricultural industry of Oman, and
covers: land usage; soil and climate conditions; methods of harvesting; and the usage
of the crops, such as wheat and barley. The areas of cultivation were given top
priority for the collection of plant genetic resources from April to July 1987, resulting
in the collection of 58 species and 510 accessions. In addition to those mentioned,
alfalfa is grown for fodder, whilst the date palm is the main crop.

1017 **Gulf agriculture: a growing success.**
Dorian Hancock. *The Middle East*, no. 153 (July 1987), p. 23-26.
A review of agricultural production in the Gulf States in 1987. Although demand had
increased, local production had declined because of government investment in
non-agricultural development. In Oman, agriculture and fisheries' share of the Gross
Domestic Product had dropped from 34 per cent in 1967 to 3 per cent by 1985.

1018 **Fishmeal and oil from lantern fish (Myctophidae) with special emphasis on protein quality.**
A. Haque (et al.). *Journal of the Science of Food and Agriculture*, vol. 32, no. 1 (1981), p. 61-70.
A discussion of the protein quality of lantern fish from the Gulf of Oman, and the additives used to reduce feed consumption and improve feed utilization.

1019 **Review of fisheries in Oman.**
A. S. A. Al-Harrasy. In: *The proceedings of the 1984 Shrimp and Fin Fisheries Management Workshop. Final report*, edited by C. P. Mathews. Kuwait: Kuwait Institute for Scientific Research, 1985, p. 125-28.
A brief examination of the Oman fishing industry, covering the various sectors and the main fish stocks of tuna, demersal species, cuttlefish and squid, lobster and abalone.

1020 **A strategy for agricultural development in the Sultanate of Oman: an environmental perspective.**
Adel Ibrahim Hindy. *Journal of the Gulf and Arabian Peninsula Studies*, vol. 8, no. 29 (1982), p. 149-88.
Examines the potential for agricultural development in Oman – which is more than 90 per cent uncultivated – from a perspective that examines such development in relation to the environment. The author argues that priority should be given to the expansion of programmes of crop rotation and integrated forage and livestock production, particularly on the Batinah coast.

1021 **Regional program for the Arabian Peninsula. Proceedings of the second annual coordination meeting of the regional program for the Arabian Peninsula.**
International Center for Agricultural Research in the Dry Areas. Aleppo, Syria: ICARDA, 1990. 87p. (Report No. ICARDA 159-EN).
The report of the meeting held at Aleppo from 27 to 29 August 1989 which deals with research and training activities and agricultural priorities in selected countries of the Arabian Peninsula, including Oman. The report also contains proposals for strengthening and developing cooperation amongst participating countries in the region and with appropriate international organizations.

1022 **Biological control of the coconut scale insect, *Aspidiotus destructor* sign Homoptera diaspididae, in the southern region of Oman Dhofar.**
M. M. Kinawy. *Tropical Pest Management*, vol. 37, no. 4 (1991), p. 387-89.
An account of the effects of the introduction of the coccinellid beetle from India in 1985 as a biocontrol agent against the coconut scale insect which infests coconut palms in Dhofar. This showed a rapid build-up of the predators and a subsequent decline in the host population.

1023   **The forest potential of the Sultanate of Oman. Report to the Minister of Agriculture, Sultanate of Oman.**
R. M. Lawton.   London: Overseas Development Agency, Land Resources Development Centre, 1980. 39p. (Report 97 Oman-03-1/REP-97/80).

The results of a feasibility study on the prospects for forestation in Oman which indicated that certain areas were suitable for planting. The report also suggests varieties that could be introduced and briefly surveys water resources.

1024   **Interviews with traditional fishermen near Sur, Oman.**
J. Al-Mamry.   Colombo, Sri Lanka: Indo-Pacific Tuna Development and Management Programme Report, 1989, p. 69-71. (FAO Report No. FAO-FI-INT/86/016).

This study of the fishing industry at Sur in Oman considers the traditional methods of fishing and the role of the industry in the social structure of the fishing communities.

1025   **Biological control of citrus blackfly, *Aleurocanthus woglumi*, in Oman.**
A. M. Al-Mjeni, T. Sankaran.   *FAO Plant Protection Bulletin* vol. 39, nos. 2-3 (1991), p. 72-74.

A study of the control of the citrus blackfly which particularly affects lime trees and lime fruit production. In Oman, a variety of pesticides and herbicides are used.

1026   **National vaccination project. Sultanate of Oman.**
In: *Conference of the OIE regional commission for Asia, the Far East and Oceania. Fish disease and hygiene of fish products. Eradication of rinderpest in Asia. Feasibility of a regional rabies eradication programme. Progress reports on recommendations of the 13th conference of the regional commission*, Colombo 29 July – 1 August 1986.   Paris: Office International des Epizootes, 1985, p. 159-64.

A report on the vaccination programme in the Sultanate of Oman. It was introduced to meet the recommendations of the conference and in line with the veterinary programme introduced by the Omani Ministry of Agriculture.

1027   **Oman adjusts goals to revenue outlook, places stress on private investment.**
IMF Survey, vol. 8, no. 13 (1979), p. 198-200.

A review of the national economy of Oman which, prior to the exploitation of oil in 1967, relied on subsistence agriculture and fishing. This area of the economy employs the largest labour force but contributes only 3 per cent to GDP. Imports provide the majority of agricultural products but steps have been taken to reduce this dependence with the introduction of extension services, the establishment of cooperatives and the development of water resources.

1028   **Oman today: agriculture and fisheries.**
Middle East News Economic Weekly, vol. 24, no. 45 (6 Dec. 1985), p. 14-19.

This survey of development in Oman is focused on farming and fishing which, between them, constituted the main source of income for about half of Oman's population. Progress in these sectors had been aided by the introduction of veterinary services, research stations, government loans and the distribution of subsidized tractors and water-pumps. A high priority was also given to manpower development and training courses were held throughout the country.

1029   **Regional fishery survey and development project, Bahrain, Iran, Iraq, Kuwait, Oman, Qatar, Saudi Arabia, United Arab Emirates. Illustrated identification guide to commercial fishes.**
J. E. Randall, G. R. Allen, W. F. Smith-Variz.   Rome: Food and Agricultural Organization, Fisheries Department, 1978. 226p. (FAO Access No. 40565).

A report in Arabic and English on fishing potential in the region, with illustrations of the fish which are considered to be commercially viable.

1030   **Land distribution and the end of oases. The example of Al Batinah coast plain in Oman.**
F. Scholz.   *Erdkunde*, vol. 36, no. 3 (1982), p. 199-207.

A German-language article reviewing the land reforms instituted in Oman after 1970. These involved land distribution, technical innovation, improved fertilizers, and significant improvements in irrigation. The effects were clearly visible, but the innovations upset the hydrological and ecological balance of the area and caused both increased salinity of the groundwater and a shrinking of the coastal plain. These problems were recognized and corrective measures were introduced by the government.

1031   **Evaluation of certain newly introduced potato and tomato cultivars for late blight disease under Oman conditions.**
M. El-Sheshtawi.   *Journal of Agricultural Sciences*, vol. 13, no. 2 (1988), p. 729-34.

Ten potato and sixteen tomato cultivars were tested under field conditions in Oman to test their susceptibility to late blight caused by *Phytophthora infestans* De Bary. The article deals with the technical results of these trials and the systemic chemicals used to treat the disease.

1032   **Status of fishery resources other than shrimp (Arabian Sea).**
Rome: Food and Agriculture Organization, Fisheries Dept, 1984. 32p. (Report no. FAO-FI-IOFC/DMG/84/5).

A report on fish stocks, other than shrimp, in the Persian Gulf, Gulf of Oman and the Arabian Sea. The report is in Arabic and English.

1033   **The future of date cultivation in the Arabian Peninsula.**
        J. H. Stevens, E. Creswell.   *Asian Affairs*, n.s., vol. 59, pt. 3 (1972),
        p. 191-97.

An analysis of the future of date cultivation in the Arabian Peninsula, including
Oman, which is seen as essential to the continuance of the oases. Cultivation is still
carried out by traditional methods and, although there are regional variations, a
distinct pattern can be determined. The article is detailed and specific, and
concentrates on two problems faced by the date industry: the decline of demand and
the long-term need to reduce the area under cultivation.

1034   **The role of major agricultural projects in the economic
        development of Arabian Peninsula countries.**
        J. H. Stevens.   In: *Proceedings of the Seventh Seminar for Arabian
        Studies.*   London: Seminar for Arabian Studies, 1973, p. 140-44.

An examination of the role of agricultural development either as a means of reducing
imports or, as in the case of Oman, providing exports. The author concludes,
however, that major projects were not feasible at that time because of the level of
technological expertise amongst the farming communities.

1035   **Pelagic and demersal fish resources of Oman. Results of the
        R/V *Dr Fridtjof Nansen* surveys in Oman 1983-84. Final Report.**
        T. Stroemme.   Bergen, Norway: Institute of Marine Research, 1986.
        98p. (UNDP/FAO Programme GLO/82/001).

A report on surveys carried out to update information on the fish resources of Oman
under the auspices of the United Nations Development Programme (UNDP) and the
Food and Agricultural Organization of the United Nations (FAO). Acoustic and trawl
survey findings are detailed and biological accounts are given of some of the main
species identified.

1036   **Oman's offshore venture.**
        Susannah Tarbush.   *Middle East*, no. 132 (Oct. 1985), p. 21-22.

A report on the Oman National Fisheries Company which was founded by the
government in 1981 with the objective of supplying 70 per cent of the Gulf States'
fish requirements by 1990. The company also recruits and trains fishermen and
operates fish-processing plants in Muttrah and Salalah.

1037   **Technical report on citrus virus and virus-like diseases in the
        Sultanate of Oman.**
        Damascus: Arab Centre for the Studies of Arid Zones and Dry Lands,
        1986. 16p. (Report no. AOAD-MF-86-CO-OM-011).

This report on the incidence of citrus virus and other diseases affecting the citrus crop
in Oman makes recommendations as to the treatment of the trees and of the fruit
when in storage. In Arabic, but with an English summary.

1038   **Transformation of rural employment structures: the example of the Sultanate of Oman, south-east Arabia.**
Applied Geography and Development, vol. 33 (1989), p. 7-26.
An examination of oasis agriculture in Oman between 1970 and 1980, primarily dealing with the date industry and its place in rural employment. The article examines the structure of employment within the date palm industry and the impact on rural employment of economic expansion in areas such as the oil industry and construction.

1039   **Spray trials against the citrus blackfly (*Aleurocanthus woglumi*) on limes in the Oman.**
W. S. Watts, M. Alam.   London: Centre for Overseas Pest Research, (1973). 7p. (Miscellaneous Report, no. 8).
A description of trials conducted in Oman with various chemicals designed to control blackfly in limes. It ends with recommendations as to the most effective chemicals to be used, the volume of spraying, and the most efficient type of spray to be used.

1040   **Honey bees in the Sultanate of Oman.**
R. Whitcombe.   Muscat, Oman: Directorate of Agriculture, 1980. 20p.
Describes the distribution of wild bees in Oman and the methods used for collecting their honey, including the colonies kept in date palm trunks in northern Oman. Results are given of a development programme to improve production, including the importing of bees from Australia and the work of the honey centre at Rustaq. The problem of educating villagers not to destroy nests by taking the honey and discarding the brood combs is also discussed.

1041   **A regional survey of the aquaculture sector in eleven Middle East countries.**
P. G. White.   Rome: Food and Agriculture Organization, 1988. 50p.
A report on a survey conducted on the aquaculture industry in the Middle East, covering eleven countries bordering the Red Sea and the Arabian Gulf, including Oman. The survey deals with the following topics: consumption of fish and shellfish and the regional markets; aquaculture of fish and shellfish in the region; local infrastructure; national infrastructure; national sector management; and regional sector management.

1042   **Sohar Ancient Fields Project: interim report no. 1.**
T. J. Wilkinson.   *Journal of Oman Studies*, vol. 1 (1975), p. 159-66. maps.
This project was established to delimit and map the area of ancient intensive agriculture around Sohar and to investigate the methods of water supply and land use. The interim report describes the physical environment and the initial land-use mapping, backed by photographs, diagrams and maps. The article also describes the *falaj* system and its method of operation, with the addition of a useful diagram of a *falaj*.

1043 **Sohar Ancient Fields Project: interim report no. 2.**
T. J. Wilkinson. *Journal of Oman Studies*, vol. 2 (1976), p. 75-80.
This second report continues the story of the Sohar project and is concerned with the mapping and investigation of the open channel *aflaj* in the Sohar hinterland, the recording of the remains of *qanat, aflaj* and numerous remains of wells in the area.

1044 **Developing fisheries in the Sultanate of Oman.**
H. H. S. Al-Yahyah. *Infofish Market Digest*, no. 2 (1986), p. 19-20.
Describes the development of the fishing industry in Oman, with coverage of the first and second five-year plans together with a list of the major fish stocks.

1045 **Rangelands in Oman: management, problems and prospects.**
T. E. Yassin, S. S. A. Alshanfari. In: *Advances in range management in arid lands. Proceedings of the 1st international conference on range management in the Arabian Gulf*, edited by R. Halwagy (et al.). London; Kegan Paul International, 1990, p. 119-30.
The physical and climatic features of Oman are examined and the crops grown and numbers of livestock are briefly reviewed. The vegetation of the rangelands of the Omani mountains in the north and the Dhofar province are also reviewed, as are the reasons for the deterioration of the rangelands. The prime reasons are the limited amounts and poor distribution of rainfall, a sharp increase in livestock numbers, the construction of a modern road system, and changes in floristic composition.

The geographical mobility of a rural Arab population: some implications of changing patterns.
See item no. 633.

Wildlife rabies in Oman and the United Arab Emirates.
See item no. 734.

Farming communities of the Oman Peninsula and the copper of Makkan.
See item no. 959.

Migrant labour in agriculture: an international comparison.
See item no. 1072.

Development of agricultural library and documentation services in the Sultanate of Oman.
See item no. 1115.

Transport and Communications

1046   Primitive watercraft in Arabia.
Richard Le Baron Bowen.   *American Neptune*, vol. 12, no. 3 (1982), p. 186-221.

A valuable contribution to the study of boat building in the area from earliest times, including the significant position of Oman. Sohar had been a major shipbuilding centre in Omani history and a maritime centre.

1047   Decade of development in the Arabian Gulf ports.
Middle East News Economic Weekly, vol. 26, no. 15 (1988), p. 18-21.

Discusses the major developments that have taken place in the Arabian Gulf ports including the expansion of cargo-handling facilities at Oman's Mina Qaboos since the Iraq–Iran war.

1048   The sealand of ancient Arabia.
R. P. Dougherty.   New Haven, Connecticut: Yale University Press; London: Oxford University Press, 1932. 203p.

An account of seafaring and trading drawn from ancient records, including those of Sumeria, which record copper trading with Makan which is believed to have been the present-day Sultanate of Oman.

1049   Communications technology: A telecommunications network for Oman.
Klaus Elfrath (et al.).   *National Development* (April 1986), p. 9-12.

Describes the telecommunications network in Oman which began operations in 1982. Closed-meshed networks with all-digital switching systems in Muscat and Salalah are linked by a 620-mile radio relay. The system is designed to be further expanded with a link to the Musandam Peninsula.

1050 **A tentative classification of Arabian seacraft.**
James Hornell. *Marine Mirror*, vol. 28, pt. 1 (1942), p. 11-40.
A very interesting and informative article which examines the construction techniques of Arab shipbuilders and the types of craft built. Hornell also considers the craft of the carver and the various embellishments lavished on ships. He deals in detail with each type of craft and its uses.

1051 **Arab seafaring in the Indian Ocean in ancient and early mediaeval times.**
George Fadlo Hourani. Princeton, New Jersey: Princeton University Press, 1981; Beirut: Khayat, 1963. 131p.
Although a slim volume, this is a valuable introduction to the influence of Arab sailors and traders, including the Omani, prior to European expansion into the Indian Ocean.

1052 **Direct sailing between the Persian Gulf and China in pre-Islamic times.**
George Fadlo Hourani. *Journal of the Royal Asiatic Society*, vol. 8, no. 2 (1947), p. 157-60.
Deals with the earliest trade of the Persian Gulf with China, which was regular and profitable prior to European trading links with China.

1053 **Dhows.**
David Howarth. London: Quartet Books, 1977. 159p.
A consideration of the history of the dhow from earliest times, its influence on the development of Arabian trade, the craft of its building, and the skills of Arab sailors. The work is well illustrated with photographs showing all aspects of the dhow's history.

1054 **Twighlight of the Arab dhow.**
Marion Kaplan. *National Geographic Magazine*, vol. 146, no. 3 (Sept. 1974), p. 330-51.
Based on the author's voyage from Kuwait to East Africa, and concentrating mainly on voyages from Oman, providing details of the various routes, goods carried, and the knowledge and customs of local sailors. Kaplan also discusses the design and construction of the ships, and reproduces drawings of various dhows.

1055 **The decline of Omani dhows.**
Esmond Bradley Martin. *Great Circle* (Australia), vol. 2, no. 2 (1980), p. 74-86.
Surveys the tradition of shipbuilding in Oman from about 2000 BC. The article focuses on the decline of both the traditional building of dhows and of dhow trade since the 1970s. This was largely due to two factors: the development of modern docking facilities which were not designed to handle dhows; and an increase in larger vessels trading in the region.

1056 **Arab navigation.**
S. S. Nadvi. *Islamic Culture*, vol. 16, no. 1 (1942), p. 72-86; no. 2, p. 192-98.
Of interest for the development of Sohar as a centre of maritime activity and shipbuilding.

1057 **Arab navigation in the Indian Ocean before the coming of the Portuguese.**
Ahmad ibn Majid al-Naydi, translated by G. R. Tibbetts. London: Royal Asiatic Society, distributed by Luzac, 1971. 630p. maps. bibliog.
A translation of the work of Ahmad ibn Majid al-Naydi which is of great interest for any study of Arab, mainly Omani, trading and seafaring in the Indian Ocean.

1058 **Public services: A shift of emphasis.**
Al Tijari (Oman), (July 1981), p. 12-13.
This report on the development of public services in 1970 covers road transport, the development of Seeb international airport, and the expansion of facilities at Port Qaboos. A telephone and telex network have been installed, postal services established, and drinking water and electricity projects given priority under the first and second Five-Year Development Plans.

1059 **Sultanate of Oman: a highway maintenance project.**
Washington, DC: World Bank, Middle East and North Africa Region, Projects Department, 1985. 75p. maps.
The project proposal was designed for the period 1986-89 to improve highway maintenance, project evaluation, training of Omani staff, highway safety and pavement management.

1060 **Sons of Sinbad: an account of sailing with the Arabs in their dhows, in the Red Sea, around the coasts of Arabia, and to Zanzibar and to Tanganyika, pearling in the Persian Gulf and life of the shipmasters, the mariners and merchants of Kuwait.**
Alan Villiers. London: Hodder & Stoughton, 1940; New York: Scribner, 1969. rev. ed. 414p. maps.
A classic account of the Arab dhow trade and seafaring in 1939-40, together with a description of various Gulf ports.

1061 **Sohar and Omani seafaring in the Indian Ocean.**
A. Williamson. Muscat: Petroleum Development (Oman), 1973. 36p.
This is a difficult publication to obtain. It deals with the role of Sohar as a major shipbuilding and maritime centre of the Sultanate.

1062   **Oman: General Telecommunications Organization (GTO) second telecommunications project.**
World Bank, Industry Department, Energy and Industry Staff.
Washington, DC: World Bank, 1988. 50p. maps.

An overview of the telecommunications sector in Oman. The project under examination was designed to enable the General Telecommunications Organization to fully manage all work in the sector by 1990. The project also aimed to expand local facilities, extend the services to 37 rural communities, and to expand the capacity for domestic long-distance and international traffic.

Employment and Manpower

1063   **Social implications of labour migration in the Arab World.**
Janet Abu-Lughod.   In: *Arab resources: The transformation of a society*, edited by Ibrahim Ibrahim.   Washington, DC: Georgetown University Center for Contemporary Arab Studies; London: Croom Helm, 1983, p. 237-65.

This contribution examines the social implications of labour migration from two sources: migration caused by war and migration resulting from the impact of oil. Oman is dealt with in the latter case and is considered both as a labour-importing and a labour-exporting nation. Tables show changes in gross domestic product and migrant populations by country of origin. In terms of the effects on society the article concludes that the Gulf States, including Oman, are maintaining a monopoly of citizenship privileges whilst being dependent on migrant labour and operating a system which uses labour as a rented commodity. At the same time they are posing the question as to the effect of such a policy on the host society.

1064   **The pattern of employment migration and labour in the Gulf countries.**
G. Beauge, M. Sader.   *Population Bulletin Economic Commission for Western Asia*, vol. 21 (1981), p. 85-104.

This study of the pattern of employment in the Gulf States, including Oman, looks at the use of migrant labour, including its significance to the economic structures of the labour-importing states. Oman is considered both as an importer and an exporter of migrant labour.

1065   **Arab manpower: The crisis of development.**
John Stace Birks, Clive A. Sinclair.   London: Croom Helm, 1980. 391p. map.

This work is a survey of the labour markets of the Arab world, evaluating them by demand-and-supply analysis and the different elements in trends of employment. The objective is to set out the socio-economic conditions which underlie the crisis of development in the Arab region. Oman is dealt with as one of the 'Pseudo-Capital-Rich States' (p. 175-91). One major problem associated with a study of Oman at that time was the paucity of demographic data such that the International Labour Office aggregated Oman with smaller countries in the area. Birks and Sinclair examine the educational system in Oman and the progress made since 1970, and study the country as both an importer and exporter of labour, with the latter aspect having a significant impact on the agricultural sector.

1066 **International migration and development in the Arab region.**
John Stace Birks, Clive A. Sinclair.   London; Geneva: International Labour Office, 1980. 186p.

This work examines the volume and pattern of international migration for employment to, from and between the Arab states of the Middle East, and provides an analysis of the underlying factors. The pattern is examined in relation to the advantages and disadvantages to both the labour-importing and -exporting countries; in the former case, the long-term consequences of importing labour from the Indian sub-continent and the Far East are considered. Oman is dealt with as both a country which supplies such labour, particularly to the United Arab Emirates and Saudi Arabia, and as an importer of labour from India and her neighbours.

1067 **The Sultanate of Oman: economic development, the domestic labour market and international migration.**
John Stace Birks, Clive A. Sinclair.   Geneva: International Labour Office, 1978. 98p. (Migration for Employment Project. Working Paper, no. 28).

A study of the migration from Oman to better-paid posts in the United Arab Emirates. It discusses the effect on economic development and problems created in the Omani labour supply.

1068 **Labour migration in the Arab Gulf States: Patterns, trends and prospects.**
John Stace Birks, Clive A. Sinclair.   *International Migration*, vol. 26, no. 3 (1988), p. 267-86.

An analysis of changes in non-national migration and employment in the member states of the Gulf Cooperation Council, including Oman. The authors examine the non-national labour force, flows of migrant workers and the outflows due to the 1986 decline in oil prices and production.

1069 **Migrant workers in the Arab Gulf: the impact of declining oil revenues.**
John Stace Birks (et al.).   *International Migration Review*, vol. 20, no. 4 (Winter 1986), p. 799-814.

This is a study of the decline in demand for immigrant workers resulting from declining oil revenues since 1981, though the reduction was less than had been anticipated because of the hoarding of labour by companies. Kuwait is used as the main focus, but the study is of relevance to all of the oil-producing states. Tables give details of work permit holders in Oman between 1979 and 1984 and government expenditure and work permit issues, 1976-84.

1070 **Asians in the Arab World: Labour migration and public policy.**
Nazli Choucri.   *Middle Eastern Studies*, vol. 20, no. 2 (1986),
p. 252-73.

An examination of the pattern of labour migration in the Arab world from 1973 to 1986 and the evolution of a policy favouring Asian expatriate labour for political reasons. The commencement of the use of Asian labour was partially motivated by market conditions as Arab labour could not fully meet the demands, but also by political considerations – Asians were regarded as passive observers in the political process rather than activists, or claimants on the welfare system and other benefits of citizenship. Oman is one of the states that was both an importer and exporter of labour, with the balance heavily in favour of imported labour. The article considers in detail the overall effects, problems and prospects associated with the use of migrant labour in the region and the significance of foreign workers' remittances to the labour-exporting Asian countries.

1071 **An explosive vote of change in Khabura, Oman immigrants fill the labour vacuum.**
R. Dutton.   In: *The Middle Eastern village, changing economic and social relations*, edited by R. Lawless.   London: Croom Helm, 1987,
p. 175-93.

Oman is both an importer and exporter of labour and immigrant labour had become a feature of rural Oman. Oil wealth stimulated change in the 1970s and the village of Khabura is used as a case-study to illustrate the socio-economic effects of these changes. In terms of employment, Omanis became unwilling to work as labourers on someone else's land and Omanis who had migrated to other Gulf States began to employ Pakistanis as labourers on their land. However, the labour is unskilled and contributed nothing to the development of agriculture. Change in Khabura has permeated all aspects of its physical structure and economy, society and culture and it appears that they have been absorbed with ease but strains may exist beneath the surface which could emerge in future years.

1072 **Migrant labour in agriculture: an international comparison.**
Philip L. Martin.   *International Migration Review*, vol. 19, no. 1
(1985), p. 135-43.

A comparative study of the social and economic conditions for migrant labourers in agriculture in twelve countries ranging from the United States, various European countries, South Africa and Oman. The focus is on the domestic policies of the countries regarding foreign workers and the social change in the host countries caused by dependency upon foreign labour.

1073   **Urbanisation and labour migration in the Arab countries of the Gulf.**
Galal Abdulla Moawad.   *Journal of the Gulf and Arabian Peninsula Studies*, vol. 13, no. 51 (1987), p. 189-94.
A study of the development of nation city-states in the Arabian Gulf, including Oman, with the capital area comprising more than 70 per cent of its population. This has been brought about by the growth of expatriate labour in response to programmes of development and the growth of the oil industry. Moawad considers the cultural and socio-economic impact of this population growth, including: pressures on urban services; conflict with the indigenous population; restrictions on female employment; and social and political threats to native Arab culture and identity.

1074   **The labour force in Oman.**
Susanna Powell.   In: *Workforce management in the Arabian Peninsula: Forces affecting development*, edited by George S. Roukis, Patrick J. Montana.   London; New York: Greenwood Press, 1986, p. 113-22.
This work examines labour forces in the states of the Arabian Peninsula as they affect development programmes in the various states. The contribution on Oman examines the structure of the labour force, considering its composition, the skills required to meet the targets of the development plan and the need for, and source of, expatriate labour. Consideration is also given to the need to absorb the new generation of educated Omani into the employment sector.

1075   **Human resources in the Arab World: The impact of migration.**
Ismail Serageldin, James A. Socknat, John Stace Birks.   In: *Arab resources: The transformation of a society*, edited by Ibrahim Ibrahim.   Washington, DC: Georgetown University Center for Contemporary Arab Studies; London: Croom Helm, 1983, p. 19-33.
This paper is in five sections: definitions and caveats; an overview of current levels of and prospects for labour migration in the Middle East and North Africa; the labour-importing countries; the labour-exporting countries; and a conclusion. Oman is dealt with as one of the labour-importing countries and the tables show the origins of migrant workers, the shares of occupations by type of occupation, and the labour-exporting countries of which Oman is one.

1076   **Manpower and international labour migration in the Middle East and North Africa.**
Ismail Serageldin (et al.).   New York: Oxford University Press for the World Bank, 1983. 138p.
The published results of a World Bank research project by specialists in manpower and education in the area. The work uses 1975 as a base date and provides information on regional labour market trends and projected manpower requirements between 1975 and 1985. Oman is dealt with as one of the Arab states which is both an importer and exporter of labour.

1077 **Expatriate labor flows to the Arab oil countries in the 1980s.**
Naiem A. Sherbiny. *Middle East Journal*, vol. 38, no. 4 (1984),
p. 643-67.

An examination of labour migration to the Arab oil states, including Oman, during the
1980s which showed that such flows were, barring economic disaster, likely to
increase for the largest users of expatriate labour. The detailed study concentrates on
the larger oil-producing states, excluding Oman, but the general section of the article
is of relevance and Oman is included in some of the statistical data.

1078 **Human resources in the Gulf.**
Roger Webster. In: *Arabia and the Gulf: From traditional societies
to modern states*, edited by B. R. Pridham. London: Croom Helm,
1986, p. 188-212.

A study of development in the Gulf States, including Oman, and in particular the
question of human resources and the lack of skilled manpower in the region. As
developing states they have similar problems to the poorer nations, with high rates of
illiteracy, infant mortality and disease, and low rates of participation in development
tasks. There is also the problem of a small but vital modern sector using imported
technology and personnel juxtaposed with stagnant traditional sectors: 'a farmer in
Oman recently pointed out . . . that he can now go to Nizwa and buy fresh European
tomatoes of a more reliable quality, and at a cheaper price, than he can afford to
produce himself . . .'. Further problems are caused by the influx of foreign workers
into the region; they made up 37.3 per cent of the Omani labour force in 1980, and
even made inroads into the agricultural sector, with labour from the Indian
sub-continent replacing Omanis as agricultural labourers.

Dissertations

1079 **Manpower planning and development in Oman.**
H. A. Ali. PhD thesis, University of Bangor, Wales, 1990.
(Available from British Library, Document Supply Centre, Boston
Spa, Wetherby, West Yorkshire, United Kingdom).

This study used a survey and fieldwork to obtain data regarding the evaluation of
manpower planning in the Sultanate. The survey indicated that in 1990 Oman would
have to rely on 150,000 expatriate workers to achieve its planned growth and that by
1995 this figure would rise to 190,000. The situation would be further complicated by
the fact that in 1995 about 80,000 educated Omanis would be on the labour market
but without the skills to match the available jobs. The author determines three major
areas to be addressed: manpower demand; manpower supply; and manpower
development, with a proposed conceptual model to address these issues which need
further detailed study.

1080 **Higher education and underemployment in Oman: perceptions of university graduates in the context of dependent development, 1970-1990.**
Asya Mohamed Suleiman Al-Lamky. PhD thesis, George Washington University, 1992. 294p. (Available from University Microfilms, Ann Arbor, Michigan, order no. AAD92-23605).

An examination of the views of Omanis with regard to their education and work experience and the obstacles which they perceive as hindering the effective utilization of their skills. This study was based on a questionnaire to 500 Omani graduates together with in-depth interviews with 35 working graduates. The author concludes that the Oman labour market had imbalances due to internal and external factors which are a manifestation of a dependent economy. The obstacles are seen as prolonging the need for expatriate workers, and 65 per cent of the graduates indicated that they were unable to replace expatriates and perceived no clear policy by the Omani government to do so.

Statistics

1081 Basic indicators.
Middle East Economic Digest Special Report (Nov. 1980), p. 4.

A series of up-to-date statistics on the Sultanate, covering imports, gross domestic product by industry, and energy supplies.

1082 Civil registration and vital statistics in selected countries in the Middle East.
Population Bulletin of the United Nations Economic and Social Office, no. 2 (Jan. 1972), p. 13-19.

This is a summary of a paper in which are discussed: the new methods of collecting demographic statistics; the traditional methods previously used in countries of the Middle East, including Oman.

1083 Quarterly Bulletin of Main Economic Indicators.
Directorate General of National Statistics. Muscat: Development Council, Technical Secretariat, 1972- . quarterly.

The official publication of the government providing economic forecasts for each of the sectors of the Omani government.

1084 Directory of socio-economic data for the Arabian Gulf countries.
Doha, Qatar: Industrial Data Bank Gulf Organization for Industrial Consultancy, 1981. 166p.

A listing of available economic and socio-economic statistical data in the Gulf States, including Oman.

1085 **Foreign trade statistics.**
Muscat: Royal Oman Police, Customs Department, 1984- . annual.
An annual publication providing details of imports and exports and including data on categories, values and government revenue from duties.

1086 **The economies of the Arabian Gulf: a statistical source book.**
A. K. McMaster. London: Croom Helm, 1983. 400p.
A source of statistical data for the area, including Oman, covering topics such as balance of payments, and labour and employment statistics.

1087 **Oman statistics.**
Middle East Economic Digest, vol. 22 (3 March 1978), p. 46-47.
Includes statistics on the balance of payments for the years 1973-77; development expenditure, 1975-77; government revenue and expenditure, 1973-77; and imports by commodity, 1973-77.

1088 **Statistical Yearbook.**
Sultanate of Oman. Muscat: Development Council, 1972- . annual
The official statistical publication of the Omani government, issued jointly by the Development Council, Technical Secretariat and the Directorate General of National Statistics. Contains a wealth of detail though, as with all such publications, it is usually at least twelve months out of date at the time of publication.

1089 **Oman at a glance.**
Sultanate of Oman. Department of National Statistics. Muscat: Department of Government Printing, 1972- . irregular.
An irregularly updated booklet providing statistical data on trade, banking, the economy and society. Designed for the general reader.

1090 **Demographic Yearbook.**
United Nations, Statistical Office. New York: United Nations, 1948- . annual.
A comprehensive publication, covering basic social statistics such as population growth rates, death rates, natality, and density.

1091 **Statistical Yearbook.**
United Nations, Statistical Office. New York: United Nations, 1948- . annual.
Subjects covered include communications, education, medicine, food production, and energy. Sources of data are given, as are notes to explain the compilation and interpretation.

1092   Yearbook of national accounts statistics.

United Nations, Statistical Office.   New York: United Nations, 1957- . annual.

The yearbook replaces *Statistics of national income and expenditure*, which appeared between 1938 and 1950. It covers aspects such as expenditure on gross national product, distribution of income, and general government revenue and expenditure.

1093   National Basic Intelligence Fact Book.

United States Central Intelligence Agency.   Washington, DC: US Government Printing Office. irregular.

An irregularly updated publication giving a small amount of data on each country. Coverage is restricted to a brief outline of the country, with a section on military capability. Oman is regularly covered.

Education

1094 **Factors influencing the recruitment and retention of literacy learners in Oman.**
T. Al-Barwani, E. F. Kelly. *International Review of Education*, vol. 31, no. 2 (1985), p. 145-54.

An investigation of factors influencing the recruitment and retention of literacy learners in the national and adult literacy programme in Oman. Based on interviews of 102 adults in the interior and capital regions of Oman, the results showed distinct regional variations in motivations for enrolling, but the 'spiritual' motive was the most significant overall. Obstacles to completion of the course varied, with men indicating that work demands were a major obstacle whilst women cited family responsibilities.

1095 **Successful education and human resource development – The key to sustained economic growth.**
John Stace Birks, C. A. Sinclair. In: *Oman: economic, social and strategic developments*, edited by B. R. Pridham. London: Croom Helm, 1987, p. 145-67.

This study focuses on the human resource development policies of Oman which have been of growing importance within the general economic development strategy. The article also discusses the replacement of expatriate workers by Omanis which is considered to be a particular responsibility of the education and training system in the Sultanate. The process of 'Omanization' of the workforce needs to be carefully handled and gradual in order to maintain the process of growth, and it must be a target in the evolution of the education system. The article examines the education system at all levels, including the school system, technical colleges, the literacy programme, pre-employment training and in-service training in both the public and private sector. The authors also consider the work and role of the Education and Training Council.

1096 **Oman: aiming at education for all.**
Alison Brown. *Middle East Economic Digest Special Report* (Nov. 1983), p. 13-14.
A report on the educational system and the significant growth in schools and numbers of pupils since 1970. At that time the majority of teachers were expatriates and spoke several Arabic dialects, a situation which created some problems.

1097 **Oman: University confounds the sceptics.**
Alison Brown. *Middle East Economic Digest Special Report* (Nov. 1983), p. 16-18.
A report on the Sultan Qaboos University following the first year of construction. The university was scheduled to provide teacher-training courses, Islamic sciences, engineering, science, agriculture and medicine.

1098 **Research facilities in the Arabian Gulf: Kuwait, Bahrain, Oman, Qatar and the United Arab Emirates.**
Jill Crystal. *Middle East Studies Association Bulletin*, vol. 18, no. 2 (1984), p. 175-81.
Presents the practical aspects of research facilities in the named countries all of which require sponsorship and visas. Material for research is available but difficult to locate, and so the article also provides a guide to available collections, including specific contacts to make.

1099 **Development of education in the Sultanate of Oman during the school year.**
Muscat: Ministry of Education, 1974- . semi-annual.
A twice-yearly report of educational developments in the Sultanate, issued in English and Arabic and including statistical data.

1100 **Improving education in the Arabian Gulf region.**
Mohammad A. Rasheed, Herbert R. Hengst. *Journal of Thought*, vol. 18, no. 2 (1983), p. 97-103.
Educational development in the Arab Gulf States, including Oman, has been stimulated by the work of the Arab Bureau of Education for the Gulf States. The focus has been on the collection of data on programmes within member states, educating Arabs about their own culture and preparing to establish a Gulf University in Bahrain.

1101 **Sultanate of Oman: third education project.**
Washington, DC: World Bank, Europe, Middle East and North Africa Region, Education and Manpower Development Division, 1987. 59p. map.
An appraisal of Oman's third education project whose objectives were: to develop key education services; train and upgrade teachers; increase access to education, particularly in the rural areas and for girls. Also provides information on the current education system and policy objectives for the sector.

Dissertations

1102 **Curriculum evaluation by assessing the degree of accordance between the designer's intentions and the implementer's perceptions of these intentions: The case of primary school mathematics and science curriculum in Oman.**
Mohamed Nabil Abdelgalil. PhD thesis, State University of New York at Buffalo, 1988. 359p. (Available from University Microfilms, Ann Arbor, Michigan, order no. AAD88-12314).

In this study evaluation was undertaken by assessing the degree of accordance between the designer's intentions, as detailed in the learning objectives, and the conception of these by the implementers, teachers, supervisors and administrators. A sample of teachers and administrators were chosen for the study and stratified to reflect the whole population, while all supervisors of mathematics and science participated in the study

1103 **A process for developing policy recommendations for the recruitment and retention of learners in literacy education programs: the Oman experience.**
Thuwayba Ahmad Al-Barwani. EdD, State University of New York at Albany, 1981. 409p. (Available from University Microfilms, Ann Arbor, Michigan, order no. AAD82-06791).

An examination of the problems faced by illiteracy programmes in attracting and retaining students. The purpose of the study was to formulate policy recommendations for the recruitment and retention of learners in adult literacy education programmes. Based on field studies in Oman, interviews, and data which were further refined by Ministry of Education officials and Islamic scholars. The main findings were that adults in the capital area were interested in literacy for its economic benefits whilst in the interior interest was more in literacy for its own sake.

1104 **The performance of Omani secondary school students on selected science practical skills.**
R. Al Busaidi. DPhil thesis, Oxford University, England, 1988. (Available from British Library, Document Supply Centre, Boston Spa, Wetherby, West Yorkshire, United Kingdom).

The results of research into the science practical skills of 17–18-year-old Omani students involving 15 schools and 378 students in four educational regions of the Sultanate. The methodology is discussed, as are the findings. These showed: that the schools were an important influence on skills acquisition, and that there was a mismatch between the perceptions of the educators, between teachers' and students' expectations of the role of practical work, and between and within science curriculum materials.

1105 **The historical development of education in Oman: From the first modern school in 1893 to the first modern university in 1986.**
Mohammed Hafied Al-Dhahab.   PhD thesis, Boston College, 1987, 365p. (Available from University Microfilms, Ann Arbor, Michigan, order no. AAD89-03984).

Traces the history of the development of education in Oman from the first school established in 1893 by the Arabian mission, to the establishment of the Sultan Qaboos University in 1986. The greatest concentration is on the post-1970 development, showing the significance of education to the new government and the problems needing to be resolved.

1106 **Human capital theory and the motivations and expectations of university students in the Sultanate of Oman.**
Muneer Mohammed Sultan Al-Maskery.   PhD thesis, University of Missouri, Saint Louis, 1992. 397p. (Available from University Microfilms, Ann Arbor, Michigan, order no. AAD92-32407).

The focus of the study was the measurement of the motivations of Omani students at the Sultan Qaboos University which proved the arguments posed by the human capital theory: that people are motivated to invest in themselves and education and training because they expect a return in career opportunities and rewards during their working life.

1107 **A comparison study of elementary teachers in the Omani schools system.**
Sharon Harriet Vuich.   PhD thesis, University of Michigan, 1987. 116p. (Available from University Microfilms, Ann Arbor Michigan, order no. AAD87-20357).

An exploratory study in investigating personality profiles of elementary teachers in Oman. Vuich argues that the presence of teachers from other Arab countries may reflect values which are inconsistent with the goals of child socialization in Omani culture. This is a serious situation for policy-makers in Oman as more than half of the teachers in Omani schools at that time were from other Arab countries (Egypt, Jordan, Saudi Arabia, Sudan, Tunisia).

Libraries

1108 Coordinated economic development and the information network.
D. K. Easton. Arlington, Virginia: Educational Resources Information Center, 1977. 9p.

A discussion of the problems faced by the Advisory Organization for Gulf Industries when it undertakes to organize an information centre to serve the needs of the Gulf States, including Oman. The second main task will be the compilation of a database of economic information and statistics covering the seven Gulf States.

1109 Censorship and librarianship in Oman.
Stan Gardner. *Library Journal*, vol. 114, no. 19 (1989), p. 56-58.

Discusses the stringent checks by the Ministries of Information and National Heritage and Culture on books and audiovisual materials selected by the Sultan Qaboos University Library. The censorship procedure is described, as are the problems of status and sexism which face librarians.

1110 The development of CD-ROM provision at the Sultan Qaboos University in the Sultanate of Oman.
Colin S. Johnston. *Program*, vol. 26, no. 2 (1992), p. 177-82.

Because of high telecommunications costs, the Sultan Qaboos University has developed the use of CD-ROM as an alternative to on-line searching. The service is open to all, but students are encouraged to undertake manual searches first as part of the educational process. Although on-line searching will be available, it is intended that CD-ROM would continue to be used for the bulk of searches with on-line searching as a top-up.

1111 **The emergence of libraries in the Sultanate of Oman.**
Bakri Musa A. Karim. *International Library Review*, vol. 23, no. 3 (1991), p. 229-36.

A report on library developments in Oman from 1971 which, despite rapid social and economic development, have not been matched in the library and information structure. At the time of writing there was no designated national library, and public libraries were few and had a limited scope. The Sultan Qaboos University Library is likely to have considerable scope as a research library and some government ministries and assisted bodies have good specialist libraries. However, school libraries are deficient in resources and there is a dearth of school librarians. Professional library training had started and the first locally trained professional librarians were due to graduate in 1991.

1112 **Archiving at the Oman Centre for Traditional Music, Muscat.**
Issam El-Mallah. *Phonographic Bulletin*, vol. 55 (Nov. 1989), p. 32-48.

Describes the founding in 1985 of the Oman Centre for Traditional Music with the objective of preserving the heritage of the music culture of Oman. The author also discusses the archiving system used by the centre, and the reasons for the lack of archives for traditional music in the Arab world generally.

1113 **In Oman there is only one librarian.**
Lilly Shehadeh. *Bibliotek 70*, vol. 6 (1982), p. 179-80.

At the time of the article the library service in Oman consisted only of the National Islamic Library in Muscat. The country's only librarian was in charge of the manuscript collection and the development of the library in general. The library was reference only and the stock consisted of 30,000 books in Arabic, 1,000 in English and 3,000 children's books.

1114 **Sultan Qaboos University in Oman.**
Harvey Varnet. *College and Research Libraries News*, vol. 45, no. 4 (1984), p. 175-77.

A discussion of the plans for the Sultan Qaboos University, with a scheduled opening date of 1986. The article concentrates on the challenges to be met, such as liaising with the architect and contractors, equipment, staffing, education and communication.

1115 **Development of agricultural library and documentation services in the Sultanate of Oman. Report of a mission (25 April – 11 May 1986).**
A. M. Woodward. Rome: FAO, 1986. 22p. (FAO Accession No. XF8878327 – available only on microfiche).

A report of a special Food and Agriculture Organization mission to Oman to advise on the setting up of libraries for the Ministry of Agriculture and with proposals for development of information services to the sector.

Dissertation

1116 **The academic library in the electronic age: The case of six Arabian Peninsula countries.**
Mekhag B. Abdo. PhD thesis, State University of New York at Buffalo, 1987. 345p. (Available from University Microfilms, Ann Arbor, Michigan, order no. AAD87-10682).

Based on a questionnaire sent to the thirteen academic libraries in the Arabian Peninsula, including Oman, to determine the nature of their automation projects. The study aimed at examining the organizational set-up of the libraries, plans for automation and regional cooperation in this area.

Culture and Customs

1117 Falconry in Arabia.

Mark Allen. London: Orbis Publishing, 1980. 134p.

A study of the art of falconry in the Arabian Peninsula, the methods and its significance in Arabian culture. There are only limited references to Oman in the text, but the book is of interest because the art of falconry was previously practised throughout the Arabian Peninsula, although it is now the purview of the rich.

1118 Indigo – An Arab curiosity and its Omani variations.

Jenny Balfour-Paul. In: *Oman: economic, social and strategic development*, edited by B. R. Pridham. London: Croom Helm, 1987, p. 79-93.

Indigo is widely used in the Arab world and this is particularly true of Oman though the traditional processes are now in decline as a specialist industry. The article considers the traditional methods of dyeing, its use in dress and in medicine, and the significance of indigo dresses when dealing with evil spirits, or the *jinn* and the *zar*. Indigo also has a significance in Omani funerals, particularly as a sign of mourning for women and as a covering for a female corpse before the white cloth is laid on.

1119 Handicrafts in Oman and their role in rural community development.

R. W. Dutton. *Geoforum*, vol. 14, no. 3 (1983), p. 341-52.

A study of traditional crafts in Oman which are being encouraged by the Omani government in rural development programmes. The article considers how the development and preservation of traditional skills can assist in the preservation of rural communities which were in danger of demise with a drift from the land and the growth of migrant labour.

1120   **Omani silver.**
Ruth Hawley.   London: Longman, 1977. 60p. map.
A well-illustrated account of the various types of Omani silver, the geographical
distribution of styles, and the craft of the silversmiths.

1121   **Folklore and folk literature in Oman and Socatra.**
Thomas Muir Johnstone.   *Arabian Studies*, vol. 1 (1974), p. 7-23.
A consideration of the folklore preserved by the Mahris and Sheris of Dhofar and the
Harasis of Oman, whose isolation was partially brought about by their retention of a
different language or dialect. The article gives an outline of the social structure of the
three tribes in question before presenting examples of the lore and literature which
has survived both in magic and in legends concerning animals.

1122   **Knots and curses.**
Thomas Muir Johnstone.   *Arabian Studies*, vol. 3 (1976), p. 79-83.
An analysis of the place of knots in the culture of many peoples, making a case-study
of the custom of knotting cords against enemies. This is a custom which survived
until recently and the study presents a Mehri account of the practice communicated to
the author in 1974.

1123   **Oath-taking and vows in Oman.**
Thomas Muir Johnstone.   *Arabian Studies*, vol. 2 (1975), p. 7-18.
Dhofar is used as a case-study to illustrate the significance of oath-taking and
vow-making in a pre-industrial society where the spoken word has not been replaced
by the written one. This aspect of ethics was vitally important for a man to move
between the territory of an unfriendly tribe, where negotiated safe conduct was
essential for survival.

1124   **Women in politics: A global view.**
Kathleen Newland.   *International Journal of Intercultural
Relations*, vol. 3, no. 4 (1979), p. 393-406.
A study of the political participation of women throughout the world and an
assessment of the discrimination which exists. Only eight countries exclude women by
law from the political process; seven of these are in the Middle East, including Oman.

1125   **The Sultanate of Oman: International Symposium on the
Traditional Music of Oman.**
Jennifer M. Scarce.   *British Society for Middle Eastern Studies
Bulletin*, vol. 13, no. 1 (1986), p. 51-54.
A discussion of the work of the Oman Centre for Traditional Music which was
established by the Ministry of Information in 1985 with the objective of creating an
archive of traditional music. In the initial fieldwork trips the project concentrated on
the documentation of traditional music and associated dances through
sound-recording, video films, and interviews with participants. The first fieldwork has
produced four archives, consisting of: 1,800 recordings of video film; a sound archive
of 3,000 tape-recordings; a photographic archive of 20,000 colour photographs and
4,000 colour slides; and a transcript archive of about 5,000 field interviews.

1126 **Orders, decorations and medals of the Sultanate of Oman.**
A. R. Tinson. London: Spink and Son, 1977. xii+100p.
A listing of the various orders etc., together with descriptions and attributions.

Tribes in Oman.
See item no. 638.

Folk-tales and folk-lore of Dhofar.
See item no. 695.

Architecture

1127 Architecture and social history at al-Mudayrit.
  P. G. Bonnefort, Salin al-Harthis. *Journal of Oman Studies*, vol. 3,
  pt. 2 (1977), p. 107-35.
A study of the domestic architecture of al-Mudayit as a means of providing a social
history of the settlement and reading the patterns of change in everyday life and the
economy.

1128 Restoration of painted ceilings in Oman: the fort of Jabrin.
  Jean Claude Bourret. *ICOMOS Information*, no. 1 (1988), p. 17-25.
The fort at Jabrin was commissioned about 1670 by Bil'arub ibn Saif, largely as a
country home, though for a short period it was regarded as the capital of Oman. The
fort is large and noted for its ornately carved doorways and painted ceilings and this
article describes the restoration work on the painted ceilings carried out as part of the
Sultanate's heritage programme. The article is in French.

**1129 The indigenous built environment of Oman – its problems and
  potentials for contemporary planning and design.**
  A. Cain, F. Afshar, J. Norton.   Muscat: Sultanate Printing Press,
  1974. 455p.
An interesting study of the problems and challenges presented by the desire to blend
modern designs with traditional architecture. Contains a wealth of material on
traditional Omani architecture and the built environment.

1130 Some notes on Omani architecture.
  D. Chritchfield.   Muscat: Ministry of Information and Culture,
  Department of Antiquities, 1976. 45p.
A useful introductory booklet to traditional Omani architecture.

1131 **Studies on the built environment of the Batinah.**

Paola M. Costa. *Journal of Oman Studies*, vol. 8, pt. 2 (1985).

This complete issue of the *Journal of Oman Studies* is totally devoted to the built environment of the Batinah coastal region and provides information on the architecture of the area as well as an insight into social conditions, the way of life and the economic activity of the population. Amongst the topics covered are: The Batinah and its built environment; The palm-frond houses of the Batinah; The Sur of the Batinah; and Bayt Na'man, a seventeenth-century mansion of the Batinah.

1132 **Sultanate of Oman: building conditions and materials.**

J. R. Crowder. Garston, England: Garston Building Research Establishment, 1986. 41p. maps. bibliog.

An account of the building industry in Oman covering the conditions faced by contractors in terms of materials available, the labour force, working environment, and the general environment in relation to the industry.

1133 **Introduction to Omani military architecture of the sixteenth, seventeenth and eighteenth centuries.**

Enrico d'Errico. *Journal of Oman Studies*, vol. 6, no. 2 (1982), p. 291-306. maps.

An introductory survey of military architecture in Oman from the sixteenth to the eighteenth century. The article describes the fortifications introduced by the Portuguese, with installations in Muscat at Jalali and Mirani and at Sohar, together with traditional Muslim fortifications at Bahla, Al-Hazin and Nizwa. The origins of the architecture of the Portuguese and Omani installations are discussed, as are the series of fortifications built by the Omanis following the expulsion of the Portuguese. The article has diagrams and illustrations of the various fortifications and a map locating the various sites.

1134 **A masterpiece of Omani 17th century architecture: the palace of Imam Bilarab bin Sultan al-Yaaraba at Jabrin.**

Eugenio Galdien. *Journal of Oman Studies*, vol. 1 (1975), p. 167-79.

A brief consideration of the palace which is situated in a small oasis at Jabrin near Bahla at the end of the first large chain of the Jabal Al Akhdar. The article describes the building, using sketches to illustrate salient features, and discusses the possible building phases. It is hoped that renovation and conservation work will enable more conclusions to be drawn concerning its history.

1135 **The early Islamic architecture of the East African coast.**

Peter S. Gorlake. London: Oxford University Press, 1966. 207p. (British Institute of History and Archaeology in East Africa, Memoir no. 1).

A study of the influence of Omani decorative styles in East Africa since the 17th century, through an examination of the styles of mosques and domestic buildings.

1136 Building for higher education in the Gulf.
Kamal El Kafrawi (et al.).   *Mimar*, no. 37 (Dec. 1990), p. 23-49.
The architectural account of the Sultan Qaboos University is described on pages
46-49.

1137 Suhari houses.
M. Karvran (et al.).   *Journal of Oman Studies*, vol. 6, no. 2 (1983),
p. 309-16.
A study of a group of houses in Sohar which were built in the nineteenth century
when the town had lost its former economic glory. Today, Sohar is a fishing village
on the Batinah coast with agriculture based on dates and dried limes. Expansion of
agriculture is planned but it is threatened by the salinity of the water table. The
houses examined show Sohar's diverse activities over the years and those examined
represent middle-class dwellings. The article then proceeds to describe the various
houses, their design, construction, materials and decoration.

1138 Medinat Qaboos: a development of character.
Muscat: Taylor Woodrow-Towell. maps.
A prospectus for the new town of Medinat Qaboos, designed as a model town
comprising private housing with central community and shopping facilities.

1139 The Islamic Garden in Oman: sanctuary and paradise.
John Alexander Smith.   *Garden History*, vol. 19, no. 2 (1991),
p. 187-208. maps. bibliog.
A study of the Islamic Garden in Oman which considers its place in Islamic society to
be that of a sanctuary from the stresses of everyday life. The design, layout, features
and flora are also described.

Mass Media

1140 **Al Akidah.**
Muscat-Ruwi: weekly.
Arabic news magazine.

1141 **The Commercial.**
Muscat-Ruwi: Oman Advertising Agency, 1978- . monthly.
A magazine of economic news.

1142 **Gulf Guide and Diary.**
Saffron Walden, England: Middle East Review, 1972- . annual.
A diary with useful data on the Gulf States and Oman.

1143 **Gulf Studies.**
London: Gulf Committee, 1976- . semi-annual.
The bulletin of the Popular Front, previously issued as the *Gulf Bulletin* from 1971 to 1975.

1144 **Historical Association of Oman Bulletin.**
Muscat: The Association, 1974- . irregular.
Mainly in English.

1145 **Journal of Oman Studies.**
Muscat: Sultanate of Oman, Ministry of Information and Culture, 1975- . irregular.
Contains a wealth of information in detailed, illustrated articles covering all aspects of Omani history, life, society, economy, and flora and fauna.

1146   **The literal text of the Gulf Information Honorary Covenant which had been acknowledged from the GCC leaders in the summit conference which took place in the state of the UAE.**
Journal of the Gulf and Arabian Peninsula Studies, vol. 8, no. 50 (1987), p. 279-87.

Reproduces the text dating from December 1986 of the Covenant on Ethics in Communications signed by the leaders of the Gulf Cooperation Council at the summit meeting held in the United Arab Emirates. The media would adhere to the values of Islam and Gulf Cooperation, and all information transmitted would be objective, exact and authentic without provocation or personal attacks. The media also agreed to support social development in the Gulf and oppose everything that might harm Arab identity in the GCC.

1147   **Advertising agencies and media in the lower Gulf.**
R. A. Middleton, Tariq Almoayyed.   Manama, Bahrain: al-Hilal Bookshop, 1977, vi+133p. map.

A list of the agencies and media throughout the lower part of the Gulf, including Oman.

1148   **Oman.**
Muscat: 1983- . daily.

An Arabic daily newspaper, not published on Friday.

1149   **Oman Daily Observer.**
Muscat: Oman Newspaper House, 1981- . daily.

An English-language daily, except for Friday.

1150   **Oman News.**
Muscat: Sultanate of Oman, 1970- .

A newsletter issued by the various Omani embassies giving up-to-date news on the Sultanate.

1151   **Al Omaneya.**
London: Powers Overseas Ltd. -monthly

A monthly Arabic-language up-market magazine for women in Oman.

1152   **The Arab press: News media and political process in the Arab World.**
William A. Rugh.   London: Croom Helm, 1979. xiii+205p. bibliog.

A study of the role and structure of the Arab media, how they function and whether they are controlled, or not, by particular governments. This study is based on interviews with journalists, editors and Arab officials working and living in the Middle East. Oman is dealt with as part of this study, with coverage of the media in general, newspapers, radio, television and the Omani News Agency.

1153 **Times of Oman.**
Matrah, Oman: al-Essa Printing and Publishing Organization, 1975- .
weekly.
The major English-language newspaper.

1154 **Al Watan.**
Muscat: Represented in UK by Powers Overseas Ltd. daily.
An Arabic daily newspaper.

Dissertation

1155 **A descriptive analytical study of regional television cooperation among Arabian Gulf countries.**
Hamza Ahmad Bait-Almal.   PhD thesis, Wayne State University, 1986. 254p.
Discusses mass media cooperation amongst the member states of the Gulf Cooperation Council which has resulted in the establishment of eight regional mass media organizations. This study concentrates on the cooperative television activities through the Gulf Television Corporation and the Arabian Gulf States Joint Program Production Institution. The study also includes an evaluation of these cooperative ventures through interviews with the General Directors of Television from the seven countries involved.

Urbanization

1156 The small towns.
G. H. Blake. In: *The changing Middle Eastern city*, edited by
G. H. Blake, R. J. Lawless. London: Croom Helm; New York:
Barnes and Noble, 1980, p. 209-29.

A study of small towns in the Middle East – their numbers had doubled during the twenty-five years before this was written. In the case of Oman it is recognized that any quantitative analysis is difficult because of the lack of accurate statistical data. In 1977 it was determined to have only two small towns of 40,000 inhabitants, representing 5 per cent of the population. However, the general study of the significance of small towns, their structure, society and role is still of relevance to Oman where urban development has since taken place.

1157 Urban planning in Eastern Arabia.
Alexander Melamid. *Geographical Review*, vol. 70, no. 4 (1980),
p. 473-77.

A consideration of plans for urban development in the United Arab Emirates, Qatar, Saudi Arabia and Kuwait. Melamid also discusses the reasons why Oman is not proposing to build any new cities.

1158 Urban centres in the Gulf during the early Islamic period: a historical study.
Farouk Omar. *Bulletin of the British Society for Middle Eastern Studies*, vol. 14, no. 2 (1989), p. 155-61.

A historical survey of urban centres in the Gulf – concentrating on Bahrain and Oman – which briefly considers the centres of Sohar, Muscat, Daba, Qalbat, and Nizwa as these fall into the category of centres which are mentioned by nearly all the geographers and historians. In addition, there is precise information as to their location, and also the data available on their political, social and economic conditions.

261

1159 Urbanization in contemporary Arab Gulf States.

Ishaq Y. Qutub. *Ekistis*, vol. 50, no. 300 (1983), p. 170-72.

A discussion of urbanization in the Gulf States, including Oman, which provides an historical background to development in these states and a projection of demographic trends. A possible future strategy is also presented.

Bibliographies

1160 **Annotated bibliography of the principal publications concerning the Middle East issued by the United Nations and its specialised agencies.**
International Social Sciences Bulletin, vol. 5, pt. 4 (1963), p. 732-52.
The listing is arranged in sections, beginning with the publications of the General Assembly, various ad hoc committees, and agencies such as the Food and Agriculture Organization. This is a useful guide, though coverage is obviously much broader than the Sultanate.

1161 **The states of the Arabian Peninsula and the Gulf littoral: a selected bibliography.**
John Duke Anthony. Washington, DC: Middle East Institute, 1973. 21p.
A useful introductory bibliography, the focus being on governmental systems, political dynamics, international relations and economics. The listing is divided into two sections, the first dealing with monographs and the second with periodical articles, each section being alphabetically arranged with no subject breakdown. Nearly 200 items are listed, of which about one-quarter are monographs, with annotations limited to this section. Only a portion of the entries are relevant to Oman.

1162 **The contemporary Middle East, 1948-1973, a selective and annotated bibliography.**
George N. Atiyeh. Boston, Massachusetts: G. K. Hall, 1975. 664p.
A very useful bibliography with brief annotations of some 6,500 entries, covering monographs, pamphlets and periodical articles, primarily in Western languages. The material is selective and orientated largely towards the social scientist, with items on history, politics, social conditions, economics and education. One section deals specifically with Oman and other references are to be found in the general subject sections.

1163 **Arab regional organizations.**
Frank A. Clements. Oxford, England: Clio Press; New Brunswick: Transaction Publishers, 1992. 198p.

There are specific references to Oman throughout the text, covering relations with the Arab League, foreign policy, and relations with the United States. However, the section of main importance is that dealing with the Gulf Cooperation Council between pages 35 and 71. All entries are annotated.

1164 **Saudi Arabia.**
Frank A. Clements. Oxford, England; Santa Barbara, California: Clio Press, 1988. 2nd ed. 355p. map. (World Bibliographical Series, vol. 5).

Useful for a consideration of items dealing with the claims of Saudi Arabia to such territory as Buraimi Oasis, also claimed by Oman and Abu Dhabi, and support for the Imamate.

1165 **Guide to research and reference works on sub-Saharan Africa.**
Helen Conover, Peter Duigrion. Stanford, California: Hoover Institution Press, 1972. 1102p.

Included for the abstracts of works on Zanzibar which cover the period of Omani influence (p. 776-79).

1166 **Bibliographie über das Sultanat Oman.** (Bibliography of the Sultanate of Oman.)
Joachim Duster, Fred Scholz. Hamburg, Germany: Dokumenations-Leitstelle Modernes Orient, 1980. xviii+141+xixp.

Although the bibliography is not annotated it is still extremely useful, covering material in the main European languages and material in Arabic in translation. The introduction is in German and English and the indexing is by running entry number. Entries are repeated at appropriate subject points throughout the bibliography.

1167 **Analytical guide to the bibliographies on the Arabian Peninsula.**
Charles L. Geddes. Denver, Colorado: American Institute of Islamic Studies, 1974. 50p. (Bibliographical Series, no. 4).

An annotated evaluation of seventy bibliographies covering the Arabian Peninsula. It includes a detailed subject index.

1168 **Index to United States documents relating to foreign affairs, 1828-1861.**
Adelaide R. Hasse. Washington, DC: Carnegie Institution, 1919. Reprinted, Kraus Reprint, 1971. 3 vols.

An extensive bibliography, with numerous references to Muscat under that and related headings.

1169   **Selected bibliography on Kuwait and the Arabian Gulf.**
Soraya Kabeel.   Kuwait: Kuwait University, Libraries Department.
1969. 104p. (Bibliographical Series, no. 1).
A highly selective bibliography with only a few references to the Sultanate (p. 66-69),
though some of the more general works on the Gulf are also relevant.

1170   **A bibliography of Oman 1900-1950.**
R. King, J. H. Stevens.   Durham, England: University of Durham,
Centre for Middle Eastern and Islamic Studies, 1973. 141p.
(Occasional Papers Series, no. 2).
A good listing of material on the natural and physical sciences, though slanted
towards readily available material. The citations are not annotated and in some cases
the bibliographical references are very abbreviated.

1171   **Bibliography of the Arabian Peninsula.**
Eric Macro.   Coral Gables, Florida: University of Miami Press,
1958. 80p.
A listing of some 2,000 items, covering all aspects of the area, though the political
content is limited. Entries are arranged alphabetically by author, with anonymous
works arranged by title under the heading 'anonymous'. Entries include books,
periodicals and works from official sources, regardless of language. Unfortunately,
the work has no subject index.

1172   **Documentation on Oman.**
J. D. Pearson.   *Journal of Oman Studies*, vol. 6, no. 1 (1983),
p. 65-76.
An attempt to record the unpublished material on Oman to be found in Great Britain
in libraries, archives and other repositories. The article provides information from the
published and unpublished catalogues of the institutions surveyed. These include the
British Library, National Library of Scotland, India Office records, Bodleian and
college libraries in Oxford, university libraries in Cambridge, Hull and Aberdeen, the
Public Record Office, the Scottish Record Office, the record offices of Greater
London, Kent and Staffordshire, and the archives of *The Times*.

1173   **Index Islamicus, 1906-1958.**
Compiled by J. D. Pearson.   Cambridge, England: Heffer, 1958.
897p. new ed., London: Mansell, 1972. (Distributed in the USA by
International Scholarly Book Services, Forest Grove, Oregon).
A catalogue of articles on Islamic subjects in periodicals, Festschriften, congresses
and other collective works. The work is arranged by subject, dealing first with general
material, and then with specific topics under headings such as art, religion and
literature. Further sections are devoted to area studies subdivided by subject. Entries
are not annotated but give author, title, bibliographical details and cross-references to
other entries. It includes an index of authors and subjects. There are supplements
1956-60; 1961-65; 1966-70; 1971-75; 1976-80 (2 vols), and quarterly updates with
quinquennial cumulations, now edited by Geoffrey Roper.

1174   **Oman and southeastern Arabia: a bibliographic survey.**
Michael Owen Shannon.   Boston, Massachusetts: G. K. Hall, 1978.
168p.
An extremely valuable publication with 988 entries, the majority carefully annotated.
The work has two indexes, one to the contents and the other to journals cited in the
bibliography. At least two-thirds of the bibliography relates to the Sultanate and the
introductory essay by the compiler is a most helpful addition.

1175   **Arabia in early maps: a bibliography of maps covering the
peninsula of Arabia printed in Western Europe from the
invention of printing to the year 1751.**
G. R. Tibbetts.   Cambridge, England; New York: Oleander Press,
1978. 175p. maps.
Useful for a study of the very early cartography of the region, compiled mainly before
detailed exploration of the area began. The compiler's introductory essay on the
cartography of the Arabian Peninsula is also very informative.

Soils of the Arabian Peninsula.
See item no. 1009.

Indexes

There follow three separate indexes: authors (personal and corporate); titles; and subjects. Title entries are italicized and refer either to the main titles, or to other works cited in the annotations. The number refer to bibliographical entry, not page numbers. Individual index entries are arranged in alphabetical sequence.

Index of Authors

A

Abdo, Mekhag B. 1116
Abir, Mordechai 771
Abdelgalil, Mohamed Nabil 1102
Abdullah, Muhammad Morsy 42, 420
Abrams, M. J. 235
Abu-Lughod, Janet 1063
Acharya, A. 804
Afshar, F. 1129
Aitchinson, Charles Umpherston 421, 595-600, 602-6, 608, 616-17, 619
Alam, M. 1039
Albright, Frank P. 343
Ali, Abdul 417
Ali, Abdul-Jaleel Kassim 831
Ali, H. A. 1079
Alison, R. J. 133
Allan, J. A. 203
Allemann, Franz 134

Allen, Calvin H. 1, 2, 422, 473, 805
Allen, G. R. 1029
Allen, Mark 1117
Allen, R. 839-41
Allfree, P. S. 474
Almoayyed, Tariq 1147
Alpers, Edward A. 452
Alshanfari, S. S. A. 1045
Anderson, David Morrill 260
Anderson, Ewan N. 204
Andrada, Roy Freyre De 411
Anthony, John Duke 3, 806, 1161
Anzi, Abdulla Meshail A. Al- 832
Arberry, A. J. 711
Arikat, Harby Mohammed Mousa 835
Arkless, David C. 548
Arnensen, E. 980
Arnold, E. N. 275
Asche, H. 236

Asfour, M. G. 716
Asfour, Taiba A. al- 135
Ashban, Abdul Aziz El-391
Ata, F. A. 981
Atiyeh, George N. 1162
Attia, Abdel Moncim 751
Autret, M. 717
Awad, H. 264
Azhary, M. S. El 877
Azri, H. Al 966
Azzi, Robert 111

B

Badawy, M. I. 265-7
Badger, George Percy 385
Badri, Kais Al- 911
Bagnold, R. A. 136
Baherna, Husain Muhammed al 752, 772-3
Bailey, Roger 276
Bailey, Ronald 374, 475

267

Karabuda, B. 571
Karim, Bakri Musa A. 1111
Karvran, M. 1137
Katz, Mark N. 19, 782
Kay, Shirley 20
Kaylani, Nabil M. 484
Kazziha, Walid W. 572
Kechichian, Joseph Albert 783, 833
Keessee, Allen P. K. 758
Keith, Arthur 644
Kelly, E. F. 1094
Kelly, John Barrett 63-4, 378, 506, 537-9, 573, 740-1
Kemball, Arnold Burrowes 435
Kennedy, Roy 247
Khalaf, Abd al-Hadi 816
Khalifa, Ali Mohammed 65
Khalil, Muhammad 485
Khan, M. A. Saleem 574
Khatib, M. Tathalla El 507
Khawlie, M. S. 964
Kieran, J. A. 467
Kilbride, A. R. 246
Kinawy, M. M. 1022
King, R. 1170
Kinnear, N. B. 310-11
Kirk, George E. 66
Kirkman, James 464
Klinghoffer, Arthur Jay 784
Konteatis, C. A. C. 261
Krogman, W. M. 644
Krupp, F. 312
Kruse, Hans 508
Kubursi, Atif A. 971
Kumar, Ravinder 436-7, 509
Kuo, W. S. 194

L

Lake, Michael 486
Lamki, F. M. S. Al- 274
Lamky, Asya Mohamed Suleiman Al- 1080
Lancaster, Joan C. 390
Landen, Robert Geran 679, 768
Larsen, Kiki 313
Larsen, Torben 313-14
Lawless, Richard 938, 1071, 1156
Lawton, J. 21
Lawton, R. M. 1023
Le Cour, G. C. 221, 645
Leanza, U. 817
Leatherdale, John 247
Lee, Marc 510
Lees, G. M. 160-1
Legros, Elizabeth 934
Legum, Colin 39
Leidholdt, R. W. 213
Lenczowski, George 67
Lennon, G. 169
Leslau, Wolf 698-9
Letts, Sally E. 207, 222, 663, 990
Levell, B. K. 951
Lewicki, Tedeuoz 709
Lewis, B. 68
Liebesny, Herbert J. 487
Linder, B. M. 721
Litwak, Robert 818
Lloyd, Michael 315
Lockhart, H. J. 575
Lockhart, Laurence 438-9
Lofchie, Michael 465
Lond, David E. 69
Loney, P. E. 153
Longrigg, Stephen Hemsley 70
Looney, Robert E. 646, 888, 972-3
Lorimer, J. G. 71
Lowick, N. 398
Luciano, Giacomo 72, 952
Luke, Harry 114
Lunde, P. 21

M

Mackay, G. 836
Mackenzie, John M. 22
Mackinnon, E. C. B. 379
Mackinnon, Kenneth 316
McKinnon, Michael 317
McLachlan, Keith 935, 986, 1005
McMaster, A. K. 1086
McMaster, D. W. 915
Macmillan, Harold 511
McNaugher, Thomas L. 785
Maamry, Ahmed Mahmoud Al- 463
Mabel, V. A. 425
Macro, Eric 1171
Mahmoudi, S. 819
Maizels, J. 223
Makhawi, Rashid A. Al- 834
Mallah, Issam El- 1112
Mallakh, Dorothea 936
Mallakh, Ragaei El 873, 889
Mallas, Ruth 100
Mamry, J. Al- 1024
Mandeville, James 318, 332
Mansfield, Peter 73
Manthri, I. A. 191
Marayati, Abid al- 512, 768
Marin, Manuela 380
Marlowe, John 488
Martin, Chrysse Perry 916
Martin, Esmond Bradley 916, 1055
Martin, Lenore G. 820
Martin, Philip L. 1072
Maskery, Muneer Mohammed Sultan Al- 1106
Mathew, Gervase 468
Mathews, A. J. 169
Mathews, C. P. 1019
Matthews, Geoffrey 510
Mauryi, Vincento 440
Mazumdar, S. 195
May, H. P. 162
Meadow, R. H. 358
Melamid, Alexander 489, 540-4, 890, 953, 1157
Mellor, P. S. 994
Melville, J. C. 319-20
Merchant, Khozem 25
Metwally, M. M. 901
Middleton, R. A. 1147
Miladi, S. 717
Miles, Samuel Barrett 76, 101-3, 647
Miller, Anthony G. 321

271

Yassin, T. E. 1045
Yorke, Valerie 944
Young, Richard 528
Yuval-Davis, Nira 736

Z

Zahlan, Rosemarie Said 87

Zwemer, Samuel Marinus 88, 110, 132

Index of Titles

M

Q

Index of Subjects

306

reduction in mortality rates
729
salination 190, 219, 226,
229, 263
social structure 1131
water mills construction
234
locations 234
water resources 234
water table 190
water usage 263
Bats: new species identified
302
Bayadir tribe
assimilation with Arab
tribes 659
role as agricultural
workers 659
social structure 659
Bayasirah tribe
client status of 659
exclusion from Arab tribes
659
Beaches
hydrocarbons 269
metal pollution 269
oil pollution 267
tar loads 267, 269
Bedouin
culture 668
effects of oil economy 667
nomadism 672
reliance on husbandry 667
social change 672
social life 120
structure 120, 637, 655
traditions 637, 667
Wahiba Sands 185, 667
Bedouin society
effects of petroleum
company 668
structure 120, 144, 638,
655
Beekeeping
research 1007
traditional 982
Bees
development projects 1040
imports from Australia
1040
Bhattias Hindu community
migration to Muscat 15th
century 473

role in economy 473
social history 473
Bibliographies 1162, 1166,
1168, 1170, 1172-74
analytical guide 1167
Arab League relations
1163
Arabian Gulf 1161, 1169
Arabian Peninsula 1161,
1167, 1171
Gulf Cooperation Council
1163
language 698
land resources 1009
Saudi Arabia 1164
soils 1165
United Nations 1160
Zanzibar 1165
Biographical sources 3, 58
Biology
Arabian oryx 307, 309,
325
Arabian tahr 325
Musandam Peninsula 149
Birds
checklists 280, 290, 311,
316, 331
collections 291, 301,
310-11, 316, 331
Dhofar 161
Jabal al Akhdar 161
new species 331
observations 291
Upcher's warbler 289
Bocarro, Antonio: chronicles
of 414
Bombay Archives 443
Booker Agriculture
International:
agricultural research
project 998
Books: censorship of 1109
Border disputes 22, 47-8, 51,
115, 374, 426, 504, 536,
538-39, 630, 772, 816,
818, 832
Abu Dhabi 481, 535, 540,
792, 795
documents 529-30, 534
Eastern Arabia 820
international implications
773
PDRY 5, 129, 575, 776

primary documents
529-30, 534, 795-6
Rub' al-Khali 128, 540
Saudi Arabia 4, 481, 531,
534, 540, 630, 795
settlement 783
significance of oil 489,
510
Borders
conflict with traditional
tribal rights 543
Iran 775, 779
Saudi Arabia 128-29, 795
Botanical Survey 277
Boundaries: offshore
delimitation 735, 772
Boustead, Hugh: Director of
Development 1958-61
476
British diplomatic
representatives: reports
377
British Political Resident
agreement for 596
responsibility for Indian
nationals 605
role in Treaty of Sib 620
British Political Residency
annual reports 381, 481
documents 390, 475
reports 491
British Residency: role of 60,
76, 626
Bronze Age
archaeology 356
arms production 10th
century 400
settlements 356, 358
Hajar mountains 356
Budget 1988 899
austerity measures 899
defence expenditure 899,
907
generation projects 907
water supply projects 807
Budget forecasts 1985-86
906
Buraimi Oasis
Abu Dhabi claim 54, 65,
516, 530, 536, 537, 546,
630, 818
archaeology 354, 356
exploration 112, 114, 122

314

threat to oil supplies 564,
579
training facilities for
guerrillas 560, 575, 581,
591
use of air power 577
Dhofari guerrillas: Imamate
question policy 515
Dhow trade 1055
economic significance 915
historical trade with China
403, 914
19th century 109
Oman-East Africa 403,
471, 915-16, 1054, 1060
Dhows 1054
construction 916, 1053-54
construction decline 1056
drawings of 1053-54
effects of modern facilities
1055
trade decline 1055, 1056
use in slave trade 12,
915-16
Diabetes
incidence of 716
priority for health strategy
716
Dialect
Kuria Muria 699
Omani 691, 693
Shihuh 702
Dialects: oral recording of
691
Dictionaries
colloquial 3, 690
cultural 3
historical 3
Diets
study of 723
traditional 732
Dilmun
copper trade 345
location of 345, 628
Diqal oasis: settlement
decline 663
Directorate General of
National Statistics:
statistical yearbook
1088
Directories 74
companies 7, 842, 870
manufacturing 974

media 1147
Disease: incidence of 723,
1078
Diversification policies 844
Divorce: women 12
Documentary Collections
Arabic 444
India Office Records 444
Documentary sources
archival material 679
Bombay Archives 443
border disputes 795-96
Buraimi Oasis dispute 534,
795
collections 481, 492-93,
795
Dhofar War 585
Ibadhism 714-15
Indian Government 432
Nizwa school 407
Portuguese rule 411
Rostaq school 407
United States 490
use of 451
Dolium variegatum:
distribution 338
Domestic architecture
al-Mudayit 1127
East Africa 1135
materials 1127
19th century 1127
Domestic life
Harasis tribe 669
Sohar 632
Downstream activities 973
Dress
al Harasis tribe 641
al Qara tribe 641
use of indigo 1118
Droughts
impact in Western Hajar
1973-5 989
impact on agriculture
988-89
pastoralism 988-89
Durham University: Oman
project 222, 673
Dutch Reformed Church of
America
missionary activities 88,
110,
Dyeing: traditional use of
indigo 1118

E

East Africa
agreement to end slave
trade 598
Al Bu Said rule 453
archaeology 403
architecture 1135
arrival of Islam 458
attacks on Portuguese
settlements 411, 419,
438
Banaadir coast,control by
Oman 452
British interests 376, 454
caravan trade 645
commerce 396
dhow trade with 1056,
1060
economic history 456
penetration of 457, 471
significance 453, 470
imperialist exploitation
456, 466
impact of Omanis on
society 466, 645
19th century conditions
645
Omani emigration to 458,
463-64, 466, 916
Omani exploitation 452,
470
Omani rule 467
Omani tribes 645
Portuguese expulsion
from Mombassa 411,
419, 458, 464
interests 376
rivalry with Portuguese
376
slave trade 376, 454, 458,
470-71, 599
spread of Islam 458-60
suppression of Omani
arms trade 610
suppression of slave trade
599
trade with 403, 915
East African Empire
British interests 376
history 422
loss of 79, 385
Portuguese interests 376

attraction of oil industry 662
attraction to nomads 649
constraints on development 886, 1073
construction industry 1038, 1132
female 12, 666, 746, 874, 1073
manpower requirements 1068
occupational patterns 632, 1064
Omanization 894
position of Omani graduates 1080
rural 672, 676, 989, 1038, 1119
skills requirement 646, 886
statistics 1086
use of migrant labour 1064, 1068
Energy: statistics 1081
Environment 144
conservation 34
degradation from Gulf War 736
Shihuh tribe 640
Epidemiological research: diabetes 716
Epigraphic survey
Al-Balid 401
Salalah 401
Erosion: alluvial 134-35
Ethics 1146
Ethiopia: security threat 813
Ethnic diversity 805
Ethnology 654
Arabian oryx 336
tribal structure 661
Eurodollar loan, 1985 853
Europe: strategic oil interests 944
European influences 1, 2, 44, 679, 771, 802
European interests 774
European powers: struggle for Africa 457
European rivalries: 17th and 18th centuries 438
Expatriate advisers: influence 1

Expatriate labour
employment as teachers 1096
growth of 107374, 1077
projected demands 646, 864, 1079
provision of 1075
reliance upon 845, 873, 894, 1079-80
share of occupations 1075
use of 1074, 1077
see also Migrant labour
Exploration 90-91, 141
Abu Dhabi 119, 122
Buraimi Oasis 112, 114, 122
Batinah coast 92, 131-32
Capital Area 92
Coastline 104
collections 89-92, 100
Dhahirah 92
Dhofar 24, 92-93, 104, 118-19, 126, 129, 245
Gharbaniat sands 121
Hajar mountains 113, 121
Hugf mountains 121
influence on images of Oman 90, 100
interior Oman 102-03, 106, 108, 130
Jabal Al Akhdar 92, 95, 101, 109, 112
Kuria Muria Islands 96
Liwa oasis 119, 122
Masirah island 121
Muscat 92, 94, 112, 130-31
Musandam Peninsula 92, 101
Muwaigh 121
northern Oman 132
Rub' al-Khali 116, 119, 122-23, 125-29
Salalah 119, 123
Sharjah 131
Sharqiyah 92
Sohar 112
topography 104
United Arab Emirates 122
Wadi Samail 112
water resources 209-10

Exploration and travel
pre-1900 93-110
20th century 9, 16, 111-32
Exports
agriculture 896
destinations 919
statistics 1085
tables 911
tables 1904-40 919

F

Fahud Geodetic Datum
background 950
usage 950
Fahud oilfield: development 933, 943
Faisal, Sultan: reign of 425, 624
Falaj irrigation system 11, 21, 130, 204-06, 212, 214, 221, 263, 1042
diagram 206, 1042
history 232, 215
maintenance 215, 27
operation 212, 222, 224-25
role of Awamir 207
significance 212, 222, 224-25
social significance 212, 231-32
Sohar 1042
see also Aflaj
Falconry
cultural significance 1117
techniques 1117
Family Health Programmes 1117
curriculum 721-22
training 721-22
Far East: historical trade 348, 380
Farm Economic Survey, 1975 879
Fauna
coral communities 331
genetic inheritance 338
Federation of South Arabia
establishment 573
impact on region 573

317

Food and Agriculture
  Organization
  fish stock surveys 1035
  mission on agricultural
    libraries 1115
  report on health services
    717
  nutrition needs 717
Food consumption:
  nutritional value 723
Food exports 896
Food imports 920
Food production 992
  prehistoric 369
  statistics 1091
Forage: production 95, 1011,
  1020
Foreign affairs 34
Foreign invasions 33
Foreign investment 847,
  921
  development needs 885
  uses in defence provision
    788
Foreign policy 25, 39, 783
  Egypt-Israel peace treaty,
    support for 797
  independence of 827, 830
Foreign relations
  bibliography 1163
  19th century 109
  representation by Great
    Britain 478, 545-46
Forestation
  feasibility study 1023
  plant varieties 1023
  water resources 1023
Forests: Wahiba Sands 185
Fortifications: history 10, 21
  Hormuz 416
  Muscat 10, 416, 440
  Omani 10, 416, 1133
  Portuguese 10, 416, 1133
  Sohar 1133
42 Survey Engineering
  Group 259
Fossil water 1005
Foxes: rabies transmission
  981
France
  exclusion of 1798 595
  Muscat doro case 493,
    760

relations with 428, 446,
  493, 624, 783
  19th century 493, 760
  rivalry with Great Britain
    45, 491, 760
  shipping flags dispute 624
Frankincense 93, 111
  trade in 11, 24
Freshwater fish
  Oman mountains 312
  Saudi Arabia 312
Funerals: use of indigo 1118

G

Gara tribe: language 688
Gardens
  architecture 350
  design 1139
  flora 1139
  Masjid al-Luqta 350
  role in society 1139
Gas
  development of new fields
    928, 931
  economic significance
    778
  exploration programme
    955
  extraction 850
  offshore potential 735
  pipeline 933
  production 850
    for local industry 955
  prospects 5
  reserves 927, 931, 954
Gas industry 24
  development 855
Gastropoda
  Arabian Sea 319
  Gulf of Oman 319
  Persian Gulf 319
Gazetteers 71, 256, 346
GCC see Gulf Cooperation
  Council
Genealogy
  Al bu Said 651
  Zanzibar Sultans 464
General Telecommunications
  Organization 1062
Geneva Convention: Law of
  the Sea 817

applicability to Strait of
  Hormuz 817, 819
Geodes
  composition 184
  formation 184
  location 184
  mineral content 184
Geodetic surveys 252
Geography 5, 7, 11, 20-21,
  23, 26-27, 31, 33, 57,
  59-60, 73, 75, 84, 93,
  201, 276, 290, 379, 521,
  654, 781, 878
  Dhofar 24, 142
  effects on development
    268
  environmental 661
  historical 380, 410
  Jabal Al Akhdar 109,
    161
  physical 74, 661, 1045
    Jabal Al Akhdar 161
  political 83
  social 70, 74
  Sohar 632
Geology 146, 150, 153, 166,
  179, 261, 263, 964
  Arabian Sea 186
  bibliography 138
  Dhofar 138, 150, 156
  Gulf of Oman 175, 926
  history 949
  Huqf mountains 154
  interior Oman 160
  Jabal Al Akhdar 155, 183
  Jabal Haqab 159
  Kuria Muria Islands 186
  mapping 235
  mountain ranges 153
  Musandam Peninsula 158,
    165, 171
  northern Oman 322
  ocean drilling 161
  oceanic lithosphere 152,
    159
  oil exploration 926, 935
  Oman ophiolite 163, 183,
    254
  Omani line 148
  Proterozoic basin 180
Geomorphology
  history of 135
  Jiddat al-Harasis 293

328

332

Map of Oman

This map shows the more important towns and other features.

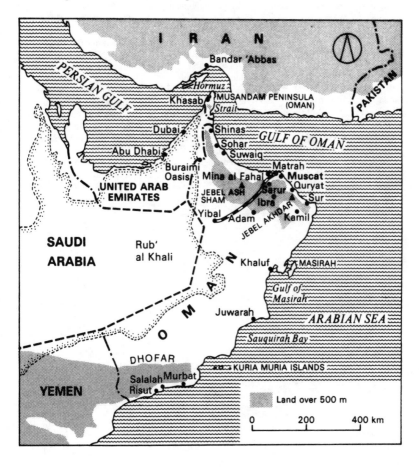

ALSO FROM CLIO PRESS

INTERNATIONAL ORGANIZATIONS SERIES

Each volume in the International Organizations Series is either devoted to one specific organization, or to a number of different organizations operating in a particular region, or engaged in a specific field of activity. The scope of the series is wide-ranging and includes intergovernmental organizations, international non-governmental organizations, and national bodies dealing with international issues. The series is aimed mainly at the English-speaker and each volume provides a selective, annotated, critical bibliography of the organization, or organizations, concerned. The bibliographies cover books, articles, pamphlets, directories, databases and theses and, wherever possible, attention is focused on material *about* the organizations rather than on the organizations' own publications. Notwithstanding this, the most important official publications, and guides to those publications, will be included. The views expressed in individual volumes, however, are not necessarily those of the publishers.

VOLUMES IN THE SERIES

1 *European Communities*, John Paxton
2 *Arab Regional Organizations*, Frank A. Clements
3 *Comecon: The Rise and Fall of an International Socialist Organization*, Jenny Brine
4 *International Monetary Fund*, Anne C. M. Salda

5 *The Commonwealth*, Patricia M. Larby and Harry Hannam
6 *The French Secret Services*, Martyn Cornick and Peter Morris
7 *Organization of African Unity*, Gordon Harris
8 *North Atlantic Treaty Organization*, Phil Williams

TITLES IN PREPARATION

British Secret Services, Philip H. J. Davies
Israeli Secret Services, Frank A. Clements
Organization of American States, David Sheinin

United Nations System, Joseph P. Baratta
World Bank, Anne C. M. Salda

Please renew/return items by last date shown. Please call the number below:

Renewals and enquiries: 0300 123 4049

Textphone for hearing or
speech impaired users: 0300 123 4041

www.hertsdirect.org/librarycatalogue
L32

Advance Praise for *The Debt* by Angela Hunt

"*The Debt* is a wonderful story that reminds us not to follow in the footsteps of men, but in the footsteps of Jesus."

—FRANCINE RIVERS,
author of *When the Shofar Blew* and *Redeeming Love*

"*The Debt* is a powerful story, captivating and superbly written. I couldn't put it down. Angela Hunt touched my heart. When I finished, I thanked Jesus for speaking to me. That's the highest compliment I can pay any book."

—RANDY ALCORN,
author of *Safely Home*

"Angela Hunt's *The Debt* is a must read! It will challenge you in many ways, and it just might shake you loose from your comfortable church pew and send you out to follow in the footsteps of Jesus."

—ROBIN LEE HATCHER,
author of *Beyond the Shadows* and *Firstborn*

"If any novel deserves to be called 'a life-changing book,' it is *The Debt*. This story not only engages your emotions—anger, sorrow, tension, laughter, and joy—but it truly resonates in your soul. *The Debt* has changed the way I look at my relationship to the world, to God, and to the people around me. When was the last time a novel changed *your* life?"

—JIM DENNEY,
author of *Answers to Satisfy the Soul* and the *Timebenders* series

"*The Debt* is a clever parable and an engaging novel about the dangers of playing church in a real world with real sinners. *The Debt* will push you out of your comfort zone and make you rethink that deceptively simple question—what would Jesus do? The answer may just change your life."

—RANDALL INGERMANSON,
Christy-award winning author of *Oxygen* and *Premonition*

"*The Debt* is a deeply moving tale of one woman's journey toward a more vital, vibrant faith. Emma's story, in Angela Hunt's skillful hands, inspires and challenges us in a way fiction rarely does."

—JAMES SCOTT BELL,
author of *Deadlock* and *A Higher Justice*

"Written from the heart, with a passion for truth that sears the pages, *The Debt* is Angela Hunt's most powerful novel to date—and that says quite a lot. This is a triumph of a novel from an author willing to challenge our preconceptions and confront the reality of where the contemporary church is today...and where it ought to be. What makes Hunt's achievement more remarkable still is that she accomplishes it with such uncommon skill and compassion."

—BJ HOFF,
author of *American Anthem* and *An Emerald Ballad*

"*The Debt* is a great book. With a timely message for today, Hunt throws open the doors of the church and encourages all believers to leave comfort and safety behind to fulfill Christ's highest command: love God, love one another. *The Debt* is a skillfully written, beautiful read that will challenge those who claim to follow Christ. If you've forgotten the thrill of his still, small voice, this parable will make you fall in love all over again."

—JANE ORCUTT,
author of *Lullaby*

"If you're ready to stop 'playing church', read Angela Hunt's *The Debt*. This amazing book shook me out of my comfort zone, and I haven't been the same since. Every Christian should read it."

—COLLEEN COBLE,
author of *Without a Trace*

"Angela's book touches upon so many relevant questions for today's Christian, but what I came away with was a new understanding about the way God sees life, and perhaps the way I have chosen not to see it. This timely parable searched my heart and I'm better for it."

—RENE GUTTERIDGE,
author of *Boo*

OTHER NOVELS BY ANGELA HUNT

The Canopy

The Pearl

The Justice

The Note

The Immortal

The Shadow Women

The Truth Teller

The Silver Sword

The Golden Cross

The Velvet Shadow

The Emerald Isle

Dreamers

Brothers

Journey

With Lori Copeland:

The Island of Heavenly Daze

Grace in Autumn

A Warmth in Winter

A Perfect Love

Hearts at Home

www.angelahuntbooks.com

THE DEBT

A STORY *of a* PAST REDEEMED

ANGELA HUNT

WESTBOW
PRESS
A Division of Thomas Nelson Publishers
Since 1798

Dedicated to the memory of Robert Briner,
who is still encouraging lambs to roar

Then Jesus told . . . this story: "A man loaned money to
two people—five hundred pieces of silver to one
and fifty pieces to the other.
But neither of them could repay him,
so he kindly forgave them both,
canceling their debts.
Who do you suppose loved him more after that?"

LUKE 7:41–42

CHAPTER ONE

*A*s the President of the United States slips his arm around my husband's shoulder, I think I might just bubble up and burst with pride. I'm standing and applauding with everyone else, of course, trying to keep my smile lowered to an appropriately humble wattage, while Abel, bless him, bows his head, obviously embarrassed by the deafening applause.

We're among the few who have been seated at the head table of the National Prayer Breakfast, and my head is still reeling from the honor. Dizzy as I am, I try to look around and gather as many impressions as I can. The support team back home in Wiltshire, Kentucky, will want me to recite every detail.

The woman next to me, a senator's wife, bends to reach for her purse and jostles the table, spilling my cranberry juice. She glances at the spreading stain, apparently deciding it's more politic to continue applauding than to help me mop up the mess.

Faced with the same choice, my heart congeals into a small lump of dread. If I ignore the stain, the president might glance over here and decide that Abel Howard's wife is a clumsy country bumpkin. If I stop to clean it up, I'll look like a woman who can't cut herself loose from the kitchen.

Fortunately, life as a minister's wife has taught me a thing or two about diplomacy and compromise. Steadfastly smiling at the president, I stop clapping long enough to pick up my napkin and drop it onto the wet linen. The senator's wife gives me an apologetic look as the applause dies down and we settle back into our seats.

"Abel Howard and his affiliated ministries," the president says, moving back to the lectern, "have provided us with an excellent example of how religious television broadcasts can promote quality in programming and restore morality to our nation. Not only does Abel Howard deliver a worship service to millions of American homes each week, he and his organization have spearheaded drives to lead our country back to its spiritual, ethical, and moral roots. In this special presentation for religious leaders, the Points of Light Foundation is pleased to honor Reverend Howard for his courage and many years of dedicated hard work."

Behind the president, Abel laces his fingers and keeps his head lowered. Beside him, the Catholic bishop who has also been honored looks at Abel with open curiosity . . . or is that skepticism in his eye? From where I sit, I can't tell.

"Abel Howard," the president continues, "and the other worthy people who stand before you today represent all we can achieve through determined effort, concentrated vision, and dependence upon God. Our nation has no official religion, no state-endorsed faith. All are free to worship or not worship, to exercise faith or sustain doubt. Yet faith, and those who practice it, brings out the best in us. Scripture describes people of faith as salt, and salt not only adds spice to a substance, it acts to retard spoilage. The men and women standing before you have decided to be salt in a society that can, at times, seem terribly decayed. I hope and pray that these men and women will be joined by thousands of others who realize that salt kept in a saltshaker is useless."

The crowd responds with another boom of applause. The president grips the sides of the lectern as he waits for the sound to fade, and I catch my husband's eye. Abel smiles, but his folded hands and stiff posture tell me he is eager to leave the platform. Abel has never minded attention, but this is a lot for a Kentucky preacher to handle.

The president clears his throat. "In a letter to a friend, George Washington once wrote, 'I am sure that there was never a people who had more reason to acknowledge a Divine interposition in their affairs than those of the United States; and I should be pained to believe that they have forgotten that agency, which was so often manifested during our Revolution, or that they failed to consider the omnipotence of that God who is alone able to protect them.'"

The president throws back his shoulders as his gaze sweeps across the crowded ballroom. "May we all remember that God can and will intervene in our affairs to keep America strong. May God bless you all, and may God continue to bless America."

As the audience rises to deliver a final thundering ovation, the president turns to shake the hands of a few people on the podium. He reaches for Abel's hand first—a fact I can't help but notice—then moves on to congratulate the nun who oversees a soup kitchen, the Muslim cleric who founded a literacy program, and the rabbi honored for his efforts to combat racism.

A host of noteworthy people stands on the platform, but the President of the United States turned to shake Abel's hand first.

That thought pleases me to no end.

Like children who've just been excused from the grown-up table, our group is relaxed and giddy as we spill out of the limo and cross the tarmac. The February day is cold, but the sun has gilded the asphalt and the gleaming white jet with "Abel Howard Ministries" painted on its side. The ministry pilots, Dan Moon and Jim Spence, are waiting by the pull-down steps, shivering in their navy peacoats. They grin and wave as we approach, then they climb the stairs.

At least a half-dozen steps ahead of me, Abel walks with Josh Bartol, his administrative assistant. While my husband rattles off a list of names and titles, Josh murmurs into the tiny tape player he always carries in the pocket of his suit coat.

Without being told, I understand what my husband is doing. The names belong to dignitaries he saw at the break-fast, and whether he shook their hand or merely glimpsed them from across the room, he'll send those VIPs a personal note within the next forty-eight hours. Abel recognized the value of networking before *networking* became a buzzword, and he has never hesitated to embrace business ideas for use in the ministry. "We're salesmen, after all," he tells young preachers who flock to his annual ministers' conference, "offering the best possible product to people who desperately need it. So why should we be any less motivated—or any less savvy—than companies peddling fancy tennis shoes and overpriced automobiles?"

Beside me, Crystal Donaldson is huffing to keep up, her boots clomping heavily on the pavement. I smile inwardly at her efforts—after nearly twenty-four years of marriage to Abel, I've mastered the long stride necessary to keep pace with him. But Crystal is new to traveling with the Reverend and probably a bit starry-eyed from riding in limos and the ministry jet. She couldn't attend the breakfast, but on our way out of the Hilton lobby I glimpsed her chatting up other staffers who couldn't get a ticket to the exclusive event.

She quickens her step. "Will we be here long?" She reaches up to grab the purse strap slipping from her shoulder. "On the ground, I mean?"

I look toward the tiny cockpit windows where I can see our pilots. "Dan and Jim are usually pretty good about moving us out. I'm sure they're as anxious to get home as we are."

"I'm not anxious to get home." Excitement sparks her eyes. "This has been absolutely incredible. Honestly. I mean, we were in the same building as Franklin Graham! And you won't believe—well, maybe you would—all the famous people I saw walking through the lobby!"

Somehow I resist the urge to pat her on the head. Crystal is probably twenty-three now, a recent college graduate, but to me she'll always be a "sunbeam" from my children's choir. I remember visiting her mother in the hospital just after Crystal's birth . . . and wishing that little pink bundle of sweetness were mine.

A few years later, after the establishment of our tentative television ministry, she became the first child baptized in a televised Sunday morning service. When she came up out of the water, wet and shivering, eight-year-old Crystal shone her blue eyes into the camera and shouted, "Thank you, Jesus!"

That single exclamation, Abel says, probably boosted donations by two hundred percent. After the sudden spurt in contributions, my husband decided God meant for us to remain in television, so we signed a contract to purchase a full year of weekly programming on our local station.

Now Crystal has come home to take her place among the scores of homegrown kids we've hired to work in the ministry. I don't know much about what goes on in the payroll department, but I suspect the average twenty-something working for us earns only slightly more than minimum wage. But they're learning as they work, gaining invaluable experience and maturity, not to mention the opportunity to list "Abel Howard Ministries" on their employment résumé.

Abel says we're teaching these young people to be servants while they follow the highest calling any believer could receive. When I see the enthusiasm in their eyes, I have to agree with him. Sometimes I'm stunned by their single-minded dedication. God has been good to bring so many committed people to our ever-expanding organization.

Crystal is working for *Purity*, our ministry's monthly magazine. She graduated from a Bible college with a degree in journalism, and as editor of the magazine, it's my job to approve her articles. She's a gifted writer, but sometimes her writing seems stilted, as though she is hesitant to write anything that might rock anyone's boat.

Her hesitation is probably my fault; when she took the job I sat her down for a frank discussion and told her that our readers could be a persnickety group. The previous month's guest column had featured the story of Gomer and Hosea, and the author happened to mention that Hosea's wife had lived as a prostitute. We're still getting mail about that issue—apparently the word *prostitute* has no business in a Christian family magazine.

I should have caught it before we went to press.

"Emma Rose," Crystal hustles to keep up with me, "mind if I ask you some questions on the plane? Impressions of the breakfast and all? I figure I can work your comments into an updated feature article about you and the Reverend."

"That's fine, Crystal."

We have reached the stairs, where Josh has fallen back to allow Abel to climb first. Wes Turner, a freelance photographer along for the ride, snaps photos of my husband striding up the steps. I can imagine the caption: *Despite a hectic schedule, the Reverend takes time to receive presidential honors at the National Prayer Breakfast in Washington.*

As Abel disappears into the cabin, Josh puts one foot on the stairs, then removes it. A deep flush creeps up from the top of his collar as he steps aside.

I grab the handrail and pretend not to notice his belated gallantry. "Thank you, Josh."

I climb into the jet and move past the cockpit. Winnie Barnes, the air hostess, gives me a warm greeting. "Mornin', Emma Rose. Did you enjoy the breakfast?"

Winnie, Dan, and Jim are the ministry's flight crew, kept on the payroll to fly wherever the Reverend Howard needs to go. Originally brought on as part-time employees, lately they've been traveling three or four times a week. The pilots don't seem to mind much, but I suspect Winnie finds it hard to leave her eight-month-old son.

I give her the grateful smile she deserves. "The breakfast was wonderful, thank you for asking. How was your rest last night?"

"Fine." Her radiant expression diminishes a degree. "Except when I called home and Charlie told me the baby has another earache."

"I'll be praying for him, then."

"Thank you, ma'am. I appreciate that very much."

I move forward, noticing that Abel has taken the seat nearest the left window. Because he didn't head to the conference table at the back, I know he's not in the mood for conversation. I slip into the seat across from him, grateful for the solidity of a window at my shoulder. If the flight makes me drowsy, as most flights usually do, I might nap on the way home.

Josh enters next, and it's obvious that his manners fell

short of extending gallantry to poor Crystal. Answering the hostess's greeting with an absent grunt, he spies the empty seat next to Abel and drops his briefcase into it, then blocks the aisle while he removes his overcoat and insists that Winnie hang it in the small closet across from her jump seat.

But he doesn't take the seat next to Abel. Understanding my husband nearly as well as I, Josh respects Abel's signal for silence. He takes the seat directly behind his boss, then hauls his briefcase from the space next to Abel.

I look away lest Josh read the irritation on my face. Abel loves the young man, says he has great potential, but I'm not so sure. Yes, he's efficient; yes, he's bright and sophisticated. But he's also brash and a little too blunt for my taste. He grew up in a well-connected political family; the father practically begged Abel to give Josh a position. Abel has not regretted a day of Josh's tenure, but I've had more experience with people, and I know Josh's type. The moment a bigger and better offer comes along, he'll be gone, leaving us to deal with whatever mess he leaves behind.

Josh just seems . . . I don't know. Sometimes I think he's giving the ministry every ounce of his intellect and energy, but nothing of his heart.

Abel thinks my fears are groundless. He says we might owe this National Prayer Breakfast honor to Josh's family. I don't know about that, but I'm content to watch and wait.

As the others troop aboard, I turn my face to the window,

hoping Crystal will follow Josh's lead and grant me a few moments of peace. I haven't forgotten my promise to give her an interview, but at the moment I want to relax and collect my thoughts.

I adore my husband, I love working by his side in the ministry. But when we are locked away in a private space with only our most trusted aides, I cherish the freedom to let my face relax, my shoulders droop.

Even the most vigilant Christian soldier needs a cease-fire now and then.

We have been airborne only a few minutes when I hear the high-pitched warble of the jet's telephone. Josh springs to answer it; both Abel and I look at him, waiting.

A faint look of disappointment flits across Josh's face as he hands the phone to me. I smile and accept it, knowing that Josh was probably expecting a call from one of the movers and shakers at the prayer breakfast this morning.

I bring the phone to my ear. "Hello?"

"Emma Rose! Good morning!"

Celene Hughes, who serves as my administrative assistant and our director of women's ministries, wouldn't have called unless something important had come up. "Everything okay, Celene?"

"Pretty much." Despite her assurance, I hear a note of worry in her voice, and my tension level rises a few points. I sink into my seat. "What's up?"

She exhales a breath that seems to whoosh straight into my ear. "It's probably nothing, just one of our usual fruit-cakes. But the young man insisted that I contact you right away. I tried to stall him, but on the off chance he really did need to talk to you, I thought I'd better call."

I shift my gaze to the window, where a quilted blanket of low clouds blocks my view of the landscape below. "What'd he want?"

"He says he wants to meet you privately. I told him you would be speaking at Sinai Church four times in the next month and you'd be happy to meet him after any of those services, but he said a public meeting wouldn't do. That's when my alarm bells started ringing. He said he had impor-tant news for your ears alone."

A soft groan escapes my lips. Last year I attracted a stalker, a lonely middle-aged man who watched the TV program every week and somehow convinced himself that I was his soul mate. His early letters went into the massive bins sorted by our mail department; when he began to mark them "personal," they came to my office. I ignored them at first, not wanting to encourage him, but when three or four letters began to arrive every afternoon, I showed them to Abel, who handed them off to Jon Stuckey, chief of security for the ministry.

After Jon wrote the fellow a terse warning, the personal letters stopped coming.

I put all thoughts of the man out of my mind until one July Sunday when a disheveled stranger began to walk up the center aisle. Though Abel saw him he kept preaching, assuming that the man wanted to pray at the altar. But when the fellow called my name and pulled a gun from his overcoat, Abel and half the choir hit the floor like wheat before the reaper.

I have a dim memory of Abel gesturing frantically, motioning for me to get down, but for a full five seconds, I couldn't think. Half-formed thoughts stuttered through my brain as my eyes registered our minister of music inchworming on the carpeted platform and my husband cowering behind the reinforced pulpit (bulletproofed in the year we launched our campaign against homosexuality depicted on television). I sat frozen beside the piano, not knowing whether to crawl beneath the Steinway or slip behind my chair, as the wild-eyed man kept coming, his eyes locked on me.

Fortunately, I didn't have to waver long. Jon and his security team—who'd probably been half-hoping for an opportunity to test themselves—rushed from pews and behind pillars and charged the platform like NFL linebackers intent on victory. While several team members covered Abel and other staff members, Jon tackled my deranged Don Juan. As they hit the floor, I glimpsed the black gleam of steel and heard the crack of the gun and an answering *chink* from one of the crystal chandeliers.

In the days to come, people often remarked on my composure. But what they took for grace under pressure was nothing more than paralyzing fear.

Within sixty seconds, it was all over. The security men hustled the man away; the choir members brushed dust from their robes and climbed back into their seats. The music director smoothed the long strands of hair atop his bald head and sat back down, though his hands trembled on the armrest.

But without so much as a tremor in his voice, Abel pulled himself erect in the pulpit and told our people that God had just protected us against a flagrant satanic attack. The congregation broke into spontaneous applause, a veritable offering of praise.

Later, after the police had interrogated the man and learned his identity, Abel drew me into his arms and asked why I hadn't crawled into the bulletproof pulpit with him.

"It all happened so fast," I answered, surprised by the question. "I never dreamed anyone would come after me."

He promised we'd be more careful about investigating suspicious letters. "It's sad to think people can't relax when they come to church," he whispered in my ear, "but this is a different world, Em, and we're charging straight into it with our weapons drawn. We might as well be prepared for trouble."

Now discreet metal detectors stand outside the entrance doors of our worship center and office complex. I'd been afraid our church members would despise the new security measures, but their reaction surprised me. "Why, look at that," one woman told me, pausing to admire the technological marvels. "Not every church draws Satan's attention. Just goes to prove you and the Reverend are making a real difference for the kingdom of God."

That supportive attitude is just one of the things I love about our church people. Outsiders, though, often worry me.

Now Celene is calling about another strange man—if he came to church, would he set off the metal detectors?

My hand tightens around the telephone. "This guy who called"—not wanting to alarm Abel, I lower my voice—"do you think you need to alert security?"

"I don't know." I can almost see Celene chewing her lip. "He seemed harmless, really. He kept saying he didn't want to bother you, he just wanted to leave his number and a brief message."

I close my eyes, imagining what the message might be. Abel gets lots of letters from well-meaning viewers who wake in the grips of a bad dream convinced God has chosen them to tell the Reverend that the world will end in forty-six days, or sixty-two, or on January 15 in the year 2005 . . .

"What's the message?"

I hear the sound of shuffling paper. "He said his name is Christopher Lewis—"

The name doesn't ring a bell.

"—and he's calling about someone whose birthday is January 6, 1976."

A sudden spasm grips my heart.

Ignorant of her words' effect, Celene continues: "This is the odd part—he told me to tell you that someone wrote an address on his birth certificate: 4839 Hillside Drive. He said it was important I tell you that."

A dark cloud sweeps out of the past and blocks my vision; the empty hand resting in my lap trembles as the life I once locked away bursts through the dam of memory and floods my heart. I have not spoken of January 6, 1976, in decades; even my husband has no idea why that date is significant.

But I know. And the young man who called has to know why I have silently marked that anniversary for the past twenty-eight years.

My voice, oddly enough, is calm when I can speak again. "That's the only message?"

"That's all. He thought the address might mean something to you."

Might. Oceans of mercy flood that word; in it I hear the possibility of saying he's mistaken, the address and date mean nothing to me, somehow he has tracked down the wrong Emma Rose Harbison Howard who once lived at 4839 Hillside Drive in Hudson Falls, New York.

But he has found me. Despite the sealing of the court records, despite legal promises and emotional assurances, he has gone through the challenging work of searching me out.

For an agonizing moment I can't decide if the thought terrifies or thrills me.

"Does it?" Celene's voice snaps at my nerve endings.

"What?"

"Does the address mean something?"

The corner of my mouth twitches. Though I experienced a dark and troubled adolescence, I have fond memories of the rectangular ranch house on Hillside Drive. Mercy House, the place was called in those days, and though its function did not appear on a single sign, no one in Hudson Falls mentioned Mercy House without adding a subtitle: The Home for Wayward Girls.

"I'm not sure why he would mention that address," I answer, taking care to wrap the truth in ambiguity. "But save the message, okay? I'll look at it when I come in."

"Fine."

Celene's voice rings with relief and I'm touched by her concern. I know when I return to my office the pink message slip will be sitting on a stack of others, arranged on my desk with a pile of carefully screened mail.

"Is that all you have for me?" I ask, looking across the plane at Abel. He gives me a tired smile, silently acknowledging the waning of the morning's adrenaline rush.

"That's it," Celene answers. "See you later today, then."

I click off the phone and drop it into the empty seat. Across the aisle, Abel leans against the curved wall to face me.

"Everything okay at the office?"

"Fine. Celene just wanted to run something by me."

"Nothing urgent, I hope. Our schedule's pretty tight for the next few weeks."

I take pains to keep my voice light. "Nothing urgent."

The message on my desk could be earth-shattering, life-changing, and completely destructive. But it can wait. After all, the stranger who called has been waiting twenty-eight years.

From the corner of my eye I see Crystal approaching, steno pad in hand. She has questions—probably a long list of them.

Despite my promise to her, I can't be interviewed now. My head is swirling with too many questions of my own.

I turn to the window and prop my brow on the molded plastic. Crystal—astute girl that she is—correctly guesses that I'd like to be left alone, for after a moment I hear soft footsteps heading toward the back of the plane where Josh has joined Wes to drink coffee and crow about the VIPs they spotted at the prayer breakfast.

I close my eyes against a sudden spurt of tears.

How completely the world can change in the space of a moment! This morning my head had been filled with sights and sounds from the powerful world of government. I'd been a little star-struck by the senator's wife sitting at my right, a little dizzied by the fact that the President of the United States wished to honor my husband.

But those memories pale in significance as other visions fill my mind. I see a reddened, squalling baby boy, pulled from my swollen belly and held aloft just long enough for a nurse to wrap in a blanket before she whisks him away.

They took him from me—at my request—but in the winding length of twenty-eight years, nothing has been able to remove him from my heart.

CHAPTER TWO

*T*en minutes out of Wiltshire, Dan Moon's voice crackles over the intercom. I haven't slept a single minute, but I open my eyes, feign a yawn, and slip my feet back into my leather pumps.

Behind the bulkhead, Winnie perches on the jump seat and snaps her belt. "A good flight," she says, meeting my eye. "Were you able to rest at all?"

I nod like a simpleton. In more than twenty years of marriage to a very public preacher, I've had to develop a gift for small talk; in the face of Celene's message that gift has vanished as utterly as morning dew. I find it impossible to babble about banalities when a particular pink message slip waits on my desk.

Leaning forward, I slip my right arm into my wool coat, then work the bulk of the material over my shoulders. The wind sliding over the mountains will be frigid, and our tiny airport offers little shelter for corporate passengers. We'll disembark on the tarmac and scurry to our cars, which will be cold and wet from melting frost.

After struggling into his overcoat, Abel glances at his watch. "We're going to have to run to make that twelve o'clock lunch meeting," he calls to Josh, who has returned to the seat behind Abel. "Is your car at the hangar?"

"Yes, sir, it is."

Abel shifts his gaze to me. "I'm sorry, Em, but I've got a Christian businessmen's luncheon down at the Ramada. Josh will take me, if you don't mind driving my truck."

Though the last thing on earth I want to do is drive my husband's bulky black Navigator, I manage a smile.

"Or," Abel gives me an exaggerated wink, "you could always join me. I'll bet the businessmen would love it if you came along."

His words reverberate along the walls of my unsteady heart, sending me back to the winter day in early 1980 when he proposed. We were both seniors at Calvary Bible College, eager and slightly apprehensive about the future. We'd been best friends for nearly two years, and though I had begun to suspect God might want me to remain by Abel's side through life, I didn't dare dream of anything specific. We were close, but I hadn't shared my secrets.

He knew I hadn't become a Christian until the age of seventeen. He knew I loved Jesus with all my heart, for I had openly declared my devotion to the Savior on the first day we met. Something in my simple speech must have either touched or amused Abel, because he frequently sought out my company. Together we talked and studied and prayed, earnestly seeking God's will for our lives.

I didn't know what God had in mind for me, and it felt dangerous to voice any assumptions. I had privately thought about becoming a social worker for a place like Mercy House. In college I learned that because God is sovereign, the darkness he has allowed to enter our lives could serve his purposes. Given my past, I figured God would put me in some out-of-the-way place, allowing me to quietly feel sorry for my sins and do what I could to prevent others from making my mistakes.

I never, ever thought that God would use me in what my fellow students called "full-time ministry." Those who had received a calling were revered on campus; even the professors looked at them as front-line warriors in training. I respected those who chose to major in ministerial studies; I studied English and psychology and prayed that someday I could make a difference in some other girl's life.

One cold afternoon in 1980, Abel walked me from the chapel to the entrance of the girls' dorm. We talked of the sermon we'd just heard, and somehow the conversation veered toward what we would do when we left school. Abel spoke of his dream of ministering in his hometown of Wiltshire, Kentucky. His father pastored a small church in that college town, but the church had suffered a split and dwindled to a handful of members. Abel wanted to resuscitate his father's ministry and encourage the local people to reach far beyond the mountainous borders of Wiltshire. Kentuckians were proud, hardworking people, he told me, and most of them were devoted to God. A man would have to be persuasive, though, to convince them to use new methods of spreading an old message.

"God can use a man who is willing to sell out," he told me, his eyes shining. "And I'm sold out to be whatever the Lord wants me to be. I expect to be serving the Lord for the rest of my life and . . . well, I'd love to have you come along on the journey."

"Really?" I joked. "As what, your secretary? I should remind you that my typing isn't all it could be and I'm an absolute dunce when it comes to computers—"

"Emma Rose Harbison." He turned, blocking my path. His gloved hand took my mittened one, pushing the boundaries of what was considered proper male/female behavior on campus. His eyes bored into mine. "I'm asking you to be my wife and ministry partner. Will you serve the Lord by my side for as many years as God chooses to give us?"

For a moment I thought he was joking. Other students walked by, their conversations blowing past us along with scattered autumn leaves. I felt a blush burn my cheek—how could he propose in the open, in the middle of the day, without any sort of warning?—but when I looked into his eyes I saw sincerity . . . and love.

With all my heart, I wanted to say yes. But though I admired Abel tremendously, appreciated his dedication to God, and loved the way he protected me, the thought of being his wife scared me silly.

"Abel," I lowered my eyes lest he see too much, "I don't think I'd be a good partner for you. We have such different backgrounds."

"Everybody's equal at the foot of the cross, Em. And I've watched you over these last two years. I know you could be a great pastor's wife. I know you could help me be the man God wants me to be. Besides"—his hand rose to lift my chin, and again I was surprised he would risk this display of physical contact in full view of professors and resident assistants—"I've learned to love you. I can't imagine going into ministry without you by my side."

I pulled my hand from his. "You have no idea what my life was like before I came here. I haven't told you about—"

"I don't need to know anything about your past, Em. Life

for a Christian begins the day we accept Christ; on that day all things are forgiven, the past is wiped clean by God's forgiveness. I don't need to know, I don't want to know what you've done. What matters now—the only thing that counts—is that you are as forgiven as I am, and just as alive in Christ."

He looked at me, his smile crinkling the corners of his blue eyes. "Honey, if Jesus can forgive the sins of this red-haired spoiled brat, he can forgive anyone. So please, Em, promise you'll marry me after we graduate."

I have never been able to resist that little-boy grin. And so, believing in Abel's affirmation and the Lord's leading, I married Abel Howard the night after graduation. Our first year held lots of adjustments and hurt feelings—mostly mine—but after a few months we learned how to live and work together. I learned that the wife of a pastor must lower her expectations; Abel learned to elevate his. I learned that I couldn't have my husband to myself every night; Abel learned that I could be trusted to handle some matters without his direct involvement.

Over the years we established a home, a church, and a television ministry. Together we toiled with God's people to touch thousands, perhaps millions, of souls.

Prayer and Praise, our weekly telecast, reaches into over forty million households every Sunday morning; each month the Prayer and Praise mailroom processes over five hundred thousand dollars in contributions. Abel's college dream has come true, and nearly every penny of the television ministry's income goes to fund some aspect of outreach extending far beyond the city limits of Wiltshire, Kentucky. The influence of television has allowed us to support missionaries in Uganda, smuggle Arabic Bibles into Iran, and feed children in the hidden hollers of Kentucky.

The thought of my husband's success softens my smile as I watch him from across the cabin. Abel likes to reminisce about his devilish childhood, but you don't have to have a Ph.D. in psychology to realize that what he and his late mother called utter depravity was nothing but typical childish mischief. My dear husband thinks he understands life on all its levels, but his understanding is intellectual, at best. He reads about horrible atrocities in *Time* and *Newsweek*, but the world's evil has never seared his soul.

And while he may be content to believe that my spiritual birth at seventeen enabled me to shed my mistakes like a butterfly casting off its cocoon, I know traces of the past remain.

One of them has just cast its shadow across my heart.

Abel pauses by the passenger seat of Josh's aging BMW and hands me the keys to the Navigator. "So you're going home, hon?"

I wrap my fingers around the keys, feeling their chilly bite.

"Eventually. I think I'll go to the church first. Celene seemed to think I should look at a few of my messages."

"I'll catch up with you later, then."

Abel slides into the car and I grab the door, not quite ready to let him go. Abel is my husband, partner, and best friend. He deserves to know that a door to my past has just sprung open.

I bend to catch his eye. "Will you be home later today? I think I might need to talk to you about something . . . and I could use your advice."

He glances at his watch. "I'm booked all afternoon, and don't forget we have that deacon dinner tonight. But I should be home at five to change clothes." A slight furrow appears between his brows when his eyes meet mine. "You okay?"

I straighten and look toward the horizon, where a cloud-bank is edging over the mountains. "Just tell me you love me."

"More than anything but Jesus." Abel gives me a wink before closing the door.

I step away as Josh starts the engine. I am burning with the desire to share my news, but it wouldn't be fair to spring this kind of surprise on my husband in anyone else's hearing. Especially Josh's.

The Navigator is cold and smells vaguely of coffee when I unlock the door and climb inside. The passenger seat is cluttered with yesterday's copies of the *New York Times* and the *Wall Street Journal*, as well as the *Wiltshire Record*. The discarded papers are a good sign—if any of the three had printed negative articles about our ministry, Abel would have stuffed the offending paper into his briefcase and spent hours working on a rebuttal. We'd have been lucky to get him out for dinner last night, but Abel had been relaxed and happy, buoyed by the thought of the National Prayer Breakfast. The sharks had been lazy and content this morning; not a single reporter had yelled out a comment about Abel's stand against homosexuality or pornography.

A tremor cascades down my spine as I slide the key into the ignition. What sort of frenzy would erupt if the press sniffed out the story behind the young man who called me? My private life is no one's business, but when an individual becomes a public figure, even ancient secrets become fair game.

Not only will I have to tell Abel about my past, I might have to tell the world as well.

He thought the address might mean something to you.

An avenue of escape still exists—I do not have to answer this young man's call; I do not have to acknowledge the past. I could ignore Christopher Lewis and live the rest of my life as if he had never reached out to me. I would never have to tell my husband the sordid story of my previous life; I would never have to face a nosy pack of reporters.

I could simply say the address means nothing . . . now. I wouldn't exactly be telling the truth, but I wouldn't exactly be lying, either.

I put the car in reverse, then glance over my shoulder. Christopher Lewis may be a thousand things, but he is a gentleman. From his carefully worded message, I know he will not hound me if I do not return his call.

But how can I ignore this man?

Crystal and Wes are standing and talking between their cars, but they pause to wave as I pull out. I never did sit for Crystal's interview, but she'll undoubtedly catch me later this week. She'll pull out her steno pad and ask a series of questions designed to elicit informative, pleasant, spiritual responses:

"Tell me about your salvation experience."

"How do you envision your role as a pastor's wife?"

"What is the greatest challenge facing Christian women today?"

In all the interviews I've given to Christian publications, no one has ever asked me to share my deepest fears . . . or my greatest sins. No one ever inquires about my life in the "before Christ" years; perhaps interviewers assume nothing that transpired back then could possibly matter to me now.

But can we pull the dark threads of our history without distorting the fabric of our lives? Surely a courageous woman would face up to her past and acknowledge the bleak days, even embrace them as part of the path that ultimately led her to acknowledge the goodness and sovereignty of God.

Unfortunately, my Bible college professors talked more

about striving for sanctification than dealing with the effects of sin.

I hand the parking stub to the gate attendant along with a five-dollar bill. He thanks me with a smile and a slight tip of the hat. He knows me as Emma Rose Howard, the Reverend's wife and a verifiable Good Woman.

He doesn't know me well.

I pull out of the parking lot, pause at the stop sign, then drive onto the main airport road. A billboard for a mobile phone company catches my eye—"Express Yourself!"

Ha! If only I could. I'd like nothing better than to announce and acknowledge my past, but I can't think only of myself. My husband and I lead a ministry that employs over three hundred people and influences thousands more. If my reputation is tainted, others will know. And possibly be hurt. And it would be better to be thrown into the sea with a millstone tied around my neck than to face the punishment in store for harming one of the young babes in Christ.

The car in my rearview mirror slants left and growls around me; the teenager at the wheel is obviously not satisfied to lag behind me on this two-lane road. I watch him roar ahead, then tap my thumb against the steering wheel. Maybe God's not satisfied with where I am in life . . . and the message waiting at the office is an invitation to swerve onto an uncharted path.

Why not turn the wheel and follow where the Lord leads? I'd be taking a risk, sure, but if God is leading, I shouldn't be afraid. After all, it's not like a gang of reporters is hounding me . . . but the press didn't care about Tammy Faye Bakker until scandal rocked the PTL ministry. Abel and I weren't on television in those days, but we couldn't help but notice how the press devoured details of that particular debacle. Mainstream newspapers reported on excesses ranging from the Bakkers' wardrobes to their air-conditioned doghouse, so that's when Abel and I decided we'd do our best to live moderately. Our church had grown to six thousand members by the time the Bakkers hit the news, and we had begun to suspect that television might be part of the Lord's plan for us.

We learned a lot from the PTL brouhaha—that's why Abel drives a Navigator while I favor a sedate Volvo sedan. We live in a nice home in a gated community, but our house is no nicer than our neighbors'. We have no dogs, therefore no doghouses, air-conditioned or otherwise, we're not into flashy jewelry, and we have no children . . .

My grip tightens on the steering wheel as I turn from the airport road into highway traffic. *We have no children . . . legally.* What will Abel say when he learns I have a son?

A huge white steeple stabs the sky as I point the Navigator up a hill. Sinai Church sits atop the mound of red rock for which it was named generations ago. The original building, a simple rectangular structure with a tin-clad steeple, served a mostly rural congregation from its completion in 1918 until May 1980, when Abel's father retired from its pulpit. That month twenty-five farming families voted to call my husband as pastor (two of the wives, I am told, dissented on account of Abel's marriage to a "Yankee from New York"), and so we arrived in the summer of 1980—newly wed, inexperienced, and eager to take on the world.

I pull into the church parking lot and wave at the security guard who has snapped to attention at the Navigator's approach. His sober expression melts into a grin when I lower the tinted window. "It's just me, Brian; the Reverend's out speaking."

He nods and waves me forward. "Good to see you, Emma Rose. Give the Reverend my congratulations on the prayer thing, will you?"

"I will." A wry smile lifts my mouth as I pull into Abel's reserved parking space. Though they are the salt of the earth, few of our local folks fully appreciate the honor Abel has just received, mainly because Abel always jokes about such events. This past Wednesday night at prayer meeting he mentioned that he had to go up to Washington to have breakfast with the president. As the crowd roared its approval, Abel sheepishly added that he was going to accept "an honor for the people of Sinai Church." That's how Abel sees it—it isn't his honor, but the ministry's. And all the glory belongs to God.

As I step out of the car, my gaze roves over a handsome white building that didn't even exist when Abel and I were first married. In the Lord's perfect timing, we arrived at the beginning of a building boom in the city. Wiltshire College had just abandoned its vocational curriculum and become a four-year liberal arts college; by 1990 it had tripled in size. The growing school attracted professors and businesses; farmers sold their land to developers who poured miles of concrete to support the shopping malls, gas stations, and grocery stores sprouting like wildflowers in a Kentucky meadow.

Fueled by Abel's determination and God's blessing, Sinai Church flourished. Abel made it a point to visit every single new professor and administrator at Wiltshire College; he bought mailing lists from the property appraiser and visited every newcomer in town. The church grew from a few families to over one hundred, then began to double every few months.

Now our complex sprawls over Sinai Hill. The original building, complete with tin steeple, has been preserved as a reception area for visitors, while our state-of-the-art sanctuary serves as a worship center and television studio. Our elevated platform is really a professional theater stage with footlights and trapdoors and curtains—all the accouterments of a regular theater.

I get out of the car, then grimace when I see a group of white-haired ladies in windbreakers and fanny packs posing beside the huge brick sign at the front of the property. They and the elderly gentleman snapping their picture are probably visiting Praise Partners, our name for the contributors who pledge twenty dollars a month to support our television ministry.

While I truly appreciate the sacrifices of our Praise Partners, this morning I don't have time to play hostess.

I duck my head, intending to make a run for the building, but I'm too slow. Before I take two steps, I hear: "Look! It's Emma Rose!"

If I ignore them, I'll hurt their feelings. If I stand and talk, I'll be trapped for at least fifteen minutes. Driving away is not an option; I need to get to my desk.

Time to exercise the diplomatic skills every pastor's wife hones to a fine edge.

Acknowledging our visitors with a broad wave, I begin to move up the hill with long strides. "Welcome to Sinai Church," I call over my shoulder. "Have a look around the grounds, and be sure to stop at the reception desk." I point toward the doorway labeled *Reception*, then smile when the visitors turn toward it like flowers seeking the sun.

While they are distracted, I hurry toward the unmarked door that leads directly to the executive offices.

Abel has always attracted single-minded, loyal people. He preaches the gospel, pure and straight, and makes no bones about Jesus being the only way to heaven. "Listen to the world and you'd think there are many ways to God," he says, "but Jesus himself said, 'I am the way, and no man comes to the Father but by me.' So it doesn't matter what Oprah or Dr. Phil or Deepak Chopra says. They don't have the keys to heaven; only Jesus holds the keys to life and death. And if he says he's the way, then he is."

In an age when everyone else is terribly concerned with political correctness, my husband's preaching is uncommonly blunt; perhaps that's the secret of his success. He doesn't need fireworks or celebrity guest stars to attract viewers. He manages very well with only a word from the Lord, a bit of humor, and a little music to warm people's hearts.

The music has been my responsibility ever since we married. I didn't even know I could sing until college—my parents certainly never encouraged me. My mother suffered from chronic migraines, so loud noises—including singing, transistor radios, and *American Bandstand*—were forbidden in our house.

I punch in the security code on the exterior lock, then slip through the doorway. Praise music immediately fills my ears, courtesy of the office intercom. I move down the carpeted hallway toward my office suite and hum along with the song playing over the office sound system.

I had never experienced the sheer beauty of vocal music until I joined the Calvary Bible College choir. My choir director singled me out one afternoon, and no one was more amazed than me to discover I had a strong alto voice. My awestruck roommate compared me to Karen Carpenter, but I didn't think my singing was any big deal until Abel told me he liked my songs. When I sang, he said, he could tell I was singing for the Lord.

I learned to play for the Lord, too. I suppose I have always been attuned to music, but in that first basic music class at college I learned there were names attached to the notes in my ear and they fitted together like black and white puzzle pieces on the piano. My piano teacher said my perfect pitch was a special gift from God, and it didn't take long before I could hear a song and reproduce it on the keyboard. I'm still not the best at reading music—there are kids in our church who read piano scores better than I do—but I seldom have to hear a song more than two or three times before I can play it.

Seeing music as worship completely changed my perspective about life and ministry. I had been thinking I had nothing to offer the world but my bad experiences, but through the avenue of music I could envision a future that involved far more than counseling troubled girls. I could sing, I could play, and I could help Abel. Everybody knew that preachers needed musicians; the two went together like salt and pepper.

Like the graceful swirls in a treble clef, my life took a new turn. Music became my means of ministry; Abel became my life. Now the Abel part often overshadows the music part, but I can still find myself swept away by the sheer beauty of a lyric or a melody. When I sing, "Oh love that will not let me go," I can't help but think about how far God's love has brought me . . . and how thankful I am that it holds me tight.

Sometimes I wonder if I even had a voice in the BC years. I know I didn't have a song.

Before turning into my office, I walk to the end of the hall and peer around the corner. Tanzel Ellers, the church receptionist, sits at her round desk before the main entrance to the office complex. Rumor has it that Tanzel is one of the two farmers' wives who voted against Abel coming to Sinai, but she's mostly all smiles these days.

"Morning, Emma Rose." An extra-cheery note resonates in her voice, probably because the tourists are now browsing the literature table against the wall.

"You take good care of those folks." I wave at the white-haired woman who has just turned to gape at me. "I'd love to have a cup of coffee with you all, but I'm going to be tied up in my office this afternoon."

The woman's eyes widen while her elbow prods the old man's ribs. "Look! She looks just like she does on TV!"

I shift my attention to Tanzel. "Anything these nice folks need, you'll see to it, right?"

She nods. "Of course."

I twiddle my fingers at the tourists, then retreat around the corner. I always feel a little guilty when I have to duck visitors because some people drive hours to visit the church they watch on TV every week. Every Sunday after services, Abel and I host a reception in the old sanctuary for anyone who wants to shake our hands or share a prayer request, but we're not set up to entertain people during the week.

I make my way down the carpeted hallway, keeping my head low in order to avoid having to personally greet secretaries for the Sunday school, education program, publications department, and physical plant office.

Another corner and I'm at the hall leading to the executive suites—home away from home for Abel, Josh, and me. I pause in the vestibule of Abel's office to greet Esther Mason, his grandmotherly secretary.

"Mornin', Esther. Have you heard from him yet?"

She heaves a frustrated sigh, then shakes her head. "The president of the businessmen's club has called twice. They're getting antsy."

"He should be there by now. He and Josh left the airport right before I did."

"Thank goodness. I hate it when I can't find him."

"I know what you mean."

Leaving her, I pass Josh's office, then stride into the soft pink suite reserved for me, Celene, and the women's ministry.

My hands are trembling when I lower my purse to Celene's desk, but she doesn't seem to notice.

I pull my gloves from my fingertips in an effort to hide my nervousness. "Anything exciting?"

She lifts a banded stack of envelopes from her in-box. "Not a blessed thing. But here's the morning mail—I've flagged the letters calling for a personal response."

My eyes dart toward the phone. "Any calls?"

"It's been pretty quiet since I talked to you. I put your messages on your desk."

I take the mail and thank her, then hesitate. "About that strange message . . ."

She looks up, her eyes wide.

"Let's keep that between us, okay? I'm going to tell Abel about it and let him decide if we need to alert security."

"No problem." She leans back in her chair, a sly grin brightening her face. "So—did you figure out who Christopher Lewis is? Could he be an old boyfriend?"

Something in me recoils at the question. "I have no old boyfriends."

Tsking, she shakes her head. "I don't understand you, Emma Rose. What were you before you married the Reverend, a nun? A woman like you should have had lots of old boyfriends."

I shake my head and walk through the open doorway, leaving her words to trail behind me. My windowless office is lit only by the tall lamp on the credenza. I drop my purse into an empty desk drawer, then pick up the tidy stack of pink messages in the center of the polished wood.

Like cream, the most significant message has risen to the

top. The "C" in the name *Christopher* has been traced several times, probably as Celene took the message and mulled over its significance.

Despite that revealing sign, I trust her completely. In the five years she has worked for me, Celene has never betrayed a confidence or committed an indiscretion. Christopher could have spilled his entire life story on the phone, and she wouldn't breathe a word of it unless I gave her permission.

Perhaps what I'm looking at *is* his life story. I read the date in Celene's loopy handwriting—January 6, 1976—and the address on Hillside Drive.

At this tangible reminder of my baby's birth date, cold, clear reality sweeps over me in a wave so powerful that my knees weaken. I sink into my chair, staring at the address where I was, in a very real sense, reborn.

The image of Mercy House materializes in my mind's eye—faint at first, then as vivid as a snapshot emerging in a tray of developer. When I close my eyes I can see Lortis June Moses, smell her honeysuckle perfume, and feel the crepey softness of her skin. Her sandpaper voice fills my ears: "There is a balm in Gilead . . . to heal the sin-sick soul."

Exhausted by the irresistible riptide of memory, after a long moment I reach for the phone and punch in the number on the pink slip. I hold my breath as I bring the phone to my ear, then my left hand, almost of its own accord, reaches over and disconnects the call.

I lean back, the receiver falling to my chest as I close my eyes against the sting of tears. I can't do this, not yet. Abel is my husband, my partner, my pastor. I can't spring this news on him as a *fait accompli;* it wouldn't be fair to involve him without warning.

Before I proceed . . . *if* I proceed . . . I must talk to Abel.

CHAPTER THREE

*E*ither by the grace of God or ingrained habit, I manage to tackle the business of the afternoon. After placing Christopher Lewis's message safely inside the Bible I keep at my desk, I sort through the other pink slips.

Abel has always delegated problems in the women's ministry to me. "I love women," he says, "and I married one. But I don't understand them, I don't think like one of them, and I sure don't know how to please them. Fortunately, my wife does."

Though I'm honored by my husband's trust, sometimes I'm not sure I do. Women—myself included—have a tendency to sprinkle blood from their wounds in wide circles instead of healing the hurt and applying a proper bandage. I am constantly encouraging our women to confront the source of their problems in a loving manner, but all too often that approach is a last resort instead of a first step.

One of my pink messages pertains to a call from Judy Rousey, who is upset because Rachel Williams criticized Judy's preschool program in a ladies' Bible study group. But instead of going to Rachel and asking how she could help solve her problem with the preschool program, Judy has written a letter to Abel, called me, and inflamed the entire preschool department staff.

I jot a note on my calendar to invite Judy and Rachel to a lunch meeting. We'll work it out over pasta and salad.

Edna Larson, a vice president of Women for a Christian America, wants to know if I'm available to speak at their national convention in July. Edna is too high-profile to risk offending, so instead of delegating the call to Celene, I will call personally to say I'm not sure about the date but will let her know within the week.

Sue Hargett, our high-school youth pastor's wife, wants to know if I can participate in what she calls an "immodest fashion show" for the teenage girls. "We're trying to make a point by showing the girls what not to wear," she tells me when I call. "We thought you'd make a great Lori Long Legs. You could wear a short skirt, you know, or shorts that are way too skimpy."

Grateful she can't see my face, I frown at my legs. The years have taken their toll, and my hose can't hide the faint blue map of varicose veins. "Um, I don't know, Sue . . ."

"We all change in the rest room right across from the chapel, so it's not like you'd have to walk around in your outfit. But I understand if you're busy. We just thought it'd be nice for the girls to see you in a different role."

Her unspoken message is coming through loud and clear—*it'd be nice for our girls to see you up close and in the flesh, not just on the platform.*

I accept her challenge and pencil the date on my calendar. "I'll be there. With a thick terrycloth robe to cover me as we run from the rest room to the chapel."

I hang up, then pencil "find a too-short skirt?" on my to-do list. Life at Sinai Church is never boring.

After responding to all my messages, I glance at my watch. Three o'clock. At least two more hours before I can talk to Abel.

I swivel my chair toward the narrow window at the side of my office. My brain knows I need to keep busy. I have responsibilities, and I ought to move on to something constructive like studying the lesson I'm supposed to teach for the Sunday morning new members' class, but my brain is spinning like a top around one fixed point: Christopher Lewis.

My son . . . and the gracious keeper of my secret.

Celene is intuitive, but she would never guess the relationship between me and the stranger who called. The entire world seems to know that Abel and I are childless, and I'd bet my last dollar that Celene and most of the church folk have joined Abel in believing I am the infertile partner in this marriage. In Scripture, after all, it's always the woman who is barren.

My husband—who has refused to submit to the procedures required for fertility testing—has accepted our childlessness as the Lord's will. He has always been honest about the heartbreak of the empty womb, freely mentioning our failure to conceive in sermons, interviews, and personal conversations. With a generosity born of ignorance, he says infertility is a shared problem, something that cannot be blamed on one partner or the other. If God chooses not to bless a couple with children, then the Lord clearly has other plans.

My gaze falls on a laminated plaque featuring an article from the front page of the *Washington Post*. The headline proclaims *Kentucky Pastor Wants to Sanitize TV for America's Children*.

I have read the first paragraph so many times I can quote it verbatim:

Abel Howard, fondly known as "the Reverend" to his extended flock, has joined with his wife, Emma Rose, to launch a crusade to clean up television, and, by extension, American society. When asked why he cares so devoutly about the nation's television viewing habits, Howard answered, "We care about television because we care about the glassy-eyed, media-hypnotized children of America. My wife and I have no children of our own. After dealing with that sorrow—through which we realized that our desire for progeny is nothing compared to the incredible yearning God feels for his errant children—we came to see that God intends our offspring to be spiritual, not biological. For the sake of our *spiritual* children—who range in age from one to ninety-two—we want to bring this nation back to the standards of decency and righteousness that once exalted us as a people."

Abel has long forgotten about the pain of our empty bedrooms. The quest for spiritual children occupies his days and nights and even his dreams, and my hopes have been swept up in his quest for souls. I love the thought of bringing children into the kingdom of God, but I can't deny that my empty arms still ache when I walk through the brightly painted nursery classrooms.

Abel mourned for our unborn children and moved on; sometimes I think he scheduled his grief in his appointment book. My grief clings to me like a shadow; it lies next to me at night, often waking me from sleep with soft groans. On those nights I lie motionless in the thrall of moments alchemized from forgotten time. In the moonlight pouring over our bed I see the nurse holding my son over my breast. This time she pauses, allowing me to count my baby's fingers and toes and study the sweet shape of his lips . . .

If I'm not careful, I'll drive myself crazy. I reach for my Bible, open it, and flip through the delicate pages until the pink message lies beneath my fingertips.

There it is again—the link to my son, my past.

I run my finger over the inked lines. What can you discern about a man from his name? *Christopher* sounds modern, elegant. More sophisticated than the Steves and Gregs and Mikes who teased me in grade school . . . and the pseudonymous Joes and Jacks who picked me up on the Lower East Side. One of those Joes or Jacks is Christopher's dad, but I have no way of knowing who fathered the child that ultimately saved me from life on the streets.

Christopher . . . the name sounds *good*. Lewis, obviously, comes from the family who adopted him. The agency never told me much about them, only that they were a Christian couple who lived somewhere in upstate New York and wanted a child. I have always imagined my boy growing up in flannel and sneakers, with a pony or a big dog at his side as he hikes through the Adirondack Mountains . . .

The image jars me. Goodness, how has he found his way to Kentucky? I bring the message closer and study the phone number—the area code and exchange are local.

Christopher Lewis did not call from New York, but from Wiltshire.

I bring my hand to my mouth as my stomach clenches.

Celene raps on the door, then opens it. "You didn't get lunch, Emma Rose. Do you want something to eat?"

I struggle to force words across my tongue. "Thanks, Celene, but I'm fine."

May God forgive the lie.

"Okay, then."

She closes the door; I lower the pink paper back to my Bible. Christopher Lewis would be twenty-eight now, a full-grown man. Perhaps he's married . . . maybe he has a child. Maybe the child is the reason for this call; Christopher might need to understand his genetic history because his baby needs a bone-marrow transplant or something.

I rake my hand through my hair. Or maybe I've watched too much television. But isn't that always the way it unfolds in movies? Adopted kids from happy families almost never search for their biological parents unless they need an organ transplant or suffer from some unusual genetic disease. Maybe Christopher is sick with some incurable illness, and I'll have to tell him he must have inherited it from his dad because I'm as healthy as a May morning. And then he'll ask who his father is, and I'll endure the excruciating agony of admitting I have no idea.

Because I was turning tricks to survive when my child was conceived. And I was seventeen. And so stoned most of the time that I couldn't even describe the men who picked me up, let alone remember their names. In those days I had no idea God had designed sex as a gift.

I bow my head and cover my face as a wave of agony rises from someplace below my breastbone and floods my face. I've been a minister's wife for nearly twenty-four years; I've been living this new life for twenty-eight. I walked the streets for no more than twenty-two months, so why have those days come back to haunt me?

God, what are you doing?

Abel says we should close our eyes to the past in order to keep sin at bay, yet something in me wants to throw open my arms and welcome this souvenir of my darkness. Is that per- verse . . . or only natural? Should I try to be human or godly?

I lower my head to the desk and close my eyes as memo- ries come flooding back.

Abel's upbringing and mine were about as alike as mus- tard and custard. While Abel played in the hills of Wiltshire, I grew up in Brocton, a small town in western New York state. My dad worked for the FBI; my mom lived for the bottle. Since we saw more of Dad's empty recliner than we did of him, Mom spent more time pouring herself drinks than car- ing about her only child.

Kids are resilient, they tell me, and I suppose I couldn't miss what I never had. As a kid I spent most of my time day- dreaming or reading. I was an A-plus student who found pleasure and affirmation in pleasing my teachers. If the summer of '74 had never come, I'd probably have graduated as salutatorian and gone to college on an academic scholarship.

But Joey Malone robbed twenty-four banks in the winter and spring of '74, and Dad was one of the federal agents sent out to track him down. Dad must have thought he'd hit the jackpot when he walked into a St. Louis tavern and discovered Malone bellied up to the bar. Witnesses said the lone agent tried to take Malone in, but Number Two on the FBI's most wanted list calmly shot Special Agent Tom Harbison in the chest, ordered a whiskey, and took the time to gulp it down before stepping over my father's body and striding out the front door.

After that, Mom wore the title *widow* like a veil, hiding in its gray shadows as she spurned public sympathy and drank even more. I kept thinking there ought to be a special word for kids who've lost their fathers, something more dignified than *poor thing*, which was all I heard from my neighbors and classmates.

Yet Ziggy Constantine, a brawny senior, whispered those words with a particular tenderness to which I eagerly responded. I didn't think Mom even cared about my dating until she came home early one night and found me and Ziggy making out on the living room couch. In a sodden rage she threw Ziggy out, then strode into my room, yanked my clothes from the closet, and flung them onto the front lawn.

Responding with the white-hot anger of a fifteen-year-old, I plucked a few things from the mess in the yard, tossed them into a gym bag, then strode back into the house long enough to grab every dollar, quarter, and dime I could find. After a confrontation at Ziggy's place, where I learned that seventeen-year-old boys are hard-wired to avoid any permanent responsibility suddenly thrust upon them, I took a bus to Manhattan. Time and poverty led me to the Lower East Side.

I wish my story were more unique. A thousand variations of my runaway experience have flashed across the nation's movie screens with both happy and tragic endings. In reality, my existence was far dirtier and hungrier than those depicted in most Hollywood dramas. I could have easily disappeared into the urban landscape, worn into nothingness like a piece of gum on the sidewalk, but God had other plans. My dreams of glamour and independence popped like a string of soap bubbles, and before two years had passed I found myself sick, pregnant for the second time, and too broke to pay for another abortion.

So I tried to kill myself. One morning I scored sleeping pills and a bottle of vodka from a pimp who worked Avenue B. Weeping over the misery of my life, I swallowed the first pill and pulled at the bottle, then swallowed the second pill and drank some more. I kept thinking death might hurt, so I wanted to be completely senseless when I took that last breath . . .

I woke up the next morning in an alley with rat bites on

my ankles and bits of gravel imbedded in my cheek. The pills had disappeared along with the bottle, and someone had pulled every last dime from my pockets.

I propped my arms on my knees and stared at the broken concrete. I was a waste of skin and bone; I couldn't even commit suicide properly. I had but one thing to give . . . and there were plenty of takers on Manhattan's Lower East Side.

A week later, I was on my way to score some drugs in Tompkins Square Park when I stopped for the light at Third Street and Avenue B. A graceless little restaurant occupied that corner, a place I'd never noticed. The paint had weathered out of the fading letters on the sign, so I could barely make out the name: Nola's Meat and Three.

I hardly ever ate when I was using, but something— maybe the baby—made me hungry. The aromas coming out of the open doorway called to me. For a long moment I stood motionless, breathing in the scents of baking bread and roasting beef. I don't know how long I stood rooted to the sizzling sidewalk, but before I could move a big woman came out, threw her arm around me with amazing tenderness, and led me inside. Two minutes later I was in a booth slurping up beef stew and gulping down biscuits that tasted like they'd been baked in heaven.

Nola Register settled into the seat across from me, her eyes beaming at me over a set of triple chins. She propped her head on her hand and watched me eat. She couldn't have been more than sixty, but her eyes looked a thousand years old. Two years before, I wouldn't have given Nola the time of day, no matter how much she fed me. Overweight and frowsy, she lumbered like a stevedore and smelled of yeast and perspiration. Something about the way her wiry hair jutted up like exclamation points made me nervous.

But her eyes shimmered with love and compassion. Those eyes caught me, embraced me, enslaved me. At that moment I was so hungry for love I'd have signed on as a potato peeler for life if she'd asked me to.

She had something far different in mind. "Honey," she finally said, "you're headed down a dead-end street. Whaddya say to a fresh start?"

I stared at Nola over a bowl of beef stew, a fountain welling behind my eyes. My vision blurred, and suddenly I couldn't speak over the sobs rising from my chest.

Nola stood up and came to sit beside me, then wrapped a meaty arm around my shoulders. "There, now," she whispered, rocking me in her embrace. "Everything's going to be all right."

Within twenty-four hours I was on a bus to Hudson Falls, a town in east-central New York; within another twenty-four hours I had been welcomed into the rectangular brick building known as Mercy House. Lortis June Moses, a woman with sharp cheekbones and silver ringlets curling on her forehead, ruled over my new home with a velvet fist. No messin', no men, and no Marlboros, Lortis told me in the front room. At Mercy House I'd find studyin', singin', and salvation—plenty to take the place of all my bad habits.

My stubborn pride rose up when Lortis June recited that speech, but within a week I discovered that the same firm love that animated Nola reigned in Lortis June.

At Mercy House I discovered a new way of life. Lortis June demonstrated that "Christian" was more than a box to check on a demographic survey. Being a Christian meant having a new birth, a new perspective, and a new life.

While volunteers helped me earn my GED, Lortis June helped me understand that God never intended me to be lost in my sin. I had been created for fellowship with God, she said, and my life would change if I decided to listen to God instead of ignoring him.

"I'm not saying your life will always be perfect," she told me. "But the trouble we Christians go through has been engineered for us, designed to bring us even closer to the Lord we love. So we can trust the trouble. We can even smile through the pain."

My love for the Lord grew as quickly as the baby swelling inside me. Within a month of arriving at Mercy House, I had chosen to give my life to God. Jesus and I enjoyed a kind of honeymoon phase until I had the baby.

After that, I didn't know what to do.

I had accomplished worthwhile things at Mercy House. I

passed the GED tests, received a high-school diploma, gave birth to a healthy baby boy, and found a loving home for him. I checked off every item on my life's "to-do" list but couldn't imagine what I was supposed to do next. I had no money for college and no means of financial support. Lortis June thought I might be able to get a partial scholarship from a Christian college, but even if I entered a work program, I'd still need financial help to complete a four-year degree. I began to think I might have to go back to Brocton and search for long-lost relatives—or Mom, God help me—but that idea appealed to me about as much as taking a voyage into the eternal night of the damned.

I was beginning to doubt Lortis June's promise that God had a plan for me when a letter arrived from Brocton. Displaying considerable ingenuity, my mother's lawyer had tracked me through the General Educational Development testing service.

My mother, he informed me, died nine months after I left home. The house had been in bad shape, but, acting under a power of attorney, he paid for repairs with the money left in her estate and sold the house within a few months. As my mother's only daughter, I had inherited the remaining estate, which amounted to just under fifty thousand dollars.

That night Lortis June sat with me in the tiny room we used for a chapel. The lawyer's letter weighted my hand, as heavy as the unshed tears in my heart. I had loved my mother with the unreasonable and unreasoning love a child feels for the center of her universe, but I had never known love from her. She had made no effort to find me.

Lortis June picked up my hand and pressed it between her work-worn palms. "The Lord moves in mysterious ways, honey." Her voice went soft with awe. "I can't pretend to know why this happened when it did, but I know you can trust our Jesus. Your mama is gone, but she's left you with what you need to get on with the rest of your life. God had a hand in that. He has a hand in everything that touches the lives of his children."

I stared at the letter in my lap. "Why couldn't God just make her love me? That would have been nicer than having money. She could have cleaned up and dried out, and then she would have helped me through school, and I could have worked to help her—"

"I've found it's best not to argue with the past." Lortis June patted my hand. "I just accept and move on. That's what you need to do."

So that's what I did. Accepted the money, went to college, met Abel Howard under a spreading oak tree. I found the love I'd been searching for and so much more. I began to forget the pain of having a mother who never even looked for me.

Blinking away bitter tears, I raise my hand to swipe the bangs from my eyes. For an instant I am startled to discover that my bangs are wispy, not the longer, heavier style I wore in college.

I am no longer a young woman. I am forty-five, old enough to be a grandmother. The paper in my open Bible may lead me to discover that I am.

The wonder of the message strikes me afresh—mostly because after Mom died, I never expected anyone to make an effort to find me.

But someone has.

CHAPTER FOUR

*U*nable to concentrate on anything more significant than the arrangement of books on my desk, I give up on work and drive home. I let myself into the house, turn off the alarm, drop the mail on the table in the study. Relieved of that small burden, I slip off my shoes and pad toward the bedroom Abel and I left only twenty-four hours ago.

When I packed for our overnight trip to Washington, our room had felt large and spacious, vibrant and elegant. Now the bedroom feels chilly and small, as if the walls have inched forward in our absence. The bed looms large in the center of the room; the other furniture cowers before it.

I drop my overnight bag onto the small bench at the footboard and stare at the smooth satin comforter. I can almost see a gulley running down the center of the mattress, the beginning of the abyss that might develop before nightfall.

Tonight when I lie next to Abel, will he reach across the chasm to touch my hair as he usually does before he says good night? Or will my news prove too much to bear? I have known couples who gradually drifted apart; others are torn apart by infidelity and betrayal. Abel would never divorce me for something that occurred before we met, but my news might destroy his love. After all, he says love is a decision you make every day.

Will he decide to love me tomorrow?

The question hangs in the cool dark silence.

Desperate for something to do, I open my suitcase and pull out the rumpled suit I wore yesterday. I carry it into the bathroom, then drop it into the hamper dedicated to the dry cleaner. My toiletries kit gets shoved beneath the bathroom sink, my toothbrush clatters back into the china holder sitting beside the faucet.

Good grief, what is keeping Abel? I glance at the small clock on the marble vanity—it's five-fifteen, and Abel promised he'd leave the church by five. Our house is only ten minutes away, so I should hear the hum and creak of the garage door at any moment.

I'll stay busy, keep my mind occupied. I pull my lingerie

from the overnight case and drop it into the regular laundry hamper, then turn the case upside down and give it a shake to make sure I haven't missed anything. Satisfied, I push it to the top shelf in our walk-in closet, then step into the bathroom.

I'd love to soak my tension away in the whirlpool bath, but the tub is a disaster. Last month we discovered a leak in the water line leading to the tub; a plumber repaired the leak two days ago. But now we need a tile man to replace the tiles the plumber had to remove in order to access the plumbing. The tile job will be larger than we expected, because the tiles on our tub match the floor tiles, and the old tiles are no longer being manufactured. So we'll have to replace all the tub and floor tiles, which means I'll have to deal with home repairs for at least another week.

Sighing, I walk back into the bedroom. I should have called a tile guy today, but Abel and I have had more important things on our minds than bathtubs.

I sink to the edge of the bed and glance at the clock on my nightstand. Five-twenty. Abel is late, but that's nothing unusual. An urgent call could have come into the office at the last moment. But now he's too late for me to tell him my news—the deacons' dinner is at six, and something like this can't be sandwiched between appointments. I had wanted at *least* a half-hour to talk to Abel; I need time to gently break my news.

I wander back to the closet. Though I would give anything

to stay home to think about the day's revelation, nothing short of a heart attack can get me out of this banquet. If I don't go, Abel will be peppered with a thousand questions about where I am and if I am well.

At least I don't have to sing. I can sit quietly at the head table, paste on a pleasant smile, and mull over Christopher Lewis's call while my husband speaks. I'll just have to remember to laugh in all the appropriate places.

I put one hand on my hip and study my side of the crowded closet. What to wear? Nothing too flashy; these are local church people, many of whom will have come straight from work. Nothing too drab, either; they are proud of their pastor and his wife; they expect us to look like television personalities. A suit is too stiff; a flowered dress too domestic.

I finally settle on a tailored pantsuit with a delicately embroidered lapel. The embellishment elevates the outfit above the ordinary, but it's still about ten degrees shy of costume.

After changing, I step to the mirror to freshen my makeup. My shoulders tighten when a quick glance at the clock tells me it's five-thirty. I swipe another coat of mascara onto the tips of my lashes and realize that if Abel doesn't come through the door soon, we'll be lucky to make it to the dinner on time.

I brush my teeth, rinse with mouthwash, check the tips of my fingernails. I am applying another spritz of hair spray when I hear the electric hum of the garage door. It's five-forty. Abel will barely have time to change his shirt before we have to leave.

I wave the hair spray away from my face, then move into the bedroom. Abel enters a moment later. "Hey, hon." He pecks my cheek, then waves a yellow envelope before my eyes. "I found this by the front door."

It's a regular envelope, hand-lettered and addressed to "Mr. and Mrs. Abel Howard." There's nothing beneath our names, but someone has written a return address in the upper left corner: Cathleen Stock, 8374 Martingale Place, Wiltshire.

The woman lives next door, and the fact that there's no "Rev." in front of Abel's name tells me she doesn't know us at all.

Shrugging out of his coat, Abel gives me a broad smile. "Hey, you look great. Ready to go?"

I drop the envelope and sink into the leather recliner across from the bed. I had so hoped to be able to unload the burden I've been carrying all day, but there's no time.

Disappointment brings a lump to my throat: "I suppose so."

"I'll just be a minute." He strides by me, headed toward the bathroom. His voice echoes in the cavernous tiled space. "Did you bring in the mail?"

I hesitate before I answer. I did grab the mail, but I was so preoccupied I dropped everything on the desk without sorting through it. Most of our mail comes to us through the ministry; only personal bills come to the house, and those are all listed under the name of "E. R. Howard," the only designation we trust. For security reasons, we never open anything arriving at the house with our own names featured in the address.

The envelope in my hand, however, looks harmless enough. I slide my thumbnail under the seal. "The mail's on the desk in the study. Haven't had a chance to look at it."

"That's okay."

As Abel takes off his shirt, I open the folded page from the envelope. My neighbor has organized a progressive dinner for all willing residents of Martingale Place. The event is scheduled for February 22, 5:30 P.M. All families who want to participate should RSVP before February 15—

It's impossible, of course. We're just too busy for this sort of thing. I consult my mental calendar. The dinner is more than two weeks away, but the twenty-second is a Sunday . . . and there's no way we can attend on a Sunday evening. Even though my husband never preaches on Sunday night, preferring to give the other staff pastors an opportunity to speak, he wouldn't think of missing a service for a social activity.

Besides, Abel really likes to be "off" when he's home. It's the one place where no one asks his opinions about politics, theology, or whether or not the Church will endure any part of the Tribulation.

Abel steps out of the bathroom, buttoning a fresh white

shirt he's pulled from the closet. "Good day, hon?"

"Hmm." I press my lips together as I slip Cathleen's invitation beneath a coaster on my dresser. "An interesting day."

Abel grins. "Trouble in the women's ministry? I saw that letter from Judy Rousey. Sounds like she's got it in for Rachel Williams."

"I'm taking them both to lunch. We'll work it out."

I look him full in the face, hoping he'll see that Rachel and Judy are the last people in the world I want to talk about. If he looks intently enough, surely he'll see the secret lurking in my eyes and ask why my voice is pinched and tight.

But he's frowning at the buttons on his shirt. "I hate these things. They always make the buttons too small."

I don't answer, and my silence makes him look up. "What's wrong, Em—oh. You wanted to talk to me about something, right?"

The right question, but not the right attitude or the right time. I nod as the lump crowds my throat again, then I swallow. "It can wait. There's not enough time to get into it."

"You okay?" A faint thread of concern lines his voice as he tucks in his shirt. The question is sincere, but his eyes are distracted.

For an instant I am tempted to open my mouth and let everything in my heart spill out. Abel could be late to the dinner, couldn't he? And it wouldn't be the end of the world if he didn't show up. We have dozens of men on staff who could step in and take his place; several of the deacons are wonderful speakers. Other men miss meetings on account of family emergencies—well, I'm Abel's family, and tonight we have an emergency.

But my husband's thoughts are not with me; they have already focused on tonight's meeting. Tonight Abel has to speak to the men and women who actually do the work of the local church. Many of them are the aging pioneers who worked alongside us when we came to Sinai Church twenty-four years ago. He'll want this night to be relaxed and open; he'll speak from his heart and relax his guard. He won't want to miss this meeting, and if I tell him my news beforehand, walls will come up behind his eyes. Our people will see. They'll know something's on his mind. And they'll ask what it is.

I can't let my troubles intrude now.

"Later, gator." I stand and reach out to touch the soft wave falling over his ruddy brow. "I want to talk to you about something personal, but it'll keep."

The line of his mouth tightens. "You're not sick or anything?"

"I'm fine." I underline the words with all the sincerity at my disposal. "I just want to talk to you about an opportunity I'm thinking about pursuing. I'd like your opinion before I proceed."

Relief floods his features. He buckles his belt, then heads back into our cavernous closet.

"What color are you wearing?" he calls, and I am slammed by the awareness that he stood right in front of me without really seeing . . . anything.

"Black." I move to the bathroom doorway and lean against the casing. "Nice to know you still pay attention to how I look."

"You always look beautiful, Em."

He steps out of the closet again, a red tie looped around his neck, then plucks a black sports coat from a hanger on the back of the door. "Ready?"

I nod, suddenly too weary for words. I had hoped to share this burden by nightfall. The thought of carrying it alone for two or three hours more makes my shoulders ache.

The banquet is a cookie-cutter copy of dozens of others I have attended in the years of my marriage. I am seated at the head table with Abel at my left and Jane Swenson, wife of the chairman of the deacons, at my right. Jane is at least eighty years old and a dear saint, but she spends the entire evening filling my ear with complaints about the "unruly hellions" our middle-grade youth pastor escorts into the worship center every week.

"Up and down, down and up; during the service they are like little rats," she says between bites of chicken breast and green beans. "Honestly, what happened to good manners? I know those kids aren't allowed to run around in school, so why does that youth pastor let them run around during worship?"

I scan the crowd for the pastor under discussion. "I'm sure he's trying to teach them," I tell Jane. "I think we should be grateful the kids are in church at all."

Chewing in the deliberate and cautious manner I have come to associate with the aged, Jane shakes her head. "I don't see what good church is doing 'em if they won't sit and listen to the sermon."

Squinting between sprays of fern that jut from the over-sized bouquet before the lectern, I finally spot Jake Simons, pastor to our middle-grades department, sitting at a table with his wife and several deacons. I hope his dinner companions aren't giving him a hard time about kids wandering through the sanctuary during worship.

As we finish our cheesecake, John Swenson stands to introduce Abel, though no introductions are necessary. My husband is greeted by enthusiastic applause as he takes his place behind the lectern, and for the next half-hour the audience is enthralled by his plans for the future—a new campaign to clean up television, a program to monitor the votes of politicians on Capitol Hill, and the publication of tracts designed for spiritually-ignorant folks like the Hollywood producer who wrote our ministry and asked for information on the gospel.

"I'm sure this fellow is still as lost as Atlantis," Abel says, grinning, "but the light of God has begun to shine upon his heart. And when the light of God shines, my friends, sin is rooted out, souls are convicted, and people come to Christ. And that is what our church is all about!"

Thunderous applause fills the room at each thump of Abel's lectern, and I know these people are thrilled to be getting a sneak peek at what God is planning to do through their church and their prophet. Looking at them, I can't help but think of the ancient Romans, who sacrificed much to train their gladiators in the field. They see Abel as Wiltshire's warrior, its captain, and their shepherd.

And he is only too happy to rise to the challenge.

He concludes his remarks with thanks for the work they do to support the church, followed by a heartfelt prayer of blessing for the men who minister to the body of believers and the women who support them. When he finally says "amen," chairs all over the room scrape across the carpet and women dive to retrieve their handbags.

Jane Swenson leans over to give me a warm hug. I return it, but something in me resists the urge to kiss her wrinkled cheek. If I had wandered into Sinai Church in my younger days, she'd probably have resented my attendance at services. I didn't know how to sit still for worship. Because my parents never took me to church, the only religious images in my mind were clips from old movies—people lighting candles, confessing to priests, and wearing somber colors while singing hymns in hard wooden pews.

As Abel steps out from behind the head table, an impromptu line of deacons and their wives forms as they come forward to speak to him personally. Ordinarily I would stand by his side or slip away in my car, but tonight we arrived in one vehicle so I can't go home now. Neither can I stand beside him—my face feels as if it is made from tissue paper and might shred with one sharp smile.

So I walk into the hallway and retreat to the ladies' lounge. No one lingers on the cushioned benches in the elegant front room, but a quick glance at the line of pale pink stalls assures me I am not alone. After visiting the wall of mirrors to check my makeup—a habit borne out of regular TV appearances— I settle onto a bench and open my purse as if I have some urgent business with its contents.

A moment later Eunice Hood, one of the deacons' wives, comes out of the stall, splashes her hands at the sink, then blows her nose. She pulls a bit of tissue from her purse and dabs at a smear of mascara beneath her eyes, then slips through the front lounge with barely a glance at my bent head. She looks as though she's been crying, but I haven't the energy to ask her if something's wrong.

As the door closes, I prop my elbow on my knee and let my shoulders slump. If not for fear of discovery, I would curl up on this bench and weep myself, for while my husband was speaking of the future, I could think only of the past.

What is God doing to me? My life has been devoted to the

advancement of the kingdom of God, yet for some unknown reason the Lord has allowed my past to rear its ugly head. Why? And why now?

I love my husband dearly, but even though he is generous and understanding, he may not understand Christopher Lewis. Abel knows about the world, but he has a hard time accepting sin and weakness in those he trusts. More than once he has quietly asked deacons to resign because of their involvement with alcohol, pornography, or adultery.

What will he do when he learns that my past includes all those things . . . and worse?

Tears brim at my eyes. I dash them away, but still my eyes sting. My mascara will be running soon, and the rims of my eyes might already be red and swollen . . .

Please, God, keep the deacons' wives at a safe distance.

In the ballroom, Abel has at least another half-hour of handshaking to perform. Each deacon present will want to personally assure "the Reverend" of his support, and more than a few will lean close to whisper words of "concern"— better translated "complaint"—into Abel's ear. But though he is bone-tired, Abel will nod, smile sincerely, and thank the gentlemen for their concern.

Later, of course, he will proceed exactly as he feels the Lord wants him to proceed. There's a fine art in leading a church—the pastor is the shepherd, Abel says, and while the sheep may love to bleat and baa and balk, the shepherd is responsible to the One who owns the sheep. Wise is the shepherd who listens to the counsel of elders, but a pastor is ultimately responsible to God alone.

I lean against the wall and close my eyes, resigning myself to a long wait. Abel loves to preach about sheep—though they are not the brightest animals on earth, he says they can be amazingly brave and assertive. They will do almost anything to follow the shepherd they have learned to trust.

It would be uncharitable, I suppose, to remind Abel that not all his sheep trust him. When people bombard our offices with petty concerns that have nothing whatsoever to do with the purpose of ministry, I am tempted to return their notes and letters with one word written across the page in bold, red ink: "BAAA."

Good grief, what is wrong with me? I'm not usually so cynical. I love our church members dearly. For years they have supported us with their prayers, and the week after my emergency appendectomy they absolutely flooded our house with flowers and food. They are wonderful, giving people . . . but most of them share a mind-set that would have trouble accepting my current situation.

I lift my eyes to the ceiling. *Forgive me, Lord, for feeling so skeptical about the people you have called Abel to lead.* A good shepherd does not hate the flock, but protects the lambs, rescues the wayward ones, and leads the sheep beside still waters.

I would give almost anything for a rest beside still waters

right now. I need my shepherd, my husband, but the bleating flock will not leave him alone.

For half an hour I wait, filling the time with a meticulous purging of my purse. After tossing away the last unnecessary receipt, scrap of cellophane, and paper clip, I check my watch, then stand, smooth my slacks, and adjust my jacket. With my organized purse on my shoulder, I walk toward the ballroom wearing a smile that feels only two sizes too small.

Abel has whittled the line down to one deacon. This last fellow, a young man who recently joined Sinai Church, is babbling about how excited he is to be involved in a ministry where God is moving, miracles are happening, and people are making a difference in the world.

After catching my eye, Abel grasps his shoulder, shakes his hand, and sends him off to bed with a heartfelt word of blessing. As the young deacon walks toward the exit, I take Abel's arm like a mother who needs to drag her reluctant young son away from the playground.

"Come on." I lead him toward the rear exit where we parked. "Let's go home."

And as we go, I realize that events have forced me to share my news in the last hour of our day. Perhaps this is how it should be. If Abel must know my deepest secret, it seems appropriate that he learn of it in our most intimate space.

While Abel showers, I sink to my vanity stool and peer at my reflection in the mirror. I've already dressed for bed and washed my face, so the eyes staring back at me are bald and bare. Faint smudges of weariness appear in the half-circles below my eyes, and all color has vanished from my cheeks.

I look like a woman whose energy went down the drain with her makeup. I am bone-tired from carrying this secret, and I will not carry it another hour. I need my husband to understand that Christopher Lewis could be my son . . . and if he is, I want to meet him.

I'm not exactly sure when I came to that decision. I spent most of the day dreading Abel's reaction. The reasons for that anxiety, however, reach beyond his discovery of my sin. Now that I am about to look my husband in the eye and open my heart, I think I have been dreading his reaction because I want to meet my son.

Abel didn't talk much on the drive home, but his silence didn't bother me. In my newlywed days I used to think that Abel's silences sprang from his unhappiness with something I'd said or done; now I know he needs a few moments to mentally flip the switch from being "on" to "off."

My husband is a great preacher, but he's also a wonderful man. Away from the public eye, he can be funny and warm and witty. He could have made a great living selling anything from computers to cars, but he answered the call of God and has never looked back. I've never had second thoughts, either.

I married him for better or worse, and after that brief period of "worse" in which we adjusted to each other and I adjusted to sharing my husband with the demands of a growing church, things got better.

Something tells me we may be headed for another bad patch—maybe the worst yet.

A cloud of steam rises from behind the frosted shower doors while a baritone voice belts out "Oye Como Va"—Abel's in a good mood if he's singing that Santana tune. He would never sing a rock song in public—especially if he had no idea what the words mean—but I think the act of venturing into unknown rock-and-roll makes him feel a little wild and dangerous.

I pick up a brush and run it through my short hair. Children would have been good for Abel; they would have loosened him up. And he would have been a great father. Sometimes I wonder if our ministry would have taken a different form if we'd had children. If Abel had to make time for T-ball games and soccer matches, if he had to attend father-daughter banquets and spend time at the mall, would his vision have centered more around home and family issues? Or would his ministry be exactly the same, forcing me to handle all the child-rearing responsibilities alone?

I drop the hairbrush, wary of debating a moot point. God knew we would not have children; he does not make mistakes when he calls men and women to ministries. He called Abel to his work; he called me to Abel.

Still, I can't help wondering about what might have been . . . if we'd been a little more flexible. I would have been willing to investigate adoption, but when Abel never mentioned it, I couldn't find the courage to approach the topic. I couldn't imagine sitting before an adoption counselor and admitting that I wanted to adopt a baby even though I'd given one away.

So I will never know what it's like to parent a child. I have acknowledged and accepted that truth many times over the years because I don't want to become bitter. I don't think I'm resentful . . . and I don't think resentment is driving my desire to meet Christopher Lewis.

The sound of running water ceases, and I'm startled by the sudden silence. The moment of revelation moves closer, and my heart begins to thump.

I've spent most of the afternoon and night imagining Abel's reaction. I'm sure he will be stunned. Even if at some point he grasped the depravity of my prior life, we have lived in a sanitized Christian bubble for so many years that the reality of my past will be shocking, perhaps even revolting.

He might flare into anger—directed at me or Christopher Lewis. More than twenty years of ministry have taught me that people often become angry when God changes the settings of their lives. Abel will probably be suspicious of Christopher . . . and he will definitely be annoyed. Though he would be the last person on earth to reveal his frustration in public, unexpected, unscheduled urgencies have always irritated my husband.

I look up as the shower door opens with a metallic pop. Abel has wrapped his damp towel about his waist, and he gives me a smile as he moves to the sink where his toothbrush waits.

At forty-five, Abel is a handsome man. Though his waist measures two inches more than it did when we married, he has not gone paunchy around the middle like other preachers I have met. He does not work out—he likes to quote the apostle Paul, who proclaimed that physical exercise profits little— but he is nearly always moving at the speed of sound, mentally if not physically.

He arches a brow as he works the brush over his teeth. "Wha diff fayne venson haf oof ay?"

From my library of prerecorded wifely responses, I summon a laugh. "Translation, please?"

He spits into the sink, rinses, then pats his mouth with a hand towel. "I said, 'What did Jane Swenson have to say tonight?' I saw her carrying on about something."

I lift one shoulder in a shrug. "She's upset because the young people tend to wander around in the service. She blames Jake, of course."

Abel laughs as he finger combs his auburn hair. "As if Jake could control them! The problem begins when parents don't bring their children to church. The kids wandering the sanctuary are the ones whose folks are home in pajamas, so the problem is only going to get worse. But the kids are in church—that's something."

"That's what I told her."

"I knew you'd say the right thing." He comes toward me, bends to drop a kiss on the top of my head, then moves out of the bathroom. I close my eyes, listening to the gentle slide of his bureau drawer. He will pull on pajama bottoms, then he will pick up the television remote and power on the TV so he can watch the news until eleven-thirty.

Unfortunately, I must interrupt his routine.

I stand and walk into the bedroom, where the situation has unfolded exactly as I imagined it. FOX News is blaring from the small set on a table, the remote lies at Abel's side, and he sits with his back against the headboard, a copy of our denominational newspaper in his hands.

Ordinarily I would lift the comforter and crawl in next to him, but now that feels . . . presumptuous.

"Abel?"

He doesn't answer, so I sit beside him, pick up the remote, and punch the power button. The TV goes black, followed an instant later by the crinkle of Abel's paper.

He peers at me over a bent corner, his face twisted into a human question mark. "What's going on?"

I lean toward him, supporting myself with one trembling arm. "We need to talk, remember? I don't think I can put it off any longer."

His eyes fill with the realization that I am not joking. Immediately the entire newspaper falls into his lap. "What do we need to talk about?"

I look away, unable to bear the brightness of his eyes. "Give me a minute, will you?" My voice is strangled again; a boulder has risen from the base of my throat to block my speech. I wait for it to dissolve, but Abel has never been content to allow anyone to hesitate if he could fill in the missing word.

"Are you sure you're not sick? Did you discover a lump or something?"

I shake my head, half-irritated by his probing. "I'm fine."

"Then what in heaven's name—"

"I got a phone call today." That much came out easily. Our phones ring a hundred times every day with people calling from all over the world.

Abel receives this news calmly and leans back against the headboard. "Who called?"

"I'm not absolutely positive . . . but I think he's my son."

My husband takes a wincing little breath. "Your . . . You had a *baby*?"

My heart thumps against my rib cage as I realize the significance of his question. For years Abel has consoled himself with the private belief that our infertility is my fault. I have unwittingly delivered news that could rattle his self-esteem, injure his masculinity, and even undermine his role in our marriage.

"Yes, but it was many years ago. Long before I met you . . . and before I met the Lord."

Abel's mouth changes just enough to bristle the reddish whiskers on his cheek, but he says nothing. So I rush to fill the silence with stories and facts he never wanted to hear. Using quicker, blunter words than I would have chosen if I weren't so frustrated, I tell the story of my past. I finish with news of Christopher Lewis, who has called my office at the church and wishes to speak to me . . . but only if I want to contact him.

Abel does not speak the entire time I am talking, but the words "church" and "office" seem to snap him out of his daze. He waits until I finish, then reaches for his newspaper.

"Ignore the message." His answer is automatic; so is his return to his reading. "Your past is done, gone, wiped clean by the blood of Jesus. It no longer exists."

He speaks these last words to the printed page, having lifted it as a barrier between us. I recognize his action for the defensive posture it is, but I'm not in the mood to humor him.

I reach for the paper and swipe it down, crushing the pages against Abel's lap. "Christopher Lewis exists, Abel. And if what I suspect is true, I am his mother."

A tremor touches his lips. "You are the biological source of his life. The woman who adopted him is his mother."

Though I know it's true, the answer stings.

"Finding me can't have been easy, and he only wants to

speak to me. He's here in Wiltshire, so he has come a long way and worked hard to search me out—"

"If you ignore him, he'll go away. If he has any consideration at all, he'll respect your need for privacy and leave us alone."

I draw a deep breath. Abel hasn't had time to think things through; he hasn't carried this knowledge around all day like a seed in the recesses of his heart. I have, and in the hours of waiting and fretting and fuming, a strong desire has taken root. With the desire came an idea—it may be an unfair slap at my son's character, but it is one sure way to convince Abel that I should call Christopher Lewis.

I look at my husband with a slanted brow. "*Will* he leave us alone?"

Abel's flat expression gives way to pained concentration. "What do you mean?"

"What if he doesn't?" I point to the crumpled newspaper in a calculatingly careless gesture. "What if he goes to the press with his story? He could, you know. He's obviously found something to link me with his history. He could track down that reporter who's always giving you so much trouble—"

Abel lifts a finger, cutting me off, as his eyes fire with speculation. Leaning forward with his elbows on his knees, he is no longer the perturbed husband, but a worried televangelist and national religious leader.

"I suppose," he finally says, not looking at me, "you'll have to call him. Sound him out. Admit nothing, but discern what his intentions are." His face clouds as irritation sharpens his tone. "For heaven's sake, what if he's planning to extort money from the ministry? This is not going to become a scandal, Em. I won't let him taint our reputation. Not a word of this story can get out."

For a moment he looks at me as if he's convinced Christopher Lewis and I have conspired to inflict harm upon his life's work. That look cuts me deeply, but I am resolved to see this through.

"It'll be okay. I have a good feeling about this." Retreating from Abel's hot eyes, I stand and move to the doorway, then press the light switch. Shadows engulf the room, but even in the darkness I can feel Abel's burning stare.

I move to my side of the bed and lift the comforter, then slide under it and turn toward the wall. "Do you want to listen?" I toss the question over my shoulder. "We could call him together, on the speakerphone."

"Heavens, no." His resentment is like a third body in our bed, a hulking, glowering presence.

The trust I've nurtured through twenty-four years of circumspect living has vanished along with the lights.

CHAPTER FIVE

*T*he rising sun floods our bedroom with a gray and watery light. I'm usually the first one out of bed, but the double doors leading into the bathroom are framed in a yellow glow, and the sound of running water breaks the stillness of the morning.

Abel never rises early unless he's had a restless night. When he sleeps soundly, nothing short of two alarm clocks and my nudging his shoulder will rouse him.

So . . . my news impacted him severely, as I feared it would.

I turn over and close my eyes, but sleep has fled with the

dawn. A thousand thoughts buzz through my brain, but the loudest and most persistent is *Today I might speak to my son.*

I know I should approach this phone call with caution and trepidation. Abel wants me to be wary, alert, and on the defensive. If Christopher asks for anything more than casual contact, especially if he solicits money, I should hang up and resolve to put him out of my mind. I entrusted my child to God twenty-eight years ago; I can certainly trust the Lord to take care of him from today forward. This young man is not my responsibility; he is not part of my present life.

But he might be bone of my bone and blood of my blood. If he is who I think he is, this stranger and I were intimately acquainted for nine months. We are bound together in a way Abel and I will never be.

Father God . . . what are you doing?

Suddenly I find myself hoping that Christopher Lewis *is* my son, that he has tackled mountains of paperwork, conquered the devils of red tape, and traveled hundreds of miles to find the woman who gave him life.

Pulling the comforter over my head, I stare into the darkness. "Please, Lord, let it be him."

Celene moves automatically toward the break room off the hallway when she sees me coming. "Coffee, Emma Rose?"

"Please."

My heart sinks when I see my office door standing open. But this is Friday, and the women who work in the executive offices always have devotions in my office on Friday mornings. Monday through Thursday they troop down the hall to the cafeteria, where one of the staff pastors leads them in prayer and shares a devotional thought; on Fridays, the task falls into my lap.

I usually enjoy this time of sharing. The ladies feel free to be themselves in my company; they talk about things they would never mention if a man were present. Celene has told us her sister is battling breast cancer; Esther Mason, Abel's secretary, is worried about her son's marriage. Crystal Donaldson, who's still single, is struggling to live a chaste life in a world where most men expect sex on a first date. These women open their hearts in the sanctuary of my private office, but today I find myself hoping they will be brief, then I am instantly smitten by guilt.

Wrong, so wrong. I need to be attentive to these women. They've come to rely on me, and I can't let them down.

I go to my desk and drop my purse into the drawer, then open my Bible and see the edge of the pink message slip peeking from its hiding place in the Psalms. I resist the urge to read the message again; one of the ladies might notice it. Besides, I have memorized the phone number.

From the moment I got out of bed I've been resisting the

urge to pick up the phone. Caution ultimately prevented me. Abel wouldn't want me to call from our home phone—Christopher Lewis, whoever he is, might trap our unlisted number from caller ID. If he proved to be a crank, we'd have to change the number again.

Besides, who wants to have a once-in-a-lifetime conversation before their first cup of coffee?

Crystal raps on my open door with a knuckle, then smiles when I gesture for her to come in.

"We never did have a chance to talk yesterday," she reminds me. "And I still have a few questions I'd like to ask for the article I'm doing."

I glance at my appointment calendar. "Can I get back to you next Monday?"

"Celene said you had a light schedule this week."

"I do—I did, but something's come up. I tell you what—drop a list of questions by Celene's desk. I'll answer them as soon as I can, and Celene can send my replies by e-mail."

Crystal nods, but disappointment flares in her eyes. She was hoping for more than written answers, but right now I'm not sure I want anyone reporting on my mannerisms, my mood, or my facial expressions. I've been burned by reporters far more skilled than Crystal—a writer for the *New York Times* visited our ministry last year and declared that I delivered my Sunday school lessons in a manner that was "quite competent, but completely perfunctory."

The criticism stung. My fleshly response was to wonder aloud if *she* could teach the same material for twenty-four years without falling into a routine, then the Spirit convicted me about my attitude and I resolved to find new approaches to teaching.

Not only had the reporter skewered me, but she'd also found fault with our worship praise team ("a group of 'Friends' clones"), our children's facility ("the church does Disney"), and our parking lot attendants ("too country club").

The most hurtful item was a picture a *Times* photographer snapped of one of our young people. Wearing a leather jacket with "I am crucified with Christ" emblazoned across the back, the young man had his picture taken while he was lifting his hands in worship. Combined with the message on his jacket, the photo seemed to imply our members literally imagined themselves crucified.

The *Times*, Abel said, tried to portray us as some kind of cult, which we definitely are not. After that disaster, he decreed that we'd allow no more secular reporters free access to the church campus. Formal interviews, fine; unrestricted freedom, no way. Members of the media reported things they couldn't explain or understand because they had no spiritual knowledge.

The arrival of Celene and Esther jars me from my memory-induced haze. I stand as they take seats on the sofa against the far wall, then nod to three other secretaries who shuffle into the room.

My smile fades as I turn away on a pretext of moving my desk chair into their circle. Nothing is as it should be this morning, everything feels slightly off-kilter. I feel the change sparking my blood; can they not see that I am pregnant with a secret? But no, they are wrapped in routine.

When my chair has bridged the gap between my desk and the guest chairs, I sit down and cross my legs in a silence broken only by the swish of my pantyhose. I am about to read from my open Bible when Josh Bartol sweeps in and drops a group of stapled pages into my lap.

"The Reverend would like you to read that," he says.

I find myself holding a two-page, typed letter, topped by one of the forms our correspondence department uses to route the dozens of letters our ministry receives each day. One of the readers in our mail department has checked the box next to "For Reverend Howard" and drawn three exclamation marks next to Abel's name.

Josh slips his hands into his pockets. "The Reverend is extremely upset about this. I think we're going to investigate and maybe call a press conference later in the week."

I glance at the letter. It's from a viewer in Atlanta who was browsing in a Books & More bookstore and discovered a book called *Your Wife or Mine?*

"This book is nothing more than a how-to guide for wife swapping," Lester Keit has written. "I was horrified, as any God-fearing man would be. I took the book to the store manager, asked him why he would sell such trash, and he said he had a perfect right to sell anything he liked. I know you can't do everything, Reverend Howard," Mr. Keit finished, "but you have tremendous influence, so I thought I should bring this to your attention. If anyone can help turn the tide of immorality in this country, Christians can. But we need you to rally the troops."

I can't stop a grimace. "Yuck."

"You're right, it's awful and disgusting." Josh opens his mouth as if he would say more, then looks around and takes a hasty half-step back. "The Reverend's going to use this, I think. We'll probably be leading a boycott of those bookstores."

I lower the letter. "Didn't one of these stores just open in Wiltshire?"

He nods. "Right across from the Wal-Mart on East Highway."

Celene leans toward the letter. "What's it about?"

"Nothing that need concern us right now." I slip the pages beneath my Bible and smile around the circle of women. "Shall we get started?"

Josh backs out of the room. "Have Celene shoot a copy of the letter, then return it to my office, will you? We're trying to call Mr. Keit for some follow-up, then we'll decide what direction we're going to go with it."

I exhale heavily as Josh exits, then flip through the pages of my Bible, searching for a marked passage. I have been leading women's devotions and Bible studies since the early days of my marriage; sometimes I think I could speak extemporaneously about anything from Absolution to Zechariah.

I pause when a highlighted passage in 2 Corinthians catches my eye. Perfect.

"'Therefore, come out from them and separate yourselves from them,' says the Lord," I read. "'Don't touch their filthy things, and I will welcome you. And I will be your Father, and you will be my sons and daughters,' says the Lord Almighty. Because we have these promises, dear friends, let us cleanse ourselves from everything that can defile our body or spirit. And let us work toward complete purity because we fear God."

I lower my Bible and look at the earnest faces of the coworkers around me. They are good women, every one of them, and they could earn more working in almost any other office in town. But because they love God and believe in Abel's vision, they have devoted themselves to this ministry.

Despite my heightened nerves, I feel a sudden rush of gratitude. I haven't felt so many strong emotions since my hormonal pregnancy days.

"Paul was warning the people of Corinth about spiritual contamination," I tell them. "He knew how easy it is for the world to corrupt our minds and thoughts. So he is reminding us to stay out of the world and avoid anything that would sully our minds."

I give Crystal a special smile. "But you already know this,

or you wouldn't be working here. The Reverend is striving hard to clean up television, movies, and"—I pull out the letter on my lap—"it looks like we're going to try to do something new to clean up our nation's immoral mind-set. We are the light of the world, but we can't do any good if we walk around with dirty lampshades. Light can't shine through an unclean vessel. So let's make sure we keep our hearts and minds pure and fit for the Master's use."

The room has been quiet, but when I close my eyes to pray, an almost tangible hush fills the circle where we've gathered.

"Father, I thank you for every woman in this room. I pray you would bless them in their work, that you would give them purity of mind and heart, and that you would touch our spirits every time we even *think* of straying from the things that are holy and pure and good. Keep us clean, dear Lord. Keep us holy. Keep us separate from the world so we can be completely blameless and fit for work in your kingdom."

A soft chorus of "amens" flutters around the room as I open my eyes. I was hoping my short prayer would end the session, but when I look up I see a small frown of disappointment on Esther's face.

"Everything okay with you, Esther?"

"My son." She pinches the bridge of her nose and closes her eyes. "He and his wife are still separated. I've been praying so hard—"

"And we'll all keep praying with you. We'll pray every time we think of you today."

I am anxious to clear the room, but I can't give these dear women short shrift. "Any other prayer requests we should know about?"

Celene waves her hand. "My sister has another chemo treatment this week."

"Okay. We'll keep praying."

Crystal gives me a bewildered look.

"I know it feels a little backward to take prayer requests after I've officially prayed," I tell the group, "but the Bible does tell us to pray without ceasing. Today when you think of Esther and Celene, please remember to breathe a prayer for their loved ones."

I wait another second, then stand. "Forgive me, ladies, but it looks like it's going to be a busy morning. Next time I promise we'll have more time for sharing."

They rise and file out, their understanding smiles softening my guilt. Celene is the last to leave. She hesitates in the doorway and asks if I need anything.

I shake my head. "I'm fine."

She lifts a brow. "Don't you want me to make a copy of that letter and return the original to Josh?"

For an instant my mind goes blank, then I remember the stapled pages in my hand. "Right, of course. But hold the copy at your desk, will you? I'd like to be alone for a while."

With a dozen questions in her eyes, Celene comes forward and takes the letter, then closes the door and leaves me alone.

I sink into my chair and prop my head on my hand. My watch tells me it's eight-twenty-six, which might still be too early to call.

But I have to speak to Christopher Lewis soon. I can't seem to function with thoughts of him running through my brain, and too many people are depending on me. I can't avoid my responsibilities for long.

I decide to call at nine A.M.

For a long while I sit with my hands folded on the desk, my thoughts chasing each other round and round in my head. The minutes stretch themselves thin as nine o'clock flutters ahead of my fingers like a summer butterfly.

Guilt rises up to accuse me in the silence. I've been short with the women, I rushed through a devotion, and I think I might have cheated to arrive at this moment. Abel doesn't want me to call Christopher Lewis. I used my influence to manipulate him just as Eve influenced Adam to take a bite of that forbidden fruit . . .

I regret my failings, but if this were Eden and that telephone forbidden, I would still lift the receiver and place this call.

I've just gained a new appreciation for the power of temptation.

The clock on the wall, a gift from the Glory Girls Sunday school class, chimes the hour.

I watch my hand pick up the phone; my fingers punch in the number. I bring the receiver to my ear and listen as the local number rings in some building probably less than a twenty-minute drive from where I'm sitting.

I consider the three possible outcomes of this effort—he will not answer, I will get a machine, or I will reach Christopher Lewis. If he doesn't answer, I will call again this afternoon; perhaps I can find time between the Missionary Union luncheon and Abel's monthly conference call to our Praise Partner state reps. If a machine takes the call, I will not leave a message . . . unless I get the machine three times, which may mean he is screening his calls.

As the phone rings a second time, another thought occurs—what if a woman picks up? He may be in Wiltshire with his wife, he may live with a roommate, he may live with—I shudder—a girlfriend. I cannot assume he is a godly Christian man; I have no way of knowing what values he holds. I know what Abel would like him to be—decent, Christian, and discreet—while more than anything I want Christopher Lewis to be . . . my son. I want him to be godly and strong and healthy and handsome, but most of all I want him to be *mine*.

The phone rings a third time. If he's still sleeping, he will be annoyed if I let the phone ring again; if he's been in the shower, he'll be irritated if I hang up too soon. My heart thumps in an odd rhythm as the fingers of my right hand inch toward the phone. I should disconnect the call; if he hasn't picked up by now, he's not in. And I don't want to summon him from the shower or the garage; when we connect I want him to be calm and rested and prepared for whatever this conversation might bring—

"Hello?"

The sudden clarity of a male voice startles my thoughts into silence.

I hear nothing but the hum of the telephone line, then his voice drops. "Emma Rose Howard?"

His words are like a slug to the center of my breastbone. Somehow I gather enough breath to speak. "Christopher Lewis?"

"That's me."

"I received . . . your message yesterday."

"Thank God. I know this hasn't been an easy decision for you."

The silence between us vibrates with tension, so I utter the first thing that pops into my head, which happens to be a completely inane remark: "How can I help you, Mr. Lewis?"

Warm, melodic laughter rumbles over the phone line. I am bathed in it, and tears—of embarrassment?—spring to my eyes.

"I'm s-sorry," I stammer. "I don't know why I said that. Habit, probably."

"Don't worry about it." He laughs again. "I'm just glad my message made sense to you."

I pull the pink slip from my Bible. "You were born on January 6, 1976?"

"Yes."

"The Hillside address was written on your birth certificate?"

"Not on the form itself, but in the margin, like a nurse's afterthought. And not my amended birth certificate, mind you, but the original."

I close my eyes as truth sweeps over me with the force of a rushing train. "How did you manage it? The records were sealed."

"That's not really important, is it? I have friends who have friends in high places. But what I wanted to say is . . . well, I wanted to say hello. I wanted to thank you for what you did for me. And let you know that I'd really like to meet you . . . if that's okay with you."

A blush rises from my collar and heats my neck. I swivel my chair away from the desk and stare at the wall behind me.

He continues, his voice like music in my ear. "I'm sure you want to proceed with caution, so let me assure you that I'm not asking for money or a job or anything like that. I don't intend to harm you in any way. I . . . just want to know you. I've come a long way to find you."

"Are you sick?" The question slips from my tongue before I can cloak it in softer words. I don't know much about legal matters, but if a young man had leukemia or some other genetic disease, his lawyer might be able to obtain a court order and open sealed adoption records.

He chuckles. "I don't need anything from you, Emma Rose, nothing at all. If you're willing, though, I'd appreciate the gift of your time. I hope you can understand . . . that I've always yearned to know you."

And I you. The words leap to my lips, hover there for a moment, then pass into vapor without being spoken. I can't unlock my heart without knowing more about his motivations . . . and not without seeing his face. It's still entirely possible that this man is someone who stumbled across my son's birth certificate and wants to wreak havoc in our ministry. If Christopher Lewis is my son, I'll be able to read the truth in his face.

I draw a deep breath, then swallow. "I'll have to discuss this with my husband. Abel's a public figure, you see, and he's very careful about anything that might . . . well, he's careful to keep our private lives private."

"I know all about you, Emma Rose—do you mind if I call you that?"

I wince as a twinge of unease tightens the back of my neck. Now he sounds like a stalker.

"Call me Emma." My heart is drumming against the sides

of my rib cage, but I try to maintain a steady voice. "People who knew me in the before-television years call me Emma."

"Really?" Laughter creeps back into his voice. "I guess I qualify, then. Well, as I was saying, I know who you are and I'm familiar with your ministry. I think it's great, in fact. I don't intend to embarrass you in any way. I'd just like to meet you, to know you better. But if that's asking too much, I can go back to New York."

I shove my wariness aside. "It's not asking too much."

How could it be, when I have yearned for the same thing? If I had spent months trying to locate him, I wouldn't give up easily.

A hopeful note fills his voice. "We can meet, then?"

"I need to talk to my husband first. He may want to meet you, too."

"I'd be delighted."

I close my eyes, knowing that *delighted* is the last word Abel would use to describe his feelings about this reunion.

I turn to look at my calendar. "All right, then. Will you be at this number? Are you here in Wiltshire?"

"Yes. I'll be working in the area for a while."

"So is this the best number to reach you?"

"It's a pay phone, but you can call any time, day or night. Someone should be around to get me or take a message."

"All right, then." I take a deep breath. I know this conversation needs to end, but, fraud or not, I'm reluctant to let him go. "I hope this works out, Christopher. I have so much to ask you."

He laughs again. "Anything you want to know, I'll tell you. I'm pretty much an open book."

"Good." My voice wavers. "I'll call again, probably tomorrow. I'm not sure I'll have an opportunity to speak to Abel until later in the day."

"Tomorrow, then."

"Good-bye . . . Christopher."

I hang up the phone, then cover my face with my hands, torn between laughter and tears. If what he said was true, the sin in my past has produced a mature, considerate man who wants to know me.

For so many years I have smiled in silence while Abel told the world that God did not bless us with children so we might bear spiritual offspring. We have borne spiritual children, hundreds of them, but now I have a son.

A man with my genes, perhaps my eyes, someone into whose face I can look and see a shadow of myself. Until yesterday, I had buried my baby so deep in the vault of memory that thoughts of him could rise and stretch only in my dreams.

I pull my desk calendar toward me and pencil his phone number on Saturday's page. I will call him tomorrow, and I will try to arrange a meeting. Until then, it's going to be hard to keep this news to myself.

I lean back in my chair and rub my stomach in a slow circle, recalling the ache in the lower back, the sensation of fullness, the flutter of life in a pregnant belly. Now these feelings flow not from a baby, but from anticipation. In a few hours I will look upon the boy I surrendered so long ago, the child I had abandoned all hope of ever knowing.

CHAPTER SIX

*E*ventually my sense of wonder fades and I find my thoughts returning to the world around me. I spring to my feet and leave my office, moving past Celene without explanation. I stride down the hall to Abel's suite, give Esther a nod and a quick smile, then step into my husband's inner office.

Josh is leaning across Abel's desk when I enter; both men are intent upon a sheet of paper in Abel's hand. My husband looks up as I approach.

"I didn't think it could get any worse." He frowns at the page as if it were a bad smell. "I asked Esther to do a search for that wife-swapping book at several other Books & More bookstores, and it's either available or can be ordered from every one of them. When Josh asked a division manager why they carried such filth, he said they were doing all they could to promote the free expression of ideas."

"I didn't talk to the CEO," Josh adds, his expression a trifle woebegone. "The quote came from the southeastern sales manager. We're hoping to get some good material from the head honcho later today."

Abel leans back in his chair. "I imagine they're circling the wagons now, trying to put together a statement for the press. They know we're interested in the story, and they know we have the capability of reaching forty million households with our message. It'll be interesting to see how this situation shakes out."

"It's a great cause." Josh is fairly glowing with excitement. "I love the political ramifications. Though we're bound to hear from the free-speech liberals, it'll be worth the risk of disturbing a Sunday service with a handful of protesters."

"Oh, I believe in free speech." Abel pressed his hands together and leaned back in his chair. "It's free speech that allows us to broadcast on Sunday mornings, and we can't forget that. But free speech doesn't give you the right to yell 'fire' in a crowded theater, either, and that's the approach we need to take. Speech that's hurtful—speech that injures the very fabric of our society—need not be given free rein in this country."

Any other day I would have perched on the edge of a chair and listened to every detail; today I want to clear the room and speak of something no one else can hear.

I sink into a chair and give Josh a pointed look. "Would you mind if I spoke to Abel alone for a few minutes?"

For an instant his eyes widen, then he recovers. "Sure. Um . . . just let me gather my notes, and I'll be out of your way."

As he fumbles for papers on the desk, I let my gaze rove over Abel's cluttered office. The bookshelf against the wall is crowded with commentaries and bestsellers about Christian living; the far corner contains a filing cabinet filled with particularly poignant personal letters he has received over the years. My husband's passion for sheep is evident in the wall art, the ceramic sculpture on the bookcase, and the collection of toothpick-and-cotton-ball lambs the children make for him every Christmas. The little fuzzy creations are scattered over the bookshelves like an errant herd.

An embroidered sampler hangs crookedly near the window, and I make a mental note to straighten it before leaving. I stitched the project myself, covering the tiny fabric squares with Abel's life verse, Genesis 4:2: "And Abel was a keeper of sheep."

After gathering his notes, Josh leaves, but not before tossing his boss a questioning look. Abel ignores it, but a cloud settles on his brow as the door closes.

He folds his hands. "Let me guess; you called that young man?"

"I did—and Abel, I think he's my son. I won't know until I see him, but all the pieces fit. Somehow he gained access to the adoption records and his original birth certificate."

"If he could do it, anyone could. So this guy could be a phony."

"But he could be telling the absolute truth."

Abel picks up a pencil and twiddles it between his fingers. "So . . . what does he want?"

"He says he wants to meet me. That's all."

Abel's warning look puts an immediate damper on my rising spirits. "That's what he says now. After you meet him, he'll want a relationship, then he'll want a job. Next thing you know, he'll want to move into the house—"

"I don't think so, Abel." I pause, drawing strength from an unfounded but strong conviction that my son could not be less than sincere. "He said he didn't want anything from me."

"And you believe him?"

"Why shouldn't I?"

Abel snorts as he exhales. "Sometimes, Em, you can be unbelievably naive. This man—whom you've never even seen—has managed to find out about your past. Maybe he ran into someone who knew you from your life on the streets; maybe he's someone you picked up."

Against my will, rage rises in my cheeks. "I can't believe you said that."

"Sorry." He lifts his hands in a gesture of surrender. He's not playing fair, and he knows it.

"Emma," he begins again, speaking in the patient voice I've heard him use with little children and aged ladies, "you need to be cautious. This man will play you like a fiddle if you're not careful. I agreed you should call him in order to protect the ministry—"

"You made your reasons abundantly clear."

"—and you say he doesn't want anything from us. Fine. So thank him for his time and tell him he needs to move on with his life."

"It's not that simple, Abel. I'm his mother."

For the first time since I entered the room, my husband looks directly into my eyes. "He has a mother; the woman who adopted him did all the hard work."

"Maybe she didn't. Maybe that's why he's looking for me." The comment bubbles up from some place deep within me. I know child rearing involves years of difficult, strenuous, heartrending work, but so does surrendering a child. After the initial agony, you wonder and pray and watch every kid who walks by to see if he even faintly resembles the baby who nestled in your womb . . .

"Don't get crazy on me, Em." Abel's voice softens. "I can imagine what you must be feeling, but this is one time you can't let your heart rule your head. This young man says he wants a meeting—if you go, I've a strong hunch he'll be wanting something else by the time you get ready to leave."

I rub my temple and exhale slowly. "I don't think this is about money."

"Of course it is! Does he know who you are?"

"Once he found the birth certificate, I'm sure it didn't take long to trace my steps."

"Does he know what you are?"

I consider the question. Christopher says he knows all about me. If he has watched *Prayer and Praise* for any length of time, he knows I'm a Christian, a pastor's wife, and a musician. He must know that Abel and I have taken a strong stand against immorality on television, in film, and in politics. He probably knows about Abel's crusades to clean up America; he might even know about the occasions we've had scores of activists marching around Sinai Church because Abel dared to protest Gay Pride Day at Disney World or profanity on television.

He has to know that our ministry takes in millions of dollars each year.

I give Abel a brief, distracted glance and force a smile. "What are you saying?"

"I'm saying," he leans toward me, "that this man is probably out to blackmail us. He knows we stand for righteousness and purity, but he is evidence of your scandalous past. He is part of the darkness from which you've been freed. You've been walking in the light for so long you have forgotten what people are capable of."

Indignation flares within me. "I know more than you think, Abel." I stand, one hand clenching against my palm. "I know more about darkness and pain than you ever will."

Leaving him speechless, I turn on the ball of my foot and retreat.

Twenty minutes later I'm back in my office. I'm supposed to be writing my monthly column for *Purity,* but I have turned away from the computer to sketch faces on a legal pad— angular faces, round faces, square faces, faces with my own pointed chin. Which face is Christopher's?

I have been trying to work, but Abel's parting words still ring in my ears. He thinks he can understand sin and its corruption by reading books and news reports, but though he's as human as any man I know, depravity has never touched my husband with its sorrowful consequences. No man but Jesus was ever born without sin, but sometimes I think Abel was born with only the barest sprinkling.

My husband has been a believer practically since preschool, having been born into a Christian family that could have written a book on holy living. His father had just entered the ministry when Abel came into the world. Abel prayed the sinner's prayer before he could read and went under the baptismal waters before he could ride a bike.

"I was young, but my experience was real," he told me the night of our first date. "I fell in love with Jesus when I was only a kid, and I've never seen any reason not to follow him. Sure, I went through the usual kid troubles, but because my parents and the church members were watching out for me, I never really wandered from the straight and narrow. Jesus yanks hard on my chain whenever I'm tempted to stray."

He shrugged as he related his testimony, and I remember thinking he was like the prodigal's elder brother, steadfast and tough and faithful. It didn't hurt that his shoulders looked broad and strong in the soft streetlights lining the road that led to the girls' dorm. I had burdens to carry in those days, and Abel seemed the sort of man who could help me bear up under any struggle.

Abel's shoulders are still broad and muscular, but is it fair to ask him to carry a burden from my past?

Not knowing what else to do, I pick up the phone and punch in a number that will be burned into my memory until my dying day. I haven't dialed this number in at least three years, but I hope the woman who owns it is still alive, well, and willing to talk to me.

Lortis June Moses is a second mother to me. In 1976 she

served as "housemother" to fourteen girls at Mercy House; the last time I spoke to her she was still living there, but no longer managing the residence. She'd been in her early fifties when I passed through the home, so she has to be at least eighty now . . .

Please, Lord, let her be there.

A young, professional voice answers the phone. "Mercy House."

"Hello." My voice is clotted, so I pause to clear my throat. "I'm looking for Lortis June Moses. Is she still around?"

The woman on the phone laughs. "I don't think we could pry her out of here with a crowbar. Would you like me to connect you with her room?"

"Please."

My chair creaks as I lean back and marvel at Lortis June's longevity. She had been a widow when I met her—a young widow, actually, but at seventeen, I thought Lortis June positively ancient. She ran a clean house, well-organized and punctual, and within ten minutes of meeting her we girls knew what would (clean beds, clean nails, clean language) and would not (messy beds, dirty nails, crude language) be tolerated. But despite her rigorous standards, Lortis June always managed to exude warmth and compassion. She welcomed us into Mercy House without asking questions, accepting us as we were . . . and I had to be one of the most messed-up girls to ever cross her threshold.

In my first three weeks, Lortis June worked with the physician to help my body rid itself of drugs. She sat with me all night, guarding the door so I couldn't slip out to prowl the streets in search of whatever pills would help me get through another day. She sat across from me in the study hall, making sure I had books, paper, and pencils; she sat on the edge of my bed and held me as I wept the pain of rejection away.

And like Nola Register, Lortis June loved to talk about Jesus. Nola had convinced me I was a wreck and needed a savior; Lortis June demonstrated how a person could live a victorious life in Christ. If I had never read Galatians 5:22, I would recognize fruits of the Spirit because in Lortis June I saw love, joy, peace, patience, goodness, gentleness, self-control . . . and mercy. Measureless mercy.

"Hello?" The voice at the other end is creaky with age, but I recognize it immediately.

"Lortis June? It's Emma Howard."

A second passes, then she cackles. "Land's sakes, child, I thought you'd forgotten all about me!"

"I'm sorry, I should call more often."

She laughs again. "Where are you, honey?"

"Still in Kentucky—we've been in Kentucky over twenty years."

"How's your husband?"

"Fine."

"And your walk with the Lord?"

Lortis June's blunt approach to spiritual issues never fails to startle me. Even Abel has learned to be fairly diplomatic in his conversational approach.

Smiling, I accept her challenge. "I'm good. Lately I've been asking the Lord to reveal himself in new ways, and I think he is. The ministry is thriving; we're seeing hundreds of people come to Christ. Yesterday Abel was honored by the president at the National Prayer Breakfast in Washington."

"The president of the prayer breakfast?"

"The President of the United States, Lortis June. Abel got to shake his hand."

"That's wonderful, honey. Hang on a minute, will you, while I turn down that blasted television."

I hear the phone clunk against something hard, then several seconds pass before the sound of the television ceases. Lortis June must be moving more slowly these days, but I'm impressed she's still living independently.

The phone clunks again. "Now, then—where were we?"

Despite the pressures weighing on my mind, I remember my manners. "How are you? I was surprised to hear you're still at the home."

"Where else am I going to go? Besides, girls these days need someone to talk to; they're even more mixed up than you were." The words fall without rancor or blame; she calls life the way she sees it. "But you didn't phone to ask about me. What's on your mind, child?"

I swallow hard as an unexpected crest of emotion rises within me. "Do you remember . . . my baby?"

"Land, that I do. I have his picture right here by the phone."

Lortis June, who had gone with me to the hospital, insisted that I be given a photo of my baby. When I left Mercy House, I wanted to give her something important. That photo was the only valuable thing I possessed.

"Prettiest baby boy I've ever seen," she says, her voice soft. "I've kept his picture safe in a little silver frame. Are you . . . missing him?"

"He called me, Lortis June. Somehow he's tracked me down, and I spoke with him this morning. He says he wants to meet me."

"Land sakes alive."

"I don't know what to do."

"Lord, have mercy."

Silence rolls over the phone line, and I tense at the sound of it. Words seldom fail Lortis June.

"Well," she speaks slowly, "if God allowed him to find you, a meeting might be his will. How do you feel about it?"

I lift my gaze to the ceiling, where small tails of dust move in the breath of the heating duct. "I feel . . . elated. Terrified. Disloyal. And unbelievably guilty."

"You don't have to feel guilty about planning an adoption for that baby. If you had taken him with you when you left . . .

well, I'm not sure you could have made it, child. You were carrying the weight of the world in those days."

"I don't feel guilty for the adoption. I feel guilty for not telling my husband about it. He never wanted to know, but yesterday I had to tell him about the baby . . . and everything else. I felt better after telling him, but he didn't exactly want to hear any of it."

Silence, then: "How'd he take it?"

"I think he's in denial." My thoughts drift to the memory of Abel hunched over his desk, his eyes fixed on reports about Books & More bookstores. "Looking at him, you'd think he wasn't giving my news a second thought, but I know Abel. When something bothers him, he heads off full steam in another direction."

"He's a godly man, Emma. I hear him preach every week, and I can't find any fault in what he says."

"That's the problem—Abel has hardly any faults at all." I offer this confidence with a whimper. "Oh, he's not perfect— he leaves his socks on the floor and forgets to check with me before scheduling things. But he lives what he preaches, no doubt about that."

"Well, that's what—" Lortis June's words are lost in a coughing fit.

My tension level rises. "You okay? Should you be seeing a doctor for that?"

She clears her throat, then cackles another laugh. "Honey, when you're eighty-one and breathing on your own, you're doing fine. Don't worry about me; this is just a cold. The Lord is going to keep me on earth as long as I'm useful, and there are lots of places to be useful 'round here."

"So." Gently, I draw her back to the topic at hand. "What should I do, Lortis June? Abel's not wild about me meeting this young man—he's afraid he has ulterior motives."

"Emma." A faint note of reproach underlines her voice. "Think about it. If you had found his name, would you call him?"

Would I? Maybe not at first. I wouldn't call if he were too young, or even still living at home. I probably wouldn't even call in his college years, because young adults are so impressionable. But if I carried the information around long enough, the desire to know him would simmer in my subconscious . . . as it has for all these years.

"Yes, I'd call. If only to hear his voice and know he was all right."

"He must have the same desires. So pray about it, then follow the Spirit's leading. Meet the young man, fill your heart with his face, and let the Lord guide you from there."

"Are you sure? A wife is supposed to respect her husband's opinion, and Abel thinks this is crazy—"

"Abel may not be thinking clearly at this point. Talk to him, see if you can help him see things the way you do. And tell me this—did you love that little boy when you released him way back then?"

"Of course I did."

"Do you love him now?"

The question slices like a scalpel, opening a chamber in my heart that has been sealed for years. Raw feeling pours out, emotions that flood my soul and threaten to choke off my speech.

Love is a decision you make every day.

"Yes," I manage to reply through a current of tears. "I love him."

"Then go to him, child. Your Abel will understand. Keep your eyes open so you can see what the Lord intends to do through this. Be as wise as a serpent and harmless as a dove, but go to him."

I thank her, promise to call more often, and hang up. And as I stare at the framed photos of Abel and me atop my credenza, I realize that I called Lortis June because she's at the top of my list of people who walk with God. Abel's on that list, too, but in the last few days our connection has weakened somehow . . .

And in Lortis June's presence, I never felt anything but love.

After giving a speech across town at the Missionary Union luncheon, I drive back to the church and hurry to my office.

Celene hands me a stack of messages as I pass her desk; I flip through them and shake my head when I realize that so many issues I thought important a few days ago now seem like trivial annoyances.

Christopher has not called. I didn't expect him to, but something in me had hoped he would.

I can't wait to speak to him again.

I ask Celene to hold my calls, close the door, and pick up the phone. After punching in Christopher's number, I slide my appointment book closer. I don't have much free time this weekend, but I'd move heaven and earth and any number of appointments to make this meeting happen.

He answers on the second ring. "Hello?"

"Christopher? It's Emma."

"Hello!" His voice rasps with joy.

At the sound of his excitement I have to blink away tears. "I'd-love-to-meet-you." The words come out in a rush, borne on an impulse I don't want to weaken by second thought.

"Great!" Again, joy vibrates in his voice. "I've been praying you'd want to come."

I nod because I can't speak.

"When are you free?" he asks.

My gaze falls upon the calendar, filled with appointments I'd happily cancel if necessary.

"You tell me what's best for you," I say. "I can move things around to suit your schedule."

"Will your husband come, too?"

Part of my brain registers his thoughtfulness; another part shrinks from the thought of Abel's involvement. I suddenly realize I want to savor this pleasure alone. Abel wasn't part of my life when Christopher was born, so why does he need to be part of this reunion?

Am I being selfish . . . or am I afraid to bring the two men together?

"I'm not sure Abel is free," I answer, glad that this much is true. "He is almost always booked, even on weekends. But if you'll tell me when and where you'd like to meet, I'll do my best to be there."

"Wonderful." His voice has taken on an almost-dreamy quality. "Well, I know your days are full, so how about an evening?"

Again, evidence of supreme thoughtfulness. Most evenings I'm out with Abel on one of his speaking engagements, but Christopher wouldn't know that. And I could easily beg out of one of Abel's fund raising dinners.

"An evening would be fine."

"Great." He hesitates. "Aw, shoot, I can't wait. How about tomorrow night? Can you make it?"

I open my mouth to agree, then glance at the calendar. Tomorrow is Saturday, and Saturday nights are sacrosanct at Sinai Church. Abel has held a contemporary worship service every Saturday night for the past twenty years. I've seen him drag himself out of bed with a fever just so he can trudge into the pulpit and proclaim that nothing short of emergency surgery can keep him from joining God's people at the appointed time for worship.

There's no way on God's green earth Abel will agree to meet Christopher Lewis on a Saturday night. But I have just finished promising that I'd come, so I will.

I close my eyes. "Tomorrow night it is. What time?"

"Nine o'clock? I know that's late, but—"

"Nine o'clock is perfect." The service is finished by nine, so maybe Abel can come after he's completed his ritual of shaking the hand of every last person who wants to talk to him. This might be ideal—I can meet Christopher in private, then Abel can join us and see that this young man poses no threat. "Where shall I meet you?"

"How about O'Shays? It's on Fourth Street."

For an instant I'm startled by the unfamiliar name, then I realize that this, too, is good. Abel wouldn't want Christopher coming to the house for this first meeting, and after services our church members tend to flock to Denny's and Village Inn. I'm less likely to run into people I know at an out-of-the-way place downtown, so I won't have to stop and explain this private meeting with a young man.

I write *O'Shays* in my appointment book. "I'll find it. And I'll be there at nine."

"Thanks."

"Um, Christopher"—I tap my pencil on the page—"how will I know you?"

His laughter is warm and rich and tickles my ear. "Considering the few people likely to be in O'Shays at that hour, how can you think we won't know each other?"

He's still chuckling when I tell him good-bye.

CHAPTER SEVEN

$\mathcal{M}$y thoughts are swarming like bees when I enter the conference room, late, for Abel's monthly call to the state Praise Partner representatives. All fifteen pastors of Sinai Church are seated in chairs around the long table, their attention focused on the black phone facing Abel. Their staff secretaries sit behind them with pens and steno pads at hand.

From her seat behind Abel, Esther Mason presses a finger to her lips as I enter. Abel is speaking in the stentorian tones he usually reserves for his sermons, so I've arrived in the middle of his monthly report.

I sink into an empty chair next to Josh and cross my arms,

trying to remember the items on the agenda for this meeting. Any other day I would be able to recite Abel's schedule forward and backward; today my brain feels like Swiss cheese.

I listen for a moment, then pull a pencil from behind my ear and scrawl, *What's on the agenda?* across my notepad. I elbow Josh, who reads my note, then smiles a grim little grin and leans to whisper in my ear.

"We managed to get forty-two of the fifty state reps on the line, so the Reverend's going to bring up the bookstore matter."

Of course.

Abel is now telling the state reps—pastors who have affiliated themselves with our ministry goals—about the book he has discovered in Books & More bookstores. "Wife swapping," he says, placing his palms on the table as he leans over the speakerphone, "is a disgrace and a threat to the institution of marriage. People who think this is fun, that it's harmless, are ignoring the thousands of impressionable young lives who will forever be scarred by people who place their personal, perverted pleasure above the sanctity of marriage. The American public has hit a new low in standards of decency. Television has taken us from *Temptation Island* to *Momentary Marriage,* and this book about so-called 'swinging' is a natural result of the garbage that's being piped into our living rooms every night.

"We're going to talk to the officials at the national office of Books & More bookstores. If they don't agree to pull this offensive title, we're going to mount our own media campaign. We're going to interview adults whose marriages were destroyed by this kind of lifestyle; we're going to interview children whose lives were scarred by parents who cared more for worshiping at the altar of hedonism than raising healthy, happy children. We have to act now, brothers, and we have to act with strength and determination. The fabric of this nation is eroding faster than we can shore it up."

Abel pauses to take a breath, but his address has been so succinct, so smooth, that the room erupts in spontaneous applause. Hearing whoops and garbled "amens" from the telephone speaker, I applaud with the others and nod at the staffers who look at me with eyes that say, *He's really going to give it to them this time!*

Drawing a deep breath, Abel pulls a handkerchief from his pocket, mops his brow, then releases the deep, three-noted laugh that has become his trademark.

"Well, friends," he grins at the speakerphone, "I'm glad to know we're united on this one. I wish I had the time to speak to each of you personally, but if you need me, please don't hesitate to call. One of us will get back to you right away."

I look at Josh, who is busy making notes on a legal pad. Unless it's a particularly urgent situation, he will field calls from the state reps. There's no way my husband can get his work done if he's on the phone all day.

"Before I close, I want to thank each of you for all your

hard work." Abel smiles around the room, assuring each person present that he's grateful to us as well as the pastors on the phone. "It may be an uphill battle, but our victory is assured. One day soon, the Lord will be exalted, the devil will be defeated, and we will gain the ultimate victory!"

The room applauds again. Just as the sound begins to fade, Josh leans forward and disconnects the call. Abel pushes back his chair, thanks his staff for attending, then retreats through a back door.

Drawn by the invisible thread that links us, I slip into the hall and hurry to Abel's office. We meet in the hallway.

"Hi there, hon." He opens the door and holds it for me. "What'd you think?"

"What I heard was great." I precede him into the room, then drop into the leather guest chair in front of his desk.

"I was a little disappointed in the turnout." He sinks onto the sofa, his hands at his sides, and for a moment he looks like a little boy who has just lost a championship baseball game.

I lean forward, propping my elbows on my knees. "Josh said you had forty-two reps on the line. That's good, isn't it?"

"I was hoping for all fifty. We'll need one hundred percent involvement if we're going to pull off this boycott on the national level. We're planning to launch a media blitz with a press conference on Sunday the fifteenth. We were hoping to have our reps do the same thing in their states, but forty-two won't cut it. Our California rep was AWOL, also the guy from New York."

"Maybe Josh can call them and get them to sign on?"

Abel frowns. "Not sure it'd do any good. That California guy was gung-ho a year ago, but I've a feeling the blush has worn off the rose. Some people just can't stay committed. If they don't see personal success coming their way, they back away and look around for a more illustrious cause to support."

Closing his eyes, he drops his head to the back of the sofa. Through the closed door that leads to Esther's office, I hear movement and the sound of voices.

"Hon, before Esther and Josh come in, I'd like to ask you something."

An expression of resignation flickers over his face, but his eyes do not open. "Hmm?"

"It's about Christopher Lewis. He wants to meet me . . . and I said yes. He invited you, too, if you want to come."

His eyes twitch behind his closed lids. "My schedule is packed, Em. With this new campaign—"

"I told him you were busy." Mingled relief and shame flow through me. "I told him I'd probably come alone."

One blue eye opens. "Are you sure about this?"

"I want to meet him."

The eyelid lowers. When he speaks, his voice is flat. "When?"

"Tomorrow night, after church. I'm meeting him at a little restaurant downtown, some place called O'Shays."

Abel's eyes suddenly blaze into mine. "You're kidding."

"What do you mean?"

"O'Shays is a bar, Emma. Everybody knows that."

I stiffen, offended by the scowl darkening his brow. "I'm sure it's a restaurant. They might serve alcohol, but so does nearly every other restaurant in this town."

"It's a bar."

"How do you know?" I realize I'm challenging my husband, but his attitude is testing the limits of my tolerance. "You've never been there, have you?"

"I don't need to visit a pigsty to know it's filled with slop. I've heard talk about O'Shays. It's a bar, one of the seediest in town. It's probably not even safe for you to be alone downtown late at night."

I straighten in my chair. "I really don't think Christopher would pick a bar for our first meeting. Besides, nine o'clock is not the middle of the night. I'll go, I'll meet him, I'll come home. Simple."

Abel lowers his chin like a bull contemplating a charge, then shakes his head. "I don't like it."

My reservoir of patience, which has been heated by the emotional boiler of the past twenty-four hours, completely evaporates.

"Abel, have I ever asked you for anything as important as

this? I have given my life to serve you and God and the people of this church. Now I'm asking you for one thing—let me meet this young man. I'll go quietly, I'll be discreet, but I'm begging you, don't deny me this opportunity. Please, honey—if you love me, you'll let me go."

He closes his eyes as if he can't bear to witness my foolishness, but he does not protest again.

CHAPTER EIGHT

*A*bel and I try to keep Saturdays free for ourselves—after all, Saturday is the Sabbath, and it's impossible for a minister's family to rest on Sunday. We usually sleep late, then go out for a late breakfast at Denny's. Without fail, though, in the restaurant Abel will encounter someone from church and have to put on his "pastor hat" for half the morning.

Today, however, I have too much energy to sleep. I rise with the sun and slip out of bed, then turn off the alarm and step outside to fetch the newspaper. A glittering veneer of ice coats our winter-bare shrubs, and I find myself believing Punxsutawney Phil's prediction of six more weeks of winter.

Back inside the warmth of the house, I wipe my slippers on the entry rug and find myself eying the foyer with the judicious eye of a newcomer. If I were to bring Christopher to the house, what would his first impression lead him to think of us?

My eye roves over the white floor tiles, the gilded foyer table, and the elaborate grandfather clock just inside the door. The dining room, which is off to the immediate right, features a chandelier dripping with cut glass and purple pendants. My prized crystal lines the shelves in the china closet; a silver tea set rests on the antique buffet.

Beyond the foyer, our living room opens to wide windows with a view of the golf course. The leather sofas are comfortable, the antiques completely serviceable, the art traditional . . . yet this is not a welcoming house.

I feel the truth like an electric tingle in my bloodstream. Not one personal item lies within my view, not a single family photo or memento. There are no keys carelessly tossed on the foyer table, no shoes kicked off by the door. No toys in the hall, no scuffmarks on the tile, not even a doggie toy beneath the table.

This doesn't look like a home, it looks like a carefully dusted, perfectly preserved museum.

A wave of self-pity threatens to engulf me, but I push it back and head toward the kitchen. I've done my best to create a comfortable home, but I can't help it if we're rarely here. We are at the church Sunday through Friday, and we're often away from home on weeknights. If Abel isn't speaking here in Wiltshire, he's taking the jet to speak for a Praise Partners fund raiser somewhere or he's preaching at a revival.

When we are home, we hardly ever have guests at the house. We scarcely know our neighbors, and we've made it a habit to meet with church people at the church. Abel says a man needs a haven away from the ministry, so our home has always been our private place . . . maybe *too* private.

I drop the newspaper on the kitchen island, then move to the coffeemaker and press the power on. While it hisses and sputters, I check to be sure there's coffee in the filter, then pour fresh water into the top.

Is it possible we've become too secluded? Frowning, I lower the empty decanter beneath the spout and wait for the fragrant flow. Abel says a minister shouldn't have close friends, because it breeds jealousy and competition within the church. My experience tends to agree with his, and while I am friendly to everyone, I couldn't say that I have any truly close friends even among our staff. If an intimate friend is someone to whom you can confide your darkest secrets, then I have no intimate friends . . . except the Lord. Abel is my closest companion, and at the moment he's scarcely speaking to me. He hasn't forbidden me to see Christopher, but he hasn't given me his blessing, either. I'd bet my bottom dollar (if preachers' wives were allowed to bet) that he's praying I'll become convicted and not go to O'Shays tonight.

As the coffee brews, I cross my arms and look out my kitchen window. My next-door neighbor, Cathleen Somebody-or-other, is training a puppy on a patch of lawn between our houses. Her dog, a long-legged gangly creature, is tiptoeing over the frosted grass as if he's not quite sure about the wisdom of walking outside on such a cold morning.

I can't help smiling, and something in me hopes Cathleen will look my way so I can wave. She'd probably faint if I did—I don't think we've said more than ten words since the morning she brought me a plate of cookies to welcome us to the neighborhood. She and her husband live alone, I think, but a steady stream of cars pulls in and out of her driveway. One night—it must have been somebody's birthday—I counted four different families who came to visit, three of them with small children. Like an eavesdropper, I sipped my coffee on the front porch and listened to the happy squeals of kids and adults at play.

I can't believe I'm envying a woman I hardly know.

I don't think Cathleen and her husband go to church—ours or anyone else's—and several times I've been tempted to go over there and invite her to Sunday services at Sinai. I don't go, though, because in my deepest heart I know what her reaction will be. She will blink in surprise, then smile and thank me for the invitation. She might even promise to think about it, but she won't come.

She needs Jesus . . . but she probably isn't aware of her need. So what can we offer that she wants and doesn't already have?

Parking spaces in downtown Wiltshire are easy to find at night. Like most mid-sized cities, our downtown has fallen upon hard times as stores have moved out to the suburbs. The only really active businesses here are the Greyhound Bus station, the Kentucky Bank and Trust, and Elmer's Hardware, in which you can obtain whatever thingamajig you need along with free advice on everything from plumbing to politics.

Making my way toward the maze of one-way streets, I try to remember the last time I ventured downtown—probably three years ago, when two of our young people were arrested for breaking and entering one of the local liquor stores. I visited the jail with the youth pastor's wife because she was too terrified to go downtown alone.

As I make my way through the heart of the city I feel a thrill of fear—darkness presses liquidly against the car windows, and for a moment I feel as if I'm piloting a submarine through an ocean of ink. But iron streetlights in the heart of town pour cones of yellow light over the sidewalks and storefronts, and an occasional neon sign glows through the gloom.

Stopping at a blinking traffic signal, I am surprised to see that several businesses still survive on these pitted asphalt streets. After proceeding through the intersection, I pass several antique stores, a consignment shop for women's clothing, a homeless shelter, and the Christian Science Reading Room, where a bright halogen bulb burns over the barred steel door.

Few people are about. Two young boys slide in and out of the shadows as they ride their skateboards over the cracked concrete. A woman hurries through the lamplight, her purse over her shoulder and both hands holding tight to the strap.

I travel down two blocks of Fourth Street before I spot O'Shays. The narrow structure stands in a thin wash of moonlight, its single window cluttered with neon signs. I put on my signal to park in front of the building, but the saving grace of second thought restrains me.

From what I can tell, Abel might be right about this being a bar. And since the back of my car is clearly marked with a Jesus fish, I should probably park several feet away to avoid the appearance of impropriety.

I circle the block again and park short of my destination. As I turn the key in the ignition, I can't help but grimace at my assumptions. I'd been thinking that O'Shays would be nearly empty because nine o'clock was late for a downtown restaurant to be open. Christopher implied it would be empty, too, but for entirely different reasons. If this bar is like the others I've known, the Saturday night party crowd won't arrive until after eleven.

Too late for commerce and too early for nightlife, at eight-fifty-five I step out of my car, lock the door with the remote, and gingerly make my way over the cracked sidewalks. Chilled by the wind, I draw up inside my coat like a turtle. Abel's warnings echo in my ears, but desperation drives me forward. *My son* wants to meet me, and I would not miss this opportunity for the world.

I have so many questions. I want to know how Christopher grew up, what his adoptive parents are like, what he's doing and where he's living. Most of all (though these are questions I probably won't have the courage to ask), I want to know if he thought of me as he grew up . . . and if the flesh-and-blood woman he's finally meeting lives up to the image he has carried in his heart.

Did his adoptive mother speak of me with love? Did she speak of me at all? It would probably serve me right if she told Christopher he sprouted in a cabbage patch. Heaven knows I probably deserve one cabbage-patch story for every time I remembered my son, then banished the memory before Abel could read the longing in my eyes.

My long stride breaks when I glance toward the shadowed walls and see a newspaper-covered bum stretched over the sidewalk. Wiltshire isn't a place where you see this kind of thing, and for a moment I feel as though I have somehow been transported to New York or New Orleans. But no, this is downtown Wiltshire, and I have just passed the cobbler's shop where I used to take Abel's shoes.

I edge toward the curb as a sudden chill climbs the ladder of my spine. I look for a policeman—surely it's against the law to sleep on the street—but there are no blue-and-white sedans in sight, nothing but streetlights and shadows and leafless trees swaying in the wind.

Panic roots me to the spot. What if this man is dead? I glance toward the body again and am struck by the stiffness of the man's curled fingers. Is that evidence of rigor mortis? I should call 911 . . .

I am just about to dig for my cell phone when the man moves. I step back as he pushes himself up from the ground. The newspaper over his head falls away, exposing a face shaped into lines and pockets of sagging flesh that are more suggestive of overindulgence than age. A quilted plaid blanket around his shoulders falls away as he props himself against the wall.

His head bobs, his gray gaze meets mine. For an instant his eyes narrow, then he seems to remember who and where he is—

"Hey, lady," he thrusts out that pallid hand, "got a dollar?"

Shaking my head, I hurry down the block. I've been where that man is; I know how the game is played. If I give him a dollar, he'll spend it on alcohol or dope. If he really wants help, he could go to the shelter on Second Street or even to the YMCA in Lexington. Street people know where to go—I always did.

I halt on the sidewalk when I spot the peeling marker above the O'Shays entrance. A glowing Budweiser sign hangs in the door, and a matching clock in the window assures me they are open. Through the glass I see a polished wooden bar and a dark-haired man standing behind it.

I don't understand why my son would choose this place for our first meeting—maybe because it's quiet at this time of night—but it's too late to back out now.

At least the place looks clean. And if they sell something as simple as sandwiches, I can truthfully tell Abel that O'Shays is a restaurant.

I lift my chin and tuck my purse more securely under my arm. I won't let the fact that they serve alcohol bother me. After all, Abel and I enjoy eating at the country club, and that dining room has a bar tucked into a side room.

Pressing my lips together, I open the door and move forward. A bell above the door jangles a welcome and my heels make tapping sounds as I cross the black-and-white-tiled floor, but only the bartender looks up at my approach. A woman sits at the far end of the bar, her head bent low, and a couple of men occupy one of the booths that line the left side of the room.

The joint isn't exactly jumping.

Giving the bartender a shaky smile, I walk slowly past the booths, only to find all the tables strewn with dirty ashtrays and unwashed glasses.

"Sorry about the mess over there," the bartender calls. "Haven't cleaned up after the after-work crowd yet. But you can have a seat at the bar."

I am about to pretend I have come seeking a rest room when the bartender leans toward me and lowers his voice. "You look a little lost, lady. Do you need help?"

"Um," I edge closer to the polished brass railing, "I'm supposed to meet someone here."

I hold my breath, half-afraid that this tall, dark-haired young man will grin and confess that he is Christopher, but he only plucks an empty glass from the soldierly row behind him. "Can I get you something while you wait?"

I'm not at all sure of the etiquette a Christian woman should use in a place like this, but I seem to remember my mother assuring me that ladies did not ever sit unescorted at a bar. But she was a drunk thirty years ago, so maybe things have changed.

The buxomy blonde occupying the bend of the bar doesn't seem to mind being alone. With one hand she supports her head, with the other she manages to hold her cigarette and absently stroke the rim of her glass. Her eyes are wide and unfocused, as if her thoughts are a thousand miles away.

I slide onto one of the stools and smooth my skirt. "Thanks." I smile at the bartender and set my purse in my lap. "I'll just wait here a few minutes."

"No problem." He winks at me. "But don't you want something to wet your whistle?"

I look at the woman and the amber-colored liquid in her

glass. I'm not sure what she's drinking, but I can smell the alcohol from two stools away.

Some odors you never forget.

I meet the bartender's gaze. "I'd love a pot of hot tea. English Breakfast, if you have it."

Mr. Bartender lifts a brow. "Tea?"

"Yes, please, whatever brand you can find."

He shakes his head slightly, then turns. "That'll take a few minutes. We don't get much call for tea."

I sit on the stool, perspiring inside my coat, but I am too self-conscious to rise and slip it off. I don't want to look like I'm staying if Christopher doesn't show. My watch tells me it is five past nine, so punctuality is not one of his virtues. That's all right; tonight I can forgive a case of tardiness. If he's as nervous as I am, he's probably pacing down the block some-place, working up the nerve to come in.

The bartender brings me a mug of hot water and a dusty packet of Lipton tea. It's not what I'd call first-class service, but it'll do.

I pull off my gloves, then unwrap the tea bag. "Do you have a menu?"

His brow lifts again, and suddenly it occurs to me that he might know my face from TV. I don't know how much Christian television he watches, but this *is* the Bible Belt.

I give him one of my brightest smiles. "I thought I might get something to eat."

"Right."

"Thank you." While he walks to the end of the bar, I drop the tea bag into the hot water. Thin streamers of darkness swirl in the mug, then I hear the clunk of something hitting the bar.

The bartender has dropped a bowl of salted peanuts next to my elbow.

Wincing, I look up at him. "You don't have a menu, do you?"

The corner of his mouth lifts in a half-smile, exposing tobacco-stained teeth. "Heck fire, lady, you're a bona fide genius. You want food, that's what we got. If you get really hungry, I might be able to find a box of goldfish crackers somewheres."

I do not answer, but pull my tea bag from the mug then drop it, still dripping, onto the bar. Since bartenders in movies seem to take supreme joy in wiping the counter, I've just given him a way to make himself deliriously happy.

Gall burns the back of my throat as I sip my tea. Abel was right about one thing—the most important meeting of my life is about to take place in a tavern. I haven't stepped inside a bar in . . . well, I can't remember the last time. I drank plenty when I was living on the streets, but because I was underage, I mostly imbibed from long neck bottles my friends handed me. Once or twice I walked into a bar with a john to pick up a bottle, but even then I knew well-bred ladies didn't sit unescorted at bars, even if they were sipping nothing stronger than tea.

I lower my gaze. What must Christopher have been thinking when he picked this dump for our first meeting? Perhaps Abel was right, and this is all a cruel fraud. Some reporter must have sniffed out my past and pretended to be my long-lost son. Now he's probably waiting outside to snap a picture of Abel Howard's bleary-eyed wife staggering out of a dilapidated tavern—

"You been stood up, sweetie?"

The throaty voice belongs to the cigarette-smoking blonde. During my momentary pity party, she has slid from her stool to the empty seat next to me, accompanied by the overpowering aroma of cheap perfume. When I glance at her, I see that she is advertising a décolletage Mae West would have envied.

Lush is the word my mind automatically supplies.

Reluctantly, I look through the lacy tendrils of her cigarette smoke. "I beg your pardon?"

"I said"—her sour breath bathes my face—"did some guy stand you up?"

"Some guy?" My brittle laugh is more like a cry of pain. "It's beginning to look that way."

She takes a sip of her drink, which has come along for the ride, then lowers her glass. Her eyes cross as she looks at me. "Fuggedaboudim."

It takes me a minute to translate. "Oh," I say, not knowing how else to reply.

She rakes her talons through her mane. "I could tell you was all dressed up for somebody."

I run my hand over my skirt. I spent nearly half an hour trying to choose an outfit that would look nice without looking gaudy. I didn't want to appear sexy, and I certainly didn't want to seem maternal. I just wanted to look . . . respectable. Nice. Pretty enough that my son would feel proud of me.

The woman finishes her drink, then drops the glass to the bar. Using the empty glass as an ashtray, she flutters her mascara-caked lashes and casts me a sidelong look. "I think I know you. You been in here before?"

I shake my head. "First time."

"Then you go to Charley's, over on Sixth."

I force a smile. "I doubt we've ever met."

She wags a finger at me, then pulls a fresh cigarette from her glittery purse. "I never forget a face, and you've got a nice one. Too nice to be left sitting here all alone."

I sip my tea. It's bitter and needs sugar, but something tells me any sugar packets this bartender might have are buried behind a ten-year-old box of goldfish crackers.

"Hey, Jim." The blonde waves her unlit cigarette at the bartender. "You asleep at your post?"

Annoyance struggles with resignation on the bartender's face as he comes over and lights her cigarette. She inhales, then tips her head back, closes her eyes, and exhales twin streamers through her nose like some ancient movie actress.

Rolling his eyes, Jim moves away.

"Hey." Her lashes lift at the sound of his footsteps. "You forgot to bring me a refill."

"You've had enough, Shirley."

"I'm not drivin', I'm walkin'. Ain't no law against walking home with a few drinks in ya."

"I don't think you'll make it home if you keep knocking them back."

I glance behind me, hoping that by some miracle the dirty tables have cleaned themselves so I can retreat from this conversation. The tables are still filthy, and no wonder. Jim hasn't left the bar since I arrived.

I glance at my watch. I'll wait until nine-fifteen, no later, then I'll slip out. I'll walk with my purse shielding my face in case there's a photographer lurking about.

Shirley taps a length of ash into her empty glass, then props one hand on her thigh and looks at me. "So—who is this bum that stood you up?"

"He's not a bum." Surprising, how easily I defend a man I've never met. I look toward the bartender, hoping he'll rescue me from Shirley's attention. "He's . . . my son. I think."

Her jaw drops in exaggerated amusement. "You *think* he's your son? Whaddhe do to get you so mad at him?"

Engulfed by frustration, I look away, hoping to insulate

myself against the woman's attempts at conversation. I should ignore her; experience has taught me it's impossible to reason with a drunk.

"I had a son once," Shirley continues, apparently unaware that I have dropped out of the conversation. "Real cute little boy. Dark hair, dark eyes, lots of curls—and smart, too. Real smart. Took after his daddy, I think, 'cause I ain't never been smart."

She reaches for her glass and tips it back, then sputters as she spits out the ash. "Aw, man!" Dropping the tumbler, she leans both elbows on the bar. "Land's sakes, Jim! You've got me drinking dirt down here! Howsabout somethin' else?"

While her attention is diverted, I stand and slip out of my coat. If Jim's not going to clean up, I might as well lend a hand. The pastor's wife in me can't stand to sit and watch when there is work to be done.

I select the least cluttered table and begin to clear it. I have just moved a pair of lipstick-smeared glasses from a table to the bar when the bell above the door jangles. This time, Jim, Shirley, and I turn to see a young man enter, a tall and slender fellow with dark hair, blue eyes, a firm chin . . . and my mother's nose.

My hand flies to my chest; my heart pounds beneath my palm. The newcomer's eyes seem to take in the long and narrow room with one glance, then his eyes fix on me. A long, slow smile brightens his face as he strides forward.

Do I hug him? Shake his hand?

For a moment I stand in terror of this intimate stranger, then his arms are around me, lifting me from the floor, and we are laughing together.

Thank you, Father, for finally allowing me to embrace my son.

Chapter Nine

A wellspring of emotions bubbles up the instant I recognize the man who was once my baby. When I look at Christopher, I am struck by an overwhelming impulse to cover him with kisses and count his fingers and toes.

I can't do that, of course. He is a grown man, dignified and distinctive. Though I know he is not yet thirty, faint creases outline his mouth and eyes, muting his youth with strength. He is wearing jeans and a sweater beneath a nice black leather jacket. The coat could be expensive; it could be a cheap imitation. I don't know much about trendy men's clothing, and at the moment, I don't care.

From beside the bar, I hear Shirley's crusty voice: "*Chris? Chris is your son?*"

"Yes." I laugh as my eyes connect with his. "I'm sure he is."

Ten minutes later we are sitting across from each other in a booth, oblivious to Shirley's droning and Jim's comments from behind the bar. Christopher is sipping a glass of ginger ale; my mug sits before me, the tea now cold and dark. Other people have begun to trickle in—a few men at the bar are talking about sports, a cluster of college kids has crowded into booths near the front door.

I don't care about any of them. The only words registering in my brain are Christopher's, the only face that matters is his. My doubts and reservations fled the moment he came through the door.

"I was beginning to worry," I tell him, unwilling to look away from his beautiful face. "I had almost convinced myself your call was some reporter's attempt to ferret out my sordid past."

He grimaces, and I immediately regret my choice of words.

"Sorry. I didn't mean to imply you are something I could ever be ashamed of—unless—well, I don't know what I mean. But I am thrilled, Christopher, to finally meet you. I never dared to dream of this day, yet here you are."

"Call me Chris, please." He reaches across the table and catches my fingers. His skin is warm and supple, his hand strong and full of promise. When I look down, I see a young man's hand entwined around a middle-aged woman's . . . yet it all seems so incredibly *right*.

Looking up, I blink in a moment of lightheadedness. "You have my mother's nose."

He laughs. "I think I have your eyes."

"You think so?" I squint at him in the dim light, trying to discover my features in his face. "I can't tell. Probably because I never really look at myself—not in an analytical sense, anyway. I'm always checking my makeup, but I never really study my face . . . as you can probably tell from my bedraggled appearance."

"You're lovely." His words bring a flush to my cheeks, and the realization that I'm blushing like a schoolgirl sends even more heat into my face.

I lower my gaze, unable to look into those probing blue eyes. He is answering all my questions, addressing needs I couldn't even begin to express, and we've only been sitting together a few minutes.

"I want to know all about you." I squeeze his hand, then release it. "I want to know about your family, if you're married, what you're doing with your life."

"I want to know about you, too. But you can have the first question."

He leans back, slouching against the wall of the booth, and suddenly I am grateful he chose this odd little place. It's getting noisy, but no one will eavesdrop here, nor will anyone chase us out until we have exhausted this opportunity.

"Are you married?" I ask.

He grins. "Not yet."

"Any prospects?"

"None on the horizon. I was almost engaged once, but the young lady wasn't comfortable with my vagabond existence."

I nod in an attempt to remain open and nonjudgmental. What does he mean? I suppose he could be anything from a sports recruiter to a full-time hobo . . .

No, he's too nicely dressed to be a bum.

I fish for an answer. "So . . . you travel a lot in your work?"

"I listen for the voice of God and I go where he sends me."

I close my eyes as an ocean of gratitude threatens to spill out through my lashes. "Your parents kept their promise, then. They said they would bring you up in a Christian home."

He smiles almost shyly through wispy dark bangs. "They're wonderful people who genuinely love the Lord. I was their only child, so they made sure I had everything I needed. They taught me about God from an early age."

"I'm so relieved. I was trusting God when I allowed the agency to place you, but I was such a baby Christian in those days. I didn't have a lot of experience with trust."

"Seems appropriate, though, doesn't it? A baby Christian placing her baby in God's hands?"

My heart turns over when he smiles. "So . . ." I struggle to maintain control of my voice. "What brings you to Wiltshire? I always assumed you grew up in New York State."

"I did. But after college I developed this incredible yearning to know you. My dad has connections in high places, so he was able to get the adoption records opened." He lowers his voice. "I don't know how he did it, and I didn't ask. But one year at Christmas I open this box, and in it I find my original birth certificate."

"That was . . . a long time ago?"

"Yeah—I think I was twenty at the time. I waited, seeking God, waiting for the right time to approach you. I'd watch you and your husband on TV . . . sometimes I got a little crazy with wanting to know you."

I can't speak. Each word that falls from his lips is like a pearl falling into my open hand, and I am desperate to catch each one.

He rubs his hand across his face, and I can hear the faint rasp of the stubble on his cheek. "Finally God gave me the freedom to come. I arrived in Wiltshire about six weeks ago, and have been working here, waiting until the time was right . . ."

When his voice trails away, I realize this meeting means as much to him as it does to me.

Seeing the shimmer of tears in his eyes, I steer the conversation toward a less emotional topic. "What sort of work are you doing?"

Please, Lord, for Abel's sake let him be gainfully employed.

"I'm a minister." A small smile ruffles his lips, then his eyes grow serious. "There are so many needs here, have you noticed?"

I gape at him in pleased surprise, knowing Abel will be hard-pressed to complain about a fellow preacher. "Why, that's wonderful! What church are you working with? Abel knows every pastor in the area, so we probably—"

"I'm doing parachurch work, nondenominational. I minister to people where I find them."

I tilt my head, uncertain how to interpret his answer. "Well . . . it's wonderful that you've received the call. Tell me about it—did God call you in seminary? Or were you only a child?"

Something that might have been humor flits into his blue eyes.

"We're all called, Emma. The moment we surrender our lives to Jesus we are called to follow him. And he leads us down paths that are as different as our personalities."

For a moment I wonder if he has gone to a real seminary—it's as if he's speaking Hebrew while I'm conversing in Greek.

"Yes, yes, I know we're all supposed to serve God. But the call to pastoral ministry—surely that was different for you."

He shakes his head. "Afraid not."

"So . . . you were never called to be a pastor?"

He glances at the ceiling, then lowers his gaze and smiles at his glass. "I was called to minister as a follower of Christ, Emma. I've been called to obey."

"But"—A chilly breeze of disappointment frosts my smile—"we're all called to do that."

"But how many of us actually follow through?"

For an instant I wonder if he is chiding me for something, but his face is clear and honest, his eyes shining in simple sincerity.

Somehow, somewhere, someone failed to teach this boy about ministry in the real world.

"The call of a pastor is a unique thing," I explain, folding my hands. "Abel was sixteen when he heard the call, and he knew his life would always be different. He stopped going to parties and school dances, he began to search for a good Christian college, he started listening to the great preachers. From that moment on, he knew what his life's work would be."

Christopher nods. "I know what my life's work will be, too."

"What?"

"Following Christ."

I bite back a sigh of pure exasperation. "God calls us to tasks. There's that verse about how God outfits the church by giving us pastors and teachers and evangelists and prophets—"

"You're absolutely right," Chris answers. "But tell me—is every Sunday school teacher at your church on staff?"

I shake my head. "Of course not."

"Yet their gift is as God-given as the pastor's. So why is one calling more sacred than another? No, Emma—we are all called to follow Christ. He has given us special gifts, and he expects us to use them as we move through the world. I used to think that being a Christian meant doing my religious duty—now I know that only God knows what my duty is from minute to minute. My job is to follow and obey."

I stare at him as my thoughts turn to my college days. My professors praised the "preacher boys" and held them up to us as examples. We women were told that God called men to ministry, and women to men.

If what Chris is saying is true . . .

The sound of breaking glass shatters my thought processes. Behind the bar, Jim is cursing his clumsiness.

When I look at my son again, I am grateful for the interruption. Somehow we have entered a debate, and a debate is the last thing I want.

I manage a weak laugh. "Do you argue with everyone you meet?"

His eyes flash above an impenitent grin. "I've never been shy about explaining the truth. I thought we were having an interesting discussion."

I lift a brow and look down at my teacup.

"Listen," Chris leans forward and grips my hand again. "I really didn't come here to talk about myself. I know I said I didn't come to demand anything of you, but there are so many things I want to know."

I smile, enchanted by the beautiful boy beaming from within the man. "What can I tell you?"

He looks down, then squeezes my fingertips. "Did you know my father well?"

I am grateful for his lowered eyes, and at this moment I would give every cent in my bank account if I could buy a purified personal history. For an instant I even consider lying . . . but I will not be false with my son. Not even to spare him pain.

"No," I whisper, wondering if he will drop my hand and walk out in disgust. "I'd give anything if I could tell you a different story, but I wasn't a Christian in those days. I wasn't even a good person. I was seventeen, a prostitute working the Lower East Side, when I got pregnant with you. I don't even know who your father was."

I brace myself for his reaction, but when his eyes lift to meet mine, I see no condemnation in them, only soft concern.

"That must have been a horrible time for you."

"I was horrible—lost, on drugs, pregnant, and broke. You were my second pregnancy . . . and you wouldn't have been born if I'd had money for an abortion. Of course, if I'd had the money, I'd probably be dead now. The pregnancy got me off the streets and into Mercy House, and that's where Jesus turned my life around. So in a way, Chris, God used you to bring me to the Savior."

His eyes, which are clear and lovely and deep, swim as he encases my hand in both his own. "So tell me about your life now."

I don't really want to talk about myself, but he's come so far it would be cruel to deny him.

I shrug. "My life is an open book. What folks see on television is pretty much the way I am. Abel and I keep busy with the church and television ministry. The church is a huge task in itself—with ten thousand members, we visit the sick, put out fires, teach, lead—all the usual things you'd expect. We have a dedicated staff and a wonderful group of deacons who help with the day-to-day feeding of the church, but still, pastoring is a big job. As far as the TV program goes—I sing, Abel preaches, and together we do what we can to clean up our little corner of the world and point people to Jesus."

"I've seen you on TV," he says, smiling, "but I want to know what you do *outside* the church. What fills your world, Emma?"

I stare at him, suddenly speechless. What else does he expect me to do?

"We have n-no children," I stammer. "So our lives revolve around the ministry."

A tinge of sadness fills his eyes. "I'm sorry, I don't mean to pry. My mother is always saying I ask too many questions."

I'm about to assure him that I don't mind, but he speaks first.

"Does it bother you if I refer to my mom?"

I prop my chin on my hand and meet his direct gaze. "I'll be forever grateful to your mother. She did what I couldn't possibly have done."

The line of his shoulders relaxes. "She's a good lady. I think you'd like her."

I accept this as an answered prayer. For years I have prayed he would be loved and cherished . . .

"What's your favorite food?"

I blink. "Food? I . . . don't really have a favorite. I eat whatever's in front of me."

"But if you had to choose."

"Well, I . . ." I rub my brow. "Okay, I like pizza. And I hardly ever get it."

Leaning back, Chris whoops with delight. "Me, too! I love pizza; I'd eat it five nights a week if I could. Mom always thought it was an adolescent fixation, but I haven't outgrown it at all."

My heart warms as the light of understanding dawns. Despite our differing viewpoints, surely genetics binds us in other ways.

"Favorite music?" I ask.

"Country in the car," he says, "but classical when I'm thinking. Sarah Brightman is the best."

I tug at my collar and shove my disappointment aside. I hate to tell him I don't know the slightest thing about country music, and I have no clue who Sarah Brightman is. Abel and I listen to Christian praise music at the office. At home we favor the TV, which is usually tuned to FOX News or CNN.

I open my hand as if I'm counting off items on a grocery list. "Favorite color?"

"Blue."

I cock my finger toward him. "Touché. Periwinkle blue for me. Love that shade."

"Favorite dessert?" he counters.

"Oh, that's easy. Key lime pie."

"That is too cool!" He slaps the table for emphasis. "I *love* Key lime pie. I'd probably rank carrot cake as my number one favorite, but key lime is right up there."

"I like carrot cake." My gaze falls to the glass of ginger ale on the table. "Favorite drink?"

"Sweetened iced tea," he answers. "The way they make it down here. I've got an aunt who puts a cup and a half of sugar into every pitcher. It's like syrup, but it's delicious."

"Uh-huh." My gaze darts to the bar, where Jim and Shirley have bent their heads in conversation. "Do you drink . . . alcohol?"

He tilts his head to meet my gaze. "Would it bother you if I did?"

I'm stunned by the question, but I shrug to hide my disappointment. "Abel and I are teetotalers, of course. And even if the church didn't expect us to abstain, my history serves as a warning. My mother was a drunk. I was following right in her footsteps, so alcohol holds nothing but bad memories for me."

A faint glint of humor appears in his eyes. "I noticed the tea. Bet Jim gave you an odd look when you ordered it."

I glance at the bartender, whom Chris obviously knows by name. "You come here often?"

"Once or twice a week."

"And when you come here—" I hesitate, hating the needling tone that has crept into my voice. This is probably not the time or place to bring this up; I don't want our first meeting to be tainted by anything negative. But this might be the only time I see him, and he needs to know how alcohol killed my mother and nearly killed me.

Wrapping myself in maternal concern, I meet his gaze. "When you come here, Chris, do you drink?"

His eyes are glowing with the clear, deep blue that burns in the heart of a flame. "Coming here bothered you, didn't it?"

I am about to shrug and feign nonchalance, then I remember my commitment to total honesty. "Yes, it did. If anyone other than you had asked, I wouldn't have come. As it was, I only agreed to come because I assumed this was a restaurant."

He lowers his head, but not before I see a grin tug at his mouth. "There are people here, Emma. I go where the people are."

"There are people everywhere," I counter. "Even at church. If you want fellowship, you should visit a more appropriate place."

"But if I want to minister . . . what better place than this?"

It is a reasonable answer, but for some reason it stings.

"Tell me," he says after a long moment, "if you didn't have your cell phone and your car broke down in front of this place, would you come inside to call for help?"

"Well . . . yes, if I had to. It'd be an emergency and it'd only take a minute."

"So, you'd set your standards aside to rescue a car? Yet how much more valuable is a person than your wheels? It is perfectly right to do good in a bar. God wants us to be merciful; he doesn't care about the little sacrifices we make to show others we're spiritual."

Only when I realize I am gaping at him do I snap my mouth shut. In my mental filing cabinet I have over a dozen homilies on the importance of avoiding every appearance of evil, but the sheer authority in Chris's answer has left me speechless.

I'm the pastor's wife, I'm the elder Christian, I'm the *mother,* for heaven's sake. So why can't I come back with a proper reply?

Drawing a deep breath, I decide to try another approach. "I admire your sincerity, Chris, but you can't honestly expect me to say it's okay for church people to spend time in places like this. Some of our people are alcoholics; some of them are too weak to resist temptation—"

He lifts his hand, cutting me off. "I'm not saying you should send those who are weak in the faith. But I have been a Christian for years, and so have you. I can be tempted"—a flush brightens his face—"but drunkenness has never appealed to me."

He picks up the napkin that had been beneath his glass and idly wipes the table. "Listen, we didn't come here to argue. I asked you to come because I want to know you. I'd love to hear about your childhood, where you grew up . . . anything you want to share."

Grateful for the change of topic, I settle back and unwind the tangled threads of my memory, reciting every story I can remember. I tell him about how I'd been proud to be the daughter of an honest-to-goodness FBI agent, about Dad teaching me things like how a real agent always offers his credentials with his left hand so his right hand is free to draw a gun.

I tell him that I didn't have a particularly happy childhood—Mom was always in her room with a headache and/or hangover; Dad was always at work or out with his buddies. Without siblings to play with, I spent my time with books, which made me a bit of a social outcast at school.

"In fifth grade, though, one of the really popular girls seemed to notice me after I answered a question in class. She turned right around and smiled at me, then made a point of hanging around with me on the playground. I couldn't believe it—I thought I had finally found a friend—until she told me her youth group was having a 'pack the pew' contest and she'd win a prize if she had the most people in her church pew that weekend. I told her I couldn't go, and after begging for a few minutes, she turned and walked away. She never spoke to me again."

I lower my gaze to the tabletop—even now, the memory of her rejection hurts.

"I'm sorry," Chris says, his voice soft. "Kids can be cruel."

I force a laugh. "My childhood wasn't completely miserable. There were some good times."

I dredge up memories I haven't unearthed in years, blow the dust off a few gems that startle me with their brilliance. Yes, things were bad after Dad died, but I knew good times, too. Laughter bubbles into my voice as I tell Chris about a mysterious admirer who once slipped an anonymous note through the vents in my eighth-grade locker.

"What'd the note say?"

My cheeks burn as I lift my eyes to meet his. "Isn't that odd? I remember every word. It said, 'I just wanted you to know someone admires you very much.'"

Christopher is examining my face with considerable concentration. "Did you ever find out who sent it?"

"No. But I never forgot it. It was . . . a gift."

I am surprised to realize that life before Abel was not

completely miserable. And while I tell the good stories, Chris sips his ginger ale, laughing when I laugh, smiling when I smile. He is suddenly my best friend and confidant, the only person to whom I have ever completely opened the doors of my past.

He does not flinch when I tell him about the dark years—about my mother's descent into alcoholism, the horrible fights that culminated in my being kicked out of the house, all the terrible things I did to numb my pain and survive on the streets.

And then I tell him about Nola, who rescued me, and Lortis June, who led me to Jesus. "Without those two women," I say, looking into my boy's beautiful eyes, "neither of us would be here tonight."

"They showed you love . . . just like the person who sent that anonymous note."

His insight startles me into silence. I knew so little love when I was growing up . . . no wonder I hungered for it.

He is the first to glance at his watch. "It's very late," he says, "and I don't want your husband to hate me for keeping you out all night. I think it's time for me to walk you to your car."

A frisson of horror snakes down my spine when I look at the time—twelve-thirty A.M. I must have assumed this working-class bar would empty out when the hour grew late, but it's Saturday night and the place is far more crowded than when I entered at nine. Jim now has a helper behind the bar, Shirley the Lush is draped over some man who is ogling her cleavage and buying her beers; the college kids at the front tables are fizzing with laughter for no apparent reason.

But I need to get home. Abel will be worried about me.

"Before we go—" Opening my purse, I frantically dig through the contents, setting my compact, pen, Altoids, cell phone, car keys, change purse, and wallet on the table before I find my packet of business cards. I slide one free, then pick up the pen.

"This reaches my cell phone," I tell him, writing the number on the back of the card. "If you need anything, don't hesitate to call."

Christopher—*my son*—takes the card, thanks me, and slides it into the pocket of his jeans.

We stand and I slip into my coat. That's when I notice that Chris has a folded *People* magazine tucked into his jacket pocket.

"You read *People?*" I ask.

He snaps his fingers. "I knew I forgot something. Favorite magazine?"

I'm a little bewildered, but I play along. "*Purity* magazine, of course."

A wide grin spreads across his face. "I like *People*. It gives me something to talk about when I meet . . . well, people."

My astonishment must be evident on my face, because Chris laughs. "Don't you read *People?*"

I take a half-step back. "Not even in the doctor's office. It just seems so . . . worldly."

"Oh, Emma." A spark of some indefinable emotion lights his eyes. "Tell me—what was the cover article in *Purity* magazine last month?"

I don't hesitate. "We featured a debate on the pre-millennial versus post-millennial Rapture. It was very well done."

"Ah." Chris waves his hand toward the row of men and women perched at the bar. "And if you were to take a poll tonight, how many of these folks would have an opinion on that topic?"

I cross my arms and bite the inside of my cheek. He's making fun of me now—gentle fun, but still . . .

"Watch this." He plucks the *People* from his pocket, slides it beneath my folded arm, then turns to face the bar. Lifting his hands, he clears his throat. "Ladies and gentlemen, may I have your attention?"

After a moment of shuffling, the roar in the bar fades. Through the blue haze of cigarette smoke I see the college kids smirking at Chris while the old men at the bar watch with befuddled expressions.

"I'm taking an impromptu poll," Chris says, "about *Boy Meets Girl*. Which woman should Martin choose? The sweet one or the hottie?"

Lowering my head, I bring one hand up to cover my face. I'm stunned, absolutely mortified, but as I look down I see the cover of the magazine in my arms: "Charlotte or Moria?" the headline reads. "Which one offers true love?"

I wouldn't have believed it possible, but Chris's question ignites a discussion unlike anything I've ever heard in Sinai Church. The young ones begin to chant Moria's name, while the old men at the bar begin to argue over whether Charlotte is genuinely nice or too good to be true. Chris stands there, grinning, while the comments fly thick and fast, then he turns and winks at me.

"See what I mean?"

"I still don't see what good—"

"I could ask that same question to almost anyone I meet on the street, and from that we could get into a discussion of what true love—God's love—is all about. It's easy to talk to people when you know what's on their minds."

I sigh. I've never raised a son, but I'm beginning to understand why the mothers of adolescents in my ladies' fellowship group wear looks of exhaustion.

"This has been wonderful, Chris, but I need to get home."

His grin fades to concern. "Sorry—let me walk you out."

He follows behind me as I precede him through the narrow aisle between the bar and the crowded booths. At one point one of the men at the bar swivels and blocks my path with his foot. "Hey," he says, leering drunkenly, "where ya goin', pretty lady?"

Instinctively, I clutch my purse to my chest. Chris steps up, one hand falling protectively on my shoulder, and something in his gaze makes the drunk lower his foot and turn away.

I can't help but shudder as we continue toward the door. The alcoholic stench of the man's breath brought back memories not even time can erase, and again I find myself questioning why Chris picked this, of all places.

"Sorry about that," he murmurs. "But don't let guys like him rattle you. I've learned not to be surprised when sinners sin."

With one hand on my shoulder, Chris guides me through the crowd. Outside, I point to my car in the distance and we walk toward it, but Chris's step slows as we pass the sleeping bum on the sidewalk.

I hurry by, unlock the car, and get in. As I close the door, Chris catches up, then places both hands on the roof and bows his head. His words are muffled by the closed window, but I hear him say something about "angels" and "protect her."

He's praying for me.

Then he brings his fingertips to his lips, presses the kiss to my window, and steps back, releasing me to drive away.

I am loath to start the engine, but even this night has to end. And Chris is right—Abel is bound to be worried. Staying longer would not be wise or considerate.

I start the car, put it in reverse, and carefully pull out of the parking space. Just before driving away, however, I look for Chris to give him one last wave, but he is no longer watching me.

He is bent over the homeless man, helping him to his feet. My eyes sting as I reluctantly drive away.

It is one A.M.—officially Sunday morning—when I finally creep through the garage door and reset the security system. A thousand thoughts churn in my mind as I move through the shadowy kitchen; my heart brims with so many feelings that one little upset is likely to cause an emotional meltdown.

Fortunately, the sink is clean, there are no half-empty dishes on the counter, and the message board by the phone bears only one post-it note: *Em—plumber called tile guy. Will drop off stuff Sunday P.M. and start work Monday morning—7:30.*

Thank heaven—one less thing for my to-do list.

I pause by the sink, arrested by the sight of a reflected woman in the window. Abel is asleep, her eyes tell me. So why didn't you stay with your son?

I should have. I had not driven a half-mile before I found myself wanting to see him again. We spent most of the night talking about me; I need another night to learn more about him.

Years ago I gave him life; tonight I answered his questions. When I surrendered my right to raise him, I know I surrendered my right to be involved in his life. Yet this brief encounter has whetted an appetite that can't be satisfied in the space of a few hours.

"Go away," I tell my reflection.

I snap off the tiny lamp burning in the window above the sink, then go to the study to check for any urgent messages that might have come in while I was out. The answering machine is empty, so I drop my purse into a chair, then slip through the hallway and into the darkness of our bedroom. Abel has left a lamp burning in the bathroom. In the rectangle of light shining through the doorway I see him, a series of mounds beneath our satin comforter. His soft snoring accompanies the electric hum of the ceiling fan over the bed.

I tiptoe into the bathroom, pull the door closed behind me, and grab a nightgown from a drawer in the closet. After brushing my teeth and running a brush through my hair (which smells of smoke, but Abel might not notice before I have a chance to shower), I creep into our bedroom and slide into bed.

I have just settled onto my side when the mountain next to me shifts. Staring into a sudden silence, I wait for him to speak.

"Well?" His tone is sharp.

Thank goodness, Abel is willing to listen. I push myself into a sitting position and face my husband in the darkness.

"I met him, Abel. He's a very nice young man, a Christian and a minister. I think you'd like him."

"What sort of minister invites a lady to meet him in a bar? I can smell the stink of the place from here."

"Oh, you cannot!"

"I can."

I reach over and turn on the bedside lamp so Abel can see I am the same woman who left him only a few hours ago.

"The place was smoky, I'll admit. But Chris didn't drink, and neither did I."

Abel props himself on his pillows, then folds his hands across his chest. "So—is your curiosity satisfied?"

I know what he wants to hear. My sweet, wary husband desperately wants to return to a time when he believed his wife's most serious failing was occasionally stumbling over the lyrics of a song she was supposed to have memorized.

I pull a pillow into my arms. "Meeting him was a thrill, of course. But he's only working here for a while, Abel, and I spent most of the night talking about myself. I didn't suggest another meeting, but if he calls again I'd love to spend more time with him. I'd like you to meet him, too."

My husband's hands slide up his arms and lock at his elbows. "I'm not sure that's a good idea."

Leaning forward, I brush his cheek with my lips. "I love you, darling. I know you love me. And you can trust me in this—with all my heart I believe Christopher Lewis means us no harm."

"You can't even be sure he's your son."

"I'm sure—he has my mother's nose. I can't explain it, but the moment he came through the door, I knew we were connected. All at once I felt as though I'd spent my entire life searching for him . . . without realizing what I was doing. I know that sounds crazy and sort of mystical, but that's just what I felt."

Abel exhales and closes his eyes. I wait a moment for his response, then I tug gently on a tuft of hair near his temple.

"Do you want to hear all about it? I'll tell you anything you want to know."

"I've a big day tomorrow, and so do you." His features have hardened in disapproval. "We've already let this thing intrude into the Lord's Day. Now we need to sleep."

I hear the rebuke in his statement, feel the snap of guilt he intends.

"Good night, then." I pull away and switch off the lamp, then lie back against my pillows. And though my husband's rebuke and pointed disinterest have drawn tears, Abel's reaction cannot diminish my joy.

After a while, his snoring once again keeps time to the whirling ceiling fan. I fall asleep thinking of the young man who listens every day for the call of God . . . and found me in the process.

CHAPTER TEN

*W*hen I wake the next morning—forty-five minutes later than usual—the house is as silent as death.

I presume Abel has already left for church. He attends a prayer meeting with the deacons each Sunday morning at seven, but he usually wakes me with a kiss before he leaves. As I slide out of the sheets and hurry into the bathroom, I can't help but wonder if Abel forgot to wake me because he was preoccupied . . . or chose not to wake me because he was upset.

I can't take shortcuts in the shower because my hair smells of cigarettes ("Smoking won't send you to hell," Abel always says, "but it'll sure make you smell like you've been there"), and I'm so distracted by thoughts of my son and my husband that I find myself squirting conditioner into my palm before I've applied the shampoo.

Out of the shower, I grab a towel, then hurry to the closet. I'm not sure what our calendar holds for the day, but Abel rarely leaves a Sunday afternoon unplanned. So I choose an outfit that will work for most anything—a gray wool skirt, a soft sweater, and a navy blazer.

I take five minutes to dab and dash on makeup; ten minutes to blow my short hair into the soft look appropriate for a woman my age. I'm out the door half an hour after waking.

After battling the long line of traffic leading into the church parking lot, I pull into my reserved space, wave my thanks to the attendants who escorted me to my spot, and hurry into the worship center.

Our first service begins at eight o'clock. I usually run through my song in the choir room before the program begins, but today there's no time for rehearsal. I slip into my chair beside the piano, then pick up the beige-colored phone that connects me directly to Mike Thomas, our sound engineer. After wishing me a cheery good morning, he asks what I plan to sing.

Guilt slaps at my soul. One of my college professors was forever saying that God blessed our endeavors according to our preparation, but I've had no time to prepare this morning. I can only hope God will honor the time I spent learning this song several years ago.

"How about 'How Great Thou Art'?" I ask. "You have the track handy, or should I do it at the piano?"

"No track," Mike says. "So we'll go with the piano. I'll have someone down to set up the mike in a minute."

I lower the phone and lean back in my chair. I ought to be relieved. I think I could sing that beloved old song in my sleep, but I hate feeling rushed on a Sunday morning. Worship services should be approached thoughtfully, reverently, and with great care.

A thin adolescent kid with spiked hair and glasses comes stomping up the platform steps, a microphone stand in his hand. "Mornin', Emma Rose," he says, setting the mike stand by the piano bench. He adjusts the angle of the cordless microphone in the clip. "This good for you?"

I nod. "Thanks."

He stomps back down the stairs as the choir comes through the double doors at the back of the choir loft. The sound in the crowded sanctuary rises at the choir's approach—almost as if worshipers are racing to finish the last of their conversations. The place is buzzing by the time Kenyon Glazier, our minister of music, climbs into the pulpit and lifts his arms.

"Welcome to Sinai Church! Let's stand and praise the Lord together!"

I rise with the others as we begin to sing "Crown Him with Many Crowns." The three camera operators swing into position, the organist makes the pipes sing, the orchestra swells the rafters with glorious brass and strings. Our local fifteen-year-old piano prodigy—a girl whose name escapes me—pounds the keys of the Steinway. They ought to hire her to play full-time, but then there'd be no reason for Emma Rose Howard to sit on the platform.

In the midst of the song, Abel emerges from a side door, Josh trailing in his wake. Josh slides into an aisle seat in the front pew; Abel climbs the steps to the platform, smiling broadly at the choir members. Finally he turns to face the crowd, his Bible pressed to his chest and his eyes closed, as Kenyon directs the ending of the song with a dramatic flourish.

Twenty minutes later—after the welcome, announcements, choir special, and Praise Partners report—the ushers march forward to take the offering. Seeing them approach, Abel climbs into the elevated pulpit.

"It is good to see you all here today." Standing in the curve of his bulletproof perch, Abel grips the dark wooden trim and beams a smile over the congregation. "I know this church is important to you, as well it should be. When you accepted Christ, you accepted the responsibility to build your life around this church and its Savior."

I want to know what you do outside the church.

Christopher's voice speaks from my memory, startling me with its clarity. My hand rises to finger the string of pearls at my neck as I peer past the piano at the congregation. I'm not sure what I expect to see, but his voice was so crisp I wouldn't have been surprised to find him crouching behind my chair.

When Abel begins to pray, I bow my head and stand, then slide silently onto the piano bench. Moments of dead air are not allowed in a service at Sinai Church; even the ushers are aware of the need to keep things moving for the sake of the television audience. As soon as Abel says "amen," I will begin to play, and I will continue singing until the last offering plate has been safely handed to the accounting committee chairman at the back of the church.

I am well into the first chorus of my solo before I turn to look out at the congregation. The television monitor sits on the floor by the first pew, and through my peripheral vision I can see that the director has called for a closeup. My entire head fills the screen, and the effect is so disconcerting that I shift my eyes to the right, sliding my gaze over the folks sitting down front. No matter where I look, from the corner of my eye I see the unblinking lens of a TV camera trained on me.

I have just begun the second verse when my eyes encounter a sight that sends shock coursing through my body like a jolt of electricity. In the fourth or fifth row, enveloped by the discreet space strangers maintain between each other, Christopher is sitting with his eyes closed. His dark head is bobbing to the gentle pulse of the song, and his mouth is moving with mine.

Sudden tears blur my vision. I lower my gaze and see my

hands on the keyboard, but they are like the hands of a stranger. I find myself grasping for the notes of a song I could have played blindfolded, but now I can't even remember what key I'm singing in and I'm terrified to play notes that will be completely, utterly wrong.

My ears are ringing so loudly I can't hear the song in my head; my fingers have forgotten how to play. I have no idea what comes next. I lift my foot off the piano pedal, muffling the last chord, and silence pours from the open lid of the Steinway.

Every person in the congregation has tensed. I can feel the pressure of hundreds of pairs of eyes; I know they are wondering why I've stopped. The cameras are staring, too—wide, curious, and intimately personal.

I cannot play. I'm not sure I can sing. But I can at least speak.

"And when I think," I whisper, lowering my trembling hands to my lap, "that God, his Son not sparing, sent him to die, I scarce can take it in."

A woman in the choir begins to sob.

"That on the cross," I close my eyes against the shame of this failure, "my burden gladly bearing . . . he bled and died to take away my sin."

Kenyon Glazier, who is sitting close enough to see that my hands are trembling, rises to his feet. Covering my breakdown with style and grace, he moves into the pulpit and soon the entire church is singing the chorus a capella, rattling the windows with an emotional chorus of "How Great Thou Art."

When the last note has died away, I slip from the piano bench and take my seat. Aware of the camera, I am careful to compose my face into peaceful, settled lines. Inwardly, though, I am roiling in a sea of turbulent emotion. While I am thrilled Christopher came to church, I am drowning in humiliation because I offered less than my best to the Lord. I have made a mistake not only in front of a national television audience, but in front of my son.

Far worse than my personal mortification is the knowledge that some people will think I lost control of my emotions because I was overcome by my love for God.

I have never felt like such a hypocrite.

Chapter Eleven

*O*n Monday morning, I sit at the kitchen counter and sip my coffee. Abel has already gone to the office, and I'm a little amazed that his departure has left me feeling grateful and at peace.

We moved through Sunday in a cautious state of truce, neither of us speaking of my son unless absolutely necessary. At lunch I truthfully explained my lapse at the keyboard by admitting I'd been thrown by the sight of Christopher in the congregation. Abel received this news silently, then asked me to pass the dinner rolls.

Neither of us mentioned Chris again. I kept my cell phone

within reach in case he should call, but our Sunday afternoon faded into Sunday evening without a word from my son.

I check my watch, then take another sip of coffee. I will be late for work today. The tile installer was supposed to arrive at seven-thirty, but it's now eight-fifteen and his pickup truck has just pulled up to the curb.

I answer the door in my stocking feet.

"Tile man," he says, glancing at the gleaming tiles in the foyer. "You want I should take off my shoes?"

I shake my head. "Don't worry about it."

The tile guy—I'm not sure I caught his name—is an older man with a grizzled white beard and ponytail to match. Beneath his denim overcoat he wears stained white pants and a white T-shirt.

I lift my hand in a "follow me" gesture and lead him through the bedroom into the bathroom. "I'll leave you to it, then." I point to the tub. "Sorry it's such a mess."

The man grunts.

"I, um, have to go to work now. If you go out for lunch, will you lock up? You can call me, and I'll come back to let you in—I work about ten minutes from here."

The man grunts again, then squats to examine the scarred plywood frame around the tub. "I don't go out for lunch."

"Well." I clasp my hands together. "Okay. I'll leave you alone so you can get started."

My practical side makes me reluctant to leave anyone in

the house when both Abel and I are gone, but I suppose that's why most construction workers are bonded and insured. I slip into my shoes and grab my purse, eager to get out of the tile installer's way.

When I reach the church office, I can tell something's in the air. By this time devotions are usually done and the secretaries are at their desks, but the place has a deserted look when I come through the front door. Tanzel has even left the reception desk unattended.

I discover why when I pass the short hallway leading into Abel's office. Josh has gathered all the women around Esther's desk, and he's distributing paperwork. I pause in the doorway to catch up on what I've missed.

"Your job, if you choose to accept it," Josh gibes, handing Celene a sheet of paper, "is to call all the Books & More bookstores on your list and ask if they're willing to order the wifeswapping book. We suspect you're going to get a positive answer; if so, you can hang up. What we're looking for is a bookstore manager who'll go against company policy. If you find someone who refuses to order that trash; let me know right away. That's the guy we want to interview on-camera."

The secretaries accept their assignments and move away. Celene makes a face when her eyes meet mine. "Nebraska." She waves her page. "I was hoping to talk to people in someplace warm like Hawaii."

"I'll trade you." Crystal Donaldson, who's been pulled

from her magazine duties, is holding several stapled sheets by the corner. "I've got three and a half pages of Books & More stores in California. I'm gonna be on the phone all day."

Grinning, Celene clutches her single sheet to her chest. "Maybe Nebraska isn't so bad after all."

I follow Celene down the hall to our offices and pause at her desk. "Sorry I'm late—had to let the tile guy into the house. Anything for me this morning?"

"As a matter of fact, yes." She shuffles papers on her desk, then offers me a memo with *From the Desk of Josh Bartol* stamped across the top. "Josh says the Reverend wants you to interview some folks whose marriages broke up on account of a swinging lifestyle. We can use previously published quotes, but they'd really like to find a few people who'll talk on camera."

"Got it."

"And Crystal dropped off a list of questions for you. Something about an interview for the magazine?"

"Um . . . hold on to those for me, will you? I doubt I'll have time to get to them today."

"Okay—and there's this." Without further comment Celene hands me a response card—one of the hundreds of forms we make available for our parishioners to fill out and drop into the comment box as they leave the Sunday service. Usually the cards contain prayer requests, notes about shut-ins who need a pastoral visit, or complaints about the music being too soft, too loud, too contemporary, or too traditional. Someone has folded this one, however, and written my name across the top in chunky letters.

I open the card. The name and address are blank, but in the comment section, a bold and masculine hand has written: "Your music blessed me. Chris."

Thanking Celene with a smile, I move into my office and pull my chair toward the desk. This is a Monday like a hundred other Mondays, yet even with a stranger in my house and a load of work on my desk, I suddenly feel as happy as a new millionaire.

Chris wasn't embarrassed by my meltdown. He understood. And he took the time to let me know I did okay.

I prop my elbows on the desk and cover my face with my hands. "Father," I close my eyes, "thank you for making something beautiful out of my mistakes. Thank you for leading Chris to church yesterday. But this morning, you're going to have to help me concentrate. Open my eyes to the things you'd have me see, lead me to the people you'd have me interview. May this work count for the kingdom, may our efforts matter in the light of eternity."

I've prayed this prayer a hundred times, but as I sit and attempt to quiet my spirit, a series of images flashes across the backs of my eyelids—I see Shirley the Lush, the homeless man on the sidewalk, and Chris, his blue eyes crinkling into nets as he smiles.

"Concentration, Lord," I repeat, breathing harder. "Not daydreams. Please, help me focus."

"Emma Rose?"

I lower my hands. Celene stands in the doorway, a manila folder in her hand. "Josh dropped these letters off for you. We have an entire file of folks who've written us about marital infidelity. He thought this would be a good place for you to start."

Of course, I should have thought of checking the correspondence files. Televangelists receive thousands of letters every week, most of them supportive. But along with checks for five, ten, and fifty dollars, people also write to us about problems ranging from explosive tempers to shopping addictions. When letters began to pour in during our first year on the air, Abel asked several Christian counselors to create form letters that could be adjusted slightly and sent as personal replies to viewers, complete with a freshly inked Abel Howard autograph provided by SigTech 4000, a top-of-the-line signature machine. Most of these replies address the problem in general terms, then urge the correspondent to seek help from a local Christian counselor. After the reply has been sent, workers in our mail department carefully file the original letters by topic.

The file in Celene's hand is bulging.

I stand to take it from her. "So many letters about swinging? I had no idea."

She snorts softly. "The file is more general than that, but

this is only one year's worth of letters from people whose spouses had an affair. We got a slew of them when that reality show about temptation aired, remember? Infidelity was a hot topic back then."

How could I forget? I thought Abel was going to burst a blood vessel last year when a national network aired *Tahiti Temptation,* a reality show where contestants wagered on the faithfulness of married couples thrust into alluring situations.

I take the file and lower it to the center of my desk. "Before I get into this, I think I need a cup of coffee."

She smiles. "Want me to bring it to you?"

"I'll get it myself. But you can lead the way if you need one, too."

"Heavens, yes. I've a hunch the Reverend's about to drag us through the mud again. I get a slimy feeling just reading about all this stuff."

As I step around the desk, I think about how uncomfortable I felt with Shirley the Lush breathing brandy down my neck.

"More than you realize," I tell Celene. "I know what you mean."

By four-thirty, I feel as wrung out as a ten-year-old washcloth. I've spent the greater part of the afternoon on the phone with women whose names I pulled from the correspondence file. While most of them were delighted to hear from Emma Rose Howard, few of them wanted to talk about the issues that spurred them to write us in the first place. Even after I promised anonymity, most of them dragged their feet.

I can't blame them; I know only too well the pain of dredging up the past. But in the last few days I have also learned that from pain can come healing, restoration, and profound joy.

So I persevere. We only need two or three volunteers, so after I jot down the third willing woman's name, I drop my pen and press my fingertips against my eyelids, grateful to be done but silently regretting that Abel has chosen this particular crusade.

Marital infidelity is a messy business, nearly as distasteful as pedophilia and homosexuality. Two years ago our ministry launched a boycott against Disney World because the head honchos at Disney decided to offer gay and lesbian employees insurance benefits usually reserved for legal spouses. We also protested the Gay and Lesbian Day held each year at Disney World in Orlando.

That campaign drew tremendous heat from believers and unbelievers alike. Even the Christian community fractured into camps, and the most outspoken of them sent representatives to Wiltshire to advertise their positions. One Sunday, representatives from the leather-clad Dykes on Bikes paraded up and down the north side of Sinai Street while the "True Believers" marched on the south side. I was dumbfounded to discover that the "True Believers," who professed to love the same Jesus I do, were holding signs predicting hell for "queers" and anyone who reads anything other than the King James Version of the Bible.

Our church people walked up the hill in silence that day, sobered by the reality of the twisted world around us. Our TV director sent the cameras outside to catch shots of the north and south sides screaming at each other, and somehow God used the entire mess. More people than usual walked the aisle that day, and our incoming mail rose fifty-two percent in the week following the airing of that program.

But the trouble didn't end after that memorable Sunday. Abel kept preaching against Disney, and as a result we were vilified in the press and even ridiculed by a late-night television comedian. I didn't see that particular show, but the NBC guy tried to portray me as a wannabe Tammy Faye Bakker. The joke fell flat, Josh informed me, probably because Tammy Faye and I are as different as salt and pepper.

By the time that campaign ended, Disney World had not changed its employment practices, the Gay and Lesbian Day continued to be held each year (Disney had never actually sponsored it), and our contributions had increased sixty-four percent.

Though Abel was privately disappointed that the boycott

did not effect a change at Disney, he was quick to point out that God did use our efforts. We gained viewers and contributors, so the gospel reached more people than ever, new people committed themselves to supporting God's work, and we had additional funds with which to continue our ministry.

I think Abel is hoping for even greater success with the campaign against Books & More bookstores. Whether or not he keeps *Your Wife or Mine?* out of those bookstores is not nearly as important as spotlighting the importance of marital fidelity, picking up new viewers, and exposing hundreds of new people to the gospel of Jesus Christ.

He hasn't shared all the details with me, but Celene tells me Josh outlined the master strategy in a staff meeting this morning. Abel is planning to publicly launch a campaign to boycott Books & More bookstores in a huge press conference to be held Sunday afternoon, right after the eleven A.M. service. He will promote the boycott in every *Prayer and Praise* program airing in the month of March, and between now and the beginning of April, Abel will grant dozens of interviews about the impact of Christian shoppers on the national economy.

In addition to the media onslaught, our viewers will be inundated with letters—at least one per week, each of them professionally designed by our direct marketing company and written in black ink with rivers of red underlining and truckloads of exclamation points. Those letters, sent to anyone who has ever written us, will bring in contributions with which we can buy more airtime to reach even more souls. Nothing will be wasted—even letters that are never delivered will be returned to us with a U.S. Postal Service change-of-address sticker, enabling us to update those all-important names on our mailing list.

"Direct mail is not inappropriate for ministry." Abel's voice rises from my memory. "We are using the tools of the world, in some cases even using the world's money, to further the cause of Jesus Christ. This is business for all the right reasons."

I am pondering the dollar value of a single name and address when I hear Mozart playing from within the depths of my purse. I dig for my cell phone. Few people have this number—only Abel, Celene, Josh, and now, Chris.

I know who's on the line even before I look at the caller ID.

"Hello?"

"Emma?" His voice sounds as breathless as mine.

"Chris!" The room swirls around me in a mad moment of panic—after all, I gave him this number for emergencies. "Is everything okay?"

"Everything's fine. I . . . just wanted to call."

I lean back in my chair as the room settles into proper perspective. My son has decided to call me. Nothing could be more natural.

"Did you have a good day?" I ask.

"Yeah." I hear a smile in his voice. "Very good. I'd love to tell you all about it in person if . . . well, if you have the time. And if you want to see me again."

"I would *love* to see you."

"Great." He chuckles, and I know I have never heard a more beautiful sound. "I don't want to keep you out late again, so are you free tomorrow morning?"

I glance at my calendar. I'm supposed to lead a ladies' Bible study in the chapel from nine to eleven, but Louise Hammel would love to cover for me. She's a natural teacher.

"I can get free."

"That's cool. Listen, I was trying to think of a way to show you the kind of ministry I do, and I think I've figured it out."

I laugh. "Don't tell me you hired a television crew to follow you around."

"Hey, that's close! But I only have a camera. So today I shot some pictures of the people the Lord has laid on my heart, and I'd love to show them to you. I dropped them off at a photo shop downtown, and I was thinking you could meet me there when they open tomorrow morning. I'll pick up my pictures, then we can walk to this little diner next door and have breakfast. My treat."

"You don't have to treat me."

He laughs again. "It's the least I can do. And I promise the diner is nice. No drunks, no smoke. Just eggs and grits and a wisecracking waitress named Annie."

Is there anyone in town he hasn't met? My gaze falls on the photo of Abel on my desk; for a moment I can see Chris's features reflected in the glass. "Sounds wonderful."

"It's Jackson's Photo on Sixth Street, and it opens at eight-thirty. Can you be there that early?"

"Wouldn't miss it. By the way, Chris?"

"Yeah?"

"I got your note . . . and thanks."

"I meant it."

We say good-bye, and as I hang up the phone I realize I'm experiencing the same fluttery feeling I used to get at the prospect of seeing Abel after a long day of classes. The situation is vastly different, but the emotion is the same.

I've fallen in love with my son, and I can't wait to see him again. I'd love for Abel to meet him, too, but he joins the Wiltshire Pastors Association for prayer and breakfast every Tuesday morning, and I know he won't want to miss the meeting.

I drop my cell phone back into my purse and make a note to have Celene call Louise about the change in plans.

CHAPTER TWELVE

S ix o'clock finds me and Abel at the kitchen bar eating dinner from takeout containers. Rarely do we eat at home, and even more rarely do I cook.

Abel is scarfing down his order of grilled shrimp and pasta because he's due back at the church in less than an hour. Esther had to schedule a counseling session with a Sunday school teacher accused of teaching incorrect theology, and though my husband would rather be planning his press conference, he will not forsake this duty. Abel, keeper of the sheep, does not hesitate to rebuke a wanderer when necessary.

I am picking at a dish of grilled shrimp and vegetables, my

thoughts a thousand miles away. Tucked beneath the cabinet in front of us, a mini-television tuned to a twenty-four-hour news channel provides background noise while we sit in our separateness.

I'm longing to tell Abel about my upcoming meeting with Chris, but the grim line of his jaw assures me he's not in the mood to discuss my newfound son.

He lifts his head, however, when the ticker for breaking news scrolls across the bottom of the screen. The camera cuts to a somber reporter standing outside a lovely home behind a manicured lawn. "We have just heard," the reporter announces as a photograph of a smiling black man appears in the upper right corner of the television, "that Joseph Greenly, newly appointed head football coach for the Cincinnati Bengals, was gunned down in the driveway of the residence behind me. A telephone tip attributes the shooting to the World Church of the Aryan Brotherhood, and police are scouring this neighborhood for clues. People here have been stunned by this cowardly act."

Abel punches the remote, lowering the volume. "I hate hearing that kind of news. Those racists give all churches a bad name."

I cannot tear my eyes away from the silent television. The screen is now featuring a family photograph—Greenly, his wife, and four stairstep children, all young and adorable. The picture dissolves to a shot of what must be the Bengals locker room, where a group of players from all races have come together to mourn the loss of a talented coach and a good man.

The image of the children floats before my eyes. I have a son, too, and at this moment I can't imagine the pain of having a family member ripped from my life.

Abel waves his hand before my eyes. "You home in there?"

I focus on him. "Sure."

"Were you able to get some names for the interviews?"

I use my fork to spear a strip of green pepper. "I found three women who are willing to go on-camera. Two of them are here in Kentucky."

"No men?"

"Men aren't as willing to talk about infidelity, Abel. I was lucky to find the women."

He squeezes my elbow. "You do great work, Em. I'm sure nobody but you could have talked those women into cooperating."

Maybe I understood something of their pain. The words are so sharp for a moment I worry that I've spoken aloud.

Five days ago I told Abel about my past, but I gave him the condensed version. I have never shared the depths of my agony. I have never known the pain of infidelity, but I've known abandonment, fear, loneliness, starvation, illness, misery, and loss. He can imagine what I must have endured, but empathy is not one of Abel's gifts. Already I can tell he has tried to put my revelation out of his mind and move on with his life. He will throw himself into this bookstore boycott, directing all his attention and zeal toward uplifting fidelity in American marriages . . . while he ignores the growing rift in his own.

I stab another bite of grilled vegetables. "I heard from Christopher today."

Abel keeps chewing, then swallows. "Whatever for?"

"He wants me to learn about the ministry he's doing. So I'm meeting him in the morning for breakfast."

He pulls the tail from a shrimp with remarkable vehemence. "I don't understand how you can just go out and *do* ministry. What is he, a street corner preacher?"

I speak in the lightest voice I can manage. "That's why he wants me to see for myself. I'm not sure I understand, either, but I'm sure there are as many different ways to reach people as there are people."

Abel's gaze shifts to some interior field of vision I can't imagine.

"I asked Louise Hammel to take my Bible study group," I continue, my cheeks burning under his simmering disapproval. "I wouldn't shirk my responsibilities, Abel."

He says nothing for a moment, then drops his fork. With his gaze fixed to the silent television, he says, "'If you love your father or mother more than you love me, you are not worthy of being mine; or if you love your son or daughter more than me, you are not worthy of being mine.'"

For an instant I wonder why he thinks that quip is funny, then the truth hits me between the eyes—he's quoting *Scripture*. For the first time in our marriage, my husband is preaching at me.

Wavering between guilt and anger, I stare at him. "Abel Harrison Howard. How dare you insinuate that I love Christopher more than God."

He tilts his head. "Who are you putting first tomorrow morning? God or your son?"

"I hardly think missing one lesson is tantamount to idolatry." Unable to believe what I'm hearing, I swivel in my chair and face him directly. "I don't know how to make you understand, Abel. I know this is confusing to you; I know you can't relate. I have found the son I thought I had lost forever, but I'd love to share the experience with you. Come with me, meet him, see what a special young man he is—"

"I can't." He shifts his gaze as words fly from his lips like shrapnel. "I won't. I had nothing to do with your past, and I won't let you drag me into it now. A minister of the gospel should remain above reproach; he should avoid every appearance of evil and especially the taint of scandal."

My cheeks are burning, but I can't speak.

Abel picks up a glass of water. "If you won't avoid this man for your own sake, you should avoid him for the sake of the ministry. This is still a relatively small town, Emma, and someone is going to see you with this kid. Bad enough that he took you to a bar, but how can you go to breakfast with a man who is not your husband? The meeting may be perfectly innocent, but our enemies in the press would love to crucify us with speculation about that relationship. One photograph—just one—could cause us to lose donors. And I don't think you want me to go public with the full explanation."

His words resonate in the kitchen, clattering harshly among the pans hanging from the pot rack. As reluctant as I am to consider his viewpoint, my mind's eye conjures up the photo Abel fears. I hate to admit it, but he's right—in an unguarded moment I might lean toward Christopher or place my hand on his shoulder. How would that look to an outsider?

For so many years I have been careful not to give anyone reason to criticize—I don't buy cooking sherry because people will think I'm drinking, I don't linger in the magazine aisle of the grocery store because *Soap Opera Digest* and *Cosmopolitan* are stacked right next to *Good Housekeeping*, I don't entertain men at our home unless Abel or Celene is also in the house. We don't subscribe to HBO because it carries programming that qualifies as soft porn; I have never joined any community women's clubs because I might be invited to a party where drinks might be served.

I don't even say "darn" because it sounds too much like something else.

I turned my back on the old life and have worked so hard to be good in my new life. I have trained myself to obey the biblical admonition to walk circumspectly, yet all those years of discipline have fallen away in the light of my miracle son.

Abel is right, of course. I must be more careful.

My cheeks are burning as I lower my head and pick up my fork. "I'm sorry, Abel, if I've caused you any distress. I'll be careful, I promise. Tomorrow I'll tell Chris that any future meetings should be in a more private place. If he's going to stay in town awhile, maybe we could introduce him in a service so people will know who he is. We don't have to say he's my son, but we could say he's a minister visiting town for a few weeks—"

Abel's face flushes. "We are *not* putting an untested, self-proclaimed preacher on the platform!"

For a moment I can only stare at my dinner, then the missing pieces fall into place. It's not Christopher's presence in church Abel minds; after all, my son's forehead is not branded with a scarlet letter proclaiming him a prostitute's child. Chris could come to church alone any time and Abel wouldn't complain.

But if he appears with me . . . that's what my husband can't tolerate. Abel is afraid of my past and maybe even of my blazing love for my son. He's afraid of Christopher's freedom and my response to it.

I lower my fork as understanding dawns. I have never seen this kind of vulnerability in my husband.

After slipping off my barstool, I move to his side then

comb his hair away from his forehead with my fingertips. "I love you, Abel, in a far different way than I love Christopher. And I will do whatever I must to be a good wife, but you can't deny me the opportunity to know my son. I've spent the last twenty-something years denying him, and I will not deny him again. Besides, he'll be leaving eventually. He told me he lives a vagabond existence."

"Can't you see?" Abel's voice is hoarse, as if forced through a tight throat. "He's calling you to relationship, Emma. He wants your heart."

"And he has it . . . as do you." The realization strikes me as I pronounce the words. "Chris was born out of my sin, but he is innocent of it. And I cannot help but love him even more for seeking me out."

I press a kiss to my husband's cheek, then move into the living room, giving Abel space to gather his composure before he must leave to solve yet another of the ministry's problems.

Sleep eludes me that night even after Abel returns from his counseling session, undresses, and climbs into bed. Within ten minutes of eleven he is snoring softly; I am wide awake.

I set aside the devotional book I have been reading and swing my feet to the floor. The study lies on the other side of our bathroom, but as I walk through the darkness I stub my toe on a bag of powdered grout the tile man has left next to the tub.

Muffling my cry of pain, I limp the length of the bathroom. I have scarcely looked at the work the tile guy did today—one glance assured me the tiles around the tub were in place, so I assume he'll do the floor tomorrow—but right now my mind is occupied with more important things. Still limping, I slip through the narrow door leading into our study.

Outside the wide window, the streets of our gated community lie silent and still. A full moon in the east splashes our lawn with silver and black, and after a moment I see the nighttime security guard glide past in his electric golf cart.

Eleven o'clock and all is well in this sheltered village.

Bracing myself against the bookshelves, I switch on the lamp, then let my gaze glide over the spines of leather volumes. Our library holds an entire shelf of Bibles, probably more than three dozen, because publishers send us copies of their new editions every year at Christmas.

I take a random volume from the stack and notice that the publisher has embossed our names on the cover: Abel and Emma Rose Howard. The coupling of our names feels inappropriate—how can you share something as personal as a Bible? The one I use most—which currently sits on my office desk—is underlined, highlighted, and scrawled with marginal notes.

I open the Bible and riffle the thin leaves, hearing the faint snap and crack of pages still bound together by a strip of gilt edging.

A book is such a powerful thing. The one I hold in my hand has changed men and nations. Within this one volume, I am holding a record of the world's history and its future. Even men and women who choose not to believe it cannot dispute its influence.

What gives books the power to change the hearts and minds of readers? I have no trouble understanding why the Bible is powerful; the Spirit of God moves upon people as they read and he is the One who effects change. But what powers energized *Uncle Tom's Cabin*, *Mein Kampf*, and *Silent Spring*? Did Harriet Beecher Stowe, Adolf Hitler, and Rachel Carson realize how their words would change history?

I sink onto the settee in the office, holding the Bible on my palm as I consider Abel's latest crusade. He is moving against a single book that endorses an immoral practice, but could he be doing more harm than good? How many people would never know about *Your Wife or Mine?* if Abel doesn't mention it on TV throughout the next four weeks?

Christians are infamous for jumping into crusades against imagined evils. Among the many files in our correspondence department are folders marked "Procter and Gamble Hoax" and "Madalyn Murray O'Hair." Over the years we have received hundreds of letters about Procter and Gamble being a satanic organization (they're not) and Madalyn Murray O'Hair petitioning the FCC to take Christian programming off the air (she didn't). Add to those hoaxes countless letters about a boy named Brian Warner becoming Marilyn Manson because members of a church youth group shunned him (not true) and photocopied petitions from people protesting the "Second Coming Project," an attempt to clone Jesus (also untrue), and I can see why the folks in our correspondence department have grown wary and skeptical.

I can't blame them. Last year when another pastor launched an environmentalist crusade by asking "What would Jesus drive?" we found ourselves lumped in with other evangelists and pilloried in the press. Weeks later, we received a flurry of petitions to restore prayer in public schools despite the fact that our current president has done more to secure religious freedom on public-school campuses than any administration in a decade.

I rub my temple, where a nagging headache has begun to announce its presence. How can I criticize other people for inflaming public opinion when we are doing the same thing?

At least Abel is careful to check out rumors before responding to them. He objects only to situations that are offensive in the eyes of God. He is absolutely right when he says this book about wife swapping can cause great harm and marital infidelity is destroying the fabric of decent society.

But it's not the only sin running rampant through

America. There's abortion, and murder, and racism . . .

I sit at the computer and slide the mouse across the desk to wake up the hibernating monitor. Thanks to a cable modem, we are constantly on-line. It's a simple matter to open the browser and type in the URL for Books&More.com.

I type *Your Wife or Mine?* into a search field, and within a minute the book appears on my screen, complete with reviews. The first review praises the book in glowing terms and oozes with gratitude that someone is finally writing about swingers with understanding and compassion.

Well . . . that's a red flag. But not all of the reviews are complimentary, and the description of the book itself gives me pause. According to the blurb, the author is not promoting the swinging lifestyle, but exploring the mind-sets and morals of those involved in the practice. The book sounds more like an academic study than promotional propaganda, but perhaps the description is misleading.

On a whim, I go to Amazon.com and type in the same title. Yes, there it is—with only two reviews, one approving, one critical. I keep typing and clicking. The book is not listed at Barnes&Noble.com, but addall.com lists over thirty on-line bookstores where the title can be purchased.

So why aren't we protesting *all* these bookstores?

The pressure in my head increases. I click back to our Internet home page and stare at the breaking headlines. News of the murdered NFL coach flashes at the top of the screen with an update—police have tracked a suspect to a truck stop and surrounded the facility. They are hoping the alleged shooter will surrender without harming any of the people inside.

A headline scrawls beneath the main story: "Neighbor Says Suspect Is White Supremacist."

Something clicks in my brain as a memory from high school surfaces. I navigate back to the bookstore pages, where I type in the words "White Supremacist." At least seven titles appear. Next, I do a search for *The Anarchist Cookbook*. There it is, a slim volume of recipes for bombs, complete with a high sales ranking, nearly two hundred reader reviews, and a letter from the author.

I lean forward to read the fine print. The author has posted a note explaining that he wrote the book as a nineteen-year-old at the height of the Vietnam War. The work was copyrighted in the name of the publisher, and when the author matured, married, and became a Christian, the publisher ignored his pleas to have the book taken out of print.

A few more clicks on related titles bring me to a volume on how to manufacture and disperse poisonous substances, including nerve gases, anthrax, ricin, and botulin toxin. A note informs me that a Japanese cult uses this book as their lab manual.

I click on other topics, searching my memory for names I have heard in the news. At nearly all the on-line bookstores I find books by noted white supremacists, black revolutionaries, and leading practitioners of Wicca. I have no trouble finding copies of *The Protocols of the Elders of Zion*, the libelous book used by Hitler's regime as justification for murdering over six million Jews, and *The Satanic Bible.*

Seeking relief, I type in the URL of an on-line Christian bookstore, but after perusing the titles I discover that Abel and I disagree with several philosophies represented on the cybershelves. There are books about prosperity theology (*Pray and Grow Rich!*), volumes both supporting and decrying Harry Potter (how can both be correct?), and biographies of preachers who cared more for expanding their earthly kingdoms than advancing the kingdom of God.

Leaning back in my chair, I stare at the glowing computer monitor. If we were to lambaste every book with which we disagreed, we'd wear ourselves out . . . and look as much like intolerant hatemongers as the racists who murdered that unfortunate football coach. If we were to boycott every bookstore selling those books, we'd have nowhere to shop.

Jesus did confront sin when he saw it . . . he was honest with the woman at the well, he did not excuse the woman taken in adultery, he did not dismiss Zacchaeus's greedy cheating . . . but in each of those cases, he was gentle in his honesty and his confrontation. As I search my memory of the Scripture, I try to think of situations where Jesus became angry or confrontational—when he chased the moneychangers out of the temple, rebuked the Pharisees, and cursed the unfruitful fig tree.

He confronted the religious people—and an unfruitful tree—with righteous anger. He met sinners with loving firmness and truth.

For the first time in our marriage, I find myself questioning my husband's methods.

The little gremlin pounding in my head increases his volume and tempo. I click back through the secular bookstore pages and close my eyes, suddenly weary of my excursion through titles sympathetic to immorality, pedophilia, rampant consumerism, hedonism, and debauchery.

Why are we surprised when sinners sin?

Christopher's question haunts me. Why, indeed?

CHAPTER THIRTEEN

The sun struggles to rise Tuesday morning; by seven-thirty it is barely glowing through a cloud-dark sky. Abel and I part after exchanging the fewest possible words. He reminds me that he needs me to proof a draft of a letter about the bookstore boycott; I counter with a promise to return to the office as soon as possible. I even promise to bring him a cinnamon roll from the diner if they have rolls hot from the oven, but not even the offer of his favorite food penetrates the tent of grimness that encloses him.

As I park at the curb in front of a boarded-up dime store, I remind myself to ask Christopher why he is so fascinated by our decaying downtown. Ten years ago the streets would have been crowded by this time on a weekday morning, but I have no trouble finding a vacant spot on Sixth Street.

Chilly fingers brush my cheek as I get out of the car and slip two quarters into the parking meter. Above me, a swollen sky sags toward the gray buildings. I would rather be meeting Christopher under sunny skies and warm breezes, but I would not exchange this moment for the world.

Careful not to overlook Jackson's Photo, I take off down the street and clutch my coat collar to ward off the frigid wind. It's not cold enough to snow, thank goodness, but in this part of Kentucky the temperature can drop in a flash if the winds change.

I am reading signs when my eyes spy a dilapidated hanging board shaped like a coffee cup—Chris said the place was next to a diner. I quicken my pace and hurry forward, looking for the photo shop, then halt in mid-step.

Jackson's Photo lies behind a wall of iron burglar bars, through which I can see a window papered with what I can only describe as movie posters featuring photos of scantily clad women. A neon sign with three X's gleams from the window, while a cheery note hangs from suction cups on the door: *Open. Come in!*

I am wondering if I have managed to wander onto the wrong street when movement from behind the glass catches my eye. A balding man in a cardigan and reading glasses is standing behind the cash register and gesturing for me to come in.

I whirl away, my cheeks burning. I don't think I've ever consciously walked past an X-rated video store, and I've certainly never entered one. This has to be a mistake.

I clutch my purse, grateful that I remembered to recharge my cell phone. It's already eight-thirty-five and Christopher is not here, which means he's probably waiting for me in front of Arnold's Photo or Johnson's Photo Shack or something similar—maybe I wrote down the wrong name. In a little while he'll call and ask where I am. I'll tell him I'm a scatterbrain, and within a few minutes he'll come running down the street and profusely apologize for embarrassing me to death.

I'm standing on the sidewalk, my eyes intent on the intersection, when the first raindrops begin to fall. Big and fat, they splat on my coat and wet my cheek, the first spits of a major deluge. I look up in time to see that the threatening cloud has darkened to the color of weathered slate, then the skies open.

Shivering, I close my eyes. I should run back to my car, but what if Christopher comes looking for me on foot? I'll never recognize him in this deluge if I'm sitting a block away; it's as thick as fog, morphing people fifty feet away into gray, faceless figures. I could retreat to the wall, where the overhang provides a thin ribbon of shelter, but the thought of standing next to pictures of nearly naked women appalls me.

While I'm debating, I hear the metallic squeak of a door, then footsteps splash across the sidewalk.

"Lady, come inside." The man in the cardigan holds his umbrella over me. "You'll catch your death out here."

I shake my head. "I'm waiting for someone."

"You can wait inside and watch through the glass."

Abel would *die*.

"Thank you, but no." I strengthen my voice. "I would prefer to wait out here."

The man sighs heavily, then presses the handle of the umbrella into my palm. "Then at least use this. I can't have you catching pneumonia on my front stoop."

I would have protested, but surprise leaves me speechless. With wide eyes I turn as the bare-headed man splashes back through the rain and ducks beneath an absolute waterfall pouring from the tattered awning above his door.

I am still gaping when I feel the pressure of a hand on my elbow.

"Emma!" Drenched to the skin, Christopher draws me into a light embrace, kisses my wet cheek, then grins as he cowers beneath my unexpected shelter. "Didn't get your umbrella open in time, huh?"

"It's, uh . . ." Floundering like a fish out of water, I jerk my thumb toward the adult video store. "It's his. This man just came running out and gave it to me."

"That's George. You couldn't tell by looking, but he's got a real chivalrous streak in him." Christopher takes my arm and leads me toward the store. For a moment I think he's just moving me to the shelter of the awning, then he *opens* the door.

"We had to see George anyway," he says, pulling me forward. "He has my pictures."

Like a shell-shocked soldier, I am led into the kind of store that didn't exist when I was living on the streets. In those days lewd old men resorted to dirty magazines, dingy theaters, and strip clubs; if the posters are an accurate indication, this place offers magazines, videos, and interactive DVDs, all the latest in pornographic technology.

Caught by my son's firm grip, I follow Christopher into the room. We are standing in an aisle facing the counter with the cash register; behind me is a half-wall topped by a glass panel. For a moment the arrangement seems odd, then I remember that state law requires children to be shielded from the sight of X-rated materials in public places. A toddler walking in here would see nothing but a beige wall; a toddler in his father's arms, however, would take in rows and rows of videos and posters and magazines.

The warning sign at the entrance to the video area should have been posted on the front door—no, at the beginning of the *block*. No one under the age of eighteen should be permitted within a mile of this place.

Averting my eyes, I stare at the floor. Seemingly unaware of the moral cesspool behind him, Christopher calmly takes the dripping umbrella from my hand, closes it, and slides it across the counter. "Thanks for the use of the umbrella, George."

"No problem. The lady looked like she was drownin' out there."

"George, this is Emma. Emma, I'd like you to meet George."

Drawn by the sound of my name, I find myself mechanically offering my hand to the man in the rain-splattered cardigan. He takes it with surprising civility, then offers me a tobacco-stained grin. "You a friend of Christopher's?"

Thank the Lord, he doesn't know who I am.

After nodding helplessly, I lower my gaze to the spot where his belly is tugging at the lower button of his cardigan.

George releases my hand. "Christopher's a good lad. The world could use a few more like him."

I am struck dumb. And my son, who has not even turned to glance over his shoulder, seems completely oblivious to the sort of establishment he is patronizing.

The vendor turns, flips through a vertical stack of rectangular envelopes, then pulls one out and slides it across the counter.

"Here you go. Twenty-four color prints."

Though this transaction is perfectly legitimate, I can't bear to watch. I step back and stare at the black and white floor tiles.

"Well, George." A note of laughter underlines Christopher's voice. "I don't see any Disney posters on your wall yet. I'm still waiting for you to see the light."

George coughs slightly, then squeaks out a forced laugh. "Ah, Christopher. You never let up, do you?"

The door opens; a woman in wet tennis shoes and jeans comes in. In a quick glance I see that beneath her raincoat she's wearing a gold T-shirt emblazoned with the Wiltshire Warhawks logo, so she must have a son on the high-school soccer team.

I keep my head lowered, mortified that a woman would voluntarily enter this place, but I can't help overhearing her words.

"These are *yours*." I hear the sound of something sliding across the counter. "I found these in my bedroom, hidden under the mattress. I'd throw them all into a Dumpster, but then you'd come after me to pay for them, wouldn't you?"

Christopher seems to be counting out bills in his wallet, but George clears his throat with a phlegmy rumble.

"Uh . . . yeah, these are ours."

"I shoulda smashed 'em with a hammer." The woman's voice is so heated I'm surprised the videos don't spontaneously combust.

George clears his throat again. "Appreciate you bringin' 'em back."

"You people make me sick." She speaks in a soft voice

laced with venom. "I kicked my husband out, you know. I can't have that kind of filth in the house, not with two teenage sons. But now I'll have to deal with them and a divorce, all because you people make this kind of stuff available to men with dirty minds and too much time on their—"

"Lady, nobody put a gun to his head," George interrupts. "It's a free country. People can do what they want, and your husband wasn't hurting nobody."

"Are you kidding?" Her voice rises to a shriek. From the corner of my eye I see Christopher place a five-dollar bill on the counter, then he edges between me and the woman.

"My husband—this filth—has destroyed everything!" She clenches her fist and waves it in George's face, then she erupts into tears as something within her breaks.

Christopher picks up the packet of photos, then takes my arm and leads me toward the door. As we pass, I look at the woman's face for the first time. I know her—the woman is Eunice Hood, wife of one of our deacons. She's one of our people . . . and I saw her just the other night at the deacons' dinner.

Eunice does not see me—her hands are over her eyes, as if she would hide her tears of anger and shame. Her face is quite pale, with deep red patches at her neck and on her cheeks. Her wedding band twinkles at me from her left hand, but if what she said is true, she won't be wearing it much longer.

I don't know Eunice well, but I am suddenly overcome

by an urge to draw her into my arms. When I hesitate, Chris halts in mid-step. I stand behind Eunice for a moment, debating my options, then lower my head and move toward the door.

A hug might have helped her . . . but merciful heavens, what would she think if she found her pastor's wife in a pornographic video store?

I resolve to catch Eunice at church as soon as possible. If I don't see her in the crowd on Wednesday night, I might have Celene call her to my office. I can say, quite truthfully, that I am worried about her and would like to know how we can pray for her family . . .

Having resolved to wait, I hurry into the rain.

The coffee shop next door is, thank goodness, clean and neat as a pin. Annie the waitress is a small, quick woman with a tight white perm. She seats us at a table near the heater, and after a few minutes in its warm breath I feel myself begin to thaw.

Annie drops two plastic-covered menus on our table, then spins off to pour coffee at another station.

Chris doesn't look at the menu, he looks at me. "You okay? You seem a little upset."

I can't deny the truth. "That woman in the video store—I

recognized her as we were leaving. She's married to Tim Hood, one of our deacons. Abel's going to be so disappointed when he finds out. We'll have to ask Tim to step away from his leadership role, of course. And if that marriage breaks up, there are two children to consider. And poor Eunice . . . well, I just don't know what she'll do. She has no training, no job experience."

Chris's eyes shimmer with sadness, but I can't tell if his sympathy is for Eunice, Abel, or me. "Has your church no programs for wounded people?"

I'm startled by the question. "Well . . . the entire purpose of our ministry is to keep people from getting into these situations in the first place. We try to make sure people honor the Lord in their marriages, and we promote righteous living. Eunice's husband should never have set foot in that video store."

It seems a natural time to add a bit of advice. Surely a mother has the right to share a little wisdom.

"Chris," I begin, carefully choosing my words, "I can't believe you patronize that store when you could get pictures developed at Walgreens. You saw what kind of place it is. And maybe it's a good thing, even a God-thing, that Eunice Hood came in when she did. Now you see what kind of damage pornography can do."

His eyes soften as he smiles at me. "I don't go there to look at posters, Emma. And I don't rent those videos."

I can't stop a cough. "How can you help but see them? They're everywhere!"

He shrugs slightly, and transfers his gaze to the gingham tablecloth. "I'm a man, yes, and those pictures bother me, so I don't look at them. I go there to see George. And people like Eunice."

Instead of growling in frustration, I scrape my nails through my hair. I didn't raise this kid; I don't know how to read him. Just when I think we've landed on common ground, he launches a comment like that one and I'm left with no answer.

"Jesus never worked himself into a moral panic when he saw sin," Chris continues, calmly moving his cup toward Annie when she approaches with the coffeepot. "We tend to be staggered by sin, but Jesus was always calm in the face of immorality. He knew people; he knew they were sinners. The situations that ticked him off were those involving egotistical mind-sets, and he found more of those in the religious people than in the fallen ones."

I stare wordlessly across the table, my heart pounding. I'm not certain, but I think I've just been rebuked. First my husband throws Scripture at me, now my son.

Annie looks at me and waves the steaming pot. "Coffee, ma'am?"

"Yes, please."

Chris dumps two packets of sugar into his cup, then stirs. When Annie moves away, he leans toward me.

"You see, God built a sense of natural law inside man. Almost without being taught, people know that it's wrong to kill and steal and be unfaithful to their marriage partners. Nearly every religion in the world acknowledges that natural law."

Nodding, I pour sugar into my own cup.

"But Jesus introduced a completely revolutionary idea. The thing that sets Christianity apart, the thing most people don't get, is that Jesus asks us to give up our rights to ourselves. When we do that, when we allow him to have complete control, then we are actually living for him and not ourselves. If we fail to do that, we are like all the other religious people who follow a list of dos and don'ts they have attached to natural law."

Feeling as though I have stumbled into quicksand, I pull the menu closer and stare at the list of breakfast selections. Christopher and I share a genetic string and a common faith, but our differences might yet come between us.

"'I'm not asking you to take them out of the world,'" he says, his voice thicker than before, "'but to keep them safe from the evil one. They are not part of this world any more than I am. Make them pure and holy by teaching them your words of truth. As you sent me into the world, I am sending them into the world.'"

I look up, unable to make sense of his familiar but misplaced words.

"Jesus' prayer." Chris answers my unspoken question. "In the Upper Room, remember? That prayer was meant for us, Emma. We were never meant to hide in our churches or in our sheltered social circles. Jesus wants us to advance into the world, not retreat from it."

For an instant I cannot believe a twenty-eight-year-old unmarried kid is preaching to a woman who has been involved in ministry more than half her life.

My defenses kick in. "I have not retreated. Abel and I have spent our lives trying to reach the world."

"Really?" His lips are smiling, but his eyes remain serious. "I don't know you well enough to judge, Emma, and it's not my place. But in my travels I've seen too many Christians cocooning as if the outside world doesn't exist. They build huge churches, Christian schools, recreation programs, even medical centers for their members—anything and everything possible to ensure they never have to venture into the world Christ wants us to embrace."

I can quote Scripture, too, and a verse springs automatically to my lips: "'Come out from them and separate yourselves from them, says the Lord. Don't touch their filthy things, and I will welcome you.'"

"There's a difference," Chris says, his eyes gentle, "between walking in the world and wallowing in it. We are the light of the world, but we have hidden our light inside our buildings and Christian programs. When the world looks at us, too often they see petty, self-absorbed people who wag their fingers and scold everyone else for misbehaviors, then retreat into ivory towers—"

"Hold on a minute." I lift my hand. "You haven't lived long enough to see the big picture. Jesus established the church and he has blessed it through the ages. I'm not sure I understand what kind of ministry you're doing, but—"

I bite my lip, suddenly realizing that I have no idea how my son has lived or ministered. And the purpose of this meeting is for me to understand the things that have made him the man he is.

"I'm sorry." I spread my hands on the table in an attitude of surrender. "I'm cold and wet, plus I didn't get a lot of sleep last night. You're not finding me at my best."

"I love you anyway."

His smile makes my heart contract like a fist.

When the waitress approaches again I order two scrambled eggs and toast, no butter, then listen as Chris orders scrambled eggs and toast, lightly buttered.

"I learned to like it." He hands the menu to Annie, then grins at me. "My mom slathers butter on everything."

As the waitress whirls away, I attempt to guide him toward the purpose of this meeting. "I'm so glad you wanted to see me again, Chris. I felt like I talked mostly about myself the other night, and I want to know about you."

"I want to know you; I want you to know me," he says

simply, and suddenly I am hearing Abel's voice: *Don't you see? He's calling you to relationship.*

Well, why shouldn't I have a relationship with my son?

Chris swipes a hank of wet hair from his forehead, then pulls the folder of photos from his coat pocket. "I've been taking pictures so you can see the kind of work I do." He opens the folder and slides the first photo from the stack. I find myself looking at a picture of a young girl, probably fifteen or sixteen, but it's hard to tell with girls these days.

"This is Melinda." He slides the picture toward me. "She's only fourteen, but she was kicked out of her home about six weeks ago. She's using drugs, drinking, suffering the abuse of practically every man who enters the crackhouse where she's staying. But the house is warmer than the street, and I've been taking her a couple of hot meals every day."

I blink. "You're working for Meals on Wheels?"

He laughs. "No. I told you, I'm a minister."

"But you don't work for a church."

"Call me self-employed and God-directed."

I digest this answer; it's one I've never heard. "If you're self-employed . . . who pays your bills?"

His features soften; his smile becomes coy.

"God takes care of my needs."

"He feeds the birds and bees, too, but people need money to pay the bills."

"Well . . . have you ever heard of Lewis and Coombs?"

Of course I have. Lewis and Coombs is the biggest maker of household products in America. The company is older and bigger than Procter and Gamble; they manufacture everything from toothpaste to foot powder.

I gasp as the reality strikes home. "You are Christopher Lewis . . . of Lewis and Coombs?"

He nods slowly. "My father is Paul Lewis, the grandson of Geoffrey Lewis, the man who started it all with Edmund Coombs. The Coombs have all died off, but the Lewis family is still going strong. I'm an only child, but I have more cousins than I can count."

I bring my hand to my mouth, but a giggle slips from beneath my fingertips. And Abel thought Christopher came here looking for money!

"So you don't need help to pay the bills."

He grins. "My father supplies everything I need."

"But isn't he disappointed that you've chosen something other than the family business?"

Smiling, he tucks a lock of damp hair behind his ear. "In Dad's eyes, what I'm doing *is* the family business. The manufacturing part is just a day job. The real work of our family is ministering to the world where we find it, when we find it." He taps the photo of the young girl. "I find kids like Melinda all over the place. Last year I worked six months in Manhattan . . . on the Lower East Side."

I lean back against my chair as an unexpected warmth

surges through me. I can see the hand of God in this—my Lord does all things well. Imagine, Chris working to rescue people where I myself had been rescued!

I'm still smiling when the waitress approaches with our breakfast. The food smells wonderful, but I am far more interested in the young man sitting across from me than food or photos.

"Tell me about how you grew up."

Chris waits until the waitress sets his plate on the table, then he pauses to give thanks. As I bow my head, I am struck by the way he prays. He uses no formality or elaborate address, just "Thank you, Father, for this food and fellowship."

I keep my head down, waiting for the customary closing words, but they do not come. When I peek through my bangs, I see Chris unrolling his napkin.

I hurry to keep up with him.

"Growing up?" he asks. "I was as ordinary a kid as anyone."

I pick up my knife and smear jelly on my toast. "I imagine you went to a nice private school."

"No, public school, kindergarten through twelfth grade."

"That can't have been easy."

"I enjoyed it. When I reached sixth grade—right about the time peer pressure increases—I told anyone who asked that I was a follower of Christ. No one ever taunted me for my faith. In some ways, I think they respected me for taking a stand. And I did take a stand—I had to, after going public like that. I debated abortion and other life issues in speech class, talked about creationism in biology, brought up abstinence and purity in health ed. Sure, I bore a few taunts for my faith, but nothing I couldn't handle."

I stare at him. I'd been thinking that it couldn't have been easy for a fabulously wealthy kid to suffer insults from his envious peers, but Chris seems to be communicating on a different wavelength.

I take a stab at bringing the conversation back to familiar territory. "I like the way you say that—a 'follower of Christ.' It sounds . . . more active, somehow."

"My dad always said that. He said the rest of the world assumes 'Christian' means 'American,' and most Americans don't have any idea what Christians are really supposed to be."

At a complete loss for words, I glance at the photos. "Who's next?"

"Oh, right." Chris lifts the next picture and holds it before my eyes. I see a wizened middle-aged man in dark blue pants and, judging by the collars at his neck, at least three flannel shirts. A blanket is wrapped around his shoulders, a quilted plaid fabric that rings a bell in my memory.

It's the bum I saw sleeping on Fourth Street.

I force down a bite of toast. "He was outside O'Shays."

"Yeah." Chris's smile is as innocent as a two-year-old's. "His name is Judd. I met him the other night, got him some coffee and solid food."

I rub the bridge of my nose. "But all Jim the bartender had was peanuts."

"Yeah, I know. So I took him to my apartment and pulled a few things out of the fridge. After a shave and a shower, Judd began to look a lot better."

I drop my fork as horror snakes up my backbone. "Chris, honey, you can't go around doing this kind of thing, even in Wiltshire. You got lucky this time, but some of those street people are dangerous. What if he'd pulled a gun or a knife or something? Why, he might have robbed you blind!"

Chris shrugs. "All he'd take is money."

"He could take your life."

Again he shrugs. But I'm steaming like an overheated radiator, so he pulls another photo from the stack in an obvious attempt to distract me.

His gesture works. I shove all thoughts of Judd aside and gape at the picture. It's the lush at the bar—what was her name?

"Is that . . . Shirley?"

"You know her?"

I transfer my gaze to Chris, convinced that this child-man is too naive for his own good. "Well, no, I don't know her, but I talked to her the other night."

"Then you know her story."

I shake my head. "We didn't get that far."

He is about to launch into what I'm sure will be a dazzling

tale of Shirley's woe when my purse begins to play Mozart. I lift a finger, silently asking him to excuse me, then I pull the phone to my ear.

Abel's calling. Josh wants to run through details of the press conference scheduled for Sunday afternoon, and they need me back at the church ASAP.

I drop the phone into my bag. "Sorry, Chris, but I need to run."

He pushes his chair back. "Want me to walk you to your car?"

I look through the glass door. The streets still gleam with wetness, but the rain seems to have stopped for the moment.

"Don't let your breakfast get cold. Eat up, enjoy it."

I reach for my wallet, fully intending to drop a twenty on the table, but Chris catches my hand. "It's my treat, remember?"

"Oh, okay." I smother a smile. "You know, I'm probably the only new mother in Wiltshire whose kid is wealthier than she is."

His grin deepens into laughter. "I don't own much more than a few books and the clothes on my back. But Dad supplies everything I need."

On an impulse, I bend and kiss his forehead. "Listen, I'd love to see the rest of your pictures and hear more about your work. And I want you to meet Abel."

"That'd be great. I really enjoyed his Sunday sermon." Chris slides the loose photos into the folder, closes the flap, and offers them to me. "I took these for you. There are some great stories behind those pictures—great needs, too."

"I'm sure there are." Touched by his thoughtfulness, I tuck the folder into the pocket of my purse, wave good-bye, and leave the coffee shop. And as I lower my head and hurry past Jackson's Photo and X-rated video store, I can't decide whether I am relieved or irritated to be called away from my sweet, naive son.

Chapter Fourteen

$\mathcal{I}$ find Abel in the TV studio at the back of the worship center. We televise our regular worship services, but for heart-to-heart messages and appeals, Abel wants our viewers to feel they are visiting with him in a more personal space. So the studio features an office set, where a pair of tall false windows look down upon a fiberboard desk artfully arranged with my photograph, a few typed pages, and a blank desk calendar.

Abel, Josh, and Celene are gathered around a TV monitor when I walk in, and over their shoulders I glimpse a scene of two couples lined up against the headboard of a king-sized bed.

Celene is the first to hear my approach. "There you are." I hear relief in her voice, and at the sound of it I realize Abel has not told her about my meeting with Christopher . . . which can only mean he hasn't told her *anything* about Christopher. If Celene's in the dark, Josh must be, too.

I give her a diplomatic answer: "I had a breakfast meeting." I lean over to squeeze Abel's shoulder, then nod to Josh. "You've been busy, I see."

Josh is as excited as a kid with a new toy. "This is an old movie—remember *Bob & Carol & Ted & Alice*? This is vintage stuff, but the visuals are just what we need to roll at the beginning of the telecast introducing our bookstore boycott. They're decent enough to air—not a lot of flesh or anything—but the idea comes across loud and clear."

I glance again at the monitor. Natalie Wood, Elliott Gould, Dyan Cannon, and Robert Culp are sitting in a bed with expressions ranging from bored to confused. I vaguely remember my mother mentioning this movie when I was a kid; the footage certainly seems dated now.

But it's just what Abel needs for his campaign—sanitized sin, perfect for driving home his point about the dangers presented in *Your Wife or Mine?*

"By the way, Emma . . ." Josh pauses to reach for a clipboard on the desk. "This just came in from the direct marketing folks. It's powerful, but I need you and the Reverend to look it over and sign off before I give them the okay for printing."

The clipboard contains a short stack of glossy double-spaced pages. The bold letterhead proclaims that the letter comes *From the Office of Abel and Emma Rose Howard*, and the Courier font is reminiscent of an old typewriter. I doubt any of our Praise Partners actually believe Abel or I typed this, but the old-style font reeks of the days when businessmen pecked out their letters on clunky old machines.

Dear Christian friend, the letter begins, *Emma Rose and I recently received the shock of our lives when we learned that a book called* Your Wife or Mine? *is being aggressively sold at Books & More bookstores, the largest retail bookstore chain in America. You probably have a Books & More store near [city-field]—I know we have one in Wiltshire, only miles from Sinai Church.*

Frowning, I reread the paragraph. I don't know that anyone is *aggressively* selling *Your Wife or Mine?* at Books & More—unless I'm mistaken, it was only one book on shelves containing thousands of titles. The direct marketing people tend to take poetic license when they lay out a case for action.

Make no mistake, the letter continues, *this book is designed to erode the fabric of our society by destroying the God-ordained institution of marriage. Such a book should never find a place in a family bookstore!*

When I called Barry Zilhoff, president of Books & More, Inc., I was told that his chain would not stop selling the book and

Books & More stores are, in fact, "committed to meeting the needs of its customers in every conceivable area."

Heavy red lines underscore the next sentence: *Do you understand what this means, [firstname]? Can you believe that the leadership of this company considers a handbook for swinging couples a "need" for our communities? This is outrageous! It is one more example of how far we have fallen away from the ideals established by our forefathers who intended that America should be a nation under God, a country committed to honoring divine principles in public and private life . . .*

On and on the letter continues. The direct marketing folks, writing under our names, go on to rail against liberal politicians, feminist mothers, delinquent fathers, television producers, and atheistic schoolteachers who *"have all contributed to the decline of American society. But ours is not a 'society' anymore—we're living in a cesspool! Emma Rose and I need your help to drain this sewer of the filth polluting our lives so we can clean up America!"*

The letter ends with a heartfelt plea for support—money to continue the fight against this sort of filth, and, if the reader is unable to contribute, we solicit their prayers.

Please, [firstname], reads the text above a replica of Abel's signature, *even if you cannot send a contribution, encourage me and Emma Rose by signing your name and returning the enclosed support card. When we see it, we'll know you have joined us in the fight against indecency, and we'll be able to tell the CEO of the Books & More chain that you are standing with us in this fight for righteousness.*

We are counting on you.

I lower the clipboard as an inexplicable sense of discomfort gnaws at my gut. That line about the store "aggressively selling" the book has to go. Such exaggeration is an outright lie. The rest of what they've written is true; I certainly can't find fault with their comments about the need for morality in our society.

But I can't help wondering what Christopher would say if he were reading this. He might say the entire letter is misleading because the average viewer has no idea that professional writers from an expensive direct marketing firm actually wrote these pages and spent hours quibbling over every exclamation point and underscore. Our viewers probably think their response cards come directly into our offices, when in fact we never see them.

And the way this letter asks recipients to reply . . . it's common procedure to request some kind of response, because that's how direct mail companies judge the success of a campaign. A ten percent response rate is phenomenal, five or six percent is pretty good. Most of the people who send in a card also enclose a check, and even small amounts add up.

I know that thousands of pieces of mail flood our correspondence department every week—hundreds of women pour out their hearts to Emma Rose Howard and receive a channel letter in reply. But how else can we handle the situation? Too many letters crowd our mailroom; there's no way I can read and respond to them all.

I close my eyes as guilt pricks at my soul. What if Christopher had written instead of calling? If he wrote a letter as guarded as his first phone message, he would never have reached me.

"So, Emma, what do you think?"

My eyes fly open. Josh stands in front of me, his hands in his pockets, a confident grin on his face.

"Well . . . the line about Books & More aggressively selling that book needs to be cut. That's just not true."

The corner of Josh's mouth tightens. "They were pretty aggressive in their defense of it when we called them."

"But that's not the same thing as aggressively selling it."

Always the peacemaker, Celene lifts her hand. "I'll bet they will be aggressively selling it once the publicity begins. They've refused to ban it . . . so once news of this campaign hits the papers, you can bet that book will be front and center in their stores."

"But is that what we want?" I look at Abel, who must make the final decision. "If we give this awful book publicity, aren't we indirectly encouraging sales? Nobody had ever heard of this title until we got that letter from Mr. Keit. But if we go on the air and talk about it, all the people who support banned books will put it at the top of their lists. People who could care less about wife swapping will buy a copy just to defend their right to read whatever they want."

Abel's brows knit together in a scowl. "You're way off base, Em."

"Am I? I don't think so." I tilt my head, thinking of all the questionable books I discovered in my Internet search last night. If we must protest a book, I can think of far more dangerous books than *Your Wife or Mine?*

I hand the clipboard to Josh, then lay my hand on my husband's arm. "Honey, I don't think this bookstore boycott will do the cause of Christ any good. It may actually hurt."

Three heads turn toward me as if they are controlled by a common string.

"What?" Josh glances at the clipboard. "What else is wrong with this letter?"

"It's not just the letter." I look to Celene for help, but she seems as puzzled as the men. "I'm bothered by the entire idea. I looked that wife-swapping book up on the Internet last night, and no, it's not a book I'd recommend to anyone. But it's no worse than dozens of other titles I found in several other bookstores. Are we going to boycott them all?"

A line appears between Abel's brows. "If something is depraved, we need to resist it. Are you saying we should sit around and keep our mouths shut?"

"No, it's just . . ."

Why are we surprised when sinners sin?

I draw a deep breath. "I'm beginning to think the world won't understand our frame of reference. A few years ago, maybe, but things are different now. I mean, have any of us even read the book? I saw a description on-line, and from what I can tell, it doesn't advocate infidelity as much as it examines the practice from a social and psychological perspective. I didn't see anything to make me think it's a how-to guide for immorality."

The line between Abel's brows deepens. "I talked to Mr. Keit on the phone, and he said the book definitely does not condemn infidelity. The author says people who do this are merely maladjusted; he takes the position that while spouse swapping may not be for everybody, to each his own—"

"Okay, Abel, but—"

"Sin is sin, Em, and I've been called to preach against it. I can't sit back and let the world change its standards just because some expert changed the terminology. Wife swapping is not maladjustment, it's adultery; abortion doesn't kill a fetus, it kills a baby; gays are not happy, they're people who distort what God intended—"

"All right." I throw up my hands, acknowledging defeat. "But I think we're going to take heat for this one. They'll accuse us of censorship."

Abel snorts. "As if they've never censored Christian books—"

Celene and Josh have fallen silent, waiting to see who will win this battle of wills. But Abel will always win because God called Abel to ministry, and me to Abel. My husband must do what he thinks God is calling him to do. As his wife, I can advise him, but then I must stand back.

I meet my husband's gaze. "I won't argue with you."

"Good."

I close my eyes as my memory flits back to the image of Chris bending beside the homeless man on the street. People respond to him, not because he's on a crusade, but because they see how he cares.

People responded to Jesus for the same reason.

"I just want to say one thing before I go." I speak slowly, spacing my words for maximum impact. "What will this campaign do to bring people into the kingdom of God? That letter"—I point to the clipboard in Josh's hand—"may result in new names, more money, and a lot of publicity, but those things will be the result of human efforts. Will this campaign make the world hunger for Jesus? Somehow I doubt it."

I turn and begin to walk away.

"It's not our job to make Jesus look good," Abel calls after me. "He's the fairest of ten thousand; he doesn't need our help. He's called me to preach against sin, Em, just as he did. Do you think the Pharisees were attracted to him when he called them snakes and vipers? No, but still he told them the truth. He never pulled his punches, never ran away from a fight."

I step outside the heavy black studio door and lean against

it, reveling in the quiet of the hallway. I'm not sure what happened in that encounter, but I feel as if I've spent the last seventy-two hours on a tilt-a-whirl.

The world may never look the same to me again.

I'm in the break room, a converted closet off the office hallway, when the door opens. Celene crosses her arms when she sees me, then lowers her gaze to the carpet.

"What's up?" I ask, recognizing the body language that always accompanies somber news. After I left, Abel may have said something to Celene and Josh about Chris . . . but I have no idea what he'd say.

"The Reverend says you've been under a lot of pressure." Celene raises her gaze to meet mine. "He thinks you need to take some time off—maybe stay home and just relax awhile."

"I see." I lower the coffeepot to the burner, then pick up my steaming mug. "Did he mention how I came to be under all this pressure?"

Celene takes a half-step back. "Um . . . I didn't ask. But, you know—" She looks at me with such open friendliness that for a moment I am tempted to let the story of my past spill out.

But for Abel's sake, I have to be careful.

"You know I consider you a friend," Celene says. "And

though I know you and the Reverend are as close as bark and a tree, I'm sure there are times when you'd like to confide in a girlfriend." She lowers her voice to a whisper. "You can trust me, Emma. I wouldn't betray a confidence."

I am honestly touched by her assurance. "I know you wouldn't, Celene, and I appreciate the offer. But I've been dealing with some issues I can't share without Abel's permission, personal matters that really shouldn't affect anyone else."

A small grimace of pain crosses her features, as though I have wounded her.

"Listen." I lean against the counter, hoping to soothe her feelings. "There's nothing I'd like better than to tell you about all the crazy things that have been happening to me lately. But, frankly, I'm not sure I'm thinking straight. The Lord is showing me things I never dreamed I'd see, leading me to places I've never been. I'm beginning to question things that always seemed right—"

"Doubts come from the devil." Celene nods, secure in her conviction. "Tell the enemy to leave you alone."

I shake my head. "These aren't doubts, Celene. I've never believed more in the sovereignty of God. Lately, though, I've begun to wonder what God really wants of me . . . and I know he's big enough to handle my questions."

Celene gapes at me like a woman who's just been told to prepare for an IRS audit.

"I'm going to be fine." I step toward the door and give her a smile. "Now, shall we go ask Louise how the Bible study went this morning?"

Obeying Abel's admonition to get some rest, I leave the church early and go home. The tile man's car is parked at the curb, so I call out a cheery hello as I enter the house. He doesn't answer, but he may not have heard me from the depths of the bathroom. Or maybe it's bad homeowner etiquette to speak to tile men while they're working.

I drop my purse on the kitchen counter and check the answering machine. Though we received twelve calls today, no one bothered to leave a message. Most of them had to be telephone solicitors who assembled our unlisted number on one of those random digit dialers.

Not wanting to disturb the tile installer, I go into the bedroom, kick off my shoes, and peek around the corner. The fellow is on his hands and knees in the bathroom, delicately placing floor tiles around the tub.

My first inclination is to honor the man's silence and back away, but a stray thought makes me hesitate. What would Christopher do, finding this man here? In the short time I've known him, I have never seen him walk by another human without trying to make contact in some way. Even at that awful video store, after I'd stepped back out into the rain, I saw him murmuring something to Eunice Hood.

I glance again at the tile man, whose white jeans are riding low and exposing more of his backside than is socially acceptable. Abel would ignore him. He'd be polite, of course, but once the man set to work Abel would maintain his distance, not wanting to interfere. If he found himself in a situation where he absolutely had to speak, he'd make small talk for a moment, then ask where the man went to church. If the fellow didn't immediately accept Abel's invitation to join us for worship next Sunday, at the completion of the job he'd find a gospel tract inserted in his payment envelope.

How many people actually read those pamphlets?

I search for a reason to speak, then pick up the shoes I've kicked into the corner. Stepping into the doorway, I lift my gaze from his receding beltline and focus on the fellow's ponytail. "Hello," I say, striving to make my voice pleasant, "will we be able to get to the closet tonight?"

"Sorry," he answers, "but I'll have to ask you not to step on these tiles till tomorrow morning."

What do you know, the man will talk to me.

"That's okay, we have other bathrooms, but all our clothes are in that closet." Goodness, did that sound pretentious?

Giving up on the closet, I drop my shoes to the carpet. "Um . . . can I get you anything? A soda, maybe? I think we might have some cookies in the pantry if you're in the mood for a snack."

Good grief, he must think I think he's poor and starving.

He turns, and his eyes are bright when he looks at me. "No, thank you, ma'am, I brought my lunch. But it's kind of you to offer."

Heat sears my cheeks. "Okay, then. If you need anything, just call, okay? I'll be in the den."

He shakes his head and returns to his tiles, but a warm feeling seeps through my belly as I reach under the bed for my slippers. He didn't seem offended, so what I said must have been okay. When and if he ever mentions that he did work for Reverend Abel Howard, perhaps he'll add that the Reverend's wife even offered him soda and cookies.

No, that's absurd. What I offered wasn't much, but it was more than I'd have offered last week.

And who can say what Christopher would have done? For all I know, his version of ministry might be befriending blue-collar workers down at the local bar where he is just one of the gang.

Why am I thinking these things about my son?

I go into the den, wrap a chenille throw about my shoulders, then sit cross-legged on the couch, reveling in a sudden sense of freedom. Maybe Abel was right; I did need a break. I can't remember the last time I sat down to watch daytime TV. Abel rails a lot about the garbage on television, but we rarely see any of it. When we do have the television on, Abel watches the news. When we were younger, he used to watch ESPN, but he hasn't had time to follow his favorite sports teams in years.

I pick up the remote and flick through channels. A series of images flickers across the screen, and my astonishment increases with every moment. On one channel I see a woman in red lace underwear and high heels slowly walking down a catwalk; another channel features a pair of big-breasted women wrestling in a mud pit. On another station a man wearing nothing but a strategically placed bow stands beside a billboard for a trendy clothing company.

The sitcoms are not much better. I flip through them slowly, trying to get a feel for each show, but as far as I can tell, they're all about twenty-somethings sleeping around, having babies, and happily accepting the lifestyles of their homo-sexual neighbors/roommates/relatives.

Abel is so right. Television is completely corrupt. The moral fabric of this country has eroded to the point that people don't know any better. Shame has all but disappeared, and public morality is now based on whatever prevalent opinion floats by on the wind. Heaven help the misguided man who kills a grasshopper on a reality show, but let's not say a word to malign the woman who candidly discusses her abortions with Barbara Walters.

Why are we surprised when sinners sin?

The thought strikes like a bolt from the blue, rattling me

to the core. I stare at the actors on a television show and hear the inane laugh track through a buzzing in my ears. Why is television corrupt? The answer is suddenly clear: because most of the people who write for it and produce it don't know any better. Because Christianity is no longer the salt preserving our nation and the remnant still following Christ has vacated the field of competition. We've withdrawn to the spectators' stands, content to complain and ineffectively boycott sponsors who can't understand why we're upset.

I was a sinner, I still *am* a sinner, and I often fall short of God's holiness. How can I hold the world accountable to a standard I don't always attian?

I'm sitting on the sofa, slack-jawed and stunned, when I hear my cell phone ring. Where did I drop my purse? I jump up and run toward the sound, praying the caller will not hang up before I can answer.

After finding my purse—and the phone—on the kitchen counter, I am delighted to discover Chris on the line. I have waited twice for him to extend an invitation; this time, I will do the asking.

"Chris! I'm so glad you called! I wanted to see you again, and I'd still love for you to meet Abel."

"I was hoping you'd say that."

I warm to the sound of pleasure in his voice. "Good. Listen, Abel and I always have Wednesday mornings off, so maybe we could meet somewhere for brunch? The Hilton serves a great breakfast buffet. If we meet before ten-thirty, I think we can catch it."

"Um . . ."

My heart sinks.

"The thing is, I promised Melinda I'd bring her some stuff tomorrow morning. We could always go somewhere after that, I suppose . . . Hey, you wouldn't want to meet her, would you? You two have a lot in common, and I think meeting you might give her hope."

Grimacing, I try to remember what he said about Melinda. She was the girl in the photo, the one who could have been twelve or twenty. I'd really rather not spend my day off talking to a runaway, but how can I say no?

"Okay." I shoehorn a smile into my voice. "I'll meet you first, then maybe we can join Abel at the Hilton. If we miss the buffet, that's okay. We'll just make it an early lunch."

"Thanks, Emma. I really do want to meet Abel, and I want to introduce you to Melinda before I go."

"You're leaving? So soon?" The words come out as an agonized croak.

"I have to go." A note of ruefulness lines his voice. "My father wants me to help him handle some family matters, and I can't let him down. But I'll stay in touch—I'll call whenever the Spirit leads."

I can't speak for a moment; disappointment weighs too heavily upon my heart. I don't know why I thought he'd be around forever; perhaps pride led me to imagine he'd be so enthralled with our relationship he'd never want it to end. I may have been secretly hoping Abel would eventually hire Chris, who would work in our church and be part of our lives forever . . .

Chris interrupts my pity party. "Let me give you the address."

I reach for a pen.

He rattles off the name of a street near the downtown district, and I scribble the numbers on a sheet of notepaper.

"Chris?"

"Yeah?"

"Thank you," I whisper, and I'm not merely thanking him for the assurance of continued contact. I'm thanking him for being the way he is, for persevering in his search, for loving me enough to overcome insurmountable obstacles. "By the way," I ask, "I've been wondering about something."

"What's that?"

"Why do you do ministry . . . well, the way you do it? You could always get a degree and work for a church."

"I have a degree in biblical studies." He names a prestigious seminary that would impress even Abel. "And don't misunderstand—though I love the body of Christ with all my heart, I don't think we can ignore those who are dying outside the body."

"People in the church are sick, too. You should listen to

the problems Abel deals with every week. Family problems, drug use . . ." My thoughts drift toward Eunice Hood and her husband's problem with pornography.

"I know church people have problems, but if they choose to trust and obey, they also have the answer. But what do people outside the church have? They're living in darkness, and most of them have no idea how lost they are."

I think of my next-door neighbor Cathleen. She's one of the people Chris is describing . . . she desperately needs Jesus, but she's completely unaware of her need. Worse yet, unless she comes to me and asks me to explain the plan of salvation, I have no idea how to reach her.

"I think I see what you mean, Chris. The church has programs to reach lost people who reach out for help, but—"

"What programs do you participate in, Emma?"

I laugh as I reach for my purse. A copy of our church bulletin is peeking from within the recesses of my bag, and it lists the more than two hundred weekly programs of Sinai Church.

With one hand I lift the bulletin and flatten it on the counter. "Well," I run my hand down the list of activities, "there's the TV program, of course. And we have Sunday school programs from the cradle to the grave. We offer a Scripture memory program for children, and our youth pastors are really on the ball with ministries for our students. There are Bible study groups for women during the day, and other groups for working men and women on most evenings. We run a summer camp for our children and teenagers, and couples weekends for married people—"

"But what do you do to reach people who aren't *in* your church?"

I make a face at the phone. "I just told you—the *Prayer and Praise* program is capable of reaching forty million homes."

"And that's good—assuming that the unbelievers in those homes are willing to watch your program. But what are you doing to reach those who aren't?"

I search the bulletin for a moment, then tap the appropriate listing. "Abel and the deacons meet every Monday night for visitation. Abel has always believed in visitation; it's how he built our church."

Christopher laughs. "So they get a lot of cards?"

"Sure, anywhere from twenty to thirty every Sunday morning. It takes fifty or sixty people to cover all the cards, plus they also try to do nonurgent hospital visits on that night."

"That's great, Emma. I would never criticize effective programs or the people who run them. But tell me this—what is your church doing to reach people who have never visited one of your services?"

My gladness shrivels like an emptying balloon. "Well . . . Abel and I used to visit all the newcomers in town."

"Do you still do that?"

Silence swells between us as I try to make sense of what he's saying. "Well, no. There isn't time. Abel has all these other visits to make. He has to constantly put out fires among the church people, he travels and speaks, and the TV program keeps us busy raising funds. Airtime is expensive, you know."

"We certainly can't expect one couple to reach an entire city. But your church is huge—how many members?"

"Ten thousand." The number is boldly printed in the bulletin, along with the offering amounts for each Sunday of the month.

"So what are those other ten thousand people doing? Surely you have programs to train your people to reach folks like Melinda and Judd and Shirley?"

Do we? We have classes that teach people how to share their testimony in two minutes . . . but how effective is a two-minute testimony delivered to a stranger? My thoughts shift to my neighbor. Cathleen could live the rest of her life next to me and die without knowing the Savior. I could, of course, go next door and deliver my two-minute testimony like a bomber delivering its cargo . . . but I'd probably be better received if I invited her to one of the special events at our church.

"We have special events." My mind fills with a series of images from our elaborate Easter pageant, the singing Christmas tree, and the Fourth of July spectacular, complete with fireworks, honor guard, and a gigantic flag that once flew above the U.S. Capitol Building. We've always said those presentations were gifts to our community, but I know the vast majority of those who attend are our own church members.

I also know there are people in Wiltshire who so resent the media attention given to Sinai Church that you couldn't pay them to cross the threshold of our worship center.

"I'm not trying to hurt you," Chris says, his voice low and soothing. "For a long time I was afraid to climb out of the nest, too. After all, it's cozy there, I was well fed, and I was happy being among friends-of-a-feather. But one day I clambered up on the edge, looked out at the world, and realized I was no longer a fledgling. I asked God to help me fly, and he's been guiding me ever since."

I remain silent as my mind reviews the list of programs Sinai Church has instituted to keep our people busy. Abel likes to brag that the lights at Sinai burn constantly, for even in the dark of night we have people working for the cause of Christ. They go to the church at all hours to stuff envelopes and attach "Clean Up America" pins to cardboard gift cards, but should they be doing more?

"Think about it," Chris says, jolting me out of my assessment. "When the average American is physically sick today, he goes to the doctor. If he's critical, he goes to the hospital. But where does he go if he's spiritually sick? The man who discovers a hole in his soul will try to fill it with anything and everything until he learns only God can fill that void. But he'll visit bars, singles clubs, the beds of other men's wives in search of meaning and fulfillment. Where are we Christians going to find those people? They're not in our churches. They're in the bars, they're in Kiwanis Clubs, they're leading PTAs and running for local office. The world's people are in the world, Emma, but too many Christians are hiding in the church."

"But the church," I pluck one of Abel's favorite sayings from the air, "is the only institution Jesus ever founded. He didn't give his life for the Kiwanis Club; he gave his life for the church."

"He gave his life for the *world*, Emma. I'm not denying that the church is our foundation, our strength. We're a body, and we need each other. But too many people are billeting at the base camp when Jesus wants us to advance onto the battlefield."

I lift my gaze to the ceiling, silently imploring heaven for help. Chris and I aren't arguing, exactly, but still I feel we're at odds again and I don't want to be at odds with my only child. "Abel understands this," I finally whisper. "That's why he's worked so hard to build Sinai Church. That's why we established a TV ministry. We are doing what God called us to do."

"God calls each of us to the same thing," Chris answers. "We are to surrender ourselves and conform to the image of Christ. By doing that, we become salt and light just as he was. I never planned to become involved in urban ministry; I just learned to see the people I encounter in my path. Along the way, I've realized that the world doesn't hunger for what most of our churches offer. The people I meet don't yearn for sermons or pageants or crusades against immorality, yet Christians do produce the one thing they desperately want and need."

I think I know what he is going to say because I've spent the last four days watching him. Still, I ask. "What?"

"Love." Ruefulness fills his voice. "Unfortunately, even in the church love is often in short supply. Christians who forget that Jesus calls us to give up our rights to ourselves are prone to wanting their own way. And where selfishness abounds, love withers."

I am suddenly grateful he can't see my expression. He couldn't possibly imagine what I've experienced in twenty-four years as a pastor's wife, but he's right. Though Scripture says the world will know we are Christians by our love for one another, I can't count the times I've had to moderate feuds between church members.

"When I meet an obedient Christian, someone like you," he says, a smile in his voice, "the human part of me figures everything's pretty cool with the world. But then I meet someone like Judd sleeping on the street, and the human part of me is depressed. But Jesus was never prone to those kinds of feelings. He knows there's hope for people like Judd, and he knows you aren't perfect. He sees us as we are, Emma . . . and that's what my ministry is. I go where the Lord leads and ask God to let me see people as they are."

I open my mouth, but no words come.

"And so," Chris continues, speaking more slowly, "whenever I meet a person and feel the tug of the Spirit, I ask myself, 'What can I do to show God's love?' Sometimes it's something as simple as offering a glass of water. Sometimes it's as easy as buying somebody a plate of bacon and eggs."

"And sometimes," my voice clots with emotion, "it means taking a man home with you and giving him your bed?"

"That's right." His voice is tender, almost a whisper. "Sometimes it means meeting your biological mother and putting her mind at ease."

With a heart too full for words, I stare at the fabric of my skirt as comprehension begins to seep through my confusion. Until this moment, Chris's behavior had baffled me; now his actions make perfect sense. Like a dandelion seed blown by the breath of God, he has drifted throughout life, sharing God's love where and when he could.

But how can people who are tied to responsibilities live that way?

"The key is being obedient," Chris murmurs. "It's not so difficult. When you see a need and hear the Spirit's voice, you obey."

Is it that easy? For him, maybe. For me . . . it's never that simple. I have too many obligations, too many demands on my time.

"I have to go." The words spring from my tongue almost

of their own accord. "Abel will be home soon, and I need to find something to make for dinner."

"All right, then. See you tomorrow."

As I lower the phone, I realize it's been a long time since I consciously stopped in my busy routine to listen for the voice of God. Oh, I've heard him pounding against the walls of my heart a few times, but how often have I missed his still, small voice?

I have spent my entire adult life doing what I thought Christianity required me to do while Chris has been walking with an ear cocked to hear the voice of God.

Such a simple concept . . . and so difficult to implement.

I'm not sure I can live that way.

Chapter Fifteen

I'm in the kitchen, taking pleasure in the aroma of sizzling bacon and buttery eggs, when Abel comes through the garage door. I wipe my hands on a towel as I greet him. "Hi, honey."

He comes toward me like a man approaching a bomb he expects to go off. "You okay?"

"I'm fine." I smile as I realize it's true—I haven't felt so energized in ages. Chris's random thoughts have done more to open my eyes than all the Bible conferences I've ever attended.

Abel places his hands on my hips and nuzzles my neck. "Bacon and eggs for dinner?"

I laugh as his whiskers brush my cheek. "It was all I had in the house—and who says you can't have breakfast for dinner?"

Actually, I cooked breakfast because after Chris's call I needed to do something with my hands. My thoughts were racing so much that I couldn't sit still, and it felt good to beat the eggs in a bowl and drop the bacon into the skillet.

Abel sinks onto a barstool and spreads his fingers over the flecked granite counter. "I think everything is finally ready for the press conference Sunday afternoon. Josh sent out the press releases, Celene gave the local stations a heads-up, and Esther organized all the quotes we've assembled from Books & More managers. The production guys are working on the video with the women you contacted, so that'll be ready on time. We'll hand out the quotes in a press kit beforehand, before you and I step onto the platform—"

"I don't want to be on the platform, Abel." I turn a slice of bacon in the popping grease. "I thought I made my feelings clear."

He lifts his fingertips from the counter. "Fine." His voice is clipped. "You don't have to be on the platform, no problem. I'll go solo on this one, and if anyone asks why you're not with me, I'll say you're taking a sabbatical."

"I'm always with you, Abel." I pull the last slice of bacon from the pan, then drop it onto a paper-towel-covered plate. "I'm your wife, so I'll always support you. I see what you're trying to do, but I don't think this is the way to go about it."

"And what would you do?"

At first I think he's being snippy, but when I look up I see honest curiosity in his eyes.

I pause to turn off the gas range. "I think I'd tackle the problem from the opposite direction. Barnes & Noble doesn't stock that book, did you know that? I think I'd begin the press conference with praise for that company, maybe even urge Christians around the country to patronize their local B&N. Economic power can be wielded both ways, so why not try urging people to spend money instead of saving it?"

"I can't tell our people to spend money at a secular company—they'll write and tell us they spent their monthly pledge money down at the bookstore. Besides, not everything at a secular bookstore is good, so if we send them there, someone's going to find a book about soap operas or rock music and raise all kinds of Cain. We'll get letters, Em; you know how our supporters love to write letters."

He shows his teeth in an expression that is not quite a smile. "We can't support anything secular. I might be able to send them to Christian bookstores—"

"There's not a Christian bookstore in this country that doesn't contain some book you'd disagree with." I spoon the still-warm eggs into a bowl. "So why not let people support what they like and not support what they don't?"

Abel snorts. "Have you taken a close look at the people around you lately? Too many Christians have developed a taste for too many bad things. They go to R-rated movies, they watch horrible TV—"

"So they need us to tell them what's right and wrong? I thought that was the Holy Spirit's job."

He gives me a look that is anything but tender. "That's not fair, Em. Some of our people wouldn't recognize the Spirit's voice if he broadcast through their microwave ovens. They're spiritual babies. We have to lead them because they don't know how to decide for themselves."

"What would you know about babies, Abel?" I speak in a light tone, but Abel flinches at the snap in my words.

"What are you saying?"

I drop the spatula and fork into the sink, then spin to face him, my hands rising to my hips. "I've never been a parent, but I've heard the purpose of parenting is to teach children how to think for themselves. And you can't shepherd your flock forever—sooner or later people have to follow Jesus and learn to listen for his voice."

Abel shakes his head. "That's easier said than done."

"Really? Well, maybe we need to listen more closely ourselves. I've looked at the people around me—what I see are a lot of nice folks trying to get through life like the proverbial monkeys that see no evil, hear no evil, and speak no evil. If we live in the world, occasionally we're going to see and hear evil. We might even brush up against it."

From some dark place deep in my memory, the image of

a drunken, abusive stranger rises into my consciousness. Despite the strong aroma of bacon, I can almost smell the whiskey on his breath.

I turn back to the sink and brace myself against the edge of the counter. If God brings another whiskey-soaked stranger into my life, will I be able to see him through the fog of unpleasant memories? If I can't handle my past, I'm the last person on earth who should be talking about brushing up against evil.

Jesus, help me.

I take a deep breath as the memory fades. With the Lord's help, I could talk to almost anyone. In O'Shays the other night, I didn't waste a thought on my past because I was too focused on meeting my son. In that video store this morning, I could have talked to George . . . if I hadn't been so embarrassed to be in such a place. If I keep my heart and mind focused on Jesus . . .

Unaware of my thoughts, Abel continues to preach at me. "We shouldn't have to live in darkness. We shouldn't have to pay good money for bad books."

Sighing, I run my hand across my face, brushing the last remnants of the sordid memory from my mind. "No one is telling anyone to buy bad books, Abel. It's just . . . well, I've been wondering if we've done our people a disservice by keeping them squirreled away in the church." I turn to face him. "If our members attended every program we offered, they'd be at the church ten or twelve hours a day, seven days a week."

"And what's wrong with that?" Abel lifts a brow. "We are to center our lives around the Lord, we are commanded to fellowship together, we are to build up the body of Christ."

"Going to church does not equal living for Jesus. Church is part of the Christian life, but it's certainly not all of it. It *can't* be all of it."

I drop the skillet into the sink, where it clatters with more noise than I expected.

"We have visitation programs." Abel lowers his gaze. "We go into the community. We visit prisons and hospitals—"

"I'm glad you go into prisons and hospitals. When I had my appendectomy, our church people nearly killed me with kindness." I pull two plates from the cupboard and set them on the table. "But I know how few community contacts are made in the hospitals. Most of the time our pastors visit our church members, say a prayer, and go on their way."

"That's not true—we visit anyone who requests a pastoral contact."

"And how many lost people even know what a *pastoral contact* is?"

The question hangs in the silence. I know the answer because I've seen the hospital visitation reports on Esther's desk. Every once in a while we will get a call from a frightened hospital patient who is reaching out for spiritual guidance, but our pastors are so busy taking care of our ten thousand church members that they rarely have time to befriend sick people who might not even know they're in need of spiritual healing.

Abel thumps the counter as I spoon eggs onto a plate. "Well, your idea about sending our people into other bookstores just won't fly. It's harder to convince people to spend money than not to spend it, and besides—if some little lady gets ahold of a book with profanity, we'll never hear the end of it. After taking such a strong stand against immorality on television, the media would fry us."

"I don't like profanity," I scrape the bottom of the bowl, then spoon the dregs onto Abel's plate, "but I don't think anybody's going to fall captive to the dark side if they happen to read a bad word. Jesus didn't walk around with his fingers in his ears."

Abel presses his lips together. "Garbage in, garbage out, Emma. Scripture tells us to think on whatsoever is lovely, true, and of good report. Furthermore, it says we'd be better off at the bottom of the sea than in a position where we cause a little one to stumble."

"A child, yes." I wave the salt and pepper shakers over our plates. "Or a weaker brother who's such a new Christian that hearing profanity or the like might tempt him to fall back into his old lifestyle. But you've been a Christian most of your life, Abel, so you're not a weaker brother."

Abel looks at me as if I have suddenly begun to speak a foreign language. "What's gotten into you, Em?"

I sink onto the stool next to his, then lower my cheek to my hand. How can I explain thoughts and ideas I don't understand myself? My life has looped backward in the last few days, and in meeting a part of my past I have begun to question my present.

I close my eyes and try to force my confused emotions into order. "I honestly don't know. I only know that lately our methods seem . . . ineffective. In our quest to be holy and pure and protected, have we closed ourselves off from the people we need to be reaching?"

His hand, comforting and strong, falls upon my shoulder. "Don't we send thousands of dollars to the mission field every year? Aren't we spending our lives in an effort to broadcast the gospel throughout this country? Over forty million people could watch our program every time it airs, Em. We've done our best to be faithful and do our part, and I'm trusting God to do the rest."

He's right, of course. My husband has always been able to slice through my emotional fog and see the heart of the matter.

I sniffle, rub my nose, and lift my head from his hand while we bow our heads for grace.

"Our Lord and Father God," he prays, "we thank you for this food and the day you have brought us through. Give us strength for the day ahead, Lord, and wisdom to know what we should do. Guide us, protect us, and keep us on the path that is straight and narrow. I ask these things in the name of my Lord and Savior, Jesus Christ. Amen."

The prayer has changed the subject, and the set of Abel's jaw tells me he has no desire to talk further about his press conference, boycotts, or books of any kind. He searches the table a moment, then walks to the refrigerator and pulls out a bottle of catsup.

I look away, squinching my nose. I've never been able to eat catsup on eggs; Abel can't tolerate them any other way.

"Sorry." I pick up my fork. "I forgot to set it out."

"No problem."

I slice off a bite of egg, then edge toward another topic Abel won't be eager to discuss.

"I got a call from Christopher today. He'll be leaving town soon"—that news, at least, should please Abel—"and he'd like to meet you. Tomorrow he's taking me to this place where he's ministering to a teenage runaway on Fourteenth Street. I thought you might like to come along."

Abel picks up a slice of bacon and bites off the end. "I thought," he mumbles around the bacon, "you and I were going to have brunch at the Hilton."

"We can still do that. If we miss the brunch buffet we can always do lunch."

His brow wrinkles, and in that instant I know he is not going to meet my son. Not unless the Lord himself comes down and gives my husband a direct command.

"I don't need to meet him." Abel reaches for the catsup. "He's part of your past and he's going away. Let's leave it at that, shall we?"

"Well . . . I think he'd be honored to meet you. He's watched the program, Abel, and he came to church Sunday morning."

Abel slams the meaty part of his hand against the bottom of the catsup bottle with a trifle more force than necessary. A slurry of catsup spits across the counter, spraying his eggs, the edge of his plate, and about six inches of my formerly clean countertop.

I take another bite of egg, knowing his decision is irrevocable.

"I don't understand," he says, speaking in the clipped, curt voice he uses when he is truly angry, "why you keep trying to force this kid on me."

"He's not a kid. He's a wonderful young man."

"Fine. But he has no claim on us."

"He's my son."

"He belongs to the people who raised him. You were only the baby factory."

He has gone too far again, and he knows it. In the abrupt silence I hear all the unspoken words that bubble behind his closed lips—questions about why I wasn't able to give him a child, unvoiced suspicions about my abortion and our subsequent infertility. But he will not say these things, because our childlessness could be his fault. That fact alone prevents him from dropping the entire burden of our empty home upon my shoulders.

"I won't mention it again." I stab my egg, then frown as a chunk of white eggshell cracks beneath the tines of my fork.

"He doesn't even treat you like a lady," Abel mutters, swiping a dishtowel across the messy counter. "Taking you to a bar! How can you think I would be glad a man like that has come into our lives?"

I am suddenly very glad that I haven't told Abel about my meeting with Chris at the video store.

"My son has always shown me the utmost respect. He looks out for me."

"You should never have been anywhere near downtown."

I lift my chin as my mind fills with images of Shirley and George and Judd, who is no longer sleeping on the sidewalk. "Maybe I should go downtown more often. Maybe Chris is doing the real work of the ministry while you're spinning your wheels."

Abel flinches as my words strike deep . . . and instantly I wish I could withdraw the barb. My husband is a good man, a godly man, and he is giving his best to the Savior. I have never seen him do anything to bring dishonor on the Lord or the church he serves.

"I'm sorry, honey." My eyes brim with tears as I reach for his arm. "You didn't deserve that; I know you're doing everything you can for the kingdom. But Christopher has done nothing to deserve your scorn."

Abel looks at me, his eyes damp with pain. "What I feel for him isn't scorn. I'm . . . I'm not sure what it is."

"I know. This has been a confusing time for all of us."

Abel drops into his seat, then picks up a fork and slices a piece of egg. "I suppose I could be a little more open-minded—after all, the Pharisees called Jesus a winebibber because he consorted with drunks. They accused him of wickedness when he socialized with sinful people. His family even called him insane."

I laugh, a wild sound that echoes crazily in our kitchen. "I've been wondering if *I'm* losing my mind, but Christopher definitely is not."

We eat the rest of our meal in silence.

I am putting the dirty dishes in the sink when I hear the three-noted beep that sounds whenever a window or door in our home has opened. I look across the kitchen to the study and see Abel's foot on a leather hassock—he hasn't moved, so who opened the door?

I go to the window and watch as the tile man lowers his tools into the back of his pickup truck. Guilt avalanches over me when I realize he was in the house—our expansive, high-ceilinged house where voices float up to the ceiling and echo to every room—while we were arguing at dinner.

Arguing over Chris. My son.

For the first time in years, an outsider has seen a chink in our armor.

I sink to a stool. Here I am, thinking of myself as Lady Bountiful because I offered the man a soda and cookies . . . now he'll go home and tell everyone that Reverend Howard and his wife fight just like other couples. If he heard us clearly, he has some powerful information.

Lord, forgive me.

I walk to Abel's study and stand in the doorway, watching him as he reads a commentary. Under the pressure of my gaze, he looks up, a question on his face.

"He had to hear us." I jerk my head toward the front door. "The tile guy."

Abel turns a page. "I'm sure he's heard worse in hundreds of other houses. Besides, he doesn't know us."

"But he knows who we are. And I was trying to—" What? My offer of a snack was a far cry from witnessing Abel Howard style.

I was trying to show concern and caring . . . and I'm sorely out of practice.

But Abel's nonchalance calms me. I'm overreacting. The tile guy doesn't care about who we are or what we've done. He probably didn't listen in to our conversation. But he undoubtedly knew we were arguing.

Leaving Abel to his reading, I turn and move toward our bedroom, weary and more than ready for my pajamas. So the tile guy saw our humanness, what's so terrible about that? Everybody's entitled to be human, right? And if he didn't hear what we were specifically arguing about . . .

No . . . I feel awful because I wanted him to see a man and woman united by God's love and his purposes for their lives—the pair our TV audience sees. But that couple doesn't live in this house, if in fact they ever did.

I breathe deep and feel a stab of memory, a broken remnant of a conversation with Christopher.

Jesus . . . knows there's hope for people like Judd, and he knows you aren't perfect. He sees us as we are, Emma.

I've been the Christian superwoman for so long, I can't imagine being human . . . yet the freedom to be human at this moment would be sheer relief. God knows my frame and its weaknesses. If I could take all the energy I invest in maintaining my virtuous image and transfer it to simple trust and obedience . . . maybe then I could leave my reputation and other people's expectations in the Lord's hands while I walk through each day with an ear cocked for his voice.

After dressing for bed, I crawl beneath the covers and lie in the soft gray glow of the television. When Abel has not come to bed by the time the clock strikes eleven, I turn off the TV and close my heavy eyes.

CHAPTER SIXTEEN

$\mathcal{I}$ don't know when Abel came to bed. When I wake Wednesday morning, I leave him sleeping while I tiptoe into the bathroom, step carefully over the perfectly spaced tiles, and head toward the shower.

Before opening the shower door, I take a moment to admire the tile man's work. Every piece is perfectly placed, with a uniform quarter-inch gap between each tile, even in odd spaces like the diagonal corners of the bathtub.

I find myself wishing I could stick around and sound out the installer when he comes in to do the grout. Maybe he didn't hear last night's dinnertime conversation . . . but the odds are against it.

I lean into the shower and turn on the hot water full force. While the water heats, I peek into the closet and find myself wishing I owned a pair of blue jeans. Jeans and a sweater would be the perfect attire for a blustery February day, but the most casual pants I own are beige khakis. I pull them from the shelf, then select a blue Oxford shirt to go beneath a cream-colored cashmere sweater I've owned at least ten years.

After a quick shower and a cup of instant coffee, I head into the garage and start the car. I keep looking toward the door, expecting Abel to stick his head out to say something—anything—but I haven't seen him since I left the bedroom.

He'll go about his business, then, without even trying to find out when I'm meeting Christopher. And I'll catch up with Chris and offer some lame excuse about why Abel couldn't come, even though he had the morning off and had nothing more urgent to do than sleep.

Then I'll take my son to the Hilton for lunch, hoping to run into Abel . . . and if he doesn't show, I'll know the breach between us has widened. We have not had a major disagreement since our horrendous first year, but this feels like the beginning of something significant.

Am I sacrificing peace in my marriage in order to pursue this relationship with my son? I shouldn't have to—a woman should be able to love her child and her husband without either one fearing the other. But unless Abel changes his heart, I'm afraid Chris will always be a thorn between us.

After turning on the radio, I find myself listening to Amy Grant as I take the interstate and head toward the downtown area. Abel doesn't approve of Amy—he thinks she sold out a few years ago when she recorded songs for the secular market, and he completely wrote her off when she remarried after her divorce—but I'd bet my bottom dollar that Christopher likes Amy Grant. A lot.

I am cautious on the highway, for last night's below-freezing temperatures left patches of ice on the overpasses and in areas shadowed by hills. The highway leads me through the timbered outskirts of town, meandering through leafless trees that stab at the winter white sky with black, bony arms.

Fifteen minutes later I catch my first glimpse of downtown Wiltshire from the exit ramp. The dingy sky hangs over this urban area like a dustsheet over threadbare furniture. Soon I'm navigating narrow, hilly streets boarded by old clapboard houses that have seen better days. I glance at the address on the sheet of notepaper—1089 Fourteenth Street lies just ahead.

A patina of grime covers the slanted house with boarded-up windows. A leafless vine clings to the clapboards and covers a window at the front, giving the place a furtive look. I park on the curb, then shiver as I look around. Not a sign of life on the block. Iron burglar bars adorn the windows and front door of the house across the street; the two-story next door nestles in the embrace of a thorny hedge, formidable even in the grip of winter.

The building at 1089 Fourteenth Street looks uninhabited. No smoke curls from the crumbling brick fireplace; no lawn beckons the visitor forward. There's no car in the driveway, no door on the mailbox, no light shining around the edges of the boarded windows.

For an instant I think I've made a terrible mistake, then experience reminds me that Christopher never does what I expect. I unbuckle my seat belt and look around, hoping to see a vehicle or any sign of civilized life. I am not getting out of the car unless I feel safe, and I definitely do not feel safe in this neighborhood.

Then I catch a glimpse of movement. I turn to see Christopher standing on the concrete slab that probably used to be a front porch. He is wearing jeans and a thin pullover sweater—where is his coat?—and he is smiling at me.

Thank the Lord, for once he has managed to arrive on time. I pull my purse out of the passenger seat, then step out and click the remote to lock the car—probably a senseless gesture in this neighborhood. After I cross a carpet of crisp dead weeds, Chris greets me with a hug.

"Thanks for coming, Emma."

I step back and give him a look of maternal rebuke. "You'll catch your death of cold out here without a jacket."

"I'm okay." Smiling, he takes my arm and leads me into the house. "Melinda's inside. I told her about you. I think she really wants to meet you."

What did he tell her? I haven't time to wonder, because he opens the door and leads me into the house. I am not sure what I expected to see, but never in my wildest dreams could I have imagined this.

Pigsty is too mild a word to describe what I see once my eyes adjust to the gloom. The scarred wooden floor is littered with newspapers, crumpled food wrappers, and brown paper bags. A man sleeps—at least I think he's sleeping—on the floor before a brick fireplace that's been decorated with profanity and obscene words. Another man sits with his back to the dark window, puffing on a hand-rolled cigarette . . . and I don't have to ask what he's smoking. A sweet, acrid aroma mingles with the sharp tang of body odor and the pungent smell of urine.

Christopher walks through the rubbish without flinching. He turns to catch my eye, then nods toward the hallway. "Melinda's back here."

A kitchen opens up off this hallway, and the room is filthier than the first. In the shadows beneath a sagging cupboard, a rat nibbles on what looks like a shriveled apple. A roach scurries into a flattened pizza box on the chipped orange Formica countertop at our approach, but the girl sitting on the floor does not move. Her hands rest on the tops of her knees while lank hair, caked with grease, straggles around her face. Her eyes are closed.

"Melinda?" Christopher reaches for a white plastic bag on the counter, the only spotless object in sight. "I've brought you some soup. You need to eat it."

Slowly, her eyelids lift, revealing glassy blue eyes. I finally recognize the girl in the photograph, the child with whom Chris thinks I can identify. She looks younger in person.

My son has lifted a foam container and plastic spoon from the bag. "It's beef and barley." He kneels on the dirty floor. "You need to eat something. Starvation is not good for you or the baby."

I take an involuntary half-step back. The baby? Good heavens, how did this child come to be with child?

Melinda looks at Chris with a slightly perplexed expression, as though she heard his voice but couldn't understand what he was saying. Finally a light gleams in her eyes. "I . . . don't . . . like . . . soup."

He flashes me a quick grin, as if getting her to respond at all is a major victory, then returns his attention to the girl. "What do you like, then?"

Even in her stoned condition, a mischievous smile quirks the corner of her mouth. "Pepperoni pizza. Thick crust."

Chris looks at me. "I think we can manage a pizza. Can't we, Emma?"

For an instant I am struck dumb and senseless, then I

understand. "Oh! Of course." I pull my cell phone from my purse, then realize I haven't the faintest idea what company to call in this part of town.

Shrugging helplessly, I hand the phone to Christopher. "I don't know who to call."

He laughs. "I do."

Standing, he punches in a number from memory, then proceeds to order a large pepperoni pizza with thick crust. As he gives the address, I walk back to the hallway and peer into the other rooms of this hellish house.

The bathroom stinks to high heaven—either the plumbing is not working or it's been months since anyone cleaned the toilet. Rust stains crowd the aqua tile, the stool has no seat or handle. Gingerly, I turn the faucet at the sink—no water. I flip the light switch—no power. A candle sits on the edge of the rusty tub, burned down to a nub.

I peek into the bedrooms. A thin, stained mattress crowds most of the floor in the first room, and the bed is occupied by a man and a woman who seem dead to the world. The woman opens her eyes as I walk by the doorway, then closes them with no more reaction than if I were only a figment of a dream. On the floor beside her, a little girl with dark hair calmly plays with a broken mouse trap. She can't be more than two or three.

Almost instantly, my mind fills with a scene from the old black-and-white version of *A Christmas Carol*. One of the ghosts who visits Scrooge shows him two pitiful children, Ignorance and Want. "Beware them both," the spirit warns in a booming voice, "and all of their degree, but most of all beware this boy, for on his brow I see that written which is Doom, unless the writing be erased . . ."

I bring my hand to my mouth as my gorge rises. It's bad enough that people make choices that degrade themselves to this point, but must their children be forced into this miserable sort of existence?

I stumble into the hall, where I nearly run headlong into Christopher.

"Hey." He catches my shoulder. "You okay?"

I can do nothing but nod.

He looks at me for a moment, then drops my phone back into my hand. "The pizza is on its way, but it'll be a while before it gets here. While I go out and watch for the delivery guy, would you mind talking to Melinda? I've been trying to get her out of here, but she won't leave." His eyes soften as he looks at me. "She doesn't trust men, but I think she'll listen to you."

Finding my voice, I gesture toward the room where the little girl is playing in filth. "What about the others? We need to do something about that situation; we can't just leave that child. We should call social services."

Chris glances toward the room, then shakes his head. "If you call social services, they'll disappear. They'll go out the back window the minute that car pulls up, and then that little girl will be living on the streets. As bad as this is, it's a roof over her head."

Frustration percolates beneath my breastbone as I stare at him.

"One person at a time, Emma." His hands, warm and steady, fall upon my shoulders. "I spoke to the Father this morning; this is Melinda's day."

My frantic restlessness calms under the power of his gaze.

"Okay." I swallow hard. "Today we help the pregnant girl. But where will she go?"

"Any place is better than this, don't you think?" His eyes are glowing with purpose and pleasure. "I'm sure the Lord will provide a place."

When he turns to leave, I am suddenly terrified by the thought of being alone in that house. "Wait, Chris." I catch his sleeve. "Do you have to wait outside? I mean, won't they bring the pizza to the door?"

He gives me a wide smile with a touch of irony behind it. "Delivery people don't like to stop in this neighborhood, Emma. You kinda have to catch them as they go by."

As he strides away and opens the front door, I take a deep breath and feel a dozen different emotions collide—fear, loneliness, irritation, hope, despair, hopelessness. For an instant I am sixteen again and standing alone in Grand Central Station, then I remind myself that the past is past. I have become an adult, I have been redeemed, I have . . . overcome. Through the love of Jesus, I have been saved from far worse than this. And I owe an unspeakable debt.

Nola Register swept me off the street and into loving arms. It's time for me to reach out and rescue someone else.

I walk down the hall and go back into the kitchen where Melinda still sits on the floor, her arms limp at her sides, her hands palms-up on the cracked linoleum. She is staring straight ahead, her eyes as remote as the ocean depths. The cup of soup sits on the floor, untouched.

I pick up the soup, slip the plastic lid back onto the container, and place it on the counter. When I've completed that small chore, I realize I have two choices: I can either begin to clean up this kitchen or sit down and try to clean up a life. The kitchen would be far easier to tackle, but Chris asked me to come here for reasons that have nothing to do with my domestic skills.

Reminding myself to buy a pair of jeans as soon as possible, I sink to the floor in front of Melinda. "You know," I link my arms around my knees, "I was about your age when my mom kicked me out of the house. My dad had died a few months before, and my mother was an alcoholic. Anyway . . . she caught me making out with my boyfriend and she couldn't handle it. Actually, I don't think she could handle anything by then. She was looking for a way to simplify her life."

Slowly, Melinda's eyes focus on my face.

"I didn't know where to go." I lean back against a sticky cupboard, realizing that this sweater will never be the same. "I was living in New York State at the time, so I caught a bus to Manhattan. Seemed like a glamorous place to go. Broadway, Madison Avenue, Greenwich Village . . . all of it sounded better than hanging around my hometown."

Melinda tilts her head slightly as her eyes drift away. I draw a breath, assuming I've lost her, then she closes her eyes. "I'm from Cason's Holler, back in the hills. My daddy"—she pronounces it *diddy*—"he took a new wife, and she didn't like me at all. So she turned me out. And my daddy didn't say nothin'."

Grief wells in me, black and cold. I am tempted to draw Melinda into my arms and weep for her, but I don't want to frighten her away. Instead I drop one hand to cover hers . . . in much the same way Nola Register reached out and comforted me.

"I hitched a ride here." Melinda finally meets my eyes. "And the guy who gave me a ride was a college boy, all sweet and nice, until we got to the school. Then he turned me out, too. But before that . . ."

Her eyes fill with tears as her voice trails away. I slide across that dirty floor to place an arm around her slender shoulders. "I know."

"He . . . he put a baby—"

"You're going to be okay, Melinda. Believe me, honey, I've been where you are, and I know you're going to be okay."

Suddenly she is holding me like a drowning girl clings to a life preserver. Her tears are coming in sobs so strong they shake her body, and I realize I am crying only when I taste the salt of my tears running into the corner of my mouth. Holding her, I rub her back and whisper soft shushing sounds while the walls of her resistance come tumbling down.

It is a small victory, but I cherish it nonetheless. I haven't led her to Christ or found her a home or helped her toward the future, but I have drawn her into my arms and shown love.

Yet if not for Chris, I wouldn't be here.

When Melinda's weeping slows to a trickle of tears, I pull away, push the hair from her eyes, and lift her chin. "You're going to get out of here, honey. We're going to find you a place to stay, and then we're going to take care of you and your baby."

She blinks, and for a moment I wonder if she has again retreated behind the wall of indifference. "Christopher says you're on TV."

I'm a little perplexed by the change of subject, but I nod. "That's right."

"What do you do on TV?"

"Well, I sing. On a program from our church. My husband preaches."

"What does he preach about?"

What do I say? He preaches about sin and morality and

indecent books and the importance of having your kid play on a Christian Little League team?

None of those things matter one whit to Melinda . . . or anyone like her.

I meet the girl's wet eyes. "He preaches about Jesus' love."

A slow, shy smile blossoms on her face like a rare and radiant flower. "I know about how Jesus died for our sins and all like that. Mama brought me up in the church before she died."

I nod again. "That's good."

Melinda wipes her nose with her sleeve. "So what else does he talk about?"

I am staring at the stained plaster ceiling, trying to come up with a truthful, useful answer, when I hear a man's groggy voice. "Hey—food's coming!"

I stand and peer around the corner into the front room. One of the men—the formerly comatose guy by the fireplace, I think—has opened the door.

I turn to grin at Melinda and hold up a finger. "You wanted pizza, right?"

She nods.

"Then wait right here. We aim to please."

Four steps take me down the hall to the front door. Our bearded and malodorous sleeping beauty steps aside as I approach.

"You hungry?" I ask.

He scratches his beard for a moment, then nods.

"Good. I'll be right back."

I step through the doorway in time to see Chris approaching a nervous-looking delivery man in a red SUV.

Chris wasn't kidding—the pizza guy has pulled over to the right and makes no move to get out of his truck. He takes Chris's money, then struggles in the confined space to wrestle a large pizza box from an insulated pouch.

Grateful for a blast of fresh, cold air, I step onto the porch. The sun is now almost directly overhead, spreading white light over the wet black roads. The surrounding houses stand like silent sentinels; if not for the smoke rising from a chimney down the street, I would wonder if other people still lived in this crumbling neighborhood. But across the street, the face of an elderly woman appears through a gap in the lace curtain, then vanishes. The SUV in front of her house must be making her nervous.

Scanning the street, I feel a sudden coldness that has nothing to do with the weather. I have read about urban blight in magazines and newspapers, but before this week I had never thought that it might be gnawing away at Wiltshire. Yet here are all the signs of inner-city decay—empty homes, frightened residents, the homeless and helpless living in a drug-induced haze to ease the pain of disconnection.

I shudder when I realize that I, who have always considered Abel a little out of touch, have passed the last two decades of my life in another sort of seclusion. If Chris had not come to town, I might never have seen these streets or met these people. We have been so intent upon reaching the world for Christ that we have forgotten about parts of our own city . . .

I am shivering, my hands in my pockets, when a rumbling truck crests the hill to my left. It's a Schwan's delivery truck, and as Chris accepts the pizza from the driver, I'm wondering which shut-in in this neighborhood orders packaged foods. As Chris begins to cross the street, the pizza delivery driver guns his engine and cuts hard on his steering wheel, attempting to make a quick U-turn in front of the oncoming truck.

My feeling of uneasiness suddenly turns into a deeper and much more immediate fear. Time slows as I shift my gaze to the driver of the delivery truck. The young man, close enough now for me to see the expression of surprise on his face, utters a one-word exclamation and braces himself against the steering wheel. I hear the squeal of brakes; I see the back of the truck swing wide. I am moving down the concrete steps and breathing in the acrid scent of burning rubber by the time the vehicle spins on the wet road.

My feet stutter to a stop on the broken sidewalk. I see the side of the truck hit Chris and jettison him across the asphalt; I watch as the pizza box flies from his hands. The Schwan's man glides by me in the safety of his cab; the front of the truck turns its pale yellow face away.

Somewhere, a drum begins to pound to the rhythm of my pulse. The young man stumbles from the vehicle, the pizza guy has left the scene, and Chris, my beloved son, lies on the pavement a few feet away.

I take a step forward, then retreat, torn between running for help, rushing to his side, and melting into helpless panic.

The delivery truck driver shocks me out of my stupor. "I'm calling an ambulance! Get him warm, lady!"

His voice is all the impetus I need. I run to Chris's side.

His eyes are closed when I first approach, but they open when I kneel and touch his cheek. He is so perfect, so unbroken, that for an instant I am certain God sent an angel to deflect the force of impact. Soon he'll stand up and laugh; he only needs to catch his breath . . .

But then he smiles, and blood trickles from the corner of his mouth. I yank at my sweater, pulling it off, then shape the cashmere into a pillow for his head. A smear of blood wets my palm as I withdraw my hand. He is bleeding from the ear, too, and something in me knows this is not good.

I sink to the road and pull his hand to my cheek. "Hang on, Chris."

His blue eyes are glowing brighter than I have ever seen them. "Mom?"

"I'm here, baby."

"I have to go home."

And he leaves me, just like that. The light in his eyes dims and after a moment I find myself staring into blank, empty windows that no longer house a living soul. Though his palm is still warm and his lips curve in a smile, I know he is no longer with me.

He is with the Lord.

"Chris—?" Pressing his hand to my heart, I rub the pale skin of his arm as if I could massage life back into his frame. "I love you, son. I love you so much."

I am still sitting there when the ambulance arrives. One of the paramedics gently lifts me up so they can take care of Chris. Though he is gone, they hook him up to machines; perhaps, I am told, his organs can be used to help someone else.

One of the paramedics, a young woman, asks if I want to ride along. I am about to say yes, but then I glance behind me.

The accident has drawn a small crowd—mostly elderly people, but also a few small children who seem to have materialized out of thin air. Melinda stands in the midst of the gaping strangers, her arms crossed over her chest, her hair whipped by the wind. I cannot see her eyes, but I can imagine what she is thinking: Someone came, someone cared, and someone left. Something bad happened again, and she is once more alone.

I can get into the ambulance and ride with a lifeless body to the hospital . . .

I spoke to the Father . . .

. . . or I can remain here with the girl Chris came to rescue.

. . . this is Melinda's day.

Somehow I find the strength to tell the paramedic I will go to the hospital later.

I walk to Melinda and slip my arm around her shoulder as tears stream down my face. And as the ambulance pulls away, I hear my heart break with a sharp, snapping sound.

CHAPTER SEVENTEEN

*F*atigue oozes from every pore as I wait for Mr. and Mrs. Lewis to arrive. I'm sitting in a pale green visitor's lounge with some ugly vinyl chairs, a sofa, and an industrial-sized waste can. The glass-and-chrome table at my knees is littered with copies of *Sports Illustrated, Guideposts,* and *Good Housekeeping,* but I have not felt like reading since my arrival.

Next to me, Abel sits silently, his ankle resting on his knee, his foot jiggling. I am grateful he has come, but I know he is not comfortable. He has waited in this room a hundred times before, always in complete control, but never has he waited to comfort the parents of his wife's son.

The scene is beyond bizarre.

My husband and I have scarcely spoken. I called him from the scene of the accident to tell him what happened and that I would not be going to the office today. I planned to wait at the hospital until Mr. and Mrs. Lewis arrived, no matter how long it took.

To his credit, Abel walked through the doorway half an hour later. He pulled me into his arms, offering comfort in the best way he knew, then took the chair at my side.

We've been sitting for three hours, not talking, not even looking at each other. When a candy striper comes by to ask if we want coffee; Abel accepts her offer and follows her in search of the coffeepot. He returns a few moments later and hands me a cup; I place it on the horrid chrome table.

The big black-and-white clock overhead is striking five when the door swings open again. A man and a woman enter, both of them pale and glassy-eyed. The man looks at Abel, the woman looks at me.

I see her see me, and I know she knows.

I push the boulder from my throat as I stand. "Mrs. Lewis—"

"I'm Georgiana; my husband is Paul. And you are Emma Rose."

"Emma," I tell her. "Call me Emma."

And then she falls into my arms and we hold each other, two weeping mothers bound by tears and love for one remarkable son. I don't have to describe the accident; through the sounds of our sobs I hear Paul Lewis explain that they heard the story from the police and came as quickly as they could.

I'm not sure how long we stand there, but eventually Paul tugs Georgiana away. They sit in the awful chairs across from me and Abel; their eyes scan our faces. It occurs to me that Abel is the only one whose eyes are not swollen from weeping.

It is time to talk, but I'm not sure how this conversation should begin.

Georgiana begins. "Thank you." She pulls a tissue from her purse and wipes her streaming eyes. "Thank you so much for being so generous with your time this past week. He kept calling with reports of how well you were getting on —meeting you has been an answered prayer. He has wanted to know you for so long."

Her gaze shifts from me to Abel, and through the thickened, awkward air I sense my husband stiffen. To spare him the embarrassment of confessing he did not know Chris at all, I lean forward to capture Georgiana's attention.

"You did a wonderful job of raising him." I give them a wobbly smile and hope they can see my sincere gratitude. "He was . . . remarkable. Truly the most unique young man I have ever met. I was so happy to know—to be able to *see*—how God answered my prayers."

Paul's chin wavers. "For so long we prayed for a son. You

answered our prayers when you chose to give him life. We will never be able to properly express our gratitude."

"You don't owe me anything." Heat enters my face as I meet their eyes. "Chris owed his life to an old woman on the Lower East Side and a widow in Hudson Falls. I owe my life to them, too."

"It's like"—Georgiana's voice breaks, but she turns the sob into a cough and continues—"God gave him to you, you gave him to us, we gave him back to you, and you gave him back to God." Her green eyes are swimming. "Though I can't believe the Lord has taken him so soon, somehow it seems right that he was with you when he went home. Like a complete circle."

I close my eyes, unsure how anything about this can seem right. I have sat beside scores of grieving parents who have lost children, and accidents like this never seem to make sense. We always assure parents that God does not make mistakes, yet this time I wonder if I'll be able to believe the standard assurances.

Is it right that God took a strong young man in the prime of his life? Chris gave so much, but he had so much more to give. Who knows what sort of ministry he could have had if he'd been allowed to live fifty more years? He might have worked at one of the nation's largest churches; he might have even joined us to work with *Prayer and Praise.*

I turn my head, unwilling to let the Lewises read whatever bitter emotions might be reflected on my face. And as I wrestle with my rebellious feelings, the rational part of my brain reminds me that Chris did not measure his effectiveness in the same way Abel and I always have. He didn't count honors or numbers or donors. I don't think he counted anything. He just . . . cared.

Georgiana opens her purse and pulls out a small photograph album, the simple plastic kind favored by middle-school girls and doting grandmothers. "I threw this together in a hurry, but thought you might like to have these . . . since you missed his growing-up years."

Gratefully, I accept the photograph album and set it on my knee, holding it to the side so Abel can see, too. He says nothing, but slips his arm around me as I flip through the pages.

Here, encased in plastic sleeves, are frozen moments of Christopher Lewis's life. On one page I see him waddling in a sagging diaper; on another he is riding a pony. Flipping through the pages, I see my son kissing the cheek of a little girl, wearing a baseball uniform and ball cap, belly-down on the carpet with a video game controller in his hands. He is handsome in a tuxedo with a pretty girl on his arm; he is the all-American boy in graduation cap and gown. He is adorable in a college sweatshirt; silly in reindeer antlers beside a glittering Christmas tree. In the final shot he's standing between Mr. and Mrs. Lewis—his mom and dad—with a diploma in his hand.

"Thank you." The words come out as a strangled croak; my throat is too tight for natural speech. I find myself wishing I had some similar token to give these people, then I remember.

"I have pictures, too." Delighted by the sudden memory, I look at Abel. "Chris took them just the other day. He said he had taken shots of all the people to whom he was ministering."

I pull my purse to my chest and sort through the pockets until I find the white envelope from Jackson's Photo.

"Here." I lift the flap and pull out the glossy pages. "I haven't had a chance to look at more than a couple of these, but maybe you can get an idea of what he was doing here in Wiltshire."

The first photo is a shot of Melinda, and my throat aches with regret as I slide it over the coffee table. "That's a fourteen-year-old pregnant girl Chris befriended at a house in the downtown district. Chris and I were visiting her when . . ." I bite my lip. "She saw the accident, and she was pretty shaken up about it. So I drove her to my assistant's house, where she'll sleep in a warm bed tonight."

Georgiana lifts the photo, then tenderly traces the outline of Melinda's face. "He always had a soft spot for outcasts."

Her gentle words stab at my heart. "Did he?" I look at Georgiana, whose eyes are soft with pain. "Did he think I rejected him? I never meant for that to happen. You've got to believe I never meant to hurt him."

"Oh, my dear." Georgiana drops the photo, then reaches forward to take my hands. "Emma, we know you had the best of intentions for him. Children don't always understand the ways God works in our lives, but in time, they learn."

Featherlike lines crinkle around Paul Lewis's eyes as he smiles. "I can't tell you he never went through hard times. Like any other kid, he had his insecurities and his questions. But he matured past all that. And after a while he wanted to find you . . . if only to tell you how grateful he was for what you did."

Georgiana picks up Melinda's picture again. "What will happen to this girl?"

I glance at Abel. A plan has been percolating in my brain these last few hours, but I haven't yet found the courage to speak to my husband about it.

"I know a place." I meet Georgiana's eye. "Mercy House, in central New York. I'm hoping to take a few days off to drive Melinda up there. She'll have the best of care, an opportunity to continue her education, and a wonderful Christian influence."

Somehow, Georgiana finds a smile. "I think I know the place. There's an adoption agency right around the corner."

Our eyes meet, silently acknowledging the bond between us. "That's the one."

Our paths crossed at Mercy House and the place changed both our lives.

Georgiana opens her mouth, then holds up a finger and

dabs at her eyes as fresh tears begin to stream down her cheeks. Her husband drapes his arm around her, drawing her close, but she looks at me and forces words through the crack in her voice.

"Despite this"—her hands sweep outward to indicate our surroundings—"I'm so glad he came to you." She swipes at her nose, then balls her tissue in her fist. "I wouldn't ever want you to think it was wrong for him to come here. All his life, he yearned to know you. I knew he loved me, so I was never really jealous. Chris just had this great big heart."

I manage a choked laugh. "Did he have you visiting street people, too?"

A look of surprise crosses her face, then she glances at the photo of Melinda and shakes her head. "We've always believed that to follow Christ means just that—we follow him wherever he leads. The Lord led Chris into the inner cities. He led my husband into the corporate world. Me, I've followed Jesus into the Junior League and the Garden Club. I was a little reluctant to join those groups because I'm not really into meetings and social events, but Chris reminded me that society women need Jesus, too."

Where have I followed the Lord? Over the last twenty-odd years, have I been following Jesus . . . or Abel?

A memory opens as if a curtain has been pulled aside. I am sitting on a bunk bed in the dorm, and I am telling my college roommate that I think the Lord might be calling me to work with teenage girls because he has brought me through some really rough waters . . .

In believing that God called Abel to ministry and me to Abel, have I missed the ministry God intended for me?

Sobs rise in my throat again, threatening my speech, and Abel, bless him, tactfully changes the subject. He nods at the other photos in my lap. "What else do you have there?"

Grateful to be distracted by the question, I look at the photos in my lap. "I'm not really sure. Chris was going to tell me about all of these people, but . . . we never finished."

I lay the stack on the table, then run my fingertips over them, spreading them like a deck of cards. We all lean forward as if we could discern the meaning of a lost life in a few glossy rectangles.

Recognizing a flip of blonde hair, I slide a photo from the row. "This is Shirley, from O'Shays. The man next to her is Jim, the bartender. And this one"—I pull out another photo—"is Judd, who was sleeping on the sidewalk before Chris took him home and gave him a bed." My voice softens. "I scolded him for that, but he said he knew he was doing the right thing."

"Chris was fearless like that." Georgiana's voice trembles. "He said as long as he was being obedient, nothing could happen to him except what the Lord willed."

Abel abruptly reaches for a photograph. "What are you doing with a picture of Eunice Hood?"

My breath catches in my lungs. The photo in Abel's hand is Eunice the way I saw her last Tuesday, her face flushed, her eyes red from weeping. She's even wearing a wet raincoat and the Wiltshire Warhawks T-shirt.

Impossible. Chris couldn't have snapped this photo before we met Eunice . . . could he?

A shiver rises from the core of my belly as I examine the scattered photos on the table. There are pictures of strangers as well as people I recognize—a photo of the little girl in the crack house, the man hungry for pizza, the frightened old woman peering at me from behind a lace curtain and iron bars. There's a shot of the cardigan-clad clerk in the video shop, a picture of some other down-and-outer on a downtown street.

And in my mind, as sharp as reality, other images form in glorious living color: my neighbor Cathleen, with her new puppy, the tile man standing beside his truck, Eunice weeping before a sink in a public ladies' room.

My mouth goes dry. I know the others are looking at me, waiting for details, but I can't begin to explain the images in front of me. Yet I can hear Chris's voice ringing in my memory: *There are some great stories behind those photos—great needs, too.*

I may never understand how or when he took his pictures, but in a flash of insight I understand why: These people and their needs are now my responsibility.

Too shaken to talk further, I push myself up from my chair. "I'm so sorry for your loss," I say, allowing habit to take over. "But I have to go. I have to get out of here . . . I need to be alone for a while."

Leaving Abel to say a proper good-bye, I push on the swinging door and hurry away on legs that feel as weak as a newborn colt's.

Somehow I find my car, unlock the door, climb into the seat and turn the key. I have to go somewhere, stay busy, do something, then maybe these hot spurts of loss will stop burning my cheeks.

I pull the car out of the hospital parking lot and head toward the interstate. The Lewises will be at the hospital for some time yet, and I need time to say a final farewell to the son I have known only a few days.

My foot feels heavy on the gas pedal, but cars are regularly whizzing by me. I watch them pass, a little amazed that so many people can go about their business as if nothing unusual has happened. A good and godly man has just left the world—how can they not sense the sorrow that shadows our city?

From the interstate I take the now-familiar downtown exit. I check my watch—five o'clock. Too early for O'Shays to be in full party mode, but Jim should be working behind the bar. And maybe Shirley will be there. Surely one of them will know where Chris was staying.

My brain sorts through the available facts as I negotiate the one-way streets. The Lewises undoubtedly have the address of Chris's apartment, but I don't want to ask them for it. He had to be staying someplace near the downtown area, because he seemed to walk almost everywhere.

I pull into an empty space across from O'Shays, then slide out of the car and stride toward the door, ignoring the parking meter at the curb. A handful of men are gathered around the bar—the after-work crowd, obviously—but Shirley is not among them.

Jim cocks a dark brow as I approach the bar. "So . . . it'll be something stronger than hot tea today, right?"

Why would he think that? Startled, I glance at my reflection in the mirror behind the bottles. The Emma Rose Howard staring back at me has mussed hair, lashless eyes, and a swollen nose.

I look like I've been licking the inside of a gin bottle for the better part of a week.

Ignoring his comment, I lean against the brass railing. "You know Chris Lewis, right?"

Jim looks at me as if he's weighing my motives, then nods slowly. "So what if I do?"

I am about to explain what has happened, but a sudden

tightening of my throat assures me I won't be able to speak of the accident without igniting a fresh explosion of tears.

I close my eyes. "He was staying around here, right? I need to know where he was—is—staying."

"Can't help you, lady."

My eyes fly open. "You can't help—or you won't?"

"None of my business. If he didn't tell you, none of yours, either."

With that he turns to answer a summons from the far end of the bar. I draw in a ragged breath, then hear a chuckle near my ear.

"Chris is a little young for you, ain't he?"

The man next to me is barely five-foot-two, with thinning silver hair arranged in a faint halo on his head. But there's nothing else angelic about him—I can smell whiskey on his breath and see its effect in the blossoms of burst blood vessels in his nose and cheeks.

I recognize him almost immediately—he's one of the men in Chris's photo collection.

"I seen you here with him," the pint-sized wino assures me. "The other night you was here with Chris."

A flurry of hope rises in my breast. "You know Chris well?"

The wino nods again. "Ought to. We're roommates. The day he came to town he saw me standing down by the bus stop and said, 'Hey, buddy. Where can a guy get a room around here?' So I took him to my place, and the landlord said we could share the room, long as we didn't light candles or anything that might burn the place down."

"Leave the woman alone, Buddy." Jim has returned, and he's frowning at the little man by my side.

"It's okay." I drop my hand to Buddy's shoulder, then lower my head to look into his eyes. "I need to see Chris's room. There's been an accident, you see, and I need to pull his things together."

Buddy squints at me for a moment, his eyes alight with speculation, but when I pull a twenty from my purse his face melts in a buttery smile.

I can't believe I'm greasing palms like a Hollywood hot shot.

"C'mon." He slides the twenty from my hand as he waddles past me. "It ain't far."

Buddy is right, the apartment isn't far away. We leave the bar and walk a few feet, then Buddy opens one of those unadorned, dark doors that downtown shoppers pass without thinking.

I follow him through a dingy hallway with a floor of chipped tiles, then we come to an elevator shaft. Buddy jerks his thumb toward the old-fashioned expanding gate. "Don't work. Never worked since I've been here."

I follow him through a swinging door clad in only a few shreds of paint. Someone has carved obscene words into the wood, but those don't alarm me nearly as much as the sight of a fat rat scuttling into the shadows behind the stairwell.

"Second floor." Buddy is wheezing now, and clings to the banister as we begin to climb. "First door on the second floor, that's our room."

I keep pace with his lagging step, though everything in me wants to turn and race out of the building. We turn the corner at a dark landing, and I'm faintly amazed that my swollen nose can still register the strong odors of sweat and urine.

Another flight of steps, another landing, another door, this one even more bare and scrawled than the first. A naked light bulb hangs by the door, adorned only by a spider and its filmy web.

"Room two-oh-seven," Buddy says, leading me down the hall. Newspapers litter the floor, and a soiled mattress sits outside one door. I'm surprised no one is passed out on the mattress, but the hour is still early.

Finally we halt outside a door. Two rusty letters hang on bent nails, a two and a seven with a space between them. Buddy fishes a key from his pocket, unlocks the door, and pushes it open.

I am suddenly aware that I am putting myself at the mercy of a stranger—exactly what I warned Chris not to do. Despite the withered condition of the man with me, the gloom in this place feels heavy and threatening.

I tilt my head toward the open room. "You first."

Shrugging, Buddy walks into the room and flips a switch. With a loud plastic crack, an overhead bulb floods the place with yellow light, revealing a square room with a sink against one wall, two beds on rusty iron frames, a small table, and an extra lamp. One of the beds has been neatly arranged with the pillow at one end, a folded blanket at the other. The other is covered by a rumpled sheet and blanket.

Buddy sinks to the rumpled bed and gestures toward the table. "That's Chris's stuff. He doesn't have much."

I move to the desk. A small suitcase sits beneath it; an open Bible, two copies of *People* magazine, and a leather journal are stacked on its surface.

"You say Chris was in an accident?"

I pull out the rickety chair and sit in the place Chris must have occupied, perhaps just this morning. "Yes."

"Somebody drop a brick on him? Bad stuff always happens to the good 'uns."

I run my hands over the leather binding of his Bible, then open it to a random page. The words have been underlined and highlighted; the margins are crowded with handwritten notes.

"He was hit by a truck. And he died."

Buddy swears softly, and when I hear the holy name he utters I am compelled to meet his gaze. "Chris was a follower of Jesus, you know."

Buddy lowers his eyes. "I know. Talked about Jesus all the time."

"Then I'm sorry I missed the respect you must have intended when you said his name."

Buddy sits in silence a moment, his hands fidgeting with the edges of his coat, then he mumbles something about having to visit the john and leaves me alone.

Running my hands over the pages of Chris's Bible, I realize I am no longer frightened. A sense of rightness washes over me, and I understand what my son meant about having no fear as long as he was in the perfect will of God.

It is right that I be here. This room is no worse than those I slept in during my dark days. My alcoholic companion is no worse than I was; in fact, he has shown kindness by bringing me here.

The Lord has shown me a kindness by bringing me to this moment.

I pick up the journal. Will I be trespassing if I read it? For a moment I hesitate, my head bowed, but the feeling of peace persists.

I open the front page, in which Chris has scrawled his name and New York address. I study his bold handwriting for an instant, then flip to a page and read what he has written:

I believe Christ calls us to be quiet followers, not heroes. When I am following him, the simple act of offering a cup of water to a thirsty man on the street is more precious to God than the preaching of an eloquent sermon that falls on mostly uncaring ears. The Lord has not called me to a platform . . . he has called me to walk among people as he did, touching them one by one.

Sometimes I look at my bio mother and wonder if the show business mentality that has invaded our view of Christian work has blinded us to the real meaning of discipleship. Believers look at people like Emma and think they have to do exceptional things for God, when that's not what the Father wants at all. I'm learning to be extraordinary in ordinary things, to be holy in unpleasant circumstances, surrounded by confirmed sinners.

This is where faith sustains me.

Pressing the journal to my heart, I ball my fingers into hard fists, fighting back the tears that swell hot and heavy in my chest. I'm tired of weeping, weary of the holy hands that keep twisting the stubbornness from my heart, but still they persist. And it hurts, dear God, it hurts.

My son has pulled the blinders from my eyes and allowed me to see myself for what I am—a sinner, cast from the same mold as the people I've met this past week. Yet until today, I was so focused on my own joys and worries that I refused to see the souls behind those strangers' faces.

Chris wanted me to see them—that's why he took their pictures. He wanted me to understand his view of the experience I glibly refer to as the "Christian walk." Now I see how blind I have been.

Jesus never meant for me to retreat from the world. I'm beginning to think he wanted me—a woman with a past as colorful as Mary Magdalene's—to grow strong in faith and love so I could reach out to people like Buddy and Jim and Shirley and Melinda and Eunice and George and all the strangers I don't yet know. They need the Savior as much as I do. None of us deserve redemption, yet still Christ calls us from darkness into light.

Still holding the journal to my chest, I lift my face to the streaked window. A week ago I thought I had honed the Christian walk to an art form. I was living a blameless life, working in the ministry, serving a church and a godly husband, doing my part to spread the gospel over the airwaves. I loved every minute of my perfectly designed calling.

But who called me, Jesus or Abel? When Abel proposed, did I automatically transfer my allegiance to him? He is a godly man, a wonderful pastor and teacher, and by following him I have managed to lead a dutiful Christian life.

But Abel is not my Lord, nor does he understand who I am. I am the woman who came to Jesus with an alabaster jar, the grievous sinner who washed his feet with her tears and dried them with her hair. I gave him all I had—a wretched, broken life—and he lifted me up to a life worth living.

I love my husband, I will honor and submit to him as the

head of our home, but I can no longer seek Abel's will when I should be seeking my Savior's and listening for his holy voice.

Over the years I have discovered that human nature and pride can handle almost anything. How long has it been since I found myself begging heaven for a touch of divine mercy because I had utterly reached the limits of my capability? Abel and I regularly invoke God's blessing on our food, our work, our home, but when was the last time we came broken to the throne, offering up a problem we could not handle?

I'm in desperate need of divine grace at this moment. My carefully arranged life has been blown to bits by the breath of God, and I have no idea how—or if—I should put it back together.

CHAPTER EIGHTEEN

*F*or the first time in twenty years, I miss a Wednesday evening service at Sinai Church. After gathering Chris's belongings, I carry them to the hospital and present them to Paul and Georgiana Lewis. I embrace Christopher's parents, thank them again through my tears, and then drive around town and stare at the winking houselights.

I don't know how Abel will explain my absence behind the piano—he'll probably mention something about a family emergency or simply say I'm not feeling well. He'll be telling the truth in either case. I don't feel well—my eyes are burning, my nose is raw from too many tissues, and a migraine has

begun to claw at the back of my left eye. Despite the lessons
I've learned in the last few hours, something in me wants to
die rather than face the loss I've suffered.

By nine-thirty I am heading home, and by nine-forty-five
the garage door opener hums to let me in.

A lamp is burning in the bedroom when I enter the house.
I drop my purse onto the kitchen table, slip off my shoes by
the mat, then slip silently through the kitchen and hallway.

Abel is sitting on the bed, his gaze downcast. As I draw
closer, I see that he is studying Chris's photographs. They are
spread over the comforter, arranged edge to edge like perfectly
spaced tiles.

Without speaking, I lower myself to the opposite side of
the bed. He acknowledges me with an uplifted brow, then
picks up one picture and turns it toward me. It's the photo of
Eunice Hood.

"How did one of our deacons' wives end up with this
crew?"

I press my fingertips to my throbbing temple. "I don't
know when Chris took the picture. And they're not a crew,
Abel . . . they're people."

"Not the sort . . . well." His voice trails away.

I gather my courage and attempt to explain. "Chris and
I were in this downtown photo store when Eunice came in
to return some X-rated videos she found in her home.
Apparently they were Tim's."

Abel shakes his head, pauses for a moment. "I had no idea."

Limp with weariness, I wave the issue away. "He's a man, Abel. Even Christian men can struggle with lust."

"I should have known." Worry lines mark Abel's face, creases that didn't exist a week ago. "A pastor should know about the troubles of his flock."

"Your flock has ten thousand members. You can't know everything."

"But Timothy Hood is one of my deacons. We ate dinner together just the other night. He was praying and testifying right along with the others."

"You can't see into a man's heart, Abel. So don't beat yourself up about it."

I curl up beside my husband and place one hand on his arm. "I love you, Abel. I know you are a righteous man who loves God. I know you try to do your best to lead the flock. But you know what? You're a sheep, too. Though the lambs can learn a lot from you, there comes a time when they have to grow up and learn to follow Jesus. He's the true Shepherd."

Abel hauls his gaze from the photographs to my face. "You were in the sort of place that rents X-rated videos?"

I close my eyes. "I wasn't there to rent anything."

"But you were there."

"Chris had befriended the owner. And you may not believe this, but I think I was supposed to be there that morning. I felt a tug at my heart when Eunice came in and started crying, but I was too preoccupied with my own embarrassment to see her need. Now I know I should have stood right in the middle of that store and wrapped my arms around her."

Surprise has siphoned the blood from my husband's face.

"I disobeyed the Spirit, Abel." I look up and meet his gaze. "I heard him, and I ignored him. And now I'm wondering how many other times I've ignored him to further my own interests."

"You've always followed Christ." Abel speaks in the raspy voice of frustration. "We've spent twenty-four years praying together, being a team—"

"We've spent twenty-four years following your vision, Abel. My prayers have been echoes of yours; my goals have always been whatever you put on my to-do list. I think it's time I asked the Lord what he wants me to do."

"He wants you to keep on being the way you are."

"No—he doesn't. He wants me to look back to where I've come from. I know that world, and I know how to help the people who are mired in it."

I send up a silent prayer for wisdom, then take a deep breath. "You reflect what you know, honey, and you've always known God as holy and pure. He is those things, but he is also passionate love—love strong enough to reach into the pits of despair and depravity. That love rescued me, Abel, and delivered me from my miserable life. In the early days, you were a great example for me to follow. But now I've matured, and it's time I learned what God wants me to do."

My husband's handsome face and bright eyes, which can intimidate most men even from a distance, are full of beaten sadness. When he speaks, his voice is rough. "I don't understand what you're getting at, Em. We've always tried to win souls to Christ. We've always worked together."

"And we'll still work together. I'm not leaving you, Abel. I just think it's time I opened my eyes to the work God might have for me *outside* the church."

He shakes his head. "What else could you do? We've never tried to limit God."

"Maybe we've been limiting ourselves." I turn the thought over in my mind, examining it from all perspectives. "I mean, think about it—we have built our ministry to be a lighthouse and we expect it to draw people like moths. But there are some valleys where the light doesn't reach. Even in Wiltshire, some people can't see it. So we need to take the light to them."

Abel considers a moment. "So you think we should go out and live in the gutters?"

"I think we should live circumspectly as we move through the world . . . being as wary as serpents and as harmless as doves. Isn't that what Jesus told us to do?"

Abel looks at the ceiling as if appealing to a higher authority, then grips his arms. "I understand what you're saying, Em, but I just don't see how it applies to us. I'm already doing all I know to do. I don't have many free hours as it is."

"I'm not saying you have to do it all, but you can train our people to think differently. Instead of inventing so many programs to keep people within our walls, let's think about sending our people out. Instead of creating Christian baseball teams, let's send our Christian coaches into the city leagues. Instead of boycotting books about swingers, let's write something to promote the ideal of a Christ-centered marriage. Let's light a candle instead of cursing the darkness."

"You've thought a lot about this."

"I've had a lot of time to think . . . and I'm not done yet."

As he slides the photos into a neat pile, I hug my pillow. "I drove around town tonight, Abel, and I asked the Lord why he brought Chris into my life. I mean, look at it from an eternal perspective—I knew Chris only four days. If God meant to take him home today—and I believe he did—then he could have just as easily kept Chris in New York with his parents. But God sent Chris to Wiltshire, and to me. The Lord used Chris to pull me out of my usual places and patterns, and he had to have a reason. I want to understand it."

He lifts one eyebrow at me, suggesting in marital shorthand that I'm overtired and in need of sleep. "Sometimes things just happen, Em."

"I don't believe that." I run my hand up his arm. "I've already figured out one thing I'm supposed to do. Tomorrow

I'm going to do whatever I must to get Melinda safely situated at Mercy House, but I can't do that for every runaway girl in Kentucky. So I want to think about beginning our own home for throwaway kids . . . girls *and* boys. And I think we need a place where alcoholics can learn about Jesus while they dry out. And we need to establish a ministry for families who have been torn apart by pornography and drug abuse. Downtown real estate is cheap, Abel, and that's where some of the neediest people are. We could buy a building there and get started by summer."

Abel scratches the stubble at his chin. "You're talking about a lot of work and money, Em."

"It couldn't be any harder than cleaning up television."

When he lifts a brow again, I know I've scored a point.

Chapter Nineteen

*T*hursday morning I rise with the sun and dress in slacks and a casual cotton sweater. While Abel stumbles sleepily to the shower, I pull a suitcase from a closet shelf and toss in lingerie, socks, a change of clothes, and a pair of pajamas.

By the time Abel comes out of the shower, I'm packed, with my purse and car keys in hand. He comes forward, scrubbing a towel through his hair, then looks at me and blinks hard.

"I'm going to Celene's house to pick up Melinda." I lift my chin. "Then I'm driving Melinda to Mercy House. I'll stay there overnight, spend a little time with Lortis June, then I'll drive back Saturday morning."

"You're driving her? Why, that's more than five hundred miles!"

I pull my purse to my shoulder. "Ten or eleven hours in the car will give us a chance to know each other. And I could use the time alone on the way back. I need to think and pray about some things."

"But—"

I rise on tiptoe to plant a kiss on his cheek. "I've already spoken to Celene. She's going to cancel all my appointments, and she's already spoken to the folks at Mercy House. So it's all settled."

I linger a moment, waiting for his reaction, but Abel seems too stunned to object. I move toward the door, then turn to blow him a kiss.

I don't know much about teenagers, but Melinda and I settle into guarded conversation as we set out. I learn she is from a small town back in the mountains, with seven siblings, a father, her evil stepmother, and "a passel of hound dogs" her father uses for hunting. Her favorite possession is an old transistor radio that looks like it was manufactured during my high-school years. Her greatest fear is that God will punish her for getting pregnant by doing something bad to her baby.

I tell her that God doesn't operate like that, but my assurances have no credibility with her now. So we stop for lunch at a Cracker Barrel and I tell her bits and pieces of my story. Her gaze keeps drifting over my shoulder, so I'm not sure how intently she's listening.

She interrupts as I'm explaining how I met Nola Register. "You know that guy who got killed?"

I nod. To speak Christopher's name would spur more tears.

"You have his eyes. The way you talk sometimes, you look just like him."

I pick up my fork and stab one last green bean. "That's probably because he was my baby."

Melinda's bushy brows shoot up to her hairline. "That ain't right. He told me his people lived in New York."

"The wonderful couple who adopted him *do* live in New York. I'm the woman who gave birth to him. I'm the girl who was pregnant and scared half to death because I was living on the streets in a big city."

Melinda doesn't answer, but her eyes stop wandering as I continue. I tell her about Nola, about how that brave woman took me in and fed me when I was hungry, and about Lortis June, who gave me a bed and a home and love when I had nowhere else to go.

Melinda eats, she listens, and when we're back on the interstate heading north, I catch her studying me with an intently curious expression.

Night has fallen by the time we pass the Hudson Falls city limit. The town has sprawled farther into the wooded hills since I left it, but Hillside Drive is still the first right after Central Avenue and Mercy House is still the first house on the left.

Melinda and I get out of the car. I reach for our small suitcases; she tugs nervously at the hem of her new shirt as we walk up the narrow sidewalk.

The porch light blazes out of the darkness, then the storm door opens with a metallic screech. "That you, Emma?"

At the sound of that voice I am seventeen again, happy to exchange my heartbreak for the security of home. I drop my suitcase on the sidewalk and run into the soft, sachet-scented arms of Lortis June Moses.

"Why are you troubled, child?"

I give Lortis June a look of skepticism. I have just finished telling her about the four days I spent with Christopher; I have wept my way through another box of tissues as I described his death. I knew I didn't have to share every detail, but something drove me to describe the smile on his face, his last words, his last look. Talking about it brought him back, if only for a moment . . .

So how can she ask me why I am troubled?

"It's just—" Unable to find the words, I wave my hand. "It's everything, Lortis June. My heart feels so heavy. Something in me wonders if I'll ever be happy again."

"That's grief, honey. You'll feel that way awhile, then the grief will ease. Part of your heart will always feel a little lonely for heaven, though."

Sighing, I rest my cheek against my palm. We are sitting in Lortis June's little room, and I can't help but wonder how many other brokenhearted females have curled up in this wicker chair and let their hurts flow into this cozy space. She sits on the other side of a chintz-draped table cluttered with silver-framed baby photographs.

Looking at the babies, for a moment I look for Christopher's face, then I decide not to try. I'd rather remember him as a man who came into my world and somehow sharpened the focus.

"I know grief," Lortis June's faint smile holds a touch of sadness, "and I know trouble. And the look you're wearing has as much trouble behind it as sorrow."

I swallow hard and blow my nose. She's right, of course—even though her eyes are weaker than they were twenty-eight years ago, she doesn't miss a trick. "It's just—" I halt when my throat clogs, then clear it and press on. "Well, Christopher worshiped and loved the same Lord I do. But he lived so differently! He talked about Jesus as though he and the Lord had breakfast together every morning. And he was so dedicated to his work, though it was the most disorganized ministry I've ever seen."

"Is that what's troubling you? His ministry?"

"Not really . . . maybe I'm jealous. Maybe I'm wondering if I've somehow missed the boat. I've always thought I was fulfilling God's plan for my life by being Abel's right hand, but now I don't know what I'm supposed to be." I hiccup a sob. "I'm a forty-five-year-old woman who has no idea what she's supposed to do with her life. I have all these ideas. . . . My mind is racing."

Silence falls between us, broken only by the clank of the radiator in the corner of the room and the pinched sound of Lortis June's labored breathing. Giggles of passing girls seep through the door, and for a moment my thoughts wing after them. I had hoped to work with girls once . . . before I met Abel.

"Not everybody is gifted to work with people on the streets," Lortis June says, "and not everybody is gifted to be a pastor's wife. But we are all called to follow Jesus, and to be lights where we are planted. If you're using your gifts, and shining your light, I don't think you have any reason to be troubled."

I know she intends to comfort me, but one phrase sticks in my mind: *If you're using your gifts . . .*

I'm using my talents—I'm playing a piano and exercising my voice. I'm using the knowledge I acquired in college to edit a magazine and teach Bible classes. I know my spiritual gifts are teaching and administration, and I am using those in our ministry.

But aren't Christ's love and mercy also gifts? And I, who have been so completely bathed in his forgiving love and grace, should be splashing that same love and mercy onto everyone I meet . . . yet I can't recall the last time I met anyone who didn't profess faith in Christ.

An image focuses in my memory. Wait—I met the tile man. And Shirley. And Jim. And George. And Judd. And Buddy. But at the time I met most of them, I was far more concerned with my own feelings than their lives. I have met my neighbor Cathleen . . . and I have repaid her kindness and her invitations with marked indifference.

God, forgive me.

I bow my head and cover my eyes with my hands. Lortis June says nothing, but begins to hum tunelessly as she picks up her crochet.

She will wait until the Lord is finished speaking to me.

I will wait, too.

CHAPTER TWENTY

$\mathcal{T}$he nine A.M. service at Sinai Church opens in predictable, comforting splendor. As the organ swells to the strains of "Holy, Holy, Holy," Abel stands beside the pulpit, Kenyon Glazier aerobically directs the congregation, and my fingers move smoothly over the piano keys.

I'm a little weary from my marathon drive, but I doubt anyone will notice. I pulled in before dark last night and caught up with Abel when he came in from speaking at a Fellowship of Christian Athletes rally.

We exchanged little more than the usual pleasantries—I asked about his meeting ("Went well, thanks"), and he asked about Melinda ("Settling in nicely, I think. Lortis June will take care of her").

I asked about his big press conference ("Everything's on schedule for tomorrow"), and he asked if I had changed my mind about joining the bookstore boycott ("No, I haven't. Thanks for understanding").

A stranger might have thought we were enjoying one of those comfortable silences long-married couples routinely share, but I knew something had changed.

Half-afraid to begin working our way through the fog between us, we went to bed early in preparation for a busy Sunday at Sinai.

Now, as my fingers automatically slip into the chords my ears have selected, I realize that though my environment has not changed, my perspective is radically different. My emotions have been rubbed raw by the harsh events of the past few days. Lortis June was a comfort as always, and so were my prayers on the long drive home. But I could not pray for consolation without asking God to open my eyes as well. The Spirit filled my heart and mind with new thoughts, and by the time I reached home, I knew things in my world were about to change.

Tomorrow morning, I'm going to talk to Abel again about beginning a different kind of ministry—something designed to get our people out of the church and into the community. That's what struck me most about Chris—everything he did was motivated by his desire to show love to a lost world. I don't want to scold or chide or challenge the world. I don't want to boycott anything. I want to dish up love to people who hunger for it because I have been a starving soul.

Even as I stand on the brink of a new adventure with Christ, the dependability of this worship service comforts me as much as the hundreds of tip-tilted faces involved in worship. I have always been moved by the power of community, but through the music and sights of this service, I feel as though this body has slipped its arms around me. I see love in the faces that occasionally glance my way and smile; I feel the strength undergirding the aged saints who are lifting wizened hands to the Lord.

The body of Christ is a mighty force, and Abel is not wrong to serve it. He is a guardian of the sheep obeying the Lord's command. He is feeding them with what he has been given, he is teaching the young ones and helping them grow strong in wisdom and faith.

But I pray I will never again cocoon in this comfort. There are too many absent from this building, too many people waking to a Sunday morning filled with despair and loss.

I relax, letting my hands slide over the keys, relishing the tension in my fingers as I manage the octave reach to emphasize the notes in the chorus. My eyes fill with tears of gratitude in the swell of the song. I am so grateful God is holy, and that the sacrifice of his blameless Son is enough to cover my past, present, and future sins . . .

When I look up, my heart does a double beat. Through my blurred eyes I see Christopher standing in the congregation, his head tipped back, his hands slightly raised as if the song has lifted him somehow. He's wearing the black leather jacket he wore the night we met in O'Shays.

My vision clears when I blink the tears away. The dark-haired man isn't Christopher at all, yet he is still familiar. I look away, puzzling over his identity, then the answer comes—the stranger in Chris's jacket is no stranger at all. Judd—the man who'd been sleeping on the sidewalk—has come to church.

After church, Crystal Donaldson stops me as I'm getting into my car. "Emma Rose?"

I hesitate, my hand on the door. "Yes?"

A blush burns her cheek. "I hate to bother you, but I still need to get your impressions of the National Prayer Breakfast. The deadline for the April issue is nearly on top of us."

I tilt my head. The girl has everything—a tenacious personality, pleasant looks, a talent for words.

"Crystal, you're a good writer. Have you ever thought about getting a job with the *Wiltshire Record*?"

The smile on her face vanishes. "Are you firing me, Emma Rose?"

I laugh. "No, honey, I'm just asking a question. When you were studying journalism, did you ever think about working for a city paper?"

She grimaces, but I can see thought working in her eyes. "Well . . . no. I always thought I should work for a Christian publication."

"Think again, sweetheart." I open my car door, then pause to squeeze her shoulder. "You're as good a writer as anyone, honey, and the world could use a few more Christian journalists. Pray about it. Stay if that's what the Lord tells you to do, but who knows where he'll send you if you're willing to go?"

When I pull out and wave good-bye she is still standing in the parking lot, her eyes alight with speculation.

After leaving the church, I stop by our local T. J. Maxx and pick out a pair of jeans. The teenage girl at the cash register stops chewing her gum when I hand her the price tag and tell her I plan to wear them out of the store. After giving me a slanted look, she runs my credit card through the register and I'm on my way.

Abel is having a special lunch for the pastoral staff before his big press conference. I was invited, of course, but I told him I needed to go back to the house where Chris died. Melinda is safely in Lortis June's care, but she wasn't the only person in need of help.

I spoke to the Father yesterday. Today belongs to the mother and the little girl.

The pieces fell into place on my long drive from Hudson Falls. Chris was right when he said the church shouldn't send young Christians into difficult situations, but I've been tested, tried, and prepared in over twenty years of hands-on ministry. Furthermore, before Chris appeared I had been praying that God would reveal more of himself to me . . . and God took me at my word.

Another paragraph from Chris's journal replays in my mind: "The things that tempt me from following God daily aren't sinful things," he wrote. "They're good things—duty to my family, to my father's company, to the people at my church. But if I am going to devote myself to following God, I must be willing to leave the good things behind as I seek the best thing—total submission and obedience."

I have been so wrapped up in good things—Christian forms, Christian functions—for so many years that the idea of breaking free is a little frightening. And yet I must do it. I'm not sure how the Lord will use me to reach the world, but I know where I can begin.

Before leaving for church this morning, I found Cathleen's invitation to the progressive dinner. Before tossing the note, I asked the Father about it . . . and received a surprising answer. So I dialed Cathleen's home and told her that if it wasn't too late, I would be delighted to participate because I looked forward to getting to know my neighbors.

Every year Abel and I attend an average of two hundred

services at Sinai Church. On Sunday night, February 22, I will obey the Lord by meeting the lost lambs on Martingale Place . . . and I hope Abel will come with me. Church attendance is a good thing, but obedience is better.

Now obedience is leading me back to the place where I lost my son. A look of decay still clings to the neighborhood when I park at the curb outside the dilapidated house. I get out of the car and hesitate at the place where Chris died. Nothing marks the spot; no gravestone or cross will ever call attention to this particular patch of asphalt.

But for me it will always be one step shy of holy ground. Christopher, the son born of my sin, brought me back into the world from which I had been miraculously, gloriously saved.

Thank God for that.

I cross the walk in a few steps, then pause on the porch. The stale odors of the house waft through a gap between the door and the framing, and I instinctively take a deep breath of clear air to fortify myself for the stench inside.

When I open the door, I find that little has changed. The pizza Chris paid for with his life has vanished, but the empty box litters a corner of the living room floor. Someone has drunk the soup Melinda wouldn't touch. The empty container lies on the counter, but at least Melinda is no longer crouching beside a cabinet.

"One person at a time," I whisper. "That's how Jesus met people."

I find the woman I'm seeking when I reach the back bedroom. On my last visit I thought she had to be at least forty-something; today, seeing her in the afternoon light, I realize she's probably in her mid-twenties. The little girl, obviously her daughter, squats beside her on the floor.

Despite the chill, the toddler's feet are bare.

Ignoring the snap and crackle of my knees, I crouch to look them both in the eye. The mother won't meet my gaze.

"I'm Emma." I reach out and touch the child's soft cheek. "I saw you here the other day."

The woman's mouth curls in a one-sided smile. "You're the one who took the girl away?"

"Yes." I sink all the way to the floor. "And I can help you get out of here, too, if you want."

"Why would I want to leave? One house is as good as another."

"Not really. I was thinking maybe you and your little girl would like a hotel room, some place with clean water and a nice bed. And then I was thinking maybe you could use some help getting a job and finding someone to watch your little girl during the day."

She gives me a guarded look. "Why would you do that for us?"

"Because someone did it for me."

I am about to offer my hand to help her up when the front door creaks. I glance over my shoulder and look down the hall—a tall man in dark slacks and a sweatshirt has come into the house, and his stiff posture sends a shiver of unease up my spine. I can't see his features in the windowless gloom, but I see him survey the room, then look down the hall toward me.

A gasp catches in my throat when I recognize his silhouette. The newcomer is my husband, a man who hasn't ventured out of the house in anything this casual in more than twenty years.

He looks around for a moment, his hands in his pockets, then lifts his chin when he recognizes me. He strides forward, glancing to the left and right, and hesitates in the bedroom doorway.

"Hi," he says softly, his gaze falling upon the little girl. "I have some food and blankets in the truck. Want me to bring them in?"

For a moment I'm too surprised to speak.

"I saw your car." He shrugs toward the street. "You weren't hard to find."

I glance at my watch. "But you're supposed to be at the press conference."

"I canceled it."

Visions of invoices and conference calls and fund-raising letters flash through my mind. "You *canceled* it?"

"I called off the entire campaign." He lowers his head a moment, then slips his hands into his pockets. "Boycotting one rotten book didn't seem very important after . . . well, after everything that's happened."

I can't stop a grin from sneaking across my lips. "I'll bet Josh didn't appreciate you upsetting all his carefully laid plans. And the direct mail people—"

"Well . . . you know what they say about the best-laid plans of mice and ministers. The direct mail people will survive; we'll just change the focus of our next campaign. And Josh quit."

I stare at him, my mouth open.

Abel shrugs. "Apparently he didn't care for the new direction of our ministry."

With an effort, I close my mouth and take my husband's arm. After escorting him out of the bedroom, I tilt my head back to study his eyes. "Are we moving in a new direction, Abel?"

Beneath the smooth surface of his face there is a suggestion of movement and flowing, as though a submerged spring is trying to break through. "I've been thinking all weekend, and while you were gone I kept looking at those pictures."

He seems hesitant to continue, but then he looks at the little girl who clings to the leg of my jeans. "This morning during my sermon, I kept thinking that it wasn't a preacher who reached you, Em. It was a cook."

I nod, remembering his morning text. In order to prepare our people for the big boycott campaign, he had preached on bearing one another's burdens and building up the church.

"Actually, Nola was a restaurateur. But mostly she was a follower of Christ."

"Right." His gaze drops to the floor. "Anyway, I realized

that in my own home I haven't been practicing what I preach. I've not been fair to you, and I have to apologize for that. I should have rejoiced when you rejoiced and wept when you wept . . . and I should have listened when you were trying to explain what God was teaching you. I forgot to sit still and listen to what God wanted to teach me. I've been all caught up in thinking that nothing we do *outside* the church is as important as what we do *in* it."

"I don't think you can separate the two." I stand and take two steps forward, moving close enough to lower my voice so my words reach Abel alone. "We don't stop following Christ the moment we leave the church property. We have to be lights wherever we find ourselves . . . even when we are led to places like this. And God doesn't call just preachers—he calls restaurateurs and dentists and real estate agents and teachers to light up the world. You're not responsible for saving the world all by yourself."

"Well . . . I know one thing. I want to help you obey the Lord."

In that moment, I realize again why I married him.

"And I want to help you." I rise on tiptoe to kiss his cheek, then melt into the circle of his arms. "I love you, Abel, and I always will. But I can't obey God through you . . . I can only follow him beside you."

He kisses my forehead, then we both look down. The little girl is clinging to Abel's leg and looking up at us with mirror-black eyes.

I hear my husband's breath catch in his throat.

"There are others like her," I whisper. "Enough to keep us busy for a long time to come."

I release my husband, then turn him toward the kitchen. "Let me get the counter cleaned off and we'll serve lunch for anybody who's hungry."

As Abel heads to the car to fetch the food, the young mother comes out of the bedroom, then lifts the toddler to her hip. She props one shoulder against the wall, then twirls a strand of hair around one finger. "I don't know you people," she says. "Why are you here?"

I have scooped up a few pieces of trash, but at her question I drop everything onto the counter so I can reach out and squeeze her shoulders. "We're here because we care about you, honey, and we want to know your name."

Distrust flickers in her eyes, hot and bright as a Kentucky sun in August, then her lower lip trembles. For the first time since my arrival, she meets my gaze. "I'm Julia, and this is Liane."

"What beautiful names." I brush a lock of the baby's hair from her eyes, then outline the curve of her cheek with my fingertip. "You can call me Emma."

Questions for Book Discussion Groups

1. Did this book shock or surprise you in any way? Why?

2. Some parts of this story are allegorical—they are meant to represent other characters or events. Which characters might be allegorical representations? Who do you think Chris represents?

3. Emma says that Christopher was born of her sin. Who was born as a result of mankind's sin?

4. *The Debt* is also intended to illustrate the parable Jesus told in Luke 7:41. How does Abel's love for the Lord differ from Emma's?

5. Why do you think Christopher had Emma meet him in such odd places?

6. Compare Emma's encounters with people at O'Shays, Jackson's Photo, and the abandoned house to Jesus' encounter with the corrupt tax collector, the woman caught in adultery, and the woman at the well. Did Jesus worry about his reputation when he dealt with people? Did he worry about his reputation at all?

7. What did you think of Abel? Is he a good Christian? A good husband? A good neighbor?

8. Has this book challenged your thinking in any way? How?

9. The Bible says that some are gifted to be pastors, teachers, and prophets—abilities that minister to the body of Christ. When Scripture speaks of our "callings," however, it speaks in general terms—we are called to be disciples, to be obedient, to follow Christ. Are those who are gifted to serve the body also called to minister to the world at large?

10. Not everyone is led to the sort of "street ministry" Christopher practiced . . . nor is everyone led to work with the body of Christ. So what are some ways you can walk in the world and shine the light of Christ to those who don't know him? When was the last time you went out of your way to befriend an unbeliever?

11. At the end of the story, Emma realizes that she has been depending upon Abel for far too much—he is not only the spiritual head of their home, but he has stepped into the role she ought to reserve for Christ. What other figures in our lives might fill the place that rightfully belongs to Christ alone?

12. Chris urges Emma to venture out of the church so she can act as "salt" in the world. As we go into the world, what must we do in order to avoid becoming "salt licks"? In other words, what things can we do to prevent our testimony from being eroded? What sort of personal standards should we establish to be sure we remain as "wary as snakes and harmless as doves" (Matthew 10:16)?

AUTHOR'S NOTE

Like Emma, I am a long way from perfect obedience, but in the past few years the Lord has brought me out of a cloistered place to a more exposed place. The cloister is safer, to be sure . . . downright cozy, in fact. When in the world, I find that I must be more vigilant, more watchful, more cautious of my words and attitudes.

In my high-school youth group we used to glibly chant, "You're the only Jesus some people may ever see."

Truths often come from the mouths of babes.

This is my third attempt at writing an author's note. I filled the first two versions with reasons and explanations, but if a story does what it's supposed to, why should explanations be necessary?

My job is simply to tell the parable. I've had help along the way, and I need to acknowledge it:

Thank you, Jesus, for tenderly teaching me what it means to listen for your voice.

Thank you, members of my prayer team, who supported this project in the heavenly realm.

Thank you, Bill Myers, for giving me advice and a great line for George's video store.

Thank you, Susan Richardson, Marilyn Meberg, and Marty Briner, for giving me excellent feedback on a rough draft.

Thank you, Bob Briner, for writing *Roaring Lambs,* a book that reinforced things I had been thinking and feeling for years. I can't wait to personally thank you in heaven.

Finally, thank you, B. J. Hoff, for telling me that love is what the lost world most hungers for . . . because that's the seed from which this story grew.

An Excerpt from the Bestselling Book

THE NOTE

BY ANGELA HUNT

CHAPTER ONE

WEDNESDAY, JUNE 13

The sultry breeze carried not a single hint that the summer afternoon would give birth to the worst aviation disaster in American history. At New York's bustling LaGuardia Airport, thousands of passengers clutched belongings, flashed driver's licenses, and gripped boarding passes before departing for far-flung destinations across the globe.

Every one of them had made plans for the evening.

At gate B-13, 237 passengers waited for a jet that would carry them to Tampa International Airport. Their reasons for traveling were as varied as their faces: some hoped for a few days of fun, others looked forward to work, others yearned to see family. A pleasant mood reigned in the lounge area despite the jet's late arrival. Chuck O'Neil, one of the PanWorld gate attendants, told jokes to pass the time. Four standby passengers smiled in relief when they were told seats were available.

PanWorld Flight 848, which had originated at TIA, touched down at LaGuardia at 2:38 P.M., almost an hour late. Two hundred fifty passengers and crew disembarked from the Boeing 767, which had developed problems with a pressure switch in the No. 1 engine. The trouble was nothing unusual, considering the age of the twenty-two-year-old plane, and Tampa mechanics had corrected the problem while others performed routine maintenance.

In the gate area, families kissed their loved ones good-bye while other travelers placed last-minute calls on their cell phones. Five passengers were PanWorld employees utilizing one of their employment perks: free travel on any flight with available seating. Debbie Walsh, a ticket agent with PanWorld, was taking her nine-year-old son to visit his father in Florida.

Forty-nine-year-old Captain Joey Sergeant of Tampa stepped out for a cup of fresh coffee before returning to the cockpit. With him were flight engineer Ira Nipps, sixty-two, of Bradenton, Florida, and first officer Roy Murphy of Clearwater. Together the three men had logged more than forty-six thousand hours of flight experience.

On the tarmac, PanWorld employees loaded the belly of the plane with golf bags, suitcases, backpacks, and two kennels— one occupied by a basset hound belonging to the Cotter family from Brooklyn, another by a ten-week-old Siberian Husky, a present for passenger Noland Thompson's grandchildren in Clearwater. While baggage handlers sweated in the afternoon sun, mechanics poured twenty-four thousand gallons of fuel into the jet.

The flight attendants boarded the waiting travelers with little fuss. Among the 237 passengers were Mr. and Mrs. Thomas Wilt, who planned to cruise the Caribbean from the port of Tampa; Dr. and Mrs. Merrill Storey, who hoped to buy a condo in St. Petersburg; and the Darrell Nance family—two parents and four children, all bound for Disney World after a day at Busch Gardens. First-class passenger Tom Harold, defensive coach for the Tampa Bay Buccaneers, boarded with his wife, Adrienne. To celebrate their fortieth wedding anniversary, the couple had taken a quick trip to New York to catch her favorite play, *Les Misérables*, on Broadway.

Forty-eight of the PanWorld passengers were students from Largo Christian School—recent graduates whose senior class trip had been postponed until mid-June to avoid conflicting with final exams. The students and their nine chaperones had missed an earlier flight, and many were openly thanking God that the airline could accommodate the entire group on Flight 848.

Shortly before 4:00 P.M., flight attendants sealed the doors, then airline workers pushed the 767 back from the gate. On the flight deck, Captain Sergeant started the four Pratt & Whitney engines. After checking with air traffic controllers in the tower, the plane taxied to its assigned runway.

At 4:05, controllers cleared the jet for takeoff. By 4:15,

Flight 848 was airborne, her wheels tucked back into the well, her nose lifted toward the stratosphere. After a short circling climb over New York Harbor, Captain Sergeant began a graceful turn to the south, toward Florida and sunny skies.

The pilots couldn't have asked for better weather. Temperatures in Tampa were in the high eighties, the humidity a sultry 70 percent. No clouds marred the horizon for as far as the pilots could see. The captain took the jet to 35,000 feet, typical cruising altitude for the 767, and held it at 530 miles per hour. Once the plane was safely settled into her flight path, he checked the passenger list and noticed that he flew with two empty seats. Florida flights often sold out at this time of year.

The passengers set about the business of making time pass as quickly as possible. They closed their eyes to nap, clamped on headphones, browsed through magazines, or peered at dusty paperbacks they'd picked up from the airport bookstore. The high school graduates in the back of the plane laughed and shouted across the aisles as they shared stories of their Manhattan adventure.

The flight attendants unfastened their seat belts and whisked out the drink carts, murmuring "Watch your elbows" with every step they took down the aisle.

One of those flight attendants was Natalie Moore. She had joined the flight in New York at the last moment, filling in for a steward who had taken ill. Before leaving New York she told a roommate she was looking forward to her first visit to Tampa. A rookie with the airline, she had graduated from flight school in Atlanta and moved into Kew Gardens, a New York neighborhood primarily populated by young flight attendants who worked out of LaGuardia and Kennedy Airports.

As the hands of her watch moved toward five o'clock, Natalie and her coworkers began to serve dinner. Passengers had a choice of entrées: baked chicken breast or sirloin steak, both accompanied by green beans and salad. As soon as the flight attendants served the last of the dinner trays, they cleared their cart and pushed it aft to begin cleanup. The flight from New York to Tampa did not allow much time for lingering over dinner, and only because Flight 848 flew during the dinner hour was a meal offered at all.

At 6:06, after nearly two hours of uneventful flight, Captain Sergeant began his descent. At 6:18, air traffic controllers at Tampa International cleared the incoming flight to drop from 15,000 to 13,000 feet. As usual, the pilot responded by repeating his instructions: "PW 848, out of one-five for one-three."

On board, passengers on the right side of the plane caught a dazzling view of Florida's Sun Coast—white beaches, pool-studded backyards, and green treetops, all bordered by the wide, blue expanse of the Gulf of Mexico.

In the galleys, flight attendants locked the drink carts into their stowed positions, getting ready to make a final pass down the aisle. Natalie Moore moved through the cabin reminding passengers to be sure their seatbacks and tray tables were in their upright and locked positions. As she waited for a rambunctious teenager to comply, she bent to glance at the horizon. The sun, slipping toward the ocean, had painted the sky in a riot of pinks and yellows.

At 13,389 feet, while Natalie and the other crew members went about their work, the torrent of air rushing past a loose screw on the fuselage outside the fuel tank created a spark. The electrical fuses tripped, and at 6:29 the plane's radio and transponders fell silent. Captain Sergeant sent a distress call, but no one heard it.

The loose screw continued to spark.

A few moments later, a man sitting in row 24, seat C, noticed three of the attendants huddled in the galley, their arms around each other. One wiped away a tear, while another bowed her head as if to pray.

"Isn't that nice." He nudged the woman sitting next to him. "Look—they've had a tiff, and now they're making up."

Their disagreement must not have been serious, for the flight attendants immediately separated. "Ladies and gentlemen," a male voice called over the intercom, "this is the captain. Please give attention to the flight attendant in your section of the plane. We have experienced a loss of power due to an electrical disruption, but we can still land safely. In order to prepare for this event, however, we ask that you remove all eyeglasses, then give your attention to the flight attendants as they demonstrate the crash position."

Leaning forward, the man in 24-C looked out the window and saw that they were descending in a curving path, moving over water toward land. Though the atmosphere in the cabin hummed with tension, he remained hopeful. The jet was coming down in a relatively smooth spiral above the choppy waters between the Howard Frankland and Causeway Campbell Bridges. The airport lay just beyond.

As the people around him fumbled to obey the flight attendants, he pulled a sheet of paper from his coat pocket and scribbled a message. Glancing out the window again, he saw the blue of the water and felt a flash of inspiration. Digging in another pocket, he produced a plastic bag, then tucked the note inside and secured the seal.

Smiling, he looked up at the pale stewardess standing in the aisle, her mouth a small, tight hyphen. "Sorry," he said, noticing that everyone around him had already bent forward to prepare for an emergency landing. "I wanted to take care of something. I'm sure we'll be all right, so tonight I'll laugh and give this to my—"

He never finished his sentence. A spark from the fuselage ignited the fuel vapors, and Flight 848 exploded. At 6:33 P.M., pieces of the plane began to rain down into the waters of Tampa Bay.

Among the shards and debris was a note.

Available from Angela Hunt

THE CANOPY
by Angela Hunt

Neurologist Alexandra Pace races to find a cure for a deadly disease that is already ravaging her own mind and body. Can she trust British physician Michael Kenway and his unbelievable story of mythical healing tribe living deep in the Amazon jungle? Are Alex and her team willing to confront the unknown dangers lurking in the dense forest? Is her faith in Michael enough to lead them through the black waters to an antidote that can save her life?

THE PEARL
by Angela Hunt

Talk-radio show host Dr. Diana Sheldon has made a career out of giving advice to irate daughters-in-law and spurned lovers. But when her whole life changes in one moment of bad judgment, the carefully built life she's built begins to spiral out of control. She'd give anything—and everything—to get her family back.

From the best-selling author of *The Note*, a heart-wrenching story about the sovereignty of God and the peace he offers he children if only they'll receive it

Also Available from Angela Hunt

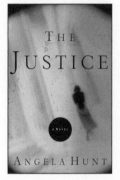

THE JUSTICE

Destiny propels Vice President Daryn Austin to the pinnacle of power when President Parker dies unexpectedly. She now controls the White House. To help her through political and legal quagmires, she hires Paul Santana, the brilliant lawyer she loved in law school. When she nominates Paul to fill a vacancy on the Supreme Court, however, her grand plans begin to crumble. After being influenced by another justice, the man she loves begins to love God, a rival with whom Daryn cannot compete. Daryn's obsession with the changed Paul leads to an emotionally charged battle of wills from which neither can escape unscathed.

THE NOTE

When PanWorld flight 848 crashes into Tampa Bay killing all 261 people on board, journalist Peyton MacGruder is assigned to the story. Her discovery of a remnant of the tragedy—a simple note: "T - I love you. All is forgiven. Dad."—changes her world forever. A powerful story of love and forgiveness.

THE IMMORTAL

A man claiming to be 2000 years old says he is on a holy mission to prevent a global cataclysm. To uncover the truth, Claudia must re-examine her beliefs as she delves into ancient legends of the Wandering Jew, biblical warnings about the Antichrist, and eyewitness accounts of the Crucifixion, the Inquisition, and the Holocaust.

The Heavenly Daze Series

THE ISLAND OF HEAVENLY DAZE
By Lori Copeland & Angela Hunt

To a casual visitor, the island of Heavenly Daze is just like a dozen others off the coast of Maine. It is decorated with graceful Victorian mansions, carpeted with gray cobblestones and bright wild flowers, and populated by sturdy, hard-working folks—most of whom are unaware that the island of Heavenly Daze is also populated with a group of unforgettable angels.

GRACE IN AUTUMN
By Lori Copeland & Angela Hunt

Authors Lori Copeland and Angela Hunt revisit the *Island of Heavenly Daze* in the second book of the highly acclaimed series about a small town where angelic intervention is common-place and the Thanksgiving feast a community affair.

A WARMTH IN WINTER
By Lori Copeland & Angela Hunt

In *A Warmth in Winter*, the unforgettable characters and humorous circumstances offer poignant lessons of God's love and faithfulness. The story centers around Vernie Bidderman, owner of Mooseleuk Mercantile and Salt Gribbon, the light-house operator, who despite the vast differences in their struggles are being taught about the ultimate failure and frustration of self-reliance.

A PERFECT LOVE
By Lori Copeland & Angela Hunt

Despite the blustery winter chill, love is in the air in Heavenly Daze. Buddy Franklin is searching for someone to change his lonely life, Dana and Mike Klackenbush are trying to reestablish the friendship that led them to marriage three years before, Barbara and Russell Higgs are contemplating babies, and Cleta Lansdown is determined to keep Barbara, her married daughter, close to home.

HEARTS AT HOME
By Lori Copeland & Angela Hunt

Edith is trying to lose weight in every way imaginable to get into a certain dress by the time Salt and Birdie's April wedding rolls around. Annie has to learn how to find God's will . . . and open herself up to a new love that's been under her nose the entire time.

W PUBLISHING GROUP™
www.wpublishinggroup.com